Lines in the Sand

Lines in the Sand

Congressional Redistricting
in Texas and the Downfall of Tom DeLay

BY STEVE BICKERSTAFF

UNIVERSITY OF TEXAS PRESS   AUSTIN, TEXAS

First edition, 2007

Requests for permission to reproduce material from this work should be sent to:
Permissions, University of Texas Press, P.O. Box 7819, Austin, TX 78713-7819,
www.utexas.edu/utpress/about/bpermission.html

∞ The paper used in this book meets the minimum requirements of ANSI/NISO
Z39.48-1992 (R1997) (Permanence of Paper).

Library of Congress Cataloging-in-Publication Data

Bickerstaff, Steve.
    Lines in the sand : congressional redistricting in Texas and the downfall of Tom Delay /
by Steve Bickerstaff. — 1st ed.
        p.   cm.
    Includes bibliographical references and index.
    ISBN-13: 978-0-292-71474-8 (cl. : alk. paper)
    ISBN-10: 0-292-71474-2
    1. United States. Congress. House—Election districts.   2. Election districts—Texas.
3. Texas. Legislature—History.   4. DeLay, Tom D., 1947–   Influence.   5. Politics,
Practical—United States.   I. Title.
    JK1343.T4B53   2007
    328.763′073455—dc22

                                                                                    2006029082

Contents

Preface

The partisan battle over the redrawing of congressional district lines in Texas in 2003 was bitter. For the first time in recent history, a political majority within a state legislature undertook to displace an existing, valid congressional district scheme with a new plan designed to maximize the majority party's power in Congress. Both political parties figuratively drew lines in the sand over which none of their members could cross.

People nationwide watched as the Republicans and Democrats of the Texas legislature engaged for six months in a historic battle to determine which party would control a majority of the state's thirty-two-member congressional delegation. Republicans targeted ten Anglo Democratic incumbents as part of an effort to add as many as fourteen lawmakers to the Republican majority in Congress as well as to marginalize the Democratic Party in Texas. The redistricting effort was driven largely by national political forces and benefited national Republican leaders, including U.S. House Majority Leader Tom DeLay and President George W. Bush.

Faced with a reality in which they held no statewide elective offices and were a minority in both houses of the state legislature, the Democrats resorted to extraordinary tactics in an effort to defeat the Republican redistricting legislation. The Texas lawmakers took themselves and their partisan fight to Oklahoma and New Mexico, and the plight of the Texas lawmakers eventually became a rallying cry for Democrats nationwide in the drive toward the 2004 elections.

This book tells the story of the 2003 congressional redistricting in Texas and the persons who played a major role in determining the outcome. These stories are told against the background of the past four decades of partisan, racial, and ethnic political change in Texas, particularly the events of 2001–2002 that made partisan redistricting possible in 2003.

For the past four decades I have been involved in election matters in Texas at the congressional, state legislative, and local government levels. First as an assistant state attorney general, then as a private attorney retained to represent governments and government officials, and most recently as a professor of law, I have represented hundreds of elected officials from both political parties and advised them on the law of redistricting. As a result, much of the historical background I provide has its origin in my own experiences. In many instances, I was there, and, for better or worse, provided legal advice to the officials responsible for redistricting decisions or represented them in court. It has been interesting for me to go back to the court opinions, official records, and news accounts over the past four decades to confirm—and in many instances to expand or correct—my recollections of past events.

I was not involved in the 2003 redistricting. I neither represented nor advised either the Republicans or the Democrats. My lack of involvement was an advantage for purposes of this book: I am free from any personal interest in how history portrays the events of 2003 and free from any attorney-client obligations that could affect the telling of the full story. In December 2004 I joined with a group of university professors who filed an amicus brief in the federal court proceedings, but I do not believe this limited involvement has affected my perspective of what happened in 2003.

A major goal of this book is to provide an accurate and dispassionate account of what happened. I find the twists and turns of the events in 2003 and the stories of the individuals caught up in the chaotic process to be fascinating. I hope that readers will find my account both entertaining and informative. Be warned, however: I have attempted to err on the side of being historically complete. As a result, portions of the book may contain too much detail for some readers, and so I have provided subheadings within each chapter to allow readers to better identify events that may be of more or less interest to them.

This book also is intended to explain the strategies that each party adopted during the redistricting process and the extent to which those strategies worked. Each move by one party generated a countermove by the other. Some moves succeeded; some did not. For over six months the Texas lawmakers from the two parties and the two national parties themselves moved with stroke and counterstroke. The Republicans ultimately prevailed; I have tried to explain why.

A third purpose is to relate and examine the involvement of national figures, such as Congressman Tom DeLay, and to show how national interests came to prevail over state interests in the final redistricting plan. The outcome in Texas was important for both national parties and for a variety of partisan interests. Party officials, activists, and major donors played a critical role in the outcome in Texas. For some, such as Congressman Tom DeLay, the final consequences were far different from what they had expected.

I have also tried to explain the importance of racial and ethnic politics in past redistricting in Texas and in the 2003 redistricting process. The final redistricting plan has a significant effect on the ability of racial and ethnic minorities to elect persons of their choice to Congress. Republicans claim that the final redistricting plan enhances minority voting strength. Most minority advocacy organizations and lawmakers argue that the plan dilutes or diminishes minority voting strength. For many minority lawmakers, the opposing tactics of the Republican and Democratic parties presented a personal dilemma as to how redistricting could best be used to enhance, or at least safeguard, minority voting power. This book examines how a few racial and ethnic minority lawmakers confronted this dilemma—in some instances, coming to entirely opposite conclusions about what was in the best interest of their minority constituents.

Another purpose of this book is to evaluate the implications of the 2003 redistricting imbroglio for the future. The Republican strategy for marginalizing the Democratic Party in Texas—mid-decade redistricting for partisan advantage—could be applied elsewhere, and if it becomes widespread, the consequences could be profound. The legislative tactic of breaking a quorum to prevent the passage of legislation is not new, but the scale and partial success of the Democratic boycott in Texas created a precedent for the possible future use of this tactic by disgruntled lawmakers.

Finally, I must emphasize that this book is not objective. By describing some events and not others out of the many thousands that took place, I am being to some extent subjective. More importantly, I have provided an informed commentary to accompany my description of the events; such analysis is necessarily subjective. However, I have attempted to be scrupulously nonpartisan and accurate. It is not my intent to demonize or lionize anyone.

I am grateful to many people who made this book possible. My research assistant, Mason Hestor, and my professional assistants, Anthony Nichols and Nelly Soriano, helped me conduct the research and prepare the manuscript. Becky Vragel helped on the research. Sherry Henry McCall provided the valuable maps. Leslie Tingle at the University of Texas Press and copy editor Kip Keller labored intensely over the manuscript as though it were their own. I am grateful to my colleagues on the faculty of the University of Texas School of Law (particularly Mark Gergen) for their encouragement and to the many participants in the events in 2003 who agreed to answer my questions. The interviews are listed under "Resources" in the Appendix. A glossary of redistricting terms is also included.

Lines in the Sand

CHAPTER I

The Significance of the 2003 Congressional Redistricting in Texas

Politics, n. A strife of interests masquerading as a contest of principles. The conduct of public affairs for private advantage.
—*THE DEVIL'S DICTIONARY,* AMBROSE BIERCE

The redrawing of congressional district lines in Texas in 2003 was one of the most extraordinary political events of the past fifty years, the culmination of a three-year effort to increase the Republican majority in the United States House of Representatives. The significance of the outcome lay not only in its effect on the relative strength of political parties in Texas or the U.S. Congress, but also in the precedent it set for political and redistricting trends nationwide.

Tales of Extraordinary Institutional and Personal Challenge

The story of redistricting in Texas in 2003 presented some of the most engaging personal tales and most interesting moments in recent Texas and national political history.

To prevent enactment of a Republican plan for partisan redistricting, most of the Democratic lawmakers left Texas to break quorum (the minimum number of legislators needed to consider legislation). Fifty-one Democratic state representatives departed in secret (most by bus) on a night in May 2003 and showed up together in Oklahoma. They remained gone until it became impossible for Republicans to pass a redistricting bill in the regular session of the 2003 Texas legislature. During a special legislative session on redistricting called by Texas governor Rick Perry, a Republican, at the end of July, eleven Democratic senators rushed from the state Capitol out of concern that they were about to be locked in the Senate chamber by Republicans intent on maintaining a quorum in that legislative body. The senators flew to New Mexico and remained there for almost forty days. Perry eventually called three special sessions of the state legislature before a quorum could be restored and a redistricting plan enacted.

Persons from both political parties were caught up in these tumultuous events and were confronted with personal dilemmas that, they now claim, made the period the most difficult of their political lives. Their stories are significant for anyone who values learning from history—from the experiences and judgments of interesting people grappling with extraordinary circumstances.

The Importance of the 2003 Redistricting to the Preservation of the Republican Majority in Congress

In 2003 there were 229 Republicans, 204 Democrats, and 1 independent in the U.S. House of Representatives. Democrats hoped that by winning as few as thirteen congressional races from Republicans in 2004, they could achieve a voting majority in the House. The 2003 redistricting in Texas effectively killed any chance of a Democratic takeover of the Congress in 2004 because it put seven Democratic seats in jeopardy.[1]

Redistricting in Texas resulted in a net gain by Republicans of twelve seats (six seats changed from Democratic to Republican control, meaning a net gain of twelve for the Republicans) in Congress, thereby permitting the Republican Party to add to its slim majority in the House and to significantly enhance the possibility that the Republicans will be able to build a larger, long-lasting majority in Congress. Because of Republican gains through Texas redistricting, the Democrats, although gaining four congressional seats elsewhere in the nation in 2004, ended up with two fewer seats in Congress. Without the redistricting in Texas, the Republican majority in the United States House of Representatives would have dropped to seventeen (225–208). Instead, the Republican majority increased by four seats, to twenty-nine (231–202, with one independent and one vacancy).

This voting margin would have powerful implications on particular pieces of legislation or policy issues. For example, before the Texas redistricting, several very close votes determined the fate of Medicare (216–215), the Head Start program (217–216), school vouchers for schools in the District of Columbia (209–208), and President Bush's $726 billion tax cut plan (initially failing by one vote, then passing by three).[2] For each vote, the Republican House leadership tried to strictly enforce party discipline to persuade House Republicans to support the leadership's position. Only a few Republicans broke ranks. After the Texas redistricting, the Republican leadership had a cushion of eleven or twelve additional votes. Moreover, those five freshman Republican congressmen (and one incumbent Democrat who switched parties to win reelection) from Texas generally have been loyal party soldiers, toeing the Republican line because they owe their election to the party's national leadership, which pushed through the redistricting plan in Texas. For example, in 2005 all five voted with Majority Leader Tom DeLay on all major legislation votes.

This enlarged Republican margin in Congress is particularly important for congressional action on budgetary, environmental, and civil rights issues. Four of the defeated Democrats were fiscal conservatives who frequently voted against what they perceived as wasteful expenditures.[3] All five were consistent votes for environmental protection, so their absence is likely to affect future congressional action on environmental issues. For example, in 2005 the freshman Republican congressmen joined with other Republicans to authorize changes to the Clean Air Act, a vote that passed in the House by only two votes.[4] To some observers, one of the greatest potential implications of the Texas redistricting is the effect a lasting Republican majority may have on the Voting Rights Act. Many minority leaders nationwide have expressed concern that Republicans either will oppose extending the act or will try to weaken its effect. The outcome in Texas increases the likelihood that House Republicans will have a strong majority for taking whatever action the Republican Party leadership wants.

The 2003 redistricting plan was designed to provide noncompetitive congressional districts. It is doubtful that many of the seats will change hands again in this decade. The twenty-one-to-eleven split in the Texas delegation after the 2004 elections will likely represent a minimum Republican majority for the remainder of this decade. The most competitive district is District 17, won by Democratic incumbent Chet Edwards in 2004. This Republican-leaning district, however, is likely to elect a Republican congressman in the future, especially if Edwards does not seek reelection. Therefore, it is possible that, by the end of this decade, the Texas delegation will consist of at least twenty-two Republicans and no more than ten Democrats.

Presidential adviser Karl Rove is generally credited with the current strategy of creating a lasting Republican majority in Congress, one equivalent to or longer lasting than the Democratic majority left as a legacy by Franklin D. Roosevelt.[5] Successfully redistricting Texas was seen as a critical step toward this goal. Congressman Tom DeLay's aide Jim Ellis acknowledged in 2003 that Republicans wanted to use gains in Texas as part of a plan to build a thirty-to-forty seat majority in Congress, explaining, "When you've got those kinds of margins, it's going to take a national tide to sweep you out. We're looking to build a long-term majority."[6] The Republican success in Texas in 2003 contributed significantly to that ambition.

Marginalizing the Democratic Party

The 2003 redistricting was significant also because it demonstrated the potential effectiveness of a long-term Republican strategy: to marginalize the Democrats as a party exclusively for losers, liberals, and racial minorities. Redistricting specifically targeted all ten Anglo incumbent Democratic congressmen from Texas. Only three of the ten survive in Congress today as Democrats. This strategy is discussed specifically in Chapter Four, but throughout the book are explanations of how the strategy evolved and how this goal was advanced.

The most obvious attempt at marginalization was the effort by Republicans to leave a Democratic Party in Texas in which, as explained by Democratic state senator Rodney Ellis, "the only elected officials left in it would be African American and Hispanic."[7] By trying to make the official face of the Democratic Party brown or black, Republicans are "branding" the party as one composed primarily of racial- and ethnic-minority voters. This impression is intended to increase the likelihood that undecided Anglo voters see a racially defined Democratic Party as inhospitable to Anglo voters and officeholders. Disaffected Anglos would then gravitate toward the Republicans.

Republicans dispute whether this branding of the Democratic Party in Texas as a party of racial and ethnic minorities was a goal of redistricting, but few, if any, of them dispute that Republicans have benefited by the branding that nevertheless occurred. Democrats made racial issues the defining and public focus of the redistricting battle in Texas, unintentionally helping Republicans. Chapter Three describes how racial and ethnic minorities have historically been excluded from the political process in Texas and how recent events have left the Texas Democratic Party now represented in Congress almost solely by Hispanics or African Americans. Only three of the surviving eleven Democratic congressmen are Anglo; two of these were elected from heavily minority districts. Thus, ironically, the racial and ethnic minorities once excluded from the political process by the Democratic Party in Texas have gained control of that same party as it has become a declining, minority political party.

The 2003 redistricting further marginalized the Democratic Party by reducing the diversity, and perceived diversity, of its voices on issues such as gun control, abortion, fiscal responsibility, etc. The defeat of the targeted Democrats bolstered the Republicans' claim that they are the only party for moderates and conservatives. Four of the targeted congressmen were members of the so-called "Blue Dog Coalition," which consists of conservatives and moderates who focus primarily on balancing the budget. These Democrats often voted contrary to the majority of their party. The elimination of such moderate or conservative Democratic representatives will make it that much harder for the Democratic Party to attract the rural moderate and conservative voters who once composed its core. As Republican consultant Grover Norquist was quoted as predicting, "[N]o Texan need grow up thinking that being a Democrat is acceptable behavior."[8]

A related effect was the likely hardening of voting patterns among conservative and moderate voters in Texas against the Democratic Party. Although Anglo voters in Texas in recent years have increasingly voted for Republican candidates in statewide races, more Texans actually continue to vote in the Democratic statewide primary than in the Republican primary. Some voters have acted more like independents, "splitting their ticket" to support some moderate or conservative Democratic candidates, particularly in local or district races. (In Texas, voters do not have to register as members of a particular party, and so can vote in either primary.) The targeted Democratic incumbents were reelected in 2002 in their heavily Republican districts precisely because of this phenomenon. The defeat of such Democratic officeholders because of the 2003 redistricting reduces the likelihood that Texans will continue to see themselves as independents capable of splitting their votes among candidates from both major parties in federal, state, or local races.

A third sort of marginalization of the Democratic Party in Texas resulted from the depletion of its leadership and influence in Congress and the national party. The ten targeted Democratic incumbents represented 128 years of seniority in Congress; two of them had each served for twenty-five years. One, Charles Stenholm, was the ranking minority member of the House Agriculture Committee. Others held ranking positions on the Transportation, Veterans' Affairs, Energy and Commerce, Space, and Homeland Security committees. Several (such as long-term congressman Martin Frost) held positions of power within the Democratic Party's leadership or in organizations such as the Blue Dog Coalition (Jim Turner). With the defeat of these senior lawmakers, Texas Democrats have become less able to effectively assist persons, businesses, and organizations wanting to influence decisions in Washington. Businesses and persons thereby necessarily will become increasingly dependent on Republican congressmen; this dependency will likely lead to campaign funding from these sources.

When asked about the state's loss of seniority through the replacement of the targeted congressmen with freshman lawmakers, Congressman DeLay explained that, in his view, the Democratic Party was essentially "irrelevant" in Congress today:

> They [the Democratic incumbents] may look at themselves as important. I look at them as rather irrelevant. The ranking members don't vote with the

majority of Texans in almost every issue that comes to the floor. They are opposed to everything. And how can you claim to be relevant if you are opposed to everything just for opposition sake and in a partisan vein? So I don't see that as a loss to Texas at all.[9]

Therefore, in DeLay's view, a loss by Texas of congressional seniority in the Democratic Party was unimportant. Other Republican officials emphasized that they were likewise unworried: since the President and many important members of Congress were from Texas, they expected the state's interests to be adequately protected. Some Republicans pointed out that Texas now has the largest Republican delegation in Congress (twenty-one members, ahead of California's twenty and Florida's eighteen) and can wield more power within the controlling Republican majority.

However, not all Republicans were thrilled with losing this seniority in Congress, or with what the Republican redistricting plan meant for rural Texans. For example, Kevin McMahon, who chairs the chamber of commerce in the Republican stronghold of Lubbock, observed, "To get rid of seasoned legislators just so we can get some freshmen Republicans, I don't think that's good for Texas. Rural Texans are a minority. There isn't any court that's going to protect the rights of rural Texans."[10] Nevertheless, despite such resistance among some of the Republican rank and file across Texas, the Republican strategy of defeating these rural Democrats and drawing districts that joined rural Texas to growing Republican suburbs went forward.

A final marginalizing effect was to leave the impression that Democratic lawmakers, and therefore the Democratic Party, were losers. The Democrats succeeded at killing redistricting at the end of the 2003 regular session by walking out of the Texas House of Representatives to break a legislative quorum. Some Republicans who otherwise were not enthusiastic about redistricting were incensed by the tactic. Others became galvanized; they felt that this embarrassing Democratic victory could not be allowed to stand. They felt that the Republican Party must "win" this showdown. Personal and partisan pride played its part on both sides.

Ensuring Republican Control of the Texas Congressional Delegation in the Future

The carefully designed redistricting in 2003 also is significant because it strengthened long-term the electoral position of the Republican Party in Texas and is likely to forestall the date when even the mushrooming growth of Hispanic population in the state can make a difference in the partisan makeup of the state's congressional delegation.

The 2003 redistricting allowed Republicans to gain seats that they probably will hold throughout this decade. The district boundaries are shaped so that it is unlikely that any district will gain enough minority voters to change its partisan leaning anytime soon. Areas expected to increase in Hispanic population are placed either in the already packed majority-Hispanic districts or in districts that are overwhelmingly Anglo and Republican, where the Hispanic population growth will not endanger the reelection of Republican congressmen in the foreseeable future. The one Republican congressman previously endangered by a growing Hispanic population was given a redrawn district that now is heavily Anglo and unlikely to change in the near future. Smaller African American communities throughout the state were shifted from districts where their support had been crucial to Democratic successes to heavily Republican districts, where their votes in congressional elections will be largely meaningless as long as they vote Democratic. As Republican consultant David Bositis acknowledged in 2003, "The next six years are important to Republicans although the immediate battle is for 2004."[11]

The Anglo population in Texas is now estimated to be less than a majority; it probably was less than a majority when redistricting occurred in 2003.[12] The Republican redistricting shaped the congressional districts in Texas so that a conservative Anglo minority (Republican activists) effectively controls election outcomes in twenty-two of the state's thirty-two congressional districts. The effect of the 2003 redistricting, however, is not limited to this decade. The redistricting puts more Republicans in Congress who, as incumbents, will be more likely to survive this decade, to have winnable districts preserved in the next round of redistricting, and to withstand challenges in the future, despite the changing ethnicity of their districts.

A Precedent for Control of State Congressional Redistricting by National Party Leaders and Other Outside Interests

National party figures and their allies wielded enormous influence over the Texas redistricting. The most visible of these national figures was Congressman Tom DeLay of Sugar Land, Texas. DeLay, a former state representative from Texas, was House majority leader until he was required to temporarily step aside in 2005 after being indicted for felony violations of Texas campaign-finance laws in the 2002 elections. He permanently stepped down as majority leader in January 2006. On April 4, DeLay announced that he intended to resign in June 2006. These developments are discussed in Chapter Eighteen.

At the beginning of 2003, a major redrawing of congressional districts appeared unlikely. Republicans certainly had a legitimate reason for wanting to increase their representation in the Texas congressional delegation. Texas Republicans had suffered from prior partisan redistricting by Democrats, who still held a majority (seventeen to fifteen) of the state's congressional districts, even though no Democrat had won a statewide election in Texas since 1994. Nevertheless, few Republican state officials or lawmakers had any enthusiasm for the divisive task of redrawing district lines at a time when the state legislature was already set to tackle several major state issues. Moreover, the congressional delegation was gradually but steadily changing (the number of Republican congressmen had increased from eight in 1991 to fifteen by 2003), and most of the surviving Anglo Democrats were being elected (sometimes narrowly) in congressional districts where the voters were overwhelmingly supporting Republican statewide candidates. It seemed to be only a matter of time before some or all of these surviving Democrats would be defeated. In the meantime, the Democratic congressmen enjoyed significant seniority in Congress and were supported by local elected leaders and by many constituents who otherwise voted Republican. Every major newspaper in Texas editorialized against redistricting in 2003. The few Republican lawmakers who longed to advance the Republican cause by redistricting were the exceptions. Most had little or no enthusiasm at the start of 2003 for a large-scale redrawing of congressional lines in Texas.

More than any other person, Congressman Tom DeLay was responsible for changing that lack of enthusiasm into a firm commitment on the part of Texas officials and Republican lawmakers to redraw congressional lines and help elect a Republican majority to Congress. Republicans ultimately accepted that redistricting changes would be a necessary "reorientation" to eliminate the effects of prior Democratic gerrymanders and to align the congressional delegation with a voter base that appeared strongly supportive of President George W. Bush and the policies of the Republican Party. Events in Texas became a line in the sand—a litmus test—for members of both parties.

Congressman Tom DeLay has been condemned and celebrated for his extraordinarily effective role in driving the final redistricting outcome in Texas. Individually and through the Texans for a Republican Majority Political Action Committee (TRMPAC), he helped elect a clear Republican majority in the Texas House of Representatives in 2002, and helped his friend Tom Craddick become speaker of that House in 2003. DeLay's success in changing the Texas House from an enemy stronghold, as it was in 2001, into his closest ally in 2003 was essential to what happened with redistricting. On behalf of the Republican delegation from Texas and the national Republican Party, DeLay formulated strategy, convinced reluctant Republicans to go along with redistricting, kept state Republican leaders focused on accomplishing redistricting despite the unusual tactics of the Texas Democratic lawmakers, and decided on the partisan results to be achieved by the final district lines.

Focusing solely on Congressman DeLay, or Karl Rove, however, would be a mistake. What happened in Texas in 2003 was not a result of the influence or planning of one person, or even a handful of persons. Instead, it was driven by a much more consequential partisan movement and was one facet of a ruthless and effective quest for power by persons and groups that share a common ideology and ambition. Activists within the Republican Party and major Republican donors played a critical role in convincing reluctant Texas Republican lawmakers to go along with an aggressive partisan redistricting plan despite their own reservations and substantial public opposition. DeLay (along with his associates) provided the focal point around which this partisan movement spiraled. Given essentially unlimited power at the end of the legislative process to design whatever redistricting plan they desired, DeLay and his allies put aside any pretense of advancing state interests or partisan fairness and greedily sought the most partisan plan that the law would allow.

National Democratic Party and elected officials did not remain above the fray in Texas. Some observers believe that the national party ultimately "captured" the Texas state senators for the benefit of the national party and used the controversy to energize Democrats nationally at the beginning of the race for the presidency. The effect was to turn an intrastate political battle in Texas into a national cause celebre. As the media spotlight shown on the boycotting Texas senators, Democratic officials nationwide, including the men competing for the party's presidential nomination, were drawn to the light. The Texas lawmakers became celebrities who, as guests of honor at Democratic rallies across the country, were used to rally the Democratic base (especially racial and ethnic minority voters) for the upcoming presidential election. As the stand-off continued, the Democratic senators increasingly focused their attacks on President George W. Bush, in what were some of the first shots fired in the presidential campaign.

The Effect of Money

The story of redistricting in Texas cannot be told without discussing money. The ability of Republicans to seize power in the Texas House in the 2002 elections was crucial to the ultimate success of redistricting in 2003. Three organizations, led by DeLay's Texans for a Republican Majority (TRMPAC), raised and spent more than $4.5 million in the effort to win Republican control of the Texas House. Over $2.65 million of this amount consisted of possibly illegal corporate funds that went unreported to the Texas Ethics Commission. A fourth organization (perhaps illegally) poured an estimated $2–2.5 million in corporate funds into Texas shortly before the 2002 elections to help Republican state legislative candidates and the Republican candidate for attorney general. Much of this money was generated through a web of associated lobbyists in an apparent effort to gain favor with Congressman DeLay.

The influence of money was also felt during redistricting itself. Some major Republican donors made it clear that any redistricting plan allowing the survival of certain Democratic congressmen was unacceptable. Republican state officials and lawmakers felt that they had no choice but to listen. These donors were driven not so much by economics as by ideology. Their clout became one of the assets available to DeLay in the quest for aggressive partisan redistricting.

Electing the Right Republicans

The events in Texas showed how certain persons and organizations can enforce a particular ideology by directly affecting a party's choice of candidates. For example, most of the attention given to the activities of TRMPAC has centered on its work on behalf of Republicans in the 2002 general election. However, perhaps its greatest impact was felt during the previous Republican primary, when TRMPAC screened potential candidates and supported those who best embodied Republican ideology, including showing a willingness to support tort reform and DeLay's friend Tom Craddick for House Speaker. TRMPAC subsequently endorsed particular candidates, contributed to those in tight primary races, and, along with its allies, sent mailings attacking their opponents. This critical involvement in the primaries changed the likely outcome of several races and ensured that the Republicans seeking election in the general election would be the "right" Republicans.

An example of this screening process: acting Lieutenant Governor Bill Ratliff was denied the Republican nomination for lieutenant governor in 2002. As the acting lieutenant governor, Ratliff was the logical person to become the Republican candidate for that office. Moreover, he had served with distinction and was very well respected by political observers and writers and by Republican and Democratic senators. However, major Republican donors and activists deemed him insufficiently partisan, so he was compelled to withdraw from the race in 2001 only days after declaring his intention to seek the Republican nomination.

The Democratic Party also expected partisan loyalty from its lawmakers and was prepared to enforce it. Only a handful of House Democrats failed to join in the boycott in May 2003. Three of them were targeted in 2004, and all three lost in the Democratic primary.

A Textbook for Partisan Gerrymandering

The 2003 redistricting plan in Texas was a textbook example of how parties can configure districts to minimize the voting strength of opposing groups while maximizing their own electoral opportunities. Chapters Five and Thirteen discuss how the plan masterfully used the techniques of packing, fracturing, dismantling, and destroying constituent-member relations.

Although the redistricting process in Texas lasted over six months and involved thousands of persons—including lawmakers, attorneys, legislative staffers, members of the general public, expert witnesses, local elected officials, and newspaper editorial staffs—the districts in the final plan were the product of a few like-minded persons at the very end of the process. This cabal felt free to disregard all that had gone on before in the process, and under national partisan pressures and the guidance of DeLay, was able to fashion a masterfully partisan districting plan.

Legal Implications

The 2003 redistricting raised several significant legal issues. It was challenged in federal court, and at the time of this writing, the case remains pending at the United States Supreme Court.

The plan was attacked as an unconstitutional partisan gerrymander. That attack was twice rejected by the federal courts and seems unlikely to succeed, given the historical dominance of the Democratic Party in Texas.

A second and more plausible constitutional attack was based on the fundamental principle of "equal representation for equal numbers of persons." This challenge raised the question whether a state or local government is free mid-decade to replace a valid election system with a new one without doing more to ensure equal representation than relying on outdated census data that it knows is wrong. In a state like Texas, with a growing and shifting population, and with a mushrooming minority population, redistricting with old census data can be used to discriminate against ethnic and racial minorities. This happened in Texas.

If upheld, the 2003 redistricting in Texas will establish a precedent for redrawing election districts at any time during a decade, despite the lack of valid population data. Officials in other states, including California, Illinois, Georgia, New York, and New Mexico, have raised the possibility of engaging in mid-decade redistricting for partisan reasons. Unnecessarily redistricting without accurate population data endangers the most basic election principle in this country—i.e., the right of equal representation for equal numbers of persons—and opens a door for racial and ethnic discrimination.

The events in Texas also demonstrate the importance of the Voting Rights Act as a constraint on partisan gerrymandering. In U.S. politics, race has become a proxy for party affiliation. Areas dominated by African American and Hispanic residents are presumed likely to vote Democratic. If unconstrained by the Voting Rights Act, Democratic-controlled legislatures in Texas would have continued to split minority communities among multiple districts to maximize the election of Democrats. In 2003, Republicans in Texas pushed (and may have exceeded) the edge of what is legally permitted under the Voting Rights Act, which compelled them to avoid blatantly reducing the number of districts in which minority voters could determine the outcome of elections (thus probably allowing Democrats to win). If unconstrained by the Voting Rights Act, Republican map drawers in 2003 easily could have reduced the number of predominately African American and Hispanic districts included in the final plan, and thereby further enhanced the number of Republicans elected to Congress. This effect of the Voting Rights Act in Texas in 2003 is evidence of the need to retain its provisions set to expire in 2007.

These legal issues are discussed in Chapter Sixteen. The Supreme Court of the United States agreed to consider challenges to the redistricting plan and heard arguments on March 1, 2006. The outcome before the Supreme Court is discussed in the Afterword to this book.

Unusual Parliamentary Tactics

The events in 2003 also set a precedent for the use of extraordinary parliamentary tactics to defeat disfavored legislation. Faced with a circumstance in which all of the state officers in Texas were Republican and both houses of the state legislature had Republican majorities, Democratic lawmakers realized that they had no chance of defeating the Republican redistricting plan on an up-or-down majority vote. Therefore, the Democrats relied on other tactics. One of these tactics was the much publicized walkout or boycott to deny the Republicans a legislative quorum. In the Texas Senate, Democrats relied on procedural rules forbidding consideration of any redistricting plan that lacked the support of at least two-thirds of the members of the Senate. Democrats also chose to not even try to compromise on a plan that was less egregious than the most aggressive of the Republican plans. The Democratic strategy is specifically discussed in Chapter Six, but the effectiveness (or ineffectiveness) of that strategy marks every stage of this story.

The Judicial Process

The 2003 redistricting in Texas tested the effect of partisanship on the fairness and impartiality of the judicial process. At least since *Bush v. Gore* (2000), courts have been criticized for functioning as tools of partisanship rather than agents of justice when dealing with politically important cases. State and federal courts frequently became involved with the 2003 redistricting; the political implications of each potential ruling were apparent to the judges and the participants in the case. How did the courts react? This book provides some insight.

The Price of Hubris?

Finally, this tale is one about the potential costs of hubris—excessive pride. When the redistricting began in 2003, Tom DeLay was at or near the height of his political power. As House majority leader, he was widely considered to be the most powerful Republican on Capitol Hill. He had acquired that reputation through the smart and sometimes ruthless use of congressional power and private money to increase the Republican majority in Congress, maintain party discipline among House Republicans, and make the lobbying community in Washington first bipartisan, then predominately Republican through the so-called "K Street Project."[13] He used these same assets in Texas. The outcome in Texas in 2003 seemed at the time to confirm and enhance DeLay's political reputation and power. There was even some talk that adding six new Republicans from Texas would allow DeLay to become Speaker of the House.

In hindsight, however, some of DeLay's actions during 2001–2002 and 2003 were foolish. They set in motion a cascade of events that ultimately brought him down. As one Democratic state senator recently mused in an interview with me, the Texas Democratic lawmakers in 2003 were like the hunters who first threw their spears at a mammoth: they may have been crushed, but their weapons inflicted the first wounds of the many that would be necessary over time "to bring the beast down." By 2006, DeLay's seemingly invulnerable position was gone, and he found himself fighting for political survival.

CHAPTER 2

Partisan Politics and Redistricting in Texas

The history of electoral politics in Texas during the latter half of the twentieth century can best be described as the story of the dominance, decline, and eventual eclipse of the Democratic Party as the state's majority party.
—HENDERSON V. PERRY (2005)

The extraordinary events of 2003 in Texas are best understood against the background of the history of partisan politics in Texas. For over 100 years, from the 1870s until the 1980s, the Democratic Party dominated congressional, state, and local elections in the state. A victory by a candidate in the Democratic Party primary was tantamount to winning election to office. Rarely, if at all, were Democratic candidates seriously opposed in any general election.

A sprinkling of Republicans began winning congressional and state legislative seats in the 1960s, but they were a feeble minority, subject to domination by Democratic elected officials on all partisan issues and to potential discrimination in the drawing of congressional and state legislative district lines. For the Republican Party, the chance to flex its power over redistricting in 2003 presented a time for payback.

Nineteenth-Century Republicans

The Republican Party did not exist as an official organization in Texas until 1867, although the provisional governor (A. J. Hamilton) appointed by President Andrew Johnson in 1865 was a Republican.[1] Under President Johnson there were few restrictions on voting or office holding by former Confederates. African American Texans, however, were still unable to vote. As a result, Democrat J. W. Throckmorton (a Unionist) was elected governor of Texas in

1866. Then the U.S. Congress stepped in. Under congressional Reconstruction, African Americans gained the right to vote, military rule was imposed, former Confederates were disqualified from voting, and Throckmorton was expelled from office. The federal military commander appointed Elisha M. Pease governor.[2] Republicans controlled the state's constitutional convention of 1868–1869 and ratified a new constitution granting full rights to the freed slaves. The state legislature was dominated by Republicans, many of whom were African American. Pease resigned in 1869 over differences with the federal military commander. The ensuing gubernatorial campaign was primarily between "Radical Republican" Edmund J. Davis and former governor (and moderate Republican) A. J. Hamilton. Davis won by a mere 800 votes. During this period, Republicans also controlled three of the state's four congressional seats and both U.S. Senate seats.

Davis was to be the last Republican governor in Texas for 107 years. In 1872, Congress restored political rights to most former Confederates.Though defeated by a two-to-one margin for reelection in 1873, he hoped to remain in office with the support of federal troops. On January 12, 1874, when the new and overwhelmingly Democratic legislature convened and the newly elected governor (Richard Coke) prepared to take office, they found Davis barricaded on the first floor of the state Capitol, protected by state troops and his own state militia. Davis was waiting for a response from President Ulysses S. Grant to an appeal for federal troops. Grant declined his request. On January 16, Davis left the Capitol by horse-drawn carriage, to the cheers of his faithful militia.

While Davis was governor, Republicans also controlled the state legislature.[3] For the remainder of the nineteenth century, the Republican Party remained largely a party of African Americans. African American Norris Wright Cuney was the party leader from 1883 to 1896. Even after Democrats assumed their control of state offices, several African American Republicans continued to win election to the state legislature through the latter part of the nineteenth century.[4] Republican congressman (Robert B. Hawley) served until 1901.

Republican Gains in Congress and the State Legislature

The first Republican elected to Congress from Texas in the twentieth century was Harry M. Wurzbach (Seguin) elected in 1920.[5] Republican Ben Guill won a seat temporarily in a special election in 1950. Voters in Dallas elected Bruce Alger to Congress from 1955 to 1965. Ed Foreman was elected to Congress from West Texas in 1962. Both Alger and Foreman were defeated in 1964 when their congressional districts were redrawn as part of a statewide redistricting.

In 1966, two Republicans, George H. W. Bush (Houston) and Robert D. Price (Pampa) were elected to Congress. These were joined by a third Republican, James M. Collins (Grand Prairie) in 1968.

A handful of Republicans won election to the Texas legislature during the period 1900–1931. The most prominent of these was Julius Real (Kerrville) who served five terms in the state senate. In 1932 the Republicans lost the African American voting bloc as a result of the policies and candidacy of Franklin Roosevelt. Between 1931 and 1951, no Republican served in the state legislature. The first Republican state representative elected thereafter was Edward T. Dicker (Dallas) in 1950; he served 1951–1953. The first Republicans were elected to the state senate in 1966. Henry Grover (Houston) served until 1973. Ike Harris (Dallas) served until 1995. These Republicans, and a few others (e.g., Senators Bob McFarland and Betty Andujar), were the isolated exceptions within a state legislature that otherwise was composed wholly of Democrats. Although the vote was growing for Republican candidates (including for president) during this period, there actually was little growth in the number of Texans who identified with the party at the state level. Texans still largely saw themselves as Democrats.

A useful date for beginning to track the partisan change among congressional and state legislative seats in Texas is 1971. The state had been compelled by the courts in the 1960s to adopt state legislative and congressional districts of essentially equal population. Not unexpectedly, the congressional districts that had in the past contained marked excesses in population included the "ever-expanding metropolitan areas of Houston, Dallas, San Antonio and Fort Worth."[6] With the state's implementation of this federal constitutional requirement for equal representation of equal numbers of persons, voters residing in insular areas of political or partisan cohesion that previously had been submerged became better able to elect persons of their choice. This meant that the increasingly Republican suburbs of the state's largest cities became entitled to their own election districts and capable of electing Republicans. The results can be seen in the election of Republicans to the state senate and to Congress in 1966.

In 1971 there were three Republicans in a Texas congressional delegation of twenty-three. Over the next thirty-one years the number of Republicans grew, despite the efforts of the Democrats to redistrict at the beginning of each decade to limit further Republican gains (Table 2.1). At all times through the 2002 election, the proportion of Republicans in the state's congressional delegation was significantly less than the percentage of votes cast for Republican candidates in statewide elections. Based on an average of the percentage of votes garnered in all statewide elections (other than president), Republican

Table 2.1. Republican gains in U.S. congressional seats, 1971–2003

Year	1973	1983	1993	2003
Republicans	4	6	9	15
Democrats	19	21	21	17

statewide strength increased from 37 percent in 1962 to 40 percent in 1982, 49 percent in 1992, 52 percent in 1994 and 57 percent in 2002.[7] According to this analysis, the "statewide voting strength" of the Republican Party varied during 1962–1988, but grew steadily in each election cycle after 1988.

The number of Republicans in the state legislature also increased over this period (1971–2001) (Table 2.2). A surge in the number of Republican lawmakers in the Texas House came in the 1970s as the state was compelled by the federal courts to abandon multimember state legislative districts in the state's most populated counties. Countywide multimember districts had permitted insular minority groups (including racial and political minorities) to be outvoted by the opposing majority. As these multimember districts were replaced with equipopulous single-member districts, Republican areas, primarily in the suburbs surrounding the largest cities, could more easily elect Republicans to the Texas House. The effect can be seen in the jump in the number of Republican House members between the 1971 (10) and 1981 (35) legislative sessions. The number of Republicans elected to the House continued to increase through the 1980s and 1990s as more voters, particularly in the previously heavily Democratic rural areas of Texas, began to vote for Republican candidates in the general elections.

The surge in the number of Republican members of the Senate in the 1990s followed the ordering by a federal court of a redistricting plan for the 1992 election in lieu of the plan adopted by the legislature. The legislature's plan had been blocked by an objection from the Department of Justice under Section 5 of the Voting Rights Act, but it was the Republicans, not racial minorities, who were the primary beneficiaries of the court plan. Thirteen Republicans won election to the Senate in 1992. By the end of the decade, the court-drawn districts had given the Republicans a majority of the seats in the state senate.

At the beginning of the redistricting cycle after the 2000 census, Republicans constituted a majority of the Texas Senate (16 of 31 senators), but remained a minority in the House (72 of 150 representatives). After the 2002 elections, the Republican majority in the Senate increased to 19–12 and, for the first time in 130 years, the Republican Party held a majority of seats in the House (88–62).

Table 2.2. Republican gains in the Texas state legislature, 1971–2001

Year	1971	1981	1991	2001
Senate	2	7	9	16
House	10	35	60	72

The battle cry of some House Republicans in 2003 was that the Democrats had controlled the House of Representatives "since God made dirt", or at least for the past "130 years", and now that Republicans at last controlled the House, it was payback time.

Republican Success in Statewide Offices

Texans have regularly voted Republican in presidential elections since 1948. Texas voters supported Republican Dwight Eisenhower in 1952 and 1956. Democrat John Kennedy carried Texas by barely 46,000 votes in 1960. Lyndon Johnson carried his home state in 1964 and 1968, but Richard Nixon won in 1972. The last Democratic presidential candidate to win in Texas was Jimmy Carter in 1976. The Republican candidate has won in each of the last seven elections.

The first Republican to win election to a statewide office in Texas after 1872 was John Tower to the U.S. Senate in 1961. Tower remained the sole Republican official elected statewide until oilman Bill Clements won a shocking victory over Texas Attorney General John Hill for governor in 1978. Clements famously tossed a rubber chicken on Hill's plate at a political function and claimed that he would wrap then unpopular President Carter around Hill's neck like a rubber chicken. Clements's victory was a result of many factors. Important for subsequent elections in Texas was the last-minute get-out-the-vote, anti-Hill effort directed at churchgoers. During the same election, Republican James A. Baker III, the future U.S. secretary of state and captain of the Bush legal team in the Florida recount in 2000, ran a well-financed but losing campaign for Texas attorney general.

Clements subsequently was defeated for reelection as governor in 1982, but ran again and was returned to the governor's mansion in 1986. Democrat Ann Richards followed Clements as governor. She was defeated for reelection in 1994 by George W. Bush.

The first Republican elected to a statewide office other than governor or

U.S. Senator was Tom Phillips, who was appointed Chief Justice of the Texas Supreme Court by Clements and won election to that office in 1988.

Texas has twenty-nine state or federal offices filled by statewide elections.[8] In 1990, most of these offices were held by Democrats. Republican Phil Gramm held one U.S. Senate seat; the other was held by Democrat Lloyd Bentsen. Justice Phillips was Chief Justice; two other Republicans served on the state supreme court. Otherwise the Democrats held the critical state offices. However, this Democratic dominance began to disappear dramatically with the 1990 election.

In the 1990 elections, future U.S. senators Kay Bailey Hutchison and John Cornyn first won statewide office, along with future governor Rick Perry. Hutchison was elected state treasurer. Cornyn was elected to the state supreme court. Perry won election as agriculture commissioner. Year after year during the 1990s Democrats were swept out of office, or Republicans were elected to replace Democrats who did not run for reelection. Democratic Lieutenant Governor Bob Bullock remained a formidable political figure for most of the decade, but, ironically, he also was a great friend of Governor George W. Bush and was his valuable ally in the Democratic-controlled legislature while Bush was governor. Bullock left office voluntarily at the end of his last term in 1999; he died soon thereafter. The other Democratic statewide officials who won in 1994 (Attorney General Dan Morales, Comptroller John Sharp, and Land Commissioner Garry Mauro) also stepped aside in 1998 to seek election to higher office. Such political musical chairs had been usual during the previous decades of Democratic dominance. In 1998, however, none of the Democratic candidates for statewide office was successful.

No Democrat has won a statewide election in Texas since 1994. A few elections have been close, particularly those for lieutenant governor and comptroller in 1998. However, the Republican margin of victory generally has been increasing. George W. Bush won the state by an overwhelming majority in the presidential elections of 2000 (64.1 percent) and 2004 (61 percent). Since 1999, Republicans have held all twenty-nine of the statewide elective offices in Texas.

The Karl Rove Factor

The transition from Democratic to Republican officeholders in Texas was not a result of the activities of Karl Rove. However, he was an important player during this change.

In 1978, Rove aided Bill Clements in his successful race for governor. In

1981, Rove set up a political direct-mail business. He continued to assist Clements and other Republican candidates. Clements was defeated for reelection in 1982, but two years later Rove worked on the campaign of Phil Gramm, who won the U.S. Senate seat that had been held by John Tower. Gramm defeated Democrat Lloyd Doggett, who in 2003 would be one of the targeted Democratic incumbent congressmen. In 1986, Rove was instrumental in the successful bid of Bill Clements to recapture the governorship. In 1988, he orchestrated the election of Tom Phillips as Chief Justice of the Texas Supreme Court.

In the 1990s, Rove was instrumental in electing many of the Republicans who won statewide office. He engineered the defeat of two promising Democratic candidates, Jim Hightower (defeated for reelection as the state's agriculture commissioner in 1990) and Lena Guerrero (defeated in 1992 for election to the railroad commission seat to which she had been appointed in 1991). He helped future governor Rick Perry win his first state office as agriculture commissioner in 1990. In 1994, Rove helped Kay Bailey Hutchison win the U.S. Senate seat previously held by a Democrat; she had first won the seat in a special election in 1993. He also was the strategist and consultant for George W. Bush in his victory over Ann Richards in 1994. By the time Rove left Texas for Washington with president-elect Bush, his former clients held the Texas governorship, both of its U.S. Senate seats, a majority of the seats on the state supreme court and most of the other statewide offices. However, Rove's involvement was not limited to statewide elections. He also was instrumental in helping Republicans win important legislative seats.

Rove's effective work on behalf of so many successful Republican candidates paid off during the redistricting effort in 2003. Many of the key players (e.g., Governor Rick Perry and Senator Robert Duncan) had been his clients. More importantly, Rove had established a solid connection with the major sources of funding for Republican causes, such as Kenneth Lay and Bob Perry in Houston and Louis Beecherl in Dallas; the latter two also played a major role in what happened in Texas in the 2002 election and in the 2003 redistricting.

Changing Parties from Democrat to Republican

To many participants in Texas politics, such as former governor Ann Richards, the growth of the vote for Republicans in Texas over the past four decades is merely a shift of conservative Democrats out of the Democratic Party. From this perspective, the battle now between Republicans and Democrats is only a continuation of a battle that has raged for the past 100 years between the conservative and liberal wings of the Democratic Party. On many issues affecting the role of government or fiscal policy, the views of the conservative Democrats of the past were often indistinguishable from the views of the Republicans. Some observers suggest that the conservative wing of the Democratic Party has merely morphed into the Republican Party.

A transition can be seen as early as the 1950s, when many prominent conservative Democrats (e.g., Governor Allan Shivers) backed Republican presidential candidate Dwight Eisenhower. Eisenhower won a majority of the vote in Texas. However, voters did not generally identify with the Republican Party. As late as 1978 (the year Bill Clements won the governorship in Texas) only 150,000 Texans voted in the Republican primary, as compared with 1.8 million in the Democratic primary.

However, as statewide voting trends continued to shift toward the Republican Party and more Texans began to identify themselves as Republican, Democratic elected officials began to switch parties. Many of the elected leaders of the Republican Party in Texas in the 1990s first ran or were first elected as Democrats, but then changed to the Republican Party. For example, U.S. Senator Phil Gramm, Governor Rick Perry, and former Governor John Connally all began as Democrats. Even Congressman Tom DeLay admits voting Democratic before running for the Texas legislature as a Republican in 1978. In 2003 one of the targeted Democratic congressmen, Ralph Hall, switched to the Republican Party and won reelection in 2004 in his newly redrawn district.

Another reason for the growth of Republican voting strength in Texas over the period 1970–2000 was the large influx of persons from other states in the United States. Economic growth in Texas attracted many persons from states where a strong Republican Party already existed. These new Texans were not burdened by decades of voting only Democratic, and rapidly found themselves at home in the Texas Republican Party. In 1981, after acknowledging the likelihood that Republicans would continue to pick up additional congressional seats in Texas, Lieutenant Governor Bill Hobby, a Democrat, joked that some of these new Texans "come from states where they didn't know that it is socially unacceptable to be a Republican. We hope to educate them to our local mores and customs."[9]

Independent Voters and Ticket Splitting

Many Texans have voted independently in the past. When John Tower in 1961 and Bill Clements in 1978 won election despite the overwhelming dominance of the Democratic Party in other races, their successes were traceable to the presence of significant ticket splitting by voters. Most voters at the time still

Table 2.3. Ticket splitting by voters in six Texas congressional districts, 2002

District	Democratic candidate	Hometown	Vote for (%)	Democratic vote for governor (%)
1	Max Sandlin	Marshall	56	39
2	Jim Turner	Crockett	61	40
4	Ralph Hall	Rockwall	59	30
9	Nick Lampson	Beaumont	59	46
11	Chet Edwards	Waco	52	34
17	Charles Stenholm	Abilene	52	28

cast their ballots predominantly for Democratic candidates, but in the cases of Tower and Clements, also cast a vote for one or more Republican candidates.

Until Kay Bailey Hutchison was elected U.S. senator in 1993, the voters of Texas had for thirty years sent both a Republican and Democrat to the U.S. Senate. The last Democratic governor of Texas, Ann Richards, also won in part in 1990 because of ticket splitting that resulted in her victory over Republican Clayton Williams, despite Republican successes in other contests that same November.

Over the past fifteen years, this ticket-splitting phenomenon apparently has declined, particularly in statewide races. Some voters continue, however, to split their vote among both Republican and Democratic candidates in other races. For example, most of the Democratic incumbent congressmen who were targeted by Republicans in the 2003 redistricting had won in 2002 because of ticket splitting by voters in districts that otherwise had gone strongly Republican at the same time in statewide races (Table 2.3).

The phenomenon of ticket splitting also continues to survive to some extent at the local level in many rural areas of Texas, where county officials frequently are Democrats in a county that otherwise consistently votes Republican in statewide races.

Even though Republicans have won every statewide race since 1994, until 2006 the Republican Party statewide primary has never attracted more voters than the Democratic Party primary. In the 2002 primaries, there were 1,003,388 votes cast in the Democratic Party primary and only 622,423 in the Republican primary. As with any election, turnout was probably driven to some extent by the number and intensity of contested races; and in fact the Democrats featured several hotly contested statewide contests and the Republicans essentially none. Also, voter turnout in the primary (1.65 million) was far less than in the general election (more than 4.5 million).

Voter participation statewide has always been less in Republican primaries, even over the past decade of Republican ascendancy in the general election. In the last five rounds of statewide elections, more votes were cast in the Democratic primary than in the Republican: in 1990, the figures were 1,487,260 for the Democrats and 855,231 for the Republicans; in 1994, 1,036,944 and 557,340; in 1998, 664,532 and 596,839; and, as mentioned above, in 2002, 1,003,388 and 622,423, and in 2004, 839,231 and 687,615. Some Democrats suggest that these primary numbers are significant: that they indicate more Texas voters continue to identify themselves as Democrats than Republicans and that Republican success in statewide races has come as a result of attracting independent voters—a reversible trend.

It appeared for a while that the 2006 Republican primary in Texas would promise an interesting test of the phenomenon of ticket-splitting because incumbent Governor Perry was being openly challenged in the press by Comptroller Carole Keeton Strayhorn; both are Republicans. In anticipation of opposing Perry in the Republican primary, Strayhorn openly appealed in 2005 for Democrats and independents to "cross over" and vote in the 2006 Republican primary to overcome Perry's strength among Republican Party loyalists; she claimed that winning the Republican primary was "tantamount to election." In 2006, however, Strayhorn changed her mind and announced that she would run in the November general election as an independent rather than challenge Perry in the spring. The fall campaign and outcome will provide an indication of whether independent voters can still affect a statewide election in Texas.

Another recent election suggests that split-ticket voting in local or district races survives. In a special election in early 2006 to fill a vacancy in state House district 48, Democrat Donna Howard won election in a Travis County district that had voted heavily Republican in prior statewide elections. Her victory caused one observer to define a moderate Republican as a conservative who cares more about adequate funding to hire a new calculus teacher for his or her child at the local public school than about hot-button ideological issues like school vouchers or the right to life.

Bipartisanship in the Texas Legislature

Texas has enjoyed an extraordinary institutional bipartisanship in its legislature, as measured by the appointment of both Democratic and Republican committee chairmen by presiding officers of the opposing party.

The first Republican committee chairman in the Senate under a Democratic lieutenant governor came in 1981 when Lieutenant Governor Bill Hobby appointed Dallas Republican Ike Harris chairman of the Economic Development Committee. Harris had previously chaired at least two subcommittees or interim committees. Republican Tom Craddick was appointed chairman of the House Natural Resources Committee in 1975 by Democratic Speaker Bill Clayton. He was the first Republican committee chairman in the House in over 100 years. Craddick continued to serve as a committee chairman under various Democratic Speakers. After Democrat Pete Laney was elected Speaker, he appointed Craddick in 1993 as chairman of the Ways and Means Committee. Craddick served as chairman until the 1999 legislative session.

Every lieutenant governor and speaker since the 1970s has followed this tradition of including persons from the opposing party as committee chairmen. This tradition continued in 2003, when new Republican Speaker Tom Craddick selected twelve Democrats among his House committee chairmen. Moreover, many other Democrats served in 2003 as vice-chairmen or chief budget officers (CBOs) of House committees. Eight of the chairmen of committees or standing subcommittees in the Senate in 2003 under Republican David Dewhurst were Democrats. Despite the extraordinary partisan rancor that occurred in 2003, most of these persons retained their chairmanships in 2005 in the House and Senate.

This history of bipartisanship within the legislative structure in Texas is highly unusual. Most other state legislatures are organized on a partisan basis, like Congress, with the majority party holding all or virtually all of the committee chairmanships. Historically, this institutional bipartisanship in Texas has played a valuable role in effectively moving legislation through the legislative process and avoiding purely partisan showdowns.

At the same time, however, there is an understandable expectation by the Speaker or lieutenant governor that any person appointed committee chairman will be a "team player." Being on the leadership team does not preclude disagreeing with the presiding officer's position. However, neither Republican nor Democratic presiding officers have regularly countenanced strongly partisan or uncooperative members of the other party as committee chairmen. An example is what happened to Tom Craddick. Democratic Speaker Pete Laney appointed Craddick chairman of the powerful Ways and Means committee in 1993, but stripped him of the chairmanship in 1999. Craddick, through a political action committee, had tried in 1996 and again in 1998 to elect a Republican majority in the Texas House and to depose Laney as Speaker.[10] Laney in 1999 understandably refused to reappoint Craddick committee chair.

Some observers suggest that legislative bipartisanship in Texas was actually born as an alliance between conservative Democrats who had been elected Speaker or lieutenant governor, and Republicans. In fact, some observers suggest that several past Democratic Speakers were selected over more liberal Democrats because of their ability to attract Republican support. For example, in 1983, Republicans were among the first to support the candidacy of conservative Democrat Gib Lewis for Speaker. This alliance also allowed conservatives to continue to prevail on many legislative issues, even as a greater percentage of Democrat lawmakers came from minority areas or from the liberal wing of the party.

Members of both the Texas Senate and House in 2005 indicated that despite at least the appearance of institutional bipartisanship, the organization and activities of the legislature were more partisan than in the past. Members of the House in particular felt that their chamber was becoming increasingly organized along partisan lines, and that party discipline was leading to party-line votes on most substantive issues. This pattern in the House left Democrats generally unable to materially affect legislation, which moved at the will of the Republican leadership.

Bipartisanship remains more prevalent in the Texas Senate. Senators of both parties credit the smaller size of the Senate, its more collegial atmosphere, and the need, in view of the two-thirds vote requirement, to gain bipartisan support for major legislation.

Past Partisan Gerrymandering of Congressional Districts

Partisanship is accepted legally as an unavoidable aspect of virtually any redistricting.[11] Republicans justified the partisanship of the 2003 redistricting by the alleged mistreatment of Republicans by Democrats during redistricting in the past. Democrats responded that they had never been as ruthlessly partisan when they controlled the process. Specifically, Democrats claimed that unlike prior redistricting plans that generally protected all incumbents, the 2003 plan was designed to defeat incumbent Democratic congressmen. Republicans responded that this is not a wholly accurate description of past redistricting, and to the extent it is correct, it is a distinction without a difference because Democrats in the past were merely trying to hold on to power in the face of increasing voter preference for Republicans. Republicans further argued that past opportunities for Democrats to target Republican seats in the midst of this growth had been minimal.

Whether a difference in the degree of partisanship existed or, if it existed, was even important is not clear. It is certain, however, that Democrats repeatedly drew districts intended to disadvantage the Republican Party. For the past three decades, the redistricting plans passed by the Democratic-controlled legislature consistently packed staunchly Republican voters, especially those in the suburbs, into as few districts as possible. The plans also apparently targeted some Republicans in rural districts for defeat, such as Republican congressmen Ed Foreman (Midland) in 1964 and Bob Price (Amarillo) in 1972.

The circumstances described below are given merely as examples of past partisan gerrymandering, without any attempt at comprehensiveness.

1963–1965

The Texas legislature in 1965 enacted a redistricting plan to comply with federal court orders to create districts of equal population. This enactment came after a roiling court battle that had been initiated in 1963 on behalf of future president George H. W. Bush, who was chairman at the time of the Harris County Republican Party. The court battle continued after the 1965 plan was revealed. The primary legal question was whether the plan met the "one person, one vote" requirement of the U.S. Constitution. However, the plaintiffs also challenged the districts drawn in Dallas, San Antonio, and Midland (the splitting of Midland County from Ector County) as being partisan gerrymanders drawn to dilute Republican voting strength. The 1963 redistricting plan—the original target of the lawsuit—had in fact resulted in the defeat of the two existing Republican incumbent congressmen (Alger and Foreman) in 1964.

Specifically, the complaint alleged that in Dallas "a vigorous Republican stronghold of demonstrated outspoken, effective, militant, articulate conservatives" had been placed "among rural people" in a district that stretched 205 miles to the west. The federal court conceded that more compact districts might have been drawn that would have given these voters greater political influence by joining them instead with "more kindred, like-minded souls" in the Dallas area. The court, however, rejected all partisan gerrymandering claims on the basis that it could find neither a partisan gerrymandering purpose nor effect in the plan.

1971

The congressional districts drawn by the Texas legislature in 1971 were challenged in federal court. The plan was acknowledged to promote "constituency-representative relations," which the U.S. Supreme Court explained as "a policy frankly aimed at maintaining existing relationships between incumbent congressmen and their constituents and preserving the seniority the members of the State's delegation have achieved in the United States House of Representatives."[12] In other words, the plan was drawn primarily to protect the twenty Democratic incumbents. Republicans allege that the plan also targeted Republican Congressman Robert Price for defeat, but Price won reelection in 1972. The plan also provided a congressional district in Houston that resulted in the election of the first African American (Barbara Jordan) to Congress from Texas in the twentieth century.

Although the legislatively enacted plan was struck down because of its population deviations, the court-ordered plan used for 1972 and subsequent elections during the decade maintained the "policy" of the legislation (i.e., keeping "constituency-representative relations" intact). This respect for incumbency minimized Republican successes. All four Republican incumbent congressmen were reelected in 1972, but despite statewide voting strength of 45 percent in the 1980 election, Republicans were still able to successfully elect only five of the state's twenty-four congressmen.

1981–1983

In 1981, the governor of Texas was Republican Bill Clements. Both the Texas House and Senate had substantial Democratic majorities. Clements vetoed the legislature's state-senate and congressional redistricting plans. The Senate districts subsequently were drawn by the Legislative Redistricting Board, composed at the time entirely of Democratic state officers. The legislature reconvened in special session during the summer of 1981 to redraw the congressional districts.

The main point of contention was Clements's demand for a majority-minority district (i.e., one in which a majority of the voters belong to an ethnic or racial minority) in Dallas. Such a district would have had the partisan effect of reducing the number of dependably Democratic voters spread among the surrounding districts in the Dallas area, increasing the possibility of Republican success in those areas. (The racial and ethnic effects of this proposal are discussed in Chapter Three.) Specifically, the Democratic congressman seen as being in the greatest jeopardy was Jim Mattox, since the Republican plan would cause his district to lose most of its minority population. After a gubernatorial veto and a special session, the legislature eventually passed legislation in 1981 that created a majority-minority district meeting Clements's mandate. However, before the 1982 primary election, a federal court dismantled the legislature's majority-minority district and adopted a plan that again spread the minority voters among several districts. Following Clements's defeat in the 1982 general election, the Democratic-controlled legislature passed legislation in 1983 essentially adopting the court plan for the remainder of the decade.

Clements's loss in 1982 marked a sharp drop in the percentage of Republican votes in statewide races that year, to 40 percent. However, the percentage recovered, and during the 1980s the number of Republican congressmen increased to eight (including the election of Tom DeLay to Congress in 1984).

1991

The Almanac of American Politics described the 1991 Texas congressional redistricting as "the shrewdest gerrymander of the 1990s . . . The plan carefully creates Democratic districts with incredibly convoluted lines and packs heavily Republican suburban areas into just a few districts." Under this plan, Democrats won twenty-one of the state's thirty congressional seats in 1992, even though this election marked "the tipping point" whereby Republicans first consistently obtained 50 percent or more of the statewide vote.

The 1991 redistricting plan was a "shrewd" redistricting with "incredibly convoluted lines" because it protected Democratic incumbents while also drawing minority-opportunity districts to comply with the Voting Rights Act. These minority districts are discussed further in Chapter Three. These minority districts were bizarrely shaped because of the legislature's use of computer technology to draw the districts literally census block by census block in a search for enough African Americans and Hispanics to fulfill the requirements both for minority voters and for equal population.

Republicans challenged the plan in federal court as a partisan gerrymander; they lost again. A later legal challenge invalidated the bizarrely shaped minority districts as unconstitutional racial gerrymanders. However, the court's remedial plan merely eliminated the most outré of the plan's urban tentacles, leaving the political effect of the plan unchanged.

Once the minority-opportunity districts were created, there were considerably fewer dependably Democratic voters remaining to be spread among the other districts. The carefully drawn districts in the 1991 plan included fewer of the ever-decreasing number of ostensibly Democratic Anglo voters. As a result, Republicans began to win in many of the districts. Several Democratic incumbent congressmen lost to Republican challengers. For example, the 1991 plan split the city of Amarillo in the Texas Panhandle in an attempt to save Democrat Congressman Bill Sarpalius, but he was nevertheless defeated by Republican William McClellan (Mac) Thornberry of Clarendon in 1994. District 23 in southwest Texas was redrawn to absorb a heavily Republican area in Bexar County, with the result that Democratic incumbent Albert Bustamante lost to Republican Henry Bonilla in 1992 against the background of press reports that the Democratic incumbent was being investigated. Bustamante later was indicted and convicted. Republicans captured three other seats in

1994 when the Democratic incumbents (John Bryant, Jim Chapman, and Pete Geren) did not seek reelection in increasingly Republican districts.

Ironically, Congressman Tom DeLay is remembered by members of the Texas legislature as urging the Democratic-controlled legislature in 1991 to "protect incumbents." The federal courts later recognized that, in fact, the 1991 congressional redistricting plan protected incumbents and that this was consistent with past state policy of maintaining member-constituent relations. All Republican incumbents won reelection, although Republican congressman Joe Barton complained in 2003 that the 1991 redistricting had taken the expensive, but as yet nonexistent, Superconducting Super Collider from his district and left him with only a portion of his hometown; Barton still won reelection in the heavily Republican district. The number of Republican congressmen increased from nine to thirteen during the 1990s. However, although some Democratic incumbents lost during the 1990s, many others survived against Republican challengers, even though the voters in their congressional districts were by this time consistently supporting Republican candidates in statewide races.

2001

In 2001, each political party controlled a house of the state legislature. Although both the House and Senate tried to pass legislation redrawing congressional and state-representative districts, they failed.

In a series of events that possibly proved consequential for 2003, acting Lieutenant Governor Bill Ratliff appointed Republican senator Jeff Wentworth chairman of the Senate redistricting committee. Known as a moderate Republican, Wentworth obtained some bipartisan support for a redistricting plan that probably would have increased the number of Republicans in the congressional delegation, but would also generally have preserved the seats of all incumbents. Critics attacked the map as being too friendly to Democrats.

To prevent the Senate from considering Wentworth's plan, Republican senators relied on the requirement that two-thirds of the senators (twenty-one of thirty-one) must agree to suspend Senate rules before legislation can be brought to the floor. (This two-thirds voting requirement is discussed in Chapter Six.) Ratliff would not allow Wentworth to try to suspend Senate rules to take up the plan unless Wentworth was able to show a commitment of support from at least twenty-one senators.[13] Wentworth was unable to gather the necessary twenty-one commitments, but told Ratliff that other senators would likely support the suspension motion once it was made. Ratliff, however, would not allow Wentworth to try. Wentworth continues to believe that the votes necessary to suspend the Senate rules to bring up the redistricting bill would have been present if he had been allowed to move to do so.[14] If a bipartisan redistricting bill had been successfully enacted in 2001, the extraordinary events of 2003 might never have occurred. On the other hand, it is far from clear that any congressional redistricting plan supported by Democrats could have avoided a veto by Governor Rick Perry.

When the 2001 regular session ended without a congressional redistricting plan, attention fell on Governor Perry and whether he would call a special session. Congressman DeLay telephoned Senator Ratliff to see whether he would insist on the two-thirds vote requirement in the Senate during a special session. Apparently DeLay felt that he could get a reasonably Republican-friendly plan through the House, but doubted that he could get the necessary twenty-one votes in a Senate that had only sixteen Republicans. Ratliff told DeLay that he would insist on retaining the vote requirement in any special session.[15] Governor Perry did not call a special session, so the task of drawing the congressional districts fell to the courts.

After several months of legal maneuvers, a congressional districting plan was adopted by a three-judge federal panel. The court's plan essentially made only enough changes from the districts used in 2000 to draw in the two new congressional districts that had been apportioned to Texas and to equalize population among all the districts. The two new districts featured strong Republican majorities. In fact, a majority (twenty) of the thirty-two congressional districts in the court plan had voted strongly Republican in statewide elections. Some Democratic incumbents were now thought to be more vulnerable than in the past to a Republican challenge. However, the plan generally left existing constituent-member relations in place by retaining the core of each existing district. Incumbents from both parties benefited.[16]

Republican congressman Thomas M. Davis III (Virginia), the chairman of the National Republican Congressional Committee in 2001, said he was satisfied with the outcome in Texas. Davis explained, "It's a win, period. But maybe it's not as clean a win, in a perfect world, that you would want. It meets our expectations. It does not exceed our expectations."[17] Congressman DeLay was not as generous. He criticized the court map as "incumbent protection" that failed to create any new minority districts or give Republicans what he considered fair representation.[18] Four years later another three-judge court (with two of the same judges as on the panel in 2001) concluded that by making only a minimum of changes, the court in 2001 had unintentionally "perpetuated much of the 1991 Democratic Party gerrymander."[19]

CHAPTER 3

Racial and Ethnic Politics

Racial and ethnic politics have always played a significant role in Texas elections. For most of the nineteenth and twentieth centuries, the Hispanic and African American voters of the state were effectively excluded from participation in the state's electoral process. As these minority voters grew in number and voting strength over the past forty years, the number of African American and Hispanic members of Congress and the Texas legislature increased. Nevertheless, on several occasions in recent decades the Democratic-controlled Texas legislature chose to forgo or even dismantle minority-opportunity districts (i.e., districts in which minority voters have sufficient voting strength to be likely to elect the person of their choice) in order to draw districts likely to preserve Anglo Democratic incumbents in office.

The role of race and ethnicity has become more nuanced, but no less important to the outcome of recent Texas elections. Some observers have even suggested that because race and ethnicity have become a proxy for forecasting political affiliation and voting (i.e., minority voters tend largely to vote Democratic), the issue now overwhelms redistricting.

In 2003 both major political parties understood the crucial importance of the race and ethnicity of voters in any district to the partisan effect of any redistricting plan. Both Republicans and Democrats attempted to exploit equity for racial and ethnic voters as justification for their disparate positions on how districts should be drawn. The truth regarding the impact of the redistricting on African Americans and Hispanics is much more complex than either party has suggested, and is best understood in the context of the evolving role of race and ethnicity in Texas elections over the past sixty years.

Racial and Ethnic Minorities in Texas

There are two significant racial or ethnic minority groups in Texas—African Americans and persons of Hispanic origin or descent.

African American Voters

Most African American voters in Texas are located within largely segregated communities in a handful of urban counties. There are exceptions. Some rural areas of East Texas continue to have a significant percentage of African Americans, many descended from African American farmers. So also, some African Americans have integrated into predominantly Anglo neighborhoods. Most African Americans in Texas, however, reside in insular, segregated communities in the most populous counties in the state. The biggest concentrations are in Harris County (Houston) and Dallas County (Dallas), but substantial African American communities also can be found in Tarrant County (Fort Worth), Travis County (Austin), and Bexar County (San Antonio). Relatively large African American communities also exist in the more populous centers of East Texas (Tyler, Longview, and Marshall), Central Texas (Killeen and Waco), and southeast Texas (Beaumont, Port Arthur, and Galveston).

These widely separated concentrations of African American voters were important in the 2003 redistricting because African American voters in Texas vote overwhelmingly (more than 90 percent) for Democratic candidates. This disenchantment with the Republican Party appears to predate even the Franklin Roosevelt era, and at times in the past has exceeded the support given to Democratic candidates by African Americans nationwide. Adding to the potential partisan potency of the African American vote in Texas was the generally high rate of political participation (i.e., organizing, registering, and voting) among African American voters. This participation rate was generally conceded to equal the rate overall among Anglo voters, but remained behind the rate found in some affluent, mainly Anglo suburban communities.

Therefore, the treatment of these insular African American communities was critical to the partisan effect of any redistricting in 2003. As Anglos in Texas continued to vote in increasing percentages for Republican candidates, the presence of a significant African American population within a legislative or congressional district was certain to affect the viability of any Democratic candidate. Predominantly African American districts were highly likely to elect a Democrat. Nevertheless, Republicans were willing to accept this virtual certainty in some districts if they could then dilute the Democratic vote in the remaining, smaller African American communities by spreading it among districts where it could be overwhelmed by the votes of Anglo, pro-Republican voters. Democrats, on the other hand, would benefit if these historically dependable Democratic voters could populate, in politically significant numbers, as many districts as possible.

The voting patterns among African Americans in the Democratic primary also were important to the 2003 redistricting process. African Americans tended to vote heavily in the Democratic primary. Since many Anglo (and a significant percentage of Hispanic) voters tended to vote in the Republican primary, African American voters could be a majority of voters in the Democratic primary even if they constituted only a minority of the voters in the district. Since African American voters also tended to vote as a bloc for the candidate of their choice, they could control the outcome of a Democratic primary. Therefore, in any district where the winner of the Democratic primary usually wins the general election, African American voters, even if not a majority in the district, could effectively determine the winning candidate. For example, in 2003, congressional districts 24 and 25 were seen by some experts as black-opportunity districts because they generally voted Democratic in the general election and a sizable African American minority in each district effectively controlled the outcome of the Democratic primary.

In 2003, this battle over the placement of African American communities in congressional districts permeated redistricting. Moreover, this battle posed a very real moral and political dilemma for the African American members of the Texas legislature: which plan would be best for African American voters in redistricting? This dilemma is discussed in Chapter Fourteen.

Hispanic Voters

Persons of Hispanic origin also historically have voted Democratic in Texas, but by a somewhat lower percentage in recent years than African Americans. (Hispanic support for Democratic candidates is usually estimated at 70–75 percent. However, some Republican polls showed Bush receiving a majority of Hispanic votes against Kerry in some areas of Texas in 2004).[1] Therefore the placement of Hispanic voters also was important to the outcome of any redistricting plan. However, there were several other specific factors that affected the ability of Hispanics to control primary and general elections and to achieve a voting strength comparable to their percentage of state population. These factors in turn affected redistricting.

Although the percentage of African Americans in Texas (10–12 percent) has remained relatively stable over the past few decades, the Hispanic population has grown. Around 60 percent (i.e., 2.33 million) of the 3.865 million persons the state added during the 1990s identified themselves in the census as being of Hispanic ancestry. By 2000, the Hispanic population had increased to 32.2 percent of the total, whereas the white, non-Hispanic (Anglo) population had decreased from 60.6 percent to 52.4 percent. Estimates from the Texas State Data Center in 2004 indicated that this trend was continuing. In 2004, the U.S. Census Bureau estimated that Anglos no longer made up a majority of the population in Texas.[2] It is possible that Anglos were no longer a majority by the time of redistricting in 2003.

Much of the growth in the Hispanic population occurred along the Texas-Mexico border, as both Hidalgo County (McAllen) and Webb County (Laredo) increased almost 50 percent in population, most of it Hispanic. According to the 2000 census, there were overwhelming Hispanic majorities in some of the most populous border counties, such as Hidalgo (88.3 percent), Cameron (84.3 percent), Webb (94.3 percent), and El Paso (78.2 percent).[3] Away from the border, and excluding the sizable Hispanic presence in and around Bexar and Nueces counties, much of the Hispanic population growth has occurred in rural counties that remain predominantly Anglo, or in urban counties, such as Harris and Dallas, where much of the growth in Hispanic population has occurred in areas that remain predominantly Anglo or African American.

This dispersion of Hispanics among predominantly Anglo or African American areas poses two problems for the drawing of congressional districts. First, the presence of Hispanics in Anglo or African American neighborhoods within a county can be misleading if it is assumed to show either an assimilation of these Hispanic persons into these other cultures or the breakdown of segregated housing patterns. Instead, what appears at a higher level of examination in census data as a dispersion of Hispanics among other racial or ethnic groups in an urban environment is generally found on closer investigation to be highly segregated, predominantly Hispanic housing (e.g., an apartment complex) in the midst of a predominantly Anglo or African American neighborhood. Many of these pockets of Hispanic residents ultimately have little voting significance because many of the residents are ineligible to vote. So also, Hispanic populations in rural counties remain largely in segregated, insular communities within less populated, primarily Anglo counties, or in smaller towns and counties that have gradually become predominantly Hispanic.

This high concentration of Hispanics in counties along the Texas-Mexico border, along with the dispersion of others statewide, further affects redistricting, complicating any effort to draw a proportionate number of districts statewide with a Hispanic voting majority. Any compact district drawn in a heavily Hispanic area of the state, such as along the border with Mexico, will invariably have a very high Hispanic population percentage (80–90 percent). Compact districts drawn elsewhere in the state are unlikely to have even a majority of Hispanics. A federal court resolved this problem in 1982 by adopting a plan that split the contiguous border counties and combined the heavily Hispanic neighborhoods with less Hispanic areas in counties farther north. This districting structure—parallel, noncompact districts stretching for hundreds of miles from the Mexican border toward Central Texas—has remained the basic structure of these districts for the past three decades.

The ability to draw congressional districts containing a majority of Hispanic voters (as opposed to population) is further complicated by the disproportionately low level of political participation among Hispanics. A district with a slight Hispanic population majority, according to the federal decennial census, is highly unlikely to have a majority of Hispanic voters. This phenomenon has three components. First, the percentage of Hispanics eighteen or older (i.e., the voting-age population, or VAP) is lower than that for the Anglos or African Americans. Second, Hispanics old enough to vote continue to register and turn out to vote in lower percentages than their Anglo or African American counterparts.

By far the most important reason, however, for the disproportionate participation of Hispanics as voters in Texas is the shockingly high percentage of the Hispanic VAP that is noncitizen. This characteristic is particularly true in the largest urban counties. For example, the census indicates that over 50 percent of Hispanic residents eighteen or older in Harris County are not U.S. citizens. Therefore, they are ineligible to register to vote. A similarly high percentage of noncitizen Hispanic VAP exists in Dallas County. This is one of the reasons why dispersed pockets of Hispanic population in these urban counties often have very little if any voting significance: the pockets are concentrations of primarily noncitizen residents.

The percentage of noncitizen Hispanics is far higher in the largest counties (Dallas and Harris) than elsewhere in the state, primarily because these centers attract undocumented immigrants to the many low-paying jobs in the construction and service industries. Noncitizenship among voting-age Hispanics generally is much lower outside of Dallas and Harris Counties.

Minority Voter Exclusion in the Nineteenth and Early Twentieth Centuries

For more than half of the twentieth century, racial- and ethnic-minority voters in Texas were excluded from the electoral process. Possibly the most startling but succinct explanation of state policy toward African American voters was embodied explicitly at one time in state law. According to a law adopted at Ku Klux Klan urging by the legislature in 1923:

> [I]n no event shall a Negro be eligible to participate in a Democratic Party primary election in Texas.

The Democratic Party at the time was effectively the only political party in Texas. Persons selected in the party's primaries almost invariably won in the general elections. The fall general election was essentially a nullity. Therefore, banning Negroes from Democratic primaries was tantamount to barring them from any meaningful participation in the electoral process.

The 1923 statute was an explicit statement of a subtler policy of exclusion that more or less prevailed throughout Texas until at least the 1960s. Other exclusionary policies and laws, such as the poll tax and the requirement for property ownership as a qualification for voting, as well as acts and threats of violence, limited African American participation even after they obtained the right to vote. Legal challenges to the exclusionary policy embodied in the 1923 statute led to a series of cases before the U.S. Supreme Court known generally as the "White Primary Cases." It was not until after 1952 that the last vestiges of this blatantly discriminatory policy were finally declared unlawful. Even then, other barriers to meaningful participation by African Americans continued.

Hispanics encountered similar impediments. Spanish and Mexican pioneer ancestors of today's Hispanic residents of Texas preceded Anglos in the territory that now constitutes the state. Many of these "Tejanos" lost their lands or were forced to flee Texas as a result of persecution after Texas became part of the United States. Tejanos remaining in Texas were largely engulfed later in the nineteenth century by continuing Anglo immigration to Texas and by emigrant Mexicans fleeing violence in Mexico. Anglos made little distinction between these traditional Tejano citizens of Texas and the flood of Mexican nationals who came to the state as a largely disenfranchised workforce. Anglos came to characterize all Hispanics as "Mexicans," and social stratification placed Anglos in dominant positions and "Mexicans" generally below. Members of the state's growing Anglo majority often looked with contempt on the Hispanics' social standing, lifestyles, religion, and values. Direct and indirect limits on voting or holding office, along with discriminatory policies in education, housing, voter registration, etc., effectively prevented large numbers of Hispanic citizens from voting or electing persons of their choice at the state or local levels. For example, at one time state law prohibited anyone from serving

Table 3.1. Racial and ethnic minorities among Texas lawmakers, 1961

Total		African American	Hispanic
Texas Senate	31	0	1*
Texas House	150	0	6
Congressional	22	0	1*

* These numbers are for the same person. Henry B. Gonzalez was sworn in as a state senator in 1961, and in a special election later that year was elected to Congress, the first Hispanic representative from Texas. Gonzalez was replaced as state senator by Franklin Spears.

as a public-school trustee unless the person could communicate in English. Hispanics were effectively excluded from "White Primaries" much as African-Americans were. MALDEF insists in its litigation that Hispanics in Texas continue to bear the effects of this prior discrimination.

Two specific election structures further diluted the impact of minority voters even as the official exclusion of these voters ended. The presence of multimember election systems made many state-representative races countywide, meaning that African American and Hispanic voters generally were unable to elect persons of their choice in the face of polarized voting by a white majority within the county.[4] Moreover, there were severely malapportioned congressional and state-legislative districts that allowed rural areas to maintain a controlling majority in the state legislature and in the state's congressional delegation, despite the shift of population away from these rural areas.[5] Because of this malapportionment, areas in which most minority persons resided were grouped into severely overpopulated (sometimes multimember for state legislative seats) districts, thereby minimizing the number of members potentially elected from areas with substantial minority population. This was the case with Harris County (with a large African American population) and South Texas (with a rapidly growing Hispanic population).

The effects of this past exclusion and lingering minority-vote dilution are reflected in the small number of persons from these minority groups who served as elected officials in Texas in the 1960s. Many African American lawmakers were elected and served as Republicans during the nineteenth century. But by the beginning of the twentieth, no African American was to be found as a lawmaker in the Texas legislature or in the state's congressional delegation. In 1961, the racial and ethnic composition of these bodies was as shown in Table 3.1.

The Emergence of Minority-Voter Participation

Effective minority participation in Texas came slowly, even over much of the last half of the twentieth century. It emerged, with rare exceptions, only through litigation and over the grudging opposition of the persons in power—the Anglo-dominated Democratic Party.

Equal Representation for Equal Numbers of Persons

The first major successes by minority candidates came with the forced redrawing of state-legislative and congressional districts in the 1960s to comply with the new court-imposed requirement for "equal representation for equal numbers of persons."

Texas was in litigation throughout the 1960s over the population inequality of its districts, but by 1970 the effects of this litigation were apparent. Under the new court-ordered redistricting plans, severely under-represented areas were now essentially entitled to additional seats in multimember districts or to districts of their own. In many instances, these newly drawn districts or apportioned seats lacked incumbents. This encouraged African American and Hispanic candidates to run for office. In some instances, the successful minority candidates (especially in the multimember urban counties) were allegedly successful only because they had been "handpicked" by influential Anglo organizations. Nevertheless, because of equipopulous electoral districts, by 1971 the Texas House of Representatives had twelve Hispanic members and its first two African American members since the 1890s.

By 1971, the state Senate also had an African American member (the newly elected Barbara Jordan from District 11 in Harris County) and one Hispanic member (Joe Bernal of District 26 in Bexar County). There were still no African Americans elected from Texas to Congress. Two Hispanics (Eligio "Kika" de la Garza [Rio Grande Valley] and Henry Gonzalez [Bexar County]) were serving in Congress from Texas in 1971.

Eliminating Multimember State Legislative Districts

Litigation in the 1970s brought even greater changes to the makeup of the Texas House. The legislature in 1971 voluntarily drew single-member districts in Harris County, but retained multimember districts for eleven other counties. Litigation followed. Texas was gradually moved by the federal courts and the U.S. Department of Justice to abandon all multimember districts in favor of single-member-district plans that included districts with enough minority voters to provide African Americans and Hispanics with an opportunity to elect the candidate of their choice without relying on Anglo votes. The effect was dramatic. By 1981, there were fourteen African Americans in the Texas House (all elected from districts in urban counties) and seventeen Hispanics. By 1981 racial- and ethnic-minority lawmakers made up over 20 percent of the House; all were Democrats.

Protecting Democratic Seats at the Expense of Minority-Opportunity Districts

Trading a Senate Seat for a Congressional Seat

By 1981, the districts drawn in 1971 had led to the election of four Hispanic members to the Texas Senate. All were elected from heavily Hispanic areas in South Texas and Bexar County. However, there was no longer any African American member of the Texas Senate.

The reason for the disappearance of the sole African American senator lay in the 1971 redistricting plans. The 1971 congressional redistricting plan had created a congressional district in Harris County (District 18) with enough African American voters to elect an African American to Congress. State Senator Barbara Jordan was expected to seek this congressional seat in the 1972 election. When it created this potentially winnable seat for an African American in Congress, the legislature also adopted a Senate redistricting plan that divided the African-American areas in Jordan's existing senate district among several other districts in Harris County. This dispersion of African American voters was a partisan strategy to allow Democrats to hang on to several Senate districts in Harris County. This strategy was largely successful early in the 1970s. However, this short-term Democratic advantage was achieved at the price of the sole Senate district previously won by an African-American.

Battling over an African American Opportunity District in Dallas (1981–1983)

The Texas legislature in 1981 remained under Democratic control. However, the Democratic majority was coming under increased pressure from the growth in Republican voting, from the demands of minority voters, and from the requirements of the Voting Rights Act.

The Texas Legislative Redistricting Board (acting after the legislature's efforts were rendered inoperative)[6] adopted plans that contained African

American opportunity districts for the Senate in Dallas and Harris counties. A congressional district in Dallas, however, was at the center of a convoluted and complicated battle among the branches of state government and a federal court.

The congressional redistricting plan passed by the legislature during the 1981 regular session retained the African American opportunity district in Harris County that had been won in 1972 by Barbara Jordan, but still did not contain such a district in Dallas County. The African American population of the Dallas–Fort Worth area remained split among several districts. The effect was to maintain districts represented by Anglo Democratic congressmen. However, although the majority of the members of the House and Senate were Democratic, the governor was now a Republican. As discussed in Chapter Two, Governor Bill Clements vetoed the pro-Democratic redistricting plan. Clements called the legislature into special session and demanded that a majority-minority congressional district be drawn in Dallas County.[7]

After an intense legislative battle, the legislature drew a congressional district in Dallas that satisfied Governor Clements. Some Democratic House members (known as the "Killer Fleas") showed their opposition to the bill and its likely effect on incumbent Democratic congressmen through a halfhearted walkout. Enough absent lawmakers, including state representative (later state senator) John Whitmire, were quickly gathered up from locations around the Capitol and downtown Austin to provide the necessary quorum in the House, and the congressional redistricting bill passed.

The battle over congressional districts in Dallas went immediately to federal court. In a strange outcome, a three-judge federal court adopted a plan that redrew the districts to favor the reelection of the Democratic incumbents, whom it considered responsive to minority needs.[8] Two judges on the panel (Fifth Circuit Justice Sam Johnson and District Judge William Wayne Justice)[9] agreed with this view. The Supreme Court later overruled this decision because the district court had never found the legislatively drawn Dallas congressional districts unlawful, but the district court nevertheless ordered the use of its plan for the 1982 election because the state agreed that there was not sufficient time to change back to the legislatively drawn districts before the scheduled primary election. In 1983, the Democratic-controlled legislature essentially adopted the court's plan, eliminating the African American–opportunity district. Clements had been defeated in the 1982 election. The new governor, Democrat Mark White, agreed with the new congressional plan and the pro-Democratic Dallas districts.

As a result, Dallas County in the 1980s remained without a congressional district in which African Americans were likely to elect the candidate of their choice. Instead, congressional districts were drawn to protect Anglo Democrats.

1991: Minority Success, but at a Cost to Democrats

In 1991, the Texas legislature under the leadership of two Democrats, Lieutenant Governor Bob Bullock and Speaker Gib Lewis, attempted to draw state-legislative and congressional districts that would both create the maximum number of minority-opportunity districts and protect incumbent Anglo Democrats. The resulting urban districts were almost uniformly bizarre in shape.

Republicans have described the 1991 congressional redistricting as one of the classic gerrymanders of all time. The partisan effect of these congressional districts is discussed in Chapter Two. However, the plan was even more effective at creating opportunities to elect minorities to Congress. It maintained the African American–dominated congressional district (District 18) in Harris County and created for the first time a similar district (District 30) in Dallas County and a new, predominantly Hispanic district (District 29) in Harris County. To some extent, the eventual configuration of these new minority-opportunity districts were achieved by the Texas legislature over opposition from the congressional delegation, particularly Martin Frost, who wished to keep part of the core (predominantly African American) of Dallas County in his congressional district. Frost's position in 1991 brought him into conflict with then state senator Eddie Bernice Johnson and led to an intense personal animosity between the two that still exists. Johnson won election to the Dallas seat in 1992. Former state senator Gene Green won the new Harris County district over a Hispanic candidate after a primary race marked by a heated election contest and a court-ordered special primary election. It should be noted that the real impetus for the creation of these new majority-minority districts came from minority members of the Texas legislature, not the Democratic Party, and they were intended to meet the requirements of the Voting Rights Act as interpreted at the time by the Justice Department.

Creating minority-opportunity districts in the 1990s came at a price for overall Democratic representation. Concentrating African Americans in single districts in Dallas and Houston and creating a new Hispanic-opportunity district in Harris County meant that fewer dependably Democratic voters remained for the other congressional districts. Throughout the 1990s, the number of Democrats in each state legislative body and in the Texas congressional delegation steadily fell as more and more Anglos voted Republican. Several Democratic incumbent congressmen were defeated by Republican challengers. After the 1990 census, Texas picked up three seats, for a total of thirty, in the national reapportionment of Congress. The congressional delegation elected in 1992, the first one chosen under the 1991 redistricting plan, contained twenty-one Democrats and nine Republicans; by 2001, those figures had changed to seventeen Democrats and thirteen Republicans.

Why Democrat and Not Republican?

The past exclusion of African American and Hispanic voters and the dilution of their voting power occurred when the powers of state government rested firmly in the hands of the Democrats. Even as late as the 1980s, the Democratic-controlled legislature found ways to split urban African American communities among existing districts so as to allow the reelection of a greater number of Anglo Democratic incumbents, who ostensibly were protective of minority interests. It might be expected, therefore, that African American and Hispanic voters would hold the Democratic Party responsible for these past impediments and offer their support to the Republican Party. Yet in 2003, of the seventeen African American and forty-three Hispanic members of the Texas House, the Texas Senate, and the Texas congressional delegation, all but two were Democrats. Two minorities (one Hispanic, one Asian) were Republican.

This possibly surprising result can be better understood by realizing that the Democratic Party in Texas over most of the past fifty years had in reality been two parties. The liberal and conservative wings of the party regularly fought over party affairs, elected offices, and state policy. Conservative Democrats usually triumphed. Studies show that African American and Hispanic voters in Texas usually were aligned with the liberal wing and supported liberal Democratic candidates, such as U.S. Senator Ralph Yarborough.

The growth of African American and Hispanic participation and voting strength in the 1960s–1980s coincided with the departure from the Democratic Party of many of its most conservative officeholders and voters. African American and Hispanic voters, however, continued to support Democratic candidates. As more and more Anglos departed for the Republican Party, racial- and ethnic-minority voters became a larger component of the Democratic vote. As a result, more and more African Americans and Hispanics became Democratic officeholders. Even Anglo Democratic officeholders necessarily owed their victories to minority voters and served only because they were the choice of one or both minority groups. However, the success of minorities within the Democratic Party coincided with the party's dramatic loss of power, thus leaving African American and Hispanic voters and officials in Texas with increasing control of an increasingly weaker political party.

After the 2000 Census

Thus, the stage was set for the redistricting of congressional districts after the 2000 census. Republicans counted nine minority-opportunity districts protected under the Voting Rights Act. An African American opportunity district existed in both Harris and Dallas counties. Each had already elected an African American Democrat to Congress: Eddie Bernice Johnson from District 30 in Dallas and Sheila Jackson Lee from District 18 in Houston. There were seven congressional districts with a majority Hispanic voting population. Hispanic Democrats had been elected in five of these districts: Solomon P. Ortiz from Corpus Christi in District 27, Silvestre Reyes from El Paso in District 16, Charles Gonzalez from San Antonio in District 20, Ciro D. Rodriguez from San Antonio in District 28, and Rubén Hinojosa from Mercedes in District 15. One Anglo Democrat (Gene Green) had been elected and was serving from the predominantly Hispanic 29th congressional district in Harris County. A Republican Hispanic, Henry Bonilla from San Antonio, had defeated a Democratic Hispanic incumbent in 1992 in another of the seven districts (District 23), this one running from San Antonio for over 500 miles across West Texas to El Paso.

Democrats and minority organizations urged that two additional districts were entitled to protection under the Voting Rights Act. The population of District 24 in the Dallas–Fort Worth "Metroplex" had a combined African American and Hispanic majority (60.2 percent). Anglo Democratic congressman Martin Frost was representing the district. The Mexican American Legal Defense and Education Fund (MALDEF), a Hispanic advocacy group, urged that District 24 should be redrawn to increase the Hispanic population from 38 percent to a majority. This district was at the center of the redistricting dispute in 2001 and 2003. Democrats also urged that District 25, straddling Harris and Fort Bend counties, was entitled to protection under the Voting Rights Act because it had a combined African American and Hispanic majority (57.4 percent) population. Anglo Democrat Chris Bell was the elected representative from District 25. Some African Americans wanted to redraw District 25 to raise the African American population above the 23.7 percent of the district as it existed in 2002 and to make it more likely that an African American could be elected.

Hispanic advocacy organizations, such as MALDEF and the League of United Latin American Citizens (LULAC), also urged that at least one of the two new districts apportioned to Texas after the 2000 census should be drawn with a Hispanic majority, given the magnitude of the Hispanic population growth over the 1990s. Moreover, although the African American population had not grown as a percentage of the state's overall population, the dispersion of African Americans in Harris County and the bloc voting of this group suggested that it might be possible to draw a second congressional district in Harris County that could be dominated by African American voters. These factors played an important part in the 2003 redistricting.

CHAPTER 4

Electing the Right Republicans:
The Republican Strategy for the 2002 Election

The one thing that binds the entire TRMPAC team and all the supporters of Texans for a Republican Majority is the sincere conviction that Republican policies hold the best promise for the future of Texas and of presenting a common vision for the growing diversity of Texas.
— TEXANS FOR A REPUBLICAN MAJORITY (2002)

Although the Texas legislature had been unable to draw new congressional districts in 2001, the heavily Republican Legislative Redistricting Board (LRB) had redistricted the state House and Senate.[1] The LRB consists of five elected state officials. Under the Texas Constitution, this board convenes only if the legislature fails to redistrict the state House and Senate in its first legislative session after release of the federal decennial census. The board has no authority to redraw congressional district lines. The LRB in 2001 consisted of four Republicans (Attorney General John Cornyn, acting lieutenant governor Bill Ratliff, Comptroller Carole Keeton Strayhorn, and Land Commissioner David Dewhurst) and one Democrat (Speaker Pete Laney). Republicans in the legislature in 2001 were under no pressure to adopt redistricting plans for the state House and Senate because they knew that Republicans would control the LRB. Predictably, the legislature deadlocked over state-legislative redistricting. In June 2001 the task passed to the LRB, which did not disappoint the Republican activists; its plans were very partisan.

The LRB's Senate plan created an authentic opportunity for the election of two or more additional Republicans and the possibility of increasing the Republican majority in that legislative body. However, it was the LRB plan for the Texas House that created the greatest opportunity. Under that plan, Republicans had a real chance to win as many as 20–24 additional House seats— more than enough to give Republicans a safe majority. Three organizations outside the Republican Party became critical to Republican success. These organizations raised and spent more than $4.5 million, including more than $2.65 million in possibly illegal corporate funds.[2] A fourth organization poured an additional $2–2.5 million in corporate funds into Texas to help Republican state-legislative candidates and the Republican candidate for attorney general.

An important vehicle for effecting this change came through Congressman Tom DeLay. By the summer of 2001, DeLay and his aide Jim Ellis recognized the Republicans' fabulous opportunity in the 2002 election. They also realized that the blueprint for this ambitious enterprise—engineering a Republican takeover of the Texas House—already existed in DeLay's national political action committee, Americans for a Republican Majority (ARMPAC), which was also known as "Leadership PAC." Since 1998 this organization had raised over $12 million (much of it corporate money) and dispensed it nationwide to Republican candidates, officeholders, and PACs. It was one of the most potent forces behind Republican campaign successes nationwide. ARMPAC also was a source of personal prestige and influence for DeLay, who chaired the PAC and largely controlled the dispersion of its funds. Ellis was the organization's executive director. (Both continued to hold these positions in 2006.) The vehicle for Texas was organized along the lines of ARMPAC, even using many ARMPAC personnel. However, Ellis told me that it also was patterned after the Texas Partnership PAC, established in the 1990s by Democratic Speaker Pete Laney to support Democratic candidates for the state House.

The possibility of a state PAC in Texas was discussed during the summer of 2001. DeLay and Ellis decided to call it Texans for a Republican Majority (TRMPAC, pronounced "trimpac"), after its federal model. TRMPAC's goals were to elect a Republican state Speaker and to advance the party's overall agenda, particularly congressional redistricting. Ellis later explained that DeLay "has a great affinity for that body [the Texas House of Representatives]. His longtime friend Tom Craddick was going to be a very strong candidate for speaker, and DeLay wanted to help both those things."[3] Ellis said that at the time TRMPAC was formed, congressional redistricting was not a "front-burner topic", but "certainly it was an issue in the back of our minds."[4] Many continue to believe, however, that for DeLay and Ellis the primary goal with TRMPAC was to achieve a Texas House that would support partisan congressional redistricting.

When TRMPAC was created in the fall of 2001, there was no assurance that the Republican candidates for statewide office or the Texas Senate would win in 2002. Therefore, in its formative stages (according to Jim Ellis), TRMPAC had the general objective of working to elect Republicans to all statewide and legislative offices in Texas. TRMPAC's mission statement reflected this purpose: "Texans for a Republican Majority PAC will help Republican candidates successfully run and win campaigns in Texas, and increase and maintain our majority of statewide and legislative offices for the next decade." Control of the major state offices as well as both houses of the legislature would be critical to any redistricting effort in 2003. It soon became apparent, however, that it was the chance for Republicans to take control of the Texas House that presented TRMPAC with its greatest opportunity.

By 2001, the Democratic majority in the Texas House was only 78–72. However, overcoming this small difference did not fully describe the Republican task ahead. The Democratic Speaker, Pete Laney, had considerable support among Republican lawmakers and could probably win reelection as Speaker if Republicans gained only a slight majority. Also, Tom Craddick, DeLay's pick for Speaker, was not overwhelmingly popular among his Republican colleagues, several of whom had emerged as possible Speaker candidates if Republicans gained a majority. This group of lawmakers became known as the ABCs, or "Anybody but Craddick." Many observers thought in 2002 that if Republicans gained only a bare majority in the House, either Laney or one of the ABCs would be speaker. Craddick stood the best chance of becoming Speaker if the Republicans could win at least eighty seats. DeLay knew the circumstances and the players well. He and Ellis had a plan that, if successful, would elect a safe Republican majority to the House, elect DeLay's friend and former colleague Tom Craddick Speaker, and pave the way for a favorable redrawing of congressional districts by the legislature in 2003.

TRMPAC

Jim Ellis initiated the meetings that led to the organization of TRMPAC. The organizers included Austinites Suzanne Sanders (Bellsnyder), accountant Russell Anderson, and lawyer Randy Ervin. TRMPAC was officially formed as an Austin-based general-purpose political action committee on September 5, 2001. TRMPAC's accountant (Anderson) said in 2005 that the organization's initial bank account was established on September 10.

Congressman DeLay (along with Ellis, future ambassador to Mexico Tony Garza, and others) appeared at a news conference in Austin on November 24, 2001 (the day following the release of the federal court opinion that drew the congressional districts to be used in 2002) to draw attention to TRMPAC's existence and purpose. DeLay's written statement declared, "We stand on the cusp of holding legislative majorities in both [legislative] chambers as well as every major statewide office."[5]

TRMPAC never had any employees: everyone was an independent contractor. TRMPAC never had a permanent office: it temporarily used the address of the law office of Kerry Cammack (husband of Texas Supreme Court justice Harriett O'Neill), on West 15th Street in Austin, as its official mailing address, but "for all functional purposes the organization was run from Russell Anderson's home office."[6]

John Colyandro (age thirty-nine) was selected by Ellis and DeLay to be the executive director of TRMPAC. Colyandro and Ellis were very good friends. They had known each other for fifteen or sixteen years. At one point Ellis had been married to Colyandro's cousin. Colyandro had previously been part of Karl Rove's direct-mail operation in Texas (1985–1989) and had worked in numerous Republican campaigns as a consultant and at several state agencies, including the Railroad Commission and the comptroller's office (where he was later dismissed as chief of staff). In a later deposition, Colyandro acknowledged that he had never raised corporate soft money for a campaign before 2002. As TRMPAC's executive director, Colyandro hired consultants, oversaw contributions and expenditures, communicated with candidates, evaluated candidates for TRMPAC support (with the help of other consultants), and generally ran the TRMPAC operation, under watchful eyes in Washington.[7]

In TRMPAC's early days, Colyandro also served as the organization's treasurer. In October or early November 2001, however, Colyandro approached Dallas businessman Bill Ceverha to become treasurer. In a letter dated November 16, 2001 (filed November 19), Ceverha was designated treasurer. He was a logical choice. Ceverha had served for twelve years as a state representative (1977–1989). For part of that time he had served alongside of Tom Craddick and Tom DeLay. Since leaving the state legislature, Ceverha had worked as a political consultant and lobbyist, particularly for Dallas investor and major Republican donor and political power Louis Beecherl. Ceverha's recognizable name among Republican activists and donors was expected to ease TRMPAC's access to these persons. As a witness at the TRMPAC civil trial in 2005, Ceverha said he performed the official duties of treasurer, but was seldom actually involved in TRMPAC's ongoing activities and never actually reviewed any of the reports filed with the Texas Ethics Commission because they were filed electronically without his signature. Ceverha claimed at the trial that Colyandro authorized some of the more controversial TRMPAC expenditures without his knowledge.

The seed money for TRMPAC ($50,000) came from ARMPAC. DeLay appeared on many TRMPAC documents as the first of a handful of advisory board members. Others included Tony Garza (then a member of the Texas Railroad Commission, later ambassador to Mexico), State Senator Florence

Shapiro, State Representative Dianne White Delisi, and Bill Ceverha. In his testimony in 2005, Ceverha downplayed the importance of the advisory board and of DeLay's role on the board. He said that the board had only two formal meetings—one for a "bus tour" during the Republican primary and one at the Republican state convention in June 2002—and that DeLay seldom participated in the board's conference calls. Despite Ceverha's testimony, however, documents and deposition testimony offered at the TRMPAC civil trial in 2005 showed that DeLay participated often in TRMPAC activities.

The Strategy

The notion of prevailing in congressional redistricting through the election of a Republican majority to the Texas House was not entirely new. Representative Tom Craddick and the Republican Party of Texas organized efforts in 1996, 1998, and 2000 to elect a Republican majority to the Texas House; the efforts failed. DeLay had helped these earlier efforts by raising money. For example, in 2000 lobbyists for the Enron Corporation advised colleagues that DeLay had sent notes to company executives "about designating portions of their contributions for use in Texas." Three days later Enron sent a check for $50,000 to the Republican National State Elections Committee (RNSEC) in Washington, along with checks from three executives totaling $25,000. The RNSEC transferred $1.2 million to the Texas Republican Party, which in turn donated $1.3 million to twenty state-legislative candidates. Some of the Republican lawmakers who had been part of this effort (e.g., State Rep. Mike Krusee) had hoped that a Republican majority in the Texas House would lead to a redistricting plan in 2001 that could bring a Republican majority to the Texas congressional delegation. However, even though the Republican campaigns in the 1990s had narrowed the numerical difference in the House, the 2000 campaign had "failed to move the mark." The primary reason had been the efforts of Speaker Laney, who had responded with his own organization (the Texas Partnership PAC) to battle Craddick's campaign to take over the House. Laney had also been successful in slowing the flow of PAC contributions to Craddick's effort by letting lobbyists and PACs know that he was watching to see who contributed to it.

The LRB's partisan redistricting plan for the House in 2001, however, created opportunities for Republican success that far exceeded any from the past. Craddick, DeLay, and other Republicans realized (and had worked for) this chance. An estimated twenty-four House districts existed under the plan without an incumbent or where the Democratic incumbent's chances of reelection were significantly lessened because of redistricting. TRMPAC's strategy was to focus primarily on the races in these districts, in hopes of gaining a clear Republican majority in the Texas House. It was not a time for a conservative, defensive strategy; it was time to attack.

Success in capturing the House depended on several factors. First, the Republican candidate in each of these districts would have to be one who could win in the general election and, if elected, would be likely to support Craddick's election as Speaker and certain party priorities, including congressional redistricting in 2003. Second, the Republican candidates had to be provided with political consultants, polling, and planning, things that most candidates normally would be unable to secure or afford on their own. Third, ample money had to be directed to Republican candidates in the targeted districts and to their campaigns. Finally there needed to be effective direct-mail and "turn out the vote" campaigns on behalf of TRMPAC's selected candidates.

One of TRMPAC's tasks was to provide a vehicle for recruiting candidates, evaluating candidates, and picking and choosing among potential Republican candidates in the Republican primary to find the best candidate. This political action committee further was a means of paying for and providing help for selected candidates. TRMPAC also was a means for raising hard dollars that could be contributed to the selected candidates. Most importantly, however, TRMPAC was a means of tapping an even larger pool of corporate money that could be raised quietly from contributors who were unwilling to openly give hard dollars to beat Democratic Speaker Laney.

As it turned out, in 2002 TRMPAC was helped along the way by the Texas Association of Business (TAB), Texans for Lawsuit Reform (TLR), ARMPAC, and the Law Enforcement Alliance for America (LEAA).

Picking the Right Republican

The first step for TRMPAC was to find the right Republican candidates. According to Colyandro, approximately "30 or so" races were considered "in play" in the Republican primary. TRMPAC's plans to recruit candidates never fully developed. However, TRMPAC played a significant role in determining who would be the Republican candidate for the general election by endorsing specific candidates, contributing money during the Republican primary, and orchestrating intense direct-mail campaigns when needed. The TRMPAC advisory board made the final selection of the candidates to be supported in the March 2002 Republican primary. The decision, however, was largely within the control of Colyandro because he made the recommendations to the board. Colyandro in turn relied in part on the evaluations of a field consultant, Kevin Brannon, who interviewed potential candidates. Brannon was a friend of Colyandro from the Phil Gramm campaign.[8] Brannon began his assessment of candidates in the fall of 2001. One of the persons he enlisted in this effort was his former client, Phil Gramm. A letter dated July 18, 2002, indicated that Tom DeLay had obtained Gramm's help for TRMPAC.[9]

Whether a candidate would support Craddick was a major factor in determining whether the candidate would receive TRMPAC support. Brannon was helped in the candidate-assessment process by his friend and employer Phil King, a Republican House member, who made "no secret that [he] wanted—wanted Tom to be speaker . . . Phil was one of his key—his key backers."[10] Representative King told me in 2006 that he was part of an ad hoc group of six to nine "young" House Republicans who organized to help elect more Republicans to the House. He says he always assumed that Craddick would win the speakership if Republicans controlled the House. So, he told me, he could not recall ever asking a candidate to support Craddick for Speaker.[11] Craddick himself participated in this "assessment and intelligence gathering" process, making recommendations to Brannon and TRMPAC on specific candidates.[12] Although Brannon testified that he did not recall whether he ever expressly asked a candidate to support Craddick for Speaker, he acknowledged that the issue was often discussed with candidates who wanted TRMPAC help because they would "volunteer" to him (Brannon) that "Oh, I am a big Tom Craddick guy."[13] Brannon would note the candidate's preference for Craddick as part of the notes of the candidate's interview. Colyandro too acknowledges discussing TRMPAC's endorsements with Craddick. Several Republican primary candidates reported Craddick contacting or trying to contact them during the primary for the apparent purpose of determining whether they were likely to support his candidacy for Speaker.

Ultimately, TRMPAC contributed at least $116,344 (including actual contributions and express advocacy mailers) to seventeen candidates and made endorsements in at least seventeen primary contests. TAB generally provided support through mailers for these same candidates. These endorsements from TRMPAC were seen by some Republicans as an endorsement by Congressman DeLay. As a result, in one instance Colyandro approved spending TRMPAC funds to send a mailer on behalf of the Young Conservatives, declaring that "Congressman DeLay" would not endorse in a particular primary runoff. Ultimately, thirteen of the seventeen TRMPAC candidates won their primary contests.

One criterion for support by TRMPAC for candidates in contested primaries was the probable electability of the candidate in the general election.

But other factors were also important. One Republican primary race provides an example. District 50 spans the conservative-leaning suburbs of northern and western Travis County. There were four Republicans competing for the party nomination in 2002. One of these was a well-known former state legislator, Bob Richardson. Richardson handily won the first round of voting on March 12, 2002. Jack Stick, a political novice unknown to most voters, reached the runoff by a mere ninety votes over a third candidate, African American businesswoman Kris Gillespie. However, Richardson had a major problem. He had enemies within the Republican hierarchy. Richardson was a trial lawyer who, some Republican leaders feared, would oppose tort reform. Moreover, despite Richardson's pledge to support Craddick for Speaker, some suspected that he was a friend of Speaker Laney and might be willing to vote to retain the Democrat as Speaker. Among Stick's early contributors was Mike Toomey, who, as a lobbyist for the TLR and a future chief of staff for Governor Rick Perry, was in a position to influence support from Republican donors and donor organizations. Money from these sources began to flow to Stick at the close of the first primary. Shortly before the primary election, two TAB mailers reached Republican voters within District 50. They attacked Richardson. These last-minute mailers and contributions were enough, in Richardson's view, to prevent him from winning the primary outright without a runoff.[14]

Shortly after the first primary, Stick received a $5,000 check from TRMPAC. (All together TRMPAC reported spending a little over $6,200 directly on Stick's candidacy.) Then, as Mike Toomey (the TLR's chief lobbyist at the time) told me in 2006, "We unleashed the dogs." Money flowed to Stick from the TLR and from numerous other major Republican donors from outside District 50. TAB flooded the district with ostensibly "issue ad" mailers accusing Richardson of being a liberal personal-injury attorney and a "wolf in sheep's clothing." The mailers charged that Richardson only wanted voters to think that he was a Republican. Some of the mailers distorted cases that Richardson had handled as an attorney. TRMPAC added its own flier endorsing Stick. On April 9, 2002, Stick routed Richardson in the runoff, winning 69 percent of the vote.

Another example was in District 89, where Republican candidates Jodie Laubenberg and Mike Lawshe were forced into a run-off. Craddick and Ceverha met for lunch with Lawshe,[15] apparently seeking his support for Craddick for speaker. Lawshe deferred; preferring to give his support to one of the moderate Republican candidates for speaker. TRMPAC and TAB came out hard against Lawshe. TAB sent mailers attacking him for being a Democrat disguised as a Republican. TRMPAC directed $25,000 to Laubenberg. In addition, TRMPAC directors Tony Garza and Florence Shapiro campaigned in District 89 on behalf of Laubenberg. Lawshe lost the runoff by 167 votes.

A similar scenario was played out in most of the other sixteen primaries in which TRMPAC endorsed a candidate. Candidates who were suspected of being too independent or of being soft on any of the major policies of the Republican Party were denied TRMPAC support or endorsement and were sometimes attacked. In some instances, these candidates were possibly the strongest and most experienced Republican candidates. Nevertheless, if they were considered a risk on any of the party's principal issues, such as tort reform or public school finance, TRMPAC and its allies swung their support to other candidates. TRMPAC provided the donations; TAB usually provided the attack mailers (e.g., "What's worse than a wolf in sheep's clothing? A liberal in Republican clothing.").

TRMPAC also supported Republican incumbents who found themselves in danger of losing. As with nonincumbent candidates, TRMPAC's support of these incumbents depended on whether the incumbent was seen as strongly partisan, committed to achieving Republican goals on issues such as tort reform, and a solid vote for Craddick for Speaker. TRMPAC threw its support behind the endangered incumbents. Two incumbent races provide an example of how this intraparty battle played out. In District 58, the incumbent, Mary Denny, was in trouble in her race for reelection. Her opponent was Clayton Downing, a well-regarded former school superintendent who favored greater state funding of public education. Early polls showed him leading. Downing avowed that he would not be "a Craddick puppet" and that he was opposed to school vouchers. Downing considered the response from the Republican establishment "vicious" and "dirty".[16] Mailers were sent to Republicans in the district attacking Downing as a "tax and spend liberal school superintendent." In District 67, incumbent Jerry Madden's reelection bid was in trouble because of alleged personal indiscretions. His opponent, John R. Roach, said in 2006 that "the speaker's race played a huge role in my race."[17] Roach credits his lack of TRMPAC support to his refusal to promise Craddick that he would support him for speaker. Moreover, according to Roach, Craddick in their meeting kept talking about "doing right for the Republican Party," which in hindsight Roach sees as an allusion to the need for congressional redistricting. Both Denny and Madden were allies of Craddick. TRMPAC contributed to both of these incumbents in the primary and paid for mailers. Interestingly, however, the TRMPAC logo was removed at the last minute from these mailers. The mailers ended up being sent with the TAB logo, although at TRMPAC's expense. Moreover, at least in Roach's race, voters received a recorded message in the final days of the primary from Governor Perry, one critical of the challenger. Denny and Madden won.

TRMPAC was aided throughout the primary by TAB. The Texas Association of Business claims to have played a part in fifty-four different primaries, including having acted on behalf of challengers in some races in which the renomination of incumbent Republicans in the ABC (Anybody but Craddick) club were contested. Twelve of the targeted Republican primary races (as in District 50, between Stick and Richardson) went to a runoff. Nine of the runoff candidates backed by TAB won. Ultimately, forty-eight of the candidates backed by TAB won in the primary and advanced to the general election. Most of the mailers in the Republican primary came from TAB rather than TRMPAC, but the two organizations coordinated their efforts. John Colyandro was generally credited later with designing the "issue ads" that were sent by TAB or by the candidate. TRMPAC paid the printer, Thomas Graphics, for the expense of some of the TAB mailers, although there was no mention of TRMPAC on the mailings. TRMPAC even paid TAB $10,200 directly in corporate money for flyers TAB sent at TRMPAC's request in two primary races (Denny and Madden). At the TRMPAC civil trial in 2005, the printer, Bob Thomas, said that TRMPAC and TAB worked together on mailings and "would come to me and say who to bill."[18]

Republican consultant Royal Masset said in June 2002 that to the best of his knowledge "this widespread active intervention in strength during the primaries [was] unprecedented."[19] Masset was referring directly to the TAB effort in the Republican primary, but TRMPAC alone spent approximately $200,000 through the time of the Republican primaries, including $116,344 in contributions to selected Republican candidates, $13,400 to the Karl Rove–linked Thomas Graphics, and $10,200 to TAB for a mailer sent by that organization in two primary races. Some of this money (other than the direct contributions) was corporate money, but from TRMPAC's view, the expenditures were legitimate, even the mailers, since they did not expressly advocate the election of a particular candidate. I have been unable to determine how much TAB spent during these months, but it sent mailers in at least twenty contested Republican primaries on behalf of candidates it (and usually TRMPAC also) endorsed. According to Colyandro, the TAB/TRMPAC mailers were sent in those primary campaigns that "were locked in a more heated battle."[20]

This screening effort in the primaries assured TRMPAC that virtually every Republican legislative candidate in the November general election was someone who had been effectively vetted on the issues important to TRMPAC, including likely support of Craddick for Speaker and a willingness to adhere to the party position on issues such as congressional redistricting. At the Republican Party state convention in June 2002, TRMPAC joined with a group of incumbent Republican lawmakers led by Representative King to interview the Republican nominees, to assess each new candidate's campaign plan, and to decide who needed help and who stood the best chance of success. TRMPAC paid for the event with corporate funds.

TRMPAC Fund-Raising

TRMPAC raised approximately $1,547,963 during the 2002 election cycle. This total included both "hard money" (approximately $803,026 from individuals and PACs), which apparently was given legally to TRMPAC for political purposes, and money (approximately $750,000) from corporate treasuries, which may or may not have been given legally. Early on, DeLay and Ellis determined that the corporate money should be kept separate from the hard-money contributions.[21] TRMPAC reported the hard-money contributions to the Texas Ethics Commission. The corporate-money contributions were not reported. The contribution of this corporate money to TRMPAC and its failure to report the contributions led later to criminal investigations, criminal indictments, criminal prosecutions, and civil litigation.

Individuals generally are free to give to a state political action committee, such as TRMPAC. TRMPAC had tremendous access to the traditional large Republican donors, such as Louis Beecherl ($35,000), Bob Perry ($165,000), James Leininger ($100,000), T. Boone Pickens ($50,000), Charles and Sam Wyly ($20,000), and John Lattimore ($25,000). Corporate PACs also can contribute directly to candidates or to an organization like TRMPAC, since the money in these PACs comes from the individual officers and employees of the corporation, not from the corporate treasury. TRMPAC's fund-raisers in Texas, some featuring prominent Republicans such as Congressman DeLay and former Florida secretary of state Katherine Harris, were aimed at least in part at attracting these hard-money donations from individuals and PACs. Individual TRMPAC board members also worked to obtain such donations through personal solicitations. TRMPAC retained Austin-based Susan Lilly to solicit hard-money contributions in Texas. In filings with the Texas Ethics Commission, TRMPAC reported raising a total of approximately $803,026 in hard money, including $25,000 from the National Republican Legislators Association and $150,000 from the Farmers [Insurance] Employee and Agent PAC of Texas. However, these hard-money contributions could have gone directly to the candidates rather than through TRMPAC. In fact, one TRMPAC solicitation letter actually gave prospective contributors the option of giving money to the Republican candidate or to TRMPAC. TRMPAC's unique function, however, was to attract money from corporations. This was a new and potentially large source of funds.

Raising hard dollars from corporations for an organization like TRMPAC is difficult. As indicated above, a corporation's PAC funds can be contributed to candidates or to other PACS, like TRMPAC, because the funds are considered hard money. Corporations tend, however, to hoard this limited resource and give it directly to candidates or officeholders so that these politicians will be aware of the support and generosity of the corporation's officers and employees. Giving PAC funds to an intermediary such as TRMPAC is often seen as a waste of such a limited resource because the corporation may end up without any recognition or appreciation from the candidate or officeholder who thus receives the corporation's money only indirectly.

Although TRMPAC attracted some substantial corporate PAC contributions (e.g., $150,000 from the Farmers Employee and Agent PAC), some corporations were reluctant to give up these "hard dollars" to benefit TRMPAC. This problem was evident at several stages of the TRMPAC experience. For example, DeLay's effort to raise individual and PAC contributions from lobbyists in Austin at the end of July 2002 was generally unsuccessful. One lobbyist explained at the time that he usually wanted to give funds from his law firm PAC directly to candidates. Similarly, when Union Pacific was asked for a contribution to TRMPAC, it instead came up with $25,000 in hard money from its PAC and agreed in August 2002 to give the funds directly to TRMPAC Republican candidate "targets" while accompanied by a "'DeLay' person." To ensure that TRMPAC received credit with the state-legislative candidates for any of these direct PAC contributions, it sent faxed notes to the candidates, advising them that the contributions were coming because of TRMPAC's efforts.

On the other hand, funds from a corporation's treasury rather than from the company's officers and employees are theoretically more abundant. However, state and federal laws have historically restricted when such corporate money can be given or used in national or state elections, out of concern that corporate (or labor union) funds could overwhelm an election, and that treasury funds belonged to the shareholders, not the officers of the company. TRMPAC was meant to provide a way for corporations to contribute funds from their treasuries so that they could be used to help elect a Republican majority to the Texas House. Texas law (*Texas Election Code,* section 253.094[a]) generally prohibits a corporation from making a political contribution or expenditure from such funds, allowing only several narrow exceptions. One of these exceptions became vital to TRMPAC's plans. Section 253.100(a) allows a corporation to "make one or more political expenditures to finance the establishment or administration of a general-purpose committee." TRMPAC was a general-purpose committee, so the legal question that was to determine the organization's role in the 2002 election, and was later to spark criminal charges and civil litigation, was what TRMPAC expenditures were allowable as administrative expenses that could be paid with corporate funds.

Ed Shack is an Austin attorney who previously served in the Office of the Secretary of State of Texas. He is known among Republicans as an expert on state election law in general and on state campaign-finance law in particular. In 2002 he advised TRMPAC, TAB, and others about the legality of their fundraising and expenditure plans. On March 22, 2002, Shack advised TRMPAC by letter that corporate funds could legally be contributed to TRMPAC and spent for administrative expenses without being reported to the Texas Ethics Commission. He cited Ethics Advisory Opinion No. 132. TRMPAC adopted a broad definition of what constituted an administrative expense on which unreported corporate funds could be expended. Essentially, it considered permissible any expense that was not direct advocacy. In subsequent litigation, TRMPAC claimed that Shack was only one of three lawyers who gave the organization legal advice in 2001–2002 about its formation and operation under state law. It should be noted that TRMPAC's organized effort to raise large amounts of corporate funds was well underway by the end of 2001, over three months before Shack's letter opinion.

TRMPAC solicited corporate money in earnest. The invitations to its early fund-raisers openly indicated "Corporate Contributions are Welcome." The printed materials for TRMPAC's Contributor Sponsorship Program explained:

> Unlike other organizations, your corporate contribution to TRMPAC will be put to productive use. Rather than just paying for overhead, your support will fund a series of productive and innovative activities designed to increase our level of engagement in the political arena.

Corporate contributors were eligible to receive certain benefits based on the size of their contribution (e.g., Platinum Level—$100,000, Gold Level—$50,000, Silver Level—$25,000, and Friends Level—$15,000). Platinum Level benefits included a "Private dinner with Board Members." The corporations were urged to contact TRMPAC in Austin or Warren Robold in Washington.

Warren Robold (WRM Consulting, Inc.) was the person primarily responsible for raising corporate money for TRMPAC. He shared an office in Washington with Jim Ellis, the executive director of ARMPAC. Robold also was the chief fund-raiser for ARMPAC and continued to raise money for ARMPAC while also doing so for TRMPAC. Robold's contract with TRMPAC provided that he would "solicit funds, particularly corporate funds" starting January 1, 2002. As later described by Colyandro, Robold raised money from "primarily corporate contributors that he had relationships with in primarily the Washington area."[22] Robold knew the Washington lobbyists and was instrumental in raising funds for TRMPAC from corporations based outside Texas and having little or no connection to the state. Almost all these corporations, however, had issues pending in Congress and were therefore susceptible to appeals by or on behalf of Congressman DeLay. DeLay's role in attracting this soft money is further discussed in Chapter Fifteen. Robold stressed to potential givers that corporate funds could be given in unlimited amounts to TRMPAC and were nonreportable under Texas law. The fact that contributions to TRMPAC were ostensibly "non-reportable" was attractive. Robold was asked to raise $600,000 in corporate money for TRMPAC; he succeeded. Virtually all of this money came from corporations seeking to sell goods or services to the federal government, or from businesses in federally regulated industries: nursing homes, HMOs, tobacco, and energy.[23] Altogether at least 37 percent of TRMPAC's funds came from out-of-state corporations with little or no apparent connection to Texas. Warren Robold was indicted in 2004 for his activities on behalf of TRMPAC.

The Texas Association of Business

The Texas Association of Business (TAB) was created in 1922. It merged in 1995 with the Texas Chamber of Commerce. TAB is not a large organization, consisting primarily of its executive director and a handful of support staff. Historically, the association has kept a low profile in state politics. For example, it spent only around $87,000 during a two-year election cycle as recently as 1998. This changed dramatically in 2001–2002.

Bill Hammond took over as president and executive director of TAB in 1998. As with so many of the key figures in the events of 2001–2003, he also had served earlier in the state legislature alongside Craddick and DeLay in the Republican minority. Since becoming the head of TAB, he had made no secret of his desire to see pro-business Republicans in control of the Texas legislature. In 2000, TAB had been a small player ($30,000) in Craddick's unsuccessful effort to elect a Republican majority in the Texas House. Like DeLay and Ellis, Hammond also recognized the unique opportunity that existed in 2002 as a result of the LRB's 2001 redistricting plan. He decided TAB would participate in the 2002 elections at "an unprecedented level" to "change the face of the Legislature." Whether Hammond directly consulted with DeLay, Ellis, or others before making such a decision is not clear.

TAB had a political action committee (the Business and Commerce PAC, or BACPAC) that could contribute directly to candidates. In 2001–2002, however, TAB embarked on a separate campaign to raise and spend corporate money in ways designed to elect favored Republican candidates to the Senate and House. Like TRMPAC, TAB turned to Ed Shack for legal advice. When testifying in the TRMPAC civil trial in 2005, Hammond called Shack "the premier election law attorney in Texas." On numerous occasions during 2002, TAB asked Shack to review particular mailers, ads, or proposed expenditures from TAB's corporate-funded "voter education program." Shack's legal advice generally was that the TAB could use corporate funds to send mailers or run ads for voter education in primary and general elections as long as the mailers and ads did not "expressly advocate the election or defeat" of a particular candidate. Therefore, these "voter education" mailers and ads in the various House races were paid for with corporate money, whereas express endorsement materials for those same candidates were left to the organization's PAC. TAB failed to report either the corporate contributions or expenditures to the Texas Ethics Commission.

TAB initially claimed to have spent approximately $2 million in the 2002 general and primary election campaigns. Only $101,821 was in the form of hard dollars distributed to candidates or spent through its PAC. TAB claimed that all or virtually all of the remaining $1.9 million (or $1.7 million or less, as now appears more likely) came from corporate donations it raised in an aggressive solicitation campaign aimed at corporate executives statewide. Hammond himself led the effort to raise corporate money. In an important memorandum dated August 21, 2002, and addressed to "Texas Business Leaders," but delivered specially to a statewide conference of insurers, Hammond hailed TAB's "highly-targeted direct mail program," which the Austin-based *Quorum Report* credited with "making a real difference in the [Republican] Primary."[24] He explained that the "voter education direct mail program . . . was made possible with corporate money." For the general election, "Our strategy is simple: to educate voters about pro-business candidates through an aggressive direct mail program." He closed with a plea for a check of $50,000–100,000 from each company—"to make a difference in the political climate in Austin"—and a promise that "Contributions for this purpose are not reportable."

Documents released in court discovery in 2005 showed (apparently inadvertently) that the insurance companies answered Hammond's request. Fifteen insurance and health providers gave TAB at least $580,000 in corporate funds for the 2002 election campaign: for example, the Alliance for Quality Nursing Home Care, $300,000; PacifiCare Health Systems, $100,000; Humana Inc., $100,000; United Health Care of Texas, $100,000; Blue Cross of California, $100,000; CIGNA Corp., $80,000; Liberty Mutual Insurance, $25,000; Metropolitan Life Insurance, $10,000; Great-West Life, $50,000; Health Insurance Association of America, $25,000; and Travelers Insurance, $25,000. AT&T also gave $300,000. The *Austin American-Statesman* traced the donations through the heavily redacted documents and cautioned that the total contributions from insurance companies are likely to be "substantially higher once the other corporate donors are identified and all the money (given to TAB) is accounted for."[25]

TAB used this $1.7–1.9 million in corporate funds to pay for an aggressive direct-mail campaign in the primary and general elections. The organization played a direct role in twelve Republican primary runoffs; nine of its favored candidates won. Its political action committee, BACPAC, endorsed 104 primarily Republican candidates in the general election. Most of these races were uncontested. TAB targeted 22 contested general-election state-legislative races for its public-education program; its preferred candidate in every race was a Republican. TAB claimed that altogether it sent over 4 million mailers—with as many as eight different mailers going to some households—in these targeted races. All but two of these races were for the Texas House. The other two were for the Texas Senate.

Texans for Lawsuit Reform

Houston-based Texans for Lawsuit Reform (TLR) has been a major source of funds for efforts to elect a Republican majority in the Texas legislature. Led by its chief lobbyist, Mike Toomey, the TLR spent $1.4 million in 2000 in an attempt to elect enough Republicans to oust Speaker Laney and to pass legislation to curtail what TLR saw as costly lawsuits plaguing Texas businesses. According to the 2005 testimony of TAB president Bill Hammond, the TLR worked with TRMPAC and TAB in 2002 to elect a Republican majority in the Texas House. During the Republican primary, the TLR aggressively fought to defeat at least five or six Republican candidates (such as Travis County trial lawyer Bill Richardson) whom it feared would vote against tort reform. TRMPAC and TAB also opposed these candidates. The TLR contributed to essentially the same general-election candidates as TRMPAC and TAB in the House races. Unlike TAB and TRMPAC, however, the TLR apparently operated only through its PAC, with hard dollars, and reported the amounts to the Texas Ethics Commission. In 2002 the TLR contributed approximately $3.5 million to candidates, most of them Republican. Its largest contribution was $389,222 to Republican Senate candidate Bob Deuell. Republican House candidates receiving large contributions, such as Sid Miller ($102,722), Martha Wong ($71,480), Mike Hamilton ($57,201), Rick Hardcastle ($62,787), and Eugene Seaman ($50,000). These candidates also were on the list of state-legislative candidates supported financially by TRMPAC and by mailings from TAB. Approximately $1.2 million of the TLR's money went to the twenty or twenty-one Republican state-legislative candidates supported in the general election by TAB and TRMPAC. Virtually all of the TLR's money came from only a few individuals. Some, such as Bob Perry ($300,000), James Leininger ($50,000), and Boone Pickens ($35,000), were also major donors to TRMPAC. No civil action or criminal investigation has targeted the legality of the TLR's contributions or expenditures.

Law Enforcement Alliance for America

Another organization made a surprise appearance late in the 2002 Texas elections. The Law Enforcement Alliance for America (LEAA) is a nonprofit corporation based in Virginia. It was started in 1991 with seed money from the National Rifle Association (NRA) at a time when the NRA and most law officer associations differed over whether the federal government should regulate so-called "cop killer bullets." The organization's budget has swelled in recent years to almost $5 million. LEAA does not routinely report the names of its contributors or the amount of its contributions and expenditures. Tax records show that the NRA continues to give some funds to LEAA. Writers in the *Wall Street Journal* have speculated, however, that LEAA now receives much of its funding directly or indirectly from the National Chamber of Commerce. As a result, the organization's issue priorities include tort reform as well as gun rights and criminal justice.[26]

Within two weeks of the 2002 general election, LEAA purchased $1.5– 2 million in media time to air ads statewide against Kirk Watson, the Democratic attorney general candidate. The ads criticized Watson for being a personal-injury attorney of the kind who has "made millions suing doctors, hospitals and small businesses—hurting families and driving up the costs of health care." The ads went on to describe the Republican candidate, Greg Abbott, as a "respected Supreme Court justice" who would do something about child pornography. The ads did not expressly solicit votes for Abbott. Specifics about the amounts spent by LEAA in the 2002 election are unknown because neither the amount nor the nature of the expenditures was reported to the Texas Ethics Commission.

John Colyandro acknowledges that he contacted LEAA official James Fotis on at least one occasion during the fall of 2002. However, the purpose and effect of his call or calls to LEAA are disputed. Colyandro was serving simultaneously as the executive director of TRMPAC and as the director of policy issues for the Abbott campaign. He claimed in a later deposition that his contact with LEAA was about the organization supporting some Republicans in state legislative races, not about LEAA funding ads attacking Watson in the attorney-general race. Testimony in the civil trial against TRMPAC in 2005 showed that Colyandro shared candidate-specific information with LEAA, that LEAA also used Thomas Graphics for at least two of its mailings, and that TAB helped design at least one of the LEAA mailings.

Watson called on Abbott to tell LEAA to pull down the ads in the attorney-general race; Abbott did not do so. Watson admitted in 2005 that the LEAA ads came as such a surprise and at such a late stage of the race that he was slow to "connect the dots." It was not apparent to him who was funding LEAA or why the organization was attacking him. Watson speculated later that the corporate money flowing through LEAA into ads targeting the attorney-general campaign might have stemmed from concerns about the potential of Watson, as attorney general, to prosecute corporate wrongdoing aggressively. Another possible concern was Watson's background as a plaintiff's attorney. However, Watson indicated to me in 2005 that on watching the redistricting events in 2003, he realized that winning the attorney-general race was vital to Republican plans for a change in congressional boundaries and that the last-minute LEAA involvement in Texas might have been intended at least in part to help pave the way for the 2003 redistricting.[27]

As indicated above, LEAA also became a participant in at least two state legislative races. In the race in District 4, LEAA sponsored mailers targeting Democratic candidate Mike Head. The ads claimed Head, a criminal defense lawyer, "is on the side of convicted baby killers and murderers." The mailers claimed that Head "is not only on the side of criminal suspects, he *GUARANTEES their bail so they are returned to the streets* where you live and work, and the schools and parks where your children spend their days" (emphasis and caps in the original mailer).

Democrats Watson and Head lost the election. In 2003 they filed a complaint in state court, accusing LEAA of using corporate funds in a political campaign in violation of Texas law. John Colyandro and undisclosed corporate contributors and conspirators were included as defendants. Buck Wood was the attorney for Watson and Head. In response to the charges in the complaint, LEAA contended that the ads were legal because they were not coordinated with any candidate's campaign and did not constitute "direct advocacy." LEAA removed the case to federal court. It resisted efforts to force it to disclose its donors or expenditures. A motion to remand the case to state court was denied in 2005. Wood indicated in 2005 that he expected to pursue the litigation in federal court.[28] LEAA has been accused by state officials in several other states (e.g., Mississippi, Pennsylvania, Illinois, and Kansas) of funding similar ads in political campaigns in violation of state law.

Coordination of Efforts

Bill Hammond, president of TAB, testified at trial in the TRMPAC civil case in 2005 that TAB, the TLR, and TRMPAC, along with "sundry" persons from other organizations, met together "numerous times" in 2002 to discuss who each organization was supporting, the "public education programs" of the various organizations, fund-raising opportunities, polling and phone-bank activities and results, direct-mail campaigns, mailing lists, and "plans about campaigns and work on campaigns." In his testimony, TAB political consultant Chuck McDonald described regular meetings between Colyandro, Hammond, Mike Toomey (TLR), and himself in which these persons would discuss "the message" and "strategy." Colyandro acknowledged in his deposition that he met "frequently" with TAB, TLRPAC executive director Matt Welch, and Toomey, but insisted that the meetings were more social than political. In his trial testimony, however, McDonald described the coordinated effort in the fall of 2002 as "massive," leading quickly to the production and mailing of huge amounts of information to voters: "We were very busy." Colyandro also acknowledged that he was regularly in touch with the Republican Party of Texas and the regional office of the Republican National Committee about the election campaigns. Republicans insist that these meetings among the PACs and party organizations were not unusual or illegal in the world of politics.

A chart from the campaign watchdog group Texans for Public Justice confirms that TRMPAC, TAB, and the TLR generally gave hard money to the same twenty to twenty-two Republican House candidates in the general election, but in amounts suggesting that the giving was coordinated so as not to waste money by unnecessarily duplicating the heavy giving of each group. As evidence that the groups operated as a coordinated partisan machine, Democrats point to all of the following: the admission by Hammond, Colyandro, and McDonald that these groups regularly met; a similarity in wording of TAB and TRMPAC mailers (both of which Colyandro apparently designed); TRMPAC's $10,200 payment to TAB for mailers sent under the TAB name; the payment ($13,126) from the TAB political action committee (BACPAC) to TRMPAC for a mailer against Democratic House candidate David Lengefeld (of Hamilton); TRMPAC's and LEAA's mailing of cards designed for TRMPAC; the sharing of polling information; TRMPAC's payment of at least one bill for the TLR; and the apparent systematic allocation of candidate expenditures and functions among the organizations. Hammond insisted in his testimony in the TRMPAC civil case, however, that though all the organizations favored the election of Republican candidates, each made its own decision about whom to support, and they did not discuss splitting the races or avoiding overlap in support.

Documents and testimony in the pending civil litigation indicate that the TLR, TRMPAC, and TAB met (usually in Toomey's offices) weekly during the final weeks of the fall 2002 campaign. Some sources report that the Toomey-led TLR was the key organizing and driving force behind these coordinated efforts.[29] Toomey was on the board of TAB and was the lead lobbyist for the TLR. Toomey is generally credited with the intelligence and skills, including being a meticulous organizer, necessary to lead the organized effort in 2002. According to Colyandro, Toomey also often met with him outside of these group meetings to discuss the campaign and politics in general. On one occasion, Toomey persuaded Colyandro to have TRMPAC pay for "opposition research" (i.e., investigation of opposing candidates, usually through online resources) by the TLR on several Democratic candidates, including Debra Danburg.[30]

In 2006 Toomey acknowledged to me that these meetings of TRMPAC, the TLR, TAB, and others occurred regularly during both the primary and general election campaigns in 2002. He emphasized, however, that the participants exercised caution not to include any candidates in the meetings, because of concern that "coordination" with a candidate would make the organizations' expenditures (including corporate funds) illegal.[31] Nevertheless, some Democrats continued in 2006 to feel that since each of these organizations was also making contributions directly or through their PACs to candidates in 2002 while these meetings were taking place, there necessarily was coordination between these organizations and the candidates.[32] However, no criminal charges were brought against Toomey, the TLR, or others for participating in these meetings.

Legal or Illegal Expenditures?

TRMPAC's accountant, Russell Anderson, testified at the TRMPAC civil trial in 2005 that he rigorously kept hard-dollar funds and corporate contributions in separate accounts. As a general-purpose political action committee, TRMPAC could accept both hard-money and corporate donations. It realized, however, that the two could not be commingled.

Expenditures of Hard-Dollar Donations

TRMPAC could use its hard-money donations for direct contributions to selected candidates or direct advocacy on behalf of those candidates. It did so. TRMPAC reported raising approximately $803,026 in hard money. It contributed at least $639,642 of these funds to twenty-one Republican state-legislative candidates in the general election and a lesser amount to selected candidates in the Republican primary. TRMPAC reported these contributions to the Texas Ethics Commission as required by state law. Apparently, the candidates also reported receiving these contributions. Altogether, the TLR ($1,141,152), TAB ($101,821), and TRMPAC gave approximately $2 million to the same general set of Republican state-legislative candidates. (This total includes amounts given by the TLR or TAB to two Republican state Senate candidates who did not receive any contributions from TRMPAC.) Other expenses on behalf of specific candidates were also paid with hard dollars. For example, TRMPAC used hard dollars to pay for at least one "direct advocacy ad" in a race, for a get-out-the-vote telephone bank in nine races, and $5,000 to Kevin Brannon for his work as a consultant for three Republican candidates. No legal challenge has been mounted to these hard-dollar expenditures.

Congressman DeLay's national political action committee, ARMPAC, gave an additional $24,000 to fifteen of these Republican state-legislative candidates (at least twelve of whom had also received contributions from TRMPAC). Some of these checks from ARMPAC funds were accompanied by letters on TRMPAC stationery that said, "We are pleased to send you a contribution of [amount] compliments of Congressman Tom DeLay's political action committee, Americans for a Republican Majority." Republicans dismiss the significance of TRMPAC, the TLR, TAB, and ARMPAC giving generally to the same Republican candidates because, they claim, it was reasonably clear which legislative races were competitive in 2002 and it was not surprising that these different organizations reached similar conclusions as to whom to support.

TRMPAC sent hard-money contributions to at least twenty-seven Republican House candidates in the fall of 2002. Twenty of these candidates were the same ones endorsed and supported with contributions by BACPAC. However, TRMPAC also gave small ($1,000–$5,000) contributions in the general election to seven Republican candidates who did not receive money from BACPAC. Most of these were incumbents in safe seats (e.g., Representative Crabb of Atascocita, who got $2,500). Both TRMPAC and BACPAC gave to at least two Republican incumbents (Hamilton and Wong) who were in close contests in the general election. TAB also sent mailers in those contests.

Expenditures of Corporate Dollars

The major controversy over TRMPAC's expenditures centered on approximately $748,562 that TRMPAC reported to the Internal Revenue Service but never reported to the Texas Ethics Commission. Most or all of this money was corporate money.

Early in its existence, TRMPAC explained to potential donors that it would be providing "message and issue development" and "market research and communications" in furtherance of its mission of helping Republican candidates win election. TRMPAC told potential corporate donors that corporate funds expended for such purposes were "administrative expenses" allowable under state law. Thus, TRMPAC concluded that not only was it allowed to solicit such corporate contributions, but it was also not required to report either the contributions or their expenditure to the Texas Ethics Commission.

In civil litigation against TRMPAC, Democrats argued that only a small fraction of the corporate funds raised by TRMPAC were spent for legitimate administrative expenses such as bookkeeping, phone bills, and legal fees. The litigation focused on the approximately $600,000 in corporate funds that TRMPAC raised in 2002 and on how these monies had been spent. Among the specific TRMPAC expenditures challenged as not being legitimate administrative expenses were payments for all of the following:

- Political consultants Kevin Brannon ($39,162) and Jim Ellis ($5,000)
- PAC executive director John Colyandro—$69,936
- Contact America, for voter identification calls—$65,175
- Fabrizio, McLaughlin & Associates, a Virginia-based polling and consulting firm—$27,000
- Hard-money solicitation expenses (e.g., Lilly & Company)—$28,524[33]
- Danielle Ferro (DeLay's daughter) and Coastal Consulting, for event planning—$30,893[34]
- WRM Consulting, Inc. (Warren Robold) for corporate-money solicitation expenses—$50,843

- Entertainment and meeting expenses (including payments to, among others, Hyatt Regency, the Barton Creek Country Club, the Headliner's Club in Austin, and the Petroleum Club of Houston)—$27,528
- Printing expenses (e.g., for mailings) to Thomas Graphics, Laguna Printing, and Texas Printing—$13,470
- Texas Association of Business for mailings in the Republican primary—$10,200
- Republican National Committee—$190,000

Among other expenditures were payments for background checks on Democratic House incumbents and the payment by TRMPAC for frequent conference calls among Republican lawmakers, organized by Phil King.

In response, TRMPAC in its 2005 civil trial insisted that the "administrative expenses" of a political action committee like TRMPAC would necessarily include the cost of services such as fund-raising, polling, etc., and that as long as these corporate funds were not spent for direct advocacy, there was no violation of state law. Altogether, TAB and TRMPAC raised and spent over $2.65 million in corporate money to affect the 2002 state-legislative elections. LEAA spent another estimated $2–2.5 million in corporate money to affect those races as well as the one for attorney general.

Contact America

The circumstances surrounding TRMPAC's use of Contact America show both how TRMPAC tried to distinguish in its expenditures between hard money and corporate money and how the organization coordinated efforts with TAB for the general election. Contact America is a polling company that uses a telephone bank to determine hot-button issues for a group of voters and to identify and segregate potential voters. According to his deposition testimony, Colyandro worked with Contact America in the fall of 2002 to identify voters likely to vote for the Republican candidates in approximately fifteen targeted House races. Colyandro also helped write the telephone script designed to determine the voter's feelings about certain defining issues. TAB then forwarded the scripts to its attorney, Ed Shack, for review. Calls were made on or about October 16, 2002. Based on responses by each household to this script, Contact America created a list of voters likely to support the Republican candidate in the election. The cost for the calls and the list preparation was $65,175. Initially at Colyandro's direction, Contact America sent its bill to TAB. Hammond approved paying the bill, and then voided the check days later. TRMPAC then paid the bill from its corporate-money account. The list was provided to

Thomas Graphics for mailings from TAB. A flyer was designed for each race based on the issues important to voters in the particular district. As with the telephone scripts, Colyandro played a major role in designing these materials. TAB used its corporate funds to pay for these "issue ad" mailings.

On the heels of the mailings (on or about October 31, 2002), Contact America again called selected voters in the districts, but this time urged them to support the Republican candidate in the House contest. These calls were part of a targeted get-out-the-vote effort. For this second set of calls (in nineteen districts), TRMPAC paid Contact America $48,039.[35] These funds came from TRMPAC's hard-money account because the follow-up calls were considered direct advocacy.

In his testimony in 2005, TAB president Bill Hammond explained that the initial telephone scripts and the subsequent "issue ad" mailings had been "very carefully crafted" in conjunction with attorney Ed Shack to be within the limits of "issue advocacy." Both organizations tried to distinguish between "issue advocacy" mailings and endorsement mailings. The distinction often became blurred for the participants. For example, in his deposition in the civil proceedings against TRMPAC, printer Thomas referred to these mailings by TAB to the Contact America list as "endorsements," but later changed his characterization of them to "issue advocacy," which was consistent with Hammond's representation. Significantly, although TAB used the Contact America list for its mailings, Hammond said that he never had any dealings with the company. According to Hammond, relations with Contact America were left to Colyandro and TRMPAC.

The TRMPAC Conveyance of $190,000 to the Republican National State Elections Committee (RNSEC)

The TRMPAC expenditure that later attracted the greatest attention was the transfer in September 2002 of $190,000 in corporate dollars to the Republican National Committee (RNC). On September 10, TRMPAC executive director John Colyandro e-mailed Russell Anderson, the TRMPAC accountant, telling him to send a blank "soft dollar account check" to Jim Ellis in Washington. Colyandro stressed that the check "[n]eeds to arrive tomorrow." Colyandro was at the Greg Abbott campaign headquarters at the time he sent the message, so a messenger brought the check to him at Abbott's headquarters to sign. Colyandro later testified in a deposition that the urgency in getting the check to Ellis was due to Ellis's meeting on September 11 with someone at the RNC. Colyandro provided no explanation as to why the check was blank.[36] Democrats alleged that, along with this blank check, Ellis also provided the RNC with a list of the names of several state-legislative candidates in Texas and a dollar amount that TRMPAC wanted the RNC to send each of them. Other testimony suggested that Ellis bargained with the RNC over the specific amounts to be sent back to the Texas candidates in return for the TRMPAC money, and that the check was blank because the amount of the transfer was yet to be negotiated. A source that has asked to remain anonymous has assured me that such a list exists and apparently came from TRMPAC. He declined, however, to identify who prepared the list. Notably, no TRMPAC official bothered at the time to obtain legal advice from attorney Ed Shack, or apparently any other lawyer, about the legality of this transfer. An RNC spokesperson said during the TRMPAC trial that the RNC had no record of who met with Ellis on September 11. A later indictment, however, names the RNC official as Terry Nelson, the RNC deputy chief of staff.[37]

The TRMPAC check, eventually dated September 13, 2002, was made out to the Republican National State Elections Committee (RNSEC), the non-federal component of the RNC. The check was deposited on September 20. Events on October 2, 2002, may prove important in the criminal prosecutions because Congressman DeLay's calendar shows that he met at his House office with Ellis at 10:30 a.m. on that day. Republican candidates and officials in Texas were getting anxious over the holdup of the expected contributions from the RNSEC; they were needed for the rapidly approaching election. Craddick had called the RNSEC (and possibly DeLay) several times, asking, "Where is the money?" The details of this meeting between DeLay and Ellis on October 2, 2002, remained disputed in 2006. At first, Ellis's counsel in the later criminal proceedings denied that the $190,000 amount was discussed at the meeting.[38] DeLay, however, later acknowledged that the subject of the money did come up, but he insisted that it arose only at the close of the meeting, as Ellis was leaving, and that Ellis merely told him that TRMPAC had sent the sum to the RNSEC. DeLay says he merely told Ellis "fine."

I do not know whether more happened at the meeting than has been admitted. Democrats intimate that DeLay possibly prodded the RNSEC on October 2, 2002, to speed up the contributions back to Texas. It is known that on that same day the RNSEC generated memoranda approving $190,000 contributions to seven Texas legislative candidates. Two days later, on October 4, the RNSEC sent $190,000 in checks to the following candidates: Todd Baxter ($35,000), Dwayne Bohac ($20,000), Glenda Dawson ($40,000), Dan Flynn ($20,000), Rick Green ($20,000), Jack Stick ($35,000), and Larry Taylor ($20,000). The checks were numbered sequentially (Nos. 7470–7476). Each candidate was in one of TRMPAC's targeted races and was considered to be in jeopardy of losing. The RNSEC actually sent $198,500 to Texas candidates on

October 4, but that total included several small amounts ($500 or less) that had been approved prior to October 2 and that were in checks not in sequence with the checks to the seven legislative candidates. Two of these small contributions went to state House candidates, but some of these contributions went to Republican candidates in local races, such as justice of the peace, constable, and county clerk. A study indicates that other than this $190,000 contribution to seven state-legislative candidates in Texas, the RNC gave a total of only $35,775 to state-legislative candidates nationwide for the 2002 election.[39] The largest of these contributions was $2,000; the smallest contribution to a candidate on TRMPAC's list was $20,000. The contributions by the RNSEC to the seven legislative candidates in Texas were clearly not routine.

The $190,000 transferred from TRMPAC to the RNSEC came from TRMPAC's corporate-funds account and had not been reported to the Texas Ethics Commission. Under state law, such corporate funds could not legally be given to a candidate. This has led to the allegation that Colyandro and Ellis, on behalf of TRMPAC, were laundering the corporate funds by transferring them to the RNSEC in return for "hard money" contributions back from RNSEC to the candidates. This transaction is the basis for criminal indictments returned (initially in 2004) against Colyandro and Ellis, and in 2005 against Congressman Tom DeLay. These criminal charges are further discussed in Chapter Seventeen.

At the TRMPAC civil trial in 2005, the election-law counsel for the RNC, Charles Robert Spies, testified that the $190,000 in checks to the state-legislative candidates was only a part of approximately $1.6 million that the RNC had sent to Texas for the 2002 election. Most of it ($1.1 million, including the checks for $190,000) had gone directly to Republican candidates, including statewide and local candidates. Most of the remainder had gone to the Texas Republican Party or its PAC. A check for $6,700 had gone to TRMPAC (which TRMPAC deposited to its corporate-money account). Spies further testified that there was no evidence that the two transactions (the gift of $190,000 from TRMPAC and the equivalent contributions to the Texas state-legislative candidates) had been related or had been a quid pro quo.

He acknowledged that the RNC often responds to outside contacts, including congressmen such as DeLay, when determining how RNC funds should be spent. He said he had no knowledge of whether DeLay may have contacted the RNC about the contributions to the Texas legislative candidates. He explained that "trading money" had been a common practice until the passage of national campaign-finance legislation (the Bipartisan Campaign Reform Act) after the 2002 election. He added, however, that he would be surprised if the RNC had agreed to swap federal funds for state funds, since unrestricted federal "hard dollars" were worth more as a commodity than the restricted corporate "soft" money. Later, after a very effective cross-examination by plaintiffs' attorney Chris Feldman, Spies seemed less confident that the transactions had been a coincidence, but said that even if such a trade had occurred, there was nothing wrong: "My comment would be 'So what! It's perfectly legal.'" He said that he believed that the transaction was legal because the TRMPAC check was deposited to the RNSEC's soft-money account (thus maintaining the nature of the funds), but the candidate contributions came from a hard-money account used for such purposes. He suggested that Kevin Shuvalov, the RNSEC's regional director for the southern region, including Texas, was the person who probably made the ultimate recommendation on the expenditure of RNSEC funds in Texas.

During cross-examination, Spies acknowledged that any trade of the $190,000 from TRMPAC to the RNSEC for hard-dollar contributions to the Texas candidates may have been a second choice for Ellis and Colyandro. Colyandro in his deposition testified that the original plan was to send the corporate money to the Texas Republican Party's Texas Victory Fund. However, that decision was contemplated within sixty days of the election, and Texas law expressly prohibits contributions of corporate money to "a political party" within that period. However, TRMPAC assumed that this provision of state law applied only to contributions to the state party, not to the RNSEC, which TRMPAC officials were later to characterize as an "out of state political action committee," not a political party under Texas law. As Colyandro acknowledged in his deposition, TRMPAC did not want to waste the $190,000. It was too late to contribute the funds to the Texas Republican Party or to use them effectively in Texas during the last days of the 2002 campaign, so the money was sent to the RNC, apparently in return for an equivalent amount in hard-dollar contributions by the RNSEC to selected Republican state-legislative candidates in Texas, in time to be used in the 2002 general election.

Helping Elect Craddick Speaker

Jim Ellis acknowledged in 2003 that one of Congressman DeLay's objectives through TRMPAC in 2002 was to help his friend Tom Craddick become the first Republican Speaker of the Texas House in 130 years. Craddick played a major role in TRMPAC's activities.[40] On one side, he helped TRMPAC raise money, including corporate funds that he could not legally have raised himself as a candidate or officeholder. On the other side, he helped TRMPAC select primary candidates who would later support him for Speaker, and he dispensed TRMPAC funds to those and other candidates to reinforce that support.

Craddick was among the headliners at several TRMPAC fund-raisers (e.g., at a San Antonio fundraiser on July 31, 2002, and at another on September 23, 2002)[41] and accompanied TRMPAC board members on fund-raising visits to important Republican donors. For example, in early 2002 he accompanied Bill Ceverha to Dallas to solicit a contribution from Pickens Oil. A few of the donations to TRMPAC came addressed to Craddick. In October 2002, Craddick met with Chris Winkle, the CEO of Mariner Health Care, Inc. (an Atlanta-based nursing-home operator in Texas), and as a result, Wink gave Craddick a $100,000 check on behalf of the Washington-based Alliance for Quality Nursing Home Care during dinner at a restaurant in Houston. Craddick's friend, lobbyist Buddy Jones, represented the organization and arranged the meeting. The association later acknowledged that it gave the corporate funds to TRMPAC at the request of two of its Texas nursing-home members. Some persons have suggested that Craddick insisted the association give $100,000 to TRMPAC after discovering that it had already given $300,000 to the Texas Association of Business.[42]

Colyandro acknowledged in his deposition that he discussed the TRMPAC endorsements with Craddick. Later, TRMPAC allowed Craddick or his office to personally dispense funds to candidates. When Union Pacific in September 2002 came up with $25,000 in hard dollars to give to eleven TRMPAC-supported candidates and wanted a "'DeLay' person" to be involved in delivery of the checks, Tom Craddick was chosen to deliver the checks. In fact, the Union Pacific checks were sent by Federal Express directly to Craddick to distribute. It is unclear whether Craddick personally delivered any of the Union Pacific checks or whether Union Pacific lobbyist Ron Olson delivered some of them.

On October 18, 2002, TRMPAC wrote $152,000 in checks to fifteen Republican state-legislative candidates. Colyandro had the checks sent to Craddick in Midland to distribute. Craddick was expected to personally hand out the checks at a fund-raiser. Craddick's attorney insisted in 2005 that there was "no quid pro quo" involved in the delivery of the checks. In fact, Craddick's lawyer said that Craddick was out of state at the time and never personally delivered the checks to any candidates, but instead had them sent by overnight delivery.

Two days after the 2002 election, Craddick held a victory press conference in Austin at the Capitol. At the bottom of the invitation to the press conference was a small notice: "Paid for by Texans for a Republican Majority." All of the winning Republican candidates earlier endorsed by TRMPAC were on Craddick's postelection list of lawmakers who had pledged to support his candidacy for Speaker. Lobbyists and corporations that had been the key to funding TRMPAC were also given the opportunity "to meet the new Speaker" at an event in Washington. Among those lobbyists was Drew Maloney, a former DeLay staffer who had been the organizer of the key fund-raiser at the Homestead in Virginia (discussed in Chapter Fifteen).[43]

The Outcome of the 2002 State Legislative Elections

The 2002 campaign was successful. Altogether Republicans won sixteen additional seats in the Texas House. As a result, Republicans would hold an 88 – 62 majority when the House convened in January 2003.

Bill Hammond could not contain his joy at this outcome. In a press release the day after the election, he was quoted as saying "Tuesday's general election can only be described as a sea change in Texas government." In the November 2002 issue of its publication the *Texas Business Report,* TAB proclaimed, "The Texas Association of Business blew the doors off the November 5 general election using an unprecedented show of muscle that featured political contributions and a massive voter education drive." TAB expected that the elected lawmakers "will hold the line on taxes . . . favor lawsuit reform, and . . . make health care affordable and accessible." TAB claimed to have sent approximately 4 million mail pieces, and in two state legislative races (those of Republican candidates Holt Getterman and Gene Seaman) to have relied on radio and television ads. Seventeen (TAB erroneously claimed eighteen) of the twenty-two state House races targeted by TAB were won by the Republican candidate it supported. Six of the defeated House Democrats had been incumbents (Debra Danburg of Houston, Tom Uher of Bay City, Ken Yarbrough of Houston, Ann Kitchen of Austin, David Counts of Knox City, and Bob Glaze of Gilmer). One Senate Democratic incumbent (David Cain of Dallas) targeted by TAB also had been defeated. Hammond's comments were carried widely in newspaper stories and television reports throughout the state. In his highly respected *Quorum Report,* Harvey Kronberg said that much of TAB's effort "came late" in the election campaign and "is credited by many for helping turn the tide in several close races."[44] The outcome gave TAB new "clout" in its battles in the Texas legislature.

TRMPAC's favored candidates were essentially the same as TAB's. Of the twenty-seven whom TRMPAC supported with contributions, only five lost. These were the same five losing Republicans supported by TAB (Nelson Balido, Holt Getterman, Dionne Roberts, Eddie Shauberger, and Rick Green). Of the seven candidates who received the late infusion of money from the

RNSEC, only Rick Green lost. However, unlike Bill Hammond, the principals associated with TRMPAC avoided any public celebration.

Those Who Discovered the Corporate Contributions and Expenditures

Many persons were shocked by the magnitude of the Republican victory in state legislative seats and statewide elections. Some suspected that something foul was the cause. Frequent telephone conversations and e-mail messages followed as information was traded among various individuals and public interest watchdog groups, including Fred Lewis, Craig McDonald of Texans for Public Justice, and Public Citizen. One attorney in particular played a major role during this time and later. Although already thirty-five years of age, Cris Feldman was a recent graduate of the University of Texas School of Law (where he was a student of mine). He had been active in numerous "good government" investigative activities even before becoming a licensed attorney. The *Texas Observer* (August 26, 2005) called him "an intense and driven young lawyer." After the election of 2002, Feldman quickly began to delve deeper into the puzzle of what had happened.

Civil Litigation against TRMPAC and TAB

By the end of November 2002, two lawsuits had been filed in Travis County against Hammond and TAB on behalf of several losing Democratic candidates. Cris Feldman had filed one. Buck Wood had filed the other. Unlike the newly licensed Feldman, Wood was an experienced election lawyer; he had begun his career in the Texas secretary of state's office in the 1970s under Bob Bullock, and became a recognized "legal expert" for Democrats on election rules over the next two decades. Wood had litigated many different election lawsuits, particularly election contests, in the past. In addition to TAB, Wood included the TAB political action committee (BACPAC), Bill Hammond, and "undisclosed corporate contributors, Joe Does and John Doe conspirators" as defendants in his lawsuit. Feldman later added these corporate defendants to his suit.

Both suits proceeded slowly: TAB fought having to disclose its contributors and insisted that it had a constitutional right to solicit and spend corporate funds for a "public information program" that did not expressly advocate voting for or against specific candidates. TAB appealed adverse discovery orders. These appeals, and the distraction of the ongoing criminal investigations and later indictment of TAB (but not Hammond), effectively stalled these proceedings. As a result of these delays, the two civil lawsuits against TAB remained pending at a preliminary stage in 2006. Both Feldman and Wood expect the cases to go forward. Wood told me in 2005 that he expected a quick resolution of these cases (probably without trial) as soon as the criminal investigations end.

In late 2002 and early 2003 the role of TRMPAC gradually became visible. The attorneys in the civil cases were led initially to TRMPAC through some documents found in the TAB litigation. A key moment, however, was when it was discovered that TRMPAC had filed forms with the Internal Revenue Service as a Section 527 corporation and shown far more in contributions and expenditures than it had reported to the Texas Ethics Commission. TRMPAC had reported only its hard-money contributions and expenditures to the TEC. A comparison of the IRS and TEC forms showed a difference of approximately $750,000 in unreported contributions. On May 8, 2003, Feldman filed a suit on behalf of several losing Democratic candidates (with changes over the next few months, the plaintiff candidates eventually became Paul Clayton, Mike Head, David Lengefeld, Danny Duncan, and Ann Kitchen), naming Bill Ceverha, individually and as treasurer of TRMPAC, as defendant. Only four days later (May 12), Wood filed suit on behalf of another losing Democrat (Jim Sylvester) against Ceverha, Ellis, and the Republican National Committee.

Both Feldman and Wood brought the cases based on the contingent recovery of attorney fees. However, in a difference that probably reflected the lawyers' differing levels of experience and the overriding approach of Feldman that "the TRMPAC litigation was a matter of principle," Wood was willing to delay litigating the cases in anticipation of obtaining fees through a settlement, especially as the criminal investigations and indictments proceeded. Feldman was eager to press forward, "to use the judicial process to disclose the wrongs" that had plagued the 2002 campaign.[45]

Both TRMPAC civil lawsuits initially named Ceverha, but both also ended up adding or naming Jim Ellis and John Colyandro as defendants. However, once the criminal indictments came down against Colyandro and Ellis on September 21, 2004, the civil proceedings could not continue against them. Wood chose to let his lawsuit remain dormant, pending the outcome of the criminal proceedings. He used the time to pursue other, unrelated litigation (such as a challenge to the state system for financing public schools) and to quietly obtain settlements, including attorney fees, from some of the corporations that had given to TAB or TRMPAC. For various reasons, including the eagerness of Bill Ceverha to get to trial and of Feldman to show how "secret corporate cash warps the electoral system," Feldman's suit against Ceverha continued, leaving Colyandro and Ellis for later.

Joe K. Crews, a partner in Feldman's law firm, was instrumental in convincing the partners to accept the TAB and TRMPAC litigation, even though the chance of recovering attorney fees was considered slight, and was an important part of the plaintiffs' legal team at trial in the TRMPAC case. Feldman and Crews recruited a third lawyer, noted election and civil rights lawyer David Richards, for the trial. Richards, age seventy-two, was semiretired and living in California. His addition to the plaintiffs' team immediately gave the litigation some recognition and credibility that it might otherwise not have received. Initially, Ceverha was represented by Andy Taylor (who was also representing the TAB defendants). By the time of the trial in 2005, however, Taylor had stepped down as the attorney for Ceverha and TRMPAC. He was replaced by seasoned Austin trial attorney Terry L. Scarborough of the firm Hance, Scarborough, Wright, Woodward & Weisbart. Much of the testimony and evidence from the trial is referenced in this chapter.

The TRMPAC case (*Paul Clayton, et. al. v. Bill Ceverha, Individually and as Treasurer of Texans for a Republican Majority Political Action Committee, et. al.*) went to trial on February 28, 2005, as a bench trial before highly respected Senior State District Judge Joe Hart.[46] The pleadings alleged civil conspiracy, the unlawful acceptance and use of corporate contributions, and violations of chapter 254 of the Texas Election Code. However, the inability to proceed immediately against Ellis and Colyandro, along with the now essentially defunct status of TRMPAC, caused Feldman to proceed against Ceverha only on his obligations as TRMPAC treasurer. As a result, the issue at the trial in February was a narrow one: whether Ceverha failed to report contributions and expenditures that TRMPAC should have reported to the Texas Ethics Commission. Under Texas law (Texas Election Code, section 254.231), the campaign treasurer of a political action committee who fails to report in whole or in part a campaign contribution or campaign expenditure is liable for damages. TRMPAC had not reported its corporate contributions (and some noncorporate contributions) or its expenditure of those contributions. The legality of the contributions and expenditures themselves was not directly at issue. Feldman and Crews insisted that their other charges would wait for the availability of Ellis and Colyandro.

The TRMPAC civil trial was marked by several dynamics or factors not immediately apparent from the pleadings or the evidence adduced at the trial. One of these was the focus of attention on DeLay. Although not a party to this civil lawsuit, DeLay was (as Scarbrough put it) "the pink elephant" in the room. Another matter was the ill will between Scarbrough and Feldman. Scarbrough was uncharacteristically critical of Feldman both to the court and in his public statements. Scarbrough, accustomed to major litigation over large amounts of money, was apparently frustrated by Feldman's relative inexperience, his altruistic intensity, and his eagerness to pursue the case (at a substantial cost in ongoing attorney fees for Ceverha), even though Ceverha did not have assets to pay a significant final judgment. The purpose and pattern of civil litigation as Scarbrough knew them did not seem to apply. Scarbrough accused Feldman of dishonesty and unethical conduct and of being responsible for the criminal complaint that Texans for Public Justice filed against TRMPAC with the Travis County district attorney (see Chapter Seventeen). Scarbrough's obvious frustration with Feldman worked against Scarbrough during the trial. Finally, it should be noted that staffers from the Public Integrity Unit of the Travis County district attorney's office attended the entire civil trial, apparently interested in how the evidence and outcome might affect the criminal proceedings.

On May 26, 2005 (over two months after the trial), Judge Hart issued his ruling by a letter opinion addressed to the counsel. He found that TRMPAC (Bill Ceverha) should have reported the corporate contributions and the expenditure of those funds. Judge Hart rejected Ceverha's argument that the funds did not need to be reported because they were not used for "express advocacy." Hart said that this constitutional protection for individuals and groups "is not necessary for organizations like TRMPAC, 'the major purpose of which is the nomination or election of a candidate.'" In regard to whether the corporations had the requisite intent to use the corporate funds for political purposes rather than administrative expenses, Hart pointed to TRMPAC's stated purpose of helping "Republican candidates successfully run and win campaigns in Texas." He concluded that "there is overwhelming evidence from which the intent of donors to TRMPAC can be fairly and reasonably inferred." Hart rejected the position that the "administrative expense" exception in the Election Code should be interpreted broadly to include expenses such as fund-raising, polling, political direct mail, political research, contributions to the national party, etc.. Hart found that $613,433 in unreported corporate and noncorporate contributions and $684,507 in unreported expenditures should have been reported to the Texas Ethics Commission.

Hart's ruling on the damages issue did not please anyone. He ruled that damages should be based on the unreported contributions and expenditures specifically related to the races of the five named plaintiffs rather than to the whole election. As a result, the total award in damages was only $196,660 (as opposed to a possible award of almost $13 million), to be split among the five plaintiff Democratic candidates. Neither party immediately asked Hart to reduce his ruling to a final judgment or to enter formal findings of fact or conclusions of law. By 2006, neither Ceverha nor the plaintiffs (who would challenge the damage award as insufficient) had undertaken the cost of an appeal yet.

All seem to waiting, partly to see the outcome of the criminal proceedings, although Feldman and his team of attorneys asked for an award of $745,849 in attorney fees. In the meantime, Ceverha had declared bankruptcy.

Commentary

One of the lingering questions about the events of 2002 is why DeLay and the other organizers of TRMPAC made such an effort to elect Republican state lawmakers in Texas when the redistricting plans drawn by the Republican-controlled Legislative Redistricting Board in 2001 seemed virtually certain to result in the election of a Republican majority in the Texas House of Representatives any way. Several reasons suggest themselves. Just electing a Republican majority would not have been sufficient to achieve the objectives DeLay sought. The winning Republicans had to be the right Republicans — committed to the ideology and goals that DeLay thought important. Among these goals was the election of Craddick as Speaker. If he became Speaker, Craddick could be counted upon to lead the Texas House in congressional redistricting.

A second goal of TRMPAC was to increase DeLay's power and influence in the national party. The money-raising and money-dispensing capabilities of ARMPAC (particularly with corporate money) had been important to Republican electoral successes nationwide. Moreover, DeLay had gained influence with the Republican congressmen who had benefited from ARMPAC. TRMPAC presented a means of achieving that same sort of success and influence, for the national Republican Party and DeLay personally, in Texas — as well as a possible model for use at the state level nationwide. According to Jim Ellis, DeLay indicated in 2002 his interest in creating organizations like TRMPAC in many other key states, thereby creating a web of organizations intended to enhance personal and national party power nationwide.[47]

Whatever happens with the civil litigation and criminal charges surrounding the events of 2002, the immediate results of the activities of TRMPAC and its allies were a spectacular success. Thirteen of the seventeen candidates who received money from TRMPAC won their contested Republican primaries. Seventeen of the Republican candidates supported by TRMPAC in targeted contested races won in the general election. Each of these Republicans had pledged to support Craddick for Speaker and followed through once they took office. All of them also voted for major legislation in 2003 designed to limit the recovery of damages in tort suits. All but two voted for the final congressional-redistricting bill.

Republicans have insisted that what TRMPAC did in 2002 was not significantly different, if at all, from what was customary in election campaigns at the time. I believe, however, that in 2002 the principals in TRMPAC were reckless. Perhaps intoxicated by the apparent success of their operations and the prospect of success in the coming election, they confused what was happening in federal campaigns with what was allowed for state election campaigns in Texas. They obtained a written opinion from Texas election-law expert Ed Shack, but only in March 2002, long after TRMPAC had begun aggressively soliciting corporate money. I found no indication that TRMPAC had fashioned its conduct to comply with the directions in Shack's opinion or had consulted Shack on day-to-day decisions, such as whether the ongoing uses of corporate funds were for allowable administrative expenses. They did not ask Shack's legal counsel on the legality of sending the $190,000 in corporate funds to the RNSEC in September in return for contributions to state-legislative candidates. Shack was TAB's lawyer. His March 22, 2002, opinion letter for TRMPAC, indicating that a political action committee could accept corporate funds for administrative expenses, seems to have been an all too obvious attempt to "paper" the record of TRMPAC's conduct—to make it appear that TRMPAC was following legal advice.

Republicans have alleged that Democratic PACs have accepted and used corporate funds in a manner similar to that of TRMPAC. Thus far, however, the Republicans have relied on only generalized claims to support this argument. TRMPAC indicated to its potential corporate contributors as early as December 2001 that it intended to use the corporate money "unlike other organizations." Specifically, TRMPAC said that rather than "just paying for overhead," the money would be used "to fund a series of productive and innovative activities." TRMPAC clearly anticipated using corporate money differently from how other organizations (Republican or Democratic) had used it in Texas in the past. Inquiries made by the Travis County district attorney at the request of Republican lawmakers in 2003 and 2004 failed to disclose similar uses of corporate funds in the past by Democratic organizations. The district attorney's inquiry into the Lone Star Fund organized by Martin Frost found "no evidence that any corporate or labor organizations funds were ever deposited into or expended from Lone Star Fund–Texas."[48] Former speaker Laney insists that in six years his Partnership PAC accepted $100,000 or less in corporate contributions and spent all of it on what he felt were clearly administrative overhead expenses (rent, utilities, etc.).[49]

Understandably, Republicans may be reluctant to take Laney's word on the conduct of his PAC, or may even be skeptical of the objectivity of an investigation by a Democratic district attorney. However, Republicans have failed to come forward with any information to contradict these representations. State Senator Robert Deuell, the Republican lawmaker who requested the investigation of the Lone Star Fund, seemed to abandon the issue after Earle released his findings by letter on July 30, 2004. Senator Deuell did so without disclosing any specific information warranting further investigation.

Republicans have further urged that TRMPAC's expenditures for things like polling, voter identification, and political consultation were common for political action committees. They are correct that political parties, under the guidelines of the Federal Election Commission, were using corporate funds in 2002 to pay for "party building" activities, such as "voter drive costs" (e.g., voter registration, voter identification, get-out-the-vote campaigns, or other activities that encourage the general public to support candidates of a particular party), and for "issue advocacy" at the federal level.[50] Furthermore, some of these voter-drive costs that the national party could pay for with corporate funds included the federal portion of such costs incurred in mixed state-federal elections.

However, Texas law and precedent did not include these same exceptions to the state's prohibition against using corporate funds in state elections. Nor had the Texas Ethics Commission given its blessing to spending corporate money for such activities. It had recognized only the limited exception of using corporate funds for "administrative expenses," generally defined as expenses incurred in the normal course of business by any active organization, whether or not it engaged in political activity.[51] In view of this difference between TRMPAC's conduct and state law, by 2005 TRMPAC's attorneys were left to argue in the civil and criminal proceedings that TRMPAC's polling, political consulting, voter-identification campaigns, etc. (i.e., its "voter drive" or "party building" activities) were really only "administrative expenses" for a general-purpose PAC. This argument is a real stretch; even federal law at the time distinguished between administrative expenses and these other costs.[52] TRMPAC's expectation that state law allowed corporate money to be spent to raise hard dollars or for voter drives or party building was a mistake.

Republicans have also suggested that exchanges of funds between state and national parties, similar to the transfer of the $190,000 by TRMPAC to the RNC, were common before the McCain-Feingold bill changed the law before the 2004 election. Although the mere existence of any such transfers in the past would not necessarily legally justify TRMPAC's actions, it would strengthen the argument that neither TRMPAC nor its principals had the requisite criminal intent. It is clear from federal records that at least since the mid-1990s both parties transferred large sums of money to and from the national party under this loophole in the federal law.[53] However, it is not at all clear that any of these transfers were analogous to the 2002 quid pro quo trade of corporate funds for hard-money contributions.

Democrats have claimed that the Republicans unlawfully laundered the $190,000 in restricted corporate dollars into unrestricted hard-dollar contributions by passing it through the RNC. Democrats have challenged the normality of this transaction by pointing out that other than this $190,000, the RNSEC gave a total of only $35,775 to state-legislative candidates nationwide, and the largest of those contributions was only $2,000. By comparison, the smallest contribution to any of the seven candidates in Texas that shared in the $190,000 was $20,000. Republicans have responded that sending more money to these candidates in Texas made sense because of the importance of winning control of the Texas House and because no comparable opportunity for Republican success existed elsewhere in the country. Republicans also have asserted that Texas has long allowed corporate money to be used for "administrative" expenses, even though the necessary effect has been to free up more hard dollars to contribute to candidates. DeLay's counsel, Dick DeGuerin, asked me in 2006, "How is this [the 2002 TRMPAC transfer] any different?" He insisted that if the TRMPAC transfer to the RNSEC freed up more hard dollars for the RNC to send to Texas, then the transfer was simply a continuation of an old and legal practice.[54]

TRMPAC mistakenly assumed that the conduct of political parties and committees at the federal level indicated what was allowable in Texas. TRMPAC was wrong: Texas law was far more restrictive. Ultimately, however, the outcome in the civil and criminal proceedings against TRMPAC and its principals will likely turn on the constitutionality of those restrictive provisions of the Texas Election Code. The U.S. Supreme Court has recognized that all government restrictions on election expenditures and contributions affect an area protected by the First Amendment.[55] The First Amendment protects the rights of political expression and political association. The Court has determined, however, that some government regulation of contributions is allowable, upholding state and federal restrictions on corporate and labor union contributions and expenditures.[56] TRMPAC has challenged the Texas provisions on corporate contributions as unconstitutionally vague, claiming that any government restrictions on the use of money in politics must be narrowly drawn and clear, and must provide adequate notice of what is or is not allowed. Otherwise, the rights of individuals and organizations to participate freely in political discourse is burdened or chilled by the uncertain fear of criminal prosecution. The Democrats responded that it is inappropriate to apply the same standard of statutory vagueness to ordinary voters and to political committees set up for the purpose of achieving certain election results. They argue that the politically savvy officials of TRMPAC knew or should have known that the extent of the organization's solicitation and expenditure of corporate funds in 2001–2002 greatly exceeded anything permitted by state law and that any question of vagueness should be determined "as applied" to these experienced actors. This issue of unconstitutional vagueness will likely determine the outcome of the criminal (and possibly civil) proceedings involving TRMPAC and its principals.

CHAPTER 5

As Partisan as the Law Allows: Republican Strategy in 2003

I'm the majority leader and we want more seats.
— CONGRESSMAN TOM DELAY, ASSOCIATED PRESS, MAY 7, 2003

Our purpose was purely political. We wanted to elect more Republicans to Congress.
— STATE REPRESENTATIVE PHIL KING, 2006

There was no single strategy over 2001–2003 attributable to all Republicans. Different ones foresaw different outcomes and had different (although often similar) objectives. The central character in the Republican drive for congressional redistricting throughout this period, however, was Congressman Tom DeLay. His goal was to elect a Texas congressional delegation dominated by Republicans. On review of the events over this period, it is fair to credit DeLay with a strategy for achieving this goal and, because of the ultimate success of that strategy, to treat it as the "Republican Strategy."

Although George W. Bush had won election as president and, on the way, had overwhelmingly carried Texas, 2000 was not a good year for the Republican effort to gain seats in Congress from Texas. All seventeen of the Democratic incumbents won reelection. This result was a setback for the Republican Party, but also was a personal embarrassment for Tom DeLay. While he was scouring the country for opportunities to add to the slight Republican majority in Congress, he was unable to win any additional seats in Texas. DeLay's critics (both Republican and Democratic) said he "had not delivered" even in his home state. DeLay set out to change that situation.

DeLay's tactics evolved as circumstances changed. In 2001 he appeared before the Texas legislature and urged it to draw compact, nonpartisan congressional boundaries in order to increase minority voting strength. He pointed out that boundary changes in Dallas could increase Hispanic voting strength there.

In 2002, DeLay's focus shifted: his goal became to elect enough of the right Republicans to the Texas House to ensure that his friend Tom Craddick would become Speaker and the last roadblock to congressional redistricting would be removed.

DeLay's goals continued to evolve in 2003 as circumstances changed. With a clear Republican majority in both houses of the Texas legislature, DeLay no longer spoke so often about increasing Hispanic voting strength in Dallas. Instead, his focus shifted to passing a redistricting plan that would maximize the number of Democratic seats that could be eliminated. As obstacles to his control of the final redistricting plan disappeared, DeLay's goal for the number of additional Republican seats increased. Given a chance in late 2003 to oversee the drawing of essentially whatever plan they wanted, DeLay and other Republican activists seized the opportunity to stretch the legal constraints and design a map that aggressively targeted all ten Anglo Democratic congressmen and aimed to elect as many Republicans as possible.

Ultimately, the only constraint on DeLay's ambition for increasing Republican power in Congress through Texas redistricting was the law, particularly as embodied in the Voting Rights Act. Even in this regard he was aided by the U.S. Department of Justice in 2003 being under the leadership of Attorney General John Ashcroft, a staunch Republican.

The Republican strategy was opportunistic and ruthless. Forces within the party and ideological fellow travelers on its fringes saw the circumstances in Texas as a litmus-test showdown between political parties and ideologies. DeLay successfully coordinated many political assets at the national and state levels to achieve an optimal final redistricting plan: redrawing Texas congressional districts was not a matter to be left to Texas lawmakers.

Rationales for Redistricting

As part of their strategy, Republicans offered several justifications for redistricting in 2003, other than the party's quest for greater partisan power. An overriding rationale was that the Texas congressional delegation should better reflect the support shown by Texas voters for President Bush. Bush had carried the state overwhelmingly in 2000, yet a majority of the congressional delegation remained Democratic and more often than not voted against Bush-sponsored legislation. Republicans urged that if Texas voters supported Bush, their representatives in Congress should do the same.

A second rationale was "political fairness." By 2003, Republicans in Texas held all federal and state offices elected statewide. In 2002, Republican statewide candidates had generally won with more than 55 percent of the vote. In one of the closest statewide races (for lieutenant governor), Republican David Dewhurst had won with slightly less than 52 percent of the vote. The highest vote getter for the Democrats in a statewide race had received only 46 percent of the vote; several Democratic candidates had not even received 40 percent. Given this strong showing by Republican candidates, Republicans argued in 2003 that it was unfair to allow Democrats to continue to hold a majority of the state's seats in the U.S. House. Moreover, the Republicans argued, the Democratic incumbent congressmen had been able to win reelection only because the Democrats had gerrymandered district lines in 1991 and the later federal-court plans had simply maintained the effects of that earlier partisan gerrymander. DeLay pointed out that "[m]ore than 56, almost 57 percent of the Texans in this state in the last election [2002] voted for a Republican running for Congress, yet we only have about 45 percent of the seats. Why? Because of the way the lines are drawn, no other reason than the way the lines are drawn."[1] Republicans urged that, as a matter of fairness, they should be entitled to undo the effects of the earlier alleged Democratic gerrymander.

Obviously the final districting plan with twenty-two (68.8 percent) heavily Republican districts out of the state's thirty-two exceeded the 55–60 percent proportion mentioned by DeLay and other Republicans during the redistricting process. The 2004 outcome (twenty-one out of thirty-two, or 65.6 percent) similarly exceeded this proportion. However, in subsequent litigation, the Republicans argued that if a political party has a voting majority statewide of above 50 percent, it should expect to control a larger percentage of a state's congressional districts. They pointed to expert analyses indicating that with a statewide voting majority of 55–60 percent, Republicans in Texas should expect to be able to control the outcome in as many as 25 of the state's congressional delegation. By example, they pointed to Massachusetts, where a Democratic majority elected all of the state's congressmen.

In a third rationale, Republicans noted that the congressional lines in effect in 2003 were the result of a court-adopted plan, and argued that it was the legislature's duty to replace the court's plan with one of its own. Congressman DeLay went a step further, suggesting that the court's plan had been intentionally drawn to protect Democratic incumbents. DeLay explained, "When the Democrats in Texas saw that they no longer were the majority party, they used judges to protect them. And they went 20 years being a minority party with a majority of the Congressional delegation. And they used judges to do it."[2] He specifically blamed District Judge John Hannah (a former Democratic state representative and secretary of state), who had served as one of the three federal judges on the panel that had drawn the congressional district lines in 2001.[3]

A Gerrymander Is in the Eyes of the Beholder

Much of the rhetoric either justifying or condemning the Republican effort to redraw congressional boundaries in 2003 relied on use of the word "gerrymander." Democrats condemned the Republican effort as a "partisan gerrymander." Republicans condemned the then-existing congressional plan as the result of a Democratic "partisan gerrymander" in 1991. It turns out that the two political parties were working with different definitions of what constitutes an offensive gerrymander.

Historically, the search for a gerrymander usually begins by looking for bizarre or irregularly shaped districts not attributable to political subdivision (e.g., county or city) boundaries or natural features such as rivers or mountains. After all, the word was coined in 1812 to describe a legislative district created for political advantage in Massachusetts by the party of then-governor Elbridge Gerry. Some thought the district looked like a salamander, and thus coined the word "gerrymander."

Shape remains a key factor for the courts in identifying election districts that have been drawn to give an unfair advantage to one political or interest group over another: an odd shape suggests that something odd is happening (i.e., that the districts are being drawn to combine geographically disparate groups of like-minded voters to maximize the voting strength of an interest group or political party). However, a party or interest group may be advantaged or disadvantaged by district lines that are not particularly unusual. It is at this juncture that the two parties in Texas reached different conclusions about the application of "gerrymander" to the 1991 and 2003 plans.

The Democratically drawn 1991 congressional redistricting plan was not an obvious partisan gerrymander as measured by the traditional test of districts drawn to combine voters across a state in oddly shaped districts to maximize or minimize political strength. Republicans challenged the plan as a partisan gerrymander in 1991, but lost before a Republican-dominated three-judge court. The 1991 plan contained several extremely bizarre looking districts in Dallas and Harris Counties, but the shape of these districts was a direct by-product of the creation in these two counties of African-American and Hispanic majority-minority districts.[4] Contiguous Republican districts in these urban areas necessarily were bizarre-looking mirror images of minority districts. These oddly shaped districts in Harris and Dallas counties were later struck down in *Bush v. Vera* as racial gerrymanders. They were eliminated in a plan drawn by the federal court that was used in all elections beginning in 1996 and that was the basis for the plan drawn by the federal court in *Balderas v. Perry* in 2001. The suburban and rural districts were reasonably compact: Democrats packed the Republican suburbs into as few districts as possible (which were safe for Republican incumbents), and elsewhere they had preserved the core of existing rural districts to protect Democratic incumbents, so districts did not need to stretch across the state in a search for like-minded voters.[5] The districts were drawn to effect the state interest of maintaining "constituent-member relations." Therefore, to Democrats the 1991 plan was not a partisan gerrymander.

To Republicans, however, the plan was a partisan gerrymander not because the districts statewide were oddly shaped, but because it had been drawn to protect incumbents, most of whom were Democrats. Republicans insisted that a "fair" congressional mirror plan would be one drawn to the voting trends of recent statewide elections. In 2003, the Republican-controlled legislature ended up with a plan in which many districts were irregularly shaped. To Democrats, the plan was an offensive gerrymander. In the eyes of Republicans, however, the 2003 plan was fair because it created districts likely to elect a congressional delegation reflecting recent statewide voting trends.

Whether or not some districts in the 1991 plan could properly be labeled gerrymanders because they were bizarre in appearance or were attempts to protect incumbents, the plan was not actually responsible for the election of most of the Anglo Democratic incumbents targeted in 2003. The 1991 plan concentrated suburban Republicans heavily in compact districts, but these districts were essentially mirror reflections of the urban minority-opportunity districts with their heavy concentrations of Democrats. The difference between the number of Republican and Democratic congressmen in 2003 lay outside of these urban and suburban areas. Most of the Democratic congressmen targeted in 2003 had won in rural districts that were voting Republican in statewide races. Many had not benefited from the 1991 attempt to protect Democratic incumbents simply because they were not incumbents in 1991. Six of the ten targeted Anglo Democrats (Sandlin, Doggett, Lampson, Green, Bell, and Turner) had been elected after 1991. Four had been first elected as late as 1996. Doggett (elected in 1994) had won in a compact district that was wholly contained within the Democratic stronghold of Travis County and never challenged as a gerrymander of any kind. It was inaccurate for Republicans to depict the targeted Democratic congressmen (with the possible exception of Martin Frost, Ralph Hall, Chet Edwards, and Charles Stenholm) as holding office in 2003 because of any congressional districts designed in 1991 to protect Anglo Democratic congressmen.

Another circumstance was critical to the survival of the Democratic rural incumbents in 2002. Most of the Republican funds in 2002 flowed to the Republican effort to win the Texas House instead of to the Republican congressional challengers. Of the six Republicans challenging Democratic rural incumbents (John Lawrence in District 1, Van Brookshire in District 2, John

Graves in District 4, Paul Williams in District 9, Ramsey Farley in District 11, and Rob Beckham in District 17), only two—Farley and Beckham—received any money at all from either ARMPAC (DeLay's federal PAC), the national Republican Party, or any related party committee. They received only $5,000 apiece from ARMPAC and only $20,000 from Republican Party committees. By comparison, the DeLay fund-raising machinery garnered over $1.5 million for TRMPAC, and the RNC sent significantly more money (partly as a result of funds sent from TRMPAC) to individual Texas state House candidates than to the party's challengers to the incumbent Democrats.

The Democrats in 2003 argued that the voters in these rural districts had a right to elect whomever they preferred (Republican or Democratic) and that Republican defeats in 2002 had been attributable to qualitative differences between the candidates from the two parties. This argument was never successful in the media or, perhaps more importantly, in federal court. Republicans successfully depicted the 1991 redistricting as a partisan gerrymander and, without addressing any specific Democratic incumbent (except Martin Frost), broadly portrayed all of the Anglo Democratic incumbents in 2003 as the undeserving beneficiaries of that gerrymander.

Effectively Utilizing Republican Assets

Congressman DeLay and his staff and associates focused on achieving a favorable redistricting. They alternately inspired, coordinated, and managed a host of Republican Party assets—including technology, lawmaker sentiment, state officials and their staffs, state-legislative majorities, the U.S. attorney general, U.S. congressmen, activists and donors, and even the White House—to achieve this goal.

Technology

To some extent, the ability to engineer a particular partisan effect in redistricting in the 2000s can be attributed to the availability of three things: census data in very small geographical components (i.e., blocks and election precincts), past election returns by precinct, and software that allows such data to be easily viewed and manipulated. This observation, however, is only partly correct.

Census data at the block level has been used for redistricting since at least the 1970s. Precinct-by-precinct election data—used to forecast outcomes in future elections—was also available in the past. Computers were being used by the early 1980s to manipulate all this data and produce redistricting plans.

In fact, the Texas redistricting plans that the federal courts struck down in the 1990s as racial gerrymanders were legally vulnerable because they had been created using computers to identify the racial and ethnic makeup of urban census blocks and then to combine selected blocks into outlandishly shaped districts that meandered block by block in an effort to "capture" enough minority voters to create majority-minority districts. Therefore, the use neither of census-block or past election data nor of computers was new in the 2000s.

The important changes for the 2000s were ones that decentralized the map-drawing process. Although computers had been used to configure districts in prior decades, such use had been largely confined to the designated staff of the state legislature (the Texas Legislative Council). Individual redistricting plans were generated primarily through central computers controlled by the legislature. Lawmakers could request the legislative staff to draw up a plan based on specific criteria, or, in the 1990s, they could access the central computer (using the Red Appl system) directly. Few persons outside the state legislative staff were skillful at using the computers to draw maps. Moreover, legislative lawyers often reviewed the plans as they were drawn and recommended modifications deemed necessary to meet legal requirements.

By the 2000s, however, much had changed. Software was more sophisticated. Many more people knew how to use computers to manipulate vast amounts of data. Virtually any lawmaker or group interested in redistricting had one or more (usually young) assistants eager to play at drawing redistricting plans on a computer. Several companies had designed redistricting software. Census and election data was available in a format that could be used on personal computers or laptops. Specialized software was available to show selected data (e.g., the location of Republican women's clubs). As a result, an essentially unlimited number of map drawers could work independently and explore the effects of an infinite number of redistricting options. The software allowed map drawers to instantly see the partisan or racial effect of each change in a redistricting plan. Any of these districting plans could be transferred to the state-legislative computer system and presented as an official plan, with accompanying color maps and detailed demographic information. In the 2000s, the state legislative staff effectively lost control of the map-making process.

These changes were crucial to what happened during the 2003 redistricting. Once the redistricting bill reached the conference committee in September 2003, the actual map drawing rested in the hands of a very small cadre of like-minded persons. There were no legislative rules constraining how the districts could be drawn. The map drawers disagreed about some districts (e.g., whether a West Texas district should be dominated by Midland, as Speaker Craddick wanted), but worked together to maximize Republican electoral success and marginalize Democratic voting strength. The map drawers had the essentially unfettered opportunity to use their PCs (more often laptops) to constantly redraw and tweak the redistricting plan until they found one that was as partisan as the law allowed. The result was a masterful Republican gerrymander.

Republican Lawmaker Sentiment for Redistricting

When asked in 2005 to explain DeLay's success in 2003, more than one Republican lawmaker suggested that DeLay had been "plowing a fertile field." Few Republican lawmakers in Texas saw congressional redistricting as a high priority in 2003, but essentially none opposed it. Some, such as Rep. Mike Krusee, had been planning and working for a favorable congressional redistricting since the 1990s.[6] In 2003, DeLay's ambitions for increasing Republican strength in Congress became the driving force that achieved redistricting. However, DeLay found many willing colleagues among Republican officials and lawmakers anxious to avenge "130 years of Democratic domination."

Republican State Officials

Crucial to the redistricting process in 2003 was the fact that all the principal state leaders were Republicans. Rick Perry was governor. He had previously served in several state offices, including lieutenant governor, and became governor in 2000 when Governor George W. Bush resigned to accept the presidency. He was elected governor in 2002. Lieutenant Governor David Dewhurst was elected to that office in 2002 after serving as the commissioner of the general land office. Greg Abbott had served on the Texas Supreme Court before being elected attorney general in 2002, replacing Republican John Cornyn, who was elected to the U.S. Senate. The Speaker and presiding officer of the House, Republican Tom Craddick, also was a key state leader. In 1968, when first elected to the Texas House, he was one of only eight Republicans in that body; by 2003, there were eighty-eight. When his colleagues chose him as Speaker in 2003, Craddick became the first Republican to hold that office in 130 years. Democrats held no state office in Texas in 2003 (and had not since 1994).

These principal state officers met several times in 2003 to discuss the Republican strategy for redistricting. Attorney General Abbott remained away from some meetings because of the potential perceived conflict of having the state's chief legal officer involved in the actual redistricting process. Often Congressman DeLay was a part of these meetings. Together these state leaders could effectively control every official aspect of the legislative and redistricting process, including appointing committees, scheduling the consideration of bills, rendering official legal advice, and even calling special sessions of the legislature if necessary to complete a favorable redistricting. DeLay's task was to convince these state leaders that redistricting should be a priority and to shore up their nerve in the face of unexpectedly strong public and Democratic opposition. He succeeded.

State-Legislative Majorities

By 2003, Republicans held a majority in both houses of the Texas legislature. As long as Republican lawmakers voted as a bloc for a partisan redistricting plan, the specifics of a final plan could be left largely to DeLay and the Republican congressional delegation. The Democrats could never win a vote. DeLay's task was to see that party discipline was enforced and that supporting an aggressive partisan redistricting plan was a litmus test for every Republican lawmaker.

U.S. Attorney General

The U.S. attorney general is important to any redistricting in Texas because the state is subject to Section 5 of the Voting Rights Act of 1965. Therefore, no redistricting plan from Texas can become effective unless first precleared by the office of the U.S. Attorney General as in compliance with Section 5 of the Voting Rights Act. In 2003 the U.S. attorney general was the highly partisan John Ashcroft. As discussed in Chapter Twelve, the voting-rights section at Justice, which was responsible for passing on the legality of redistricting plans in Texas, ultimately answered to persons aligned with the Republican administration.

Republican Congressmen and Their Staffs

Every Republican congressman played a role in what happened in Texas in 2003. They agreed in late 2002 that another redistricting should occur, helped develop an agreed-upon redistricting plan (one that would alter their own districts in the interest of defeating their Democratic colleagues), intervened with the state legislature to push for an aggressively partisan plan, and eventually signed off on the final configuration of their districts. DeLay assigned each congressman a state senator (usually one whose district overlapped the congressman's) to monitor and influence during the legislative process. The congressmen called Texas legislators at critical times during 2003; many came to Austin, especially during the final stages of redistricting, to exert pressure on their state counterparts. Republican Congressman Kevin Brady is credited by one Republican state lawmaker as being present "24/7" during the final stage.

At least one staff member from each congressman's office participated in an ad hoc network that regularly communicated the status of redistricting at any moment (based on their contacts with state lawmakers and their staffs). As with most able congressional staffers, these generally young persons worked enthusiastically and energetically to achieve the goal of their congressman and their party. In this instance, that goal was to pass a redistricting plan that would defeat Anglo Democrats and elect Republicans. This congressional-staff network engaged Republican activists and party officials across Texas to bring pressure on Texas lawmakers. DeLay and his aides were at the center of this network.

The Staffs of Republican State Officials

The public focus during redistricting seldom fell on the staffs of state officers. However, these persons were much more than implementers of state officials' wishes. They had worked alongside one another for years. Some had served in elected positions in the past and were not reluctant to recommend or even to make policy decisions. They were most adept, however, at smoothly and efficiently carrying out these decisions. They, too, generally were committed in 2003 to achieving the Republican partisan strategy and provided the infrastructure that made the Republican juggernaut possible.

Mike Toomey, who was Governor Perry's chief of staff in 2003, had served in the Texas legislature (1983–1989) along with Tom Craddick and Tom DeLay. As a legislator, he was particularly active on state finance matters and was considered effective at battling tax increases. Toomey left the House to serve as deputy chief of staff for Republican governor Bill Clements during the 1989 session. An extremely smart and intense attorney, Toomey in 1990 became the chief lobbyist for a new organization, Texans for Lawsuit Reform (TLR), created to promote legislation designed to curb lawsuits against Texas businesses. The TLR donated approximately $1.4 million to candidates (mostly Republican) for the 2000 election. Toomey was a key participant in the 2002 meetings with TRMPAC and TAB on behalf of Republican candidates. Well known among Republicans in Texas and Washington, he readily and easily directed the governor's office when Perry was absent from the state during the final stages of redistricting. Toomey needed no convincing of the merits of an aggressive plan for defeating Anglo Democratic congressmen.

Bruce Gibson, chief of staff for Lieutenant Governor Dewhurst in 2003, had also served with Craddick and DeLay in the state House (1981–1992); however, he had served as a Democrat. Gibson was consistently named one of the state's best legislators by various publications, and is generally respected as a smart, diligent, and capable attorney and public official. He was appointed executive assistant to Democratic lieutenant governor Bob Bullock in 1992. Gibson returned to the business world in 1994. Over the next nine years he served consecutively as president and chief executive of the Texas Chamber of Commerce, vice president of Houston Industries, Inc., and senior vice president and lobbyist for Reliant Energy. Gibson proudly acknowledges his friendship with many Texans in the White House (e.g., Karl Rove and Karen Hughes), but insisted in 2005 that he never discussed redistricting with Rove in 2003. Gibson also had ties to TRMPAC. On September 9, 2002, TRMPAC fund-raisers Susan Lilly and State Rep. Beverly Woolley met with Gibson in Houston. Gibson's employer at the time, Reliant Energy, soon contributed $25,000 of corporate money to TRMPAC. Gibson insisted, however, that although he does not recall the specific meeting, he has always observed a strict policy of never discussing legislation and contributions together.[7] Gibson is generally credited with playing a major role in the sometimes moderate stance taken by Lieutenant Governor Dewhurst in 2003.

This important group of state staffers also included Barry McBee, first assistant Texas attorney, who had worked as Rick Perry's chief of staff (while Perry was lieutenant governor and governor) after having served as chairman of the Texas Natural Resource Conservation Commission (now the Texas Commission on Environmental Quality), a post to which then-governor George W. Bush had appointed him. In 2003, McBee proved to be a dedicated partisan, coordinating the activities of the state attorney general's office and bringing its power and authority to bear when necessary to ensure that the Republican redistricting plan succeeded. For example, in May 2002 he attempted to obtain assistance from the U.S. Department of Justice in finding and returning the boycotting Democratic House lawmakers. Assistant Attorney General Don Willett and Texas Solicitor General Ted Cruz also played key roles during 2003. Willett was the chief liaison between the attorney general and the map drawers during the redistricting process. He was later named by Governor Perry to a vacant seat on the Texas Supreme Court. Solicitor General Cruz was the assistant attorney general most likely to later have responsibility for actually defending the final redistricting map in court. His view of whether a particular plan could achieve preclearance from Justice and be upheld in court was critical.

John Colyandro, who was executive director of TRMPAC in 2001–2002, served at the same time as director of policy issues for Greg Abbott (the Republican candidate for Texas attorney general) and as a political consultant for David Dewhurst (the Republican candidate for lieutenant governor), the Texas Conservative Coalition (a group of Republican state lawmakers), the

Young Conservatives of Texas, and at least one state-legislative candidate (Ben Bentzin, a Republican candidate for the state Senate). After the 2002 election, he served on Abbott's transition team when Abbott took over as attorney general. Colyandro's background and role on behalf of TRMPAC in 2002 are discussed further in Chapters Fifteen and Seventeen. Ellis told me in 2005 that Colyandro was the executive director of the Texas Conservative Coalition and played no role in the 2003 redistricting.[8] However, Ellis stayed with Colyandro when in Austin during 2003 and on at least one occasion used Colyandro's computer to send a message on redistricting to a network of congressional staffers. Moreover, one of Colyandro's employers in 2002 and 2003, the Texas Conservative Coalition, is a caucus of Republicans in the Texas House, all of whom supported redistricting.

The ties among these staffers were not necessarily apparent to outsiders in 2003; their actions in aid of redistricting largely remained out of public view. However, they played an important role: Jim Ellis acknowledged to me in 2005 that one of his tasks was to interact with them (other than McBee) and with other designated staffers.[9]

Attorney Andy Taylor

In an event as infested with capable lawyers as the 2003 redistricting process, it is unusual to recognize one attorney as having played a particularly significant role. Andy Taylor, however, deserves that recognition. He was critical to each stage of the redistricting story. As first assistant to Texas attorney general John Cornyn in 2001, Taylor was instrumental in seeing to it that the Legislative Redistricting Board (LRB) drew the partisan districts that made it possible for Republicans to elect a majority of the Texas House in 2002. Later in 2001, as a private attorney retained by the attorney general, he was the lead counsel in defense of the LRB districts and in the lawsuit over congressional districts. After the 2002 election, Taylor chaired the transition committee for the new attorney general, Greg Abbott. When TRMPAC and TAB officials first faced possible civil liability or criminal prosecution for their actions in the 2002 election, Taylor was their attorney of choice. In 2003, Taylor spoke out early in favor of redistricting and authored an op-ed urging legislative action. Later in 2003, Abbott retained Taylor to advise on redistricting during the legislative sessions and to defend the redistricting plan when it was challenged in court. Republican senators indicated that Taylor met with them at least once in a private caucus while redistricting was pending and offered legal advice on redistricting.

Not surprisingly, Taylor was often criticized by Democrats during 2003 and

2004, both because of the very large fees he was charging the state and because of the impression of conflict created by his representation of multiple clients. Taylor at least temporarily survived his critics and continued until early 2005 to represent the state in the redistricting litigation. Taylor litigated aggressively on behalf of his clients, TAB and Bill Hammond, during the civil and criminal proceedings arising from the 2002 election. After the Texas Supreme Court overruled his First Amendment–based attempts to block discovery in those proceedings, he became much less visible in this litigation.

Republican Party Activists, Party Officials, and Major Donors

For many ardent Republicans, ensuring the passage of an aggressively partisan redistricting plan in Texas was a righteous mission. Defeating Anglo Texas Democrats to elect more Republicans to Congress meant "winning big time" in the ongoing partisan battle nationwide and securing a Congress that would support George W. Bush and the party's conservative agenda. Several Republican lawmakers interviewed in 2005 acknowledged that they had been surprised at the number and intensity of the contacts they received at critical times in 2003, urging passage not only of a redistricting plan, but of the most aggressive plan possible. One of these lawmakers indicated that most of these telephone calls, letters, personal visits, and e-mails came from what he described as the "radical right" or "right wing" of the Republican Party.

A second (but sometimes overlapping) category of Republicans who played a role in the events of 2003 consisted of Texas Republican Party officials. The state party was instrumental in orchestrating a public response to Democratic claims. It was local party officials, however, who generally were credited with exerting the most effective political pressure on reluctant Republican lawmakers during the 2003 session.

Of equal or greater importance was the active participation of the largest Republican donors. Dallas investor Louis Beecherl, Houston builder Bob Perry, San Antonio physician-turned-businessman James Leininger, Dallas oilman T. Boone Pickens, and McKinney businessman John Lattimore, are well known in Texas for their substantial support of Republican candidates and causes. Their support is as much ideological as economic. Major donors like these contributed substantially to TRMPAC in 2002 to elect a Republican majority in the Texas House, and some contacted lawmakers and Republican state officials in 2003 to encourage adoption of an aggressively partisan redistricting plan.

These activists, officials, and donors were important assets for use by DeLay in 2003, particularly for encouraging Republican officials and lawmakers to overcome Democratic tactics and opposition and for convincing Republican lawmakers to pass an aggressive redistricting plan. He didn't have to persuade these actors that passage of an aggressive congressional redistricting bill was desirable. Rather, he had to coordinate their actions for maximum effect, especially when it became necessary to convince reluctant lawmakers or state officials to go along. Ellis and the network of congressional aides played an important role in this coordination. Once it became clear that a redistricting plan was going to be adopted and that Republicans could control its design, Republican activists willingly sprang forth to push for the best possible partisan result.

The White House

Many persons will disagree whether DeLay used members of the current administration as assets in 2003, or whether he was a tool used by the administration to achieve its own goals. The role of the White House is discussed in Chapter Fourteen. It is enough to note here that the chief justification offered by Republicans for redistricting in 2003 was that more Republicans were needed in Congress to help George W. Bush achieve his goals, and that several current or former members of the administration (e.g., Karl Rove and Karen Hughes) played roles in Texas during the 2003 redistricting.

One of Karl Rove's acknowledged goals in 2003 was to build a long-lasting, dominant Republican majority in the Texas legislature and in Congress, and no state was as important to control of Congress as Texas.[10] Many of the state officials and lawmakers in Texas were former Rove clients. As mentioned above, John Colyandro was a veteran of Rove's direct-mail business. Many of the key state officials considered Rove a friend as well as a professional acquaintance. Therefore it is not surprising that Rove appears throughout this story. Few, if any, can honestly doubt his interest or involvement in the outcome. Nevertheless, Rove largely remained in the shadows—a telephone call here (e.g., a call on May 10, 2003, to discuss redistricting with Lieutenant Governor Dewhurst,[11] or one on June 15, 2003, to discuss it with State Senator Bill Ratliff), a meeting there (e.g., with State Senator Bivins in early July), an encouragement when needed (e.g., for Governor Perry).[12] Republican state officials and lawmakers in Texas acknowledge that they spoke or met with Rove on numerous occasions during 2003. However, they consistently downplay the importance of these occasions, or indicate that the discussion of redistricting was brief, general, and secondary to a discussion of other issues (e.g., exemption of the state sales tax from the national income tax). Even when the contact from Rove was acknowledged to be primarily about redistricting, the Texas lawmaker in question insisted to me that while Rove explained the importance of the Texas redistricting to the president, he did not specifically ask for the lawmaker's vote.

Targeting Ten Democratic Incumbents in 2003

The Republican redistricting strategy in 2003 included targeting all ten Anglo Democratic incumbents in Congress. Republican Congressman Joe Barton declared in September 2003 that the sooner these Democrats were defeated, the better: "That doesn't mean that they're bad people. It doesn't mean that they're bad congressmen. But they are not a protected minority. . . . And now that there's no longer a Democratic majority in the House and the Senate or a Democratic governor, they can't be protected politically."[13] Republicans avoided targeting any of the seven Democratic minority members of Congress.

The ten targeted Anglo Democrats generally fell into two categories that ultimately determined the specific Republican strategy for their defeat.

Max Sandlin

Congressman Sandlin was first elected to Congressional District 1 in 1996. The largely rural district was located in 2003 in the far northeastern corner of the state. A lawyer, Sandlin had previously won election as county judge of Harrison County. In 2002 he became the chief deputy whip of the Democratic Party leadership in Congress. In 2003 he was serving on the Transportation and Infrastructure, Financial Services, and Ways and Means committees. He was a member of the fiscally moderate group the Blue Dog Coalition. Sandlin lost his bid for reelection in 2004 in a redrawn District 1.

Jim Turner

Congressman Turner was first elected to Congressional District 2 in 1996 after the famous incumbent Charlie Wilson declined to seek reelection. The largely rural district was located in 2003 along the Texas-Louisiana border and consisted of all or part of over fifteen counties. An attorney from Crockett (in Houston County), Turner had previously served in the Texas House (1981–1984), as mayor of Crockett (1989–1991), and in the Texas Senate (1991–1995). He was highly respected by his congressional colleagues and his constituents. He won reelection in 2002 with 61.4 percent of the vote, even though Democratic candidates for statewide office in the same election received an average of only 42.1 percent from precincts in District 2. In 2003 Turner was serving on the Armed Services Committee and was ranking minority member of the Committee on Homeland Security. He also was a member of the Blue Dog Coalition and the New Democrat Coalition. Turner did not seek reelection in 2004.

Ralph Hall

Congressman Hall (from Rockwall County, outside of Dallas) was first elected to Congress from District 4 in 1980. The district in 2003 consisted of rural and suburban counties and communities northeast of Dallas. Hall was an attorney. Prior to running for Congress, he had served as county judge of Rockwall County (1950–1962) and as a state senator (1968–1972). He ran unsuccessfully for lieutenant governor in 1972 before being elected to Congress. In 2003, Hall was ranking minority member on the Energy and Commerce Committee and the Science Committee. Possibly the most conservative of the incumbent Texas Democrats, he often voted with the Republican majority in Congress. Republican redistricting plans in 2003 did not target Hall for defeat by a Republican. In fact, Republicans usually counted him as an add-on to any Republican successes through redistricting. On January 2, 2004 (after redistricting), Hall announced his switch from the Democratic Party to the Republican. He was elected as a Republican in 2004. Following the switch, he was appointed chairman of the Energy and Air Quality Subcommittee of the Energy and Commerce Committee.

Nick Lampson

Congressman Lampson was first elected to Congress in 1996 from District 9, which has its core in Jefferson County in the southeast corner of Texas. Lampson had previously served as Jefferson County tax assessor for nearly twenty years. In 2003 he was on the Science Committee and was the ranking minority member on its Subcommittee on Space and Aeronautics. Defeated in his try for reelection in 2004, Lampson won the Democratic nomination in District 22 to run against Congressman DeLay in 2006.

Lloyd Doggett

Congressman Doggett was first elected to Congress from District 10 (Austin) in 1994. An attorney, Doggett had previously been elected to the Texas Senate (1973–1985) and the Texas Supreme Court (1989–1994). Doggett generally was considered one of the most liberal and outspoken members of Congress and a thorn in the side of the Republican congressional majority. Doggett won reelection in a different district (District 25) in 2004. He served on the House Ways and Means Committee in 2005.

Chet Edwards

Chet Edwards was first elected to Congress in 1990 from District 11, which includes Waco (McLennan County). In 2003, the district encompassed the counties of McLennan, Coryell, and Bell, and included Fort Hood and the surrounding communities where military families and supporting businesses were located. Edwards won reelection in 2004 over a Republican state House member. He continued in 2005 to serve on the Budget and Appropriations committees. In addition, he continued as the ranking minority member on the Military Quality of Life Subcommittee, the second-ranking member on the Energy and Water Appropriations Subcommittee, and a member of the Homeland Security Subcommittee. He cochaired the bipartisan House Army Caucus. During redistricting in 2003, he garnered considerable support even from Republicans because of his years of seniority on the powerful Appropriations Committee and focus on funding for military issues such as veterans programs and soldiers' health care. Edwards is facing a strong Republican opponent in 2006 in what remains a heavily Republican district.

Charles Stenholm

Congressman Stenholm was first elected to Congress in 1978 from District 17, which includes Abilene (Taylor County). The district in 2003 consisted of all or part of thirty-five sparsely populated counties in central West Texas. A thirteen-term congressman, Stenholm was considered one of the most conservative Democrats in the House and was a leader of the Boll Weevils, a conservative group, in the 1980s. He often clashed with President Bill Clinton, but was also a severe critic of the Bush administration's fiscal policy. In 2003, Stenholm was the ranking minority member on the Agriculture Committee. He was defeated for reelection in 2004.

Martin Frost

Congressman Frost was first elected from Dallas County (District 24) in 1978. The district in 2003 included largely African American and Hispanic areas of northwestern Dallas County and central and eastern Tarrant County. Frost, an attorney, was the second Jewish congressman elected from Texas. In 2003, he was the ranking minority member on the Rules Committee. Frost generally was considered the spokesman for the Democratic congressional delegation from Texas and the leader of the delegation in prior redistricting efforts. Republicans were often outspoken in their dislike of Frost. He was considered a personal enemy of Congressman DeLay, and had some long-lived disputes with other members of the Democratic congressional delegation. Frost was defeated for reelection in 2004.

Chris Bell

Congressman Bell was first elected to Congress in 2002 from Harris County (District 25). He previously had been elected to the Houston city council (1997–2001). He was defeated in his reelection bid for Congress in 2004. In 2006 he became the Democratic nominee for governor.

Gene Green

Congressman Green was first elected to Congress from Harris County (District 29) in 1992. Green, an attorney, previously had served for twenty years in the Texas House and Senate. In 2003, he served on the Energy and Commerce Committee, including four of its subcommittees. Elected from a predominately Hispanic district, Green was also a member of the Hispanic Caucus. He was reelected from that same district in 2004.

Designing a Plan to Defeat the Most Anglo Democrats and Elect the Most Republicans

The Republican redistricting plan finally adopted in 2003 is a textbook example of how to design districts to maximize the election of candidates from one political group and to minimize the election possibilities for selected candidates from another political group. The plan does more than simply use the traditional techniques of packing opposing voters into the fewest possible districts or spreading them thinly among several districts. It is useful at this point to understand why some Democratic incumbents were winning as well as the Republican strategy for defeating them. Maps of the final redistricting plan are provided in the Appendix of this book to assist the reader.

Defeating Democrats Who Had Won in Republican Districts

Six of the targeted Democrats resided in districts that voted heavily Republican in statewide races. They had won reelection in these districts in 2002 even as Republicans swept every statewide race. Specifically, based on the weighted average of all statewide elections, including those for governor, lieutenant governor, and comptroller, the Republican vote in the six districts was as follows:

District	Congressman (Hometown)	Percent Republican
1	Max Sandlin (Marshall)	57.9
2	Jim Turner (Crockett)	56.4
9	Nick Lampson (Beaumont)	52.2
11	Chet Edwards (Waco)	62.8
17	Charles Stenholm (Abilene)	67.2
4	Ralph Hall (Rockwall)	68.1

Adding more Republicans or removing Democrats from these districts would not guarantee the incumbents' defeat. In fact, for some of the districts, such as District 17, there was scarcely any way to make the district more Republican.

Democrats saw these incumbents' continued success as a testament both to the weakness of the Republican congressional candidates and to the quality of the job being done by the congressmen. Republicans, however, saw it simply as a residual effect of earlier Democratic gerrymandering. The Republican strategy in 2003 was to eliminate the benefits of incumbency for these Democrats.

Specifically, the Republican strategy was to redraw these districts so that the incumbent Anglo Democrats would have to seek reelection, if at all, in districts that not only tended to vote heavily Republican but also consisted largely of areas and voters the incumbents had not represented before. For example, Congressman Turner garnered over 61 percent of the vote in 2002 in a district (District 2) that otherwise voted only 42.1 percent for the Democratic statewide candidates. The Republican solution involved three steps. The first was to place Turner's county of residence (Houston) in a new district (District 6) along with only 4.4 percent of the voters from his old district. The second was to spread the remainder of Turner's old district among four other congressional districts. Finally, to further prevent the popular Turner from winning again, the plan paired him against an incumbent Republican congressman (Joe Barton) in a district designed for that Republican's success.

Similar tactics were used on the other incumbents. Congressman Stenholm's residence and home county (Taylor) were placed in District 19, and he too was paired with a Republican incumbent (Randy Neugebauer). Only 30.9 percent of the constituents from Stenholm's old district were in his new one. Congressman Edwards was left in a new district (District 17) with only 35.2 percent of his previous constituents. Although Edwards was not paired with a Republican incumbent congressman, he was expected to lose to a Republican state lawmaker, Arlene Wohlgemuth, who resided in his new district. Congressman Sandlin's residence was left in District 1, but the final districting plan left him with only 40 percent of his prior constituents.

The Democratic incumbents had little opportunity to establish a relationship with their possible new constituents or to seek election in a district other than the one in which their home county was placed: the redistricting plan was finally approved only weeks before the filing deadline. And not only did the redrawn districts include only a portion of their former constituents, but the excluded portion of the previous district generally was fractured among several others, so no other district offered an attractive alternative.

Although members of Congress are not required to live within their districts, incumbents in multicounty rural districts find it very difficult to win reelection if they do not. In an urban county with multiple congressional districts, such as Harris County, where the media routinely cover several members of congress, an incumbent may have name recognition throughout the county and may be able to run successfully in a district that is wholly or partly in the county, even if his or her home is carved out of the district. A relocation of only a few blocks may place the member back in a district alongside his former constituents. For an incumbent from a rural area, the problem is much greater. Few, if any, can readily move dozens of miles to a new district to follow the majority of his constituents when his resident county is separated from the remainder of the previous district. Nor is it easy to establish a sufficiently close relationship with his potential new constituents in time to win an upcoming election. Once deprived of the core of his or her district, a rural incumbent is vulnerable to defeat, especially when pitted against an incumbent from the other party in a district in which the overwhelming majority of the voters tend to support the opposing party and may even be the opposing incumbent's prior constituents. Republican strategists knew this reality of political survival. The final redistricting plan maximized the difficulties for the rural Democratic incumbents.

Democratic Incumbents in Democratic Districts

The other four targeted Democrats had won in 2002 in districts that had voted Democratic in the statewide elections:

District	Congressman (City)	Percent Republican
10	Lloyd Doggett (Austin)	40
24	Martin Frost (Dallas)	42
25	Chris Bell (Houston)	48.5
29	Gene Green (Houston)	33

The Republicans had to devise a different strategy for defeating these incumbents. Maps of these districts in Travis, Dallas, Tarrant, and Harris counties can found in the Appendix.

One of these districts (District 29) was a minority- (Hispanic) opportunity district protected by the Voting Rights Act. So there was essentially nothing that could be done legally in 2003 to significantly alter the district itself. However, in an effort to strike at the Anglo incumbent, the final plan moved Congressman Green's Harris County neighborhood into a heavily Republican District. Republicans saw this change as creating a new opportunity for the election of a Hispanic to Congress.[14]

In two of these four districts (Districts 24 and 25) neither African Americans nor Hispanics were a majority of the residents, but the two groups together constituted a majority. The African American population in each district was sufficient, however, to generally allow African American voters to control the outcome of the Democratic primary. Nevertheless, in 2003 both districts were represented by Anglo Democrats (Frost and Bell). Whether the districts were protected by the Voting Rights Act was a significant legal issue in 2003. The final redistricting plan was predicated on an assumption that it was legally acceptable to dismantle these districts. The dependably Democratic minority population of District 24 was either spread among four or more heavily Republican districts or added to the already very heavily minority District 30 in the center of Dallas County. Frost could either not seek reelection or run in a heavily Republican district. The final plan preserved District 25 (renumbered as District 9) as a majority-minority district, but with a significantly larger percentage of African American voters. Chris Bell, however, was left paired with a Republican incumbent in heavily Republican District 7.

The final targeted Democratic incumbent was Lloyd Doggett in District

10. The district is in Austin (Travis County), which remains a Democratic stronghold even though it is predominantly Anglo. Home to the University of Texas and most state government offices, Austin has a well-deserved reputation for historically voting much more liberal than most of the rest of Texas. To minimize the effect of Democratic votes in Travis County, the final redistricting plan split the county among three congressional districts. Two of them, including the redrawn District 10 (running 160 miles from Travis County to Harris County), were heavily Republican and effectively submerged the Anglo Democratic areas of Travis County in a sea of Republican voters. The largely minority areas of Travis County were joined with Hidalgo County, 320 miles to the south, in a district (new District 25) that is only 21.9 percent Anglo. The drawing of this district, besides fracturing a Democratic stronghold, combined African American and Hispanic Democrats in Travis County with Hispanic voters from South Texas to create a Hispanic-majority district under the Voting Rights Act. It was also meant to spell defeat for Lloyd Doggett, whose District 10 was now heavily Republican.

Altogether, the final plan created an opportunity for six (not including Hall's district) new Republican candidates to win in districts with heavily Republican voting majorities. It also paired three incumbent Anglo Democrats with incumbent Republican congressmen in districts designed to elect the Republican, and it left six incumbent Democrats unpaired with a Republican incumbent, but in substantially redrawn, heavily Republican districts.

Other Republican Goals in 2003

Within the context of passing a redistricting plan that would defeat the Anglo Democratic incumbents, Republican leaders had other goals in 2003. One was to draw districts that would be dominated by suburban voters. As a result, in some districts that had consisted almost wholly of rural counties, suburban and rural areas were combined, when possible, in a way that would allow suburban voters to prevail in most future elections. If rural areas were consistently voting Republican, why stretch districts out over vast distances to combine rural areas with suburbs and dilute the rural vote?

For several reasons. First, rural areas still were not as dependably or staunchly Republican as the suburbs. Rural voters had reelected the incumbent Democratic congressmen in 2002 even while voting heavily Republican in statewide elections, and sometimes they voted in the Democratic primary or for local Democratic candidates or moderate Republicans, such as Senator Bill Ratliff.

Combining the rural areas with the dependably Republican suburbs was expected to allow the suburbs to elect one of their own staunchly Republican candidates in the primary, who then would win the general election when the rural voters again voted overwhelmingly Republican, thus preventing the election, or even the nomination, of moderate or independent Republicans from the rural areas—much less the election of any Democrats.

Also, some Republican officials felt that suburban voters had been treated unfairly in the past by being clustered in compact districts; during the 1990s these districts had become badly overpopulated compared to other districts, particularly the rural ones. Combining rural and suburban areas was a way to overcome this past unfairness and ensure that the suburban areas would maintain or increase their political influence as their population grew. As a by-product of Republican efforts to reach this goal of combining suburban and rural areas, very few districts ended up being compact. Compactness was sacrificed to achieve certain interparty and intraparty goals. The statewide maps in the Appendix allow the districts in 2002 and 2004 to be compared.

Another secondary goal of redistricting reflected the principle of "to the victor go the spoils." There are certain institutions, facilities, and communities that are considered particularly desirable to have in a congressman's district. Some are merely prestigious. Others are the source of sizable potential campaign contributions. For example, in Harris County, the facilities of the National Aeronautics and Space Administration (NASA) Johnson Space Flight Center are such a prize. In 2002 they were in Congressman Nick Lampson's district; after redistricting, they ended up in Tom DeLay's district. The Texas Medical Center in Houston, which includes the University of Texas M. D. Anderson Cancer Center and the Baylor College of Medicine, is considered important also. At Congressman John Culberson's request, the medical center ended up in his district (District 7).[15] In Travis County, the University of Texas main campus and the headquarters or facilities of some of the county's major technology firms were moved into the district (District 21) of incumbent Republican Lamar Smith. DFW Airport was taken from the district represented by African American congresswoman Eddie Bernice Johnson (District 30) and placed in the redrawn and heavily Republican District 24, to which Republican Ken Marchant was elected in 2004. Similar moves were made statewide. Many of the conspicuous tentacles or bubbles in the 2003 plan (especially in the urban and suburban regions) are a result of this Republican goal of including or excluding certain areas and parceling the spoils among its incumbents or expected winners.

As Partisan as the Law Allows

The overall strategy of designing and passing a congressional redistricting plan to maximize Republican victories and Democratic losses faced three legal hurdles, which the Republican strategy accounted for.

First, the Constitution requires that congressional districts be as equal in population as practicable. All Republican redistricting plans in 2003 met this standard with absolute precision, according to population enumerations from the 2000 census. Attorneys for the Republicans advised the legislature to use these enumerations; in 2005–2006, this decision became a major legal issue affecting the constitutionality of the new plan in arguments before the U.S. Supreme Court.

Second, the Voting Rights Act of 1965 prohibits redistricting that discriminates against protected minorities, including African American and Hispanic voters. Specifically, Section 5 of the act forbids a redistricting plan to cause a retrogression (i.e., a worsening) in the voting strength of certain protected minority groups. At each stage of the redistricting process, Republican strategists paid heed to the likelihood that one plan or another might be disapproved by the U.S. Attorney General under the Voting Rights Act. The final plan, however, aggressively enhanced partisan Republican interests even at the risk of violating the Voting Rights Act. Chapters Thirteen and Fifteen discuss the Justice Department's consideration of the Texas redistricting plan and the possibility of partisan influence on the review process.

Third, the Constitution possibly prohibits a redistricting plan that is too partisan. The Supreme Court has split on whether an alleged partisan gerrymander is justiciable (i.e., is a legitimate basis for a lawsuit). Republicans in Texas in 2003 chose to ignore the possibility that their redistricting plan might be ruled invalid for being impermissibly partisan. For over four decades Texas Republicans had repeatedly filed lawsuits challenging Democratic redistricting plans as too partisan. Each lawsuit failed. Republican lawyers were not concerned in 2003 with a Democratic challenge based on a particular plan's partisanship. Instead, Republican lawmakers repeatedly and openly proclaimed that their objective was "to elect more Republicans," thereby helping deflect any allegations of racial discrimination.

Democratic lawyers meanwhile were encouraged that in 2003 the Supreme Court had agreed to hear a partisan gerrymander case from Pennsylvania (*Vieth v. Jubelirer*). The Democrats hoped that acceptance of the case meant the Court was prepared to put some teeth into a constitutional limitation on partisan gerrymandering. Some of the same lawyers who were advising Democrats in

Texas in 2003 were also representing the Democrats in the Pennsylvania case, which they expected to win. These Democratic attorneys were surprised at the openness of the Texas Republicans in claiming a partisan objective. The Democratic attorneys thought that this Republican admission, combined with a favorable ruling in the Pennsylvania case, would set the stage for a successful legal challenge to any highly partisan Republican redistricting plan.

The final redistricting plan maximized the likelihood of Republican successes and Democratic defeats whenever practicable, unless it was clear to Republican lawyers that such maximization violated existing law. The final plan was as partisan as the Republicans thought the law would allow.

CHAPTER 6

Playing Defense:
Democratic Strategy, 2001–2003

The Democrats were compelled by necessity in 2001–2003 to fight a defensive battle. The 1991 congressional redistricting plan, a defensive holding action for Democrats, had been only partly successful. The number of Republicans in the state congressional delegation had increased from eight to thirteen over the decade. Nevertheless, seventeen congressional seats remained in Democratic hands after the 2000 election, despite the tide of Republican successes in state-wide elections.

The task of maintaining those seventeen seats in Congress was formidable. Texas had been apportioned an additional two seats after the 2000 census, but Republicans held all the state offices and a majority of the seats in the state Senate. Democratic hopes for holding a majority of the state's congressional seats were faint, but not dead.

The Democrats still controlled the state House and remained optimistic that the 2002 elections would bring Democrat successes in the important statewide races. These factors affected the Democratic redistricting strategy in 2001 that led to the federal court-ordered plan under which all seventeen incumbents survived in 2002, even as Republicans again swept the statewide elections.

This chapter describes the Democrats' strategy in 2001 and 2002 and provides the background for the parliamentary requirements and maneuvers that became the focus in 2003.

Democratic Strategy in 2001

State Legislative Districts

The major redistricting battle in 2001 was fought over the state's legislative districts, but that outcome would determine what happened to congressional districts in 2003. Passage of plans to redistrict the state House and Senate seemed unlikely in 2001, given that the Democrats controlled the House and the Republicans controlled the Senate. Both Democrats and Republicans knew that if the legislature failed to pass redistricting plans, the task would pass under the state constitution to the five-member Legislative Redistricting Board (LRB). Four board members (the lieutenant governor, attorney general, comptroller, and commissioner of the general land office) were Republican; Speaker Pete Laney was the only Democrat. Therefore, if the LRB drew up the districts, the result would almost certainly be highly favorable to Republicans.

The events that determined the drawing of the state legislative districts are themselves worthy of an extended telling. For purposes of this book on congressional redistricting, however, the critical event was the outcome. The Texas legislature was in fact unable to pass a redistricting bill in 2001 for the state House or Senate. The LRB convened in June 2001 and adopted state-legislative redistricting plans that heavily favored the election of more Republicans.

The Democrats' Litigation Strategy for Congressional Districting

Democrats now acknowledge that though open to the adoption of a congressional redistricting plan in 2001, they felt no pressure to see that the legislature did so. The Republican-controlled LRB had no jurisdiction over congressional districts. Therefore, in the absence of a legislatively enacted plan, the task of drawing districts for use in the upcoming 2002 election would pass to the state and federal courts.

Democratic lawyers in 2001 expected that a court-drawn plan was likely to be more favorable to Democrats than any plan that could pass the legislature and avoid veto by Republican governor Perry. They knew that the guidelines for federal courts prevent them from engaging in partisan politics when drawing redistricting plans. Instead, a court is bound to follow legitimate state policy as embodied in a state's adopted redistricting plans. In Texas in 2001, that "state policy" was embodied in the existing, 1991 congressional-districting plan. Therefore, Democratic attorneys expected that any court creating a plan for the 2002 elections would be likely to maintain the core of existing districts. A redistricting plan preserving the core of existing districts was exactly what the Democrats wanted.

Democrats began their legal jockeying even before the legislature convened in January 2001; the first redistricting lawsuit was filed in December 2000. Republican and minority plaintiffs maneuvering for a friendly judicial forum soon followed with other suits. Some of these lawsuits were dismissed as premature, but they clearly showed that both parties (the Democrats in particular) thought that the battle over congressional districts in 2001 would be resolved in court.

As discussed in Chapter Two, the federal court in *Balderas v. Perry* finally adopted a plan in the fall of 2001 that, as Democratic attorneys had predicted, was a "status quo" plan. Twenty of the congressional districts were predominantly Republican, based on statewide election returns, but the plan retained as nearly as possible the core of each existing district. This result benefited the Democratic incumbents.[1]

Democratic Strategy in the 2002 Elections

Democrats realized after the outcome in federal court in 2001 that Republicans might try to adopt a more Republican-friendly congressional districting plan in 2003. However, there were numerous reasons why this effort might not happen, or if initiated, might not succeed.

Democratic election strategy in 2002 was not, of course, driven by the prospect of further congressional redistricting. The Texas Democratic Party was optimistic that the statewide Republican trend could be reversed. The 2002 election was the first since 1996, and only the second since 1992, in which George W. Bush would not be at the top of the ballot (as a candidate either for governor or for president). Bush was a popular and potent candidate. The Democrats hoped that without Bush on the Republican ticket, they could once again attract a majority of the state's voters.

Also, the Democratic Party was encouraged because its candidates for statewide office in 2002 were well qualified and represented the diversity within the party. A Hispanic businessman, Tony Sanchez, was the candidate for governor. An Anglo former state senator and statewide candidate, John Sharp, was running for lieutenant governor. An African American former mayor of Dallas, Ron Kirk, was the Democratic candidate for the U.S. Senate. An Anglo former mayor of Austin, Kirk Watson, was the candidate for attorney general. Democrats hoped that this diverse group of candidates would generate a high and favorable turnout among the party's constituent groups. The Republicans sarcastically referred to the Democratic candidates as "The Democrats' Dream Team."[2]

Insofar as Democratic representation in Congress was concerned, the primary objective in 2002 was for the seventeen Democratic incumbents to win reelection. This happened. Twelve of these incumbents faced Republican challengers, but all won reelection, even though six (Hall, Turner, Sandlin,

Stenholm, Edwards, and Lampson) ran in districts that voted heavily Republican in the statewide races.

Democrats knew that virtually any Democratic success in the 2002 election, either in one of the major races for state office or in a sufficient number of state House races, could block a Republican attempt at redistricting in 2003. Democrats were particularly hopeful that John Sharp would win election as lieutenant governor. He had narrowly lost the race for lieutenant governor to Rick Perry in 1998. If elected lieutenant governor, Sharp could prevent passage of a new redistricting plan through the Senate. However, he lost to Republican David Dewhurst (47.1 percent to 52.9 percent). The other Democratic candidates for statewide office (except Paul Hobby in his run for comptroller) lost by even larger margins than Sharp. Moreover, the Republicans swept to victory in many of the contested state legislative races, winning 88 of the 150 seats in the state House. After the 2002 election, Republicans occupied every elected state office and were a majority in both houses of the state legislature.

Democrats lacked the votes or official positions in 2003 to defeat a Republican redistricting effort. However, they could still try to use public opinion to dissuade the Republicans from going forward with redistricting, and there were parliamentary maneuvers available to defeat any redistricting legislation.

Democratic Parliamentary Tactics: Breaking a Legislative Quorum

Much of the national attention on Texas in 2003 came when Democrats broke a legislative quorum to stop the pending Republican redistricting bill. Breaking a quorum to prevent action on legislation is not a tactic unique to Texas, or to congressional redistricting in 2003. The events in Texas, however, were unprecedented in their scope, their organization, and the international attention that they received. Fifty-one members of the Texas House fled to Oklahoma (and another to Mexico) for four days in May 2003 to kill a partisan redistricting bill during the regular legislative session. Eleven senators tried in the summer of 2003 to duplicate this success by going to New Mexico for approximately forty days.

A quorum is a specific number (usually more than a majority) of members of a legislative body who must be present before the body may conduct any business. Without a quorum, the legislative body has no authority to take up or pass legislation. A quorum of the Texas House of Representatives is two-thirds of its membership (i.e., 100 of 150 members); a quorum of the Senate is also two-thirds of the members (i.e., 21 of 31).

Attempting to block legislation by breaking or denying a quorum has been used many times in the history of this country. For example, in 1787–1788, the tactic was used by state lawmakers who opposed ratification of the constitution that had been proposed for the United States of America. To become law, the proposed constitution had to be ratified by the state legislatures in at least nine of the thirteen states. The four most populous states (New York, Pennsylvania, Virginia, and Massachusetts) were particularly important. In Pennsylvania, the Federalist legislators favoring ratification were a clear majority, but the absence of a legislative quorum stymied their efforts. Opponents of ratification in the Pennsylvania legislature knew that they lacked the votes to defeat ratification, so they simply stayed away, thereby denying the state legislature a quorum. Two absent legislators were found and physically carried to the legislative chamber to create the necessary quorum. Similarly, absent members in Massachusetts were rounded up and brought to their desks in the state legislature. In both instances, the return of the absent legislators created the needed quorum and allowed the Federalist majority to ratify the Constitution.

In 1840, Abraham Lincoln joined other Whigs in supposedly jumping from a window of the Illinois statehouse in an attempt to prevent passage of legislation weakening Whig control of state banks. The House clerk apparently recorded the Whigs as present anyway, and the quorum remained unbroken. In 1988, U.S. Senate Republicans staged a walkout to stall a campaign-finance bill. Several of them were rounded up and returned to the Senate; Capitol police carried Senator Bob Packwood feet first into the chamber. The Senate majority leader, Democrat Robert Byrd, was unapologetic for ordering Packwood brought back to the Senate, saying senators are "paid to vote . . . not to hide."[3]

In Texas, legislators have walked out or stayed away from the legislature on several occasions.[4] Some of these efforts lasted only a few hours, serving primarily to emphasize the seriousness of the members' opposition to pending legislation. The most notorious occasion of Texas lawmakers breaking a quorum came in 1979. The Senate voted on May 15 to suspend its regular order of business and take up an apparently innocuous election bill, then some senators realized that the bill could be amended to separate the dates of the two party primaries (i.e., break up the dual primary) in order to benefit Texas favored son John Connally in his ultimately unsuccessful effort to win the Republican nomination for president. (The measure would have allowed conservative Democrats to vote for most races in the Democratic primary, and then vote for Connally in a separate Republican presidential primary.) A filibuster followed. However, when it became apparent that those opposed to the bill could not stop it using the two-thirds vote requirement, twelve Democratic senators remained away from the Senate beginning on Friday, May 18, to break quorum and block further consideration of the election bill. The senators were rumored to have left the state, but many hid out in a converted garage apartment in Austin. They became known as the "Killer Bees." Their walkout lasted four days (over a weekend) and ended when Lieutenant Governor Hobby agreed that any amendment to split the primaries would have to be supported by a two-thirds vote. The amendment was never offered. The Killer Bees are still celebrated today by some factions of the Texas Democratic Party.

A lesser-known and unsuccessful walkout occurred during a special session in August 1981, when the legislature was considering a redistricting bill to create a majority-minority congressional district in Dallas County, at the potential cost of defeating one or more Democratic incumbents. Many Democrats in the legislature fought against the plan, seeing it as a partisan ploy by the Republican governor, Bill Clements. Finally, however, the adoption of such a plan seemed unavoidable. The bill passed the House on second reading at 11:45 p.m. on August 9. Final passage was temporarily blocked at 2 a.m. on August 10 when approximately fifty Democratic lawmakers disappeared from the House. A call was placed on the House. Enough lawmakers were found around the state Capitol or in downtown Austin to establish a quorum, and the redistricting bill was adopted by the House at 4:40 a.m. This short-lived walkout earned its participants the label "Killer Fleas."

Walkouts or threatened walkouts have sometimes succeeded, especially when the affected governor or legislative leaders were willing to compromise in order to bring the dispute to a close and move on to other business. However, in 2003 the circumstances were very different. The issue was wholly partisan. The pressure on the Republican lawmakers and leadership was coming from many different state and national sources, and the Republican governor, lieutenant governor, and Speaker each had important personal, partisan reasons for not backing down on the redistricting legislation. The Democrats too were under significant state and national partisan pressures. As it turned out, there was little or no room for compromise on either side.

Democratic Parliamentary Tactics:
Reliance on the Two-Thirds Vote Requirement in the Texas Senate

Democratic strategy throughout 2003 relied heavily on a Texas Senate tradition: most legislation can come up for consideration only if two-thirds of the members present (usually twenty-one of thirty-one) agree. If the twelve Democratic senators voted as a bloc in 2003, they could prevent consideration of any redistricting bill. The Democrats' attempt to use this vote requirement to defeat the redistricting legislation is discussed in Chapters Nine and Ten. The attempt failed. Understanding why it failed requires understanding the nature of the two-thirds vote requirement.

Many media accounts of the 2003 redistricting mistakenly referred to a "Two-Thirds Rule" that governs the consideration of legislation in the Texas Senate. There is no such rule. The need for the affirmative vote of two-thirds of the members present before a bill can be brought up for consideration is an indirect result of the combination of several Senate rules and the existence of certain factual circumstances.

The Senate has no calendar committee to set legislation for consideration.[5] Instead, as soon as a bill is reported from a Senate committee, it goes directly to the bottom of the list of bills on the calendar for consideration. In other words, there is no prohibition in Senate rules against taking up legislation without a two-thirds vote. Rather, the rules explicitly contemplate that the Senate's regular order of business is to consider legislation in the order in which it is reported from committee and appears on the Senate calendar.[6]

During a session, there often are hundreds of bills on the Senate calendar at any one time. Many of these bills have little or no possibility of actually being enacted. Therefore, to ensure that the Senate's time is not wasted debating unimportant bills or those that have little chance of passage, important contested bills are "jumped ahead" of less critical ones.[7] Minor, uncontested bills are placed on the Local and Uncontested Calendar and generally passed quietly during the early-morning hours by agreement. Contested legislation without even minimum support is left on the calendar to die.

By virtue of this procedure, the lieutenant governor is able to control which legislation reaches the Senate floor for consideration. In most legislative bodies, the presiding officer exercises this control by wielding influence on the calendar committee that sets legislation for consideration. Since the Texas Senate lacks such a committee, the lieutenant governor controls the taking up of legislation, both by recognizing (or failing to recognize) a senator trying to suspend the regular order of business and take up a particular bill, and by influencing the votes regarding such a motion.

Historically, the lieutenant governor has seldom acted personally to win consideration of legislation, leaving a bill's sponsoring senator with the task of securing the necessary votes. Occasionally, however, the lieutenant governor has intervened to see that important legislation reached the Senate floor for consideration. In such circumstances, the lieutenant governor has almost always been able to obtain the necessary votes (if he wishes) by using his considerable power over committee appointments, bill referrals, appropriations, etc., to influence senators to vote to take up the bill.

In a regular session with hundreds of pieces of legislation, the two-thirds vote requirement is necessary: there are almost always bills on the Senate calendar ahead of important legislation.[8] Nevertheless, it has become usual for the lieutenant governor (as presiding officer of the Senate) to ask the chairman of the Senate Administration Committee to sponsor a bill (that the senator is willing to allow to go unpassed) that will sit atop the calendar for the remainder of the session. This bill has become known as a "blocker bill."[9]

As a practical matter, the circumstances in a special session are different. The rules remain the same, but there are ordinarily few if any bills on the Senate calendar. Since only legislation on the specific subject or subjects of the special session is eligible for consideration. House and Senate lawmakers introduce only a handful of bills, and there may be no "unwanted" legislation to sit atop the calendar as a blocker bill. As a result, important legislation may work its way to the top of the calendar and be considered without needing the support of twenty-one senators. In such a circumstance, the passage or defeat of the bill is determined by a majority of those senators voting on the bill. There have been numerous instances in the history of the Senate when a bill has been considered directly from the top of the calendar without a two-thirds vote, particularly during a special session.

For most of 2003, Dewhurst saw no reason to avoid the two-thirds vote requirement because he expected to persuade enough Democratic senators to vote with the Republicans to get the needed twenty-one votes and bring up redistricting. Seldom in the past had lieutenant governors been unable to muster the needed votes when they set out to do so. However, as 2003 proceeded, Democrats portrayed the two-thirds vote requirement as a normative Senate tradition designed to protect the interests of a political minority; any Democrat voting along with the Republicans to reach the twenty-one-vote requirement was condemned as a traitor to the Democratic Party and minority voters statewide. The lieutenant governor's usual ability to get the needed votes was nullified. Eventually, Democrats were able to firmly secure the necessary eleven votes to defeat any consideration of a redistricting bill. Therefore, for a short time in July 2003 it appeared that a coalition of ten Democrats and one Republican could forever block redistricting in the Texas Senate. However, Republicans countered by looking for a way to circumvent the two-thirds vote requirement.

At Lieutenant Governor Dewhurst's request, the secretary of the Senate researched the history of the two-thirds vote requirement. She determined that no blocker bill had been used during eighteen previous special sessions. However, she also found that on several of those occasions a vote to suspend the regular order of business was taken even though the bill in question was at the top of the calendar and no suspension of the order of business was required. On at least three occasions (special sessions in 1971, 1981, and 1992), congressional-redistricting legislation was taken up without a vote suspending the regular order of business because the bill was at the top of the Senate calendar or because the Senate had earlier passed a resolution allowing a redistricting bill to be set on special order without a two-thirds vote.

Democrats emphasized that although only an indirect result of what some would call an "arcane" set of Senate rules, the two-thirds vote requirement had become a valuable Senate tradition. It meant that a senator had to compromise or negotiate before his or her bill could be considered, and that on important issues (e.g., taxes, school finance, tort reform, parole, judicial pay, etc.), and even on unimportant ones, a minority could force itself to be effectively heard in the process so long as the minority's view could at least momentarily garner enough votes to prevent legislation from being considered. The presence of this dynamic had been useful at one time or another to almost every senator, whether Democrat or Republican. In conversations with me in 2005, both Republican and Democratic senators generally favored the two-thirds requirement for consideration of legislation in the Senate. However, Republicans drew an important distinction between purely partisan legislation, such as redistricting, and other legislation on which support and opposition was a matter of a member's personal policy judgment rather than a litmus test of party loyalty. Republican senators generally felt that a requirement like the two-thirds requirement was inappropriate for controlling redistricting legislation.

Democrats tried to characterize Dewhurst's elimination of the two-thirds vote requirement during the second and third 2003 special sessions as an inexcusable breach of Senate tradition and even as evidence of racial discrimination and a violation of the Voting Rights Act. Democratic strategy counted on using this vote requirement to defeat redistricting. Ultimately, however, like the filibuster tradition in the U.S. Senate that generated such controversy in 2005, the tradition for a two-thirds vote in the Texas Senate proved not to be iron-clad in the face of a determined lieutenant governor and Republican Senate majority.

No Compromise

Another component of Democratic strategy in 2003 was not to compromise on the specifics of a redistricting bill. The final bill was designed to elect twenty-two Republicans; it elected twenty-one. At various times during the process,

Lieutenant Governor Dewhurst or Republican lawmakers proposed other plans that, as described at the time, were designed to elect fewer Republicans. Compromising on the specifics of legislation is ordinarily how differences are resolved. However, Democratic lawmakers refused either to engage in sanctioned compromise discussions or to put forward an alternative redistricting plan.

One reason for the Democrats' refusal to compromise was an unwillingness to decide which Democratic congressmen would be sacrificed or saved. The Democratic congressmen had themselves committed as early as 2001 that they would "live or die together." The Democratic senators kept this same posture. As Democratic senator Leticia Van de Putte remarked in response to an offer of compromise from Lieutenant Governor Dewhurst, "That's like asking me to choose which one of my children to give up."[10]

A second reason for refusing to compromise was that Democratic activists saw any such compromise as a deal with the devil. The extreme partisanship of most of the Democratic lawmakers' districts meant that it would likely have been political suicide to be seen as dealing with the Republican devil over the political futures of the Democrats in Congress. Another reason was the national significance of any compromise that would significantly increase the Republican majority in Congress. A compromise in Texas that resulted in the election of new Republican congressmen would be a significant defeat for the Democratic Party. Possibly saving one or two congressional seats seemed a slight reward for such humiliating appeasement. Republican redistricting plans that preserved the districts of a few Democratic incumbents (e.g., Frost and Doggett) but likely meant the defeat of most others were not seen as an acceptable basis for compromise.

A fourth reason was that the Democrats doubted that any compromise plan would survive through the legislative process. Democratic lawmakers feared a "sham" compromise. They worried that if they allowed a compromise redistricting bill to move through the legislative process, Congressman DeLay and the Republican majorities in the two houses would later substitute a more aggressively partisan plan. Memoranda from Jim Ellis to Congressman DeLay during 2003 show that the notion of "cobbling together" a plan to win sufficient support in the Senate then later substituting a more acceptable partisan plan was a tactic the Republican leadership considered. Lieutenant Governor Dewhurst insists that his many efforts in 2003 to attract Democratic senators to a "fair" compromise plan were genuine and that he would have resisted later efforts by DeLay and others to change the plan.[11] The question whether any such compromise could have survived the intense partisan pressures that ultimately dictated the aggressiveness of the final plan will never be answered.

Dewhurst in 2005 told me that if Democrats had given him only two additional votes as late as the conference-committee proceedings in October, he could have won approval of a "fair" redistricting plan that did not try to achieve twenty-two Republican victories. His comment to me was that "I found that I ultimately had no constituency" for this position.[12] Democrats refused Dewhurst's entreaties for negotiation. It was not that they necessarily doubted Dewhurst's good faith; they doubted his ability to hold firm in the face of pressure from DeLay, Perry, Craddick, Republican activists, and major donors. When I interviewed him in 2006, Dewhurst said that the possibility of an agreement surviving in the Senate was much greater during the regular session and the first special session in July than in October after five months of often hostile confrontation. The Ellis memoranda to DeLay support this conclusion. In 2006, Dewhurst reluctantly expressed doubt whether he could have held an agreement together against the pressures brought to bear on Republican lawmakers in October.[13]

A final reason for the Democrats' refusal to compromise was the advice of their attorneys. A core group of able lawyers were advising the senators, including Paul Smith and Sam Hirsch of the Washington firm of Jenner & Block, J. Gerald Hebert representing the congressional delegation, and Austin attorney Renea Hicks. Several of these attorneys advised the Democratic Senators that an aggressive Republican plan would not stand up in court. In fact, the attorneys suggested that the more brutal and vengeful the Republican redistricting plan, the better it would be for the almost certain legal challenge. Compromise on a less egregious plan, on the other hand, would almost certainly have undercut the merits of a court claim. Therefore, for some Democrats, "worse was better."

This Democratic legal strategy depended for success, however, on several factors beyond the control of the attorneys. On the one hand, they were hopeful that the Supreme Court in the then-pending case of *Vieth v. Jubelirer* would strengthen the constitutional limitations on partisan gerrymandering. A favorable ruling in *Vieth* would have set the stage for a successful challenge to a ruthless Texas redistricting. The attorneys also expected that any court challenge would be heard by the same friendly three-judge panel that had established the existing districting plan in 2001. The panel included two judges appointed by Democratic presidents. However, by the summer of 2003 the rumor spread that one of the judges, District Judge John Hannah (who had served as Texas secretary of state under Democratic governor Ann Richards) was seriously ill.

Ultimately neither of these expectations panned out for the Democrats. The Supreme Court rejected the partisan gerrymandering claim in *Vieth*, and instead of strengthening constitutional limits on partisanship in redistricting, a majority of the Court almost held that partisan gerrymandering claims are not justiciable at all. Judge Hannah withdrew from the federal court panel in July 2003; he died on December 8. His place on the panel was taken by District Judge Lee Rosenthal from Houston. Judge Rosenthal had been appointed to the federal bench by President George H. W. Bush meaning that the court now had a majority of Republican appointees.

CHAPTER 7

You Gotta Be Kidding!
The 2003 Regular Session

*At a time when Texas is grasping for pennies to immunize Texas children,
legislators don't need to waste resources giving booster shots to political power plays.*
—HOUSTON CHRONICLE, FEBRUARY 2, 2003

Dave McNeely of the *Austin American-Statesman* has for four decades been one of the most astute observers and prophets of legislative conduct in Texas. In December 2002 he saw that the forces were converging that could make congressional redistricting a reality in 2003. He noted that after winning all of the statewide races in 2002 and a majority in both the state House and Senate, Republicans still were not a majority of the Texas congressional delegation. According to McNeely, this "sticks in their craw," especially since the Democrats' best vote-getter statewide in 2002, lieutenant-governor candidate John Sharp, had won a majority in only twelve of the thirty-two congressional districts.[1]

The regular session of the Texas legislature convened on January 14, 2003. It promised to be interesting. Republicans for the first time in 130 years controlled both houses. However, a serious budget shortfall, a perceived home-insurance crisis, tort-reform legislation, and the need to reform the state's education and tax systems seemed to be more than enough to occupy the legislature during its constitutionally limited 140-day session, leaving scant room for a divisive issue such as redistricting. Democrats promoted this position by distributing packets of information to the major newspapers, urging them to take an editorial position against redistricting. In a meeting with Democratic senators at an Austin restaurant, Ruth's Chris Steak House, in December 2002 Lieutenant Governor David Dewhurst was quizzed whether the Senate would take up redistricting. According to Democratic senator Eliot Shapleigh, Dewhurst said at the meeting that redistricting would not be considered, because it was too controversial.[2] Dewhurst recalls that his position was that the Senate would not move first on redistricting.[3]

A rumor soon circulated around the Capitol that Republicans might attempt to "reopen" congressional redistricting. The *Quorum Report*, an online political newsletter, noted that "political junkies are abuzz at the possibility" of redrawing at least a few congressional lines.[4] However, for many seasoned observers, serious redistricting seemed unlikely. Texas had never before attempted a major redistricting unless legally required to do so. Any attempt to redraw congressional districts would be politically divisive and would distract lawmakers from other, more important matters.

Therefore, it was not surprising that newspapers statewide quickly came out against congressional redistricting and that state Republican leaders appeared to publicly rule out the possibility that an attempt at redistricting was likely in 2003.

A Terrible Idea?

Once speculation about the possibility of redistricting surfaced in 2003, every major newspaper in Texas came out against it. Seldom have editorial boards been so united on a subject.

On January 30, the *Dallas Morning News* called redistricting a "terrible idea." The *Houston Chronicle* on February 2 warned, "At a time when Texas is grasping for pennies to immunize Texas children, legislators don't need to waste resources giving booster shots to political power plays." The *Austin American-Statesman* followed on February 23: "Redistricting again? Texas has enough troubles." The *Dallas Morning News* on February 24 repeated its admonition that redistricting was a "terrible idea" and added that the legislature had a "fair and square crack" at redistricting in 2001, but had ducked. Now, "it is time to move on." The *San Antonio Express-News* on March 4 urged the legislature to "ignore the push to redraw congressional districts." On April 19, the *Fort Worth Star-Telegram* observed, "You gotta be kidding," and attributed the possibly of redistricting to "the gall of national leaders."

Most of the state's major newspapers continued their editorial stance against redistricting throughout 2003. Some newspapers, such as the *Fort Worth Star-Telegram*, regularly printed editorials opposing the redistricting process. Smaller papers, such as the *Waco Tribune-Herald, Beaumont Enterprise, Laredo Morning Times, Lubbock Avalanche-Journal, San Angelo Standard-Times, Amarillo Globe-News, Longview News-Journal, Corpus Christi Caller-Times, Abilene Reporter-News, Valley Morning Star, El Paso Times,* and *Bryan–College Station*

Eagle also objected to the distraction of unnecessary redistricting. Even national newspapers, such as the *New York Times, Washington Post,* and *Wall Street Journal* were critical of plans for redistricting in Texas. As the year passed, however, although the tone of the newspapers remained critical, they increasingly acknowledged that some new redistricting plan would probably pass.

In early 2003, Republican state leaders were quoted as ruling out redistricting as a subject for legislative action. Lieutenant Governor Dewhurst said, "Congressional redistricting is almost as attractive as contagious flu."[5] Governor Perry compared redistricting to physical agony and cautioned, "It's like, 'Do you want to go run your wind sprints again?'"[6] Perry pledged that he would not call a special session on the topic.[7] Even Speaker Craddick was portrayed as not sounding "too eager" about the possibility, although he appointed a House redistricting committee.[8] Lawmakers sounded equally negative tones on the subject of redistricting. For example, Republican senator Kip Averitt (McGregor) stated, "My attitude is it probably doesn't need to happen."[9] Republican senator Wentworth went further, indicating that redistricting is the "most partisan matter that the Legislature can take up—we don't need it." Wentworth went so far as to indicate that existing congressional districts were "fair" because Republicans will win when Democrats retire and Democrats will win when Republican Henry Bonilla retires in District 23.[10]

Behind the Scenes

Despite the public impression that redistricting was unlikely in 2003, the story behind the scenes was very different. Once the 2002 elections were over, Congressman DeLay's attention shifted to the task of redrawing Texas congressional districts. In December, the Republican members of the state's congressional delegation met in DeLay's Washington office. They all agreed—redraw the districts to defeat the Anglo Democratic incumbents.[11]

As the legislative session approached DeLay spoke separately with each of the principal state officials to urge them to support congressional redistricting. DeLay arrived in Austin on January 14 to attend the swearing-in of Craddick as Speaker and to meet with Craddick, Governor Perry, and Lieutenant Governor Dewhurst. Dewhurst recalled in 2006 that he was apprehensive about meeting with DeLay, but believed that he was "noncommittal" with DeLay on whether he would pursue redistricting.[12] Ellis recalls that DeLay also met with newly elected attorney general, Greg Abbott, during this time. DeLay felt that he left Austin that January with an assurance from these state leaders that they would push congressional redistricting through the legislature in

2003.[13] He also left Jim Ellis, the director of his national PAC, Americans for a Republican Majority (ARMPAC), in Austin to meet with Republican officials or their staffs to raise the level of support for redistricting, particularly among senators, and to further explore strategies for passing a redistricting plan. By memorandum to DeLay on February 5th, Ellis reported that he had met with Senate staff and expected "no major problem keeping the Republicans in line (with the exception of Ratliff and Wentworth, as we know from our previous meetings.)" Even Senators Chris Harris and Robert Duncan of the Jurisprudence Committee were not expected to present a problem.

While Craddick's public comments were perceived as having a "negative tone," his actions were "positive and proactive." Ellis pointed out that "[t]he Redistricting Committee he appointed is everything for which we could have hoped and we will have no trouble getting a proper hearing and a bill to the floor." Representative Krusee (a Republican member of the House Redistricting Committee) recommended moving a bill out of the House early in the regular session. Ellis advised, "[I]t is clear that we are on the negative side of the PR spin and we need to implement some counter-offensive tactics."

Dewhurst's chief of staff, Bruce Gibson, told Ellis that, despite his public comments about "the flu," Dewhurst was "committed to getting the map through the Senate with the 21 votes." Gibson believed that the Democratic senators most likely to vote to bring up redistricting were Eddie Lucio (Brownsville), Mario Gallegos (Houston), and Ken Armbrister (Victoria). Other senators (Republican senators Troy Fraser and Mike Jackson) would approach each of these senators, but Gibson wanted DeLay to call the Democratic senators directly. Acknowledging that all nineteen Republican senators had to be onboard to secure the needed twenty-one votes in the Senate, Ellis indicated that "Ratliff and Wentworth will require attention, particularly the latter."

In 2006 several current and former state officials explained to me that this contrast between public and private positions in early 2003 was a result of the Texas officials being unwilling to tell DeLay no. They suggested that only Craddick was gung ho for redistricting. Governor Perry and Lieutenant Governor Dewhurst were described to me as "reluctant," given the many other issues to be addressed. However, the officials who spoke to me agreed that DeLay was reasonable to believe that he had a commitment to take up redistricting at least once the legislature had dealt with the other major issues in the session. If Governor Perry, however, began 2003 reluctant to pursue congressional redistricting, he showed no such hesitation as the year moved on. By the end of the first special session, Perry was locked in a public contest of wills with the Democratic lawmakers—a contest that he was determined to win.

Ellis busily worked at achieving a redistricting map that could be supported by all Republican members of the Texas delegation in Congress. An initial plan was presented to them in DeLay's Washington office, but several objected to the shape of specific districts. Ellis worked to address the objections and reported his progress to DeLay. Each Republican member had an opportunity to accept or reject the proposed changes to his or her existing district. In his memos, Ellis reported that some agreed to be paired with incumbent Democrats "under certain circumstances" (i.e., in districts that the Republicans could win). Others (specifically Reps. Lamar Smith, Mac Thornberry, and Michael Burgess), according to Ellis, were willing to make their districts less Republican so that Republican voting strength could be increased in other districts. Ellis listed over thirty state legislators (including some Democrats) as having made specific requests to him regarding the map (e.g., "Sen. Wentworth only wants Travis County cut into just two districts," "Rep. Wilson wants an additional African American district in Houston," and "Sen. Zaffirini wants Webb County kept whole"). The Associated Republicans of Texas as well as the Republican National Committee submitted map proposals to Ellis.

In the original plan presented to the Republican congressmen in DeLay's office, the Hispanic percentage of District 24 in Dallas was increased.[14] This plan essentially embodied the request of Hispanic groups. However, Rep. Sessions objected. He thought Martin Frost could win reelection in such a district and pushed for a plan that would defeat him by breaking up the district. A redrawing of District 24 to break up the Democratic stronghold was approved by the congressmen affected by the change. Later plans incorporated this version of the Dallas–Fort Worth districts, and, according to Ellis, the change had a ripple effect that "forced significant changes in the eastern and central part of the state." These changes resulted in the proposed pairing of Democrats Lampson and Sandlin in an East Texas district along the Louisiana border that was expected to elect a Democrat.

The objective of this process overseen by Ellis was to arrive at a "final" consensus plan that would unseat as many Democratic incumbents as possible without jeopardizing Republican incumbents. An Ellis memorandum specifically listed the "targeted" Democratic districts at the time as Districts 2 (Turner), 4 (Hall), 11 (Edwards), 17 (Stenholm), and 24 (Frost). In prescribing rules for future changes to the plan, the memorandum also listed eight districts that could not be changed; these were the districts thought protected by the Voting Rights Act. By memorandum on April 5, 2003, Ellis urged DeLay to personally inform the governor, lieutenant governor, and Speaker "when the map is finalized." At the time, three different maps were under consideration.

The partisan result preferred by Ellis (and DeLay) was a plan that would result in as many as six or seven additional Republican seats—including District 1 (Hall), which "would be Republican when the incumbent retired."

Each proposed configuration of districts was duly run through software that used past election data (available by election precincts statewide) to determine the likely partisan outcome of any future congressional race. Data from several different past elections were used, but the most conservative guideline was considered to be the 1998 race for lieutenant governor in which Rick Perry narrowly beat John Sharp. The overwhelming Bush victories for governor in 1998 and president in 2000 were seen as being less reliable for predicting possible Democratic success in future congressional races.

Republican Efforts to Counter the Negative PR Surrounding Redistricting

DeLay and Ellis recognized that an effort was necessary to counter the statewide "negative PR" for redistricting. DeLay issued statements arguing that redrawing congressional districts to replace incumbent Democrats with Republicans was a matter of "basic fairness," given that the Democrats held the majority of seats even though a majority of Texans were voting Republican in statewide races.[15] He blamed federal judge John Hannah for the court-approved redistricting map under which all of the Democratic incumbents had won reelection in 2001.[16] On a more general level, DeLay challenged the role of the courts in redistricting: "All over this country, courts are drawing the districts. That is unconstitutional in my eyes, and you have to stop it by standing up and accepting your responsibility as called for by the Constitution." Later he added, "I think it is the responsibility of the Legislature. The constitution's [sic] very specific as to who's supposed to do redistricting and apportionment—not the judges."[17] Ellis was quoted as saying that redistricting was necessary "because (the current map) underrepresents Hispanics, African-Americans and Republicans."[18]

Other Republicans joined the PR campaign by publishing opinion pieces in the major newspapers. Congressman Pete Sessions published an op-ed in the *Dallas Morning News* (February 8, 2003) urging the legislature to redraw congressional districts: "Establishing fair and proportionate representation not only is the fundamental right of the Legislature, it is a constitutional duty." He claimed that "a Democrat-controlled federal judicial panel drew the current partisan interim map." He pointed out that in the 2002 congressional races, Republican candidates garnered 2.3 million votes to the Democrats' 1.9 million, but that Republicans held only 47 percent of the congressional seats from Texas: "The bottom line: It is the responsibility of the Legislature to redraw the congressional districts to accurately reflect the will of the people of Texas." Acknowledging that the legislature has "a long list of issues it will need to address in the coming session," Session concluded that "none will be as important as the constitutional duty of finalizing the congressional map for this decade."

Similar opinion pieces appeared elsewhere in the state. For example, Republican attorney Andy Taylor argued in the *Houston Chronicle* (March 2): "Let's do right by minority Texans." He asserted that the state had failed to discharge its "constitutional obligation" by failing to adopt a redistricting plan in 2001, and that "we will have another missed opportunity if we don't act quickly, while our Legislature is in session." Otherwise, "the minorities of this state will have to wait another decade before their voices will be heard in the Congress." Taylor's article was countered by one from African American congresswoman Sheila Jackson Lee (*Houston Chronicle,* March 15). Congresswoman Lee said that Taylor's arguments were "false and misleading." She said that the objective of redistricting in 2003 would be to increase Republican power in the U.S. House of Representatives, not to help minorities: "Sending six additional right-wing Republicans to Congress would seriously harm the interests of African-American and Hispanic voters." She concluded, "They [Republicans] want to pretend to be the friends of minorities as a ruse to send more Republicans to Washington to vote against everything minorities care about."

Asking the Texas Attorney General Whether Redistricting Is Necessary

Rep. Joe Crabb chaired the House Redistricting Committee in 2003. He also received funds from TRMPAC. Early in the session he gave contradictory indications whether redistricting would occur. When appointed chairman, he was quoted in the newspapers as saying that congressional redistricting was "highly likely."[19] By early February, however, he was echoing the negative comments of Speaker Craddick and indicating that redistricting, if it occurred, was likely to deal with only minor changes.[20] Democratic state representative Richard Raymond (Webb County) has stated that Crabb told him early in the session that taking up congressional redistricting was the last thing on his mind and the last thing he wanted to deal with.[21]

On February 11, Crabb officially asked the Texas attorney general, Gregg Abbott, about the legal rights and responsibilities of the Legislature in connection with congressional redistricting. Specifically, he wanted to know whether the congressional districts adopted by the court in 2001 could remain in effect

for the rest of the decade or whether lawmakers have a "mandated responsibility to enact a permanent map for the electoral period 2003 through 2010." [22]
Crabb is quoted by the *Houston Chronicle* as indicating in April that he had no
intention of taking action on redistricting unless the attorney general "tells him
he has to do so." [23] Richard Raymond in 2005 recalled Crabb making a similar
statement to him.

An affirmative answer to Crabb's question about a mandated responsibility
to redistrict would certainly propel the process forward. On April 23, Attorney
General Abbott issued his letter opinion (No. GA-0063). The writers of the
opinion apparently tried to give Crabb an affirmative response. The opinion
emphasized repeatedly that redistricting is primarily the responsibility of the
state through its legislature or some other body authorized to redraw districts,
and that no federal court could restrain a state from doing so. The opinion
states: "This federal court-drawn map, however, is only effective unless and
until the Texas Legislature redraws it—that is, unless and until lawmakers
'renew and continue efforts to fulfill their constitutional duties.'"

Much as the opinion authors apparently tried, however, they could not tell
Crabb that redistricting was legally mandated. There was no legal reason why
the court-approved plan could not remain in place for the remainder of the
decade. In fact, although not mentioned in the opinion, Texas had conducted
elections for various congressional and state-legislative seats under court-
ordered plans through the three preceding decades. However, the opinion also
did not give Crabb's question a clearly negative response. Instead, the opinion
reframed the question and concluded that

> the Texas Legislature has the authority to adopt a congressional redistricting
> plan for the electoral period 2003 through 2010, but it cannot be compelled to
> do so. . . . Unless and until the legislature adopts such a plan, the map drawn
> in 2002 by the three-judge court in *Balderas v. Texas* will continue to be the
> congressional redistricting plan for Texas.

Although not the clarion call for redistricting that some Republicans had
wanted, the attorney general's opinion provided an impetus for the legislature
to act. In Crabb's description, the opinion "seems to say that we should, but we
don't have to." He said he would ask Craddick how to proceed. [24]

DeLay returned to Texas at the same time that Abbott released his opinion.
It is reasonable to assume that the timing of the two events had been coordinated. [25] The ostensible occasion for DeLay's visit was Speaker's Reunion Day,
a get-together for former Texas lawmakers. However, on April 24, the day
following release of Abbott's opinion, DeLay was busy meeting about redis-

tricting with state officials and Republican state representatives. Many Republican lawmakers met individually with Congressman DeLay in the office of Rep. Dianne Delisi, on the ground floor of the Capitol. Each was asked how the current redistricting plan could be changed to meet his or her preferences and whether Congressman DeLay could help with any issues in Washington.[26] DeLay's primary sales pitch for redistricting was simple: most Texans support President Bush, but the incumbent Democratic congressmen are voting against the president's proposals and must go.

Congressman DeLay also met again with Governor Perry, Lieutenant Governor Dewhurst, and Speaker Craddick on this trip.[27] After the meetings, DeLay said he had the support of the state leaders: Perry "is more than anxious to get a bill to his desk so that he can sign it, and he will be helpful in any way to try to garner the votes that are necessary," and Speaker Craddick had told him "that the committee is ready to move, and he is more than supportive in moving the bill out of the House . . . He said he's going to move a bill through the House."[28] Craddick said that he supported the "notion" of redistricting, but that he would "not push it."[29] Dewhurst indicated that he would bring a redistricting bill to the Senate floor only if it first passed the House.

Several newspapers again editorialized against redistricting. On April 26, the *Houston Chronicle* reaffirmed its opposition to redistricting. A day later, the *Fort Worth Star-Telegram* did the same. On May 2, the *Austin American-Statesman* reiterated that the "push for redistricting is wrong and offensive; it should be defeated." None of these opinions had any effect. Speaker Craddick confided, "To be blunt, on the Republican side, the leadership has changed and so has the agenda."[30]

When told that the Black and Hispanic caucuses in the House opposed redistricting, DeLay said that any minority sentiment against his proposal could be motivated only by partisan interests. He added, "If they [minority lawmakers and organizations] turn it down, they are more Democrat than they are minority. And they are representing the Democratic Party and not their people."[31]

Turmoil around the House Committee on Redistricting

While waiting for the attorney general's opinion, Representative Crabb introduced a redistricting bill. The bill merely contained the districts from the existing, court-approved plan, and if passed, it would have simply maintained the status quo. However, the bill provided the necessary legislative "vehicle" for a substantive redrawing of congressional districts.

At a committee hearing on the bill on April 10, the partisan sniping began. Representative Raymond requested that the committee conduct some hearings on redistricting outside of Austin. He particularly wanted a hearing scheduled in his hometown of Laredo because he knew that many of his constituents opposed redistricting. Chairman Crabb rejected the request.

In April, rumors spread that a map circulating among Republicans was DeLay's preferred redrawing of the congressional districts. In a letter to Crabb, Representative Raymond called for release of the proposed maps. Crabb said that no one had given him any maps. On April 22, Republican map drawer (and Craddick staffer) Scott Sims reported that his leather folio and maps had been taken from a House committee room.[32] The now infamous "DeLay Map" that Ellis had prepared in conjunction with the Republican congressmen was purportedly in the missing folio. Jim Ellis accused a "[Congressman] Frost staffer" of stealing the folio and map. Although he did not name anyone at the time, Ellis apparently was accusing attorney Gerald Hebert, who was representing Congressman Frost and the Texas Democratic congressional delegation. Hebert "categorically" denied the accusations. Frost acknowledged having a copy of the alleged map, but said that he had received it from a "high-ranking" Republican friend.[33] The Texas Department of Public Safety was asked to investigate. A surveillance videotape allegedly showed three men (including possibly Hebert) leaving the committee room, but Sims's folio was not visible. The DPS interviewed lawmakers and their staffs. The portfolio and map were never found. This bizarre incident died a quiet death.

Chairman Crabb announced on April 24 (the day of DeLay's visit to Austin) that he had concluded that it was the legislature's "constitutional duty" to move forward with redistricting and that he would hold a hearing on a redistricting bill. He denied having met with Congressman DeLay or having seen any redistricting plan.[34]

The committee hearing on redistricting came on May 2. Over 200 witnesses signed up to testify. Virtually all were opposed to redistricting, but many were confused about whether being against changing the existing districts meant that they should register as "for" or "against" the pending legislation that merely enacted the existing district lines. The beginning of the hearing, scheduled for 5:30 p.m., was delayed as the committee members waited for a plan that would be substituted for the existing court-ordered plan in the bill that Crabb had filed. The hearing finally began at 9 p.m. It lasted until 5:30 a.m. the following morning, and was continued periodically for several days thereafter.

At the hearing, Representative Raymond tried to direct the committee's attention to the wording of the attorney general's opinion and to its finding that the legislature was not mandated to take up redistricting. Raymond tried to raise the issue in questions to Chairman Crabb. The chairman refused to recognize Raymond for his questions or for a parliamentary inquiry. It was at the conclusion of the testimony at 5:30 a.m. the next morning that Crabb finally recognized Raymond for his question about the opinion. Crabb conceded that the opinion did not say that the legislature was mandated to redistrict, but indicated that the committee was going to move forward anyway. Crabb also denied ever having told Raymond or the press that the committee would not take up redistricting.[35]

Another heated partisan exchange had erupted around 2:30 a.m. as the tired lawmakers continued hearing witnesses. Representative Raymond renewed his request that the committee conduct hearings outside of Austin, specifically in Hispanic areas of the state. Chairman Crabb responded that such hearings were inappropriate in part because, "There are only two people I know of on the committee that speak Spanish. The rest of us would have a very difficult time if we were out in an area—other than Austin or other English-speaking areas—to be able to have committee hearings or to be able to converse with people that did not speak English."[36] Raymond was stunned by the chairman's response. He explained to Crabb that the residents of Laredo spoke English and that, if necessary, there were plenty of interpreters there. Crabb would not relent.[37]

Concerned that Crabb's actions (including failing to post a notice in Spanish for the hearings) might have violated the Voting Rights Act, Raymond hired Austin attorney Renea Hicks, and on May 8 sent a letter to the Department of Justice, complaining about the notice-posting oversight and the lack of redistricting hearings in Hispanic areas of the state.[38] Raymond learned a few days later that DeLay had purportedly told House Republicans that he would get the complaint dismissed by Monday, May 12, the day the redistricting bill was to be debated in the House. Raymond elected to withdraw his complaint. His attorney faxed a letter to Justice on Sunday evening, May 11, withdrawing the complaint because Raymond had "received reliable information that the normal processes of the Department of Justice for complaints have been circumvented under pressure from Congressman Tom DeLay of Texas." Congressman DeLay's aide Jonathan Grella responded that "Raymond's strategy all along was to garner headlines for himself, and his decision to drop the inquiry is further proof that he wasn't serious."[39] On May 12, Hicks filed a lawsuit for Raymond in federal court, asserting essentially the same claims that had been included in Raymond's Justice Department complaint. Raymond later decided to voluntarily dismiss this suit. Whether the hearings and notices in question were legally required is doubtful, but including them would have been very good policy, and historically they have been used by Texas in any redistricting process. The legislature decided later in the summer of 2003 to hold hearings at several locations outside of Austin, including hearings in predominately Hispanic areas of the state, and to post notice of such hearings in Spanish as well as English.

DeLay aide Jim Ellis was conspicuous by his continuing presence in the offices of the House Redistricting Committee. According to Richard Raymond, Ellis "camped out in the back room of the committee and was working on a map that could be used for new districts. Jim Ellis made no bones about his role: it was to make sure the map that was drawn and passed was the one that Tom DeLay wanted."[40] Ellis, and House Republican Phil King undertook to redraw the plan that had been presented on May 2. Ellis in 2005 insisted that he never actually drew any maps (i.e., operated the computer "mouse"), but that he attended a great many private map-drawing sessions. Ellis worked directly with King in a partnership that would be important over the next five months of the redistricting process.[41]

Even though the hearing that had started on Friday, May 2, went until 5:30 on Saturday morning, there were still witnesses waiting to be heard. The committee recessed until 10 a.m. and then reconvened to continue to hear testimony; it heard witnesses until approximately midnight. Still more were waiting to be heard. The committee reconvened on Sunday at noon; testimony lasted until 10 p.m. The committee met again on Monday. Finally the hearing was completed.

The House Redistricting Committee convened again on Tuesday, May 6. Chairman Crabb announced that he was unsure whether the committee would act then to adopt a redistricting plan and report the bill, as substituted, to the House floor. As Raymond recalled later, he surprised a chagrined Crabb by reading to the committee a news report indicating that DeLay's office in Washington had issued a press release moments earlier saying that the Texas committee would adopt a redistricting bill that day.[42] Raymond sarcastically suggested to Crabb that perhaps he had just not been told of DeLay's plans. Still, the committee members waited around. Ellis and others were busy obtaining the Republican congressional delegation's approval of a final plan for the committee to consider. At midnight the new plan from Representative King emerged. Democrats complained that this plan had been "intentionally hidden" until late at night to avoid public review or comment. Their complaints went unaddressed. Ellis, who had participated in drawing the map, explained, "Our goal is to elect more Republicans."[43] The bill (with the so-called "midnight plan") was finally "kicked-out" of committee by a post-midnight vote on Wednesday morning.

CHAPTER 8

No Better Option:
The Democrats Break the Quorum
in the House of Representatives

The Chicken Ds that did this ought to be ashamed of themselves. There is disgrace in running and hiding . . . I've been in the House for 35 years and I've lost some, but I've never walked off the floor like these Chicken Ds.
— SPEAKER TOM CRADDICK, *DALLAS MORNING NEWS*, MAY 13, 2003

As he sat in his legislative office in the state Capitol, State Rep. Jim Dunnam was in a terrible quandary.[1] The date was Wednesday, May 7, 2003. At 12:30 a.m., the House Committee on Redistricting had adopted a plan for redrawing the boundaries of all thirty-two congressional districts in Texas. The bill's Republican sponsor claimed that the plan would elect at least five additional Republican congressmen from Texas. As the head of the Democratic Caucus in the House, Dunnam's task now was to determine what additional action, if any, the Democratic members could take to stop the Republican juggernaut.

Dunnam had been the chairman of the Democratic Caucus only since the beginning of the 2003 session, when it became clear that Democrat Pete Laney had ended his bid for reelection as Speaker. Historically, the Speaker of the House also served as the de facto leader of the Democratic majority in that chamber. After the Republicans elected a majority of the House members in the 2002 election, it became probable that for the first time in 130 years the Speaker of the Texas House would be a Republican. When Laney finally withdrew his candidacy, it became imperative that the Democrats find new leadership in their unfamiliar role as a minority in the House. Dunnam, an Anglo state representative from Waco, was their choice.

Early in the session, it had appeared to Dunnam and others that redistricting was not going to be one of the session's major headaches. At the beginning of the year, none of the elected Republican state leaders publicly supported a redrawing of congressional district boundaries. Some Republican House members had even told their colleagues that redistricting would not happen. Over the past few weeks, however, Dunnam had watched the situation change. By May 7, despite the newspaper editorials and the testimony at the public hearings against a redistricting bill, the legislation was out of committee and on its way to the House floor for consideration and certain passage. Dunnam weighed the options.

Weighing the Options

As the Republican redistricting effort gained momentum, various Democratic representatives began to discuss how to deal with it. Was any effort to stop the redistricting bill truly worthwhile, or was the Republican redistricting inevitable? Was it better to try to work out a compromise that could at least save a few of the targeted Democratic incumbent congressmen? Would the Republicans even be willing to compromise for less than what they otherwise could achieve through the exercise of their legislative majority?

The frequency and intensity of these informal discussions increased sharply as it became evident that the Redistricting Committee was likely to act favorably on a redistricting plan. At the Democratic Caucus meeting on Tuesday, May 6, Rep. Richard Raymond, who was still fighting to stop the redistricting bill at the committee level, urged that only a walkout by Democratic House members to break a quorum would stop the bill. He asked everyone at the meeting if any of them thought that breaking a quorum "would not be a good idea." No member raised his or her hand to indicate objection.[2] Representative Senfronia Thompson said, "My first thought was that it couldn't work. As I began to think about it, I thought it was worth a try."[3] Still, no final decision had been made and no plans existed for a walkout. Democratic House members awaited word from their caucus leader.

As he considered the situation a day later, Dunnam saw no attractive alternatives. Now that the bill was out of the Redistricting Committee, it was certain to proceed quickly through the calendar committee and would probably be set for consideration by the full House as early as Monday, only four days away. Any vote on the bill, or on any substantive amendment to the bill, was certain to be along partisan lines, and Republicans would win every vote. There were no apparent legislative rules violations that might allow the bill to be sidetracked by a legislative point of order. With Speaker Craddick favoring adoption of a redistricting bill, there was no assurance that, as presiding officer, he would grant any unfavorable point of order, even if one existed.

Meaningful compromise seemed unlikely. However, even an attempt at compromise seemed fraught with danger. Many Democrats were concerned that the current bill was only a stalking horse for a harsher and more partisan plan that would be substituted later in the Senate or in a conference committee. To allow the bill to pass even in a compromised form would mean that House Democrats would be virtually powerless later to prevent passage of a more aggressively partisan plan.

There were a few positive circumstances. The regular legislative session was nearing its end—June 2.[4] Moreover, legislative rules impose restrictions on when certain kinds of legislation can be considered during a session. One such rule prevents the House from considering its own bills after the 123rd day of a (140-day) session. The rule is to prevent the House from wasting time on legislation that the Senate would not have time to pass. The rule can be suspended, but only by a two-thirds vote of the members present. Dunnam knew that the Democrats had enough votes (62 out of 150) to prevent the rule from being suspended in order to allow consideration of the redistricting bill. Therefore, the redistricting legislation could apparently be blocked if consideration of it on the House floor could be delayed until past adjournment on Thursday, May 15, after which the rule against consideration of House bills would become enforceable.

Another positive circumstance for the Democrats was that House Democrats were relatively well organized and mutually trusting. Several of them had significant legislative leadership experience; many had been ousted from their committee chairmanships at the beginning of the 2003 legislative session when Speaker Craddick appointed new chairmen who were less affiliated with former Speaker Laney. Democratic representatives such as Pete Gallego, Scott Hochberg, Garnet Coleman, Richard Raymond, Senfronia Thompson, Yvonne Davis, and Ruth McClendon had years of legislative experience and had proven resourceful during the 2003 session in combating Republican-backed legislation they deemed harmful to societal interests.

A second reason for the Democrats' unity was that Craddick's style of governing in the House had become a focal point for Democrat opposition. As former Speaker Laney explained, "He (Craddick) has done more to unite the Democrats than I ever could."[5] Democrats could not understand how the House Republican leadership could be pushing redistricting while claiming that no time remained in the session for addressing more important topics, such as public-school finance.

Another key reason for Democratic unity was Dunnam's light-handed leadership style. He had guided the Democratic Caucus through collective decision making, involving many different Democratic members. By the end of May, the members of the Democratic Caucus were generally willing to cooperate toward common goals. Dunnam in 2005 emphasized to me, however, that the unity and trust among Democrats in 2003 was, as with any group of individually elected officials, fragile and uncertain. There was never, in Dunnam's mind, a certainty that the group could stay united long enough to block the redistricting bill.

It was clear to Dunnam on May 7, 2003, that successfully achieving a walkout of at least fifty-one members of the Texas House would severely test his leadership, the strength of the caucus, and the mutual trust among Democratic members. Dunnam convened a meeting the next morning to discuss the options. Dunnam, along with Raymond, Coleman, and Rep. Ryan Guillen (Rio Grande City) were together. Dunnam quickly added Rep. Pete Gallego to the group. Dunnam then grabbed ten additional members from the House chamber and the group went to an office downstairs in the Capitol. The participants discussed the options and generally agreed that a walkout might be necessary. However, a walkout would not be required if the Democrats in the Senate could block a redistricting bill once it passed the House.

Lieutenant Governor Dewhurst had announced publicly that he had told the Speaker and governor that he did not have enough votes to pass a redistricting bill in the Senate, and that, therefore, the House would have to pass a redistricting bill before the Senate could take it up. Senator Gonzalo Barrientos (Travis County), the leader of the Democratic Caucus in the Texas Senate, seemed to agree with Dewhurst's assessment; he had been quoted on May 7 as claiming that he had enough votes in the Senate to block a Republican redistricting plan.[6] However, these same newspapers also reported that the House sponsor of the redistricting legislation, Rep. Phil King, was claiming that the partisan legislation would pass the Senate.[7] Dunnam needed to know if Senator Barrientos and the other Senate Democrats had the necessary votes to defeat a redistricting bill once it passed the House.

On the afternoon of Thursday, May 8, Dunnam and Raymond went to the Senate side of the Capitol to meet with Barrientos. The Republican majority in the Senate (nineteen to twelve) was certain to pass a partisan redistricting plan if Senate rules could be suspended to allow its consideration. Barrientos had been saying publicly that he had pledges from thirteen senators to vote against any redistricting legislation. Suspending the Senate rules to take up the redistricting bill would require the affirmative vote of twenty-one senators; thirteen negative votes would be more than enough to block redistricting. In private, however, Barrientos now explained to Dunnam and Raymond that he actually had commitments from only eleven senators and that at least one of those eleven was "soft." When asked if he could "guarantee" that the Senate would not pass a redistricting bill that came from the House, Barrientos said he would check again with the senators and call Dunnam on Friday with a final count of firm votes. Dunnam and Raymond agreed that the news from Barrientos meant that a walkout was the best remaining hope for stopping the redistricting legislation.

A meaningful walkout would require at least fifty-one House members to be safely gone by Monday, May 12, when the redistricting bill was set to be taken up. According to Dunnam, "There was no real plan. On Thursday I said 'I have to get off my rear and start talking to people.'"[8] The walkout plans were underway when Barrientos confirmed on Friday that there were not enough solid votes in the Senate to block a redistricting bill. He said that the House Democrats should go ahead and do whatever they needed to do.[9]

May 7–10: Organizing a Walkout

One of the first issues to be decided was whether each of the fifty-one members should be free to make (or not to make, as the case might be) his or her own plans for hiding during a walkout. The Democratic planners feared that allowing members to make their own arrangements would almost certainly lead to one or more being found and returned to the House chamber. The return of as few as one or two could allow the Republicans to achieve the necessary 100-member quorum. Dunnam and others also saw a need for the walkout participants to stay in touch and cooperate. Therefore, it was agreed that at least fifty-one Democrats had to go together to a single site where, as Representative Gallego explained, "everybody could see everyone's cards."[10]

Any location in Austin, or even in Texas, would leave the Democrats subject to being found and forced to return to the House. Nuevo Laredo, Mexico, was suggested, but there was little enthusiasm for being seen as having left the United States, especially given the number of Hispanic Democrats likely to participate in the walkout. Someone suggested Lake Charles, Louisiana, as a possible destination. However, Keith Hampton, the legislative chair of the Texas Criminal Defense Lawyers Association, pointed out that the governor of Louisiana was Republican and might, pursuant to a contact from someone at the White House, be willing to cooperate in an effort to force the Democrats back to Texas. Raymond added that Louisiana allowed gambling, and it would be detrimental to the Democrats' purposes if they were portrayed in the media as being at the gambling tables of Louisiana instead of at their desks in the House chamber.[11]

The governors and attorney generals of Oklahoma and New Mexico, however, were Democrats and probably would not cooperate with any Republican effort to force the Democrats back to Texas. To be sure about the anticipated hospitality, discreet inquiries were made to officials in those states. Austin political consultant Dean Rindy spoke directly to the Oklahoma attorney general and to the governor's chief of staff. Rindy's wife, Cynthia Miller, made similar calls to officials with the New Mexico attorney general. Both sets of responses were encouraging: neither Oklahoma nor New Mexico officials were likely to cooperate in the extradition of Texas lawmakers.

Dunnam preferred Oklahoma. He was personally familiar with Ardmore, Oklahoma, because his wife's grandparents had once resided outside of the town. He knew that it was a pleasant community, but he was sure that Ardmore was unlikely to be seen by the media or voters as a vacation spot like Louisiana. Therefore, Dunnam decided on Ardmore, Oklahoma, as their destination. It was agreed, however, to keep this a secret even from their Senate Democratic allies and most of the other Democratic members of the House until the walkout actually began.

Numerous logistical arrangements remained to be made. Rep. Trey Martinez Fischer indicated that he could arrange for buses from a source that did not need to know the destination beforehand. Raymond offered the use of his credit cards. The caucus's chief staff member, Hugh Brady, contacted the Holiday Inn in Ardmore and reserved a block of twenty-six rooms under his name. Consultants Ed Martin and Matt Angle provided advice and assistance.

The critical task was getting at least fifty-one Democratic members to agree to walk out by Monday. Any fewer would be meaningless, since the Republicans needed only 100 of the 150 members to establish a quorum and permit passage of the redistricting bill. Moreover, each member who promised to walk out had to be willing to remain gone until May 16 to finally kill the bill. The worst possible scenario as seen by Dunnam and the other planners was one in which almost all of the fifty-one members left, but one or two either remained behind or were found by the Republicans in time to allow the quorum to be established and the redistricting bill passed. Under that scenario, the redistricting bill would pass, and the members who had walked out could face criticism from constituents and retribution from the Republican House leadership. It was even possible under that scenario that a member who broke with the Democratic Caucus to give the Republicans a quorum would be rewarded handsomely by the Republican leadership for his or her actions.

Dunnam, along with Representatives Raymond, Coleman, Gallego, Thompson, and Rick Noriega (Houston) began on Thursday, May 8, to meet systematically with small groups of Democrats while the House was convened. The meetings occurred in Representative Coleman's legislative office (GW.17, on the western ground floor of the Capitol) because it was directly below the back of the House chamber and could be conveniently reached by an elevator behind the chamber. The lawmakers generally were called together in groups of friends or persons who shared common interests. The routine in each meeting was essentially the same, even as the participants changed. Dunnam and one of the other planners would go over the options for stopping redistricting and explain why none appeared to hold much, if any, chance for success. Ultimately each member included in the meetings agreed that only a walkout would prevent a Republican triumph. Dunnam insisted to me in 2005 that the meetings in May 2003 were not a hard sell.

One of the first groups to be corralled in these meetings was the so-called "WD-40s." These were the "white Democrats over 40." The members of this group had willingly adopted the label (complete with oil-can lapel pins) after it was offered good-naturedly by Representative Raymond earlier in the legislative session. Now Raymond in particular was concerned that these members might be unwilling to boycott the session because they were potentially more vulnerable to a backlash from their constituents. To Raymond, it was important to confirm the support of these Democrats before going further. Dunnam met alone with most of this group in Representative Barry Telford's office (GW.12). After hearing the options, each of these members agreed with the walkout strategy, and all of them subsequently participated in it.

Another group of Democratic members created a special dilemma. A handful of African American and Hispanic Democrats had broken early with the ill-fated Speaker reelection effort of Pete Laney. They had sided with the eventual winner, Republican Tom Craddick, and had been rewarded with positions of responsibility as committee chairmen or vice chairmen. These representatives sometimes were called the "Craddick Ds" (or, more unaffectionately by some, the "cross-dressers"). One African American representative from Harris County, Sylvester Turner, had become president pro tempore of the House. Some of these Democrats had an allegiance to Speaker Craddick that would make their participation in a walkout politically and individually problematic. Also, there was a risk in communicating anything about the walkout strategy to some of these members because one or more of them could feel obligated to alert Speaker Craddick to what was being planned.

Nevertheless, these lawmakers were still Democrats and generally shared many of the same concerns as the other Democrats. Therefore, each of these members was approached either by Dunnam or by one or more of the other walkout planners and given a chance to participate in the walkout. For example, Dunnam and Rep. Craig Eiland met on Saturday at the Texas Chili Parlor (a restaurant near the Capitol) with Harold Dutton to advise him of the planned walkout and ask him to participate. Representative Coleman spoke with President Pro Tempore Turner. Other members from this group were approached "back channel" through constituents. Some of these members agreed to join the walkout. Others declined, but were asked to keep the matter secret. Some reportedly agreed to walk out and then did not do so. Dunnam told me in 2005 that only Rep. Ron Wilson was avoided altogether because it was assumed that he would not have participated in the walkout and would have immediately warned Craddick.

Dunnam insists that every Democratic representative except Ron Wilson was told about the walkout strategy and asked to participate. At least one of the other representatives (Vilma Luna) who stayed behind said at the time, however, that she was never asked to participate in the walkout.[12] On the other hand, Wilson insists that he (and the Republican leadership of the House) knew beforehand about the walkout and were not surprised by the absence of Democrats on Monday, May 12.[13]

At one stage the planners put the names of Democratic House members on a blackboard and marked each name as either certain to leave or doubtful. Some planners hoped initially to leave three loyal members behind because, under House rules, it would take three members to demand a record vote. They wanted to prevent the Republican House leadership from trying to pass the redistricting bill by voice vote even in the absence of a quorum. It soon became apparent to the planners, however, that there were no members to spare to leave behind in Austin. Dunnam initially planned to remain behind alone because of his knowledge of House rules. Ultimately, however, it was decided that media coverage would prevent the Republicans from bypassing House rules and that Dunnam should lead the exit to Ardmore.

By Friday, May 9, thirty Democrats had agreed to join a walkout. By Saturday, the number had risen to enough to break the quorum. Dunnam told me in 2005 that he believed a major reason for the Democrats' willingness to agree to such an extraordinary step as a walkout was the general feeling that their views on important issues such as the state budget, school finance, insurance reform, and tort reform had been ignored all session. Specifically, Dunnam told me in 2005, "We would not have gone to Ardmore but for the way that they (the Republicans) handled the budget." Many Democrats reportedly felt "irrelevant" as a result of the way that the House was being run under Republican leadership. Hugh Brady recalled in 2005 that some Democratic congressmen called reluctant Texas lawmakers and encouraged them to join the walkout.[14] Whatever the reasons, Democrats were committing to the walkout. Moreover, logistical plans for the departure were falling into place. It increasingly appeared that the walkout would come off.

Communications among Democrats at the Capitol and in the House chamber during these few days were "like secret communications in a prison camp" (as in the movie *The Great Escape*).[15] Participating Democrats were told on Saturday that the departure would be on Sunday. In some instances, individual members were assigned to watch over other lawmakers and to coordinate bringing them to the designated meeting place. Eventually on Saturday some of the members were told where to meet on Sunday. Even up until the moment the Democrats crossed the state line into Oklahoma on Sunday night, Dunnam was anxious that their plans and destination might become known and that they might be "apprehended" by House or law enforcement personnel sent to bring them back. The senator closest to the House Democrats, Rodney Ellis, did not know of the plans until the walkout had occurred.[16]

On the occasion of a smaller, impromptu walkout in 1981, some House members had improperly voted electronically from the desks of absent lawmakers to suggest that the lawmakers were in the chamber. Hugh Brady, considered an expert on House rules, suggested to the planners in 2003 that as a means of officially showing the lack of a quorum and preventing their Republican colleagues from possibly casting votes from the absent Democrats' desks, the Democrats draft a letter to the clerk of the House, asking the clerk to lock the requesting member's voting machine.[17] A separate letter was prepared for each Democrat. Since the House was in session on Saturday, each participating member was asked to come quietly to Representative Coleman's office to sign his or her letter. The signing of this letter also served as a ritual commitment by each member to join in the walkout as long as the necessary fifty-one members were participating. Some Democrats hesitated to sign. However, everyone who had committed earlier to walk out also eventually signed a letter. Only one of the members (Harold Dutton) who signed this letter ultimately did not participate in the walkout. These letters were kept by Dunnam's staff, to be delivered together on Monday, May 12, as an official announcement of the walkout.

A Sunday Departure

The secret departure plan called for all the participating Democrats to meet on Sunday, May 11 (Mother's Day), at 6:30 p.m. in the parking lot of the Embassy Suites hotel on north Interstate 35 in Austin. Members began to gather early. The buses were waiting. The early arrivals waited anxiously for their colleagues. Doubts remained that fifty-one or more members would actually leave town. Gradually over the next three hours the number of House lawmakers in the parking lot grew. Cell-phone calls were made often to confirm that other members were en route. Each new arrival was greeted and cheered. Rep. Rene Oliveira (Brownsville), who was ill, stopped by the parking lot to say farewell before leaving for Mexico.

An example of the unity among these Democrats was the decision of Juan Escobar. He had just been elected in a special election to replace longtime state representative Irma Rangel, who had died of cancer. Scheduled to be sworn in as a new representative in an official ceremony on May 12, Escobar settled for an impromptu ceremony earlier so that he could join his colleagues on the trip to Ardmore.

Eventually forty-seven Democratic House members were gathered in the parking lot. Rep. Robert Puente was one of the last to arrive. Representative Raymond, however, recalls that the last to show up was Rep. David Farabee from Wichita Falls. Representative Oliveira's immediate departure for Mexico made forty-eight. Another four Democrats had earlier announced that they were traveling separately to Ardmore. One of these was the former speaker, Pete Laney, who had indicated an intention to fly his private plane to Ardmore. Rep. Steven Wolens was driving his car from his home in Dallas. Rep. Kevin Bailey was driving his car from his home in Houston. Rep. Paul Moreno from El Paso (who is confined to a wheelchair and is less able to travel by air) would cross the state line from El Paso to New Mexico, but possibly would join the others in Ardmore later. If all of these fifty-two Democrats were successful in leaving the state, the Republican majority, lacking a quorum, would be paralyzed. Dunnam said, "Everyone was important. If everyone had not gotten on the bus, nobody would have gotten on the bus." [18]

Only one of the members who had signed a letter to the House clerk, Harold Dutton, was neither at the buses nor reportedly on his way to Ardmore or elsewhere out of state. Calls to his cell phone went unanswered. There was no reason for the Democratic lawmakers to wait longer. A van was left behind in the event that Dutton arrived later. The forty-seven Democrats at the Embassy Suites parking lot finished boarding the two buses around 9 p.m. Many of the lawmakers still did not know where they were going. The buses headed north on Interstate 35 toward Oklahoma.

The bus ride to Ardmore took approximately five hours. Initially, the members were jovial and full of excitement. Rep. Ismael "Kino" Flores called Representative McClendon on the bus. He was in the Rio Grande Valley and wanted to know if enough Democrats were leaving to break the quorum. He said he too would stay away from Austin. His absence meant that fifty-three Democrats were participating in the boycott. A fifty-fourth, Norma Chavez, remained in El Paso.

As the bus headed north, some of the passengers saw irony in the fact that the movie shown on one of the buses was the adventure thriller *Catch Me If You Can*. As with most such long trips, however, many of the travelers were mostly tired, bored, and restless by the end. Their excitement was renewed when, at shortly after midnight, the buses crossed into Oklahoma and out of the reach of Texas state troopers. Although the plan included staying out until after Thursday if necessary, most of the lawmakers expected to return sooner. Even Dunnam failed to take enough clothes for what became a four-day stay in Oklahoma.

The buses arrived at the Holiday Inn in Ardmore at around 1:30 a.m. No official notice had yet been given of the lawmakers' departure from Austin. The lawmakers were housed two to a room. The members registered under assumed names. The motel personnel had no idea who they were. Some members hoped that they could remain completely hidden from view for the next four days while filing press reports "from somewhere in Oklahoma." However, within twenty-four hours the attention of the media throughout Texas and much of the country was focused on Ardmore and these "runaway lawmakers."

The Republican Reaction in Austin and Washington

On Monday morning (May 12), the press corps at the Texas Capitol gathered at 9:30 a.m. for what they understood to be a press conference by Representative Dunnam and other Democrats about the redistricting bill set to be considered by the House later that day. Neither Dunnam nor any other Democratic member of the House appeared. Instead, Dunnam's chief of staff, Tamara Bell, quietly handed out copies of the fifty-one letters advising the House clerk that the members would be absent and asking him to cut off their voting machines. It was clear that most of the House Democrats were gone. When asked, the members' staffs denied any knowledge of their whereabouts.

The Texas House of Representatives was scheduled to convene at 10 a.m. Republican members began to gather on time. They mingled in a strangely empty chamber. It was clear that most of their Democratic colleagues were absent. The 81 members present were well short of the 100 necessary for a quorum. Word of the letters and the walkout spread quickly through the chamber.

Republican leaders said afterward that they were not surprised by the Democrats' departure. It is clear that rumors of such action had circulated around the Capitol during the previous week and had been the source of speculation in at least one newspaper. However, the confused actions of the Republican leaders on Monday, May 12, indicated that they were embarrassed by and unprepared for what had happened. The chance that the walkout might seriously endanger passage of the redistricting bill did not seem as important to some Republicans at the time as how the walkout might seem to reflect badly on their ability to govern.

In hindsight, Republican leaders have regretted some of the steps taken in response to the walkout, but at the time, such extraordinary measures seemed necessary. The first official step by Speaker Craddick was to lock down the House chamber shortly after 10 a.m. to keep the other members from leaving before a quorum was established. Under House rules, a "call" was immediately placed on the members; this allowed House personnel to search for the missing lawmakers and bring them to the chamber. A search of the Democrats' offices confirmed that they were not in the Capitol. Democrats later viewing the video of Craddick at the dais during this time were fond of saying that he looked "shell-shocked."

Speaker Craddick and other state officials immediately set about trying to find the absent Democrats and compelling them to return. The House sergeant at arms issued a "warrant" on House stationery for each of the suspected boycotters. The document was addressed to "any Peace Officer of the State of Texas," and directed the officer to arrest the named lawmaker and return him or her to the "Hall of the House of Representatives and there secure and retain that person." The Texas Department of Public Safety (DPS) was contacted. Attorney General Abbott assured the DPS (by letter) that it had the authority to secure the attendance of the absent lawmakers, including the authority to arrest them. At noon, Craddick announced to reporters at the Capitol that the DPS had been asked to find the missing Democrats and that DPS officers were entitled under existing reciprocity agreements with neighboring states to cross state lines to arrest the Democrats if necessary.

According to Perry's chief of staff at the time, Mike Toomey, "everyone" was caught up in trying to find the Democrats. Since one rumor at the time was that the Democrats had fled to New Mexico, Governor Perry's office (ostensibly at the request of Speaker Craddick) made inquiries to officials in New Mexico about the possibility of arrests in that state. However, the Democratic officials of New Mexico quickly rejected the notion of New Mexico peace officers tracking down and arresting the Texas Democrats. The Democratic attorney general of New Mexico, Patricia Madrid, responded publicly by joking that the police of New Mexico "were on the lookout for politicians in favor of health care for the needy and against tax cuts for the wealthy." She added more seriously that the dispute was "an internal political matter to be handled by Texas government officials."[19]

Attorney General Abbott (through his first assistant, Barry McBee) asked for assistance from the United States Department of Justice. McBee called

John Sutton, the U.S. attorney for the Western District of Texas (which includes Austin). McBee asked whether the U.S. Attorney had jurisdiction to help find and return the absent Democrats. He told Sutton that a Justice Department lawyer had done some research on this matter and that Sutton should call that attorney. As it turned out, this lawyer (whom Sutton later called) was a former Justice Department attorney now serving as counsel for Congressman DeLay. McBee also asked Sutton whether the FBI could assist. Sutton responded that he doubted that there was any federal interest in this matter, but that he would check. McBee called a second time at approximately 5:30 pm on May 12. Sutton explained that "after a quick review" he doubted whether there were grounds for filing a complaint under the Fugitive Felon Act. He said, however, that he would "bounce it off people in D.C."[20] Sutton called DeLay's counsel and gave him a similar response. McBee called Sutton again early on May 13. He paged Sutton, who was at the Dallas/Fort Worth airport. Sutton called back and confirmed that his office would not become involved.[21]

The DPS set up a "command post" on the 12th in the dining room in Speaker Craddick's suite of offices. At various times it was staffed by three to four DPS officers as well as the state's Homeland Security liaison person. McBee seemed to some to be the person in charge. Rep. Mike Krusee participated on behalf of the Speaker. First, they added the missing lawmakers to the list of persons in the Texas Crime Information Center (TCIC) bulletin sent to local, state, and federal peace officers statewide. The bulletin stated that the "following fifty-three legislators . . . are subject to immediate arrest."[22] The bulletin listed the names of each of the missing legislators, his or her date of birth, driver's license information, and last known address. This bulletin caused some law enforcement officers to be reassigned to find their local legislators. Some were assigned to conduct surveillance at locations where the legislators might appear (e.g., scheduled speaking events). One DPS sergeant in Corpus Christi contacted an FBI special agent with whom he regularly worked. Newly elected lawmaker Juan Escobar was a former border agent and colleague of the special agent. The FBI special agent had known Escobar for twelve years. At the DPS officer's request, the special agent called Escobar's cell phone. Escobar answered and, in an exchange of brief telephone conversations with the agent over the 13, confirmed that he and Corpus Christi Representative Gabi Canales were in Oklahoma.[23] However, by this time the location of the Democrats was well known. The TCIC notice was rescinded at 8:30 p.m. on May 13.

One of the first persons alerted on May 12 to the Democrats' disappearance was Congressman Tom Delay. Speaker Craddick personally called DeLay and asked for help. As a result, DeLay too began trying to find a means to locate the Democrats and return them to Texas. His office contacted the Justice Department and the Federal Aviation Agency (FAA). In response to questions from the press, a representative of DeLay's office charged: "The people elected their representatives to cast difficult votes, not to run away from them. . . . It's a good thing these Democrats weren't there during the Alamo."[24] Although the nature and extent of Congressman DeLay's involvement in the search for the Democrats would not become known until later, Craddick acknowledged publicly on May 12 that the possibility of having the Democrats arrested under authority from the federal government was "being worked on."[25] The specifics of DeLay's involvement at this stage are discussed in Chapter 15. In Austin, DeLay's aide Jim Ellis accused the Democrats of operating in the interest of the Democratic Party rather than the state.

Although the DPS had been asked to find the absent Democrats, DPS spokesman Tom Vinger acknowledged by Monday afternoon, "We don't believe we have explicit power to go across state lines in this specific instance."[26] DPS officers, however, continued their search, even across state lines. Several weeks later, a state district court in Travis County (visiting judge Chuck Campbell) ruled that the DPS lacked authority to search even within Texas for the absent lawmakers.

Republicans were critical of the missing Democrats. In response to media claims that the missing Democrats were "Killer Ds," Speaker Craddick countered that the Democrats were "Chicken Ds" (or as some Republicans preferred, "Chicky Ds"): "The Chicken Ds that did this ought to be ashamed of themselves. There is disgrace in running and hiding." He added, "I've been in the House for 35 years and I've lost some, but I've never walked off the floor like these Chicken Ds."[27] Governor Perry compared the Democrats to "pouting children" and called them cowardly.[28] From Washington, DeLay called the absent legislators "fugitive Democrats."[29] Perhaps the harshest comments on Monday, however, came from fellow Democrat Ron Wilson, who called the Democrats' actions in bringing the House to a standstill "tantamount to a criminal act."[30]

Someone at the DPS command post suggested that former Speaker Pete Laney might be using his private plane to ferry Democratic lawmakers into hiding. DPS Lieutenant William Crais called a federal air-interdiction service (the Air and Marine Interdiction Coordination Center in Riverside, California), which is part of the Department of Homeland Security, in an effort to locate the plane. Initially these efforts were unsuccessful. However, with the help of DeLay's office in Washington, Texas Republican officials finally learned Monday afternoon (about 4:30) that Laney's Piper Cheyenne was expected to land momentarily in Ardmore, Oklahoma. Unbeknownst to the Republicans at the command post, there were no legislators on the plane; the plane was merely ferrying legislative staff to Ardmore. The plane apparently then left Ardmore. Republicans thought it was headed back to a small airport outside of Austin, raising hopes that if Laney was returning to Austin to pick up additional Democratic lawmakers, these lawmakers (and possibly Laney) could be apprehended at the airport and brought to the House chamber to restore the quorum. A group of DPS officers was dispatched to the airport to wait for Laney's plane. The plane, however, never arrived. Instead of flying to Austin, the plane had been flown to Wichita Falls because the pilot was going to see his mother. When the plane failed to appear as expected in Austin, the Department of Homeland Security was contacted and asked to find the aircraft; it contacted the FAA; the FAA began a search. In an interview in 2005, Representative Krusee insisted that Homeland Security was contacted only because of concern that Laney's missing plane had crashed: it could not be found. Laney vigorously disputes this claim. Nevertheless, this information from the FAA provided Republicans with a clear indication that the absent lawmakers were likely to be in Ardmore.

Late on the afternoon of May 12 an FBI special agent in Ardmore received a call advising him that the attorney general of Texas wanted to speak with him.[31] The agent thought that the call was a prank. A moment later, the special agent received a call from Jay Kimbrough, a deputy attorney general of Texas. Kimbrough was in the Speaker's office at the time. According to Kimbrough, he called the FBI agent at the direction of Speaker Craddick, who had told him that a game warden whom Craddick knew in Oklahoma had said that he knew an FBI agent who said that he could help because the Democratic lawmakers had crossed the state line. Kimbrough told the FBI agent that the Texas lawmakers had been tracked to Ardmore. He asked if the FBI could arrest them. The special agent later told Justice Department investigators that he responded, "It did not sound like there would be much the FBI could do, but he said he would check." Kimbrough faxed the sergeant at arms' letter ("warrant") to the agent. The agent discussed the letter with his supervisor and the FBI's Oklahoma Division counsel. He then called Kimbrough back and indicated that the FBI could not be involved, since the incident was not considered a federal matter.

At 9:45 p.m. on Monday evening Speaker Craddick announced that "40-plus" of the Democrats had been located "about five minutes ago" by Texas state troopers at a Denny's restaurant in Ardmore, Oklahoma.[32] He suggested that federal officers might help return the lawmakers. At the same time, however, he held out an olive branch to these absent lawmakers. He acknowledged that there was no way to arrest the members outside of Texas, but offered to fly the Democrats back to Austin and assured them that there would be no sanctions for their actions. He implied that some House Democrats might be returning from Ardmore. Finally, however, at around 10 p.m. Craddick told his House colleagues that it did not appear that any Democrats were coming back. As a result, he said, "I think that there is no reason for us tonight to punish y'all for their inability to do what's right for the state."[33] There were ninety-two members present as the House closed down on Monday evening.

Under a "call" on the House, the doors of the chamber are locked and the lawmakers are forbidden to leave, but Craddick gave lawmakers permission to temporarily leave the House chamber for the night. He then called some Republican House members together in a private late-night meeting to discuss the situation.

Over the next several days the Republicans in Austin and the Democrats in Ardmore traded shots in the media in an ongoing battle for public opinion. Craddick spoke with many news organizations, including CNN, CNBC, NPR, and radio and television stations in Texas. Regular press statements were released at the Capitol. Craddick even gave an interview to his hometown newspaper, the *Midland Reporter-Telegram*. This battle over public opinion is discussed below.

The Democrats in Ardmore faxed a letter to Craddick, offering to return if an agreement could be reached to not take up a redistricting bill in the time remaining in the session. Craddick refused to compromise. Democrat Robert Puente, chairman of the House Natural Resources Committee, telephoned Craddick in an attempt to discuss this compromise. Craddick did not accept or return the call.

Early on Wednesday, Speaker Craddick met at the governor's mansion with Governor Perry, Lieutenant Governor Dewhurst, and Comptroller Carole Strayhorn in their usual weekly breakfast meeting. No staff attended. By this time it was clear that the Democrats were beyond the reach of the DPS and that none of them were willing to return to Austin to permit a timely vote on the redistricting bill. These Republican officials considered the alternatives for continuing with the effort at redistricting. The House bill was dead. It was unlikely in the time remaining that a redistricting bill could originate in the Senate and come to the House for concurrence. Therefore, redistricting almost certainly was dead for the regular session. There were other issues requiring attention, such as the state budget. Nevertheless, Perry, Dewhurst, and Craddick remained committed to redistricting.

The DPS command center disappeared. At 9:39 a.m. on May 14, the DPS destroyed its records from the command center and the search for the absent Democratic lawmakers. The DPS later explained that the destruction of documents was routine because the matter was now closed, even though the House had not yet adjourned. A House committee subsequently reviewed videotapes of the rear hall of the House to determine who helped with the command center. The video showed that DeLay's aide Jim Ellis made an appearance at the Speaker's office during this span. However, Ellis later insisted to me that he was not there while the DPS command post was in operation and neither offered to help in the hunt nor discussed the hunt in detail. Subsequently, the Texas House Committee on General Investigating and Ethics, under Democrat Kevin Bailey, announced that it would investigate the involvement of the DPS and the destruction of records, but the committee never conducted hearings or issued any report. An investigation by the district attorney of Travis County also ended quietly, without criminal charges.

The House of Representatives technically remained in session, subject to a call on its members, from Monday morning until Wednesday. Republican House members met in a closed meeting on Wednesday morning for forty-five minutes. Craddick was back from his breakfast meeting at the governor's mansion. At 11:25 a.m. the House finally adjourned for lack of a quorum. This adjournment meant that members for the first time could leave the chamber without a note of approval from Craddick. It also meant that DPS troopers no longer were engaged in a manhunt for the absent Democrats. Craddick's office announced that "there's no plan to ambush [the Democrats] with a redistricting plan" once they return.[34]

The Democrats Who Remained Behind

Fifty-two of the sixty-two Democrats in the Texas House of Representatives left the state to break the legislative quorum. Two others were in Texas, but away from Austin. Eight remained behind. Of the Democrats who remained in Austin two are Hispanic, and the other six are African American. The lawmakers were Vilma Luna (Corpus Christi), Sylvester Turner (Houston), Roberto Gutierrez (McAllen), Al Edwards (Houston), Glenn Lewis (Fort Worth), Harold Dutton (Houston), Helen Giddings (DeSoto), and Ron Wilson (Houston).

The individual circumstances for each of these members varied. Most in 2003 were committee chairmen (and continue to be) and, therefore, had a closer relationship to Craddick than some of their Democratic colleagues. However, this fact alone is insufficient to explain why they stayed behind, since several other Democrats holding similar positions participated in the walkout.

Wilson, Luna, Gutierrez, and Turner showed up on the morning of Monday, May 12, when the House was scheduled to convene. Turner and Luna were both on the committee working on the state budget and said that this was one reason why they stayed in Austin. Craddick implicitly criticized the absent Democrats by commending these four for being "more interested in what's best for this state than what's on the 10 o'clock news."[35] Edwards, Lewis, Dutton, and Giddings were absent from the House, but were not with the other Democrats in Ardmore or elsewhere outside Austin.

Rep. Sylvester Turner is Speaker pro tempore, a position that he owes to Speaker Craddick. Nevertheless, Turner on Tuesday, May 13, asked Craddick to remove the redistricting bill from the calendar so the House could move on to "more pressing matters", such as the state budget. As he pointed out, "Congressional redistricting is not a must-do thing. The budget is number one."[36]

Also on Tuesday, three other Democrats who had remained in Austin returned to the House; one, Helen Giddings, arrived in the custody of a state trooper. She had called Craddick on Monday and asked to meet privately with him on Tuesday. However, as she neared her car on Tuesday, she was approached by a state trooper, who then accompanied her to the House chamber. Giddings later met with Craddick on Wednesday and again on Thursday. Al Edwards and Harold Dutton also joined the House on Tuesday. All three explained their Monday absences by indicating that they had been ill or had business away from the Capitol (i.e., they were not participating in the walkout). However, all three joined Turner in his call for removing redistricting from the calendar. Glenn Lewis remained at an apartment in Austin, but apparently did not return to the House chamber during this period. Some Democrats claim, however, that Lewis remained in constant contact with Speaker Craddick and would have been available to create a quorum if needed.

Craddick stood firm against the request that he drop redistricting.

Life in Ardmore

The Democrats' hope for remaining hidden in Ardmore ended on Monday night with the arrival at the Holiday Inn of a reporter from the *Dallas Morning News*. Around 9:30 p.m., four Texas Rangers (apparently from the drug-enforcement section) showed up at the hotel. Most of the Democrats were in a meeting at the time. The Rangers tried in vain to coax one or more of the lawmakers back to Austin by asking whether any lawmakers were being held against their will. No lawmaker took the bait. The Rangers were soon followed by Ardmore police officers, who had been called to the hotel to ensure that there was no trouble for the lawmakers. The Rangers stayed at the hotel or at the Denny's next door before giving up and leaving empty-handed at midnight.

Late on Monday night, Representative Moreno arrived from El Paso, thereby raising the Democrats' total to fifty-one. After his arrival, the lawmakers relaxed; in 2005, *Austin American-Statesman* reporter Laylan Copelin recalled that Moreno's arrival was a key moment. Until then the Democrats had been "tense and skittish," patrolling the hotel in pairs, trying to reassure themselves that no lawmaker would leave or be captured. With Moreno's arrival, the quorum break was secure as long as the Republicans could not convince any of the members in Ardmore to return to Austin before Friday. Some Democratic lawmakers began to celebrate. Moreno cried at the warmth of his reception. Republicans still tried to lure one or more of the absent lawmakers away before Friday. At least one member (Timoteo Garza from Eagle Pass) claimed to have received a call from Governor Perry, asking him to "be a hero" and return to Austin.[37] However, no Democrats in Ardmore broke the boycott.

By Tuesday, May 13, the Oklahoma authorities openly acknowledged the presence of the Democratic legislators from Texas. The state's Democratic-controlled House adopted a resolution commending them, while rejecting a Republican-sponsored resolution calling for Oklahoma officials to assist in returning them to Texas. The sheriff of Carter County (in which Ardmore is located) acknowledged that "we're glad to have them here."[38] The sheriff stationed an officer near the hotel to help deter any effort to compel their return to Texas.

The Democrat's initial press conference was on Tuesday morning. Twenty-three television cameras recorded the words and faces of the missing lawmakers. Afterward, some of the Democrats set about using their cell phones to contact every media outlet that came to mind. Spanish members conducted press conferences and interviews in Spanish. This effort to win public opinion continued every day thereafter.

Some of the day-to-day life in Ardmore was exciting: the national attention and, on Tuesday night, the need to spend time in the hotel cellar as a tornado passed over Ardmore. But it wasn't all excitement. Democrats could be found milling around the motel's spacious courtyard, hanging out at the adjacent Denny's, talking to family, staff, or allies on cell phones, huddling in the conference room, or trying to work on legislation. The motel pool was soon off-limits because of concern about the possible negative image of the lawmakers lounging around the water. Many Democrats across the country supported the boycotting lawmakers with gifts: Florida Democrats sent a crate of oranges; Congressman Charles Gonzalez (D–San Antonio) sent copies of *Pro-*

files in Courage for Our Time (Caroline Kennedy); and entertainer Willie Nelson sent red bandanas and whiskey, along with a note: "Stand Your Ground."

Rep. Pete Gallego increasingly became a public spokesperson for the Democrats in Ardmore. He continued describing the Republican redistricting as "excessively partisan," but he also called for both sides to tone down their rhetoric. He emphasized that the Democrats would join with Republicans in suspending the necessary rules to get important legislation passed in the legislative session, including bills affecting health and education, once the redistricting legislation was killed.

The Battle for Public Opinion

Democrats

The absent Democrats aggressively sought to win public support for their extraordinary action. Even as he rushed to board the buses for Ardmore, Representative Dunnam carried initial drafts of possible press statements. One was to be used if the buses were stopped short of Oklahoma. The other was to be issued to explain the Democrats' actions if they made it to Oklahoma. A final version of this statement was released in Austin on May 12 by Democratic senator Rodney Ellis. It claimed: "We did not choose our path, Tom DeLay did." The statement described the Republican redistricting as a "misbegotten plan" that is "a monument to Tom DeLay's ego, appetite for power and disregard for our constitutional rights." It concluded, "At a time when we are told there is no time to deal with school finance, and when we must still resolve issues like the state budget crisis and insurance reform, the fact that an outrageous power grab sits atop the House calendar is unconscionable."[39] This statement was a brew with many cooks.

The foundation of the Democratic position in this first press statement (and later ones) was that by allowing DeLay to drive the legislature toward an unnecessary and unfair redistricting, the Texas Republicans were failing to address other, more important state issues, such as school finance. This position was an attempt at both offense and defense. Democrats knew that the Republicans would blame them for the inability of the legislature to take any action on pending legislation, especially the state budget, so putting the blame for their walkout on the "reckless" and "unnecessary" actions of the Republicans was a preemptive strike. Also, however, it appeared from earlier editorials and stories in the state's newspapers that the notion of DeLay directly interfering in state legislative business and causing time and resources to be spent on unnecessarily redrawing existing congressional districts was generally unpopular, even among Republicans. Therefore, it made sense to the Democrats to focus on DeLay as the most villainous architect of the redistricting effort instead of focusing on state Republicans, who might be more likely to find support from other Republicans across the state.

Another element of the Democrats' strategy to win public opinion was to be publicly conciliatory, offering to return promptly if the redistricting bill were pulled. Also the Democrats immediately decided to pay for the trip themselves and agreed to forfeit their $124 daily state allowance during their absence. They emphasized these facts publicly again as a preemptive strike. Dunnam criticized the continuing manhunt by state troopers in Texas, which had resulted in DPS officers allegedly following Democrats' family members even after it was clear that the Democrats were in Oklahoma. On Tuesday, May 13, he wrote a letter to Craddick, asking him to "[p]lease stop having our loved ones followed and staked out by law enforcement."

The Democrats regularly telephoned news reporters and other persons in their districts to make certain that their story was being told. Some members wrote comments that were published by their local papers.[40] National newspapers, such as the *Wall Street Journal* and *New York Times,* and national news networks, such as CNN, covered the developments in Ardmore. The lawmakers' actions were featured on Comedy Central's *Daily Show* and were honored as ESPN's "Play of the Week." Nine of the Democrats explained their position in an opinion piece that was published May 14 in the *Houston Chronicle.*

The *Houston Chronicle* had written on May 13 that the walkout was "not a bad strategy given the realities of the GOP juggernaut on the divisive and bad redistricting plan." The paper also recognized, however, that the Democrats might only be delaying the inevitable. Other papers generally treated the walkout as a "stunning event," but since virtually all of them had editorialized against redistricting, they generally blamed the Republicans slightly more than the Democrats for what had happened. For example, the *Fort Worth Star-Telegram* offered, "While the Democrats deserve a scolding for resorting to such a drastic tactic, so do the Republicans."[41]

Although winning wider public opinion was an important task during the walkout, many of the Democrats were also playing to their constituents. The African American and Hispanic members in particular had been elected from districts in which the voters were primarily Democrats. The walkout played well in those districts. In fact, a show of firm partisanship by such members was a political asset. Rep. Pete Gallego explained, "In Spanish we say '*Es bastante* (It's enough).' You get to a point when you draw a line in the sand on principle. We've reached that point."[42]

Democrats elected from more competitive districts, however, faced not only the potential criticism of the public generally, but also specific partisan ad and telephone campaigns designed to weaken them politically in their districts. The battle for public opinion was particularly important to these members. Dunnam shared a concern that one or more of these Democrats might be defeated in 2004 because of their participation in the walkout. None was defeated.

Republicans

As anticipated, the Republican strategy was to blame the absent Democrats for killing important legislation unrelated to redistricting. Craddick claimed that the walkout "killed over $630 million worth of revenue measures [needed] to help the state of Texas in balancing the budget."[43] Governor Perry pointed out that with less than three weeks remaining in the session, "legislators have yet to send me a balanced budget, meaningful homeowners' insurance reform that lowers rates and a medical malpractice bill that will protect patients' care in Texas."[44] Democrats promptly responded that even if the Democrats stayed away until the deadline on Friday, May 16, House rules could be suspended to pass these other bills.

Some House Republicans explained their side of the dispute in the newspapers. One in the *San Antonio Express-News* decried the Democrats' "crybaby approach to government."[45] Another, by Rep. Fred Hill (Richardson), explained that the legislature had a "duty" to redraw congressional district lines since it had been unable to do so in 2001 and that "Republicans have been in the minority for 130 years in this body and now they are in the majority and the Democrats can't accept it."[46] Phil King, sponsor of the redistricting bill, said that he would not withdraw it because to do so would simply mean that Democrats could "begin to walk every time they think they're going to lose a vote."[47]

Governor Perry took the offensive on television through a video statement in which he set out the Republican position and then pleaded, "My Democrat friends, it's time to come back to work."[48] Additional attention was drawn to the dispute when House Republicans came out with a deck of fifty-two playing cards, each with the image of one of the missing Democrats, similar to the playing cards issued by the coalition forces in Iraq in their search for officials in the Saddam Hussein regime.

Much of the criticism of the Democrats came from persons outside of state government. For example, one radio talk-show host in Fort Worth (Mark Davis) described the Democrats as acting with the "petulance of third-graders who can't handle the rules," adding, "Winning is easy. Losing with grace is harder, and takes character."[49]

By Tuesday, a radio ad was running in the districts of three Democrats (all Anglo), including Patrick Rose (Dripping Springs), attacking these absent lawmakers. The ad in Rose's district claimed that he specifically by name had "failed to execute his responsibilities on legislative business" and had "taken flight." The ad claimed that Texas state troopers had been "ordered to find and arrest Representative Rose." Listeners were asked to call the DPS "if you have any information on the lawmaker's whereabouts."

Returning to Austin

The Democrats in Ardmore indicated on Wednesday, May 14, that they would return to Austin on Friday, May 16. Numerous noncontroversial House bills on the Local and Consent Calendar, as well as numerous Senate bills, awaited immediate action on the return of the Democrats and the reestablishment of a quorum. But Democrats were confident that Republicans could not suspend House rules to allow a redistricting bill to be considered in the time remaining in the session.

Even as the inability to pass a redistricting bill during the regular session became clear, Governor Perry, Speaker Craddick, and Lieutenant Governor Dewhurst in a joint news conference on May 14 reiterated that they had no intention of backing off their push to get a redistricting bill through the Texas legislature. Perhaps to add an exclamation mark to this statement, a bill identical to the House redistricting bill was filed in the Senate that same day by Republican Chris Harris at the request of Dewhurst. However, the mere filing of a bill was insufficient to begin the process for consideration of a bill. To be officially introduced so late in the legislative session, the bill would need the permission of four-fifths of the membership of the Senate (twenty-five votes). Dewhurst acknowledged that the bill did not have the necessary support in the Senate to win a suspension of this requirement.[50]

One way around the vote requirement for introducing Harris's redistricting bill was for Governor Perry to send an official message to the legislature declaring redistricting an emergency. Perry did not do so. But Democrats were sure that in the remainder of the legislative session they could block any consideration of a redistricting bill in the Senate, even if a filibuster were to prove necessary.

Therefore, attention shifted from redistricting to other important subjects. Governor Perry acknowledged that there was enough time to consider other major legislation, including the budget. When asked by the press about the possibility of later calling a special session to consider redistricting, he responded that such a session was "not even on my radar screen" at this point.[51]

On the afternoon of Thursday, May 15, Speaker Craddick adjourned the House to meet again on May 16. This adjournment officially ended the time under House rules when a redistricting bill could be considered without a suspension of the rules. The redistricting bill was dead, along with several other controversial House bills. Speaker Craddick acknowledged the result and added, "Hopefully, we'll be back to business as usual."[52] He promised not to retaliate against the Democrats.

On their final night in Oklahoma, the Democrats gathered to tell stories and to entertain one another. Among the highlights was a magic show put on by Dallas representative Steve Wolens. Plans to leave for Texas were moved up because of tornado warnings around Ardmore. At 10:45 p.m., the fifty-one Democrats boarded the buses for their trip back to Austin. As they crossed into Texas, the legislators applauded, cheered, and joked.

Following a 7 a.m. rally on May 16 at the Capitol, the Democrats returned to the House chamber at 10. The welcome from their Republican colleagues was cool, but generally not hostile. The lawmakers of both parties set about addressing other legislative matters, including trying to resolve issues affecting the state budget, before the session ended on June 2.

Commentary

The Democrats' walkout was a legislative success, defeating the Republican redistricting effort in the 2003 regular session of the legislature. Just getting over fifty-one lawmakers to join in such a risky maneuver was an amazing and unprecedented achievement. Many things could have gone wrong before the Democrats left Austin or before they reached the relative security of Oklahoma. A loss of nerve by only one or two of them would have allowed the Republicans to establish a quorum and would have marooned the other Democrats in a substantively meaningless and politically dangerous boycott. But fifty-two Democrats left the state and held firm until the redistricting bill was dead; another two remained hidden in Texas. Representative Dunnam and the other leaders of the Democratic Caucus had shown the leadership necessary to successfully bring the Republican-controlled House to a standstill. The Democrats were justly proud of their achievement.

The walkout was also a success because it brought the Democrats together at least temporarily into an effective, cohesive team and set a precedent for action that must continue to be respected. This cohesion is attributed by Representative Dunnam to the deep resentment they felt about the new Republican leadership ignoring the Democrats' views on issues such as education and the state budget. Republicans respond that such perceived "slights" were not intended or "real." Some Republicans attribute the rough spots during the 2003 legislative session to the newness of the parties' minority and majority roles and to Craddick's initial stumbles as Speaker, rather than to any Republican conspiracy to render the Democrats' wishes irrelevant to the legislative process. Moreover, Republicans claim that the Democrats had themselves caused many of the difficulties because of their lack of cooperation and their partisan attacks on Craddick and the new Republican House leadership.

For Republicans, the battle for public opinion was at best a draw. Many feel that the Democrats effectively won the battle by attracting worldwide attention to the extraordinary events in Texas and to the "villain" Tom DeLay. Unlike the later walkout by Texas Democratic senators, this one ended quickly, with a clear Democratic legislative victory and without becoming ensnarled in charges of racism. Republican efforts to portray the absent lawmakers as "cowards" or shirkers were effectively countered by the Democrats' energized efforts to influence press reports across the nation. The attention of the media and much of the public was momentarily fixed on the audacity and apparent success of the Democrats' actions. Whether this favorable public response could have lasted if the boycott had gone on for a month or more, as occurred in the Texas Senate, seems doubtful, but in May 2003 the walkout was a media hit.

The Republican leaders performed poorly over those few days in May. They had intentionally delayed consideration of redistricting until near the end of the session to give them time to marshal Republican support for the bill and to minimize the effect of the divisive issue on consideration of other important matters. Because of that delay, however, a walkout of only four days was able to kill redistricting. Also, despite almost certainly knowing that the Democrats had discussed a walkout before May 12, the Republican leadership appeared shocked by its actuality. Moreover, Republicans quickly realized that unless enough absent lawmakers could be immediately located and returned to the House, the Democrats would prevail on redistricting. Once the Democrats were across state lines, the Republicans actually had very few weapons to use against them in the remaining days of the session.

The initial missteps and miscues by the Republican leadership on May 12 appear cartoonish in retrospect. Possibly from embarrassment at being caught unprepared by the successful Democratic departure, or at losing control of the House after leading it for only a few months, or at being subjected to Republican constituents' cries of "Do something!" the Republican officials bolstered their appearance of ineptness by a spasmodic series of overreactive measures seemingly lifted from some terrorist thriller. No proper explanation has yet been given for why DPS officers should ever have been in a "command post" at the state Capitol, why state troopers should have been engaged in an almost comical manhunt over at least three states, or why federal officials should ever have been asked to help with the search. This spectacle aided the Democrats in attracting favorable attention nationwide. Subsequent court and federal-agency decisions questioned whether these uses of state and federal resources were legal. The true adverse effect at the time, however, was not so much due to the possible illegality of these steps, but to their unintentionally making the Democrats into popular heroes and media darlings.

Republicans' attempts to benefit politically by portraying the Democratic walkout as an abuse of public responsibility failed. Republicans targeted Anglo Democratic House members in competitive districts, mounting telephone campaigns that accused the lawmakers of breaching the public's trust by walking away from their duties. Subsequent efforts to defeat these Anglo Democrats in 2004 failed. The Democrats exacted payback from Democratic lawmakers who were considered overly supportive of the Republican majority during the 2003 conflict over redistricting. Reps. Ron Wilson, Roberto Gutierrez, and Glenn Lewis were specifically targeted in the 2004 Democratic primary and defeated.

Although the Democratic walkout was a legislative success, the success was temporary. More importantly, the ultimate effect may have been negative for Democrats. DeLay aide Jim Ellis in 2005 claimed to me the walkout unified Republicans:

> It [the walkout] was exactly what we needed. It certainly galvanized our side. They challenged the Republican control of the Legislature. What had been a vote to increase Republican seats in Congress became a leadership challenge, because them running away made it a challenge to the Speaker, lieutenant governor, and governor. It drew a line in the sand.[53]

Ellis even suggested that he and DeLay had been concerned that if the redistricting bill had died a natural death at the end of the regular session there might not have been enough support for a special session to take up redistricting. Ellis claims that the Democrats' walkout changed that likelihood.

Other Republicans, including Dewhurst's chief of staff, Bruce Gibson, disagree. Gibson believes that a special session would have been called with or without the Democrats' walkout.[54] Nevertheless, even moderate Republicans, such as Senator Jeff Wentworth, were caught up in the greatly intensified partisan atmosphere created by the walkout. Wentworth said, "We Republicans felt we were mistreated by the Democrat majority in the redistricting in 1971, 1981, and 1991, but 'run and hide' was not, in our judgment, a legitimate response to our being outvoted by the majority political party at the time."[55] Democrats in the House said in 2005 that they never expected the walkout to end the matter of redistricting. Instead, they said that they had hoped the walkout would give Democratic senators a chance and a reason to kill redistricting. The House Democrats added that they never thought that the two-thirds vote requirement in the Senate would be "bypassed."

CHAPTER 9

Personal Dilemmas:
The First Special Session

Every now and then, Godzilla eats the city.
— STATE REP. JIM DUNNAM, *AUSTIN AMERICAN-STATESMAN,* JULY 8, 2003

Many Democrats and Republicans faced personal dilemmas over redistricting during the summer of 2003. Each Democrat who took a firm stand against the Republican juggernaut did so only by risking his or her own personal status in the Senate and, ultimately, their own personal financial and political well-being. No one, however, faced a greater dilemma than three Republicans.

Lieutenant Governor David Dewhurst

Lieutenant Governor Dewhurst is a tall (six feet five) slender man, with salt-and-pepper hair, expensive attire, and a seemingly perpetual tan from working at his ranch—a distinguished appearance.[1] Independently wealthy from his success as a businessman, Dewhurst was elected lieutenant governor in 2002 after serving as commissioner of the state's General Land Office. He had never served in the Senate before becoming its presiding officer. Dewhurst was absolutely critical to the success of any Republican redistricting effort. Without his help, redistricting would have been impossible. Dewhurst, however, indicated publicly early in 2003 that he was concerned about going along with redistricting because such a controversial issue could needlessly divide the Senate along partisan lines and damage his efforts to work with all senators, to maintain the bipartisan cooperation necessary for the chamber's productive operation. However, Dewhurst also had ambitions for higher office. He agreed that the Democrats' seventeen-to-fifteen advantage in the congressional delegation was unfair, and he knew that being perceived by Republican activists and major donors as responsible for killing the redistricting effort would almost certainly mean killing his own political ambitions.

Senator Bill Ratliff

Republican senator Ratliff too faced a particularly difficult dilemma.[2] He had been a member of the Senate for thirteen years. An engineer by training, Ratliff was very interested in the equity of public schools. Consistently recognized as one of the state's top legislators, he was highly respected by his Republican and Democratic colleagues. His Senate colleagues selected him to serve as acting lieutenant governor during 2000–2002, when then-Lieutenant Governor Perry became governor after George W. Bush resigned to run for president. Ratliff was Republican, but was never strongly partisan. In an earlier run for the Senate he had explained that he was a Republican "for the same reason I'm a Methodist. I agree with them at least 51% of the time."[3] At the end of the 2001 regular session, Ratliff announced himself a candidate for the Republican nomination for lieutenant governor, but withdrew his candidacy only a few days later after it became clear that he probably would not garner the support of major Republican activists and donors in a race against Dewhurst (and possibly future attorney general Abbott). Ratliff acknowledged to me in 2005 that his inability to garner this critical support was due in part to his refusal as presiding officer of the Senate in 2001 to engage in "breaking some arms" to pass an aggressively partisan congressional redistricting plan. One influential Republican donor told him, "Redistricting is not *an* issue, it is *the* issue."[4]

Ratliff's independence in 2001 on redistricting and other issues (e.g., his support for hate-crime legislation) brought an aggressive challenge to his Senate reelection effort in the 2002 Republican primary from a right-wing group called The Free Market PAC (FreePAC). This organization targeted Ratliff and a handful of other moderate Republican incumbents with mailings containing vicious personal attacks. Ratliff responded with his own barrage. On March 6, 2002, standing before a group of approximately twenty-four lawmakers of both parties, Ratliff publicly condemned the group and its supporters for engaging in "hate mongering" of the type "now being practiced by the al Qaeda and the Taliban."[5] Bill Ceverha, who was the secretary of TRMPAC at the time, criticized Ratliff and called for an apology. Ceverha said he was "not defending the content of the FreePac mailings", but challenged Ratliff's choice of words comparing the FreePac organization to those who "harbor and finance terrorists."[6] Ratliff and the other targeted Republicans won renomination (Ratliff with 72 percent of the primary vote) and reelection in 2002.

Ratliff continued to feel very strongly about the traditions, especially the historical bipartisanship, of the state Senate when he met with me in 2005. He saw the 2003 redistricting as a needless threat to the institution of the Senate and the particular redistricting plans as a threat to the interests of his constituents in northeast Texas. Republicans in 2003 knew, however, that without Ratliff's support, a redistricting bill could die. They counted on him to allow the Senate to consider redistricting. Ratliff faced the dilemma of choosing between party loyalty or acting to preserve the institution and relationships that he valued.[7]

Senator Robert Duncan

Senator Duncan has served in the Senate since 1997, after serving two terms in the Texas House.[8] He is an attorney from Lubbock, in West Texas. Although a relatively young man, Duncan is greatly respected by his colleagues as a person of humility, gravity, and integrity. In 1993 he was named Republican Freshman of the Year in the House. Two years later the National Republican Legislators Association named him legislator of the year. The *Lubbock Avalanche-Journal* described him as "soft-spoken, polite, logical and deliberate. He is an effective voice in the Senate for our area and keeps a cool head in circumstances that are prone to cause tempers to flare. He has a reputation in Austin of being a mediator—someone who brings opposing parties together."[9]

As chairman of the important Senate Committee on Jurisprudence, to which any redistricting bills would be assigned, Duncan was vital to passage of a redistricting plan. He announced publicly early in the process that he would keep an open mind on redistricting.[10] Personally, he saw no need for redrawing congressional districts, especially in West Texas. He explained that all of the wrangling over redistricting was distracting the legislature from other legislative functions, such as monitoring the budget and implementing legislative changes to state programs: "All of these things take a back seat whenever you have such a divisive issue."[11] Most of his constituents were strongly against redistricting in 2003.[12] Even Republicans in his Senate district generally favored keeping the existing congressional district lines and the existing congressmen, including Democrat Charles Stenholm. Also, like Senator Ratliff, he felt strongly about preserving the bipartisanship and cooperation that he saw as important to the Texas Senate as an institution. Nevertheless, as chairman of the Senate committee with responsibility for redistricting, he was expected to produce a redistricting map that could win approval. Four months later, as the process ended with passage of a redistricting plan different from the one he preferred, he explained, "[W]hen you have a seat at the table, you're responsible for moving the process forward and you can't be selfish and only handle your own district. You have to be responsible for the whole process."[13]

As Republicans, each of these men faced a personal dilemma. They were under significant pressure to put aside any personal concerns they might have about redistricting. They were asked to accept that these concerns were outweighed by a need to repay Democrats for past gerrymanders and by the partisan benefits that could be achieved at the national level by the defeat of the incumbent Anglo Democratic congressmen. Each man's resolution of his personal dilemma had significant implications for redistricting in 2003 and for him personally.

The Regular Session Ends

As the regular session ground to a halt in the days before its required adjournment sine die on June 2, Governor Perry acknowledged that he probably would recall the legislature in special session later in the year to consider school finance. At the same time, he denied rumors that he had already decided to recall it for a special session on redistricting. However, a contrary indication was heard from Washington, where Congressman DeLay indicated, "I understand Governor Perry will hold a special session."[14]

On Thursday, May 28, Republican congressman Joe Barton met with Governor Perry. Later, Congressman Barton was seen in the House chamber carrying redistricting maps. Congressman Barton freely acknowledged that he had urged the governor and the legislature to take another stab at redistricting. He cautioned, however, that his trip to Austin was purely a personal one to visit his girlfriend, who worked at the University of Texas, and that the maps he was carrying were of the existing congressional districts, not new ones.[15]

Partly in response to Congressman Barton's visit, fifty-five Democratic members of the House sent a letter to Governor Perry on Friday, May 29, asking that congressional redistricting not be included in any special session. Having just successfully defeated Republican redistricting in the regular session, the Democrats by this letter seemed to be making a request and issuing a warning. The governor offered no comment.

As the regular session ended, the lawmakers dispersed from Austin. Most sought some normalcy after dealing with contentious and often intractable state issues for five months. The continuing call from Washington, however, was unmistakable. Jim Ellis explained, "It's clear we have the votes. Normally in the legislative process the will of the majority carries the day."[16]

Republican Plans Take Shape: The Critical Meeting on June 16

In the first weeks of June, the governor continued to deny that he had decided to call a special session on redistricting. In meetings with editorial boards for the *San Antonio Express-News* and *Dallas Morning News* on June 10, Lieutenant Governor Dewhurst reiterated his reluctance about redistricting: "I have said over and over again that I see no consensus [in the Senate] for a redistricting measure. I am not going to take the lead on redistricting." Dewhurst's visits to the editorial boards were part of a generally triumphant postsession period for the lieutenant governor. He was being lauded for his performance during the session. He even won favorable reviews from many moderate and liberal sources for his independence from the other Republican officials and for how he had presided over the Senate. The premier political arbiter of Texas politics, *Texas Monthly,* had surprisingly recognized him as one of the "Ten Best Legislators" from the session, even though, as lieutenant governor, he was not actually a legislator.

This public indication of reluctance about continuing with redistricting contrasted with what Congressman DeLay was being told was the mindset of state Republican officials.[17] Jim Ellis reported that the state leaders were committed privately to continuing with redistricting. A crucial meeting occurred on June 16 among DeLay, Perry, Dewhurst, Speaker Craddick, and Attorney General Abbott. These five "principals," accompanied by their chief staffers (Mike Toomey, Bruce Gibson, Barry McBee, and Jim Ellis), met at the governor's residence at 5 p.m. The governor wanted all five principals together in a single room "to agree on a legislative strategy and calendar." The governor and Speaker specifically wanted DeLay to get Dewhurst to commit to "get a bill out of the senate." Ellis told DeLay that there would be a "concrete calendar" by the time of the June 16th meeting, but "Craddick believes the Governor will announce the special session on Wednesday, June 18th." Ellis added, "The votes appear secure in the House. The Senate teeters around the 21 mark, but success appears very realistic. The Speaker does not believe the Democrats will try another run to Oklahoma."

According to Ellis, the meeting was essentially "a discussion of where we go from here. Was a special session viable?"[18] Dewhurst was determined to continue to require a vote of two-thirds of the Senate to bring a bill up for consideration, even in a special session. If the principals were to go forward on the basis of this "21-vote strategy," they felt that Dewhurst must be committed to securing the necessary votes in the Senate.[19] So long as all nineteen Republicans voted together, only two Democrats would have to vote to take up the redistricting bill. The Republican officials had already identified at least two "swing" Democrats and several other "approachable" Democrats who might give the necessary votes. Dewhurst was confident that he could obtain at least two Democratic votes. It was imperative, however, that all nineteen Republican senators support the final plan.

DeLay had a plan to ensure that the Republican senators would vote together for redistricting. A Republican congressman had been assigned to "cover" each Republican senator. Senators "needing attention" would receive it from state leaders, congressional officials, and other sources until a firm commitment was obtained. Once each senator had committed to moving forward on redistricting, they would be persuaded to support a specific plan. At least twelve of the nineteen Republican senators were considered firmly in favor of redistricting; others needed attention. Two Republicans in particular were considered "swing" senators: Senator Ratliff and Senator Wentworth (San Antonio). However, it was assumed that Wentworth was concerned only about how the districts would be drawn, not whether redistricting should happen. On the other hand, the meeting participants were concerned about Ratliff; help was needed to ensure that he was onboard.

On the following day (June 17), Karl Rove called Ratliff.[20] Several participants in the previous day's meeting have suggested to me that Rove called Ratliff at the suggestion of DeLay. Ratliff acknowledged later to the newspapers that Rove asked whether the Senate (and Ratliff individually) would go along with a "fair" redistricting plan and indicated that redistricting the Texas congressional seats was important to the president.[21] Ratliff told Rove that the chances of the Senate's passing a plan (under a two-thirds vote requirement, as Ratliff assumed) would be close, depending on how "severe" the plan and how big the change from the current districts. Rove asked Ratliff if it would make any difference if "the president calls." Ratliff said, "I'm always happy to speak with the president." Ratliff told me in 2005 that he still did not know if Rove had been serious about the president being willing to call about redistricting.[22] Ratliff told Rove that he personally would consider a fair redistricting plan. This conversation reassured Republican leaders that the necessary twenty-one votes could be found. The path forward to a special session seemed cleared.

The Governor Calls a Special Session

On June 18, Governor Perry ended any suspense about whether he intended to call a special session for redistricting. He also tried to blunt criticism, declaring to reporters in Houston, "This isn't a White House issue. This isn't a congressional issue . . . This is between the [Texas] House and the Senate."[23]

The governor announced that he would call the legislature to convene in a thirty-day special session beginning on June 30, 2003. The subject would be limited to redistricting, although the governor indicated that he would open the special session to other "unfinished business", such as funding for two health-care programs important to South Texas and the region of Texas bordering Mexico, once work on redistricting was completed. This not so subtle attempt to win over Democratic lawmakers from that region was lambasted by Laredo representative Richard Raymond: "It is the most blatant and worst type of political blackmail I have ever seen, and I'm from Duval County."[24] The governor filed the proclamation on June 23, calling a special session for the 30th.

The numbers of Republicans and Democrats in the House and Senate had not changed since the regular session. Republicans had majorities of eighty-eight to sixty-two in the House and nineteen to twelve in the Senate. A highly partisan Republican redistricting bill was virtually certain to pass both houses and be signed into law by Republican governor Rick Perry unless it could somehow be blocked from consideration. Speculation began early about what tactic, if any, the Democrats might use.

Hearings

Once it was clear that the issue of redistricting would probably reach the Senate during the special session, the Senate Jurisprudence Committee on June 23 announced that it would set public hearings across the state.

Republican Robert Duncan chaired the committee. He indicated that he had not discussed redistricting with Congressman DeLay and that "I'm really going to try to keep an open mind 'til I see the entire map."[25] Duncan had, however, discussed redistricting with Speaker Craddick in late May. Craddick showed Duncan maps that would center a new district on Midland while maintaining two other districts for West Texas. Duncan acknowledged to me in 2005 that he agreed with Craddick at the time—Craddick's arguments for the West Texas configuration were attractive—but Duncan insisted that he explained the need to vet the plan with Randy Neugebauer, the congressman from Lubbock, and to his own constituents. On doing so, Duncan found strong opposition to the plan.[26]

Following the Senate's lead, the House also scheduled hearings statewide. Eventually, over several days in late June, House and Senate members fanned out to Houston, San Antonio, Dallas, Lubbock, Brownsville, Laredo, San Angelo, and Nacogdoches. The House and Senate held their hearings separately.

The hearings generated considerable testimony. Most of the testimony was opposed to redistricting and the Republican proposals. A House subcommittee hearing in Brownsville on June 26 was halted when a noisy crowd shouted, "Shut it down! Shut it down!"[27] Some Democratic House members (e.g., Reps. Kino Flores [McAllen] and Richard Raymond [Laredo]) complained that they had been sent to hearings far from their constituents in retaliation for earlier helping break quorum in the House.

In Harris County, the House hearing became bitter. Over 400 people, mostly Democrats, attended. African American representatives Garnet Coleman and Ron Wilson exchanged blunt words. Wilson accused Coleman of putting the interests of the Democratic Party ahead of the interest of African Americans, noting that Coleman had taken payment from the party in 2002 for coordinating a get-out-the vote effort in Harris County. In response, Coleman pointed out that Wilson, a Houston lawyer, drove a Lamborghini and was "shilling" for the Republicans. Many in the crowd yelled "sellout" at Wilson.[28]

The Senate hearings proceeded somewhat more peacefully, although these hearings too encountered some turmoil, especially in heavily Hispanic areas. Senator Duncan kept each hearing going until every person who wanted to testify was allowed to do so. In Dallas, the lawmakers were treated to the sight of a large inflatable rat in the bed of a pickup truck. The rat was identified variously as representing Governor Perry or Congressman DeLay.

Following a hearing in San Antonio, two senators representing different parts of Travis County (Republican Jeff Wentworth and Democrat Gonzalo Barrientos) actually reached apparent agreement that Travis County should not be divided among four congressional districts, as had been proposed during the regular session.[29] House sponsor Phil King predicted that Travis County would not be split four ways and that "when everyone looks at it, you'll say, 'Oh, that's not so bad.'" He later predicted only "minuscule" changes to the existing district in Travis County.[30] In a Senate hearing in Houston, however, Democratic African American congresswoman Sheila Jackson Lee accused Republicans of "playing the race card" by including her photograph in e-mails intended to encourage Republicans to attend the hearing to testify in favor of redistricting.[31]

Both political parties accused the other of trying to rig the hearings. Democratic state party chairwoman Molly Beth Malcolm and several local Republican Party chairmen sent e-mails to party activists, suggesting wording for editorials or testimony at the hearings. The two parties packed vans to boost friendly turnout at the hearings. Republican state party chairwoman Susan Weddington put two dozen audio files on the party's Web site for downloading and playing on local radio stations.

Although most of the testimony at the hearings was opposed to redistricting, Republicans claimed (with some justification) that the testimony had been orchestrated by the Democratic Party. After claiming that many of the hundreds of witnesses against redistricting had been "bused in," Representative King explained, "But in the end, this is the right thing for Texas."[32] Senator Duncan later lamented to me in 2005 that Republicans supporting redistricting had failed to turn out at the hearings.[33]

There is no indication that the testimony at these hearings affected the lines drawn in the final congressional redistricting plan. Senator Duncan told me in 2005 that he believed that the senators at the hearings were influenced by some of the testimony and that the Senate redistricting plan and the later efforts at compromise embodied the lessons of these hearings.[34] However, the input that ultimately determined the districts in the final plan did not come from these hearings.

The House of Representatives Passes a Redistricting Bill

Newspapers correctly speculated that it was unlikely that the House Democrats could again walk out to break a quorum. Some of the Democrats who had left in May were reluctant to do so again because of concern about voter backlash.[35] A number of lawmakers felt that constituents had overlooked or even supported their earlier walkout, but that many of these same constituents were less likely to do so again. The biggest factor, however, was that time was now on the side of the Republicans.

It was one thing for the Democratic Caucus to organize and maintain a successful walkout of at least fifty-one lawmakers for four days; it would be entirely something else to do the same for thirty days. Moreover, it was now clear to the Democrats that the Republican state leaders were prepared to call successive special sessions until redistricting was achieved.

Republicans did not take the unlikelihood of a second House walkout for granted. Democratic state representative Patrick Rose reported that during June his constituents received anonymous automated telephone calls criticizing him for participating in the May boycott and urging the constituent to "Please call Patrick Rose . . . and tell him this time, don't run away."[36]

At the critical meeting on June 16, Republican leaders considered whether the Senate should act first. Dewhurst maintained that it should not. Once it was settled that the House would move first, Craddick was determined not to make the same mistake as before: delaying consideration of redistricting until late in the session, when a walkout of only a few days could kill it. The redistricting bill was immediately set on a very fast track for passage by the House.

The special session convened on June 30, 2003. The redistricting bill (House Bill [HB] 3) by Rep. Phil King was immediately assigned to the Redistricting Committee. This committee was convened by its chairman, Republican Joe Crabb, on Tuesday, July 1. King at that time presented his map for consideration by the committee. The meeting was interrupted by catcalls from the public attendees. Several expert witnesses raised concerns about the impact of the plan on minority voters. A day later King withdrew this plan because it contained district lines that potentially violated the Voting Rights Act.[37] He explained, "I am not saying this puppy is dead. It's just sick."[38]

King and other Republican sponsors of redistricting worked on developing a new plan with advisers (including DeLay aide Jim Ellis), in a room with newspapers taped over the glass door for privacy. A wall projector was used to show the map changes to the meeting's participants. On July 3, King presented a new map to the committee. He said that he was confident that this plan would meet legal concerns. Among other changes, it kept District 24 (Martin Frost) essentially in its 2002 form out of concern that elimination of the majority-minority district would potentially violate minority voting rights. Committee member Richard Raymond angrily shouted his objection to this map as a "phony": "There's no way Tom DeLay will ever let a map get out of here [the legislature] that lets Martin Frost get reelected. He hates him that much."[39]

A slightly altered version of this plan was unveiled before the committee on Saturday, July 5, by Republican representative Ken Grusendorf (Arlington). Again Raymond blasted the new map, this time because the committee had not had time to debate it. Nevertheless, the plan easily won adoption (ten to four), including the support of two Democrats. Surprisingly, the plan as adopted left the districts of Democratic congressmen Frost, Lloyd Doggett, and Republican Henry Bonilla virtually intact. King predicted that the plan would elect as many as twenty-one Republican congressmen. The bill was immediately set for consideration by the full House on Monday, July 7.

Without another walkout as a viable option, Democrats were without any means of blocking or materially changing the partisan bill now headed to the full House. Democrats resigned themselves to speaking out against the bill during floor debate. Some of them hoped that by doing so they could help any later litigation by making an official record of the adverse effect of the plan on African American and Hispanic voters. Therefore, as one Democrat after another asked King questions or spoke against the redistricting bill, the primary topic was its alleged racial and ethnic implications.

At King's request, the Republican members of the House remained silent throughout the floor debate.[40] They knew that there was no reason to be drawn into any dispute with the Democrats or the Republicans leadership. No amount of debate could change the outcome on the bill or any amendment to it. Moreover, Republicans understood from past experience and the advice of legal counsel that the Democrats wanted to entangle Republicans in official oral exchanges about race and ethnicity for possible later use in litigation. As Republican state representative Mike Krusee explained:

> It's a tar baby because, once you get into it, they just start lobbing grenades at you, and it becomes very vitriolic very quickly. It takes a lot of restraint because our voters in the suburbs have been disenfranchised for decades.[41]

The wisest policy for the Republicans under the circumstances was silence. They stuck with this policy.

Although the outcome in the House was never in doubt, the debate continued for ten long hours. There were several interesting moments.[42] For example:

- The public gallery contained a block of persons with hand puppets intended to reflect their opinion that the members of the Republican majority were acting as puppets for Congressman DeLay.
- African American representative Senfronia Thompson (Houston) offered an amendment pairing Republican congressmen with Democrats in Democratic districts, including pairing Congressman Tom DeLay in a predominately African American district with incumbent congresswoman Sheila Jackson Lee. The amendment was tabled on a motion by King.
- Rep. Ruth McClendon proposed an amendment returning to the current congressional districts. It was tabled 83–59.
- Democrat Jim McReynolds (Lufkin) pointed out that the redistricting plan would significantly lessen the number of congressmen elected from rural areas in East Texas, and if the incumbent Democratic congressmen were defeated, Texas would lose the ranking Democrats on the Transportation, Veterans' Affairs, Agriculture, Energy and Commerce, Space, and Homeland Security committees.
- Democrat Barry Telford (DeKalb) called the redistricting plan "vindictive."

- Democrat Mike Villarreal (San Antonio) placed a twelve-inch stack of witness statements alongside a one-inch stack of statements to show the relative number of witnesses who had testified against redistricting as compared to the number who had testified in favor.

As sponsor of the legislation, King spoke as necessary for the legislation, answered questions, and, by his comments on proposed amendments, showed the Republican majority how to vote. He retained his calm through all the Democratic attacks.

King emphasized repeatedly that it was the legislature's obligation to redistrict in 2003 since it had not done so in 2001, that this plan was politically "fair" since Republicans were underrepresented in Congress under the existing one, and that the proposed plan protected racial and ethnic minorities in the state. He avoided being drawn into the exchange that Democrats wanted over the racial and ethnic implications of the plan. At one point he explained, "Race had nothing to do with the drawing of the district lines. Our purpose was purely political."[43] Each Democrat thrust was blunted.

The House also went through the choreographed consideration and predetermined rejection of two amendments offered by Republicans.[44] This practice is common when members personally need "cover" from their constituents on an issue, but do not really want or intend to have their amendments adopted and thereby possibly upset the balance embodied in the legislation. These two amendments, however, showed that redistricting in 2003 was not overwhelmingly popular, even among Republican constituents. Many Republicans didn't want a change, especially in rural Texas. Rep. Arlene Wohlgemuth (Burleson) and Rep. Carl Isett (Lubbock) faced concern from their constituents about how the proposed plan would change their congressional districts. Each representative offered an amendment to restore the congressional district in his or her area to its shape in 2002, explaining "I am doing this at the request of my constituents" (Wohlgemuth) and "What I heard from my constituents is that they wanted to keep the 19th district the way it is" (Isett). Neither amendment stood a chance of adoption, but they allowed the lawmakers to show that they had tried to keep the existing districts intact. These two lawmakers voted in favor of the bill on final passage. Only five Republicans voted against passage. One, Rep. Bob Hunter of Abilene, explained to his Republican colleagues that his constituents did not want their district redrawn: "I was inundated everywhere I went—parades, going to the store, at church."[45] Two Democrats voted for passage, including Rep. Ron Wilson.

The redistricting bill easily passed on second reading at the end of the day on July 7, 2003. Rather than adjourning to return the next day, as is customary at the end of a legislative day, the House remained in session until after midnight. This permitted it to consider the bill on third reading and to pass it on another legislative day, as required by the Texas Constitution. At only a minute or two after midnight, the House voted 84–61 to pass the redistricting bill. By 12:03 a.m., the bill was sent to the Senate. The date was July 8, only nine days after the special session had begun.

The chairman of the Democratic Caucus in the House, Jim Dunnam, explained, "Every now and then, Godzilla eats the city."[46]

The Senate: Hope for a Democratic Blockade

Since the House Democrats were helpless to stop a partisan redistricting bill, it was clear to both sides early that the critical battle would be fought in the Senate. Democrats had reason to be optimistic that they could stop the redistricting legislation there.

The future of redistricting in the Texas Senate in 2003 would depend on whether the Senate adhered to its two-thirds vote requirement and, if two-thirds support were required, whether the Republican majority could muster twenty-one votes. The nature of this two-thirds vote requirement is discussed in Chapter Six.

The lieutenant governor, David Dewhurst, was generally positioned to control the circumstances that determine whether twenty-one votes are needed for consideration of any bill, by controlling whether a "blocker bill" sits atop the calendar. However, once circumstances are allowed to develop so that a bill is effectively blocked by other legislation from being considered at the top of the Senate calendar, the lieutenant governor cannot thereafter disregard the requirement that the bill must receive the vote of two-thirds of the senators to be considered ahead of the other bills.

Dewhurst preferred to keep the tradition, or historical practice, of the two-thirds vote requirement in place even during the special session. He had worked successfully during his first regular session as presiding officer to run things fairly and with a relatively light hand. He prided himself on being the leader of the Senate, not necessarily its boss. Senators of both parties were accustomed to having the requirement for twenty-one votes, and Dewhurst did not want to needlessly endanger his relationship with them by arbitrarily discarding the two-thirds vote requirement.[47]

In early June 2003, Dewhurst announced that he would adhere to the two-thirds requirement for suspending Senate rules to take up redistricting legislation. Once the Senate convened, a bill was reported from committee to occupy the position of blocker bill at the top of the calendar.

Democrats did not take Dewhurst's pledge to honor the two-thirds vote requirement for granted. Even though a blocker bill was in place, Democrats moved bills out of committee and onto the calendars so that they could control consideration of any redistricting bill. By July 17 there were five House bills[48] on the Senate calendar above HB 3, the redistricting bill. One of these, House Bill 53, was sponsored by Democratic senator Rodney Ellis and was unlikely to move so long as it blocked the redistricting bill. So also there were several Senate bills already pending, including one by Democratic senator John Whitmire. Therefore, no redistricting bill could be considered in the special session without the vote of two-thirds of the senators to suspend the Senate's regular order of business.

Can Republicans Find The Necessary Votes?

Dewhurst's decision to adhere to the two-thirds vote requirement was not an attempt to prevent passage of the Republican redistricting plan. Instead, he hoped to win general Democratic support of a "fair" bill, but if not, he and other Republican leaders expected that the twenty-one votes could still be found.

One tactic included by planners as a subject for the meeting of the Republican leaders on June 16 at the Governor's Mansion was the possibility of cobbling together "any map that would get us (the Republicans) 21 votes" and then amend the bill later in the House to a more agreeable partisan form.[49] As Jim Ellis pointed out to Congressman DeLay before the June 16 meeting, this tactic would require only a majority vote in the Senate for concurrence with the House amendments and adoption of the final bill. The possibility of this "bait and switch" was precisely what had worried Democratic House members during the regular session and would worry Democratic senators during the special sessions—i.e., that Republicans would sponsor a less partisan bill at an early stage, but substitute a more aggressive redistricting plan later, when the legislation could be amended and finally approved by a simple majority. Democratic opposition at that point would be essentially irrelevant. It is clear that at least some Republicans had exactly this tactic in mind.

The Republican expectation of acquiring the necessary twenty-one votes gives the events of mid-June a new importance, and could help explain Dewhurst's later anger at Senator Bill Ratliff. One objective of the June 16 meeting was for DeLay to win a commitment from Dewhurst that he would pass a redistricting bill through the Senate. Dewhurst agreed, but only with retention of the two-thirds vote requirement. Without the necessary twenty-one votes, a special session would be a waste of time. It was imperative that all Republican senators vote to take up the redistricting bill, so the commitment of Bill Ratliff was critical. It was unimportant whether Ratliff actually voted for the final bill so long as he voted with other Republicans to suspend the order of business to allow the bill to be considered. After a call from Karl Rove on June 17, Ratliff apparently satisfied the Republican leaders that he would vote to suspend the rules.

On June 18, when Governor Perry announced that he was calling a special session on congressional redistricting, one of his advisers indicated that the governor was confident that Republicans had the necessary votes in the Senate. In fact, the newspaper quoted the adviser (on the condition of anonymity) as saying, "It's a done deal."[50]

The Republicans had good reason to believe that with Ratliff's vote at least twenty-one votes could be gathered in favor of taking up the redistricting bill. There were twelve Democrats in the Senate, one more than the eleven necessary to prevent the order-of-business rule from being suspended. However, one Democrat, Senator Ken Armbrister (Victoria), already had announced that he might vote with the Republicans to allow consideration of a redistricting bill.

Republican state representative Kenny Marchant acknowledged that Republicans might try to lure reluctant Democrat senators with favorable congressional districts for themselves or minorities.[51] Several Democratic senators later indicated that they had been approached by Republicans with an offer for a winnable congressional seat in return for an affirmative vote to take up redistricting.[52]

Two Hispanic senators were reported by the press as likely votes in favor of considering the redistricting bill. Senator Eddie Lucio (Brownsville) had indicated as far back as the fall of 2002 that he might vote for a redistricting plan that included a congressional district favorable to him in any possible future run for Congress.[53] In May 2003 he again expressed his interest in such a district and described himself as a "soft no" on redistricting.[54] Ellis's memoranda to Congressman DeLay earlier in the year showed that the Republicans saw Lucio as a probable vote for consideration of redistricting. Lieutenant Governor Dewhurst even insisted privately to the Republican map drawers in January that any plan must include a vacant Hispanic district in which Senator Lucio could run.[55] Another senator, Frank Madla (San Antonio), also had hinted publicly that he might vote for consideration of a redistricting bill if the governor allowed the special session to take up specific legislation he favored.

To Republicans, the needed twenty-one votes seemed assured.

The Redistricting Effort Stalls in the Senate

Even as the legislature convened, there were signs that the Republican effort to find the necessary twenty-one votes in the Senate had stalled. Public and private statements from House members and Democratic Party officials during the latter part of June had made it harder for any Democratic senator to trade a vote on redistricting in return for other legislative favors. For example, Representative Coleman said publicly, "We know they [the senators] won't take anything as a bribe, or 30 pieces of silver . . . and sell out their constituents because they are good people who have been elected to represent their constituents. And therefore, they can't be bought."[56] Democrats, including San Antonio state representative Ruth McClendon, worried publicly about a Republican "bait and switch." Dunnam cautioned, "Anyone who votes to suspend is culpable for the final bill."[57] Democratic senator Whitmire declared, "This is a defining vote."[58]

The three Democratic senators under the spotlight as possible affirmative votes for a redistricting bill cautiously expressed greater reservations about casting a vote with the Republican majority. Lucio announced on June 30 that he would vote against redistricting unless the Latino organizations MALDEF and LULAC (League of United Latin American Citizens) endorsed the map. Madla indicated that he was "praying for guidance." Even Armbrister showed some hesitation after he saw the adverse effect of the plan on rural areas in his senatorial district. Nevertheless, none of these statements committed the respective senator to unequivocally vote against consideration of the Republican redistricting plan.

The House redistricting plan (HB 3) was referred to Senator Duncan's Committee on Jurisprudence on July 8. Congressman DeLay said from Washington that the House plan was a "good start." Specifically, he lauded the House map because, as he explained, it was important to the people of Texas "to be properly represented, and that means more Republican seats, more Hispanic seats and more African-American seats."[59] It was immediately clear that the Senate Republicans would come up with their own districting plan. Senator Chris Harris (Arlington), who was designated Senate sponsor of the redistricting bill, responded to the House plan by saying, "I don't want something jammed down my throat."[60] Republican senators Steve Ogden (Bryan) and Kip Averitt (McGregor) complained that the House plan split their home counties (Brazos and McLennan, respectively). Averitt called the House plan "a silly map."[61] Republican senators Robert Duncan and Troy Fraser (Horseshoe Bay) objected to the proposed districts for West Texas. Fraser said, "I will not vote to suspend [the rules to allow debate] on a plan that adversely affects Abilene, that Abilene could lose its seat to other parts of West Texas."[62] Republican Bill Ratliff expressed concern about the House plan, but added that he was also troubled by the possibility that senators might vote to suspend the rules to put the process in motion without "knowing that it's not going to come back from conference looking like the house map."[63] A hearing on the House map in Dallas brought forth signs saying "Scrap the Map" and "Don't Dance with DeLay."[64]

Republicans were finding it difficult to draw equally populated congressional districts that would add the desired Republican seats while addressing local concerns from Republican constituents. Some of the opposition among Republicans grew from the splitting of areas that had been intact under the existing district plan. Other Republicans opposed losing the seniority that would be forfeited if Democrats such as Chet Edwards (ranking Democrat on a House committee key to military funding for bases like Fort Hood in his district) and Charles Stenholm (ranking Democrat on the House Agriculture Committee, whose post would go to a representative from Illinois) were defeated through redistricting. The Waco city council on July 4 adopted a resolution against redistricting. Thirty West Texas mayors met in Austin with Fraser, Duncan, and Dewhurst to oppose redrawing the congressional districts in West Texas.

Tension also simmered between Dewhurst and Craddick. It had grown throughout the regular session over issues other than redistricting. Soon after the House acted rapidly to pass a redistricting bill during the special session, Dewhurst publicly complained that "we had asked to be involved in the process of the House drawing the map,"[65] but had not been included. Such intraparty spats, however, were unlikely to mean defeat for a partisan redistricting bill, as suggested by Dewhurst's later, artfully diplomatic statement that he was not "complaining" about the House's actions, but just noting that Craddick must have been too busy to respond to the lieutenant governor's request.

The suspense over what would happen in the Senate continued to build as some of the Democratic votes earlier thought likely to be for suspension, now seemed problematic. Lucio, who was recovering at home from recent heart difficulties, was quoted by his hometown paper as saying that he was now a "solid no" on the redistricting bill.[66] Armbrister remained a probable aye. Madla, however, acknowledged that he was "on the fence." Madla was indebted to Dewhurst for the chairmanship of the Senate Intergovernmental Relations Committee. Madla expressed his concern that by voting with the Democrats, he would be jeopardizing his standing with the state's leadership (especially Governor Perry) and possibly his ability to help his constituents, in a district that stretched hundreds of miles from San Antonio to El Paso.[67]

Meanwhile, Republican attempts to persuade other Democratic senators to support consideration of redistricting had been unsuccessful. For example, Senator Rodney Ellis was approached by a Republican colleague (Senator Craig Estes) in the Senate lounge during the special session and asked directly whether he was interested in a favorable congressional district in return for voting to consider redistricting.[68] Senator Mario Gallegos of Houston also was approached about trading his vote for changes to District 29 that might attract him into a race for Congress.[69] Both Ellis and Gallegos said no.

Senator Harris explained that he would be working over the weekend to come up with a map for the Senate. Chairman Duncan scheduled a meeting of the Senate Committee on Jurisprudence for Monday, July 14, on redistricting, but then canceled it because the new plan was not yet ready. The lieutenant governor remained optimistic and predicted that a redistricting bill could reach the full Senate for consideration. He continued to believe that he had firm commitments from twenty-one senators, including Ratliff, to wait and see a final plan before declaring their support or opposition to redistricting.

Disturbing sounds for the Republicans, however, were coming from East Texas. The *Texarkana Gazette* reported on July 11 that Senator Ratliff believed that there was widespread disapproval of the House map and that "The general reaction is, this is distasteful." Ratliff said that he did not necessarily have a problem with drawing districts to increase Republican representation, but that he objected to the manner in which it was being done. Specifically, he objected to combining rural northeast Texas with suburban Dallas: congressmen elected from such districts would probably not be from rural areas. He explained that the people he represented were not happy with this possibility, "And they won't be happy with me if I let it happen, and justifiably so."[70] In Austin, Dewhurst took Ratliff's statements as a negotiating tool in what he saw as Ratliff's continuing effort to win satisfactory congressional district lines for his area of the state.[71]

Dewhurst miscalculated. Ratliff was not negotiating for better districts. On Thursday evening, July 10, Ratliff dined in Austin with three other Republican senators.[72] The conversation was about redistricting. None of the four senators favored it. The three other Republican senators asked Ratliff to publicly declare his opposition to redistricting. They suggested that he could do so because he was "bulletproof" and that by siding with the Democrats against suspension of the Senate rules, he could prevent redistricting from proceeding. Ratliff agreed with their request. In later describing Senator Ratliff's dilemma, Democratic senator Whitmire reported that at least four Republican senators "think that their service (in the Senate) is in jeopardy if they go forward with a redistricting plan."[73]

Eleven Senators Take a Stand against Redistricting

Senator Ratliff called Senator Whitmire, the Democratic dean of the Senate, and asked him how many votes he had for not bringing up redistricting. Whitmire said he had ten. Ratliff indicated, "If you can give me those written in blood that they will not vote to suspend the rules, I will be your eleventh."[74] Whitmire set out to draft a letter and to secure the necessary signatures.[75] He first called Senator Lucio to make certain that he would sign such a letter; Lucio said yes. A call to Senator Juan Hinojosa in Mission ended with Hinojosa offering to take the letter to nearby Brownsville for Lucio's signature. The other Democratic senators were contacted. Senators Barrientos and Shapleigh initially balked at signing the letter, but then reconsidered. Barrientos was the last of the Democrats to sign. By shortly after 10 a.m. on Monday morning the letter had been signed by ten Democratic senators when Senator Hinojosa brought it to Senator Ratliff. Ratliff's signature made eleven, enough to block suspension of the Senate rules.

Senator Ratliff then went to Dewhurst. He told him that he had a letter signed by eleven senators committed to voting against consideration of a redistricting bill. Dewhurst in 2006 said that Ratliff did not show him the letter. According to Ratliff, he told Dewhurst that Dewhurst could either announce that he (Dewhurst) was in receipt of such a letter and that redistricting was dead, or Ratliff would go ahead and make the announcement; Ratliff left the option with Dewhurst.[76] According to Dewhurst, he asked Ratliff to give him twenty-four hours in which to deal with the matter before Ratliff spoke with the press. Ratliff told me in 2005 that he did not recall any such request.

Dewhurst held a press conference on Monday afternoon and explained that he had spoken with Ratliff, whom he hoped would "honor his earlier commitment to keep an open mind on redistricting" until an agreement had been reached on a plan by the Senate. Upon learning that Dewhurst apparently did not intend to announce that redistricting was dead, Senator Ratliff followed Dewhurst's press conference with one of his own in the same room. He released the letter from the eleven senators. Political tremors shook the Capitol. The letter, which was addressed to Lieutenant Governor Dewhurst, indicated the "unalterable opposition" of those eleven senators (Senators Ratliff, Barrientos, Lucio, Van de Putte, Shapleigh, Gallegos, Whitmire, Ellis, Hinojosa, Zaffirini, and West) to considering any redistricting map on the Senate floor, along with their intention to "oppose any motion to bring such a redistricting bill to the Senate floor for debate." Neither Armbrister nor Madla had signed the letter.

Asked by the news media to explain his action, Ratliff repeated his concerns about how the House map affected rural areas and how witnesses had testified in opposition to redistricting, but added that he was acting in part to safeguard his Republican colleagues, whom he felt were being asked "to fall on their swords" for the Republican Party when their constituents were opposed to redistricting. "As the senior Republican in the Texas Senate I felt this mantle fell to me," Ratliff explained straightforwardly. He also expressed concern that a political battle over redistricting would undermine the Senate's bipartisan atmosphere.[77]

In an interview in 2005, Ratliff reiterated that he had not acted out of partisanship. He said that this period in 2003 was his most difficult in the Senate. He felt that the redistricting plans considered in 2003 were not fair to his constituents or to East Texas. He said, "In East Texas, it is possible to draw two to three rural districts . . . So long as this [the adopted plan] is in effect, the people that I represented in northeast Texas [as a senator] will be represented in Congress by someone from the Dallas suburbs." He pointed out that the districts are drawn to be Republican (which he felt was fine), but that the majority of the Republican voters lived near the Dallas Metroplex. As a result, this area will disproportionately control the outcome of the Republican primary, and since the district is likely to vote Republican in the general elections, will ultimately control the outcome of the general election.[78]

The chairwoman of the Democratic Caucus in the Senate, Senator Leticia Van de Putte, hailed Ratliff's stand and said that the eleven votes on the letter were "as solid as the granite in this Capitol."[79] News reports suggested that Ratliff's decision provided the "clincher" vote to block Senate action on the Republican plan.[80]

Dewhurst was furious; he felt betrayed.[81] Dewhurst explained at a later press conference that twenty-one senators, including Ratliff, had assured him they would seriously consider a fair redistricting map. He felt that Ratliff had reaffirmed this position only days earlier by indicating that he would not decide until after he saw the plan that came out of the Senate Jurisprudence Committee. Dewhurst felt that Ratliff had reneged. Ratliff responded: "I said I would consider. I did consider."[82] Dewhurst tried to change Ratliff's mind by showing him new drafts of the plans. Ratliff's vote at this point, however, was solidly against considering any redistricting.

Another aspect of what had happened was eating at Dewhurst. At the June 16 meeting with DeLay, Perry, Abbott, and Craddick, Dewhurst had told the other Republican leaders that he expected to be able to get the necessary twenty-one votes. Perry had called the special session with this expectation.

Now, however, it appeared that because of the position of a member of his own party, Dewhurst would be unable to deliver on his promise so long as he continued to require a two-thirds vote to bring up a redistricting bill.

Republican Efforts to Save the Session

Speculation began immediately on whether the governor would call a second special session if redistricting failed in the current one. Dewhurst confirmed that Perry had told him that he would do so. This public acknowledgment of the possibility of another special session put added pressure on the eleven senators who were blocking the redistricting bill, since no one enjoyed the specter of this battle going on indefinitely into the summer.

Perry made an unusual visit to the Senate chamber on July 15 while the Senate was in session to try to muster support. He indicated that he remained optimistic that action would be taken during the current special session: "I didn't call them here for an exercise in futility." [83] Nevertheless, there was no sign that any of the eleven senators would change. Instead, after advising Dewhurst that pressure from constituents and from within the Democratic Party had become "unbearable," Senator Madla joined his Democratic colleagues, making twelve senators opposed to taking up redistricting.

Dewhurst was not willing to accept that redistricting was dead. He pleaded, "If we stay cool, continue to work together, continue to come together, that we'll be able to reach consensus on a map." [84] At the same time, he considered other options, including means for getting around the need to suspend the Senate order of business. He explained that it might be too late in the session to turn back: "If we find that some of our members have changed their minds, it's incumbent [on me] to consider all options." [85]

But the time for dispensing with the two-thirds vote requirement had passed. HB 3 remained in the Senate Jurisprudence Committee. Democratic senators Whitmire and Ellis had smartly placed bills on the calendars ahead of any likely redistricting bill. Republicans might move to consider their own bills on the calendar and move them out of the way, but neither of these Democratic senators was likely to do so for theirs. Therefore, these bills were effectively blocker bills, and the requirement for suspending Senate rules was firmly in place.

Nevertheless, there was speculation that Dewhurst might try to find a way around the two-thirds requirement or to dispense with it in a second special session by forestalling any potential blocker bill. Such possibilities brought immediate and vigorous response from Democrats such as Senator Royce West, who described the two-thirds vote requirement as a "tradition" that had made bipartisan support necessary to get anything done.[86] Senator Ratliff added that dispensing with the two-thirds vote requirement "would be a serious mistake—maybe the most serious mistake he [Dewhurst] could make."[87] Even Senator Armbrister cautioned that he "would lead the exodus" of senators if the two-thirds requirement were abandoned.[88]

Dewhurst was boxed in. If he continued in future sessions to require a two-thirds vote, the Republican redistricting effort would be dead and he would be blamed. Dewhurst's political career as a Republican officeholder probably hung in the balance. Although redistricting was not generally popular, Republican Party officials, key Republican donors, and Republican activists had made clear that it was crucial—a litmus test for party loyalty.

On July 17, Dewhurst announced at a news conference that he would honor the two-thirds vote tradition in the current special session, but not in a second one.[89] He explained that leaving a seventeen-to-fifteen Democratic majority in Congress was "unfair." Taking a cue from suggestions made earlier that day by Karen Hughes[90] about how to present the new position publicly, Dewhurst justified scrapping the two-thirds requirement by explaining, "The majority of voters here in the state of Texas support George Bush and his policies. The majority of the congressional delegation does not."[91] Dewhurst said in 2005 that he had thought if Democrats were faced with the prospect of losing the advantage of the two-thirds vote requirement, they would "come to their senses," realize the futility of continuing to oppose all redistricting, and agree to a "balanced" redistricting plan.[92] Again, he had misjudged the seriousness of the Democrats' position and statements.

New Redistricting Plans in the Senate

Despite the apparent impasse over redistricting, the Senate Jurisprudence Committee continued devising a Senate plan to replace the House version. The process, however, took another bizarre turn when the Senate sponsor of the redistricting legislation, Chris Harris, abruptly stepped aside.

On July 16, Harris described to reporters two plans that he was prepared to present as options for replacing the House plan. When he made his appearance minutes later at the Senate Jurisprudence Committee, however, he instead explained that a "computer glitch in the software" used to draw up the plans had left them susceptible to legal challenge.[93] Harris explained that he was withdrawing the two plans given him "by the AG."[94] In apparent frustration, he said, "At this point, I am out of the map-drawing business. Senator

Staples now has that privilege." Chairman Duncan observed, "I don't know if he [Staples] wants that." Harris responded, "Well, he's got it."[95]

Senator Staples, who was also a member of the committee at the time, expressed surprise at what had happened. Senator Florence Shapiro (Plano) then announced that she and a dozen Republican colleagues (many from around the Dallas–Fort Worth area) had come up with another plan. She indicated that it was still being prepared. The committee recessed several times during the day while waiting for a plan on which public testimony could be heard; none was forthcoming. The lieutenant governor's office explained that "technical glitches" were delaying preparation of the map. The Republican leadership huddled. Afterward, Senator Staples announced that he would rework the map overnight. The committee finally adjourned at 7 p.m.

Staples unveiled his new map on Thursday, July 17. He had had less than twenty-four hours to cobble together Harris's and Shapiro's maps. He explained, "I am the pilot, not the mechanic on this thing," and referred questions from the Democratic senators to the Senate's lawyers.[96] Staples and Dewhurst indicated that the new plan probably contained eighteen safe Republican districts and three toss-up districts. Democrats saw a much harsher plan—one with twenty-one Republican districts.[97] According to Senator West, "They're killing off Anglo Democrats, pure and simple."[98] The Senate committee heard testimony from invited experts on Tuesday, July 22.

Dewhurst hoped that the new redistricting plan, which he saw as offering "two new minority districts," would win over some Democrats.[99] But the reaction from Democrats and minority activist organizations was negative: they saw no increase in minority voting strength.

Dewhurst tried to sweeten the pot by offering his support for the funding of programs such as a new Regional Academic Health Center in the Rio Grande Valley. Democrats publicly denounced the new plan and the lieutenant governor's funding proposals as tantamount to an attempted bribe. Democratic senator Juan Hinojosa responded, "We are not going to sell out for two pieces of silver."[100]

Many of the Democrats suggested that the crisis in Texas had been caused by Congressman DeLay, who responded: "The Democrats have a strategy that's very weak, quite frankly. They're trying to make me the poster boy of redistricting and therefore scare Republicans from doing their jobs. It's not working."[101] Republicans in July generally downplayed DeLay's involvement. For example, on July 17, Dewhurst spokesperson Dave Beckwith said "I know it's fashionable to blame Tom DeLay for everything and to demonize him and make him like the string-puller and the puppet master. The fact is, he has very little to do with it."[102]

Democratic Thoughts Turn to Compromise or Walkout

As the governor spoke more often about an additional special session and the lieutenant governor spoke about abandoning the two-thirds vote requirement, Democratic senators privately and publicly discussed walking out to break a quorum, as had occurred in the House. Senator Hinojosa explained on July 17: "If they're going to sell out the Senate, we're going to walk. We've got 11 senators willing to break quorum."[103] When asked if he was willing to spend several weeks in hiding, Senator Gallegos said, "I've spent time in the firehouse for 30 days. I can."[104] Lieutenant Governor Dewhurst met frequently with Democratic senators individually and as a group.[105] He urged them not to stage a boycott. He claimed that a "fair" compromise plan fashioned along the district lines drawn for the state Senate could be worked out, resulting in Republicans holding nineteen or twenty congressional seats "plus Ralph Hall."

To entice the Democrats to cut a deal, Dewhurst emphasized the inevitability of redistricting: "We're either going to come up with a fair plan now or we're going to come up with a fair plan later. It may be in August. It may be in September, but we will come together."[106] Senator Van de Putte, who had become chairwoman of the Democratic Caucus in the Senate after the regular session (replacing Senator Barrientos), responded, "No one wants to go to any extremes. We are continuing to dialogue. To be sure, the governor needs to understand we're immovable." On the issue of a series of special sessions, she said, "I think at some point, the people of Texas will say this is a waste of taxpayers' money."[107]

One Republican senator seriously sought settlement by proposing another plan.[108] Senator Wentworth presented a map that he said would defeat as many as five incumbent Democrats, but guarantee Republicans only sixteen congressional seats, and include three "Republican-leaning" but competitive seats. He explained that the lower number of safe Republican districts in his plan (down from the twenty-one in the current Senate version) reflected that "this state is not a 70 percent Republican state. It's about 55 to 60 [percent Republican]."[109] According to Wentworth, he took the plan to Van de Putte near the end of July as a possible compromise. She rejected the compromise: she needed "to bring her people [the Democratic senators] a victory" like the one achieved by the House Democrats.[110] In an interview in 2005, Wentworth acknowledged that any such compromise (even if approved by the Senate) probably could not have survived the later conference committee.

Dewhurst also faced Democratic charges that by not following the two-thirds vote requirement in a second special session, he would be abandoning a Senate tradition that had made bipartisanship possible by protecting political minorities. This claim was repeated by Democrats across Texas and picked up in many news stories. Dewhurst responded with opinion pieces in several major state newspapers[111] explaining how prior Democratic lieutenant governors had not adhered to a two-thirds vote requirement for redistricting bills taken up in a special session.[112] He argued that unlike other matters that were historically dealt with nonpartisanly, redistricting was always a partisan issue and had been addressed by majority vote even in the past. In an opinion piece in the *Houston Chronicle,* editorial writer Bill Coulter challenged the Democrats' suggestion that resistance to redistricting was a noble cause: "It's not the Alamo. It's politics." On July 23 the Senate Jurisprudence Committee, on a party-line vote of 4–3, advanced the new plan to the full Senate.

The final chance for possible compromise in this special session was at hand. Dewhurst was optimistic: "I see some movement by Republicans and Democrats in coming together." In my interviews with Dewhurst in 2005 and 2006, he focused on this first special session, especially before the release of the letter by the eleven senators on July 14, as the optimum opportunity for Republicans and Democrats to have reached a compromise. Dewhurst insisted that if a "fair" plan had been negotiated during the first special session, he could have presented it to the other Republican leaders as "the best possible plan." He said that DeLay and the Republican congressional delegation would have accepted a plan likely to elect four or five new Republicans (along with Ralph Hall) rather than continue the battle.[113] Dewhurst told me that he had no doubts such a plan could have been maintained through a conference committee. However, he said, "Timing is everything." As time passed during the summer of 2003, the possibility of compromise became like "milk left outside: it began to sour."[114] Dewhurst admitted to uncertainty about his ability to hold a compromise through conference committee by the time of the third special session.

Despite the heated rhetoric, some Democrats pondered whether it would be better to allow the Republicans to pass the worst possible plan and challenge it in court, or try to compromise with Senate Republicans on a plan that might save a few incumbent Democratic congressmen. Senator Whitmire enjoyed a good relationship with Dewhurst and spoke with him almost every day about how to avoid what both men saw as an impending crisis. Several Republican senators, including Wentworth, Duncan, Ratliff, and others, seemed willing to work toward a compromise plan.

There were several obstacles, however, to any serious consideration of a compromise. The Democrat's legal advisers claimed that the Republican plan was "blatantly illegal" and would be struck down by the courts; they argued that compromise was unnecessary. Moreover, Democratic senators had little confidence in the viability of a compromise: they doubted whether the Republican congressional delegation or the House would go along with one, or whether it could survive a conference committee. Finally, just as passage of redistricting had been made a litmus test for Republicans, defeating its passage now became a litmus test for Democrats. The Democrats drew a line in the sand.

Dewhurst told me in 2005 that he had met every weekday of the last half of the first special session with Democratic senators Whitmire, Van de Putte, West, and Zaffirini in an effort to find a compromise. He tried repeatedly to convince them that compromise was the best route and that he would not yield to any later effort by DeLay or other Republicans to undermine the settlement with a more aggressively partisan plan. He said he offered several possibilities, including a possible rule change to prevent consideration of any later redistricting plan that was substantively different from the agreed-upon plan. If Democrats were unwilling to vote for a final plan, he said that he was willing to allow them unlimited time to debate the reasons for their opposition as long as they would agree to set aside the two-thirds vote requirement. Senator Van de Putte in 2005 said that she did not recall Dewhurst ever offering a rule change as a possibility.[115] As the end of the session neared, Dewhurst pleaded, "Join us. Let's work together and come out with a new map."[116]

Neither side was willing to budge. Dewhurst's hopes for compromise in this first special session finally ended. Senator West proclaimed, "This is dead this legislative session. It's dead, it's dead, it's dead, it's dead."[117] Dewhurst reluctantly acknowledged on July 23 that he would not attempt to stage a procedural vote to bring the redistricting bill up for debate in the current session. On the 25th, he agreed that "[i]n essence, redistricting in this session is dead."[118] At the same time, however, he warned Democrats that the plan adopted by the Senate Jurisprudence Committee would be the starting point for the next special session.

Therefore, even though the special session was not scheduled to end until July 29, the possibility of passing a redistricting bill ended on July 25. Bills on some other subjects continued to be considered and passed. House Bill 3, however, remained pending on the Senate calendar, blocked from consideration by bills controlled by Democratic senators Ellis and Whitmire. These same bills were still atop the calendars when the Senate adjourned sine die on July 28, 2003.

Commentary

The first special session was primarily a tale of personal decisions made in the midst of public partisan turmoil. There were many such stories; I have focused on only a few.

Senator Ratliff has received significant recognition, including an award from the Kennedy Foundation, for his thoughtful and conscientious action in crossing party lines to do what he thought would preserve the institution he loved and prevent a redistricting effort that he felt endangered that institution and harmed his rural constituents. He deserves respect for his courage in doing what he felt was right. It can be argued that the partisan pressures on him in 2003 were lessened because he no longer aspired to state office and was therefore relieved of some of the pressures applied to Lieutenant Governor Dewhurst and Senator Duncan. However, in 2001, when his candidacy for statewide office turned on whether party officials and activists considered him sufficiently partisan, Ratliff bravely showed his independence even at the cost of the Republican nomination for lieutenant governor. On November 20, 2003, after the close of the sessions on redistricting, Ratliff announced his intention to retire from the Texas Senate.

The predicament of Lieutenant Governor Dewhurst in 2003 was particularly fascinating. Dewhurst remains an enigma to me. Throughout the summer and fall of 2003 he was caught between two motivations. On the one hand, he had gained respect among senators and statewide for his fairness and independence, and he wanted to preserve this reputation. On the other hand, he was politically ambitious and committed to surviving the redistricting battle in order to remain a viable candidate in future Republican campaigns. The perception of Dewhurst as more moderate or reasonable than other state Republican leaders had followed him into the redistricting fray. For example, the *Amarillo Globe-News* on July 20 called on Dewhurst to "Stand tall," adding,

Only the lieutenant governor, it seems, has kept his wits about him. [The other state leaders are] marching in lock-step to the machinations of Washington politicians rather than heeding the advice of Texans here at home. . . . But Dewhurst is feeling the heat to be a good Republican and force the Senate to decide this issue once and for all.[119]

Dewhurst was "feeling the heat."

A government professor at Southern Methodist University, Cal Jillson, explained the predicament: "(Dewhurst) believes he has a future in the Republican Party of Texas. He can't ignore the party's sense that they deserve a majority of seats in the Texas delegation. If he can get [redistricting] done without blood on the floor than I think he is in good shape."[120] Congressman Jim Turner offered the Democrats' view: "It's hard to understand how the lieutenant governor could have attempted to establish himself as a bipartisan leader in the regular session and now move away from that and try to polarize the state through this partisan redistricting."[121] Former speaker Pete Laney added the observation in 2005 that he saw no evidence that Dewhurst ever really "fought very hard" to find an outcome acceptable to the Democrats.[122]

Dewhurst's announcement that he would no longer require a two-thirds vote before the Senate could consider redistricting was ultimately to prove determinative of the outcome in 2003. The decision rendered a repeat of Ratliff's actions meaningless. Dewhurst clearly had the legal right and power to do away with such a vote, but he also had the legal right and power to retain it. His decision meant that as long as Governor Perry was willing to call additional special sessions, a redistricting bill would eventually pass. Senator Whitmire explained Dewhurst's change: "(Dewhurst) believes that if he doesn't take care of the hard-core partisan voters, he won't be [in office]. I argued that he could withstand the pressure from the right. I kept telling him that they couldn't touch him—he's got great name identification, wealth, looks, smarts."[123] Such pleas were insufficient in the face of what Dewhurst and his advisers saw as the stark reality of Republican politics.[124]

CHAPTER 10

Is There a Democratic Endgame?

It's a waiting game with all the cards on our side. We will pass a map. Time is on our side.
—JIM ELLIS, AIDE TO CONGRESSMAN TOM DELAY, *NATIONAL JOURNAL*, AUGUST 1, 2003

The Democrats in the Texas House of Representatives had successfully killed the Republican redistricting bill during the regular session by leaving Texas and denying the Republican-controlled legislature the quorum needed for legislative action. The Democrats in the Senate, along with Republican senator Bill Ratliff, had successfully killed redistricting in the first special session.

At the end of July 2003, as the first special session drew to a close and a second special session appeared likely, the unanswered questions were whether Democratic senators too would try to break a quorum, whether they could organize themselves and flee Texas, and whether such a boycott would ultimately stop the Republican redistricting offensive. Senators historically are more independent than their House counterparts. There are only thirty-one senators, each representing approximately 672,639 persons (more than the number currently represented by members of the Texas congressional delegation). The likelihood of the twelve Democratic senators staging a walkout appeared small to many observers, requiring an unachievable level of mutual trust, coordination, and individual and political will.

The possibility of a walkout had been discussed among the Democratic senators from the time the first special session had convened in June. During the last week of the session, however, Democratic senators began to meet regularly in small groups and together as the Democratic Caucus to seriously consider the possibility. As the calling of a second special session became a certainty, the Democratic senators decided to prepare for a possible boycott, which would break quorum and prevent the adoption of a Republican redistricting plan. The first discussions were about merely staying hidden away somewhere in Austin for a few days, as the Killer Bees had done in 1979. It soon became apparent, however, that something more dramatic might be necessary.

Planning a Boycott

The Senate Democratic Caucus authorized its president, Leticia Van de Putte, to make the logistical arrangements for the walkout. She looked for a state near Texas, one where the governor was a Democrat, and a destination city with a good heart hospital (given Senator Lucio's recent heart ailments).[1] No senator particularly wanted to go to Oklahoma, where the House Democrats had gone. Van de Putte considered six destinations, including three states and Mexico. She decided on Albuquerque, New Mexico, but kept this destination secret from her colleagues.

The Democratic senators were being advised during this period by several outside consultants and attorneys. One, Keith Hampton of the Criminal Defense Attorneys Association, warned Republicans publicly that it would be illegal for the DPS or the Senate sergeant at arms (or any private security officers hired by the Senate) to force senators to the Senate floor for a vote. He indicated privately to the Democratic senators that he thought he could quickly obtain a court order barring the arrest of the Democrats if they broke the quorum. Austinite Harold Cook provided staffing for the caucus and valuable logistical support. Attorney Gerald Hebert and consultant Matt Angle were present from Washington, representing the Democratic congressional delegation. Ed Martin, of the Democratic Party of Texas, also was present. Nevertheless, the Democratic senators insist that the decision to boycott was solely their own.

The overriding question for the Democratic senators was how long to stay gone to achieve victory. There was no consensus. Because the House Democrats had beaten redistricting through a walkout, it was difficult for these senators to now refuse to try to do the same. But the circumstances were very different: there was no constitutional deadline equivalent to the one that had benefited the House members. Senator Whitmire was particularly persistent in asking how long the senators would have to be gone and what they hoped to achieve. He had said publicly, "I'm ready to walk,"[2] but later cautioned, "If you break a quorum, ultimately they get everyone back in."[3]

There were no certain answers, but there were several positive possible scenarios:

- Some Democratic senators speculated that a show of unity over only a few days would be enough to convince Lieutenant Governor Dewhurst to refrain from abandoning the two-thirds vote requirement, allowing the senators to return. They knew that Dewhurst had been reluctant in the beginning to join in the partisan redistricting effort. These senators now hoped that to keep his reputation for independence, the goodwill of the senators, and the important traditions of the Senate, Dewhurst would decide to reinstate the two-thirds vote requirement. After all, the Killer Bees had won after being absent for only four days. Surely Dewhurst would relent after a few days, as Lieutenant Governor Bill Hobby had done.

- Some senators were hopeful that the pressure of a public outcry over the waste of money on unnecessary special sessions would convince the governor and other Republicans that pursuing redistricting was against public opinion and potentially politically costly.

- Some senators were encouraged by the idea that it would be possible to obtain a court order preventing them from being forced to return to the Senate chamber to vote; such an order would allow the Democrats to safely carry on their boycott while remaining and working in Texas away from the Capitol.

- Some senators were encouraged by the indication from attorneys (especially Gerald Hebert) that the lieutenant governor's failure to continue to require a two-thirds vote to bring legislation up in the Senate was a change in an election practice under Section 5 of the Voting Rights Act and could be successfully enjoined and possibly prevented under the act.

- Some senators felt that by raising the profile nationwide of the redistricting dispute and focusing attention on the implications of the Republican plan for racial and ethnic minorities, the possibility for favorable Justice Department or court action could be increased.

- Most senators felt that after the fall of 2003 it would be impossible for Republicans to implement any new districting plan. Lawyers speculated about when the deadline might be. Some senators said, however, that they would stay away for thirty to sixty days or longer to exceed this uncertain deadline and block the Republican redistricting. Not everyone agreed that staying away that long was feasible.

Any of these results could mean victory for the Democrats. The senators generally acknowledged, however, that they needed to be prepared to stay gone for at least the thirty days of a second special session.

It was clear early that the maximum number of senators likely to participate in any boycott was the minimum needed to break a quorum. Democratic senator Ken Armbrister had said publicly that he would not participate in a boycott. Although Republican senator Ratliff had joined the Democrats in opposing suspension of the two-thirds vote requirement, no one expected him to boycott the Senate. Senators Lucio and Madla were onboard, but that still meant that only eleven were willing to boycott: Gonzalo Barrientos (Austin), Rodney Ellis (Houston), Mario Gallegos (Houston), Juan Hinojosa (McAllen), Eddie Lucio (Brownsville), Frank Madla (San Antonio), Eliot Shapleigh (El Paso), Leticia Van de Putte (San Antonio), Royce West (Dallas), John Whitmire (Houston), and Judith Zaffirini (Laredo). Two of these senators are African American, two are Anglo, and seven are Hispanic. The failure of any of them to leave the state would prevent an effective boycott; a return by any of them would end the boycott.

The Democratic senators were advised by Senator Van de Putte to be ready to leave on only a few hours' notice: it was feared that Governor Perry might immediately call a second special session in an attempt to trap the Democratic senators in the Senate chamber. Senator Whitmire expressed this concern as early as July 24, when he said, "You get a strong paranoia or concern that they are going to *sine die* [adjourn] at noon and call us back an hour later so they can lock us up in here."[4] On Sunday, July 27, Senator Van de Putte, based on what she later called "mother's intuition," told the senators "to pack [for Monday] as if they were leaving for a couple of days."[5]

A False Alarm

Apprehension over the possibility that Republican officials might adjourn the current special session and immediately call a second one resulted in a false alarm during the latter part of July.[6] Caucus staffer Harold Cook sent two colleagues to Albuquerque to prepare for the arrival of the Democratic senators and called for moving two private planes to Austin. However, the plans became unnecessary as the perceived urgency of the moment passed. The caucus staffers remained in Albuquerque for two days, scouting possible hotels for the future. They suggested the Marriott Pyramid North because its rooms offered high-speed Internet access.

A Hurried Departure

The thirtieth and last possible day of the special session was Tuesday, July 29. The Republican leadership, however, had agreed on an aggressive strategy to prevent the Democratic senators from successfully breaking a quorum in any second special session. Governor Perry, Lieutenant Governor Dewhurst, and

Speaker Craddick secretly agreed to adjourn the special session a day early and to immediately call a second special session before the Democratic senators and House members could bolt from Austin.

On Monday morning, July 28, the Democratic senators met in a Senate conference room at the southeast corner of the Senate third-floor gallery to decide on a course of action.[7] The collective mood was in favor of a boycott if necessary. Dewhurst twice joined the meeting that morning in an effort to avoid a walkout. He said he was willing to retain the two-thirds vote requirement for future sessions, but only if he could be confident that the redistricting bill could get the necessary twenty-one votes. He continued to seek Democrat compromise on a "fair" plan. His efforts failed to produce an agreement. When he left the meeting for the last time, Dewhurst hugged Senator Van de Putte. She speculated later that Dewhurst knew then that the Democratic senators were going to leave. After Dewhurst left the meeting, the Democrats met with their lawyers. One lawyer said that the Republicans were "dicing minorities." Whitmire claimed that Gerald Hebert specifically told the senators that in a "worst case scenario" the Democratic lawyers could get a temporary restraining order in three to seven days against the change in the two-thirds vote requirement.[8]

Initially, the Democratic senators expected to leave, if at all, on Monday night or Tuesday morning. But about a half hour before the session on Monday was scheduled to begin, a cell-phone call from a Republican House member to Senator John Whitmire interrupted the Democrats' meeting and brought word that the Republican leadership planned to suddenly adjourn the special session later that afternoon—on the 28th rather than the 29th—and that the governor would immediately call a second special session. The assumption was that an immediate call on the Senate after the new session was announced would mean that the Senate doors would be immediately locked to trap one or more Democratic senators in the chamber, or at least in the Capitol.[9] The presence of even one of the eleven senators would be enough to establish a quorum. If this tip were true, it was imperative that the Democratic senators not return to the Senate chamber on the 28th.

Whitmire told his fellow Democrats about the telephone call. The senators looked at each other. However, according to Whitmire, there was no discussion of what to do.[10] Instead, the senators seemed to silently and quickly reach a consensus that they had to leave immediately. Van de Putte explained that Senator Hinojosa had arranged for two jets to be waiting at a private terminal at Austin-Bergstrom International Airport. The senators agreed to leave the Capitol immediately and meet at Van de Putte's Towers of Town Lake apartment. They began leaving around 12:30. Some whispered the code words "Town Lake" to one another, denoting Van de Putte's apartment. Senator Madla, who was at the governor's office on another matter, was advised of what had happened and agreed to join the exodus.

Van de Putte and caucus staffer Harold Cook had planned well. The departure went smoothly. Cars were waiting at the Capitol. The Democratic senators gathered initially at Van de Putte's apartment before going to the airport. They were joined temporarily by several House members, including Rep. Richard Raymond. Vans and cars carried the senators from Van de Putte's apartment to the airport. The senators worried during the drive that they might be stopped by DPS officers dispatched to catch them. Two private jets were waiting. Senator Hinojosa had arranged for the aircraft from two constituents, Joe La Mantia, a McAllen beer distributor, and David Rogers, an Edinburg banker. Hinojosa, however, had flown up from the Rio Grande Valley on Monday morning on a commercial flight, had missed the earlier meeting at the Capitol, and was the last to reach the airport. The other ten senators waited nervously: the five or ten minutes before he arrived were excruciating for some as they imagined DPS cars speeding to the airport to stop their departure.

After Hinojosa's arrival, the senators boarded the jets and took off. Most still did not know their final destination. Harold Cook told me in 2005 that he had instructed the pilots to file flight plans for Amarillo and asked that the flight plans be changed to Albuquerque only after the planes were airborne. As the planes headed west, most of the senators realized for the first time that they would be going to New Mexico. The atmosphere was festive.

Adjournment and a New Special Session

The House of Representatives convened at 10 a.m. on July 28. With forty-nine members listed as absent, some Democrats questioned whether a quorum was present. Craddick, however, proceeded with House business and a bill was passed. The House later broke for lunch, and then at 3 p.m. adjourned sine die for the special session. The members were told to wait a few minutes for a proclamation from the governor.

The Senate was scheduled to convene at 1 p.m. However, Lieutenant Governor Dewhurst from his position at the front of the Senate chamber officially suggested that there was not a quorum present. A roll call confirmed it. Unable to secure a quorum to approve legislation sent over from the House, the Senate adjourned sine die for the special session at 2:30 p.m.

At 3:15 p.m. the governor's office delivered a proclamation to each chamber, calling the legislature back into a second special session. The House immediately convened, but with only 85 of 150 members present, it lacked a quorum, and so adjourned until 10 a.m. on the following day, Tuesday, July 29. The Senate convened for the second special session at 3:55 p.m., but was still without a quorum. The Senate at 4:07 p.m. was directed to stand at ease until 10 a.m. on the following day. But the Republican senators present, on a motion by Senator Staples, voted to place a "call" on the Senate. Pursuant to this call, the Senate doors were locked and the sergeant at arms was directed to "send for and compel the attendance of all members whose absence is not excused, for the purpose of securing and retaining their presence."

When the House convened on the 29th, it acted quickly to pass the same redistricting plan it had passed in the first special session. The House secured a quorum and then acted 75–26 to suspend the constitutional requirements that bills go through public hearings and three days of floor action. The same redistricting plan that in July had been the subject of ten hours of debate was now adopted in twenty minutes. The process was speeded when Democrat Ron Wilson moved to cut off debate. Republicans, and some Democrats, saw the quick action on the redistricting bill as appropriate, given that the House had passed an identical redistricting plan only three weeks earlier.

Many Democrats stayed away from the House chamber. Some were critical of the extraordinary action by the House on the redistricting bill, but few, if any, could stomach another lengthy, futile fight on the House floor.

After completing its action on the redistricting bill, the House adjourned for a week. House parliamentarian Steve Collins acknowledged several days later that this adjournment probably violated the state constitution because neither house of the legislature is entitled to adjourn for more than three days without the permission of the other house. Without a quorum, the Senate could not have granted the House permission. Under the circumstances, however, this possible violation was inconsequential.

The Republican Reaction to the Senators' Departure

Lieutenant Governor Dewhurst gave a relatively low-key response to the Democrats' departure. After all, he had been meeting with the Senate Democrats shortly before they left, and was not as surprised as Speaker Craddick had been at the departure of the House Democrats. Dewhurst told the press: "I've got to share with you that I'm disappointed, very disappointed."[11] He joked that he had given the Democrats some advice before they left town: "I told them that I quite frankly thought that if they went to a vacation spot they would lose the public relations battle even more." When asked whether Albuquerque was a vacation spot, Dewhurst answered, "I certainly think it's more of a vacation spot than Ardmore."[12]

Although not surprised by the Democrats' departure, Dewhurst immediately triggered a search by the Senate sergeant at arms, Carleton Turner, for any absent senators. Dewhurst, through his spokesperson Dave Beckwith, later denied, however, that he and the governor had intended to trap the Democrats in the Senate chamber.

Some Republican senators were furious at the Democrats. They predicted failure for the walkout. Senator Jane Nelson (Lewisville) said, "They [the Democratic senators] can't hold out long enough to defeat redistricting because the governor has the right to call a special session over and over again. And they can't stay away 30 days, 60 days, 90 days." She later added that, "I think the public understands exactly what happened, and that is that these senators did not show up for work, and the public does not like that."[13] Some Republican senators, such as Todd Staples, took a more conciliatory tack (described by newspapers at the time as a "good cop–bad cop" approach) by inviting his "colleagues to return to Texas."[14]

Governor Perry responded as he had when the House Democrats had walked out. He called on the senators "to come back . . . so that we can address not only congressional redistricting, but the other very important pieces of legislation in front of us." He specifically implied that the absence of the Democrats jeopardized $800 million in new federal funding available for Medicaid. Dewhurst and Craddick joined in this attack, accusing the Democrats of preventing the legislature from finishing important work that would have generated additional funds to help Medicaid payments for home-care services, pregnant women, and health care for the children of working families.[15]

The Democrats responded to these charges by indicating that there had been plenty of time to pass such legislation during the first special session if the Republican leaders had actually wanted to do so. The Democrats suggested that "we would have left a long time ago" if a boycott could cause the governor to pay attention to education and health and human services.[16] Democratic representative Pete Gallego pointed out that the governor and the Legislative Budget Board already had authority under the appropriations bill to spend the federal funds. Eventually, after an affirming legal opinion was obtained from the attorney general, the funds were allocated without further legislative action.

Several rumors circulated around the Capitol. One claimed that Perry and Dewhurst were trying to find a way to declare the Democratic senators' seats vacant by virtue of their absence. Dewhurst acknowledged to me in 2006 that this option was considered. He indicated, however, that no legal means were found to declare the seats vacant.[17]

The One Who Stayed Behind

Senator Ken Armbrister was the lone Democrat to stay in Austin. Early in the first special session he had said that he would lead a walkout if the lieutenant governor did away with the two-thirds vote requirement. He later retracted that pledge, explaining that he was now convinced that Dewhurst was not changing the Senate rules but following precedent. Armbrister now said that he was staying in Austin to ensure that rural Texas had a voice in the redistricting process.

Life in Albuquerque

The planes carrying the eleven Democrats landed in Albuquerque on the afternoon of July 28.[18] The senators were greeted at the private terminal by the two caucus staffers who had gone ahead as an advance team. The staffers had rented large SUVs to transport the senators. The Democrats traveled to the Marriott Pyramid North hotel. At 8 p.m. the senators held their first news conference; Senators Van de Putte and Barrientos were the primary spokespersons. Van de Putte said, "This is not about Democrats. It's about democracy."[19]

Although warned days earlier by Van de Putte to be packed for a stay of several days, many senators, because of the hurried departure, arrived in Albuquerque without anything but the clothes that they were wearing. One of the first tasks for some senators was a trip to the mall to purchase essential personal items. Senator Ellis, who had been focused the prior week on the impending birth of his third child, had had his Capitol staff gather a few items for him as he sped to the airport in Austin. In Albuquerque, however, he joked that his "shirt was standing up." Senator Shapleigh had nothing but his laptop-computer case. Each senator set about calling home or shopping locally to obtain the necessary clothes and personal items for a possibly extended stay in New Mexico.

New Mexico Governor Bill Richardson

One reason that New Mexico was selected as the destination was that its governor, Bill Richardson, was a Democrat. Richardson had just been named chairman of the 2004 Democratic National Convention. Richardson also was a friend of Senator Van de Putte's from their work together on Hispanic issues. He greeted the Texas senators as "heroes." His public comments were a combination of humor and partisan accusation. He indicated that, "This is a wonderful time of the year to visit the Land of Enchantment. New Mexico has a long history of helping people on the run—and should these legislators decide to stay awhile, I will be proud to have them."[20]

Richardson later turned his comments to the Republicans at the national level, such as Congressman DeLay and Karl Rove, and accused them of putting "undue political pressure to force these legislators to succumb to political manipulation." Standing along with the eleven senators in front of a Texas flag, Governor Richardson said that he "would urge Governor Perry to cease the effort to impose redistricting" and to focus instead on other issues, such "as our common water problems."[21]

Richardson's support drew criticism from Austin and from some constituents in New Mexico. His providing New Mexico state police to guard the hotel in Albuquerque was specifically targeted. Richardson explained that this incurred no additional costs because none of the officers assigned to the hotel were on overtime. The officers were later removed after it became clear that Dewhurst did not intend to use Texas DPS officers or "bounty hunters" to capture the senators in New Mexico. Richardson stood by the Texas senators throughout the boycott, however, and made it clear that he would intervene in any attempt to forcibly return them to Texas.

Not on Vacation!

One Texas newspaper described the living conditions at the Marriott Pyramid North as being of "obvious comfort" in "one of Albuquerque's finest hotels," with cocktails at the foot of a two-story waterfall and "graceful" glass elevators "wafting classical music."[22] One reporter for *Texas Monthly*, however, was disappointed by her visit to the hotel after the "big buildup" when she found "plastic greenery and faux waterfall."[23] To avoid giving the impression that they were on vacation, the senators adopted the same policy as their colleagues had in Ardmore—no lounging around the hotel pool.

Sensitive from the beginning about possible charges of being on vacation, the senators made a point of adhering to a schedule that brought them together in the hotel's Taos conference room each morning at 8:30 am to discuss the redistricting situation and other legislation pending in Austin. Most senators dressed in suits or their equivalent for these meetings. Even when senators later traveled to other parts of the country for meetings or rallies, they generally called in to participate in these daily meetings by telephone.

The senators met around a single table, each usually occupying the same place. The meetings began with each senator explaining what he or she had learned over the past twenty-four hours from conversations with Republican senators or others back in Texas. Senator Whitmire says he was the first to acknowledge that he had spoken with Dewhurst. He stated, as he had done often over the past months, that Dewhurst did not want to redistrict. Now, however, he was criticized by his colleagues for continuing to talk to Dewhurst. Occasionally some or all of the senators would meet again in the evening to discuss what they had heard during the day. As Whitmire put it in 2005: "We were the meetingest sons of bitches."[24] One effect of these frequent meetings was to solidify the senators into a group and to harden their resolve into a principle. The senators drew their own line in the sand that none of them could cross.

The Democrats' "command and control center" was the Taos Room at the Marriott. A Texas state seal was taped to the door and a facsimile of the "Come And Take It" flag from the Texas revolution hung on the wall. The senators adopted as an official logo an outline of Texas inside a Zia Pueblo sun symbol. Shortly after each morning business meeting, the senators would hold a news conference. At one stage, political consultant George Shipley brought equipment that allowed the senators to record their own video messages for distribution back home.

Some staff members followed the senators to Albuquerque. At least three Democratic Caucus staffers and half a dozen aides to individual senators "rotated" being in Albuquerque and handling a barrage of cell-phone calls and logistical challenges, such as reviewing news stories, preparing statements for the senators, and scheduling trips. The caucus staffers were paid $30 a day from caucus funds, but the aides (as state employees) used their vacation time to be in Albuquerque. All staffers and aides spent mostly their own money on clothes, food, etc. Matt Angle from Congressman Frost's office remained in Washington but was in constant contact with Harold Cook, chief staffer for the Democratic Caucus.

Eventually, the senators were required to leave the Marriott Pyramid North because of the arrival of a large military convention. They relocated to the Albuquerque Marriott. Even after the move, however, the senators tried to maintain a regular meeting routine.

Some senators also kept busy with trips to universities, prisons, Indian reservations, a Hispanic cultural center, and state agencies in New Mexico, or by dining with state and local officials, such as Albuquerque mayor Martin Chavez and New Mexico Lieutenant Governor Diane Denish. The occasions were sometimes described as "fact finding" visits regarding legislative issues in Texas. The hotel's exercise room and the city's bike trails also saw use. Senator

Zaffirini was up typically at between 3 and 5 a.m. for a daily walk on the tread-mill in the hotel gym. Senator Whitmire allegedly was spotted on at least one occasion at the gambling tables of a local casino.

The senators tried to travel through the surrounding area, such as to nearby Santa Fe, especially on the weekends. One senator took his family to Las Vegas, New Mexico, only to see his family disappointed that the town of under 15,000 was clearly not the entertainment capital of the world. Senator Van de Putte traveled to Colorado to meet her husband. Senators Ellis and West traveled to Washington, D.C., to participate in the "Million Man March" in that city. They went on to New York.

The reality, of course, was that staying in a hotel (even a relatively nice one) away from home, family, and work for an extended period was not a vaca-tion. Each senator faced some financial hardship from being separated from clients, businesses, or jobs. The senators agreed to forgo their $600 monthly senatorial salary and their daily stipend; they paid for the hotel and the costs of the boycott themselves. Room costs exceeded $160 a night at the Marriott Pyramid. Senator Barrientos left the hotel because of the expense. In the end, the senators estimated the cost to be approximately $7,500–10,000 apiece for the stay in New Mexico, including expenses for conference rooms, Internet access, attorneys, staff, telephone calls, and the travel of family members to New Mexico.[25] Eventually, most of these costs were covered by the Democratic congressional delegation and private donors.

No senator tried to reenter Texas during the boycott, so any visit with fam-ily or friends occurred in New Mexico or another state other than Texas, or by telephone. Senator Ellis went weeks without seeing his newborn daughter. All senators worried about family. For some, the financial effect of the boycott was significant.

No Negotiations

The senators also were anxious to avoid any perception that negotiations were ongoing with Dewhurst or any Republican senators. Dewhurst was quoted by a news source soon after the senators' arrival in Albuquerque that he had spoken with two of them. Democrats feared that such contacts could be perceived as an ongoing negotiation to resolve the boycott, could undercut their stand, and could possibly destroy their unity. In response to Dewhurst's statement, Van de Putte stated emphatically on July 31: "There are no negotiations. Our strategy is for winning, not losing."[26] Nevertheless, it appears that some Democratic senators continued to speak privately over the coming weeks with Dewhurst or other senators in Austin about finding a way out of the standoff.

At one point Dewhurst and two Republican senators agreed that a secret trip to Albuquerque to talk in person with the Democrats might be worthwhile.[27] Dewhurst paid for the private plane. Republican Senators Robert Duncan and Todd Staples arrived on August 6 in Albuquerque early in the morning. They had tried unsuccessfully before leaving Austin to confirm a meeting with the Democratic senators. It was apparent that some of the Democrats were not anxious to see the Republicans come to Albuquerque. The Republican senators were left to "cool their heels" at the private air terminal. A meeting finally occurred there in the afternoon with Senators Juan Hinojosa, Royce West, and Leticia Van de Putte. The brief meeting failed to produce any progress in resolving the standoff. Senator Hinojosa later called this visit by the Republican senators and proposed compromise a "setup" and "sham," since the following day Governor Perry and Lieutenant Governor Dewhurst filed a mandamus action at the Texas Supreme Court in an attempt to compel the Democratic senators to return to Austin.[28]

The two Republican senators' efforts at secrecy were foiled when they were recognized by news media. The senators refused at the time to acknowledge whether Dewhurst or Perry knew about their trip. Bad weather prevented them from returning to Austin until the next morning. Once the meeting between the Republican and Democratic senators became public, Juan Hinojosa said that the Republicans' trip was intended to be used as evidence of Republicans' attempt to negotiate a resolution before filing suit.[29]

The Republicans' proposal for compromise is worth understanding. According to Duncan, they offered, on behalf of the lieutenant governor, to allow each senator individually to object to changes in a redistricting plan that would affect the areas in his or her own Senate district. Moreover, Dewhurst was willing to agree not to allow the Senate to take up a conference-committee report on a redistricting bill without the sponsor showing him that the report had the support of at least twenty-one senators. If firm, this proposal was extraordinary. However, the Democratic senators did not respond to it.

Senator Duncan subsequently went back alone to Albuquerque on August 17 to present this proposal to the full Democratic Caucus. The Democrats again refused to discuss the specific proposal or any compromise.

Public Support and Criticism

During their stay in New Mexico, the senators became celebrities in Texas and nationwide. They were flooded with e-mails, phone calls, flowers, food, and care packages from supporters. "Texas 11" T-shirts appeared. Guitarist Steve

Brooks came to Albuquerque to entertain the senators with his new song, "The Killer D's of Texas" (sung to the tune of "The Yellow Rose of Texas"). Seven members of the American GI Forum of Texas joined the senators in criticizing Governor Perry for cutting funding for certain special training programs (allegedly because of the group's opposition to redistricting). As with the House Democrats, Willie Nelson was among the well-wishers.

Nationally, Democrats were adopting the boycotting lawmakers as heroes in a fight against alleged Republican abuses of power in general. Former Texas governor Ann Richards claimed she would have been "run out of the state" if she had acted like Perry when she was governor. A delegation of Colorado legislators arrived in Albuquerque on August 13 to show their support and to call attention to a similar attempt by Republicans to redraw congressional districts in Colorado. The Colorado lawmakers blamed Karl Rove for engineering the Republican action in Colorado, but acknowledged that they lacked any direct evidence of Rove's involvement.[30]

A Web-based organization, MoveOn.org, launched a fund-raising appeal with a $1 million goal to produce television and radio ads denouncing the Republican redistricting effort.[31] Also, senators were invited by Democratic organizations in several states to appear at party fund-raisers. Several did so. Senators Gallegos, Shapleigh, and Hinojosa journeyed to Florida for a Democratic gathering. Senators Shapleigh and Barrientos went to Denver on August 28 for a fund-raiser. Over the weekend of August 23–24, several Texas House Democrats, including Terri Hodge (Dallas), Lon Burnam (Fort Worth), and Ruth Jones McClendon (San Antonio), arrived to discuss strategy. They brought bad news. Some of the senators had harbored hopes that the Democrats in the House might stage another walkout and remain gone for the next thirty days, allowing the Democratic senators to return. The House Democrats explained that it would be impossible to secure the agreement of fifty-plus House Democrats to stage another boycott.[32]

Some of the public's messages to the senators were critical and laced with profanity and racial slurs. Republican protesters eventually appeared around the hotel. The Texas Republican Party chair, Susan Weddington, sent the Democratic senators a care package that included diapers and baby toys. Radio ads critical of the Democratic senators' absence from Austin played in some of their home districts. Radio ads run in Senator Hinojosa's district accused him not only of failing to meet his duty in Austin, but also of opposing (Hinojosa says falsely) the Pledge of Allegiance and health-care appropriations. Hinojosa found the ad's actors (who used exaggerated Mexican accents) demeaning to Hispanics.

Dewhurst Raises the Stakes in the Standoff

Throughout August, Dewhurst both courted the absent lawmakers with proposals for compromise and steadily ratcheted up pressures on them for their return.

Dewhurst remained in regular contact with several senators: some of them took care to avoid alienating Dewhurst in case he decided to restore the two-thirds requirement. They commended Dewhurst on his conduct. Royce West said, "I cannot tell you there are no wounds here, but the wounds can heal as long as this does not get personal. The lieutenant governor has handled the disagreement in a professional manner. As long as he continues to do that, it won't cause long-term problems."[33] Leticia Van de Putte said, "He [Dewhurst] has been an excellent lieutenant governor, and we would hope that . . . we can convince him we need that restored."[34] In Austin, Ken Armbrister also praised Dewhurst: "He [Dewhurst] has been very open about wishing we didn't have to deal with this. . . . Given a choice of walking through hot coals or doing this, I think he would probably take the hot coals."[35] Other Democratic senators, however, continued to harbor ill feelings because they thought that Dewhurst had lied to them earlier in 2003 when he said that he would not bring redistricting up. They thought that Dewhurst "has succumbed to the pressure of right-wing leadership out of Washington."[36] Dewhurst insisted to me in 2005 that he was consistent in his position throughout 2003 that the Senate would never take redistricting up *first*.

Dewhurst remained hopeful: "We started this session with 31 friends and colleagues, and we will end this session with 31 friends and colleagues."[37] Some of the Republican senators, however, were less forgiving. In the beginning, many Republicans expected that the Democrats' walkout would last "a couple of days." Republican senators suspected that the Democrats would leave, but, as explained by Senator Troy Fraser, many assumed that they would "get a little national press, get their pictures in the paper and come back."[38] Dewhurst spokesman David Beckwith went so far as to attribute their unwillingness to return to their having been "captured by the Democratic National Committee blowing smoke up their rears and telling them what great Americans they were."[39] Senator Juan Hinojosa denied that he had had any contact with the Democratic National Committee and disputed Fraser's comments as well: "We told everyone we'd be gone 30 days, no more or less until the two-thirds rule was put back in place."[40]

There was a general feeling that both sides had underestimated their partisan colleagues. Senator Van de Putte claimed, "Republicans did not think we were tough enough." [41] *Dallas Morning News* staff writer Gromer Jeffers, Jr., concluded:

> Republicans might have underestimated the resolve of their opponents, most of them Hispanic, that stems, in part, from a scrappy brand of South Texas politics that extols the noble fight. Democrats might have underestimated the GOP's willingness to resort to scorched-earth tactics in a battle closely followed by National leaders. [42]

The newspaper concluded that the unexpected resolve on behalf of both groups was at least partly explained because this was the "ultimate fight" over political power and survival. On the other hand, Senator Ratliff observed, "The real tragedy is that it was all predictable and avoidable. But each step that's taken, just by one more step, destroys the Senate that I knew." [43]

As the Democratic senators remained in Albuquerque, however, Dewhurst and other Republicans in Austin became frustrated. The Senate was under a call, so the senators were not free to return to their homes. The Senate would convene each morning, then stand at ease until the next morning or the next Monday. Initially Dewhurst said that the expectation was that the senators would remain within the Capitol twenty-four hours a day "until the renegades returned." This policy soon became untenable, so senators were allowed to request (and were given) permission to return to their Austin residences; this was cynically labeled a "hall pass." Outside pressure quickly increased from Republican activists, who demanded that Dewhurst and the Republican senators "do something" about these "runaway lawmakers" and teach them a lesson. On August 6 (the same day that his two Senate ambassadors were in Albuquerque to present a proposal for compromise), Dewhurst said that the Senate and the public were losing patience and warned of the possibility of unspecified legal action against the absent senators. He explained, "I am not threatening anyone. All I'm saying is that we're going to be criticized by the people of Texas if the Senate does not act to bring back its absent members . . . Enough is enough." [44] Also on the 6th, Dewhurst met behind closed doors with thirteen Republican senators and afterward repeated his warning that, as presiding officer, he would have to act. Republicans began calling the situation a "constitutional crisis." [45]

The next day, (August 7) Dewhurst and Perry filed an application for a writ of mandamus, asking the Texas Supreme Court to compel the senators to return. The application argued that the senators were under a duty to attend legislative sessions and that the Supreme Court was best situated "to defend the Texas Constitution" by ordering them to return. The court directed the

Democrats to respond by noon on the following Monday, August 11. The simple Democratic response was that the court should not involve itself in a political dispute involving another branch of government. Before the end of the day on Monday, the Supreme Court in a one-line ruling denied the Republicans' request.[46]

The Senate then turned to other measures to put pressure on the Democratic senators. The Republican senators voted on Wednesday, August 13, to give the Democrats forty-eight hours to return or face a fine to begin at $1,000 a day and escalate each day thereafter, up to $5,000 a day. The action was hammered out in a closed meeting of the Republican Caucus. The fines were then approved in an open meeting by a vote of seventeen of the Republican senators. The next day, the Republican senators circulated a proposal to enforce the fines by disallowing parking privileges, cell phones, travel, floor privileges, and certain supply purchases by the staffers of the absent senators. One sanction gained special attention: the absent senators were no longer entitled to give their constituents flags that had flown over the Capitol. The forty-eight-hour deadline passed. In the words of one newspaper, the stalemate "loomed over the ornate but empty senate chamber."[47] On Friday, the Senate voted 15–1 (Armbrister cast the single no vote; Ratliff did not vote) to make the penalties official—in an act described as "tough love"—to bring their colleagues back. Democrats in Albuquerque attacked the penalties as "an incredible abuse of power" and as amounting to a "poll tax."[48]

In interviews conducted in 2005, two Republican senators and the lieutenant governor had different recollections of the Senate's motivations for imposing the fines and sanctions. Senator Jon Lindsay (Houston) recalled that the penalties were "almost tongue-in-cheek": "We never expected the Democratic senators to pay the fines or to do without parking on their return." According to Lindsay, Republican senators at the time needed to appear busy in response to outside pressures and to be seen as "doing something" in Austin. Lieutenant Governor Dewhurst said in 2006 that, in his mind at the time, the penalties were designed to give the Democratic senators an excuse to come back and were not adopted with any thought that they would actually pay the fines. On the other hand, Senator Ratliff recalled that the mood among the Republican senators was one of "frustration and anger. A real vitriolic sense of 'We must levy a severe punishment on these deserters so that this can never happen again. What can we do to them (or their staffs) which will be the most painful and therefore make them return?'" Dewhurst added that he now saw the fines and other sanctions as a mistake that he wished had never happened.

Republican senators tried to maintain a show of public unity behind this show of force. In private, however, there was consternation among the senators about taking such action against their colleagues. Ratliff epitomized this concern by walking out of the Wednesday caucus meeting and by his subsequent unwillingness to be present in the Senate chamber when the fines and enforcement penalties were approved. He expressed concern about whether a Senate without a quorum had authority to adopt such fines and said, "I will not be a party to any of this."[49] Dewhurst asserted that the Texas Constitution (article 3, section 10) authorizes the legislature "to compel the attendance of absent members, in such manner and under such penalties as each House may provide," and that this allowed the remaining members of the Senate to adopt the fines despite the lack of Senate rules specifically authorizing such an action.

Despite concern among some Republican senators about the potential long-term adverse effect of the fines and penalties on bipartisanship in the Senate, even moderate senators endorsed the measures. Republican senators were driven in part by their own pride. As Senator Wentworth explained, "They're [the Democratic Senators are] saying, 'If you will just raise the white flag of surrender, then we'll come home.' We're not going to do that."[50] Similar words of pique, pride, and recalcitrance came from the Democrats in Albuquerque.

Whether the Republican senators actually had authority to adopt the fines and penalties, or thought that the fines would ever actually be paid or the penalties fully imposed, is doubtful. However, these actions served both to satisfy Republican constituents who complained that the Republican senators were not taking steps against the Democrats and to provide a bargaining tool for use against the Democratic senators, who could not be absolutely certain that the fines and penalties would not be enforced.[51]

A potentially more significant risk was the possibility that the Republican-controlled Senate could (after a quorum was restored) adopt new rules doing away with the two-thirds vote requirement altogether.[52] Such a change would significantly affect the operation of the Senate and the ability of any minority, including the Democratic Party, to block legislation or to win compromises in the future. Republican senator Troy Fraser raised the possibility of completely doing away with the requirement because "the majority should rule."[53] Many Republican senators disagreed, including Duncan, who thought that the requirement "promotes consensus."[54] However, Fraser was not the only Republican senator to feel that the two-thirds vote requirement should be discarded. As the stalemate dragged on, additional Republican senators said that they would consider eliminating the two-thirds requirement and adopting a new means of setting legislation for passage.[55] Governor Perry publicly endorsed this idea.[56] Dewhurst made use of this possibility in his dealings with the absent senators, suggesting that if they continued to stay gone and were unwilling to work toward a resolution of the redistricting dispute, the two-thirds vote tradition would be in jeopardy for the future and that the senators "may have won a skirmish or two but lost a big war."[57]

The Democrats' Favorable Endgame Scenarios Fail to Materialize

After the senators' departure, the news media focused on whether the Democratic senators had a winning endgame. Republicans said no; Democrats said yes. Austin political consultant Bill Miller in August 2003 discussed the Democrats' strategy thusly, "I think that leaving the state is a dramatic play and can be effective. But it's not a long-term strategy. And that's the weakness."[58]

The Democratic senators were not without hope that one or more scenarios might play out to give them a victory. Over time, however, each of these potentially favorable scenarios failed to materialize.

Senate Authority to Apprehend the Senators

One Democratic hope was that a court might find that neither the DPS nor the Senate sergeant at arms could force absent senators to return to the Senate chamber. Such a ruling would allow them to continue their boycott, but from their homes or offices in Texas.

In a case brought earlier by Rep. Lon Burnam (Fort Worth), State Judge Chuck Campbell had issued a preliminary ruling that the DPS had no power to hunt for the House lawmakers. At a hearing in that case on July 28, Democratic lawyers asked the judge to extend the ban to the absent senators. Judge Campbell delayed his final ruling in the House case, but made clear that his final order would not include a ban on hunting senators since no senator was a party to the litigation.

After the judge's oral ruling, first assistant attorney general Barry McBee said that he would advise the DPS to go after the absent senators. McBee also sent Dewhurst a letter, advising him that the Senate sergeant at arms or any officers appointed by him "have full legal authority to arrest absent senators wherever they may be found."[59]

Despite the ruling, Dewhurst said he would not use DPS officers for the search. He held open the possibility, however, of directing the Senate sergeant at arms to hire private security personnel or off-duty police to look for the Democrats. This led some Democrats to allege that Dewhurst was intending to use "bounty hunters." The lieutenant governor's spokesperson downplayed such a possibility, but initially did not absolutely deny it. So also, Senate sergeant at arms Turner initially noted that he had no "present plans" or instructions to look for anyone in New Mexico.

Dewhurst addressed the "bounty hunter" claim by indicating that there is always some "comic relief" in any situation and that there were no bounty hunters headed for New Mexico.[60] He said, "You're not going to see senators brought back in handcuffs as long as I'm lieutenant governor." At the same time, however, he reaffirmed his view that Senate sergeant at arms had an absolute right (within Texas anyway) to "present a warrant of arrest . . . and compel the return of an absent member."[61]

Lawyers for the Democrats tried again in court by filing suit on Thursday, August 7, asking a Travis County district court to rule that the senators could not be arrested if they returned to Texas. Democrats claimed that a governor could call a special session only under extraordinary circumstances, and that partisan redistricting did not meet this constitutional requirement. This state lawsuit was later voluntarily dismissed when Democrats tried unsuccessfully to add the claims to a lawsuit that had been filed in federal court in Laredo.

The Democratic senators decided against attending the hearing of the federal lawsuit on August 27 because of the risk of being confronted by the Senate sergeant at arms or other officers authorized to return them to the Senate. The second special session had ended, but rumors existed that the governor would quickly call a third while the senators were at the hearing, thereby allowing them to be arrested.

Dewhurst acknowledged to me in 2005 that he had considered sending Senate sergeants to the August 27 hearing but decided not to after conferring with his staff. Dewhurst said, however, that Senate sergeants were sent to the home of some Democratic senators or their family members. He insisted that the sergeants were authorized only to ask the senators to call Dewhurst, not to arrest anyone. On August 29, Senate sergeants were sent to watch the homes of at least three Democratic senators in expectation that they might return for the Labor Day holiday. Since the legislature was not in session, the sergeants had no authority to compel the senators to return to Austin. There was speculation at the time, however, that if any Democratic senators were spotted, the governor would quickly call a special session, and with a minimum of six senators present, the Senate could place a call on the Senate chamber and reauthorize the sergeants to make an arrest. The lieutenant governor's office did not comment on its strategy. The surveillance came to naught, since none of the Democratic senators appeared.

The effect of these events was to dispel any hope that the senators might continue their boycott while at home and on the job in Texas. As a result, throughout their boycott the Democratic senators remained concerned about the possibility of being "captured," even in New Mexico. Any return to Texas by any senator would have risked the success of the boycott.

A Dewhurst Agreement to Adhere to the Two-Thirds Vote Requirement

At their first news conference in Albuquerque, Senator Barrientos set forth the basic bargaining position of the Democratic senators. They would return when Dewhurst agreed to adhere to the requirement for a two-thirds vote on the redistricting bill. Dewhurst, however, was showing no willingness to do so except in conjunction with an agreement by enough Democrats to vote to take up a redistricting bill. Instead, he stated publicly: "If I read the tea leaves correctly, we will pass a fair redistricting plan now or later. It is hot outside, I prefer to pass it now."[62]

Instead of backing away from his decision about the vote requirement, Dewhurst seized the initiative. He wrote opinion pieces that appeared in several state newspapers, arguing that there was no right of senators to break a quorum.[63] Moreover, he urged that he was honoring Senate tradition and precedent by not requiring a two-thirds vote on legislation in a special session: "Tradition must be set aside on redistricting, particularly in special session." He pointed out that a two-thirds vote had not been required to take up redistricting in the 1971, 1981, or 1992 special sessions. He based his public statements on a detailed historical memorandum prepared by Patsy Spaw, secretary of the Senate.

Although Democrats disputed Dewhurst's historical account of the vote requirement, the hope that Dewhurst might back down was clearly fruitless. The two-thirds vote requirement would not apply during any future special sessions in 2003.

Avoiding Additional Special Sessions

One Democratic hope was that the walkout and a subsequent public outcry against unnecessary redistricting and special sessions might cause Governor Perry to refrain from calling additional special sessions. If that happened, the senators' thirty-day stay in Albuquerque would end the dispute.

Senator Van de Putte explained, "We hope that the governor understands we're firm in our commitment and decision that redistricting is not in the best interest of Republicans." Each special session was estimated to cost $1.7 million. Democrats accused the governor of spending over $5 million on unnecessary special sessions. The art of "gerrymandering" soon became known by Democrats as "Perrymandering." Several newspapers criticized Perry for his alleged "lack of leadership" in allowing partisan redistricting to take priority over other state business.[64]

However, despite the Democrats' media efforts, no public outcry against either redistricting or Perry ever arose. Polls (e.g., the Scripps Howard poll) suggested that the public in general was unhappy with both sides. While Perry's overall approval rating dropped (six points in August, to 44 percent), his rating among self-identified Republicans remained high (65 percent), and the majority of Republicans supported him in the redistricting battle.

Perry remained firm, stating by August 15 that he would call additional special sessions as necessary to secure passage of the redistricting. He explained the need for additional special sessions in part by claiming that there was other business that the legislature could not finish until the Democrats returned. Whether these other matters needed legislative action or warranted a special session was disputed by the Democratic senators and by some sources in Texas, but the governor's claim successfully deflected some public concern about the costs of additional special sessions.

Any hope that the governor might back away from calling a third or fourth special session disappeared.

Enjoining a Change in the Two-Thirds Vote Requirement

Several of the attorneys advising the Democratic senators believed that by deciding not to continue the two-thirds vote requirement, Dewhurst had made a change in an election practice or procedure without first preclearing it with the U.S. Department of Justice under Section 5 of the Voting Rights Act. If so, the change could be enjoined by a federal court.

The Democrats filed a lawsuit (*Barrientos v. Texas*) on August 11 in Laredo to enjoin the alleged election change. The Democrats hoped to be heard before U.S. District Judge Keith P. Ellison, a Democratic appointee, and expected the forum to be a friendly one. Judge Ellison, however, recused himself, and the case passed to District Judge George P. Kazen. He too had been appointed by a Democratic president, Carter.

Trying to short-circuit any adverse court decision on the vote requirement, the attorney general and the secretary of state of Texas on August 19 submitted the issue to the Justice Department and asked either for preclearance or for an opinion that Dewhurst's decision not to require two-thirds vote in the special session was merely "an internal operating rule" not covered by the Voting Rights Act. On learning of the Texas request, Democratic counsel Gerald Hebert (himself a former Justice Department attorney) wrote Justice urging that it "not fall prey to the considerable political pressures that will be brought

upon it by Republican office holders in Texas, national Republican Party officials and even the Political Director of the White House." Essentially, Hebert's
letter was intended to persuade the department at least not to rush to judgment
on the issue.

On August 20, the Democrats attempted to amend their complaint to add
a claim challenging the right of the Senate sergeant at arms to arrest the senators as well as the right of the Republican senators to impose fines, penalties,
and other sanctions, the latter being an infringement of the senators' right of
freedom of speech. In addition, the amended complaint asked the court to determine whether Governor Perry had the right to call a special session, arguing
that redistricting was not an "extraordinary" circumstance under the Texas Constitution. The Democrats also complained that the attorney general of Texas
was "disingenuous" for contending before the federal court that Dewhurst's
decision to not require a two-thirds vote was not an election change under the
Voting Rights Act while in "secret" simultaneously asking Justice to preclear it.

Despite the letter from Gerald Hebert and contrary to the expectations of
many attorneys, who were surprised by the speed with which the department
acted, Justice sent a letter on August 26 indicating that Dewhurst's decision
was not an election change requiring preclearance under the Voting Rights
Act. This decision bode badly for the scheduled federal-court hearing.

Judge Kazen heard the Democratic and Republican arguments on Wednesday, August 27, for ninety minutes at the federal courthouse in Laredo. Under
federal law, he could temporarily enjoin a change in election laws, but otherwise was severely limited in his authority as a single judge hearing an action
under Section 5 of the Voting Rights Act. He could dismiss the action only if
it was wholly insubstantial or obviously frivolous. Therefore, he did not. He
said he agreed that drawing a new map was a "bad idea," but made clear that he
was very skeptical about the Democrats' legal argument.[65] While he lamented
the loss of civility and bipartisanship in the legislature, he found no merit in
the Democrats' argument that the Republicans' actions (i.e., the search for the
senators and the imposition of fines and penalties) were forbidden by the U.S.
Constitution. He implied that the Democrats were sore losers: "The fact is, in
a legislative body, you win some and you lose some. I know the senators represent people, but if they're in the minority, they're going to lose votes. That's
how the country works. The majority wins."[66]

The Democrats' lawyers should have been discouraged, but they found
some hope because Judge Kazen had not dismissed the suit and because he
had suggested that the governor should give senators seventy-two-hour notice
of any new session to prevent their surprise arrest. Reporters were allowed to
listen in on part of a teleconference between the senators and their attorneys in

which the attorneys reportedly gave a "rosy view of the judge's statements."[67] However, when attorney Renea Hicks filed pleadings on Thursday asking Kazen for an order requiring such notice, Kazen was gone. A similar plea to the governor went unanswered. Instead, Attorney General Abbott immediately filed a written opposition to the motion before Kazen asking for notice.

As required by federal law, Kazen convened a three-judge court to hear the Voting Rights Act claim. Two additional judges, Patrick Higginbotham of the Fifth Circuit Court of Appeals and Lee Rosenthal of the Southern District of Texas, were assigned. Judge Higginbotham had served on the three-judge panel that had drawn the congressional redistricting plan in 2001. Higginbotham and Rosenthal had been appointed to the federal bench by Republican presidents, Higginbotham by Ford and Rosenthal by George H. W. Bush. The three-judge panel heard the Democrats' argument on September 11. The judges were skeptical about the merits of the Democrats' arguments. For example, Judge Higginbotham said, jokingly, "I suggest that taking away parking in Austin is a federal question."[68] Attorneys for the Democrats admitted that they were "disturbed" by the court's skepticism: they saw it as "a dead-on case" and hoped that "on further reflection" the judges would agree with the senators.[69] The next day, however, the federal court decided unanimously against the Democrats and dismissed the litigation.[70] The Democrats' fight to retain the two-thirds vote requirement had failed.

Staying in Albuquerque Past a Legal Deadline

The ultimate strategy if all others failed was for the Democrats to remain absent long enough to prevent the Republicans from adopting and implementing a new districting plan in time for the primary elections scheduled for March 2004. This tactic would allow the senators to take advantage of anticipated delays before the Department of Justice and the federal courts, as well as existing state statutory deadlines, to prevent a new redistricting plan from being used to elect congressmen in 2004.

Any redistricting bill would have to obtain preclearance from the Justice Department, which has sixty days to review the plan and enter any legal objections to it. The department generally takes the full sixty days for its review. Based on this timeline, at least one newspaper speculated that a new redistricting plan would need to be approved by the legislature and signed by the governor by mid-September. Another suggested that the plan would need to be submitted to allow enough time for Justice Department action before December 3, when candidate filing was scheduled to begin, or at least before January 2, when candidate filing was scheduled to close.

If the new redistricting plan was precleared, litigation could further delay implementation. Therefore, there was a hope that by staying "a couple more months," the Democratic senators could prevent any new redistricting plan from taking effect for the 2004 elections. Some Democrats were quoted as believing that any plan passed after September 1 would have little chance of gaining the required Justice Department approval.

Unfortunately for the Democrats, no clear legal deadline existed. Generalizations about how much time is needed to implement redistricting, or about the sanctity of state statutory deadlines, are not applicable in a major redistricting. Both the Justice Department and the federal courts have historically acted expeditiously when necessary to allow state elections to go forward under new redistricting plans. Statutory deadlines and requirements have been suspended in the past to allow elections to proceed smoothly.

Although as a general rule Justice review may take sixty days or longer, I am aware of the department having precleared redistricting plans in less than twenty-four hours when necessary to avoid interfering in important elections. So also, federal courts have frequently expedited litigation and changed state statutory deadlines, such as filing dates, to accommodate implementation of new redistricting plans. Justice Department officials and federal judges generally are aware of major redistricting disputes as they develop—long before the disputes reach the court—and of the need to reasonably accommodate the actions of state legislatures. Such awareness certainly existed in 2003 in the Justice Department under John Ashcroft and among judges in Texas who were watching the redistricting dispute head inexorably for the courts.

Republicans in the state legislature also had a strategy for countering the Democratic hope for delay. Rep. Phil King filed a bill in the second special session to allow the secretary of state to postpone the state's filing deadline long enough to buy more time to stave off court challenges. King predicted that such a change would allow the legislature to act as late as November to finally approve a redistricting plan. Even though no action could be taken on the bill in the second session, the bill constituted a warning that the Republican legislative majority could change the election timetable, including the filing deadline or even the timing of the spring primary itself, to accommodate a late-passed redistricting bill. King acknowledged that the change in the filing deadline was intended to "take away any chance of victory" for the Democrats by delay.[71] Although such a bill would require preclearance under the Voting Rights Act, Justice would almost certainly try to expedite its decision under the circumstances.

Therefore, any Democratic hope that victory would come from Republicans' running out of time was always problematic. There was no deadline beyond which success was assured. Even staying away until late in the year (e.g., through October or November), however, did not guarantee that Republicans could not find a means of changing the filing and primary schedule to allow the 2004 general elections to be conducted under a new redistricting plan.

In hindsight, it can be suggested that the boycott would have been more effective if it had come later in the year, after the Republicans had fought among themselves over West Texas. There was little or no way, however, for Democrats to know on July 28 that Republicans might spend weeks or months battling among themselves over the congressional boundaries. On the other hand, faced with less time to act, the Republicans might have reached agreement sooner.

Democrats Play the Race Card?

After the Democratic senators departed from Austin, their comments in the media increasingly contained accusations that what was happening in the Senate had racial and ethnic overtones. Some of this increased emphasis on racial and ethnic issues was undoubtedly due to the media's desire to portray the boycott as more than a partisan dispute.

Nevertheless, the rhetoric from the senators in Albuquerque became tinged with suggestions of racial discrimination. The comments were directed not only at the Republican redistricting plan, which raised serious issues of illegal vote dilution, but also at the steps that the Republicans had ostensibly taken to try to trap the Democrats in Austin at the beginning of the second special session, to change the two-thirds vote requirement, and to impose fines and other penalties on the absent senators. For example, on arriving in Albuquerque, Senator Van de Putte described how the proposed redistricting plan would defeat Anglo Democrat congressmen, meaning that "over 1.4 million minority Texans will have no advocates because their homes will be drawn into districts in which they will have no voice in choosing their member of Congress."[72] She described the alleged Republican plan of calling a second session immediately and locking the senators in the Senate chamber as having been taken by "white Republicans" to harm her minority constituents. Subsequently, she called the action by the "white" Republicans "unconscionable."[73]

In regard to the fines and penalties, Senator Zaffirini said, "It is very clear: All of the Anglos who are representing Anglo districts are in Austin taking unprecedented illegal, immoral actions against all of us who are either minorities or represent minorities."[74] Senator Whitmire explained on August 13 that "I can dance around it all I want to, but it is a color issue": the dilutive effect of the plan, the attempt to limit the right of minorities to affect legislation by rescinding the two-thirds vote requirement, and the fines levied against the senators for "voting with their feet" through the boycott.[75] Dewhurst professed to be upset by this emphasis on race: "At the end of the day this race card is sheer Democratic, partisan baloney. It is wrong. Here in Texas we all believe in protecting all voter rights, including minority rights."[76]

The Democrats' effort to cast the standoff in racial and ethnic terms is understandable.

- First, the proposed redistricting plans were designed to maximize Republican voting strength while minimizing Democratic voting strength. Since racial and ethnic minorities in Texas voted overwhelmingly Democratic, the plans overall worked against minority voting strength except where Republicans were bound for legal reasons to do otherwise.

- Second, any successful legal challenge to a final redistricting plan would likely rest on proving racial or ethnic discrimination, so a Democratic portrayal of the dispute as racial instead of partisan had potential long-term value.

- Third, state and national media were attracted by the "race" aspect of the standoff, so a catchy comment implying or alleging racial or ethnic discrimination was more likely to attract media attention.

- Fourth, all the eleven senators but one were from districts in which racial or ethnic minorities made up at least 62 percent of the population.[77] Therefore, Democratic senators "could play to their constituents" (just as the Republicans in Austin were doing) by emphasizing the adverse effect on minorities of what the Republicans were doing.

- Fifth, as national media turned its attention to the senators, the race issue became not only catchy but, for the National Democratic Party, a means of "energizing its base" nationwide for the upcoming 2004 elections.

- Finally, however, perhaps the biggest cause of the Democratic senators' increased mention of race was that the African American and Hispanic senators were becoming more and more incensed that Republican officials and senators (all white, relatively wealthy, and from largely segregated communities) had the audacity to be publicly telling the minority senators what was best for minority voters. Every time some Anglo Republican claimed that redistricting was for the benefit of minority voters, the minority Democratic senators would become livid. Senator Van de Putte said that some of the minority senators who traditionally had been the most likely to vote with Republicans in the Senate became the most rabid in their adverse reaction to Republican comments.[78]

Although perhaps understandable, the emphasis on racial discrimination ultimately had a negative effect on the Democrats' ability to win the dispute in Texas.

Some constituents were turned on by such rhetoric, but some of the senators' constituents were turned off. The greater problem, however, was in predominately Anglo areas outside of these senators' districts. Some Republicans welcomed the Democrat strategy. GOP consultant Royal Masset said, "They'll fire up Hispanics in the Rio Grande Valley. But racial polarization will basically swing more Anglos to (the Republican) column."[79] Masset put the Democratic use of race in frank terms, indicating that the message being sent by the Democrats "gets Bubba to be more Republican."[80] Republicans viewed their risk of alienating Anglo voters on the issue as minimal. The increased emphasis on racial and ethnic discrimination did not generate public pressure on the lieutenant governor or governor to stop the redistricting process.

To the extent that the Democrats' rhetoric caused Anglo voters statewide to increasingly identify the label "Democrat" primarily with complaints about racial discrimination, the strategy unintentionally furthered the Republican objective of branding the Democratic Party in Texas as a party primarily for racial and ethnic minorities.

A Democratic Effort to Hold Bush Responsible

Another element of the Democratic strategy emerged in early August. The senators sent a letter to President George W. Bush on August 10, asking him to intervene. The letter said, "Your continued silence is being interpreted by thoughtful Americans as complicity or as tacit approval." The letter indicated that the actions of Karl Rove, Tom DeLay, and Texas Republicans have "cast a shadow over your legacy here."[81] A White House spokesman dismissed redistricting as a Texas issue and said that the president would have no response.[82]

Bush's responsibility for what happened in Texas is a legitimate issue. As I discuss later, I believe that the president bears ultimate responsibility for what happened. However, the Democratic senators could not have reasonably expected that Bush would respond favorably to the public scolding in their letter, which was seen by many at the time as having been instigated by the national Democratic Party in an attempt to gain political advantage nationwide for the 2004 election by embarrassing the president.

Whatever its potential advantage to Democrats nationally, the letter struck a negative note in Texas. Most Texans, especially Anglo Texans, strongly supported Bush, even if they did not favor redistricting. Bush had twice won election as governor and won the state handily in his race for president in 2000. Texans who were possibly prepared to believe the worst about DeLay and even the Texas Republican leaders were upset about the Democrats' attack on Bush. For example, an Amarillo paper that previously had editorialized against redistricting and had criticized DeLay for "sticking his nose in state business" excoriated the Democrats "for wanting the partisan poison to spill all the way to Washington, D.C." The paper said that cajoling Bush to become involved in an "embarrassing chapter in Texas history" was inappropriate.[83]

Democrats aggravated the situation by making the challenge to Bush personal. Senator Zaffirini was quoted as saying, "Will he [Bush] be man enough to do the right thing, will he be man enough to call off the political attack dogs, will he be man enough to say to Karl Rove, his brain, 'Back off, you are wrong.'"[84] Dewhurst dismissed the Democrats' attempts to blame Bush as being "shameful, partisan spin."

The Democrats' attempt to shift responsibility for the redistricting dispute to President Bush backfired.

Public Opinion Shifts

From the moment the Democratic senators departed, both sides were engaged in a public-relations spin contest. Over time the rhetoric became stale, and public support shifted away from the Democrats.

The main Republican theme was to shame the Democrats into returning by claiming that they owed it to their constituents to show up for work. In 2005, Jim Ellis credited Governor Perry with first stating that the Democrats had no winning strategy. Ellis recalls that Perry urged his fellow Republicans to just "sit tight" and let the public and press attention fade.[85]

The Democrats said that the Republican redistricting was unnecessary, punitive, mean-spirited, and short-sighted—and expensive, at $1.7 million a special session. They pointed out that many editorials statewide earlier in the year had opposed redistricting as unnecessary and that an overwhelming number of witnesses had testified against it. They cited the Senate Jurisprudence Committee report that 89 percent of the 2,620 persons who testified at the redistricting hearings spoke against redistricting; only 8 percent supported it. Republicans dismissed the hearing testimony as party-driven. According to Dewhurst, "Obviously, a lot of time when you're having public testimony different political parties try to get their activists turned out."[86]

Both sides tried to publicly exude confidence. Senator West on August 4 said, "If I were a betting man considering a wager on how long we'll continue, if we'll hold or if we'll fold, I'd place my chips on the Texas 11."[87] Around the middle of August, Democratic senators claimed that they were winning on the public-relations and tactical fronts and were confident that political and legal momentum was on their side. They saw the fines approved by the Republican senators as illegal and a "sign of desperation."

Other observers saw the situation differently. Dr. Cal Jillson, a political science professor at Southern Methodist University said, "The public is sitting back, sort of bemused at this point."[88] Republican pollster Mike Baselice in Austin predicted that the downsides to a partisan standoff were minimal for Republicans: "The general public does not see it as that powerful a deal. The public views redistricting as a political issue that does not affect paychecks or quality of life."[89] The *San Antonio Express-News* on August 9 noted that voters were "tuning out the remap flap" and that the subject was "losing their attention fast."

As the summer progressed and the partisan and racial rhetoric increased, a shift of opinion was discernible in most newspapers. Many that had earlier strongly editorialized against redistricting began, by August, wishing for the whole "mess" to end. On July 31, the *Fort Worth Star-Telegram* carried a staff opinion piece claiming that neither side of the political war was telling the truth about what was at stake. On August 3, a senior writer with the same paper lamented the continuing game of "political chicken" in an article entitled "The humor of the redistricting squabble is wearing thin." The *Texarkana Gazette* on August 14 called it "The silly season." Even largely Democratic Travis County was becoming restive, as the *Austin American-Statesman* suggested: "The facts seem to indicate that there is plenty of blame to go around for this mess. Both parties share guilt for twisting and spinning"; activist Robin Rather added, "Redistricting is so far down the list of things people care about now that it wouldn't make the top 10,000."[90]

This shift by the newspapers was not one in favor the state's Republican officials or redistricting. For example, the *Lubbock Avalanche-Journal* on July 30 indicated that it was "stunned by his [Governor Perry's] lack of leadership and cavalier attitude concerning redistricting." It cynically asked whether Perry had been offered a cabinet post in the Bush administration if "he presses forward." The paper finished with a plea: "Mr. Perry, it's time to stop this nonsense and move on to making Texas a better place for Texans." *The El Paso Times* on August 17 suggested that the Republicans should consider redistricting Mars because it had not been redistricted in "possibly hundreds of thousands of years" and is "probably Republican anyway." However, the paper concluded that, for now, "both sides should take a break from their little (science) fictions and return to Earth, Texas—and reality."

Nevertheless, the weariness of the public and the newspapers with the running political battle worked against any Democratic will to remain longer in Albuquerque. An opinion piece in the generally Democrat-friendly *San Antonio Express-News* on August 21 agreed that the Democratic senators earlier had no choice but to "vote with their feet" by leaving the state, but concluded

> Now they have no choice but to come home and fight what is obviously a flawed redistricting plan at the U.S. Justice Department and in federal court. . . . So now everyone's pointing the finger at race. . . . The Democrats have made their point. . . . But the summer is coming to an end. The schoolchildren in Texas are back at their desks. Texas Democrats have fought a good fight. Now they ought to get back home and throw themselves at the mercy of the federal courts.

A final stroke against the Democrats on the public-opinion front came with the release of a poll on the issue. On August 25, a survey was released of Texans polled during August 7–21.[91] It showed that 62 percent now opposed the Democrats' boycott. The survey by the Scripps Data Center in Abilene showed that those surveyed opposed the redistricting effort by 46 to 40 percent, but that only 29 percent supported the Democrats in their walkout. Forty-seven percent supported Perry calling another special session and 40 percent were opposed; of those supporting the calling of a special session, 30 percent changed their minds when told the cost would be $1.7 million. Republican West Texas appeared to be a bastion of opposition to redistricting: 57 percent opposed the governor's decision to call a second special session. The survey was of 1,000 adults statewide, and had a margin of error of plus or minus 3 percentage points (or more in the subgroups). Democrats questioned the validity of the poll and expressed their confidence that "people are opposed to redistricting."[92]

Dewhurst's public position hardened. Initially hesitant about redistricting, Dewhurst by late August seemingly smelled blood and triumph over the wayward senators. His representative David Beckwith said, "Every Republican I know believes the state's congressional delegation should reflect the voting patterns of Texas, which are solidly pro-Bush. Our current congressional delegation opposes President Bush and his policies. It's an outrage."[93]

The Democrats lost the public-opinion battle in Texas. Their effort to generate enough public indignation over the Republican redistricting effort and the expense of the multiple special sessions failed. They could not budge the Republicans' resolve.

No Easy Way Home

By August 16, at least one Democratic senator was wondering publicly about how the boycott would end. Senator Whitmire commented, "I don't know how it will end. I know it will end. I assume we must return sooner or later. We've got members out here at great personal hardship: new babies, sick parents, jobs, clients."[94] The senators' public comments increasingly shifted toward a timetable for staying in New Mexico until the end of the thirty days. Senator Hinojosa on August 16 acknowledged, "I wish I was in Texas, but we will be here for the 30 days and then we will consider our options."[95] Whitmire said a few days later, "I am homesick. But I'm going to do what it takes." Other Democrats tried to present a different face. Senator Zaffirini said, "If we're going to be here until Christmas, some of us are going to learn to ski."[96]

Dewhurst seemed to have a heightened sense that the boycott would soon end. On August 22 he suggested that there should be a "cooling-off" period for Senate Republicans and Democrats before the next special session.[97] Dewhurst said he was optimistic about the Democrats' possible return based on recent conversations between Republican and Democratic senators.[98] On Monday the 25th, Dewhurst spoke by videoconference with the senators in Albuquerque. In his interview with me in 2006, he recalled that he again told the Democrats that he wanted a "fair" redistricting plan that both Democrats and Republicans could support. He said he pledged to remain committed to any such agreed-upon plan. He may even have offered to put his pledge in writing or to cement it by a rule change. The Democrats offered no response. To Dewhurst, the conference showed that the Democratic senators were waiting for the result of the federal court hearing in Laredo. To the Democrats, Dewhurst had not said "anything new." Some dispute whether Dewhurst ever offered a rule change.

The governor did not publicly accept Dewhurst's notion of a cooling-off period, but he refrained from immediately announcing any call for a third session. He said, "I'm chilling right now. We're out of session."[99] The second special session ended quietly on August 26 at 10 a.m.

Following the disappointing hearing in Laredo before Judge Kazen on the 27th, spirits sank in Albuquerque. Democratic lawyers still professed confidence about the strength of their case. Many senators, however, began to see the stark reality that there was no winning endgame to the boycott. Senator Whitmire said, "If Rick Perry is willing to call unlimited special sessions and use every means available, it [redistricting] would be difficult to stop."[100] Divisions began to show publicly among the Democratic senators.

Whitmire admitted to reporters that he was homesick and would be going home to Houston for the Labor Day holiday.[101] He said that the standoff "may be the worst waste of human or political energy that I've seen in my 30 years in the Legislature" and that "I would be less than candid with you if I did not express that I am concerned about the ultimate endgame." Now speaking from a distinctly third-person perspective, he said that he regretted that both sides were "dug in" and "working toward their base and they don't want to make it look like they're blinking."[102] Senator Van de Putte reacted sharply to Whitmire's comments, and was reported to have said in a closed meeting of the senators that "Whitmire has poured us out."[103]

Later on August 28 as some senators began to leave Albuquerque for Labor Day, Senator Van de Putte sought to downplay the schism: "John Whitmire will be here on Tuesday [when the senators were to gather after the holidays]. He's a rock. He's the dean of the Senate."[104] Senator Whitmire too sought to underscore Democratic unity by indicating that he was not going back to Houston and that "[t]here is no split in our solidarity."[105] Some senators were fearful of going to Texas even though the Senate was no longer in session because there were rumors that their homes were being watched by Senate sergeants.

Despite his statement of solidarity, Senator Whitmire did travel to Houston for the Labor Day holiday. In 2005 Whitmire told me that while there he spoke with Lieutenant Governor Dewhurst.[106] Dewhurst confirmed that this discussion took place. Neither Whitmire nor Dewhurst, however, would disclose to me the substance of this discussion. However, Whitmire said he also received a telephone call from Tony Sanchez, the unsuccessful Democratic candidate for governor in 2002. Whitmire recalled that Sanchez indicated that he wanted to move all of the Democratic senators from Albuquerque to Washington, D.C. Whitmire said that he had considered Sanchez's proposal "crazy." While in Houston, Whitmire visited with aides and friends. He told me that he found that people back in his district had long ago given up caring about why the Democratic senators were in Albuquerque or what could be gained or lost by their continued absence. Despite a call from Van de Putte, Whitmire made up his mind that it was foolish to continue the boycott.

Whitmire returned to Albuquerque briefly on the following Tuesday before leaving New Mexico for Texas and effectively ending the boycott. He told his colleagues, "After being in my district for five days, I have concluded my constituents are opposed to redistricting, but they also believe that the fight should be on the Senate floor."[107] While in Albuquerque, Whitmire tried to convince his Democratic colleagues to follow him back to Texas; they refused. By Tuesday night, September 3, Whitmire was back in Houston.

The mood at the Albuquerque hotel was somber as the other senators expressed disappointment with Whitmire's decision. No Democratic senator announced on September 3 that he or she would end their stay in New Mexico, but with Whitmire's return to Texas and expected presence in the Senate for the next special session, the continued absence of the ten remaining senators became irrelevant to the passage of redistricting legislation.

The boycott was effectively over.

Commentary

The Democratic senators' boycott was a personally brave and costly act. Senator Van de Putte said that walking out on the Senate and staying away to break a quorum was "[t]he bravest thing that I have ever done."[108] Staying away for over four weeks meant lost income and missing out on family or personal relationships. However, the Democrats all along lacked a viable endgame. As discussed above, there were several possible scenarios that could have ended with a Democratic victory. By the summer of 2003, however, none was realistic. The legal theory behind enjoining the two-thirds vote requirement was never a winner. In reality, the fundamental Democratic strategy was predicated on either convincing Dewhurst to reinstate the two-thirds requirement or making the Republicans back down. The strategy failed. As the Democrats hardened their position against returning, state Republicans hardened their position for passing a partisan redistricting. Both sides underestimated the will and determination of the other. It was the Republicans who ultimately and predictably had the upper hand, with their control over the Department of Justice, all of the state elective offices (including a governor who was committed to calling special sessions), and the state legislature (with the ability to move state election dates back to allow late passage of a redistricting plan). The federal court that heard the Democrats' challenge to the two-thirds vote requirement was dominated by Republican appointees, but even the lone Democrat on the court dismissed the Democrats' arguments. Behind it all, the Republicans had Tom DeLay and the national Republican Party committed to not allowing the Democrat Anglo incumbents to survive.

The boycott did not stop the Republican redistricting. However, for some Democratic senators it ultimately paid a dividend because it brought national attention to DeLay and his "ruthless quest for power." They credit the attention given to events in Texas as the beginning of the series of problems that later confronted the congressman, prompting him to step aside as majority leader and to resign from Congress.

CHAPTER 11

Republican Triumph in the Senate

We're here, and finally we've got a quorum. The Democrats have shown up, and we can do the business we were all elected to do.
— LIEUTENANT GOVERNOR DAVID DEWHURST, SEPTEMBER 15, 2003

By the first week in September, only ten Democratic senators remained in Albuquerque. The number was insufficient to prevent Republicans from gathering a quorum in the Texas Senate. It seemed only a matter of time before these senators too would return to Austin.

Although the end of the boycott was proclaimed by some news sources as "Perry's Famous Victory," the person most responsible for the Republican success had been Lieutenant Governor David Dewhurst. Dewhurst had been patient but persistent throughout the walkout, and he had largely avoided being drawn into personal conflicts with the absent senators. By alternately publicly pressuring the Democratic senators and privately coddling and entreating them, Dewhurst and his chief of staff, Bruce Gibson, had successfully piloted the Republicans through the rough waters of the summer. Dewhurst continued to gently but relentlessly urge the senators' return: "They fought a good fight. It's time for them to come back."[1]

By September 2003, Republicans began to focus on reaching agreement on a redistricting plan and having it in place for the March 2004 primary elections. It had been clear since early summer that Republicans did not fully agree among themselves about the specifics of a final redistricting map. Efforts to resolve those differences over the summer had largely been neglected because of the distraction of the boycott. The biggest difference between the House and Senate versions concerned the districts in West Texas. This disagreement and others lingered unresolved. However, neither Congressman DeLay nor his allies were prepared to allow such difficulties to derail a final plan.

Regrouping in Albuquerque

After Whitmire's departure, the ten Democratic senators in Albuquerque re-grouped to consider their options. The senators now called themselves "The Texas 11 Minus One."

Their battle was now being fought on two fronts. To actually block re-districting in Texas, there remained only three possibilities. If another senator could be convinced to leave Texas, the quorum could still be broken. Sena-tor Rodney Ellis called and asked Bill Ratliff, but the Republican senator was not prepared to join them. The second possibility was that at least fifty-one members of the Texas House could be persuaded to join the senators or to leave Texas in their own boycott. Democrats in the House held out no hope for such a walkout. The third possibility was that despite their obvious skepti-cism about the Democrats' arguments under the Voting Rights Act, the three judges on the federal panel might still rule in their favor and enjoin Dewhurst from eliminating the need for a two-thirds vote in the upcoming third special session. None of these possibilities seemed promising.

The second front was national. The absent senators had become the focus of national and international attention. This fame came during the beginning of a national presidential campaign in which Democrats were out to defeat Presi-dent George W. Bush. Democrats nationwide tried to build on the plight of the Texas senators. Even with Whitmire's departure, planned visits with seven of the senators by presidential hopefuls Howard Dean, Dick Gephardt, and Joe Lieberman went ahead on September 3.[2] Senators Leticia Van de Putte, Eliot Shapleigh, and Rodney Ellis joined some Texas congressmen in Wash-ington at the National Press Club on September 4.

The Texas senators became part of an eight-city "Defending Democracy Tour" organized and financed by MoveOn.org.[3] The tour, along with radio, TV, and newspaper ads, was directed at states considered important to the outcome in the presidential election and specifically at cities with large Latino populations (e.g., Phoenix, Miami, Chicago, and Los Angeles). The cam-paign's slogan was "Don't mess with Texas. Don't mess with democracy." At least one of the Texas senators was the marquee speaker at each rally. Senator Zaffirini was invited to present the Democratic Party's weekly radio response to the president. Senators Mario Gallegos, Juan Hinojosa, and Eliot Shapleigh were together in south Florida to talk about "recount, recall and redistricting, the new three R's of Republican extremism."[4] This national campaign report-edly cost MoveOn.com approximately $1 million, which it raised in essentially one week through an Internet appeal to its members.

The Democratic senators responded to this national attention by directing their public attacks increasingly toward President Bush and Karl Rove. For example, on September 3 in conjunction with the visit of Democratic presidential hopefuls Dean and Gephardt, the senators issued a statement: "We intend to force the President's hand. He may either own up to his behind-the-scenes involvement or he can make the phone call that will stop this sham process."[5]

Spokesmen for Karl Rove and President Bush dismissed the claims of White House involvement in Texas redistricting as "baseless." White House press secretary Scott McClellan indicated that the president is "always concerned about Texas. It's his home. It's a matter for Texas."[6] Dewhurst's office countered the Democrats' allegations by claiming that the only coordinated national effort "is coming from the national Democratic Party and liberal left-wing forces" such as MoveOn.org.[7]

MoveOn.org continued its interest in Texas redistricting even after the legislature convened in its third special session. The organization ran TV ads in Texas attacking Governor Perry for wasting taxpayer money on redistricting. Perry's office responded by pointing out that he had included items such as transportation, trauma centers, and rural schools within the subjects for the session. Even as the third special session drew to a close in October, the Democratic senators continued to receive support from celebrity sources. On October 7, actor Alec Baldwin came to Austin to raise money for the Democrats. At the event, he criticized Karl Rove and, holding up a box of dog biscuits, said, "I wanted to give this to Tom DeLay's lapdog, Rick Perry." He said that the Republican Party "has been taken over by a lot of extremist, right-wing wackos."[8]

Most of the Democratic senators reentered Texas on September 10 for the first time since leaving Austin on July 28. Most of them went to Laredo on September 11 for the hearing before the three-judge court in *Barrientos v. Texas*.

Criticism and Compliments for Whitmire

The Democratic senators in Albuquerque also had harsh words for Senator Whitmire, who had made comments of apparent unity as late as Labor Day. Senator Gallegos rebutted Whitmire's claims that he had acted on behalf of his constituents: "He is listening to the Republican Party. That's the only constituency he is listening to."[9] Some Republican Senators generally applauded Whitmire's decision as courageous. However, the *Dallas Morning News* saw the situation as one in which Whitmire was "snubbed by Republicans and scorned by Democrats."[10]

After his return to Texas, Senator Whitmire began a "parade" of press conferences to explain his apparently sudden decision to split with his ten colleagues. At the Capitol on Friday, September 5, he was compelled to speak in the Senate chamber because the pending fines and sanctions against him meant he was not eligible to use a Senate conference room.

Whitmire adopted several themes over several days to explain why he had left Albuquerque. First, redistricting was inevitable. He pointed to the growing expectation among the Democratic senators that the federal court was going to reject their claims and leave them without a winning endgame. He blamed the Democratic lawyers for telling the senators to be optimistic, even after Judge Kazen's ruling. Specifically, he charged, "Somebody really did one on us. We were told in no uncertain terms to be optimistic."[11] He added, "They've [the Republicans have] got the gavel. They've got the numbers. If they're willing to use it, they can outlast us." Second, he feared that the Democrats in Albuquerque were becoming "pawns" manipulated by the national party. He specifically pointed to the attacks on President Bush as a mistake.[12] He said, "This is some of those people's 15 minutes of fame, and they are having fun doing it."[13] A third theme was that staying longer outside Texas when there was no hope of winning could push Republicans to scrap the two-thirds vote requirement permanently.[14] Finally, he concluded, "We failed. You've got to know when you've done the best you can."[15] He encouraged the other senators to return to Austin and work vigorously to "build a record" to defeat the Republican maps in federal court.

Whitmire also claimed that he, along with several of his Democratic colleagues, had committed to staying gone only thirty days. He explained that as time dragged on, the senators developed a "hostage mentality" that led to a perceived need to always appear unified.[16] He claimed that some of the senators who were now publicly criticizing him for returning to Texas had earlier privately encouraged him to do so to end the standoff.[17] The other Democratic lawmakers denied this claim. Senator Barrientos commented on Whitmire's appearance at a news conference by saying, "He [Whitmire] looked like he was grasping for a rationale for what he's doing. Frankly, it's kind of sad to me."[18] Given Whitmire's public statements, Democrats took steps to make clear that he was acting on his own and did not speak for the remaining ten senators. Barrientos said, "I find it rather painful to watch. He [Whitmire] certainly has some kind of delusions of being the great leader that brings everything together. The 10 of us remaining, we speak for ourselves."[19]

Some of the criticism (not necessarily the public remarks by his colleagues) directed at Senator Whitmire was personal. He was accused of betraying his colleagues, the Democratic Party, and minority voters throughout Texas. Angry Democrats suggested that Whitmire was influenced by his law firm, Locke,

Liddell & Sapp, and its relationship with the White House and Republican clients.[20] Whitmire answered "absolutely not" to this charge. Some suggested that he was given an ultimatum to return by Houston Astros' owner Drayton McLane, Jr., who was perhaps his most important client. Others suggested that Whitmire was showing more concern for his own well-being than for the party's. His senatorial district is potentially one of the most competitive in the Senate, and he has accepted contributions from some of the state's major Republican donors. Some looked to Whitmire's reputation for an explanation of his actions. Whitmire is known for being frenetic, a senator likely to change his mind, or "boogie," on important issues. Houston city councilwoman Carol Alvarado, a longtime friend who was upset over Whitmire's leaving Albuquerque, said, "We had joked that they better watch him the closest in New Mexico because he'd get bored and leave because he has political attention deficit disorder."[21] Whitmire acknowledged this last criticism: "You're talking to a guy who flunked the first grade because he couldn't stay in his chair. Now put me in a hotel for 30 days."[22]

In 2005, Senator Whitmire told me, "The day we left we were cooked. We were scrambling for legal arguments and forum-shopping like hell." He lamented that he had been "hacked" after his return by so many Democrats whom he had helped in the past. In regard to his decision to leave Albuquerque, he insisted that several more of the eleven senators were ready to return and that some had expressly urged him to break the boycott. Whitmire regretted that these same senators have since denied any such sentiment.

Republicans Begin a Search for a Final Plan

While the Democratic senators were away, Jim Ellis continued his effort on behalf of Congressman DeLay to secure Republican support for an aggressively partisan redistricting plan. By memorandum to DeLay on August 17, Ellis indicated that the plan passed by the House "was not a favorable plan" for the congressional delegation because it left districts in which Frost, Edwards, and Doggett could win and because it did not increase Republican voting strength for Congressman Bonilla in District 23.

Jim Ellis's memoranda to DeLay show that DeLay, the Republican congressional delegation, and state Republican leaders were considering several concepts (with potential variations in specific district lines for each concept).[23] The designation of the plans depended on how each treated District 23 (Bonilla) and the minority-influence districts (Districts 24 and 25). Ellis ranked the concepts according to the likelihood that plans based on them would obtain Justice Department preclearance.

Ellis and DeLay favored the most aggressively partisan alternative. This plan was denominated the 8–3 plan, with "Frost eliminated; Bonilla improved" and a gain of "6 seats + Hall" (i.e., a total of twenty-two Republican seats, including Hall). This plan, however, faced opposition from "key" state senators and representatives who "do not like [the] impact on their areas." Also, importantly, this plan ran the greatest risk of Justice objection. Nevertheless, it was the plan DeLay preferred. Ellis urged, "We must stress that a map that returns Frost, Edwards, and Doggett is unacceptable and not worth all of the time invested into this project." The competing 7–2–2 plan (seven Hispanic, two African American, two combined majority-minority districts) was less likely to violate the Voting Rights Act, but it left Frost's and Doggett's districts essentially intact and left Bonilla's district with a Hispanic (potentially Democratic) voting majority.

Shortly after Senator Whitmire returned to Houston, Republican senators began meeting in earnest about alternative redistricting plans. Sentiment in the Senate remained against the House map, especially over how the West Texas districts were drawn. The disputes that had appeared among Senate Republicans during the first special session remained unresolved, but there was also opposition to Delay and Ellis's 8–3 map. Staples had advised Ellis in August that a 7–2–2 concept had "somewhat more support within the caucus than the 8–3" because of the perceived risk that the latter could violate the Voting Rights Act.

Senator Wentworth again urged a compromise that he thought would result in the election of eighteen or nineteen Republicans rather than twenty-two. In statements that would come back to haunt him, Wentworth said a plan intended to give a 22–10 advantage to Republicans "would be a power grab" and that he still hoped that his Republican colleagues would not "over-reach."[24] Even Wentworth's compromise plan, however, was a difficult sell to Democrats. The Democrats continued to focus on defeating the redistricting effort altogether, not on settling for a less egregious alternative. Some Democratic senators, however, speculated privately about "horse-trading" for "nay votes" with Republican factions that were concerned about specific parts of the House map.

On Monday, September 8, Perry met privately with Dewhurst and Craddick. There was no immediate announcement of a third special session. The next day, however, Perry stated that the legislature would be called for a third special session on redistricting and on legislation to move the primary election. Senator Whitmire indicated that he would attend the session and, by doing so, make a quorum. The following day, the ten Democratic senators in Albuquerque announced that they would return to Texas "to fight the Whitmire map."[25] Dewhurst again sounded a conciliatory note: "With all of the Democrats' legal options exhausted, it is now time to come together."[26]

The Noisy Return of the Democratic Senators

The legislature convened for its third special session on Monday, September 15.

The Senate chamber is a large, stately room. The floor is covered by a deep carpet. Each of the thirty-one senators has a desk with a microphone. The desks are widely spaced on either side of an aisle running from the double doors at the entrance to the desks of Senate administrative personnel (e.g., the secretary of the Senate) and the raised dais where the presiding officer stands behind a podium. The official "floor" of the chamber, where the senators' desks are located, is encircled by a brass rail that officially separates the press and staff from the senators when the Senate is in session. The ceiling rises at least forty-five feet, and is elegantly adorned with two large star-shaped brass chandeliers, with "T E X A S" spelled in lights, and beveled-glass recessed panels bearing the state seal. Midway between the chamber floor and the ceiling is a public gallery encircling the chamber.

On September 15 this dignified chamber became a scene of confusion. The gallery was filled with approximately 350 people, most of whom were supporters of the Democratic senators. A few wore T-shirts reading "QUITMIRE," mocking Senator Whitmire for his return from New Mexico. The Senate convened as planned at "high noon." The secretary of the Senate called roll. Twenty-one senators (a quorum) were present. All of the boycotting Democrats except Senator Whitmire were still absent, but were poised around the Capitol to make a final show of unity by entering the chamber together. Dewhurst officially declared, "A quorum is present," and then immediately entertained a motion to adjourn the Senate in an effort to prevent the crowd from making a show by cheering the Democrats on their return. Whitmire made the motion (as is customary for the dean [senior member] of the Senate), and the Senate adjourned amidst booing, hissing, and shouts of "you are acting like Nazis" from the crowd. Republican senators retreated to the hallway behind the east end of the chamber. Dewhurst remained at the podium and pounded his gavel in an effort to restore order. The crowd ignored him. Soon Dewhurst too left the chamber.

The remaining ten Democratic senators had stayed at nearby offices or condominiums until it was clear that a quorum had been established. Then, after forming together outside the Senate chamber, they entered slowly in front of the frenzied gallery and fifty TV cameras, photographers jostling for position around them. The mob of senators and press spilled on to the Senate floor. The Democratic senators gathered in a circle in the middle of the chamber, held hands, and turned their heads upward toward the chandeliers and gallery. The crowd responded with more cheers and screaming. Most of the Democrats then gave speeches, many emphasizing that their fight was long from over. Senator Van de Putte said, "Thank you, Texas." Some emphasized that the dispute was about more than partisan politics. Senator Gallegos made fun of his absent Republican colleagues: "If they were so eager for us to come back to work, where are they?"[27] The speeches went on for twenty-five minutes, to the delight of the crowd. Then the microphones went silent.

Some of the Republican senators gathered in the hallway had been disturbed by what they saw as an "inappropriate and tasteless pep rally."[28] Dewhurst was likewise concerned by conduct that he considered unbecoming to the Senate. The chairman of the Senate Administration Committee, Chris Harris, issued an order to shut off the microphones. In one sense, however, the silencing of the microphones came too late. As Senator Ogden observed, "They [the Democratic senators] kind of spoiled our plan."[29]

Despite the celebratory nature of the Democrats' return, the reality was much more somber. A quorum was present; redistricting could move forward.[30] Many of the Democratic senators were to spend much of their time in the coming weeks trying to put their business and personal affairs back together after being away from jobs, family, and friends for approximately forty days.

The House Moves First Again

On the same day that the legislature convened, the House Redistricting Committee by 10–5 reapproved the same plan from the earlier sessions. No hearings occurred. Consideration of the bill by the full House was set for the next day, September 16.

On the 16th, Democrats for two hours vainly protested the plan in what one newspaper called "an occasionally ugly reprise of the well-honed redistricting debate."[31] The bill passed on second reading, 77–60. The House, in a repeat of the process followed during the second special session, again waited until after midnight to finally pass the bill and send it to the Senate. Seven Republicans voted against passage of the plan. The approved plan in House Bill 3 was sent to the Senate.

The Senate Deals with Fines and Sanctions

Existing Fines and Sanctions

When the Democratic senators returned to the Senate chamber on September 15, 2003, each of them faced $57,000 in fines and other sanctions, such as a loss of parking spaces and cell-phone privileges, because of their absence during the boycott. Several Republicans believed that the fines were appropriate because the Democrats had "broken state law" by walking out of the Senate. Nevertheless, even before the session began, there were signs that the penalties probably would not be assessed if the Democratic senators "behaved."

On the first day of the session, the Democratic senators were issued citations for parking in their privileged parking spots. On the second day, September 16, large orange barrels were placed in their parking places to prevent them from parking there at all so long as the sanctions remained in effect. However, Chris Harris, chairman of the Senate Administration Committee, declared that since the senators were back together and the fines had been adopted without any specific authorization by the Senate rules, the Senate should "do away" with the fines. Harris's comments clearly came with the approval and at the direction of Dewhurst, who earlier in the day had said that it was best to "have this matter behind us."[32]

Dewhurst was upset that the issue of fines did not go away: "I don't think that [collecting money from Democrats] was the intent of any of the Republicans on Day One."[33] He met with former lieutenant governor Hobby for forty-five minutes at the Tuesday Club in Houston.[34] Hobby urged that the fines be rescinded, and Dewhurst seemed to agree. On Wednesday, September 17, however, the Republican Caucus met behind closed doors to discuss the issue; some members felt strongly that the Democrats should "make some payment."

On Thursday, September 18, Republican senator Kyle Janek (Houston) proposed readopting the motion that had imposed the fines and sanctions on the Democratic senators. He also proposed a "state of probation" for the fines and restoration of the lost privileges. The proposed probation would last until the convening of the legislature on January 11, 2005. Democrats balked at being put on probation. They continued to contend that the fines were unlawful because they had been adopted without a quorum and because no Senate rule had authorized such fines. Senator Barrientos raised a point of order challenging the fines as a violation of Senate rules, since no legislation was pending when the call was made on the Senate in the second special session. Dewhurst overruled him. Senator Ellis prepared an amendment to provide for elimination of the fines. Before Ellis's amendment could be offered, however, Senator Harris called for the previous question and a vote on Janek's motion. It passed 13–10, with eight senators absent or not voting.

Upon passage of the motion, Dewhurst ordered Senate officials to remove the orange barrels from the Democratic senators' parking places. The fines were suspended and the sanctions lifted, but some Democrats were unhappy with being "probationers." Zaffirini called the Senate's action "official oppression."

At a news conference, Senator Madla compared the Senate's actions on the fines and sanctions to his first taste as a boy of "white supremacy."[35] Dewhurst called such remarks "simply cheap, distasteful, juvenile partisan spin."[36]

In October, Senator Van de Putte sought to reinforce Madla's comments by recounting an episode that she said occurred on September 18, after the Democratic senators had returned from Albuquerque. She indicated that during a private casual meeting in the Senate lounge, she had been told by an unnamed Republican senator that if the Democrats were "going to act like Mexicans," they "will be treated like Mexicans."[37] The meaning to Van de Putte was that if she was going to act like a second-class citizen, then that was how the Republican majority would treat her. Senator Wentworth said that he tried to discover who made the comment to Senator Van de Putte, and is convinced that the episode never happened.[38] Dewhurst too believes that the incident never occurred. (Van de Putte withdrew the allegation several days later, saying the senator had apologized and the matter was closed.)[39]

The battle over the fines and sanctions continued acrimoniously on September 19 when Senator West raised the same point of order Senator Barrientos had brought up the day before. West pointed to Senate precedent, reiterating that the call (and therefore the fines and sanctions) was invalid and lamenting the refusal of the presiding officer to enforce Senate rules. Dewhurst again rejected the challenge. Senators West and Gallegos had their written personal-privilege statements published in the *Senate Journal* for September 19. For at least one senator, there remained hope that the current hard feelings would not affect the future. Senator Duncan expressed his wish publicly: "Sometimes these vacations from hell turn out to be the things that they say bond families together. Well, I think we've been on a vacation from hell, and I quite frankly hope it works to bond us together as a body in the future."[40]

A final effort by Dewhurst to end the Democratic senators' probation came after the final redistricting plan was adopted on October 12. His effort failed. After a twenty-minute meeting of the Republican Caucus, the Senate decided to leave the probation in place until January 2005. Dewhurst explained, "I was told there were the votes to pass the motion [ending probation], then one of the votes came to me and said they were changing their vote."[41] Democrat Armbrister tried one last time on the final day of the third special session after the redistricting bill had been enacted. The Republican Caucus considered and rejected a proposal for eliminating the probation. The probation remained.

Changes in Senate Rules

When Senator Harris suggested doing away with the existing fines and sanctions, he moved to amend the Senate rules to plug the gap that had left the validity of the existing fines in question. The Senate Administration Committee discussed proposed rule changes that would allow senators absent without permission to be sanctioned with a loss of privileges. These rule changes were discussed in a closed-door caucus of the full Senate on September 17. A resolution (SR 30) embodying the proposed rule changes was introduced on Friday. On Monday, September 22, the Senate Administration Committee endorsed the rule changes and adopted a committee amendment adding a $1,000 a day fine in the future on senators who boycott to break a quorum.

On October 2, the Senate debated the proposed changes. The new rules would strip the seniority from a senator who was absent for more than seventy-two hours without the Senate's permission. They would also require a lieutenant governor to ask the Supreme Court to issue a writ of mandamus to compel an absent senator to show up. The committee amendment to add a fine of $1,000 a day was presented by Senator Wentworth; it was defeated 16−12. Debate on the amendment and the new rules was at times rancorous as Democrats questioned the motives behind the changes. Dewhurst was largely successful in persuading Republican senators not to respond publicly to the Democrats' attacks. SR 30 passed 15−13.

The Senate Finally Adopts a Redistricting Plan

The Senate moved almost as quickly as the House on redistricting. The Committee on Jurisprudence met on Wednesday the 17th to conduct a hearing on a Senate redistricting plan. On the 19th, the committee approved the plan as a committee substitute for the House plan in HB 3. The committee then approved HB 3, as substituted with the new plan, on a 4−3 party line vote. Discussion again centered on the racial implications of the plan. As Senator West remarked to the Republican members of the committee, "I don't see any of you as racists. Have you been insensitive? I think you have been."[42] Among Republicans, Senator Harris urged that, if it could do so legally, the Senate plan should dismantle District 24 in Dallas to ensure the defeat of Martin Frost. However, the Senate plan left Frost's district essentially intact.

Senate Republicans claimed that the redistricting plan adopted by the committee "guaranteed" Republicans a gain of only three seats (i.e., the defeat of Democratic incumbents Sandlin, Turner, and Lampson). Charles Stenholm, Chet Edwards, Ralph Hall, Chris Bell, and Martin Frost were considered likely to win reelection in the districts drawn by the committee. Lloyd Doggett's district in Travis County and Republican Henry Bonilla's district in southwest Texas remained essentially unchanged. The proposed plan paired only a single Democrat (Jim Turner with Republican congressman Jeb Hensarling). Even Sandlin and Lampson were left unpaired, although in heavily Republican districts.

The new Senate plan embodied the 7–2–2 concept instead of the 8–3 concept favored by Congressman DeLay. Overall, the plan was far less detrimental to Democrats than either the plan approved by the same committee in the first special session or the House plan. Democrats, however, remained focused on defeating redistricting in its entirety. For minority voters, the new Senate plan reflected the status quo. Hispanic voting strength was left essentially unchanged from the existing congressional plan. The new plan left Bonilla's district (District 23) unchanged, but did not contain either a new Hispanic district in South Texas or in Dallas/-Fort Worth as MALDEF wanted. African American voting strength too remained essentially unchanged in the largest urban areas, including potential influence districts in the Dallas/Fort Worth area (District 24) and Harris County (District 25), but was diluted in other areas of the state in an effort to defeat the rural Democratic incumbents.

The floor fight on redistricting was preceded by an exchange over parliamentary matters. On Friday, September 19, Democratic senators peppered Dewhurst with questions about the process to date and about the possibility of personal-privilege speeches on the redistricting bill when it came up. These questions and the anticipated personal-privilege speeches themselves apparently were intended to help build a record for later litigation challenging the redistricting bill. Dewhurst saw the questions and potential speeches as dilatory, but dismissed their importance because he saw it as "mechanically" impossible for the Democrats to stall redistricting to death. He said that he would recognize Democrats for personal-privilege speeches on redistricting as long as they remained in line with Senate tradition. He said, "We're not aware of any speech that's gone longer than 20 minutes, 30 minutes."[43] Democratic senators on Monday, September 22, tried to prevent any cap on the time allowed to speak on the redistricting bill, but were defeated.

On Tuesday, September 23, HB 3 as substituted with the new Senate redistricting plan was debated by the full Senate. Even though the new plan was far less damaging to Democrats than other plans that had been seen, the Democrats resisted passage. Senator West vowed to raise "every point of order I can think of."[44] Democrats alternated between parliamentary challenges, intense questioning of the bill sponsor (Todd Staples), and lengthy speeches of opposition.[45] Democrats also offered several amendments, but all were defeated. Republican senators generally remained silent, voting in accordance with Senator Staples. Many Republican senators, however, "agonized" over whether to support a plan that left the much-disliked Frost with a district that he could win.

Republican senators from the Dallas–Tarrant County area, particularly Chris Harris, Jane Nelson, and Kim Brimer (Fort Worth), wondered whether they could return home and face their constituents if the plan did not target Frost. By September 24, however, the Republican senators had generally coalesced around the new plan supported by Dewhurst and Duncan and had accepted that redrawing District 24 to defeat Frost was unacceptable for legal reasons.

Among the noteworthy moments from the four-hour debate on September 24:[46]

- Democrats successfully objected to the presence on the Senate floor of the redistricting attorneys who were assisting Senator Staples in answering questions about the plan.
- In an apparent effort to enhance the official record for any subsequent legal challenge, Senator Royce West, the acknowledged lead legal strategist among the Democratic senators, persistently asked Staples questions about the factors considered by the drafters of the map. Left without the assistance of an attorney, Staples sidestepped most of the questions and gave only very general answers, commenting later, "I am going to leave this to our attorneys to argue this before the court."
- Staples countered attacks on the plan from minority senators by pointing out that they had opposed the Senate plan from the first special session—one designed, by Republican accounts, to boost minority clout at the expense of Anglo incumbent Democrats.
- Staples repeatedly defended the new map as "fair and balanced" for Democrats and Republicans. Compared to what finally passed the legislature, this Senate plan could more plausibly be described as "balanced."
- About midway through debate, Dewhurst turned the gavel over to designated senators so he could fly to Nacogdoches for a Farm Bureau speech and fund-raiser. Such practice is common.
- Senator Robert Deuell (Greenville) defended Governor Perry against Democratic criticism and afterward said that the racial discrimination claims by Democrats "flew right in the face of what Martin Luther King had to say."[47]
- The Democrats built a case that in seven districts (other than those with a majority of Hispanic or African American voters), minority voters provided the margin of victory for the winning (Democratic) candidate and that these districts were coalitional or influence districts protected by the Voting Rights Act.
- Staples offered an amendment that made some changes in the districts of East Texas in an effort to address Senator Ratliff's concerns about the loss of power by the rural areas there. It was adopted.

One other significant amendment was adopted by the Senate. Jeff Wentworth proposed to split Webb County, removing half of it from District 23 and replacing it with portions of Bexar County and smaller counties to the south of Bexar. The amendment was adopted. This amendment caused only a minor drop in the Hispanic voting-age population in District 23 because the population added to the district was only slightly less Hispanic than the portion that had been reassigned. According to Wentworth, this change was intended to make District 23 safer for Henry Bonilla's reelection.[48] The splitting of Webb County irritated Senator Zaffirini, who a day later claimed that the action was in retaliation for an investigation by Webb County district attorney Joe Rubio (ostensibly at the urging of Zaffirini's husband) into the legality of the fines imposed on the Democratic senators. Senator Harris later was reported to have conceded that the amendment (in his mind) was intended to punish Zaffirini for "not reining in her husband."[49]

HB 3, as substituted and amended, passed the Senate on second reading by 18–13, largely along party lines. One Republican, Teel Bivins (Amarillo), and all Democrats including Ken Armbrister, voted against passage. Senator Bivins opposed passage because he preferred the House plan. Senator Ratliff voted for the bill. The bill won final approval by the Senate on September 24. The House voted immediately not to accept the Senate amendments, and the redistricting bill headed to a conference committee of five senators and five representatives.

The *Dallas Morning News* editorial board on September 24 offered the opinion that "Senate Republicans aren't as greedy as the House in carving out congressional districts for their party." The paper recommended that the conference committee "use the Senate map as a guide."

CHAPTER 12

Redistricting by Cabal:
The Final Redistricting Plan

Well, it seems to me that this map doesn't look anything like the map we voted out of this chamber.
— SENATOR JUAN HINOJOSA, OCTOBER 10, 2003

With a redistricting bill now through both the Senate and the House, Democrats had little or nothing that they could do to determine the specifics of the final plan. The district lines in the redistricting plans were entirely mutable, like lines drawn in the sand. The configuration of the final plan would rest with the conference committee, the leaders of the House and Senate, and the governor, subject to partisan pressures from Washington and outside of the Texas legislature. As a result, the final redistricting plan was developed in secret by a small group of like-minded persons committed to maximizing Republican voting strength in 2004 and the future. Looming over the drawing up of the final map was the partisan aggressiveness of Congressman DeLay, the Republican congressional delegation, and other outside forces that ultimately influenced the shape of the final map.

Disputes Between Senate and the House Republicans: Congressional Districts in West Texas

Several points of contention existed between the House and Senate plans:

- There were conflicts over Central Texas, where civic leaders from Waco, McLennan County, Bell County, and Killeen protested the splitting of their area by the House map. The Senate plan tried to address this issue by keeping Waco and Fort Hood in one district.

- Rural residents of East Texas complained that the House plan allowed the Dallas and Houston suburbs to dominate their regions. Senator Ratliff continued to express his concern about the loss of East Texas influence. The Senate plan tried to address his concern.

- The House plan included a district in North Texas that gave a clear shot at a congressional seat to one of its members, Kenny Marchant (Coppell). The Senate plan made it more difficult for Marchant unless he ran against a Republican incumbent.

- The Senate map, as amended by Wentworth, split Webb County to aid the reelection of Congressman Henry Bonilla. Representative King indicated that the House had not made any changes to District 23 because of concerns that they might violate the Voting Rights Act. King said that the Senate change might have to be taken out of any final plan in order to win Justice Department approval.[1]

- The Senate map appeared to be less devastating for incumbent Democratic congressmen—the House plan paired eight incumbent Democrats and the Senate plan only one.

By far the most visible dispute between the Senate and House, however, remained the configuration of districts in West Texas. It was, in the view of Dewhurst, "the elephant in the room."[2] It was a direct confrontation among several senators, including the chairman of the critical Senate Jurisprudence Committee, Robert Duncan, and the Speaker of the House of Representatives, Tom Craddick.

The area generally denominated West Texas is a vast region, encompassing in excess of 135,000 square miles (an expanse almost as large as Wisconsin).[3] The area consists of many geographically large counties (one, Brewster County, is larger than Connecticut) with small, widely separated communities (fifty-four West Texas counties have fewer than seven people per square mile). Only a handful of the towns and cities in the region have a population of 50,000 or more. Parts of the region depend primarily on ranching, other parts depend primarily on farming (e.g., cotton), and some West Texas cities are primarily centers for oil and gas exploration and production. In 2003, the area generally (not including El Paso, which had its own district at the far western end of the state) was encompassed within four congressional districts, each consisting of twenty to thirty counties. Historically, the congressmen from these vast districts came from in or around whichever of the handful of large cities or population centers were within the district. Therefore, each district was often described as "dominated" by a particular city or cities.

Speaker Craddick was elected from a state legislative district comprising

Midland County, the prior hometown of both President George W. Bush and President George H. W. Bush, and four other contiguous or nearby counties. Midland in 2003 was located in Congressional District 19, which had two major population centers: Lubbock and, a hundred miles to the south, the sister cities of Midland and Odessa. Republican congressman Randy Neugebauer from Lubbock had just defeated Republican K. Michael Conaway of Midland in a special-election runoff to fill a vacancy caused by the retirement of the sitting congressman.

Every redistricting plan passed by the House in 2003 contained a congressional district that could be dominated by Midland and Odessa voters. Craddick insisted that the Midland–Odessa area had been split in a bizarre fashion by Democrats in the past to keep the longtime Republican stronghold of Midland from dominating a congressional district. Craddick explained how Republican congressman Ed Foreman was elected from Midland–Odessa in 1962, only to lose in 1964 after the Democratic-controlled state legislature broke the sister cities apart in a redistricting plan passed in 1963. He recalled how future President George W. Bush had run unsuccessfully for Congress from Midland in 1978 against then-Democrat Kent Hance of Lubbock.[4] It was time, Craddick insisted, for Midland to be able to elect its own congressman. Craddick also claimed that drawing a district that could be dominated by Midland–Odessa would mean a congressman from an area that depends largely on oil and gas exploration and production. Putting Lubbock in another district would allow its congressman to focus on agricultural issues.

Craddick's proposed district was drawn without an incumbent, which meant that the other districts in West Texas were reconfigured to pair two incumbents, freshman Republican congressman Neugebauer and twenty-four-year veteran Democratic congressman Charles Stenholm from Abilene (from District 17). Craddick expected that any new plan would defeat Stenholm, the only remaining Democrat in Congress from West Texas (other than Silvestre Reyes from the Hispanic center of El Paso). Also, it was expected that the winner in the new district for Midland would be K. Michael Conaway, who, besides having just lost narrowly to Neugebauer in the special election, was a longtime friend of President Bush.[5]

Midland–Odessa voters probably favored Craddick's proposal; the other affected counties, communities, and voters largely opposed it. Neugebauer and his Lubbock constituents in District 19 opposed the change because, by pairing him with Stenholm, it threatened his reelection and the loss by Lubbock of a resident congressman. Voters in Stenholm's district, the 17th, also largely opposed the change. District 17 stretched across thirty counties, but the two major population centers were Abilene and San Angelo, and voters there did not want to be put under the sway of Midland–Odessa. Stenholm remained very popular in the district, even among Republicans. He was the ranking Democrat on the House Agricultural Committee and continued to win reelection, even though the voters in the district consistently voted heavily (around 70 percent) for Republican candidates in statewide and presidential races.

State Senator Robert Duncan, chairman of the Senate Jurisprudence Committee, was from Lubbock and represented some counties from both District 17 and 19. His constituents looked to him to stop the redrawing of those districts. Witnesses at the Senate's hearings in San Angelo in June 2003 testified overwhelmingly against redistricting. West Texas officials continually made their opposition known to lawmakers in Austin. Several journeyed to Austin to meet with Dewhurst and the senators to voice their concerns. Abilene Mayor Grady Barr and Taylor County Republican chairman Paul Washburn held a press conference in Austin on September 19 specifically to denounce the House districting plan and its Midland-based district.

Most of the West Texas newspapers (other than the *Midland Reporter-Telegram*) had editorialized in early 2003 against redistricting. They continued to do so during the summer. For example, the *San Angelo Standard-Times* warned Senator Duncan that Dewhurst might try to "pick off" senators opposed to changing the existing West Texas districts by arguing that no dispute over West Texas should stop the Republican redistricting from going through. The paper concluded that, "We expect Duncan to wage a hard fight to ensure that doesn't happen."[6] The newspaper reminded Duncan that he and other senators "heard San Angeloans and other West Texans explain clearly and persuasively during a hearing at Angelo Sate University why they want to keep the current 17th Congressional District as it is." Even the *Amarillo Globe-News*, in the heavily Republican Texas Panhandle, got into the act by criticizing Craddick for his "power play."[7] The El Paso newspaper, referring to state officials and lawmakers, noted, "They've all made a spectacle of themselves and the state."[8]

Some Republican members of the Texas House also opposed Craddick's proposed changes. Rep. Bob Hunter of Abilene said, "Democrats, independents and Republicans are very happy with the districts we have. People in our area are against congressional redistricting of any kind."[9] These House members voted against HB 3, but had no chance of stopping Craddick's plan from being adopted.

Given this degree of opposition, it is not surprising that the Senate plan preserved these districts, thereby leaving Midland in the same district as Lubbock and Neugebauer as its incumbent congressman. A showdown was inevitable with Speaker Craddick.

Craddick and Duncan tried repeatedly to resolve their differences. They first met on the subject in May, before the House Democrats staged their walk-out. Craddick invited Duncan to look at a map of Craddick's plan for West Texas. Duncan initially responded favorably to the plan, but later learned that his constituents opposed the idea.[10] Craddick accused Duncan of reneging on a deal. Duncan said that he had told Craddick in June that there was never a deal. In September, Congressman DeLay met with Craddick, Duncan, and Senator Staples (sponsor of the Senate plan) in Austin over the West Texas impasse. Still, no agreement was reached.

In one attempt to resolve the dispute, Duncan called Congressman Stenholm and asked if he would be interested in retiring to take an endowed chair in agriculture at Texas Tech University. Stenholm's retirement would avoid a pairing that could defeat Neugebauer. Stenholm said that he was not interested in retiring. Duncan even traveled to Washington to meet with Stenholm and Neugebauer, but failed to find a compromise.[11] In 2005 Duncan told me, "Charlie Stenholm just did not want to retire."

The presiding officers of the House and Senate also continued to quarrel, with the dispute over West Texas as the backdrop. Dewhurst complained that Craddick refused to negotiate a compromise on the sticking points in the redistricting maps. Craddick accused Dewhurst of failing to attend the September meeting hosted by DeLay. Dewhurst said he had never intended to be present.[12]

On September 22, Rep. Phil King presented a compromise for West Texas on behalf of the governor. The districts in the western half of the state generally stayed west of Interstate 35. One district could be dominated by Midland, and Neugebauer and Stenholm would not be paired. King said that the Speaker would accept the plan. Senators were momentarily encouraged. The plan, however, made drastic changes in many other existing congressional districts. These effects brought immediate opposition from Bivins, the powerful senator from Amarillo, because of its effect on District 13 in the Panhandle, and from Senator Kip Averitt from Waco because of its effect on the area around Bell and Coryell counties in Central Texas. The King compromise was soon dropped.

Another possible compromise over West Texas appeared on October 1 from Rep. Arlene Wohlgemuth, who proposed a district that combined Midland with Abilene, thus putting Stenholm against any candidate from Midland. Duncan embraced the West Texas solution in the plan because it left Lubbock and Congressman Neugebauer in a separate district. Craddick, however, said that Wohlgemuth had not spoken to him before submitting the plan and that the plan was not being presented on behalf of the House. Putting Midland in a district with Stenholm was unsatisfactory to Craddick, and the proposal was dropped. However, Wohlgemuth's redistricting plan also marked a change toward a much more aggressively partisan map that would dismantle District 24 to defeat Congressman Frost.

As discussed below, Lieutenant Governor Dewhurst finally acquiesced at the end of September in Craddick's concept for a Midland–Odessa-based district without an incumbent, thus leaving Neugebauer and Stenholm paired in District 19. The final sticking point for West Texas was how to make the redrawn 19th safe for Neugebauer. All the counties composing the district were heavily Republican, so the difficulty was not in finding Republican voters. Instead, the fear was that if the redrawn district contained too many of Stenholm's current constituents, he could defeat Neugebauer. The strategy was to dismember Stenholm's existing district as much as possible. Several counties (Castro, Hale, Floyd, and part of Archer) were moved from the Amarillo-based 13th District into the redrawn 19th in exchange for areas nearer Stenholm's hometown of Abilene. The new areas were considered more likely to support Neugebauer.

The focus finally fell on little-known Deaf Smith County. Neugebauer wanted the sparsely populated (18,500) but heavily Republican county moved from the 13th to the 19th District. Republican state representative John Smithee from Amarillo has Deaf Smith County within his state legislative district. His Deaf Smith County constituents did not want to be switched out of District 13. With support from two other nearby state legislators, Smithee fought the change. He held it off for four days in October, thereby delaying final agreement on a plan, but ultimately yielded.

Craddick's vision of a congressional district that could be dominated by Midland prevailed. Many constituents of the 13th and 19th Districts were unhappy. Nevertheless, as one West Texas paper noted, the area had had its "moment in the spotlight."[13] Senator Duncan won significant praise from West Texas newspapers and officials for having vigorously fought a good fight against a powerful Speaker supported by the governor and majority leader of Congress. In defending the final map, Duncan said, "[I]f you take away the personalities, you take away and you look not only seven years down the road but 17 years down the road, that this configuration is a good configuration for West Texas."[14]

Redistricting by Political Cabal

The legislative body officially entrusted with resolving the differences over HB 3 and submitting a final redistricting plan for approval by the House and Senate was a conference committee composed of five senators and five state representatives. In actuality, however, the final redistricting plan in 2003 was crafted in secret by a small, highly partisan group.

Jim Ellis acknowledged to me in 2005 that early in 2003 he had established with the House parliamentarian that "[a]nything could come out of conference. The key was to get it there." Under normal circumstances, a conference committee is bound simply to resolving the differences between the two versions of a bill. Unlike other legislation, in which a reconciliation of differences must come within the parameters set by the two bills, however, any significant change in any district of a redistricting plan necessitates changes in other districts. Therefore, the potential configuration of districts is infinite. The lines drawn by the House and Senate were entirely mutable—no more than lines in the sand. As the House sponsor and chairman of the House conference committee, Phil King, explained, the final map would "be shaped like Texas," but "everything is on the table."[15]

A conference committee actually consists of two committees—one from the House and one from the Senate. The members are different for each bill in conference. Each committee has five members appointed by the Speaker or the lieutenant governor. A majority of both the House and Senate members must sign any report approving a bill. The members of the Senate conference committee on HB 3 were Senators Duncan, Lindsay, Nelson, Staples, and Hinojosa. The House committee consisted of Representatives King, Crabb, Hamric, Grusendorf, and Wilson. Senator Hinojosa and Representative Wilson were the only Democrats. Hinojosa, an attorney from McAllen, had participated in the Senate boycott. Wilson, an attorney from Houston, was a supporter of the redistricting plan and had not participated in the House walkout.

The conference committee never met.[16] Legislative rules require a notice to be posted showing when a committee will meet and require most meetings to be open to the public. The meeting of less than a quorum of a committee, however, is not required to be posted or open to the public. The sponsors (Representative King and Senator Staples) of the redistricting bill conducted the conference committee's business without any quorums present or any formal meetings.

Such behavior by bill sponsors or conference-committee chairmen is common, even usual, under most legislative circumstances. Generally, conference-committee negotiations are left to private meetings between the two sponsors of a particular bill. This procedure makes sense for most legislation, especially during a hectic regular session, because other members of a conference committee often are not intensely interested in the subject of the bill or know little about its specifics. Since lawmakers are often busy elsewhere on other legislative matters, trying to convene a quorum of a conference committee can be impossible to achieve. Moreover, the only changes a conference committee is normally allowed to make are those necessary to reconcile differences between the House and Senate versions. Other changes are normally subject to a valid point of order against the conference-committee report. Finally, the sponsors of legislation are expected to battle in conference to preserve the version passed by his or her chamber.

These reasons for private meetings between bill sponsors were inapplicable for the conference committee on HB 3. Many lawmakers and members of the general public were interested in the specifics of the redistricting bill. There was no other official legislative business to conflict with possible conference-committee meetings. Also, there were no parameters limiting the scope of possible changes to the redistricting map, and the bill sponsors were not wed to the versions passed by their chambers. Still, legislative rules and traditions allowed for Staples and King to meet privately to design a final redistricting plan. No public notice was posted of the meetings. Senator Duncan accompanied Senator Staples at some of the meetings. However, the other legislators and the public largely waited for word of developments.

Although members of the conference committee and the general public knew little about the timing and progress of Staples and King's private meetings, several of which occurred in the Ben Ramsey Room in the governor's suite of offices at the Capitol, Jim Ellis was very much aware of them. Congressman DeLay's key aide knew about the meetings, sometimes attended them, regularly coordinated with Representative King on any issues before the committee, and helped develop the redistricting maps being considered.

In their meetings, the two bill sponsors were often joined by representatives from the governor, lieutenant governor, attorney general (usually Don Willet), and Speaker, as well as by Ellis, DeLay, or Congressman Kevin Brady. Occasionally other congressmen or representatives from the national Republican Party were present.[17] This group discussed the "big issues." They examined maps, discussed agreements and disagreements about the plan options, and considered alternatives; at subsequent meetings they would discuss the acceptability of any further changes and perhaps consider a new map. At each stage, the principals needed computer-generated demographic and election data for any plan to help them deal with potential legal and political ramifications. Most importantly, each plan had to achieve absolute population equality based on the 2000 census data.

The time required to generate such plans, with the accompanying maps and data, often caused the meetings to be spaced hours, or even a day or so, apart. Staff members, such as Deirdre Delisi (deputy chief of staff to Perry), Scott Sims (redistricting aide to Craddick), and Bob and Doug Davis (redistricting aides to Dewhurst), were at most of the meetings and facilitated the preparation of the needed demographic and political materials. Several persons credit Bob and Doug Davis with actually drawing the maps on the computers.[18] The governor, lieutenant governor, and Speaker were regularly briefed about changes being discussed, and these officials held strategy sessions with their teams. Essentially, each Republican member of the Texas congressional delegation came to Austin to meet with state officials and the principal map drawers and to vet the maps as they affected him or her.[19] DeLay was briefed by Ellis and spoke regularly with the state officials. This process went on for almost three weeks.

The major dispute over districts in West Texas was resolved in theory after only a few days. As September ended, Dewhurst agreed with Craddick on drawing a district that would be dominated by Midland and Odessa. Duncan explained to his constituents that it would be expending too much "political capital" for West Texas to kill redistricting and the special session over the shape of the West Texas districts.[20] This agreement was a major step forward, but still left the thorny issue of whether the districts could be drawn to avoid pairing Neugebauer and Stenholm. Senator Duncan acknowledged publicly the difficulty of finding a solution for this conundrum. Although the issue of districts in West Texas grabbed the headlines, the major focus of the map drawing during this period was on honing the partisan effect of the map. This small, wholly Republican group could almost endlessly try new configurations or tweak existing ones to improve the expected partisan result.[21]

Growing Pressure to Produce a Plan

As a final redistricting plan was being worked out in the conference committee, some Republicans began to worry that agreement on a final plan could come too late for the bill to take effect in time for the scheduled primary. In Texas, a new law cannot become effective for ninety days unless approved by two-thirds of the House and Senate. Republicans knew that they could not achieve that vote. Therefore, Governor Perry on September 26 set a ten-day deadline (October 6) for passage of a redistricting bill as "somewhat of a drop-dead date" to avoid having to move the date of the primary from March 4, 2004.[22] As insurance, however, the Senate had already passed a bill delaying the primary date. The political situation was further stirred by Republican comptroller Carole Keeton Strayhorn, who chided Governor Perry about his focus on redistricting instead of the state's beleaguered system for funding public schools. She said that the state leaders were "climbing up hills when we have a mountain [public school finance] looming out there."[23]

Frustrated by the lack of progress, Dewhurst accused the House of changing its demands at the conference committee. He said that Craddick and the House had for months set only one condition for a new Republican redistricting plan, i.e., a district that could be won by someone from Midland. Now, Dewhurst asserted, Speaker Craddick was negotiating like an "Iranian cabdriver" because the House leadership had waited until the last minute to pile on additional demands.[24] He also said that Craddick was holding other legislation hostage by not allowing conference committees on other legislation to meet until the West Texas redistricting issue was resolved. Craddick responded that it was difficult to negotiate with senators because they would not respond to settlement offers. He conceded that there were major differences in how the plans dealt with the Dallas area (i.e., District 24). Dewhurst's office apologized for his "poor choice of words" since he has the "utmost respect for Iranian-Americans."[25]

Pressure for a New Partisan Aggressiveness

As soon as there was an agreement to carve out a congressional district that could be dominated by Midland, the more important partisan issues emerged.

Both the House and Senate bills had essentially preserved the districts in which Democrats Martin Frost (District 24), Chet Edwards (District 11), and Lloyd Doggett (District 10), as well as Republican Henry Bonilla (District 23), had won reelection in 2002. District 24 in Dallas–Fort Worth and District 23 in southwest Texas had been left intact because attorneys had advised that it could be a minority-opportunity district protected by the Voting Rights Act. District 10 had been left intact because of opposition in Travis County to having the county needlessly split among three or four different districts, as had been proposed in an earlier House map. So also, the core of District 11 had been left intact in the Senate plan because of local opposition to the area being split up. Congressmen Frost had been "drawn out" of District 24, but there was little doubt that if the districts remained Democratic, Frost, Edwards, and Doggett would run in them and probably be reelected, whereas Bonilla might lose to a Democratic challenger.

This possibility of these election results was unacceptable to DeLay. On August 17, 2003, in a memorandum to DeLay, Jim Ellis indicated, "We must stress [to the senators] that a map that returns Frost, Edwards, and Doggett is unacceptable and not worth all of the time invested into this project." On August 19, Ellis sent an e-mail to a network of congressional staffers, explaining, "[I]it is very important that the congressional members talk to their [state] Senators" to urge adoption of a redistricting plan that would "eliminate" Frost,

Edwards, and Doggett. Despite this congressional pressure, Dewhurst initially persuaded the Senate not to agree to the changes sought by DeLay. As a result, the Senate had passed a 7–2–2 plan (i.e., preserving the existing seven Hispanic, two African American, and two combined majority-minority districts, but also leaving the districts of Doggett and Edwards largely intact).

At the conference committee, however, the circumstances were very different. Representative King and Speaker Craddick, along with Governor Perry, were now supporting Congressman DeLay's aggressive plan. They pushed DeLay's so-called 8–3 plan (eight Hispanic and three African American districts, counting a redrawn District 23 as a minority district because Bonilla is Hispanic[26] and counting District 9 as African American because of increase in the African American voting-age population there),[27] even though it was substantially different from either of the 7–2–2 plans adopted by the House or Senate. This aggressively partisan plan also substantially altered the districts that had elected Doggett and Edwards and paired most of the Democratic incumbents with Republicans. To Senator Duncan, the new partisan aggressiveness came on like a "lightbulb" one weekend.[28] Governor Perry's chief of staff, Mike Toomey, recalled in 2006 that the final "brouhaha" in 2003 was over the "Frost district" (District 24), when DeLay and the Republican congressional delegation insisted that the redistricting effort "would not be worth it" unless Frost was defeated.[29]

Dewhurst and Duncan initially resisted the change. Dewhurst believed that although the Senate plan probably would elect slightly fewer Republicans than DeLay's plan, the 7–2–2 plan was the surest to win quick approval from the Department of Justice. He also believed that it was fair. King acknowledged on October 4 that lawyers advising him also had qualms about dismantling District 24.[30] They feared that the enhancement of African American voting strength in District 9 might not be legally sufficient to offset a comparable loss in District 24. The participants realized that the more aggressively partisan plan posed a "high risk" of being ruled discriminatory. However the Texas attorney general's office now played a critical role by providing assurances that the 8–3 plan could be successfully defended before Justice and in the courts. The lawyers advising the legislature had consistently warned against reducing the minority presence in either District 23 or District 24. By contrast, the lawyers for the Texas attorney general advised otherwise.[31] There were several lawyers involved (including Andy Taylor, Ted Cruz, and Don Willett), but it was Attorney General Abbott himself who, from his wheelchair, specifically expressed confidence of success.[32] Moreover, a rumor spread among the participants in the conference-committee meetings that Congressman DeLay had given his assurance that the aggressively partisan plan would receive Voting Rights Act preclearance. The map drawers were emboldened.

Outside Pressure Decides the Outcome

Outside pressure to adopt the more aggressive plan greatly intensified during the last week of September and the first week of October. Dewhurst told me in 2005 that he does not recall a period of greater partisan pressure. Officials, activists, and donors within the Republican Party pressured the lieutenant governor and Republican senators to accept DeLay's plan for defeating Democrats Frost, Edwards, Doggett, and their Anglo Democratic colleagues. As explained to me in 2005 by Senator Ratliff, "DeLay brought pressure to the table. Not from him, but from those who supported what he was doing—the whole panoply of influence that he represented." Republican congressmen called and visited state senators and the lieutenant governor, pushing for the most aggressive possible partisan plan. Congressman Kevin Brady was especially important in these final days, remaining in Austin almost "24/7." Publicly he lamented whether a "fair plan should remove every Anglo Democrat" and whether his "good friends" among the Democratic congressmen "might not make it through."[33] At the same time, he was lauded by Republicans, including Ellis, for helping push the final aggressive redistricting plan.

Local, state, and national Republican Party officials and Republican Party activists bombarded the senators and lieutenant governor with telephone calls, faxes, and letters. Dewhurst in 2006 described this effort to me as "grassroots" lobbying that changed the attitude of the Republican senators. As explained at the time in 2003 by Senator Duncan, "The Republican congressional delegation decided it wanted a more aggressive map. The heat was being turned up on (Texas Senate) urban members, on their constituencies, to pursue a line on their request."[34] Duncan later told his Lubbock paper that the situation changed when the Republican congressional delegation became more involved: "It appeared obvious the opportunity was here to achieve certain goals they had in mind and they felt the effort needed to be more aggressive."[35] Duncan confirmed this sentiment to me in 2006. Jim Ellis offered a similar explanation for this sudden increase in outside pressure: "People began to pay attention because they decided that 'this is going to happen.'"[36] In effect, Republican activists realized that Republicans had the power in the conference committee to do whatever they wanted in the final plan.

Some of the most effective pressure came from major Republican donors. Several Republican senators told me in 2005 that they had received very clear messages directly or indirectly from these major donors in 2003 that the obstructionist Democrats (e.g., Frost, Doggett, and Edwards) had to go. These messages were delivered through telephone calls and personal visits. DeLay, Ellis, and other Republican organizers (such as Ceverha) were critical to activating this push. The senators were certain to listen to these major donors because in the 2002 election cycle they (using the top ten individual contributors to TRMPAC as a measure) directly gave Republican senators over $700,000. For an elected official to offend such important Republican donors could mean virtual political suicide. Put simply, the issue for the senators had become "Do I risk my political future as a Republican to possibly save Martin Frost?" The almost universal answer was "NO!"

Dewhurst explained to me in 2005 that senators came to his office in late September and early October 2003 to tell him that they could no longer support the plan adopted by the Senate. In a span of only three or four days they had changed their position in response to this outside pressure and now wanted an aggressive plan that targeted a maximum number of Democratic incumbents. But Dewhurst reemphasized to me in 2006 that his effort to achieve a "fair plan" was also undermined by the Democrats' continuing refusal to support even the plan passed by the Senate. In Dewhurst's words, the Senate's moderate plan "was left without a constituency."

Dewhurst himself was not immune from such outside pressures. For example, the same major contributors who had given money to TRMPAC to elect the right Republicans to the House gave $860,000 to Dewhurst's campaign fund during the 2002–2004 election cycle. The largest contributors to Dewhurst during this period were James Leininger ($100,000), Louis Beecherl ($50,000), Bob Perry ($250,000), and T. Boone Pickens, Jr. ($100,000).[37] Moreover, supporting the final aggressive redistricting plan ultimately was seen by Dewhurst and his advisers as a political necessity. It became, as Dewhurst told me in 2005, a "litmus test" of party loyalty for him and all Republican senators.

According to Jim Ellis, this final push was a "team effort."[38] Eventually Lieutenant Governor Dewhurst and the Senate yielded to the pressure.[39]

The Conference-Committee Plan

On October 3, Dewhurst and the Senate conferees embraced the more politically aggressive 8–3 plan. Senators were briefed on the implications of the plan: the existing African American and Hispanic majority in District 24 would be dispersed among several districts, and the African American percentage in a similar district in Harris County (District 25, to be renumbered as District 9) would be significantly increased. The partisan effect was to trade two Democratic districts for one with an increased opportunity for victory by an African American. African American leaders in Fort Worth (Tarrant County) sent Craddick a letter asking that he reconsider his plan, since by dispersing the minority communities of District 24 among heavily Republican districts, the plan would "destroy the political strength of southeast Fort Worth, the third largest concentration of African-American voters in Texas." However, as Representative King explained to me in 2006, "all the Republican members" on the conference committee wanted to eliminate Congressman Frost: "We wanted to try to make that to where Martin Frost could not get re-elected."[40]

The aggressive plan now taking final shape also made significant changes to District 23. The intent was to make the district more hospitable politically for Republicans, including incumbent Republican congressman Henry Bonilla, by eliminating the Hispanic voting majority in the district. The changes to District 23 came in conjunction, however, with the creation of a new majority-Hispanic district (District 25) running from the Rio Grande Valley northward for approximately 350 miles (comparable to the distance from Washington, D.C., to New York City) to include southeast Travis County. The effect was to split Travis County among two now heavily Republican districts and a third district that, although Democratic, was predominately (63.4 percent) Hispanic and most of whose population (69 percent) lived in counties other than Travis. The plan was clearly intended to make it difficult for Democratic Congressman Doggett to win reelection. Doggett's residence in Austin was left in District 10, now a heavily Republican district stretching from Travis County to Houston. To win reelection, Doggett would have to run in the new District 25, probably against a Hispanic candidate from Hidalgo County in the Valley. DeLay was specifically credited in 2003 with convincing Republican leaders to support splitting Travis County rather than the Republican stronghold of Williamson County. Senator Wentworth, who previously had opposed splitting Travis County, now accepted the change: "That's not a deal killer for me."[41]

Farther north in Central Texas, the conference-committee plan dealt a blow to Democratic congressman Chet Edwards by taking Fort Hood and the surrounding Edwards-friendly communities out of what was now renumbered as District 17. This change also was specifically credited at the time to DeLay. The new District 17 was heavily Republican, having voted 64 percent Republican in the 2002 statewide races, and consisted largely of areas not in Edwards's previous district. Edwards was expected to lose in this new district.

It appeared that this conference-committee plan achieved DeLay's goals. The plan left Frost, Edwards, and Doggett in heavily Republican congressional districts. Doggett might run in the newly created Hispanic-opportunity district (District 25) that was partly in Travis County, but if so, he could be vulnerable to a Democratic or Republican Hispanic challenger from the Valley. Republicans also saw any decision by Doggett to run in the new District 25 as another example of an Anglo Democrat depriving a Hispanic of an election opportunity. However, Frost and Edwards would have no option except to run, if at all, in districts designed for their defeat. The plan saved District 23 for Republicans and Bonilla from future defeat by a Democrat. Moreover, the plan paired four incumbent Democrats with Republican incumbents in districts designed to assure the election of the Republican, and it paired two other Democratic incumbents (Lampson and Green) against each other in a district that was heavily Republican and lacked the constituency of either congressman. Republican staffers labored to convert these "big issue" decisions about the map into specific district lines that would satisfy the affected Republican congressmen and the need for equality in population. The configuration of each district needed to be vetted by the affected Republican incumbent, and, if he or she had concerns, to be refined until it met with the incumbent's approval.

On October 2, Speaker Craddick traveled to Midland, where he told the *Midland Reporter-Telegram* that he had been "haggling" over congressional redistricting maps until 5 a.m. and was heading back to Austin for another meeting at 10 p.m. He complained that the plans kept coming—he had seen five on Wednesday night. By the following day, the logjam seemed to break, as the Senate acquiesced in the 8–3 concept. At long last optimistic that the conference committee would reach accord, the House and Senate tentatively scheduled sessions on Sunday, October 5, to consider the possible conference-committee report. However, negotiations broke down again on Saturday over the specific configurations of the districts for West Texas.

With no redistricting plan to be considered, Craddick expected the House chamber to be empty on Sunday, when he intended to recognize Representative King for a perfunctory adjournment until Wednesday. However, a dozen Democrats unexpectedly showed up. When Craddick recognized King for a motion to adjourn until Wednesday and routinely asked if there was any objection, the Democrats shouted "We object, we object," and several sprinted toward the front of the House. The Democrats apparently had planned to try to bring the session to a halt by offering a substitute for King's motion with one for adjournment sine die. Craddick ignored them and gaveled the adjournment to Wednesday, October 8. Democrats complained that Craddick had no regard for House rules.

Another Crucial Visit by DeLay

Since it appeared that the final redistricting plan was again hung up on the West Texas issue, DeLay scheduled another trip to Austin. He reportedly had told Craddick several times by telephone that he did not want the fight over the

West Texas districts to kill the entire map. Now he was coming back to Austin; there was far too much at stake to stay away.

By memorandum on October 5, Ellis laid out the situation, noting that they had achieved the goals of "helping Bonilla and eliminating the Frost district." West Texas remained unresolved. Ellis was also concerned that even though the aforementioned goals had been achieved, "major adjustments must be made to ensure that the map reflects the priorities of the congressional delegation and not the legislature." He lamented that the map still was flawed with "largely insignificant state legislative agendas." Ellis advised DeLay that in a meeting scheduled with the governor for Monday, DeLay should insist that the governor "exert leadership to gather the principals in one room and solve the fundamental problems with the map and process." He emphasized to DeLay that the RNC, the National Republican Congressional Committee (NRCC), and ARMPAC, as "the entities that will have a large responsibility for running the campaigns[,] are all comfortable with the [congressional delegation's] map. The plan has been researched and vetted for months." He also suggested that Dewhurst "should be thanked for changing positions on the 8–3 concept, thereby helping Bonilla," but should also be convinced to adopt the stronger African American district in Houston and to exert leadership to "help solve the west Texas problem." Ellis closed by indicating, "We need our map, which has been researched and vetted for months. The pre-clearance and political risks are the delegation's and we are willing to assume those risks, but only with our map."

DeLay met for several hours on Monday morning with Dewhurst and Senators Staples and Duncan. He then spent most of the afternoon meeting with Craddick, Perry's chief of staff, Mike Toomey, and his deputy chief of staff, Deirdre Delisi. Perry had aligned himself with Craddick on the redistricting fight over West Texas, but was in New York on an economic development tour. Throughout the evening, DeLay shuttled between Craddick's office and Dewhurst's office.

DeLay's efforts continued over the next two days. He told the news media that he would remain in Austin as long as necessary. He observed that "until you reach some sort of deadline, it's hard to get people to move," but that now "we're moving."[42] DeLay's three days of cross-rotunda "shuttle diplomacy" was seen as important in part because of the strained relations existing between Dewhurst and Craddick. Final approval of a plan also was delayed to allow Perry to return from New York and to give the final plan his blessing.

Another urgent reason pushed the Republicans toward a final resolution during the first week of October. Important as the Republicans' desire for redistricting might be, another Texas obsession, the love of football, was becoming a factor. The crucial football game between the University of Texas and the University of Oklahoma was on Saturday, October 11, 2003. Further delays in adoption of a conference-committee plan could make it necessary for the legislature to meet over the weekend and for members possibly to miss this important sports showdown.

By Wednesday, October 8, an agreement had been reached "in principle" on how to draw the map for West Texas. The final piece to the statewide redistricting puzzle was the shift of Deaf Smith County from the 13th District to the 19th. This final plan contained the Midland-dominated district sought by Speaker Craddick. Craddick claimed that the "West Texas plan was very close to what we originally drew back in May." [43] It also embodied the congressional delegation's preferences for the other districts. Newspapers statewide claimed a major victory for Craddick. However, newspapers also continued to be critical of redistricting and the process that had produced the final plan. In a series of editorials, the *Fort Worth Star-Telegram* criticized the "Redistricting Wrongs": "Ego is the disease of politics and the leadership of the Texas Legislature is eaten up by it." [44] In the Midland paper, Craddick was congratulated for standing firm for Midland despite pressure to come up with a map for the March 2 primary. [45] With an agreement in hand, the lieutenant governor and speaker forecast that the House and Senate could take up the final bill on Friday, only two days away.

Congressman DeLay was "ebullient." As he indicated, "Yes, you could say I'm very satisfied." He added, "It's very important for the nation, for the president, for the House of Representatives, for the state of Texas." [46] In a tour of triumph on Wednesday, DeLay moved back and forth between the House and Senate chambers, visiting primarily with Republican members of the two bodies. He explained, "I am having a great time" and pointed to the desk in the House chamber where he had sat in the early 1980s. [47]

DeLay was credited by House and Senate Republicans with making the final bill possible. Dewhurst said, "The majority leader was instrumental." [48] Senator Staples said that DeLay was "the key to resolving the West Texas problem." [49] The negotiators also acknowledged that it was DeLay who had pressed lawmakers to target key Democratic incumbents, including Martin Frost. [50] However, Jim Ellis in 2005 insisted that "the media [especially the Austin paper] got it all wrong," and that it was the state officials, not the congressional delegation, who wanted to "go further." [51]

Although praised by Republican leaders, DeLay was criticized by several newspapers for his unprecedented role. The *Bryan–College Station Eagle* commented on October 8: "We didn't need redistricting in the first place, but if we are going to have it the least DeLay can do is keep his nose out of internal state politics." The *San Antonio Express-News* asked, "What does it say about leaders in Austin that they would allow DeLay to take over the process?"[52] The *Beaumont Enterprise* offered on October 9: "There is something unnerving about U.S. House Majority Leader Tom DeLay roaming the halls of the capitol building this week trying to broker a compromise between stubborn legislators." The *Waco Tribune-Herald* suggested on October 10 that in recognition of DeLay's role, the state should build "a plush De facto Governor's Mansion for he who rules from afar."

Democrats saw DeLay's final role in Austin and the lines in the final plan as vindication of their predictions that the "real" redistricting map would not emerge until the last minute, when DeLay could achieve his aggressively partisan goals by controlling a conference committee. Unfortunately for the Democrats, vindication of their predictions left only a sour taste. As Republican sponsor King explained, this final plan was designed to "defeat as many Democratic incumbents as possible."[53]

Moving the Statutory Election Timetable

As early as the first special session, Republicans had considered moving congressional-candidate filing deadlines as necessary to implement any new districting plan.

As the redistricting bill remained pending in the third special session, the Republicans considered the need for also delaying the primary election itself. Only a few months earlier during the regular session, the legislature had moved the primary from March 9 until March 2, the same date that several other large states, such as California, New York, and Ohio, also held their primaries. Democrats objected that now moving the primary away from March 2 would diminish the state's importance in choosing the Democratic nominee for president.

Texas Secretary of State Geoff Connor told lawmakers that it would be necessary to pass a redistricting bill by October 6 to avoid changing the date of the primary election. While in Austin on October 7, Congressman DeLay indicated that moving the primary would be worth the expense and inconvenience: "Whatever it takes to make sure that this redistricting is effective in 2004 is really important to me."[54]

Friday, October 10, the House (77–52) and Senate (19–12) approved a bill moving the filing deadline for congressional candidates from January 2 to January 16 and moving the primary election from March 2 to March 9.

Final Passage

The final redistricting plan was unveiled publicly by the conference committee on Thursday, October 9. It was unlike either of the plans passed earlier by the House and Senate. The new plan shifted 9.8 million people among the state's thirty-two congressional districts, and it was a disaster for Democrats. Representative King said of the plan that he was sponsoring, "My goal was to defeat as many Democratic incumbents as possible in order to give us five or six additional seats."[55] As many as seven Democratic seats in Congress could be lost under the plan. Minority organizations too announced their opposition. However, neither Democrats nor minority-advocacy organizations saw any remaining strategy for killing the bill.

Earlier in the third special session, House Democrats had joked about "not being here for a vote on a conference committee report." Rep. Paul Moreno had quipped, "Ardmore or Acapulco."[56] But in October 2003, reality was harsh and glaring for the Democrats. Lawmakers from both parties were exhausted. Rep. Garnet Coleman acknowledged that any quorum-busting walkout by House Democrats would be "fruitless."[57] As a result, "Everyone plans on being here," said Democrat Dawnna Dukes (Austin).[58]

In the Senate, there was some speculation that a senator, perhaps Gonzalo Barrientos, might try to kill the redistricting bill by filibustering until the end of the special session. However, the session could last until Tuesday, October 14. Even if a filibuster could be maintained that long without Republicans finding a way to shut it down, the governor would be sure to immediately call another session, the same redistricting bill would be passed immediately by both houses, and the statutory deadlines would again be moved as necessary.

Some Republicans from West Texas remained upset over the final plan and announced their intention to vote against it. Senator Troy Fraser explained, "My position continues to be that all 21 of my counties have been adversely affected because of the fact that Midland has stolen a congressional seat from Abilene and the Big Country area."[59] Several House members, including Bob Hunter of Abilene, also indicated that they would vote against final adoption of the plan. Hunter was disappointed because he felt that a district combining Lubbock and Abilene could have been achieved in a "more favorable way."[60]

On Friday morning, October 10, 2003, after about four hours of debate, the bill containing a redistricting plan that had been public for only one day passed the House 76–58. The Democrats once again attacked the effect of the plan on minority voters.[61] Garnet Coleman presented a detailed written analysis of the plan's impact on minority voters. The Democrats had the debate along with lawmakers' written comments included as part of the *House Journal*. As before in June, the Republicans largely remained silent as Democrats attacked the plan. Representative King explained, "My objective, and I've been consistent, is to elect more Republicans."[62] Six Republicans (Mike Hamilton, Bryan Hughes, Bob Hunter, Tommy Merritt, Geanie Morrison, and John Smithee) voted against the bill, and two Democrats (Vilma Luna and Ron Wilson) supported it.[63]

In the Senate, the consideration of the redistricting bill went on through the morning and much of the afternoon on Friday.[64] The Democratic senators generally challenged the purpose and effect of the redistricting bill through the common Senate tactic of asking the sponsor, Todd Staples, questions about the bill. The dispute centered on whether the plan diluted minority voting strength or, as claimed by Republicans, gave minorities two new opportunities to elect minorities to Congress. Senators pointed out how much the conference-committee map differed from the one the Senate had passed. Senator Zaffirini called attention to the split of Webb County. Senator Mario Gallegos accused Republicans of packing minorities into districts in Dallas, Houston, and South Texas, and referred to these areas as three "Noah's arks."[65] Republican senator Steve Ogden responded that Democrats believe that minorities can be represented only by Democrats, and challenged this assumption by pointing to the presence of three statewide (Republican) officials who are African American and to Congressman Henry Bonilla.

Throughout the questioning, Senator Staples nimbly avoided directly answering most of the Democrats' questions. At times he relied on humor or the "club atmosphere" of the Senate to cloud the issues or deflect senators' inquiries. He explained away changes made by the conference committee vaguely as the result of the committee taking all the numerous issues into consideration and coming up with an appropriate plan. Staples frequently reiterated his views that the disputes were partisan, not racial, and that retrogression under the Voting Rights Act would be measured on a statewide basis, not for individual districts. As the end neared, several of the Democratic senators (West, Gallegos, Barrientos, Zaffirini) delivered a prepared statement against passage of the redistricting plan. Gallegos lamented that after a "session longer than any other session in history," the legislature was bowing down to the wishes of Washington and ignoring "the priorities and the will of the majority of Texas."[66]

A number of Republican senators who supported the redistricting plan indicated that they would not vote for HB 3 until the House approved an unrelated but controversial government-reorganization bill that was still pending. Dewhurst was prepared to delay final action on the redistricting bill to meet the senators' concerns, but he wanted to be sure that debate on the redistricting bill was finished so no Democrat could later try to filibuster. The last speaker on the redistricting bill on Friday was the bill's sponsor, Senator Staples. With debate now closed, Senator Staples postponed the vote on the bill until 8:15 p.m. on Friday to allow the House time to act on the reorganization bill. However, by the afternoon, the House had lost many of its members (some of whom were en route to the UT-Oklahoma football game in Dallas), and a motion to suspend House rules to take up the reorganization bill failed. At 11 p.m. the House gave up trying to bring up the bill and adjourned until Sunday at 2 p.m. Shortly afterward the Senate adjourned until 6 p.m. on Sunday, the redistricting bill still pending.

There were rumors on Friday that as many as four Republican senators might vote against the bill because of the effect of the plan on their constituents. If so, and if all Democrats voted against the bill, the redistricting bill would fail to pass (15–16). The *San Angelo Standard-Times* urged Senator Duncan to take another look at voting against the redistricting bill.[67] Governor Perry was seen in the Senate chamber on Friday and was rumored to be twisting arms to obtain the necessary votes.

On the evening of Sunday October 12, the Texas Senate quickly ended the suspense. As Democratic Senator Eliot Shapleigh said, "We ran out of options."[68] There was no debate because the debate had been closed on Friday night. By a vote of 17–14, the Senate approved the redistricting plan. Two Republican senators, Troy Fraser and Bill Ratliff, voted against final passage.

On Monday October 13, Governor Perry signed the new redistricting bill into law. He savored the victory, proclaiming, "My taste is sweet in my mouth."[69] On the same day, the governor's political arm, Texans for Rick Perry, distributed an e-mail entitled "urgent appeal for action," asking citizens to send Perry and Republican lawmakers thank-you letters for their redistricting efforts. The e-mail included a fill-in-the-blank form saying that the state of Texas owed Republicans a debt of gratitude.

Democrats quickly filed suit in Tyler, in the federal Eastern District of Texas. They had file-stamped their lawsuit only minutes after the Senate finally approved redistricting. The federal court received the pleadings on Monday. Other parties, including LULAC, the GI Forum, and the NAACP, soon joined with their own challenges to the redistricting plan.

Republican Victory Celebrations

Republican congressmen were quick to celebrate an overwhelming victory. In a moment of unguarded glee, Joby Fortson, an aide to Congressman Joe Barton, proclaimed "ha ha ha ha ha ha ha ha ha ha ha ha ha ha" for Doggett and "ha ha ha ha ha ha ha ha ha" for Frost in an e-mail to fellow Republican staffers.[70] Congressman Barton was so confident of passage that he sent invitations in September to an October fundraiser dubbed a "Victory Celebration for Republican Redistricting."

Preclearance by the Department of Justice

The bill enacting the new redistricting plan was immediately submitted by Texas secretary of state Geoff Connor to the U.S. attorney general for review under Section 5 of the Voting Rights Act.[71] The staff of the Voting Section within the Civil Rights Division of the Justice Department had been watching the developments in Texas closely, and they were prepared to begin reviewing the new plan immediately. One of the largest groups of career professionals (eight attorneys and analysts) ever assigned to review a submission under Section 5 was assigned the job. Soon, various groups, including minority lawmakers from Texas and minority advocacy groups (such as LULAC and MALDEF), submitted written comments in opposition to the plan. As is usual in its review process, the staff met with groups from Texas, including officials and attorneys for the state, to discuss each group's support for or opposition to the redistricting plan. Even the Democratic congressional delegation submitted written comments and met with Voting Section staff to express their view that the redistricting plan put minority voters in a worse position than under the existing court-ordered plan.

In response to a charge by Democrats that Attorney General Ashcroft was partisan and that the redistricting plan needed to be reviewed by career attorneys, a Department of Justice spokesman said that the plan would undergo a "thorough, full and complete review by professionals who know the law and how the things need to be reviewed under the Voting Rights Act, and a determination is made on those facts, not on politics. . . . there is never a place for politics in the work of the Justice Department."[72] Soon, however, rumors spread in Washington and Austin that Congressman DeLay and the Bush White House had intervened with the Justice Department to see that the state submission was approved. One rumor was that the professional staff within the Voting Section had recommended against approving the Texas plan but had been overruled by the political appointees. Texas attorney general Gregg Abbott dismissed such rumors, commenting, "There's no truth or evidence to support aspersions such as that."[73]

The assistant U.S. attorney general for the Civil Rights Division (R. Alexander Acosta) without explanation recused himself from taking part in reviewing the Texas plan; his principal deputy, Sheldon Bradshaw, assumed his role. Meanwhile, a sharp dialogue on whether the Texas plan violated the Voting Rights Act was ongoing between the career professional legal staff of the Voting Section and the Civil Rights Division's political appointees. Bradshaw and deputy assistant attorney general Bradley Schlozman were among the political appointees who participated in this dialogue. One of the principal persons asserting that the plan did not violate the act was Hans von Spakovsky, counsel for the assistant attorney general.

By 2003, von Spakovsky had emerged within the Justice Department as the chief administration voice on voting rights. Before being picked to work at Justice, von Spakovsky had served on the board of advisers for the Voting Integrity Project. This politically conservative organization had gained notoriety among election lawyers nationwide because of its past efforts to curtail alleged voter fraud by sending observers to watch the polls in largely minority areas. Voting-rights groups accused the organization of trying to intimidate minority voters. The organization also had pushed for the purge of felons from state voting lists, and some accused it of being largely responsible for the felony-list fiasco in Florida before the 2000 election. During the 2000 postelection legal battle in Florida, von Spakovsky worked as part of the Bush legal team. After Bush's inauguration, he was hired for the Voting Section and soon was promoted to be counsel for the assistant attorney general heading the Civil Rights Division. In that role, von Spakovsky worked primarily on directing and overseeing work in the Voting Section.[74]

Although the dialogue within the Justice Department was intense, the outcome of the Texas review seemed to some participants to be clear and predetermined. Under department guidelines, any final decision on a statewide redistricting, such as the proposed plan for Texas, must be made at the assistant-attorney-general level or above. In other words, the final decision whether to object to the state's redistricting plan or to preclear it and allow it to become effective rested with the department's political appointees. As is customary, the career legal staff of the Voting Section prepared its recommendation based on the effect of the plan on protected minority voters. The recommendation, contained in the staff's seventy-three-page memorandum, dated December 12, 2003 was unanimous. The eight career professionals who had reviewed the redistricting plan did not see a close call. They recommended that the attorney general object to the redistricting plan as being retrogressive, in violation of Section 5 of the Voting Rights Act, because of its effect on Districts 23, 24, and 25 specifically, as well as on other districts around the state. Under past practice, any such unanimous recommendation by the reviewing legal team would almost certainly be followed. It was essentially unprecedented for such a recommendation to be overruled by the department's political appointees. However, on this occasion, the political appointees exercised their right to make the final decision. Within a week of receiving the recommendation (i.e., on Friday, December 19) acting assistant attorney general Sheldon Bradshaw sent the Texas secretary of state a letter containing the simple standard wording for a preclearance letter: "The Attorney General does not interpose any objection."

The internal memo from the Voting Section was held under tight wraps for two years.[75] The Department of Justice essentially placed the officials and employees who worked on the case under a gag order. Although rumors persisted that the internal memorandum existed, it did not surface publicly until November-December 2005. In an article on December 2, 2005, Dan Eggen of the *Washington Post* reported on the existence of the memorandum and on the staff's recommendation. He noted that the memorandum said that DeLay traveled to Texas to attend many of the meetings that produced the final map. The memorandum said that the changes made in the conference committee, out of public view, fundamentally altered acceptable redistricting proposals approved separately by the Texas House and Senate. The memorandum concluded that "it was not necessary" for the plans to be altered at the conference-committee stage except to advance partisan goals. In a concurring opinion that accompanied the memorandum, the head of the Voting Section at the time, Joe Rich, concluded: "This result [the 2003 redistricting plan] quite plainly indicates a reduction in minority voting strength. The state's argument that it has increased minority voting strength . . . simply does not stand up under careful analysis."

Preclearance was the critical stage legally. Under Section 5 of the Voting Rights Act, the government submitting the redistricting plan bears the burden of showing that the plan has neither the purpose nor the effect of worsening the voting position of minority voters. Once an attorney general acts to preclear a plan, the decision is final. Established federal law prevents any appeal or challenge of the decision. Therefore, with preclearance, the Texas redistricting plan became effective. Moreover, the existence of preclearance is invariably valuable to any government having to defend a redistricting plan in court. So it was to Texas in 2003.

Democrats and racial- and ethnic-minority advocacy organizations still hoped that a federal three-judge district court in Texas might block the plan as violative of the Constitution or Section 2 of the Voting Rights Act. In *Session v. Perry,* however, the legal issue was no longer whether the plan worsened minority voting strength, but whether it unlawfully diluted that strength. The heavy evidentiary and persuasive burden rested now with the plaintiffs, not the state. The court panel hearing the challenge consisted of two of the three judges who earlier had dismissed the Democratic senators' claims challenging the elimination of the two-thirds vote requirement. These two judges (Higginbotham and Rosenthal) had been appointed to the federal bench by Republican presidents; the third judge (Ward) had been appointed by a Democratic president.

I have chosen for purposes of this book not to relate in detail the events before the federal court in 2003. In general, the plaintiff Democrats and minority organizations made the same arguments outlined above, which had been made during the legislative process, about the discriminatory effects of the plan. The Texas attorney general, through private attorney Andy Taylor, responded that the Texas legislature had a right to adopt a mid-decade redistricting plan that drew districts to enhance the Republicans' partisan position. The plan did not discriminate against racial or ethnic minorities in violation of the Constitution or Section 2 of the Voting Rights Act, because, Taylor argued, any dilution of racial or ethnic voting strength was merely a result of partisan decisions, not intentional discrimination against any minority group. Moreover, Taylor argued, any possible dilution of minority voting strength in one part of the state (e.g., in Districts 23 and 24) was offset elsewhere (e.g., in Districts 9 and 25). Taylor insisted that the legislature had a right in its discretion to choose how best to recognize the voting strength of minority populations within Texas and had no obligation to maximize such voting strength. A majority of the court accepted Taylor's arguments. The court by 2–1 upheld the redistricting plan. The plan was used in the 2004 party primaries and general election.

Commentary

For decades a dispute has existed in this country over the best state institution to engage in redistricting—an independent commission or a state legislative body. Texas found a third alternative, redistricting by cabal. A cabal is a small group of like-minded persons secretly united to bring about major changes in public policy through the usurpation of the powers of the legitimate official bodies or individuals. In Texas, the state legislative bodies were empowered to draw congressional districts for the benefit of the residents of the state. In 2003, neither the residents of the state nor the members of the Texas House or Senate had any significant impact on the final redistricting plan. That plan was drawn in secret by a handful of persons with a common objective, working under pressure from outside partisan interests: to maximize the number of Republicans in Congress from Texas while defeating as many Anglo Democratic incumbents as legally possible. After five months, the final redistricting plan (looking very different from the plans passed earlier by the House and Senate) became public only hours before it was passed by an emotionally exhausted state legislature. The cabal had succeeded. In the words of one Republican lawmaker who had been caught up in the pressures of the final days, the "process had been corrupted" by partisan outside forces.

Under traditional measures of retrogression, the final redistricting plan was clearly violative of Section 5 of the Voting Rights Act. The critical analysis and recommended objection by the career staff of the Voting Section was no surprise to experienced election lawyers. However, by law, Section 5 preclearance is wholly within the discretion of the U.S. attorney general; there is no appeal.

Once the political appointees within Justice overruled the career lawyers and approved the Texas plan, any hope of stopping the Republican redistricting plan from taking effect for the 2004 elections essentially disappeared.

Republican officials, activist groups, and lawyers long complained about this absolute power within Justice because in prior years it has meant that state and local governments have been compelled to bend to please Justice's career staffers (attorneys and analysts) or face the possibility of having a redistricting or other election law unilaterally stopped from ever taking effect. This would have happened again in 2003 if the career staff within the Voting Section had had their way. The political appointees in Justice would have nothing of such a result.

Instead of bringing balance to the Section 5 review process, the Bush administration has co-opted the unilateral power of the Justice Department to further Republican objectives and interests. The administration has engaged in a house cleaning of the "liberal bureaucrats" whom it saw as controlling the Civil Rights Division. Experienced, capable, caring attorneys and analysts have been either forced out, or moved aside and replaced by persons selected for their ideology as much as for their legal acumen, and perhaps more. Moreover, Section 5 review has become highly politicized, since individual outcomes are driven by the timing and partisan implications rather than by the discriminatory purpose or effect of the election change. The original purposes of the act have been lost amidst the Republicans' drive for revenge against the professional staff within Justice. These issues are discussed further in Chapter Fifteen.

CHAPTER 13

The Effects of the Final Plan

The maps are now official. I have studied them and this is the most aggressive map I have ever seen. This has a real national impact that should assure that Republicans keep the House no matter the national mood.
—JOBY FORTSON, A MEMBER OF CONGRESSMAN JOE BARTON'S STAFF, IN AN E-MAIL TO REPUBLICAN CONGRESSIONAL STAFFERS, OCTOBER 9, 2003 (SPELLING CORRECTED FROM ORIGINAL)

The effects of the 2003 redistricting will be felt not only for the remainder of this decade, but for the foreseeable future. The final redistricting plan (Plan 1374) is a masterpiece of partisan engineering. It is the most carefully designed and effectively gerrymandered plan that I have ever seen.

Neither the Republican lawyers nor the final Republican map drawers in 2003 were worried about using the Republican political advantage to the maximum extent possible to draw partisan districts that would defeat Anglo Democrats. They felt that any subsequent court challenge by Democrats on the basis of partisanship would be unsuccessful, just as the Republicans' challenges in the past had been unsuccessful. Instead, the Republican leadership focused on how best to insulate a final redistricting plan from a legal attack based on racial or ethnic discrimination.

Since most actions directed at minimizing Democratic voting strength would also affect minority voters, given the extent to which African American and Hispanic voters vote Democratic, Republicans in 2003 walked a narrow line. They were cautious throughout the process to explain and to justify redistricting plans as being beneficial to racial- and ethnic-minority interests. They dismissed complaints by minority organizations to the contrary as partisan, even if these organizations lacked any direct or indirect tie to the Democratic

Party and even if Democrats opposed the organizations' positions. This Republican strategy worked.

The Partisan Effects

Chapter Five describes the strategy the Republicans used to try to defeat the ten incumbent Anglo Democratic congressmen. If the strategy had been fully successful, the Texas congressional delegation after the 2004 election would have consisted of twenty-two Republicans and ten Democrats, with all of the Democratic congressmen being African American or Hispanic. Incumbents in rural districts were separated from their constituents in the existing districts and paired with a Republican incumbent in districts specially redrawn to elect the Republican. Incumbents in urban districts were moved into heavily Republican suburban districts. This Republican strategy worked.

Of the Democratic incumbents elected previously from predominately rural districts, one, Jim Turner, decided against seeking reelection after he was paired with Republican congressman Joe Barton (and Martin Frost) in a district containing only 4 percent of Turner's prior constituents. Three other Democratic incumbents (Sandlin, Stenholm, and Lampson) ran for reelection in their redrawn districts, but lost. A fifth Democrat (Hall) changed parties and won reelection as a Republican. Only one of these six Democrats, Congressman Chet Edwards, ran for reelection in his redrawn district (District 17) and won.

Houston congressman Gene Green was drawn out of his predominately Hispanic district (District 29). His new district was also partly in Harris County, however, and Green sought and won reelection in District 29. Similarly, Lloyd Doggett in Travis County abandoned his now heavily Republican district (District 10) to run for reelection in the now predominately Hispanic District 25, where he won in the Democratic primary over a Hispanic candidate from Hidalgo County and won again in the general election over a Republican Hispanic candidate from Hidalgo County. It was unlikely that candidates from Travis County could continue to win in District 25 once Congressman Doggett was gone. So also, it reasonably can be expected that at some point Congressman Green will be replaced by a Hispanic candidate.

District 24 in the Dallas–Tarrant County area was dismantled. If the Democratic incumbent, Congressman Martin Frost, ran for reelection, it would be in a heavily Republican district. Frost ran and lost. District 25 in Harris County was redrawn and renumbered District 9. It was left as a probable Democratic district, but with a larger percentage of African American voters, who were better positioned to control the Democratic primary. Anglo incumbent Chris Bell was drawn out of the redrawn district, but nevertheless sought reelection in District 9. He lost in the Democratic primary to African American Al Green.

The Republican strategy had targeted all ten of the Anglo incumbent Democrats; only three returned to Congress after 2004 as Democrats. The effect was a gain of six Republican seats, and the makeup of the Texas delegation changed from 17–15 in favor of the Democrats to 21–11 in favor of the Republicans. The net effect was to increase the Republican majority in Congress by twelve and to preserve an additional endangered Republican seat (District 23).

The Effect on Racial and Ethnic Minority Voters

Although the Republicans claimed that increasing minority-voter participation was both a purpose and an effect of the 2003 redistricting, an analysis of what actually happened tells a different story.

The Republican Claim of Increasing Minority-Voter Participation

A Republican pro-minority justification for redistricting was established early. When he testified before the Texas legislature in 2001 about congressional redistricting, Congressman Tom DeLay indicated that a redrawn plan should enhance minority voting strength. He specifically endorsed the MALDEF proposal for making District 24 more Hispanic.

On March 2, 2003, Andy Taylor, the attorney who had represented the state in redistricting in 2001 and was already actively representing Republican interests in several civil and criminal actions arising out of the 2002 campaign, claimed in the *Houston Chronicle* that redistricting in 2003 was necessary to "do right by minority Texans." As he argued: "The most compelling reason to have lawmakers in Austin redraw Texas congressional lines during this legislative session is to immediately increase minority representation instead of having to wait another decade for this to happen." Taylor pointed out that as the counsel for the state in 2001, he had asked the federal court to adopt a plan that would have created "an additional African-American district in the Houston area and an additional Latino district in the Dallas–Fort Worth area." He concluded that such a plan could be drawn by the legislature in 2003 and that "I feel strongly we will have another missed opportunity if we don't act quickly, while our Legislature is in session."

Congressman Tom DeLay and other Republicans continued during 2003 to justify the redistricting effort by promising new safe seats for minorities. On July 8, after the House had passed a redistricting bill during the first special session, DeLay explained, "I would just hope that the house and senate come together and understand how important it is to the people of Texas to be properly represented, and that means more Republican seats, more Hispanic seats and more African-American seats."[1] Lieutenant Governor Dewhurst said that the Republican plans would add two minorities to Congress. He said that Republicans wanted to increase minority voting participation and any contrary claim was "political spin."

The actual Republican approach is better represented in Congressman Joe Barton's explanation to Governor Perry in late May: "[L]et's protect blacks and Hispanics and in the rest of the state let's draw lines that reflect the voting patterns of the state [referring to Republican's recent electoral successes]."[2] Whenever given a choice between enhancing or maintaining minority voting strength or legally increasing the probable number of Republicans in Congress, the Republicans always chose to increase the number of Republicans. DeLay aide Jim Ellis admitted to me in 2005 that this was the result, but he still believed that the final plan benefited minorities—but at "the expense of Anglo Democratic incumbents" rather than Republicans.

During the redistricting process, Republicans characterized minority districts as "performing" or "nonperforming." A minority district was "performing" if it elected an African American or a Hispanic. It was "nonperforming" if an Anglo was elected. Although judging the merits of a district based only on the race or ethnicity of its representative rather than on the ability of minorities to elect the candidate of their choice is a dubious legal analysis, the view was offered by Republicans to explain why a "nonperforming" district (such as District 24) was not entitled to Voting Rights Act protection and why the Hispanic voting population in a district (such as District 23) could legally be significantly reduced, since the district would still "perform," i.e., be likely to reelect a minority (Republican congressman Bonilla). Moreover, this same rationale helped explain why Republicans moved Anglo congressman Gene Green from District 29 (an existing Hispanic-opportunity district) and then sometimes counted District 29 as a new opportunity for the election of a minority candidate. The specific affected districts are discussed below.

District 24

As it existed before the 2003 redistricting, District 24, straddling Dallas and Tarrant counties, had a total minority population percentage of 60.2 percent (22.7 percent African American, 38 percent Hispanic).[3] The district combined

Hispanic areas in both counties with the African American community in southeastern Tarrant County, the third largest in Texas. The district's status under the Voting Rights Act, however, was uncertain—was it protected or not? Most lawyers, including those of the Texas Legislative Council, advised that even though no single minority group could control the outcome in the district, District 24 was probably a protected minority-opportunity district. In their memorandum objecting to the Texas redistricting plan, the career lawyers and analysts of the Justice Department's Voting Section agreed that District 24 was a minority-opportunity district, one effectively controlled by the black voters.

Both Congressman DeLay and attorney Andy Taylor publicly endorsed the MALDEF idea of making District 24 a majority Hispanic district. However, the dilemma for Republicans was that the foremost target among Democratic incumbents, Martin Frost, was the incumbent in District 24. To leave the district as a Democratic district would almost certainly ensure that Frost would win reelection, even if his residence were moved outside the district. This outcome was likely even if the Hispanic percentage of the district were increased, because of Frost's advantages as an incumbent and because low Hispanic voter eligibility, registration, and turnout would impair a challenge from a Hispanic candidate. To DeLay and the Republican congressional delegation, a redistricting plan that did not result in the defeat of Frost was not worth the effort. Therefore, District 24 had to go if legally possible.

Republicans struggled with whether the legislature could legally dismantle the district; neither the House nor Senate was comfortable with entirely eliminating it. As a result, as much as the Republicans wanted to eliminate Frost, neither the House nor Senate plans that went to the conference committee substantially altered the racial and ethnic makeup of District 24. However, neither plan made the district majority Hispanic, as sought by MALDEF.

When the conference committee ultimately succumbed to the aggressive plan pushed by DeLay, it disregarded the outcomes in the House and Senate, as well as DeLay's earlier promotion of a Hispanic district in Dallas, and instead dismantled the district. It concluded that the district was "nonperforming" (because it did not elect a minority) and therefore was not entitled to protection under the Voting Rights Act. The final districting plan spread the minority areas of District 24 among several districts. Many of the Hispanics in the district were placed (Democrats claim "packed") into the predominately African American district of Congresswoman Eddie Bernice Johnson (District 30), thereby increasing its minority population percentage by 4 percent, to 76.1 percent; or they were placed (Democrats would say "fractured") into one of the five Republican districts in the area. The African American voters were split among three heavily Republican districts. Under the final plan, none of these minority communities from the previous District 24 was likely to be able to affect the election of congressmen in the foreseeable future, as long as they vote predominantly for Democratic candidates.

District 23

District 23 stretches for 500 miles from San Antonio to El Paso across the sparsely populated counties of far West Texas. The incumbent in 2003 was Republican Henry Bonilla from San Antonio (Bexar County). He had initially won election in 1992 by beating the Democratic incumbent in a district that had been redrawn in 1991 to absorb a heavily Republican area in San Antonio.

In the 2002 election, Bonilla had received significantly less than a majority of the Hispanic vote in the district, and the percentage of Hispanic population in the district was growing. MALDEF claimed that in 2002 only approximately 8 percent of Hispanic voters in District 23 supported Bonilla's reelection bid. As a result, Bonilla came within 6,488 votes of losing the election to a Democratic challenger, Henry Cuellar from Webb County. Mr. Cuellar (who won election to Congress in 2004 in redrawn District 28 by defeating the incumbent congressman in the Democratic primary) actually led Bonilla in election returns until late on election night, when the heavily Republican (and Anglo) precincts of northern Bexar County reported their results. Jim Ellis told me in 2005 that the Republican delegation conceded that in an open race, District 23 would go Democrat.

Therefore, one of the Republican objectives in 2003 was to redraw District 23 to reduce its percentage of Hispanic (Democratic) voters, making the district safe for the continued reelection of Congressman Bonilla or another Republican. According to Ellis, the Republican congressional delegation was united behind "shoring up" Bonilla.[4] Nevertheless, because of concerns that reducing the number of Hispanic voters in the district could violate the Voting Rights Act, neither the House nor Senate redistricting plans significantly altered District 23.

The outcome at the conference committee was very different. District 23 was redrawn to reduce the percentage of Spanish surnamed registered voters (SSRV) from 43–44 percent. Predominately Anglo counties (Kerr, 77.4 percent Anglo; Kendall, 80.5 percent; and Bandera, 84.1 percent) in the Hill Country of south-central Texas were added to the district, and 99,776 people (according to the 2000 census), most of them (96 percent) Hispanic, were removed by reassigning half of Webb County, the political base of the candidate who had almost defeated Bonilla in 2002. The changes made the district one in which Republican statewide candidates won an average of 56.8 percent of the vote in 2002 and Al Gore received only 36.3 percent of the vote for president in 2000.

To many Republicans, however, District 23 remained a Hispanic district after the 2003 redistricting because it had been left with 50.9 percent Hispanic voting-age population and because, as Republican Senator Todd Staples explained during debate in the Senate, "Henry Bonilla is Hispanic," even if he is not the choice of a majority of the Hispanic voters in the district. Therefore, although District 23 no longer had a Hispanic voting majority able to elect a candidate of its choice, Republicans consistently included it among the eight Hispanic districts in what was designated the 8–3 plan.

District 15

District 15 was one of the parallel districts running northward from the southern tip of Texas. Its population was 78.3 percent Hispanic, with a 74.3 percent Hispanic voting-age population, and 67 percent SSRV. In the 2003 redistricting plan, some of the heavily Hispanic areas in the district were shifted to make District 25 a Hispanic-opportunity district. As a result, in the final redistricting plan the percentage of SSRV dropped to 56.7 percent. More importantly to Democrats, the Democratic voting percentage, as measured by 2002 state election results, dropped to near 55 percent. In fact, in the 2004 presidential election, Bush carried newly redrawn District 15, along with two other heavily Hispanic congressional districts (Districts 27 and 28). However, for MALDEF attorney Nina Perales, the decline in the Democratic voting percentage was not a legitimate reason for objecting to the change in District 15, because it remained one in which Hispanics had an opportunity to elect the person of their choice, whether Republican or Democrat.[5] The disagreement over the changes to District 15 was an issue that divided MALDEF and the Democrats. Moreover, the Voting Section of the Justice Department concluded that the changes to District 15 were not a reason to object to the Texas Section 5 preclearance submission.

District 25

District 25 was located in Harris and Fort Bend counties before the 2003 redistricting. It had a combined majority population of 52.3 percent based on the 2000 census. Most of the area previously in this district was included in the redrawn District 9, discussed below.

The District 25 of the 2003 redistricting plan was a new district stretching in a narrow strip from Travis County to the Rio Grande Valley. Its population was 68.6 percent Hispanic. The voters of the district in 2004 elected incumbent

Anglo Congressman Lloyd Doggett, who abandoned his now overwhelmingly Republican district (District 10) to run in the sole Democratic district still partly in Travis County.

To Republicans, District 25 was a new Hispanic district that added to Hispanic voting strength in Texas. Although Senator Staples claimed that the Senate plan was similar to one supported by MALDEF, Hispanic organizations found the plan with the redrawn District 25 unacceptable: MALDEF saw the district as merely a legal justification for the loss of District 23, not as an increase in Hispanic strength. The configuration of the redrawn District 25 resembled a district included in a plan proffered by Perales on behalf of MALDEF during the session, but MALDEF's plan also retained District 23 unchanged. As long as the new District 25 was tied to a loss of District 23 as a Hispanic-opportunity district, she was not willing on behalf of the GI Forum or MALDEF to support the final plan.

District 9 (redrawn District 25)

District 25 as it existed for the 2002 election was predominately minority (52.3 percent), but was not clearly a district protected under the Voting Rights Act. Republicans concluded that the district was "nonperforming" because it had elected an Anglo (Chris Bell) in 2002. The area in and around former District 25 was shifted among several districts in the redistricting. Most of former District 25 was placed in District 9. Senator Staples characterized the new District 9 as likely to be a "strong performing African-American district."[6]

District 9 in the final redistricting plan was legitimately an enhanced opportunity for the election of an African American candidate of choice to Congress. The combined minority percentage of population in the district was raised from 52.3 to 66.2 percent. The percentage of African American voting-age population was increased from 22.0 to 36.5 percent. In 2004, the voters in the district elected Al Green, who became the third African American now serving in Congress from Texas. Whether Green (the former president of the Houston NAACP) or another African American candidate might have won in 2004 or later in a district with fewer African American voters is disputed among African American Democrats in Houston. However, the increase in African American VAP enhanced the opportunity for African American voters to elect the candidate of their choice. Representative Ron Wilson is justifiably entitled to credit for pressing for this increase.

District 9 also served at least two partisan purposes. First, as redrawn, it probably defeated the Anglo incumbent Chris Bell. The district left Bell's residence in a heavily Republican district. Even when Bell switched districts and ran for reelection in District 9, he was vulnerable to a challenger who could appeal more effectively to the increased percentage of African American voters, as Al Green in fact did. It is clear that this defeat of another Anglo Democratic incumbent, even though the district remains Democratic, is counted as a success by the Republicans who planned and pushed redistricting in 2003.

A more important partisan purpose behind the creation of a district with an increased opportunity for the election of an African American was the cover it provided for any legal challenge. Republicans asserted that the changes in District 9 created a "new" minority-opportunity district. From the Republican legal viewpoint, the presence of this district in the final redistricting plan could be used to offset the loss of minority voters' opportunity to elect the candidate of their choice, including Martin Frost, in District 24. As Jim Ellis put it to me in 2005, the redrawing of District 9 offset the redrawing of District 23 (Bonilla), even though one change increased African American voting strength while the other decreased Hispanic voting strength. The career legal staff in the Justice Department's Voting Section concluded that District 25 as it existed in 2002 was an effective minority district, even though Anglo Bell had been elected, and that the increased African American percentage in District 9 did not change the district's basic nature (i.e., it remained a minority-opportunity district).

From a partisan perspective, the changes to District 9 were a political wash. They did not result in creation of an otherwise avoidably Democratic seat; the District 25 from which Bell had been elected had been a Democratic district; and the comparable district in both the House and Senate was Democratic. The effect of the increase in the African American percentage in District 9 probably affected who might win the Democratic primary, not which party was likely to win the general election. Therefore, to the extent that the changes in District 9 potentially justified making the redrawn District 24 strongly Republican, the ultimate result was a gain of another Republican seat in Congress.

For Representative Wilson, it was unimportant that creating an enhanced election opportunity for an African American also provided a partisan benefit to Republicans. He felt that the Republican redistricting was a train that was moving inevitably toward its destination. He believed that it was better to "catch a ride on that train" and gain another African American–opportunity district than "to stand in the middle of the tracks and be run over."[7]

Dilution of African American and Hispanic Voter Influence Statewide

The congressional districting plan from 1991 had placed the scattered African American communities in Tyler, Longview, Port Arthur, Waco, Galveston, and Beaumont, along with the smaller African American communities of East Texas, into districts in which the African American vote ultimately proved important in the Democratic primary and the general election. This effect survived the adoption by the court of a redistricting plan in 2001. In fact, many of the Anglo Democrats targeted by the Republicans in 2003 would not have won reelection in 2000 and 2002 except for the support of these minority communities.

Democratic Congressmen Turner, Sandlin, and Edwards testified at trial in 2003 that the vote from these dispersed minority communities (mostly African American) had been determinative of the election outcomes in 2002, and that the congressmen must be responsive to such critical voters. A similar effect on election outcomes was shown for the Hispanic voters dispersed throughout Districts 11 and 17. The Republican dilemma was that in order to defeat the targeted Democratic incumbents, it was essential that, whenever possible, these African American and Hispanic communities be placed in districts where this dependably Democratic vote could be overwhelmed by the expected staunchly Republican vote. Therefore, one after another, these smaller African American and Hispanic communities around the state were placed into districts where they could do little partisan harm.

As a practical matter, the creation of neither the predominately African American District 9 in the Harris County area nor the predominately Hispanic District 25 affected how the other, smaller African American or Hispanic communities statewide would be treated in any final redistricting plan. Both districts were geographically separate from these other areas. The political reality, however, was very different. The creation of Districts 9 and 25 left the Republican majority better positioned legally and politically to disregard the dilutive effect of the plan on minority voters statewide.

To Republicans, this process was a matter of partisan politics. Submerging these smaller minority communities in Republican districts was simply the best means for ensuring the greatest number of Republican election victories. The NAACP and the African American members of the Texas legislature (other than Wilson) saw things differently. They saw the movement of these African American communities into districts in which they had no likelihood of affecting the election outcome for the foreseeable future as retrogressive and dilutive of minority voting rights, in clear violation of the Voting Rights Act. The Hispanic lawmakers and advocacy groups expressed similar concerns about the dilution of Hispanic voting rights statewide.

In a conversation with me in 2005, a former Justice Department official responsible for reviewing the 2003 redistricting said that he felt this submergence of the smaller African American and Hispanic communities statewide posed one of the most serious legal problems in the redistricting.

Table 13.1. The ten majority-minority districts formed by the 2003 redistricting*

District	Voting-age population (%)				Total minority population (%)	Predicted Democratic vote (%)
	Anglo	Hispanic	Afr. Amer.	Minority		
9	20.7	30.3	36.5	66.2	70.4	69.2
15	31.9	64.0	3.3	67.1	71.8	55.7
16	20.1	74.8	3.4	77.8	80.7	64.4
18	23.4	32.2	40.3	72.2	76.1	74.0
20	26.9	63.6	7.1	70.3	74.1	62.3
25	26.7	63.4	8.0	71.1	76.2	69.8
27	31.5	64.2	2.8	66.8	70.7	55.6
28	32.0	60.1	6.8	66.6	70.7	58.9
29	21.9	61.8	9.9	71.3	76.0	64.2
30	21.9	34.2	42.3	71.4	76.1	77.3

Note: The percentage of total minority VAP sometimes is less than the total of Hispanic and African American VAP because some people indicate in the census that they are black, but also of Hispanic origin.
The predicted-vote percentages are based on returns from 2002 statewide races, when all Democratic statewide candidates lost. It is possible, therefore, that this chart understates the possible Democratic vote in these districts.
*The remedial plan adopted by the federal court in 2006 changes these figures for Districts 15, 28, and 25. See the Afterword.

Packing Minority Voters

The final redistricting plan created ten districts with a majority of minority voters. However, consistent with a redistricting strategy of "packing" the votes of a partisan opponent into as few districts as possible, these ten minority districts contained an overwhelming majority of minority persons and Democratic voters. The racial-ethnic breakdown of the districts and their predicted voting percentage for Democratic candidates are shown in Table 13.1.

Moreover, the 2003 plan designed these districts so that they will almost certainly become even more heavily minority through the remainder of the decade.[8] By contrast, the twenty-two "Republican" districts essentially "spread the wealth" of Republican voters uniformly statewide to secure Republican control over future elections. Virtually all these districts have an expected Republican vote (based on the 2002 statewide election results) of 64–68 percent, and although some are likely to become somewhat more Hispanic and Democratic over the remainder of this decade, none seems likely to become Democratic.[9]

Longer-Term Republican Strategy in Texas

The redistricting in 2003 served another important Republican objective. Republicans were aware that as the number of Hispanic voters continued to grow, Texas would become a majority-minority state, and if current voting patterns held, would become more Democratic. According to the federal census bureau, Anglos by 2004 made up slightly less than half of Texas's population. This significant turning point may have been achieved by the time of the 2003 redistricting.

The Republican redistricting was drawn in part to offset even this anticipated Hispanic voter growth further into the future. At the time of redistricting in 2011, the Republicans elected under the 2003 plan will be incumbents, and thus better able to protect themselves in the redistricting process and in subsequent elections, even if challenged by Hispanic candidates. Senator Zaffirini described this purpose as an attempt by Republicans in 2003 to "solidify their gains" through redistricting so that they will be in control of redistricting in 2011 and "so they will be fortified [as incumbents], so to speak, before the Hispanics become a majority."[10]

In other words, the effects of the 2003 redistricting are likely to be felt in Texas for at least the next two decades. The districts drawn in 2003 effectively negate any chance that any further growth in Hispanic population over the remainder of this decade will add a Hispanic congressman at the expense of Republicans. Hispanic voter growth in Districts 25 (Doggett) and 29 (Green), or the decision of one or both of these Anglo congressmen to not seek reelection, is likely to result in an additional Democratic Hispanic in Congress by the end of the decade, but not at the loss of a Republican. Moreover, the 2003 redistricting gives Republicans (and previously endangered Republican congressman Henry Bonilla) a district (District 23) that, with its SSRV lowered to 44 percent, will be safely Republican even in the face of future Hispanic population growth. The significance of the court-drawn remedial plan (2006) is discussed in the Afterword.

Commentary

What can I say? The partisan design was masterful.

The Dilemma for Racial- and Ethnic-Minority Lawmakers and Advocacy Organizations

I know I'm going to upset some Democrats with this, but there are things about redistricting worth supporting. I would have to look closely.
— STATE REPRESENTATIVE HAROLD DUTTON, MAY 27, 2003

Since most African American and Hispanic voters continue to vote for Democratic candidates in Texas, it sometimes is difficult for minority lawmakers and advocacy groups to escape criticism that their choices in redistricting are driven by partisan interests. In reality, most minority lawmakers and minority-advocacy organizations confront an ongoing quandary of how best to support the Democratic Party and be properly responsive to their constituents and their advocacy mission.

The redistricting process in 2003 posed serious dilemmas for the minority-advocacy groups, especially the Hispanic organizations. Hispanic groups had not obtained in 2001 the increase in Hispanic-majority districts in the Texas congressional delegation that they thought should accompany the Hispanic population growth that occurred between the 1990 and 2000 censuses. Some of the blame was placed on the Democratic Party's fight to protect its Anglo incumbents. In 2003, these organizations saw a new opportunity to achieve this increase in Hispanic political opportunity, but the adversary had become the Republican Party.

For minority lawmakers, the dilemma was an old one—are the interests of a minority community better served by a redistricting plan that draws the maximum number of districts in which the minority group is likely to control the outcome of an election, or by a plan that gives the minority group the greatest influence on the decision making of the legislative body at stake? Although an old dilemma, it took on added significance in 2003 as the number of minority Democratic elected officials had increased, while the number of Democratic

Anglo officials had declined at the state and national level. Minority lawmakers in 2003 held differing opinions. The stories of these lawmakers and their conflicts are an important part of what happened in 2003.

The Hispanic and African American Advocacy Organizations

In prior decades, several organizations played an important role through legislation and litigation in increasing representation for racial and ethnic minorities in Texas. Although these organizations try to maintain a bipartisan stance and sometimes oppose Democratic legal and political positions, many Republicans consider these organizations to be Democratic partisans.

Mexican American Advocacy Groups

Hispanic advocacy organizations, such as the Mexican American Legal Defense Fund (MALDEF), the American GI Forum of Texas, and the Texas League of United Latin American Citizens (LULAC), have played a major role in redistricting for four decades in Texas. All were active in the congressional redistricting process during 2001 and 2003 on behalf of the creation or maintenance of districts that contain a Hispanic voting majority. Ultimately their organizations' redistricting goals were largely unrealized in 2003: the Republican majority saw adding or maintaining those districts as unnecessary to meeting Voting Rights Act requirements and as reducing the number of districts that could be expected to vote Republican. As a result, Republican lawmakers tended to dismiss the organizations' proposals as being partisanly Democratic. This was a mistake.

In 2003 Nina Perales was regional counsel for MALDEF in San Antonio. She retained that position in 2006. Ms. Perales has consistently argued since 2001 that with the phenomenal growth in Hispanic population between 1990 and 2000, Hispanics are entitled to more opportunities to elect representatives to Congress, especially since the two additional seats Texas was apportioned after the 2000 decennial census were largely due to that Hispanic population growth. MALDEF demonstrated how districts could be drawn to achieve this result.

LULAC and MALDEF's objectives during congressional redistricting in 2001 were to preserve the existing seven Hispanic-opportunity districts; to create a new Hispanic opportunity district in south-central Texas; and to refashion the 24th District in Dallas–Fort Worth so as to raise its Latino voting-age population above 50 percent. This first objective was relatively easy to achieve in 2001, especially since the Voting Rights Act prevented any retrogression in Hispanic voting strength. In 2001, however, the Democrats opposed the other two objectives because, first, of the potential that drawing a new Hispanic-opportunity district in south-central Texas could have a ripple effect that would adversely affect the district of Democratic incumbent Charlie Stenholm (District 17), and, second, because Democratic incumbent Martin Frost (District 24) opposed major changes to the districts in Dallas County.

The federal court plan in 2001 (from the *Balderas* court) did not create any new Hispanic-opportunity districts. The two congressional districts newly apportioned to Texas were drawn in suburban areas around Dallas and Houston and were won in 2002 by Anglo Republicans. As a result, the 2001 court plan actually had the effect of reducing the percentage of Hispanic-opportunity districts from 23.3 to 21.8 percent of the state's congressional districts.

In 2003, MALDEF's objectives remained essentially the same as they had in 2001.[1] It was now the Republicans, however, who directly opposed the changes they sought. In its final redistricting plan, the Republican-controlled legislature dismembered the 24th District entirely in its effort to defeat Congressman Frost, spreading the Hispanic voters in Dallas and Fort Worth among six districts. The final plan also materially reduced Hispanic strength in District 23 (West Texas) from 43–44 percent Spanish surnamed registered voters (SSRV). This change made District 23 much more strongly Republican, but MALDEF's objection to the change was that it eliminated a district in which Hispanic voters had an opportunity to elect the person of their choice. The final plan also created a new Hispanic-opportunity district in District 25, but with the reductions in District 23, the number of districts with a Hispanic voting majority—seven—remained unchanged from 2001.

In his February 5, 2003, memorandum to Congressman DeLay, Jim Ellis noted that Lieutenant Governor Dewhurst wanted MALDEF and LULAC onboard for the Republican redistricting plan. MALDEF was approached later by Dale Oldham, the redistricting counsel for the Republican National Committee. Oldham met with Nina Perales in San Antonio after the end of the regular session. He asked her to agree to support a new Hispanic-opportunity district that would run generally from South Texas to Travis County. His map showed only this one district (which Perales recalled in 2006 as having the same basic shape as that of the new District 25 in the final redistricting plan). Perales rejected this district in isolation from the other districts in Texas because she wanted to know the overall effect of any plan on Hispanic voting opportunities elsewhere, especially in District 23. Agreeing to a new Hispanic-opportunity district while losing District 23 would leave Hispanic voters without any gain. Oldham could not offer any assurances that District 23 would not be changed from a Hispanic-opportunity district. He left without MALDEF's agreement. DeLay had expected this rejection and credited it to MALDEF's interest in obtaining attorney fees from 2001 and to its being "more Democratic than Hispanic." In the first special session Dewhurst again hoped MALDEF and LULAC would support the Republican plan. When the groups criticized it instead, Dewhurst joined DeLay in crediting the criticism to partisanship.

When she spoke to me in 2005, Perales had a very different perspective on the events.[2] To her, "Both sides [the two political parties] are using race to meet their ends. What's more important to us [MALDEF] is if minority voters prefer that person, then it's their right to elect them." She added, "We are a nonpartisan organization. We only focus on Latino voters' ability to elect their candidate, whoever that person is." She pointed to the fact that MALDEF did not share the concerns of the Democratic Party about the changes to District 15 because, at 56.7 percent SSRV, the district remained one in which Hispanics could elect the person of their choice. MALDEF had proposed a similar change in its redistricting plan as necessary to create an additional Hispanic-majority district. Her objection, however, was that the Republican plan did not create a net additional Hispanic-majority district because of the retrogression of Hispanic voting strength in District 23.

After evaluating the final redistricting plan, MALDEF, LULAC, and the GI Forum filed suit in October 2003, challenging the plan as violative of the Voting Rights Act and the Constitution. The organizations, however, sought different remedies. LULAC pushed for a return to the districts used in 2002. MALDEF and the GI Forum sought a new remedial plan that would maintain District 23 as a Hispanic-opportunity district, but also add an additional Hispanic-opportunity district (such as District 25).

National Association for the Advancement of Colored People (NAACP)

The president of the NAACP in Texas testified at a hearing in Houston (June 28, 2003) that blacks throughout Texas would be harmed if Democratic incumbents were defeated. The NAACP emphasized that the organization's legislative report card for the last two congressional sessions indicated that the targeted Democrats were more than three times more likely than Republican congressmen from Texas to support issues important to blacks.

In 2001, the Association of Black Democrats proposed the creation of a second predominantly African American district in Harris County. District 9, as adopted in 2003, was similar to that district. Nevertheless, like the Hispanic activist organizations, the NAACP concluded that any gain in Harris County was nullified by the other changes made by the plan statewide.

Shortly after the final redistricting plan was adopted in 2003, the NAACP also challenged the plan in federal court. The organization continued its opposition in court even though the former president of the NAACP chapter for Houston, Al Green, won election to Congress from the redrawn District 9.

The Dilemma Confronting African American and Hispanic Lawmakers

Hispanic lawmakers remained essentially united in opposition to the Republican redistricting. In fact, it was largely the Hispanic members of the House and Senate who led the walkouts. In the House, Rep. Richard Raymond was an early advocate for breaking the legislative quorum and played a major role throughout the redistricting fight. Other Hispanic House members, such as Pete Gallego (chairman of the Latin American Caucus in the Texas House), also took a leadership role. The overwhelming majority of House lawmakers who walked out were Hispanic; only two remained in Austin. In the Senate, Leticia Van de Putte was the president of the Democratic Caucus. She made the logistical arrangements for the walkout to New Mexico and was the primary spokesperson for the Democrats while they were in Albuquerque. Seven of the eleven senators who went to Albuquerque are Hispanic. Hispanic senators Mario Gallegos, Judith Zaffirini, Gonzalo Barrientos, Frank Madla, and Juan Hinojosa also were prominent in the redistricting battle. No Hispanic senators broke with the Democratic boycott.

African American lawmakers on the other hand were deeply divided. Six of the thirteen African American members of the House stayed in Austin when the House Democrats broke quorum. They remained behind partly because of a split over how these lawmakers could best represent their constituents. As the final redistricting plan took shape, the most divisive issue arose. It was the importance of creating a district (District 9) with a higher African American VAP (up from 22 to 36.5 percent), leading to the increased possibility that an African American was likely to win election to Congress. Was the creation of this district a sufficient reason to support redistricting and the final Republican redistricting plan? African American representative Harold Dutton of Houston explained, "I know I'm going to upset some Democrats with this, but there are things about redistricting worth supporting." Eventually, all but one of the African American lawmakers in the Texas House and Senate decided against supporting the final redistricting plan. However, the issue was not an easy one.

This dilemma facing African American members of the Texas legislature is well exemplified by comparing the positions of three lawmakers—Senators

Rodney Ellis and Royce West and Rep. Ron Wilson. All are successful attorneys, all are Democrats, and all have been in the Texas legislature for at least twelve years as officials elected from predominantly African American districts in Harris or Dallas county. All are African American and have been part of the battle for African American voting rights since the 1970s. Each traces his views and allegiances back to the respected African American elected leaders of the 1970s in Texas, including Barbara Jordan, Mickey Leland, and Craig Washington. Nevertheless, despite these similarities, Ellis and West's views contrasted sharply with those of Wilson as to what was in the best interest of African Americans in 2003.

Senator Rodney Ellis

Senator Ellis was first elected to the Texas Senate from Houston in 1990. Before that he had served three terms as a member of the Houston city council and as chief of staff for U.S. Congressman Mickey Leland; in his youth he had been an assistant at the Capitol to Lieutenant Governor William P. Hobby.[3] Ellis is a capable, articulate attorney who seems very comfortable with his status as a senator. He is affable and moves easily among politicians, members of the Senate, and outside groups. He is also active with his law practice (primarily major transactions and investment banking) and other interests, including aiding his alma mater, the University of Texas School of Law, and participating in causes affecting his African American constituents and civil rights. He was generally recognized as one of the leaders of the Senate and had consistently served as a committee chairman, even under Republican lieutenant governors. Ellis was chairman of the critical Finance Committee under acting Lieutenant Governor Bill Ratliff and continued to be a close friend of Ratliff's. In 2003, Dewhurst appointed Ellis chairman of the Committee on Government Organization, anticipating that government reorganization would be a major issue during the legislative session.

Ellis seems driven most by the goal of winning on what he sees as critical social issues. In 2003 his overriding concern was not to push for another congressional district that was likely to be won by an African American, but to work for a redistricting plan that could elect the most congressmen likely to vote favorably on issues affecting the African American community. He knew that the election of African Americans to office was important, but felt that there was a point at which drawing election districts to achieve that purpose was foolish if it meant losing the ability to control or influence the legislation and public policies themselves. As he explained to me in 2005, "I can count. If we do not have a sufficient number of the right people in Congress to vote the right way on issues that are important to us, it makes no difference whether we have one more African American in Congress."

As an attorney, he was worried about the implications of the arguments being made by Republicans on behalf of their redistricting plan. In an op-ed in the *Houston Chronicle* on December 18, 2003, he warned, "This fight is not about political careers—it's about the rights of voters." He cautioned that the Republicans were trying to legally justify racial discrimination as "purely politics": they claimed it was okay for a redistricting plan to violate the voting rights of racial and ethnic minorities "as long as minorities vote for Democrats." Ellis also questioned the Republicans' argument that diluting African American voting strength statewide was somehow legally justified by the strengthening of African American voting power in District 9. He described the Republican argument as "the insulting notion that it's OK to take away the rights of minority voters in Forth Worth or Laredo or Beaumont if you provide an 'offset' that makes up for it elsewhere." He closed his op-ed by asking, "[W]ill the Voting Rights Act survive this attack in Austin?"

Ellis felt specifically that the Republican plan to increase African American voting strength in District 9 was both unnecessary and a ruse to divert attention from the overall effect of the redistricting plan on African Americans statewide.[4] During the redistricting process and later in court, he insisted that a well-funded African American could win in the district as it existed in 2002 without the increase in African American voting-age population that marked the final Republican plan in 2003.[5] Representative Wilson disagreed.

As occurred with several other minority Democratic senators in 2003, Ellis was approached by Republicans with the offer of a congressional district likely to elect him if he would provide a necessary vote for reaching the critical twenty-one votes in the Senate. In 2005, DeLay aide Jim Ellis told me that he was unaware of any such offer being authorized by the Republican leadership. Senator Ellis refused the offer.

Senator Royce West

Senator West (Dallas) was first elected to the Texas Senate in 1992 to replace Eddie Bernice Johnson, who was elected that same year to Congress from a newly created, predominantly African American congressional district (District 30). West is a large burly man with an imposing presence. He is a well-spoken, able attorney who served as a chief felony prosecutor for the Dallas County district attorney from 1979 to 1984. His primary interest in and out of the Senate is public education. In 2003, he served as the vice chairman of both the Senate Committee on Education and the Subcommittee on Higher Education. In addition, he held posts on the critical Committee on Finance and two other committees.

West often was a spokesperson for the boycotting Democratic senators in New Mexico. As he explained at one point from Albuquerque: "The Republicans need to understand that the race game is no longer the game that we're playing as legislators. We want people of color representing us, but we also recognize that there are anglos who can represent us too, and they have done so effectively."[6] During Senate debate on the redistricting bill, West further explained, "I'd rather have four or five votes at the table that will work with me on issues than to have someone who looks like me."[7] In the final debate, on October 10, 2003, he said, "When it comes to issues of importance, that ethnic minorities view important in Congress, we now [as a result of the redistricting bill] have fewer seats at the table of power in order to articulate our position in order to see it through." He acknowledged that "there were times when the Democratic Party in this particular state weren't friends of ethnic minorities," but "right now our Democratic colleagues in Congress, they are, in fact, dependent upon the ethnic minority community in the State of Texas" and "all of them must listen to the vote of the ethnic minority population of their districts."[8] In an interview with me in 2005, West reiterated that: "We can count. It makes no sense to trade six votes for one vote, no matter the color of the office-holder."

During the legislative session, West took the lead among Democrats in parrying with Dewhurst and Senator Staples over legal and parliamentary issues that he thought might affect the plan in court. The Republicans either gave stock answers to West's inquiries or refused to be drawn into a debate about legal issues or racial discrimination. At one point during Senate consideration of the final redistricting bill on October 10, 2003, West told Staples, "See you in the courthouse"; Staples answered, "See you there."[9] In later court testimony, West worried that the legislature uncharacteristically ignored the will of the people of Texas by passing a redistricting bill overwhelmingly opposed by the witnesses at the public hearings. He expressed particular concern about the effect that dismantling District 24 would have on the African American community of Tarrant County.

State Representative Ron Wilson

The vocal advocate for the opposite view was Rep. Ron Wilson, an African American Democrat from Harris County. Wilson worked in the 1970s for then–state representative Mickey Leland. At the time of the special session in 2003, Wilson had served in the House for twenty-seven years from a heavily African American district (District 131) in Harris County.

As Wilson told me in 2005, his view was that he should "distill from the system as much as possible for his constituents." He believes African Americans are better served by another African American than by a white Democrat. He said that during three decades of redistricting he had consistently spoken in favor of creating districts in which African Americans were a large proportion of the voting population and likely to control the election—rather than spreading African American voters among several districts "to reelect Anglo incumbents." Although elected as a Democrat, he said he found it easy to support Speaker Craddick and the Republican redistricting effort in 2003 because the Republican plans created "another opportunity district in Harris County." He held liberal Democrats responsible for not creating such a district sooner. He explained, "The [black] population has always been there, and they [Democrats] would never draw it. They [Republicans] have finally drawn it." Wilson told me that he went to the Democrats first with the idea in 1991, but was turned down because creating a second predominantly African American district in Harris County "would have forced white Democrats to run against Republicans." He says that Democratic leaders, such as Martin Frost and former state party chairman Bob Slagle, tried in turn to draw him out of his legislative district in 1991 because he was "off the reservation."

Wilson's differences with the Democratic Party went beyond redistricting. He was critical of some Democratic colleagues for their lack of support on social service issues, criminal justice reform, and utility rate reform. Public education was a particularly hot issue for Wilson. He pointed out, for example, that the Democrats had held power in the past but had done nothing to solve the serious problems in the public school system. He said that Democrat-controlled legislatures in the past had left education in general, and the schools in the African American sections of Houston in particular, "sucking eggs." In the debate on redistricting, Wilson responded to claims that the Republican redistricting plan discriminated against minorities by exclaiming, "I'll show you segregation, you want to look at the public school system in this state—that's real segregation." Wilson's reasoning on the needs of public schools, however, also led him to support school vouchers, another idea probably not endorsed by most of his former constituents.

Wilson supported Speaker Craddick—one of the first Democrats to do so—even before the beginning of the legislative session in 2003. In 2005 he explained this decision to me by referring to the actions of two African Americans whom he admired and who were leaders in the fight for African American representation in Texas—Mickey Leland and Craig Washington. Both served with distinction in the Texas legislature in the 1970s before winning election as congressmen from Houston. (Leland won election to Congress in 1978 to replace the retiring Barbara Jordan. Washington won election to replace Leland after Leland died in a plane crash in Ethiopia in 1989). Wilson recalled how Leland and Washington as members of the Texas House in 1975 swung their support for Speaker to conservative Democrat Bill Clayton at a critical moment to defeat liberal Democrat Carl Parker. Clayton was grateful and gave Leland and Washington "clout." Wilson's point was that he believed he could do more for his constituents on a variety of subjects by working with the new Republican majority rather than opposing it. Craddick in 2003 rewarded Wilson with appointment as chairman of the powerful Ways and Means Committee.

Wilson acknowledged, however, that Leland and Washington probably would not have agreed with his position on redistricting in 2003. He recalled how Washington and Leland in 1981–1983 had accepted a split of the African American community in Dallas to reelect two moderate Democrats. Wilson told me that he had disagreed with them then. However, it appears from a review of the newspaper accounts from that time that Wilson was one of the Democratic lawmakers (along with Leland and Washington) who walked out of the House in the "Killer Fleas" boycott episode in 1981 to protest the redistricting plan that drew a predominantly African American district in Dallas but endangered the incumbent Anglo Democrats. This walkout is discussed in Chapter Six.

Some critics dismissed Wilson's role in 2003 because (they said) an increase in African American strength in a Houston congressional district had been part of virtually all congressional plans (including those presented to the federal court) under consideration since the 2001 redistricting litigation. These critics claimed that Wilson was simply used by Republicans in 2003 to give an impression that the Republican redistricting plan had minority support and that it enhanced minority voting strength in Texas. Wilson acknowledged to me in 2005 that the Republicans probably used him to achieve their partisan goals, but answered that he also used the Republicans to achieve what he thought was most important for his African American constituents (i.e., another congressional district in Houston that could be dominated by African American voters). During the 2003 redistricting, Wilson called on the image of past African American leaders of the civil rights movement: "When you look at what Dr. King did and Stokely Carmichael and H. Rap Brown and the Black Panthers did so we can be at the table, how can I say, 'I got mine?' Those leaders would come back and whip my butt."[10] When I asked in 2005 whether the eventual winner in District 9 (African American Al Green) could have won in

2004 without the changes, or could win as an incumbent if the district reverted to its 2002 shape, Wilson said no. In an interesting additional observation, Wilson suggested that if a Hispanic lawmaker had been willing to take the same risks as Wilson by working with the Republican leadership, they might have been able to secure an equivalent addition to Hispanic voting strength in the final redistricting plan.

Wilson also offered his comments to me on the role of Congressman Delay during redistricting. He said, "Tom is not the devil. It would miss the whole damn point and be intellectually dishonest to hold him responsible." Wilson said that it is necessary to look in a broader sense to the historical shift in power. He described DeLay as "kind of a cheerleader or spokesman for the whole movement." Wilson said that DeLay was able to "maximize the power of his party." It was in this context that Wilson spoke with pride to me about how he (Wilson) was able to similarly "maximize" the power of his constituents by creating the increased African American percentage in District 9. He insisted emphatically, "I drew it. They took my idea. I drew the damn thing. We should have done it a long time ago." He saw the achievement as having a long-term effect. He thought that since the African American population in Texas is holding steady or declining as a percentage of the whole population, there might never be another such district drawn in Texas. He thought that now, since the district has been drawn, it will be easier to maintain the district as an African American one, even with a decline in the proportion of African Americans statewide. He admitted to me that most of his constituents would not "recognize" what he had done in 2003, but "that is all right. History will judge me."

African American voters in 2004 ousted Ron Wilson from the state legislative seat he had held for over twenty-seven years. The Democratic Party had worked actively for his defeat. In Tarrant County the African American voters of District 95 ousted State Representative Glenn Lewis, who had remained in Austin while his Democratic colleagues had fled to Ardmore and who had been ineffectual in preventing the African American community in Tarrant County from being placed in the heavily Republican 26th congressional district. A Hispanic representative who remained in Austin during the walkout, Roberto Gutierrez (McAllen), also lost his seat in the Democratic primary.

The Role of Congressman Tom DeLay, Republican Activists and Donors, and the White House

[W]e believe DeLay puts his situational principles and win-at-all-costs lust for power first, to the detriment of the city.
—*HOUSTON CHRONICLE*, MARCH 9, 2002, ON NON-REDISTRICTING ISSUES AFFECTING HOUSTON

Much has been written in recent years about Congressman Tom DeLay. Some of it has been scathing, some of it highly complimentary. After reading some of these materials, I found that the only apparent consensus was that DeLay elicits strong feelings: people tend to love him or hate him; there are very few who are ambivalent.[1]

DeLay served in the Texas legislature from 1979 until he was elected to Congress in 1984. He was in the Texas House alongside many other actors in the 2003 redistricting, including Tom Craddick; former Speaker Pete Laney; TRMPAC treasurer Bill Ceverha; Governor Perry's chief of staff, Mike Toomey; and Lieutenant Governor Dewhurst's chief of staff, Bruce Gibson. Few if any of his colleagues from the Texas House recall DeLay as being a significant actor while in that legislative body.

In Congress, DeLay became a major partisan force. He was elected deputy majority whip in 1988 and became majority whip in 1994. DeLay was credited by many as being more responsible than any other Republican congressional lawmaker for consolidating the gains of the "Republican Revolution of 1994" and "institutionalizing an enduring Republican majority in Congress."[2] During the Clinton era, he was a pivotal figure in the Republican fight for impeachment and against health-care reform. Under George W. Bush, DeLay was responsible for maintaining discipline among Republican lawmakers and support behind Bush's legislative program, including the major tax cuts.

Frustrated in his efforts to become Speaker, DeLay in 2002 became majority leader of the U.S. House of Representatives. To some observers, he was "easily the most powerful Republican on Capitol Hill."[3] This power extended beyond Congress to a large network of former staffers who were lobbyists in Washington. Notwithstanding this power, DeLay had been gently warned in the past by his fellow Republicans that he was repeatedly pushing the legal limits of rules applicable to members of Congress.[4]

As majority whip and later as majority leader, DeLay was expected to be an effective force for electing Republican congressmen in order to maintain and enlarge the Republican majority in Congress. DeLay's national political action committee, Americans for a Republican Majority (ARMPAC), existed specifically for this purpose. By 2001, however, DeLay's success in his own state of Texas had been disappointing. Even with George W. Bush carrying the state overwhelmingly in 2000, all of the Democratic incumbent congressmen won reelection. The continuing Democratic control of the congressional delegation from Texas was not only a material problem for Republicans in Congress, it was a personal embarrassment for DeLay.

Tom DeLay was not likely to accept defeat or personal embarrassment easily. He was committed to making Republicans a majority of the Texas congressional delegation. However, as long as the Democrats held a majority in the Texas House, the state legislature was unlikely to pass a redistricting plan favorable to Republicans. DeLay's solution was to take advantage of a unique opportunity in the 2002 election to eliminate that Democratic legislative majority and to install his friend, Tom Craddick, as Speaker.

However, even with the state offices and both houses of the legislature in Republican control, there were serious obstacles. Every major newspaper throughout Texas in 2003 was opposed to redistricting. Many Republican lawmakers found their constituents opposed to redistricting. Nevertheless, DeLay's presence in and influence on the redistricting process in 2003 rendered this opposition ineffectual. Most Republican legislators who opposed redistricting ended up feeling obligated to go forward with it in 2003 for the benefit of national partisan interests. Once redistricting was underway, many Republican state lawmakers, especially in the Senate, toiled in good faith, trying to be responsive to their constituents and the general public, fair to their colleagues, and responsible under the law. DeLay's control over the final redistricting plan rendered such efforts meaningless. Measured by the substantial partisan change in the Texas congressional delegation after the 2004 election, his work in Texas was enormously successful.

2001: Congressman DeLay's Plea for a Nonpartisan Plan to Help Minorities

In 2001, Congressman DeLay represented the Republican congressional delegation during the redistricting battle. His objective was to increase the number of Republican congressmen. However, the Texas House of Representatives remained dominated by a Democratic majority. In addition, Republicans had only a single-vote majority in the Senate, and acting Lieutenant Governor Bill Ratliff did not support an aggressively partisan redistricting plan.

Therefore, DeLay's approach was to assume a nonpartisan, "good government" stance. Along with Congressman Joe Barton, DeLay appeared before a joint redistricting committee and urged adoption of a plan that was drawn on the basis of neutral factors, consisted of compact districts, and preserved communities of interest. He urged changes in District 24 (Dallas) to make it more Hispanic. He denied any knowledge of a Republican plan to target Democratic incumbents. In response to suggestions from some state lawmakers, DeLay said that he would attempt to come up with a plan that could be endorsed by all members of the state's congressional delegation. There is no indication that he ever attempted to work out such a plan.

In June, after the regular legislative session ended without the adoption of a congressional redistricting plan, DeLay asked then–acting lieutenant governor Ratliff if he would suspend the Senate's two-thirds vote requirement so that the Republican majority (sixteen of thirty-one senators) might push through a favorable congressional redistricting in a special session.[5] As DeLay aide Jim Ellis acknowledged to me in 2005, "It was not totally out of the question" that a congressional map to the GOP's liking could have been passed through the House. The greater obstacle in 2001 was the lack of twenty-one votes to suspend the two-thirds vote requirement in the Senate. Ratliff told DeLay that he would not agree to dispense with the two-thirds vote requirement in a special session.[6] As a result, a congressional redistricting plan to maximize Republican voting strength was unachievable. Governor Perry declined to call a special session.

2002: Electing the Right Republicans to State Office

Once it became evident that a favorable congressional redistricting plan could not be passed through the Texas legislature in 2001, DeLay's focus turned to alternatives for increasing the number of Republican congressmen from Texas.

The pending congressional-redistricting litigation, *Balderas v. Perry,* held the promise of possibly giving Republicans control of the two new congressional seats allocated to Texas after the 2000 census, but DeLay saw little likelihood that the federal court (consisting of two Democratic- and one Republican-appointed judges) would redraw the existing congressional districts so as to overcome the advantage of the seventeen Democratic incumbents. A much more certain route to Republican success lay in winning control of the Texas House. DeLay realized that if Republicans could take advantage of the redrawn state districts to win a majority of seats in the Texas House, they could unseat their nemesis Pete Laney, elect DeLay's friend Tom Craddick as the new Speaker, and set the stage for a favorable redrawing of congressional districts in 2003. Under this scenario, outcomes of both the pending federal court case and the 2002 congressional races in Texas were essentially meaningless to whether Republicans could eventually gain a majority of Texas congressmen. Therefore, DeLay and Ellis agreed that the focus should be on electing Republicans (and the right Republicans) to the Texas House.

The model vehicle for electing more Republican state lawmakers in Texas already existed at the national level in ARMPAC. DeLay and ARMPAC's executive director, Jim Ellis, decided to create a state political action committee, Texans for a Republican Majority (TRMPAC), to help elect a Republican majority in the Texas House. The circumstances surrounding this organization and its effect on the 2002 election are discussed in Chapter Four. However, DeLay's involvement in this extraordinary enterprise is clear, including:

- Originating, along with Ellis, the idea of TRMPAC as a means of electing a Republican majority to the Texas House and securing a favorable forum for congressional redistricting;[7]
- Suggesting that TRMPAC could be a model for similar organizations in other key states;[8]
- Participating in the formation of TRMPAC, including announcing the creation of the organization at a November 2001 news conference in Austin: "We stand on the cusp of holding legislative majorities in both [legislative] chambers as well as every major statewide office. That's our opportunity";[9]
- Serving as a charter member and (according to some reports) chairman of TRMPAC's advisory board;
- Authorizing Ellis to play a key role in TRMPAC;
- Authorizing his ARMPAC fundraiser, Warren Robold, to raise money from Washington-based corporate lobbyists for TRMPAC;
- Allowing the transfer of $50,000 from ARMPAC to TRMPAC for that group's initial organizational expenses (John Colyandro indicated that

the funds were provided "because of the congressman's interest . . . in the organization and our success");[10] a second payment of $25,000 arrived from ARMPAC in late 2002;

- Actively raising money for TRMPAC from national and state sources through personal telephone calls and requests: many messages within TRMPAC noted the importance of having DeLay call potential contributors—for example, Robold suggested that he would call potential large donors first, and then "I would then decide from the response who Tom DeLay . . . should call";[11]

- Accepting contributions for TRMPAC. For example, former DeLay staffer Drew Maloney noted in a memo, "I finally have the 2 checks from Reliant. Will deliver to TD next week";[12]

- Journeying to Texas on at least five occasions on behalf of TRMPAC;

- Participating as an attraction at TRMPAC events and fundraisers: for example, on August 12, 2002, DeLay was the featured "special guest" for a fund-raising luncheon for TRMPAC at Houston's Petroleum Club, at which donors were asked to give $15,000 to be considered a cochair and $25,000 to be listed as an underwriter—major contributors were entitled to meet privately with DeLay as designated "members of the TRMPAC finance committee"; DeLay was an attraction at other TRMPAC events, including ones on January 16, 2002, in Austin featuring former Florida secretary of state Katherine Harris, and on July 29, 2002, when TRMPAC promised a "private meeting" with DeLay;

- Helping TRMPAC secure assistance from leading political strategists (e.g., contacting former U.S. senator Phil Gramm for help for TRMPAC);

- Helping TRMPAC secure help from national Republican Party and administration officials: for example, Robold reported to Colyandro on September 27, 2002, that U.S. energy secretary Spencer Abraham was willing to plan a trip to Texas to meet with energy-company officials and "seemed quite sincere at helping out in any way they could to support Congressman DeLay"; Robold was to put together a letter focusing "on TRMPAC and DeLay's role as well as the strong energy support in Texas"[13] (Abraham indicated later that the trip to Texas for TRMPAC never happened);

- Helping TRMPAC secure direct contributions to its favored candidates: for example, in a memo dated August 12, 2002, TRMPAC fundraiser Susan Lilly wrote that "through DeLay's . . . efforts," Union Pacific Railroad had "identified $25,000 worth of TRMPAC targets that [a company representative] is supposed to individually go and give checks to," however, the Union Pacific representative wanted "a 'DeLay person'" to accompany him; Union Pacific agreed to donate to eleven candidates after it refused to contribute directly to TRMPAC, and these Union Pacific checks were among those to be given to Republican candidates by Speaker candidate Tom Craddick;

- Being given credit with Republican state candidates for contributions from ARMPAC that were sent with letters on TRMPAC stationery, stating, "We are pleased to send you a contribution of [amount] compliments of Congressman Tom DeLay's political action committee Americans for a Republican Majority";[14]
- Helping select the Republican candidates who would receive TRMPAC monetary assistance;
- Possibly participating in the decision to transfer $190,000 from TRMPAC to the Republican National State Elections Committee (RNSEC) and from the RNSEC to seven Republican candidates for the Texas House.

TRMPAC hired Congressman DeLay's daughter, Danielle DeLay Ferro, and her firm, Coastal Consulting, to organize fund-raising events for the political organization. Ms. Ferro and her company were paid $30,893.

In court in 2005, DeLay's attorneys acknowledged the obvious: TRMPAC was DeLay's idea. In addition, it effectively was his organization—modeled after his own national PAC, led by his own trusted aides, and committed to his purpose of electing state lawmakers who would select DeLay's friend Tom Craddick as Speaker—and Craddick would favor redrawing congressional districts in 2003.

TRMPAC's ability to raise over $1.5 million for the 2002 elections was a direct result of its association with DeLay. The principals in TRMPAC readily admitted the importance of DeLay's involvement and assistance and even emphasized it as a means of assuring potential donors of the value to them of contributing. For example, in a pitch to Boone Pickens, TRMPAC advisory board member (and state representative) Dianne Delisi emphasized TRMPAC's connection with DeLay, indicating that DeLay "has agreed to help us and has been an ardent advocate for us by raising money, making phone calls, serving as a special guest at events and providing assistance with the leading strategists." Pickens personally contributed $5,000, and his company contributed $50,000. Jack Dillard, a Philip Morris official, sent $10,000 to TRMPAC on July 22, 2002, with a letter expressing his thanks "for the invitation to meet Congressman DeLay in Austin next week." The Williams Companies, an Oklahoma-based energy provider, sent its $25,000 contribution to TRMPAC with a letter addressed "Dear Congressman DeLay." In an effort to encourage San Antonio lawyer James Jonas to finish calling potential TRMPAC donors, Colyandro directed, "Please tell him how important he is and how important this is to TD."[15] Donor Harlan Crow was told, "On behalf of Congressman DeLay . . . we thank you for all that you can do."[16]

DeLay's effect on TRMPAC's money raising was most apparent in the organization's success in obtaining contributions from corporations having more of a connection with legislation in Washington than in Texas. Former DeLay staffers, such as Washington lobbyist Drew Maloney, organized fund-raising events in Washington and recommended companies that might contribute to TRMPAC.[17] Notable among the corporate donors were several clients and associates of Washington lobbyists (and convicted felons) Jack Abramoff and Michael Scanlon,[18] as well as Perfect Wave Technologies, a California company owned by Brent Wilkes.[19] Corporations were given the option of contributing to the "non-reportable" TRMPAC.

An executive for Kansas-based Westar Energy understandably wondered why the company was giving money to DeLay in its effort to insert a crucial provision into the pending energy bill. In an internal company e-mail on May 20, 2002, Westar executive Douglas Lake asked, "Delay [sic] is from TX what is our connection? . . . I am confused."[20] The company's vice president for public affairs, Douglas Lawrence, explained (in another e-mail) that the company had a package of $31,500 in hard money and $25,000 in soft ("corporate") money to be donated to politicians. DeLay was the House majority leader, and his agreement was needed before the House conferees (including DeLay, Billy Tauzin [of Louisiana], and Joe Barton [of Texas]) on the energy bill could push for the wording sought by Westar to exempt it from certain federal utility laws. The amendment would potentially mean billions of dollars to Westar. Shortly thereafter, Tauzin, Barton, and other congressmen received hard-money contributions from Westar, and TRMPAC received $25,000 in soft money. In June 2002, Westar executives, along with top officials from other energy companies, joined DeLay for a fund-raiser at a golf resort (the Homestead) in Virginia. It was at this fund-raiser (organized by Drew Maloney) that Westar made its $25,000 contribution to TRMPAC. Other participating corporations followed suit. Ellis, Colyandro, and officials from other corporations that eventually contributed to TRMPAC (e.g., Reliant Energy and El Paso Energy) participated in this golf outing.

Most of the other out-of-state corporations that donated to TRMPAC also had business before Congress or with the federal government, and came from highly regulated industries such as nursing homes, HMOs, or energy companies. For example, the donors Questerra Corporation (Virginia; $50,000) and Diversified Collection Services (California; $50,000) were federal contractors. Other major out-of-state corporate contributors included Old Country Store,

Inc., i.e., Cracker Barrel (Tennessee; $25,000); Constellation Energy Group (Washington, D.C.; $27,500); Philip Morris Management Corp. (New York; $25,000); Perfect Wave Technology (California; $15,000); Sears, Roebuck and Co. (Illinois; $25,000); and Bacardi USA, Inc. (Florida; $20,000).[21] Some of the organizations (e.g., a Boston-based trade group, Alliance for Quality Nursing Home Care; $100,000) also had an interest in state legislation (e.g., tort reform).

However, even those corporate donors with some apparent connection to Texas (e.g., Alliance for Quality Nursing Home Care, AT&T [$20,000], Belmont Oil & Gas Corporation [$25,000], Burlington Northern Santa Fe Railway [$26,000 in 2002 and $25,000 in 2003], and El Paso Energy [$50,000]) gave sums that were not readily explained by their having an interest in a state PAC committed only to helping elect Republican state representatives. Twelve of the corporations that gave to TRMPAC also gave to ARMPAC. Many of these companies are energy companies and, like Westar, gave at a time when Congress was actively considering an important energy bill. TRMPAC offered a unique opportunity for corporations to use corporate funds anonymously (or so it was thought) to gain the favorable attention of both Congressman Tom DeLay and the probable new Speaker of the Texas House, Tom Craddick.

DeLay's aggressive effort to raise money for TRMPAC contrasts starkly with the paucity of his work in 2002 on behalf of Republicans running against the Democratic congressional incumbents in Texas. Even though the five rural districts with Democratic incumbents (Districts 1, 2, 9, 11, and 17; there was no Republican opponent for Ralph Hall in District 4) were considered heavily Republican based on statewide election results, the Republican candidates running against those Democratic incumbents received a total of only $10,000 from ARMPAC: $5,000 to Farley in District 11, $5,000 to Beckham in District 17, and zero to the other three (who also received no funds from any Republican Party committee). Raising funds to help Republican candidates for Congress would ordinarily be a primary focus of the party's majority leader. But in 2002 DeLay decided that the best way to obtain Republican dominance of the Texas congressional delegation lay through the Texas House of Representatives. DeLay's strategy was to defeat the Anglo Democratic congressmen by redrawing them out of office.

Whether DeLay also played a role in the fund-raising efforts of the Texas Association of Business in 2002 is not clear at this time because the records in question are not yet publicly available. However, as explained in Chapter Four, TRMPAC and TAB appear to have carefully coordinated their election activities.

On June 15, 2004, Democratic Congressman Chris Bell submitted a complaint to the House Committee on Standards of Official Conduct (the Ethics Committee), alleging that DeLay's actions in the 2002 election violated the federal bribery statute (18 U.S.C. Sec. 201[b][2]), U.S. House rules, and Texas campaign-finance laws. Count 1 of the complaint alleged that DeLay solicited and accepted contributions for TRMPAC in return for his promise to provide legislative assistance. Specifically, the complaint alleged that the $25,000 contribution from Westar was in return for DeLay's support of an amendment to the pending energy bill, and therefore constituted bribery. Bell was defeated for reelection in 2004 in the Democratic primary. In July 2004, Texas Democratic Party chairman Charles Soechting asked that Marc Racicot, a director of Burlington Northern Santa Fe and then head of the Bush reelection campaign, be added to the inquiry.

The House committee on October 6, 2004, acted on this count of Bell's complaint. The committee acknowledged that the action sought by Westar (i.e., insertion of the critical wording in the legislation) had occurred. The committee concluded, however, that applicable law, rules, and standards of conduct prohibited a member from acting on behalf of a contributor *only* if there was a clear quid pro quo, i.e., taking official action "solely or substantially on the basis that a person has made a contribution." After describing the sequence of events as it understood them, the committee found that DeLay did not improperly solicit funds from Westar or take action on behalf of Westar that would constitute an impermissible favor. The committee sent a letter of admonition to DeLay for his "participation in and facilitation of [the] energy company fundraiser in June 6, 2002." The committee found DeLay's actions "at a minimum created the appearance that donors were being provided special access to Representative DeLay regarding the then-pending energy legislation." The letter of admonition imposed no further penalties on the congressman.[22]

Count II of Bell's complaint alleged that DeLay used TRMPAC to funnel corporate money to state legislative candidates in violation of state law. The House committee deferred action on this count pending further developments in the Travis County district attorney's investigation of TRMPAC.

As discussed in Chapter Four, three of DeLay's associates (Jim Ellis, Warren Robold, and John Colyandro) were indicted in 2004 for their activities with TRMPAC. On September 28, 2005, DeLay was also indicted. The nature and status of these criminal prosecutions and their affect on DeLay's status as majority leader and a member of Congress are discussed in Chapters Seventeen and Eighteen.

DeLay's Effort to Find the Missing House Democrats

When the Democratic House members left Texas to break a quorum, there was a period on May 12, 2003, when the Republicans in Austin did not know where the absent lawmakers had gone.[23] There remained a hope at the time that if only one or two Democrats could be persuaded or forced to return to the House chamber, a quorum could be reestablished and the redistricting bill passed. Republican leaders were anxious to find the missing Democrats.

Congressman DeLay and persons in his office played a major role in the search for the Democratic lawmakers. After receiving a call on May 12, 2003, from Speaker Craddick asking for help finding the absent Democrats, DeLay enlisted the policy director of the majority leader's office, Ms. Juliane Sullivan, in an effort to help. On May 12 she asked the Federal Aviation Administration (FAA) to locate the plane of former speaker Pete Laney. Laney was suspected by the Republicans of using his plane to shuttle Democratic lawmakers out of the state. That afternoon she called David Balloff, the FAA's assistant administrator for congressional relations, with the tail number of Laney's plane (N711RD) and, without giving a reason, asked that the FAA find the plane. Through a series of telephone calls to different facilities, the FAA was able to locate Laney's twin-engine Piper Cherokee. The FAA assistant administrator for government affairs and industry advised DeLay's staff that the plane was expected to land in Ardmore, Oklahoma, "in about seven minutes." This information was relayed to Speaker Craddick in Austin. It was through this call that Republicans in Washington and Austin became aware that the Democratic lawmakers were probably in Ardmore.

Sullivan's inquiry did not end there. She asked the FAA where the plane had been on the previous day (May 11), apparently to ascertain whether the plane had been ferrying persons to Ardmore. To answer this inquiry, Balloff initiated a series of calls to FAA flight centers. Later on the 12th, Ms. Sullivan was advised by the FAA that Laney's plane had left Ardmore, apparently headed back to an airport near Austin. DeLay advised Craddick. DeLay later explained, "I was told at the time that that plane was in the air coming from Ardmore, Oklahoma, back to Georgetown, Texas, and I relayed that information to Tom Craddick."[24] Based on this information from the FAA, Republicans expected Laney's plane back in Austin from Ardmore on Monday. When it did not show up, the FAA was again asked for help in finding the aircraft. The FAA instituted a full-fledged safety "alert" for the region covered by the Dallas–Fort Worth Control Center, but could not find the plane.

DeLay also asked the legal counsel for the Office of the Majority Leader to contact the Department of Justice for assistance. Very early on the morning of May 13, the counsel (Carl Thorsen, a former Justice attorney) left a message for Assistant Attorney General William Moschella in Washington. When Moschella called back, Thorsen asked whether the department had the legal authority to assist state officers in enforcing the "arrest warrant" issued to bring the legislators back to Texas to vote. Thorsen said he already knew what the answer would be; Moschella took this comment to mean that Thorson expected a negative response. Moschella also anticipated that the answer would be no. Nevertheless, Moschella initiated a review of the question within the department, beginning with an e-mail to Edward Whelan, acting assistant attorney general in the department's Office of Legal Counsel. This e-mail was the first of a series of e-mails and telephone conversations. Within a few hours of receiving Thorsen's call, Moschella called back to say that there was nothing that Justice could do. Later, in response to a departmental inquiry into these contacts, Whelan said that the idea of the department getting involved in the matter struck him at the time as "wacko." Thorsen told investigators that his inquiry to Moschella was "constituent service" on behalf of Texas officials. As mentioned in Chapter Eight, Thorsen also discussed the possible use of federal officers with Barry McBee of the Texas attorney general's office and U.S. Attorney John Sutton.

On May 14, several Democratic members of Congress requested that the inspectors general at the Departments of Homeland Security, Transportation, and Justice be required to release their records about their role in the manhunt. The House Judiciary Committee, after a rancorous hour of debate, rejected the request. Congressman Gene Green on June 19, 2003, filed a resolution (HR 288) to direct the Transportation Department to transmit all relevant documents and electronic records to the U.S. House of Representatives. The department provided the information without the resolution being adopted. Eventually all three departments issued reports, and all three reports found that personnel within the various agencies had been asked for assistance in tracking or returning the Democratic lawmakers. In most instances, the requests had been answered quickly in the negative. In others, such as the FAA inquiries, the department's investigation concluded that the information provided was public (e.g., on the Internet), that air safety had not been compromised, that federal resources had not been misused, and that agency personnel had not violated any department rules or regulations. Homeland Security in a report issued in June said that the search had involved "only minimal use of its resources," even though there had been a forty-minute search by the Customs Bureau Tracking Center.

DeLay acknowledged on May 14 that he wanted the federal agencies to be involved "because this is a federal issue, these are congressional seats."[25] He also acknowledged that his office contacted the Justice Department on May 12 to determine "the appropriate role of the federal government in finding Texas legislators who have warrants for their arrest and have crossed state lines."[26]

Congressman Bell's complaint (discussed above) to the House Committee on Standards of Official Conduct also included a charge that DeLay had violated House rules prohibiting members from contacting government agencies to further partisan goals. This charge was based on the calls made by DeLay's staff on May 12 and 13 to the FAA and Justice regarding the AWOL House Democrats. In its October 6, 2004 report, the House Ethics Committee recommended that the count concerning DeLay's contacts with Justice be dismissed because the department had never been asked to take specific action. In regard to DeLay's contacts with the FAA, however, the committee recommended a letter of admonition "that sets out the serious concerns that those contacts raise under House standards of conduct that preclude using governmental resources for a political undertaking." The committee concluded that DeLay's actions raised "severe concerns about the fundamental concepts of separation of powers and federalism" and that it was inappropriate to use "federal branch resources to resolve a partisan dispute before a state legislative body." The committee warned DeLay that his actions "went beyond the bounds of acceptable conduct."

Bell did not escape criticism from the committee. By a letter dated November 18, 2004, it advised him that his complaint "contained innuendo, speculative assertions and conclusory statements" in violation of U.S. House Committee Rule 15(a)(4). The committee suggested that "there is no purpose for including excessive or inflammatory language or exaggerated charges in a complaint except in an attempt to attract publicity and, hence, a political advantage."

James Ellis: DeLay's Eyes, Ears, and Facilitator for Redistricting

Jim Ellis has served as the executive director of ARMPAC, DeLay's national PAC, from 1998–2006.[27] In that time, ARMPAC has raised over $12 million, and most of this money has been used for building a Republican majority in Congress. Ellis remained executive director of ARMPAC in 2001–2002, but played a critical role in the operation of TRMPAC (discussed in Chapter Four). His specific actions throughout the redistricting process are discussed in the chapters describing the events of 2003. He spoke with me in 2005.

As a general matter, Ellis's primary role following the 2002 election was as redistricting liaison from DeLay and the Republican congressional delegation to the Texas legislature and state officials. He continued to be paid by ARM-

PAC, but spent about half of the year in Austin. During that time he provided DeLay with regular updates on events affecting redistricting, assessments of how to move the redistricting effort forward, and a strategy for meeting with state officials and pushing through an aggressive redistricting plan. He told me that he called DeLay whenever anything "important" happened, including "frequently" when the Democratic lawmakers fled to Ardmore. Ellis met with some state lawmakers, but generally communicated with the staffs or aides to the various lawmakers and state officers. The major exceptions were on the House side, where he met often with Speaker Craddick and other Republican lawmakers, especially Rep. Phil King; the two worked together closely once King became the House sponsor of the redistricting plan.

Ellis was crucial to the outcome in Texas. He worked with Republican congressmen to come up with a consensus plan that would defeat the Anglo Democratic congressmen and protect any endangered Republican congressmen. He oversaw or participated in the drawing of various maps and communicated with Republican congressmen to ensure that any changes were acceptable. Perhaps most importantly, he was the hub of a network of congressional aides, Republican Party officials, activists, and major Republican donors who worked together to produce a united and coordinated partisan effort. It was during the final stages, when redistricting was pending before the conference committee, that Ellis's efforts paid their greatest dividend.

2003: Controlling the Process

As majority leader of the U.S. House, DeLay was expected to be in Washington continually while Congress was in session, so any absence by him was extraordinary. Nevertheless, DeLay missed many roll-call votes in Congress while traveling to Austin (on at least five occasions in 2003) to push redistricting along. As Senator Bill Ratliff explained, "DeLay was omnipresent."[28] Even DeLay's staff in Washington acknowledged that he "has been spending an extraordinary amount of time and energy on redistricting." However, DeLay's expenditure of time and energy was not haphazard. With Ellis's help, DeLay knew when his presence in Austin or a call to a lawmaker or state official would be important to the redistricting process.

Presession

In December 2002, the Republican members of the Texas congressional delegation met in DeLay's Washington office. They agreed to push for passage of an aggressive redistricting plan in 2003. Telephone conversations also occurred during this period between DeLay and the newly elected Republican state officials.

January–February

In January, DeLay came to Austin for Craddick's swearing-in as speaker on January 14. He met with Craddick, Governor Perry, Attorney General Abbott, and Lieutenant Governor Dewhurst. According to my conversation with Ellis in 2005, DeLay left Austin after these meetings with an understanding that he had a commitment from the state leaders to proceed with congressional redistricting. However, Ellis was left in Austin to meet further with state lawmakers and officials. Ellis soon met with "about half of the state Senate staffs, Rep. Mike Krusee, a member of the House Redistricting Committee, and the lieutenant governor's staff." By memorandum to DeLay on February 5, Ellis reported that despite some public comments from state officials about the undesirability of redistricting, he was confident that they were still committed to passing a redistricting bill. Ellis provided DeLay a senator-by-senator breakdown showing the likelihood of each supporting redistricting.

March–April

Ellis worked with each Republican congressman to come up with a consensus plan that could be presented to the state legislature for adoption. The issues and discussions surrounding that plan are presented in Chapter Six. Ellis regularly advised DeLay of the stage of the plan's development, and DeLay himself met with the Republican congressmen to discuss the specifics of the plan. By memorandum on April 5, Ellis forwarded several alternative plans to DeLay. All were designed to defeat at least five Democratic incumbents, including Frost, and to significantly increase the percentage of Republican voters in Congressman Bonilla's district (District 23). By a separate memorandum on the same date, Ellis advised DeLay that a decision on a plan was needed "from the entire delegation next week" and that "it would be good for you [DeLay] to personally inform the Governor, Lt. Governor and Speaker when the map is finalized."

April 24, 2003

By late April, circumstances were ripe to push redistricting forward. The Republican congressmen had agreed on a redistricting plan, and on April 23, 2003, the Texas attorney general had issued a letter opinion indicating that the legislature could adopt a congressional redistricting plan to replace the existing court-ordered plan. The opinion was distributed to lawmakers on April 24, and coincided with DeLay's arrival in Austin for Speakers Day. According to Ellis, there still was no consensus at this time among Republicans in the House for proceeding with redistricting; as he put it to me, "We weren't there." DeLay set out to change this situation. He met separately on the 24th with each of the state leaders and one by one with many House Republican lawmakers. His task was to generate enthusiasm for redistricting.

DeLay's message to the Republican lawmakers was clear—the president and the Republican Party needed more Republican congressmen, so redistricting in 2003 was critical to the Republican control of Congress. DeLay explained, "I'm the majority leader and we want more seats."[29] Some House members asked for "favors" in the meetings on April 24. For example, Representative Gary Elkins (Houston) and others pressed for federal legislation making sales taxes deductible. DeLay ostensibly replied that if the lawmakers produced more Republican seats, he could accomplish it. Senator Eliot Shapleigh said later, "Tom DeLay came to the Texas Capitol in March [actually April]. Since then, nothing has been the same. He has galvanized a tiny band of extremists."[30]

May

DeLay traveled quietly to Austin again during early May. On May 7–8, he again met with many House Republicans about the redistricting bill that had been reported from the House committee and was scheduled for consideration by the House on the following Monday. Democrats saw his presence in Austin as a sign that Republican leaders thought that they might not have enough votes to win House approval of the plan. It was during this trip that DeLay allegedly told Republicans that he could block Justice Department action on the complaint filed by Democratic lawmaker Richard Raymond, claiming that the Voting Rights Act had been violated by the failure of the House Committee on Redistricting to post notices in Spanish and to conduct hearings in Hispanic areas of the state. It also was during this time that several newspapers criticized DeLay for missing fifteen roll-call votes because of his trips to Texas. DeLay was back in Washington by Monday, when he was startled to learn of the flight of the House Democrats to Oklahoma.

DeLay's efforts to assist in finding and returning the absent lawmakers are discussed above. At a press conference in Washington on May 12, DeLay lashed out at the "fugitive Democrats" as being "disloyal" for leaving Texas: "Representatives are elected and paid for by the people with the expectation that they show up to work and do the people's business and have the courage to cast tough votes."[31] He added, "I have never turned tail and run. Even when I'm losing, I stand and fight for what I believe in. It is so Texas contrary."[32] DeLay explained, "What's at stake here is the most effective and accurate representation for Texans. Republicans are the majority party in both Washington and Austin and are best able to deliver on Texans' priorities and represent their beliefs."[33] DeLay emphasized at the press conference that "[t]he U.S. Attorney was looking into" whether U.S. marshals or the FBI could be enlisted to apprehend the Democrats, adding, "If it is legal for them to do so, I think it would be nice for them to help out the Texas Rangers and the Texas troopers."[34]

In Austin, Ellis also criticized the absent Democrats. He claimed that the Democratic lawmakers were acting in the interest of the national party rather than the state: "It's unconscionable for them to shut the House down on their narrow partisan agenda, clearly on orders from Democratic leaders in Washington [Congressman Frost] and San Francisco [Congresswoman Nancy Pelosi]."[35]

Also at this time DeLay indicated that he had shared his redistricting plan with President Bush at the end of a GOP congressional-leadership meeting. DeLay explained that, "As I was walking out, I said [to Bush], you know, that redistricting is ongoing. And he said 'Well, good, I'd like to see that happen.'"[36] DeLay also acknowledged (according to one newspaper) that he had shown his redistricting plan to the President and that Bush liked the plan.[37]

Once it was clear that the Democratic walkout had killed the Republican redistricting bill in the regular session, Congressman DeLay answered, "I'm not giving up. And I will not be intimidated. This is not over yet."

June 16, 2003

On June 16, DeLay met at the Governor's Mansion in Austin with Governor Perry, Lieutenant Governor Dewhurst, Speaker Craddick, and Attorney General Abbott. This was a crucial meeting: the five affirmed that the redistricting effort would continue and agreed on a strategy for passing a redistricting plan. This meeting is discussed further in Chapter Nine. Several Republicans have suggested that after this meeting DeLay asked Karl Rove to call Senator Ratliff to determine if he would vote to bring up redistricting. Two days after the meeting, Perry announced that he would call a special session on congressional redistricting.

Ellis was with DeLay in Austin. He met with the governor's staff at 3 p.m. on June 16 to confirm the agenda for the meeting at the Governor's Mansion and then accompanied DeLay to the meeting. Later that week he said that the Republican leadership was sure that it could pass redistricting in the House and that he was "comfortable" that he would get the votes in the Senate. As he explained to the media, "We [the members of DeLay's team] have been as upfront and out front as we could be. We are going to see it to the end."

July–August–September

DeLay generally praised the map passed by the House early in the first special session. He expressed optimism about the outcome in the special session. When Senator Ratliff joined with ten Democratic senators to block consideration of redistricting, DeLay downplayed the event: "[Ratliff] has grave concerns that he wants to see met and he's sort of exercising his prerogative as a state senator and publicly airing those concerns."[38] He said that the lack of twenty-one votes in the Senate "may be a temporary setback that the lieutenant governor has to deal with, but the process is going on."[39]

After the Democratic senators left for New Mexico, however, DeLay's tone changed. He said, "We in Texas have prided ourselves on honor, duty and responsibility. Unfortunately, the Democrats in the state legislature don't understand honor because they're violating their oath of office to support the United States Constitution."[40] Senator Mario Gallegos responded from Albuquerque: "He's full of Christmas turkey."[41]

Ellis was in Austin off and on during the summer. During August he worked on a Senate version of a redistricting map and kept DeLay and the network of congressional aides advised about the situation in Austin. By memorandum on August 1 he indicated that "representatives from the key state offices (House, Senate, Governor) all believe that the Democrats will stay in New Mexico until the end of this second special session, which ends a [*sic*] midnight on Aug. 27." On August 19 he explained that Governor Perry would call a third special session after Labor Day, adding, "Preparations are underway in case the House Democrats decide to walk again in the third session. Vulnerable D's will be hit with radio ads prior to the call, thus making it clear they will pay a political price if they abandon their responsibilities yet again." He urged Republican congressional aides to have their respective congressmen "talk to their Senators" to urge adoption of the "8–3" plan in the third special session as "the only way to eliminate Frost, Edwards, and Doggett."

Ellis warned DeLay: "The West Texas dispute between Speaker Craddick and Sen. Duncan continues to be a major problem that must be solved before a map will be passed." This intraparty dispute over the West Texas districts loomed large. Once it became clear that a third special session was likely, DeLay returned to Austin in early September to meet with Speaker Craddick and Senators Duncan and Staples in an effort to resolve the dispute. According to Duncan, there was progress but no resolution. Craddick attacked Dewhurst publicly for skipping the meeting. DeLay made no public comment.[42]

On September 25, Governor Perry met in Washington behind closed doors with the state's fifteen House Republicans, including DeLay, to discuss redistricting. Afterward, Perry acknowledged to the press that the Republican congressional delegation had a map. He also acknowledged that he was resisting suggestions to keep Democratic congressman Chet Edwards because he sat on the House panel that oversees military construction.[43]

October 5–8, 2003

During September and early October, substantial outside pressure was brought to bear on Dewhurst and the Republican senators to accept a conference-committee report with an aggressively partisan plan. This is discussed in Chapter Eleven. By a memorandum to DeLay dated October 5, 2003, Ellis advised, "We have been successful in arriving at an 8–3 footprint that will achieve two of our three goals—helping Bonilla and eliminating the Frost district." The West Texas dispute remained unresolved. Ellis warned DeLay, "Though the 8–3 concept has been accepted, major adjustments must be made to ensure that the map reflects the priorities of the congressional delegation and not the legislature." A problem from Ellis's perspective was that some of the districts in which Democratic incumbents were paired with Republican incumbents were "thin" districts: "No incumbent [should be] paired in a district with less than a 58% [Republican vote in] Lt. Gov' 98 number."

Ellis's October 5 memorandum was in anticipation of DeLay's meetings the following day with Governor Perry and Lieutenant Governor Dewhurst. Ellis urged DeLay to get them to agree to the final changes in the map sought by the Republican congressional delegation: "We need our map, which has been researched and vetted for months. The pre-clearance and political risks are the delegation's and we are willing to assume those risks, but only with our map." DeLay met with state officials on Monday, October 6, and again over the next several days. He largely avoided the public. However, he explained, "I'm a Texan trying to get things done."[44] At one point he added, "It is very important to get this done, and that's why I'm here."[45] Eventually, the "West Texas problem" was solved, and the state officials and the legislature agreed to what was essentially the congressional delegation's desired version of the final map. DeLay praised the result: "Yes, you could say I'm very satisfied."[46]

DeLay's involvement in the redistricting process is obvious from public records of the events in 2003. However, those records also show glimpses of even more indirect, behind-the-scenes involvement through telephone calls to state officials throughout the year. No one denies that such calls occurred or that redistricting was a subject of at least some of these calls, but I have no means of quantifying either the number or the effect of such communications.

The Public Response to DeLay's Role

The Democratic response to Congressman DeLay's role was predictable. Representative Dunnam said, "All in all, Texas GOP leaders treated the people's government like a branch of the Republican Party."[47]

However, newspapers statewide also were critical. The *San Antonio Express-News* on October 9 charged:

> DeLay crosses the line in Texas' redistricting. . . . It is by no means uncommon for members of Congress to lobby state lawmakers during the redistricting process. But DeLay has pushed the practice beyond reasonable limits. The majority leader is not merely lobbying; he has become the deal-maker. . . . What does it say about leaders in Austin that they would allow DeLay to take over the process?

The *Bryan–College Station Eagle* on October 8 noted:

> We didn't need redistricting in the first place, but if we are going to have it the least DeLay can do is keep his nose out of internal state politics. Surely he has enough to do in Washington. And he already has cost Texas taxpayers millions of dollars for three pointless and unproductive special sessions.

The *Beaumont Enterprise* on October 9 added,

> DeLay may have figured there was no use pretending that he wasn't ramrodding this whole mess. Republicans have never claimed that congressional districts are being drawn for the benefit of voters. From the start they've made it clear that the goal is to send more Republican congressmen to Washington.

Other newspapers echoed these criticisms. I found no newspaper that praised either the redistricting result or DeLay's participation in the process.

White House Involvement

The ultimate beneficiaries of the 2003 redistricting in Texas were in the White House. President Bush obtained a greater Republican majority in Congress to support his programs, and Karl Rove moved a step closer to leaving a legacy of a Republican majority in Congress that could rival the Democratic Congresses begat by FDR. Democrats felt that the White House ultimately was behind the redistricting effort. Senator West on July 17 claimed, "Washington is exerting a lot of influence on this particular process, to the extent where the influence it is exerting may very well implode this body."[48] U.S. senator Joseph Lieberman said, "Mr. Bush could end this in a minute . . . the buck stops in the oval office."[49] Even some Texas newspapers wondered about White House involvement. For example, the *Waco Tribune-Herald* on September 7 speculated, "As sure as the sun rises and sets, the White House has been pulling every string at its disposal in Texas to increase Republican representation in Congress. That the White House would be coy about it is an insult to all involved." Nevertheless, direct evidence of substantial involvement by the president or administration personnel is thin.

DeLay and other Texas congressmen acknowledged speaking on several occasions with President Bush about the redistricting. As noted above, DeLay even acknowledged that at one point he had shown his redistricting plan to Bush at the end of a GOP leadership meeting in Washington and that the president had liked it. This meeting apparently occurred in early May, when it appeared that a redistricting bill would pass during the regular session.[50] DeLay acknowledged later that Bush and Rove had voiced approval of the result of the redistricting.[51] The participants in these conversations with the president universally implied to the media that these conversations involved only nonsubstantive, momentary, passing mentions of redistricting. For his part, President Bush took the position publicly that redistricting is "a matter for the state of Texas to address" and that he would not become involved. Press secretary Scott McClellan on September 3 said that the president is "always concerned about Texas. It's his home. It's a matter for the state of Texas."[52] During a meeting with journalists on September 16, President Bush reaffirmed that he saw redistricting as a state issue and dismissed accusations that he was behind the redistricting plan: "I get blamed for a lot of things."[53]

Karl Rove was somewhat more visible than the president. Rove has acknowledged his desire to be part of (or responsible for) a fundamental, long-term partisan realignment of American politics. In this context, it is virtually impossible not to see the 2003 redistricting effort in Texas as part of a larger national plan fostered by Rove and others in the party hierarchy to achieve a new period of GOP dominance in Congress and Texas for a generation or more. Since Rove had crisscrossed the country to help boost GOP fortunes one candidate at a time, it seems foolish to think that he would not be involved in furthering a redistricting effort in Texas that could mean a net gain for Republicans of as many as fourteen seats in Congress. It also is easy to imagine Rove in the White House, hunched over redistricting maps to see how his favorite spots in Texas and least favorite Democratic congressmen were being treated. In fact, it is very hard to imagine that Rove would not have taken a direct and substantial interest in the Texas redistricting, given what was at stake, his personal knowledge of the state, and his closeness to Republican officials and lawmakers.

Still, Rove was visible at only a few points in the story. The timing of his acknowledged appearances suggests coordination with events in Texas. For example, in early May, as the House prepared to take up a redistricting bill (also as the Texas House Democrats made preparations to leave for Ardmore), Rove called Lieutenant Governor Dewhurst.[54] Senator Ratliff acknowledged getting a call from Rove on June 17, 2003, the day following a strategy meeting between Congressman DeLay and state officials at the Governor's Mansion. Rove asked Ratliff whether a "fair" redistricting plan might pass the Texas Senate. Rove said that he thought that a redistricting plan "would be good for the president." He even asked Ratliff if his position on redistricting would be different if the president called him.[55] White House spokesman Scott McClellan did not dispute that the call had been made, but said that it was routine: "Karl keeps an active interest in what's going on in Texas. He talks with officials in Texas from time to time on various issues. This is one of those times."[56] Ratliff says that Rove never asked him to take any specific action, such as vote for a redistricting plan.

Other Republican officials, including Lieutenant Governor Dewhurst,[57] acknowledged to me that they spoke with Rove on other occasions during 2003 and that some of the conversations concerned redistricting, but each of these officials insists that redistricting was only a secondary topic. Senator Teel Bivins visited with Karl Rove in Washington over the July 4th holiday. Rove indicated in a later telephone interview that he and Bivins "may have exchanged a word or two about redistricting," but "nothing of substance."[58] Senator Wentworth discussed redistricting with Rove when both were attending a private nonpartisan gathering in California. Wentworth even showed Rove the redistricting map he was proposing, but Senator Wentworth later indicated to me that the conversation had been brief and that Rove had offered no substantive comment on the proposal.[59] Rove also spoke with Governor Perry, Speaker Craddick, and several other lawmakers. I do not know the substance of those conversations.

Democrats generally saw Rove playing a much larger role in what happened in Texas. Senator Hinojosa claimed, "Karl Rove is in constant contact with the leaders in the Senate and the House. What they are doing now is, they don't want Bush to get tainted."[60] In their letter on August 10 to President Bush from New Mexico, the Democratic Senators charged, "We have received information that your Chief Advisor, Karl Rove, has played a significant behind-the-scenes role in this divisive and unfortunate overreach of legislative power." On September 4, White House spokesman Taylor Gross disputed allegations of involvement by Rove or the President as "baseless."[61] Senator Rodney Ellis countered, "When Karl Rove makes a call from the White House, it's not like a call from your house. A call from the White House is equivalent to a thousand calls from any other house, and there is no plausible deniability by the president of the United States."[62] Texas officials tried to downplay any Washington involvement. David Beckwith, a spokesperson for Dewhurst, responded to Democratic claims by saying, "DeLay has been down there once or twice. I think Karl Rove has got plenty of other things to worry about other than this situation."[63] Several Texas newspapers suggested that Rove was a driving force behind the redistricting. For example, the *Waco Tribune-Herald* on September 7 suggested that Rove (along with DeLay) was "at whip" and that the White House's insistence on redistricting being a state matter was "about like saying the earth's rotation is a local matter."

Former presidential adviser Karen Hughes too met with state officials. Dewhurst's chief of staff, Bruce Gibson, acknowledged inviting Hughes to meet with him and Dewhurst in July to suggest a "public message" that might be used to better explain the Republican position to the general public.[64] Shortly afterward, the lieutenant governor announced that he would not require a two-thirds vote to take up redistricting in any subsequent session. On October 1, after meeting again with Dewhurst in Austin, Hughes told the media that it would be good for President Bush if Republicans erased the Democratic hold on the state's congressional delegation: "Our congressional delegation frequently votes in a way that is opposed to what the president supports and to what the people of Texas, polls show, support."[65] She was in Austin for a women's conference and said she was speaking for herself, not the president. Even Vice President Dick Cheney offered his views after the redistricting bill was finally enacted, indicating that the new redistricting bill was "righting some wrongs."[66]

Throughout the summer of 2003, Democrats claimed that the redistricting effort in Texas was being driven from the White House. For example, incumbent congressman Stenholm claimed in May that there was "credible evidence that calls [on redistricting] were coming from the White House."[67] As discussed previously, Texas senators accused President Bush and his staff of instigating or intervening in the Texas process. A spokesman for the White House called these allegations of involvement by Rove or the president "baseless."[68] President Bush explained his noninvolvement by claiming that "I've got a lot on my agenda," implying that he had no time to give to events in Texas.

It probably is fruitless for anyone to search for a time and place when President Bush or Karl Rove personally directed that the Texas redistricting effort be made, asked Texas officials or lawmakers to take specific action, or commanded that the final plan be as partisan as possible. Politics is seldom so transparent. Expectations are often conveyed in much subtler ways than by direct spoken or written command. For example, when someone perceived as close to the president says that a particular result is important to or favored by the president, the message almost certainly will be taken as tantamount to a clear direction or request for action from the president himself. Such messages are not easily ignored, particularly within a group as disciplined as the Republican Party. Neither President Bush nor Karl Rove is unaware of the potency of saying that a certain action is important to the president. Republican state officials and lawmakers in 2003 knew that the national party and the White House saw adding congressional seats from Texas as crucial to maintaining or enlarging Republican strength in Congress. Positive action by Texas Republicans was expected, and the added pressure from other outside forces made this clear. No explicit request or command from President Bush or Karl Rove was necessary. Whether any occurred, I do not know.

The other effect of this indirect word from the president was that it answered whether Bush opposed action in Texas that would unseat Speaker Pete Laney and harm the "bipartisanship" that had proved valuable to Bush in his 2000 campaign for president. Appealing to voters as someone capable of creating a bridge across the gulf of party identification, Bush sought out Democrats in Texas in 2000 to attest to the bipartisanship that he had shown as governor. Pete Laney joined Bush at an important appearance in Austin in 2000 immediately after the Supreme Court enjoined the Florida recount. Laney politically embraced Bush at the dais of the Texas House to add reality to Bush's claims of bipartisanship. Therefore, to some Texas lawmakers the real question about Bush's actions in 2003 was why he didn't intervene to prevent the unseating of Laney as Speaker or the divisive partisan effects of redistricting. Democratic representative Barry Telford reflected this view when he said,

> The man that purports to love Texas, the man that purports to love a bipartisan Legislature, has set back on his duff, not made one telephone call to say don't destroy an institution that I was allowed to be introduced to the nation from by a Democratic House speaker.[69]

President Bush could have ended the redistricting push in Texas with a single scowl, motion of his hand, or indication that he was not in favor of what was happening. His lack of action was tantamount to an endorsement of the redistricting effort. Congressman DeLay reported that soon after the redistricting bill was enacted, he was in a meeting at the White House with the president, Karl Rove, and congressional leaders. According to DeLay, the President and Rove "just congratulated Texas."[70]

Politicizing the Department of Justice Review Process

The Bush administration has politicized the Department of Justice. As a result, the department's review of election changes under the Voting Rights Act has become ineffectual.[71] Even more importantly, however, the changes made by the Administration in the core professional staff of the department seem designed to permanently alter and impede enforcement of the act in the future, even if Democrats again win the presidency and control of the political appointments to Justice.

For thirty years I have represented state and local governments on election changes under review for compliance with the Voting Rights Act. My relationship with the Justice Department generally has been adversarial. There have been many occasions when my clients (both Democratic and Republican) and I disagreed with the department in its application of the act. On several occasions these disagreements resulted in litigation in Texas or the District of Columbia. Some of this litigation ended up before the U.S. Supreme Court. Nevertheless, despite my past disputes with Justice over its interpretation and application of the Voting Rights Act, I have never felt over those thirty years, under four presidents (two Republican and two Democrat), that its decisions were being driven by partisan considerations.

The career legal staff of the Voting Section (within the Civil Rights Division) of the department has been the heart of the review process. Ever since the Voting Rights Act was passed in 1965, a group of career attorneys and analysts has provided continuity and competence in the review of thousands of sometimes complicated election changes each year. In the past, these professionals have always appeared to be motivated by a sincere desire to aid minority voters, not to advance a partisan agenda. Although I have often disagreed with how the staff has gone about trying to achieve the goal of protecting minority voters, I have never doubted the good faith of its motives. This circumstance has changed under the Bush administration. The manner in which Justice handled the 2003 redistricting in Texas is only a single example of how partisanship has become the department's dominant consideration in enforcing the Voting Rights Act.

The increased partisanship within the department in general and the Voting Section in particular is reflected in several ways. For example, some of the political appointees under the Bush administration, such as Hans von Spakovsky, came to the department with a history of openly and aggressively opposing Justice's voting initiatives. Others had essentially no experience in enforcing voting rights or managing a large organization. Their one common qualification was that they believed in the Republican ideology. They felt that the department's career legal staff reflected a "bureaucratic" liberal mindset, or "tilt," that could not be trusted and must be changed. Once in power, these appointees set out to change the department's culture that in the past (under Republican and Democratic presidents) had respected the independence of the professional legal staff. Instead of leaving the staff alone to independently analyze election changes, the Bush appointees took a direct, day-to-day interest and involvement in the analysis process, at least for major election-change submissions such as the Texas redistricting.

This ongoing personal involvement meant an increased opportunity for partisan influence on the process. Moreover, increasingly, the ultimate decisions in the Civil Rights Division (including the Voting Section) were made in isolation by the political appointees and communicated as orders. Any effort of staff attorneys to propose alternatives or to engage in a discussion of the political appointees' decisions was seen as proof that these staff attorneys did not believe in the Republican goals and could not be trusted. Attorneys thus viewed as "disloyal" were removed from positions of responsibility and replaced with others who accepted the new ideology. Attorneys accustomed to handling civil rights cases were shuffled off to other Justice divisions or sections. Morale in the division, particularly in the Voting Section, plummeted.

One result of this partisan intervention and fear of career punishment was that it drove longtime Justice voting-rights employees to leave. Over the last nine months of 2005, the Voting Section lost at least a third of its three dozen lawyers. Many of the section's best lawyers (some with over twenty years' experience) were driven to leave. Altogether almost a fifth of the lawyers in the Civil Rights Division left in 2005, most as part of a "buyout" program that some of the affected lawyers believed was aimed at pushing out those who did not share the administration's conservative views on civil rights laws. The voluntary departure of these attorneys drained the department's talent. However, for the Republican faithful, it was a welcome means of changing the culture and perspective of the department, since the department's political appointees installed persons more in tune with the ideology of the Republican Party. These new career employees, like their predecessors, are protected by civil service requirements, and, therefore, may determine the stance of the Voting Rights Section long after the Bush administration leaves office.

Another change within the department—further evidence of the desire of the Bush administration to permanently alter the Civil Rights Division and the Voting Section—concerns hiring decisions. In the past, career legal-staff positions have been effectively filled by a hiring committee consisting of career attorneys from throughout Justice. This committee reviewed resumes, traveled the country, interviewed attorneys, and made recommendations to hire new attorneys under the attorney general's Honor Program. The process was extremely competitive. In past decades, the committee's recommendations were almost always accepted by the various assistant attorney generals without substantial further examination. This process changed dramatically in 2003. The hiring committee was abolished. Since then, political appointees have reviewed incoming resumes and interviewed applicants for the honors program and for higher-ranking slots in the department. As a result, career attorneys who headed a unit within Justice were often merely advised that attorneys whom they had never met would be reporting for work. This change in the hiring process paved the way for the hiring of attorneys according to their partisan affiliations, political connections, or ideology, rather than their credentials or any interest in enforcing civil rights.

Finally, in response to the public attention given in 2005 to the 2003 internal Justice Department memoranda recommending rejection of the Texas redistricting (discussed in Chapter Twelve), the department has banned staff attorneys from making specific recommendations on election changes. This change reverses a forty-year precedent designed to ensure objectivity and insulate politically charged decisions from partisan influence.

The effect of these changes has been to cause a serious decline in the ability and willingness of the Justice Department to enforce the Voting Rights Act. Moreover, the enforcement decisions have become distinctly partisan. The Voting Section interposed far fewer objections under Section 5 in the 2001–2004 period, when most redistricting decisions were made, than in the same period during prior decades. On the other hand, career staff attorneys at Justice believe that in at least one instance (in Mississippi), political appointees held up the department's decision to preclear a redistricting plan that favored Democrats long enough to allow a federal court to impose a different plan, which favored Republicans. (A majority of the Supreme Court later determined that the department's action was not frivolous.)

In a controversial decision in 2005, political appointees at the highest levels of Justice disregarded a joint recommendation of career legal staff and political appointees in the Civil Rights Division that the attorney general object under Section 5 to a recently enacted Georgia voter-identification law. The law required voters to show photo identification before voting and to pay a $20 fee for a special card if they did not have a photo ID. The department precleared the Georgia law as having neither the purpose nor effect of racial discrimination. A federal district judge ultimately enjoined enforcement of the law as unconstitutional. The district judge compared the law to a "Jim Crow–era poll tax." A federal appellate panel upheld the ruling.

In the past five years, Justice has filed only seven lawsuits to enforce Section 2 of the Voting Rights Act (which applies nationwide and prohibits election procedures or practices that result in the racially discriminatory denial of the right to vote). One was on behalf of Anglo voters in the department's first reverse-discrimination complaint. Even more telling is that only one of the seven lawsuits involved the rights of African American voters. This case was prepared under the Clinton administration and filed by the Bush administration in early 2001 during the transition between administrations and before the current partisanship took hold.[72]

Historically, one of the most important factors affecting Section 5 decisions has been the views of the affected minority groups, lawmakers, and voters about election changes. This factor is expressly identified as a consideration in departmental rules. In 2003, minority-advocacy organizations, minority lawmakers, and minority voters overwhelmingly opposed the redistricting plan. The Voting Section memorandum recommending an objection to the Texas redistricting plan pointed to the importance of Texas minorities' views and to consideration of them as being consistent with past application of the act. However, to the political appointees at Justice, the opposition of the minority groups and lawmakers was merely partisan sour grapes, and the staff analysis showing retrogression in minority voting rights was merely a predictable bureaucratic response. Since the power to approve the redistricting plan rested with the political appointees, the outcome was probably never in doubt. Certainly, rumors of DeLay's assurances of Justice approval at the final stages of redistricting were key to what ultimately happened in Texas.

While several of the career attorneys within the Voting Section believe it likely that Congressman DeLay or persons in the White House directly influenced the department's decisions on Texas redistricting, none with whom I spoke was personally aware of such contacts. In reality, however, such direct contacts by DeLay or the White House probably were unnecessary (except perhaps as a means of reassuring nervous partisans). The political appointees at Justice controlled how the department would handle the decisions surrounding Texas redistricting, and none of them with any ambition to remain active in this Republican administration or in the Republican Party could dare allow any departmental action to delay or to block it.[73] Loyal service would be rewarded. Hans von Spakovsky, who led the battle within the Civil Rights Division to approve the Texas redistricting in 2003, was appointed by President Bush to the Federal Election Commission in 2006. The appointment was an interim appointment not requiring U.S. Senate confirmation.

With all that was at stake in the Texas redistricting, it is difficult to believe that neither Congressman DeLay nor the White House directly or indirectly contacted Attorney General Ashcroft or the political appointees at Justice to ensure preclearance of the Texas plan. It is possible that such contacts occurred at the time in early October 2003, when Republicans meeting in secret decided suddenly to go with the most legally risky but most highly partisan plan. Or contacts could have occurred later, when the redistricting plan was under review at the Department of Justice. If any such contact occurred, however, it remains a tightly held partisan secret. Nevertheless, even if such contact occurred, it probably was unnecessary to ensure a favorable outcome. By 2002, the politicization of the Justice Department ran deep, and was not limited to review of the Texas redistricting.[74]

Commentary

Congressman DeLay's involvement in Texas congressional redistricting over the span of 2001–2003 was extraordinary. Never before had a congressman taken such an active role in the redistricting process in Texas or exercised such enormous influence on the outcome.

In the past, the dominant policy in all previous redistricting efforts had been incumbent protection through plans that generally retained the core of existing congressional districts and maintained "member-constituent relations." Congressmen were most interested in preserving the core of their own districts. However, whatever an individual congressman's role in the past, it was largely at the will or indulgence of the state legislature and its leadership, since state government is responsible for drawing district boundaries. Those boundaries are supposed to be drawn to serve bona fide state interests. This did not happen in Texas in 2003.

Virtually every Republican official whom I interviewed for this book agreed that "but for" DeLay's effort to achieve redistricting in 2003, the issue would not have come up. Jim Ellis's memos show that DeLay's strategy included the possibility of passing at an early stage in the legislative process whatever redistricting plan was necessary to obtain initial legislative approval, knowing that a final plan could be drawn and approved later in the process to achieve the goals of DeLay, the Republican congressional delegation, and national partisan interests. To the extent that the state's lawmakers tried in good faith to make decisions in the interest of Texas or their constituents, their efforts were meaningless if they conflicted with DeLay's partisan goals. As the final map was being prepared at the conference-committee stage in early October, Ellis stressed that the plan must reflect "the priorities of the congressional delegation and not the legislature." Substituting a final, aggressively partisan plan at the end of the legislative process not only misled Democrats and the public, but was also a breach of trust with the Republican lawmakers.

DeLay's ruthless and hypocritical tactics are possibly understandable, even justifiable to some, when directed at the Democrats: in the minds of many Republicans, including DeLay, the Democrats were the enemy because they obstructed the programs and policies favored by Republicans. It is much less understandable or justifiable, however, for DeLay to have broken trust with his fellow Republicans. DeLay made the final redistricting outcome a function of certain national and private interests and his own personal and partisan aims instead of the result of the will, insight, and judgment of the Texas legislature, or even the Republican members of that body.

DeLay's influence on the redistricting process and the final plan was so profound that it rendered the function of the state's elected officials largely meaningless. These state officials did indeed become puppets, not so much for DeLay as an individual, but as part of a larger partisan movement that put the interests of the national party above bona fide state interests. Two Republican lawmakers told me that the process was "corrupted."

As for President Bush, the question of his direct involvement in what happened in Texas probably will not be answered until Karl Rove or someone else close to the president writes about it. However, President Bush's claim that the 2003 redistricting in Texas was only a state matter and thus something in which he was not involved is nonsense. State officials and Republican lawmakers as a group were reluctant from the beginning to undertake redistricting in 2003. For most of them, there was little or no value to interjecting the divisive issue into an already overburdened legislative session. Redistricting was driven from Washington in Bush's name. Whether the redistricting itself was "good" or "bad" for Texas or the nation may possibly be debated, but it was never simply a state matter.

CHAPTER 16

The Legal Implications of the 2003 Redistricting

The redrawing of congressional district lines in Texas raised numerous legal issues; it is not the purpose of this book to examine them. However, there are several constitutional implications that deserve brief discussion. These are (1) whether the redistricting was a partisan gerrymander in violation of the Constitution; (2) whether it violated the constitutional mandate for districts of equal population, since it was an unnecessary mid-decade redistricting based on inaccurate population data; and (3) whether the experience in Texas demonstrates that the Voting Rights Act is no longer an effective means of protecting minority voting rights.

Partisan Gerrymandering

Partisanship and lawmaker self-interest are inevitably part of the redrawing of any congressional, state legislative, or local-government election boundaries. The placement of each boundary line can affect the electability of certain candidates and the representation of partisan or other interests: it can affect who will run for an office, who is likely to win, or what group of like-minded voters has the best opportunity to elect a person of their choice. Therefore, lawmakers, political parties, and interest groups historically have tried to manage the outcome of elections through the drawing of district boundaries.

The courts have consistently recognized that the presence of such partisanship or lawmaker self-interest does not invalidate a redistricting plan so long as the plan meets other applicable legal requirements (e.g., adheres to one person, one vote; does not violate the Voting Rights Act). The U.S. Supreme Court has several times considered whether excessive partisanship can itself invalidate a redistricting plan. The question has been a difficult one for the Court to answer. The Court in *Davis v. Bandemer* (478 U.S. 109 [1986]) found that political gerrymandering claims are justiciable, but the justices could not agree on the standard for determining when a constitutional violation occurred. For the following nineteen years, courts struggled unsuccessfully to establish such a standard. No case finally resulted in a redistricting plan being invalidated because it was found to be an unconstitutional political gerrymander.

Republicans in Texas in 2003 knew firsthand the difficulty of prevailing in any claim of partisan gerrymandering. Republicans had challenged congressional and state-legislative redistricting plans in Texas since the 1960s. They lost every time. So when in a position of power in 2003, Republicans were unconcerned about the possibility that the Democrats could successfully challenge any redistricting plan as too partisan. The Republican lawyers felt that the only real basis for a successful legal challenge might be found in a racial-discrimination claim under the Voting Rights Act. So Republican lawmakers openly acknowledged throughout the 2003 redistricting process that they were redistricting for the purpose of electing more Republicans to Congress. Consistent with this same legal strategy, Republicans rejected any claim that they were acting to minimize or dilute any racial or ethnic group's voting rights and, instead, described the redistricting plans as enhancing minority voting strength.

The Republicans' open admission that the 2003 redistricting was intended to elect more Republicans to Congress seemed to the Democrats to be an invitation to litigation. It led the Democrats to attack the redistricting plan as unconstitutional because it was enacted "solely" for a partisan purpose.

In 2003 a three-judge federal court in *Session v. Perry* (298 F. Supp. 2d 451 [E.D. Tex. 2004]) rejected legal challenges to the 2003 Texas redistricting. This is discussed at the end of Chapter Twelve. The Democrats and minority organizations appealed to the U.S. Supreme Court. While the claims were pending on appeal, the law affecting partisan gerrymanders took a sharp turn. In *Vieth v. Jubelirer* (541 U.S. 267 [2004]), four members of the Court voted to end any search for a workable constitutional standard, indicating that the legality of partisan gerrymanders is not justiciable. This plurality would have reversed the earlier decision in *Bandemer*. Four other justices dissented from the dismissal of the claim from Pennsylvania in *Vieth*, but each justice offered a different possible standard for judging a constitutional claim of partisan gerrymandering. The ninth justice, Anthony Kennedy, voted to affirm the dismissal of the claim in *Vieth*, but declined to join the four-justice plurality to overrule *Bandemer*. Kennedy refused to abandon the search for a manageable standard for determining an unconstitutional partisan gerrymandering.

The U.S. Supreme Court remanded the Texas case in 2004 "for further consideration in light of *Vieth*." On remand, the three-judge district court on June 9, 2005, again rejected the Democrats' claim. In doing so, the court not only rejected the claim that a redistricting could be unconstitutional because done "solely" for a partisan purpose, but also questioned whether the 2003 redistricting was even "substantively unfair." The court described how prior Democrat-controlled redistricting plans had minimized Republican electoral success in congressional races despite a growing Republican dominance in statewide races, and how the 2003 redistricting corrected this underrepresentation.

The 2003 plan that elected twenty-one Republicans and eleven Democrats in 2004 replaced a plan that the district court in 2005 described as having "entrenched a minority party" by allowing Democrats to continue to hold a majority of the state's seats in Congress even though no Democrat had been elected to statewide office for nine years. The new redistricting plan may have been unnecessary, or ruthless, or dominated by national-party interests, but it was not so "substantively unfair" as to be unconstitutional, even if enacted solely for a partisan purpose.

The Democrats, along with the various minority plaintiffs, appealed the district-court decision back to the U.S. Supreme Court. The Court heard oral argument in the case on March 1, 2006. In their final briefs to the Court, the Democrats shifted their attack somewhat by focusing on the unique aspect of the Texas redistricting (i.e., replacing an existing valid plan) and asking whether a legislative body can replace an existing valid plan for solely partisan reasons.

Mid-decade Redistricting

The 2003 redrawing of congressional districts in Texas also is significant because it established a precedent: inaccurate population data could be used to redraw election districts in the middle of a decade to displace an existing valid districting scheme for the purpose of achieving partisan or other interest-based objectives.

The possible implications of such a precedent are huge. Following the Texas lead, partisan state leaders from both major parties announced that they were considering similar redistricting actions in several other states, including California,[1] Maryland, Illinois, Louisiana, New Mexico, and Georgia. The implications of mid-decade redistricting do not stop at the state level; if allowable, it has implications for thousands of cities, counties, parishes, school districts, and other forms of local government nationwide that elect members to a governing board from districts.

There are reasons why even when a potential exists for partisan rewards, that a state or local government may choose not to engage in redistricting except to remedy an invalid plan. Redistricting is possibly the most divisive issue that a legislative body can confront. In the past, most legislative presiding officers have strongly opposed any contested legislation designed to unnecessarily redraw state or congressional district lines because of the expected effect of the pendency of such legislation on the overall atmosphere and efficiency of the legislative body. So also, there has been very little public support for the partisan and messy spectacle that generally accompanies any redistricting effort. Therefore, although the possibility of mid-decade redistricting for partisan reasons has existed in the past, it rarely if ever has happened. Whether the Texas precedent will change that pattern is not clear.

In Texas in 2003 neither the reticence of legislative presiding officers nor the overwhelming opposition of the general public and newspaper editorial boards statewide halted the DeLay-led effort to replace Democratic congressmen with Republican congressmen. The partisan stakes in Washington were deemed too high. Republican leaders effectively wagered that whatever negative response was generated by redistricting would be soon forgotten by the state's voters, and that increasing or protecting a Republican majority in Congress outweighed the potential for any residual negative response from Texas voters. Republican activists viewed redistricting as a triumph; for many Texans, however, it was unnecessary and a state embarrassment.

In some states, the state constitution or state law allows redistricting only once a decade (at the beginning) to remedy the now unequal districts drawn in the prior decade. For example, in 2003 the Supreme Court of Colorado found that the Colorado constitution imposed such a limitation. In most states, however, no such limitation exists under state law. So it was in Texas. In 2003 the state attorney general concluded that nothing in the state constitution prohibited the legislature from redrawing the state's congressional districts, even though the state's existing districts were valid.

There is, however, a possibly serious impediment under the U.S. Constitution to unnecessary mid-decade redistricting. Every legislative body has a fundamental obligation to act in good faith to provide equal representation for equal numbers of persons. This so-called "one person, one vote" principle generally requires that, in the absence of adequate justification, legislative and congressional election districts must be drawn as equal in population as practicable.

Since at least the 1960s, states have become dependent on the data of the federal decennial census to meet this fundamental constitutional requirement. The U.S. Supreme Court has suggested that the federal census may, as a practical matter, be the only usable data for redistricting because it is a comprehensive, uniform, specific, and systematically and objectively ascertained enumeration. Nevertheless, the federal census "is at best an approximate estimate of a state's population at a frozen moment in time."[2] That moment in time is April 1 of the last year of the previous decade (e.g., April 1, 2000). From that moment onward, populations and racial and ethnic demographics throughout every state and local jurisdiction are constantly changing, often at different rates. Census enumerations are outdated even before they are published.

Ordinarily, this inaccuracy in federal decennial census data does not affect the constitutional merits of districting plans using such data because (1) most districting plans are enacted within the narrow window between the release of census data (e.g., in early 2001) and the deadline for having new districts in place for primary and general congressional and state-legislative elections (e.g., 2002); and (2) the new districting plan is replacing an existing unconstitutional or unlawful districting scheme. Census data, though flawed, are the best and perhaps only lawful tools in such circumstances for redistricting; there is no real alternative. Once adopted, these remedial plans remain constitutional (unless violative of other legal requirements) for the remainder of the decade—until shown to be unconstitutionally malapportioned by the next federal decennial census.

However, the mid-decade replacement or change of a lawful existing redistricting plan with a new plan based on now older and even less reliable census data, as occurred in Texas, raises constitutional concerns. As time passes after a census is taken, the census enumeration becomes increasingly inaccurate and provides an increasingly unreliable means for determining the relative equality of districts. (In Texas, for example, the state's population was estimated by the state data center in 2004 to have grown by almost 1.3 million persons from 2000 to 2003; some counties lost population and others gained 25 percent or more.) This increasing inaccuracy and unreliability of previous census data is evident to members of state and local legislative bodies and to all participants in any redistricting process. Therefore, any jurisdiction that redistricts using such data is doing so without any reliable guide as to the real effect of the enactment on the equality of the district populations. The legislative body is essentially doing little more than hoping that the new districts will be no more unequal in population than the existing districts. The legal question is whether, under such circumstances, the districts in the new enactment should be presumed to be the result of a good-faith effort to achieve the fundamental constitutional goal of equal representation for equal numbers of people.

It is possible, of course, that a new districting plan based on old census data will not be more unequal than the existing one. Through some bizarre coincidence, population deviations among the new districts could be smaller than those among the current districts. On the other hand, it also is possible that the new plan may be grossly more malapportioned than the existing one. The currently inaccurate census data provide no reliable answer. Under such circumstances, it is the legislative body that should bear the burden of demonstrating that any new enactment does not unnecessarily jeopardize the constitutional right of each citizen to districts of as nearly equal population as practicable and does not unfairly discriminate against a group based on its race or ethnicity. Since the right is a fundamental right, the legislative body's burden is to show by clear and convincing evidence that the new plan does not worsen the real population equality of the existing districts, or the legislative body must show that the new plan meets a compelling state interest and is narrowly tailored to meet that interest.

Using unreliable federal decennial census data for mid-decade redistricting also allows district boundaries to be redrawn so as to unfairly discriminate against certain categories of voters. More current but incomplete information—such as population estimates (including new estimates of racial and ethnic residents within specific locales), minority-voter registration, or minority turnout—that is unacceptable as a basis for drawing district boundaries may be used selectively during redistricting to discriminate against identifiable racial, ethnic, or political groups, the results being disguised through the use of old census enumerations. Even discrimination against such groups based on real population inequality among new mid-decade districts can be disguised by gerrymandering the new districts to produce misleading results based on old census data.[3] This possibility of disguising discriminatory mid-decade redistricting through the use of old census data is of particular importance in any state like Texas in which the racial and ethnic makeup is changing rapidly due to the phenomenal growth of the Hispanic population.

A specific example of this discriminatory effect was shown in the 2003 redistricting in Texas. Congressional District 23, covering a vast area of southwest Texas, has experienced a rapid growth in Hispanic population since 2000. Along with the growth in Hispanic population has come an increase in the percentage of Hispanic registered voters. For example, between the 2000 and 2002 elections, the percentage of Spanish surnamed registered voters (SSRV) in District 23 increased from 53.8 to 55.3 percent. As a result, the district was becoming more Democratic. The Republican incumbent congressman, Henry Bonilla, barely won reelection in 2002 against a Hispanic Democrat. The redistricting plan enacted in 2003 resolved this partisan problem by making District 23 safer for a Republican. The plan reduced the percentage of SSRV from 55.3 to 46.3 percent by removing much of fast-growing, heavily Hispanic Webb

County and replacing it with several slower-growing, predominantly Anglo counties to the north. This change relied on old census data for balancing the populations of the respective districts. The same result could not have been achieved (without having substantial ripple effects elsewhere in the state) if the increased populations and changed demographics of these areas had been known and used. By using old census enumerations, the Texas redistricting plan ignored the continuing growth of the Hispanic population in this part of Texas and effectively avoided the political changes in District 23 that otherwise would have occurred with the passage of time under the existing districting plan.

The 2003 plan achieved a similar dilutive result statewide by using old census data in conjunction with current political data. By the time of redistricting in 2003 it is likely that Anglos constituted less than half the population in Texas. Yet the 2003 redistricting plan was purposefully designed to give that portion of the state's population that is Republican and overwhelmingly Anglo control over twenty-two of the thirty-two congressional districts and to effectively eliminate for the remainder of this decade the possibility that any growth in Hispanic and other minority populations could change the political balance of any district. There was no district in the 2003 congressional redistricting plan that could realistically be expected to become Democratic or predominately Hispanic within this decade, notwithstanding the anticipated growth of this state's Hispanic population. Heavily Hispanic districts will become increasingly Hispanic. Heavily African American districts will become increasingly African American or Hispanic. Moreover, the 2003 redistricting places smaller minority communities throughout the state in districts where any population growth in those communities will be submerged in an overwhelmingly Anglo Republican population.

Enhancing the strength of a partisan group is not a state interest, much less a compelling state interest. Although political considerations may not be avoidable in redistricting, they cannot justify any deviation from population equality among districts. Nor should the objective of enhancing a group's partisan position justify an unnecessary redrawing of lawful district lines using inaccurate population data.

Some legislators have wondered about using more recent estimates of population for mid-decade redistricting in lieu of outdated census data. Estimates are not usable for redistricting. The census is an enumeration, not an estimate. It essentially is a "fact" that exists on the day the census is taken. Estimates are opinions based on assumptions. Speaking with the benefit of thirty years of trial experience in complex litigation, including redistricting lawsuits, I can say that experts are likely to disagree on the assumptions (e.g., immigration, emigration, births, deaths, voting-age percentages, etc.) used for population estimates, so the prospect of experts dueling over the critical population base becomes a certainty. Every party interested in the redistricting process (and in court) can be expected to have their own experts and their own opinion of the size, dispersion, and racial and ethnic makeup of the state's population. Even geographical regions, such as cities or counties, can be expected to fight over estimates of population that affect their representation in a legislative body. Moreover, estimates lack the uniformity statewide (e.g., an expert is unlikely to know specifically for each county or community statewide whether local factors, such as gained or lost businesses, economic upturns or downturns, etc. could affect the expert's assumptions regarding population trends) or specificity (e.g., knowing the estimated number of persons within a multidistrict county, such as Harris County, is a far cry from knowing how that population is spread among blocks or precincts around the county) required for drawing districts of equal population statewide. However, perhaps the biggest drawback to using estimates is the potential for manipulation of the estimates to benefit one political or racial group. Census data is objectively gathered. Estimates are no substitute.

The practical and legal effect of saying that a legislative body is not free to use outdated census data for unnecessary mid-decade redistricting is to make such redistricting unlikely to occur except for carefully considered minor boundary changes intended to serve specific, bona fide state purposes. Major partisan redistricting efforts, such as in Texas, would become virtually impossible. A careful, comprehensive state or local census enumeration might give reliable data for redistricting, but could be accomplished only with great expense and after years of planning and training. No state is likely to undertake such a project.

If the 2003 redistricting in Texas ultimately is upheld despite its reliance on outdated census data, it is likely to provide a significant legal precedent for similar periodic redistricting nationwide to benefit partisan or other interests. In the words of several observers, the game of periodic redistricting as a partisan "tit for tat" would mean that "[i]nstead of voters selecting representatives, it's representatives selecting voters."[4] Some suggest that this amounts to "rolling redistricting." Republican lawmakers in Texas in 2003 argued that mid-decade redistricting is unlikely to be a problem in other states because it should arise only when the majority party changes between the time of the initial redistricting and mid-decade. However, other states already have shown an interest in following the Texas lead, and Supreme Court Justice Stephen Breyer has noted, "By redrawing districts every 2 years, rather than every 10 years, a party might preserve its political advantages notwithstanding population shifts in the State."[5] Attorney General Abbott has conceded on behalf of Texas that if the state prevails in the federal court challenge to the 2003 redistricting, the precedent will mean that a political majority in a legislative body could redistrict at the end of a decade (e.g., in Texas in 2009) and thereby maximize its strength in the next legislature (e.g., the one beginning in 2011), which will redraw districts after the next census.

A two-judge majority of the district court in the Texas case in 2005[6] held that a state legislature should be allowed to rely on the "legal fiction" that census data remains accurate throughout a decade, even when replacing a valid existing redistricting plan. These judges concluded that a restraint on using old census data would effectively mean that voluntary mid-decade redistricting could not occur. In their view, such a result was inconsistent with precedent recognizing that a state is free under federal law to redistrict at any time. The third judge (who concurred with the outcome of the case) disagreed on this point. He concluded that allowing a state to rely on outdated federal census data to *"facilitate"* its voluntary efforts at partisan gerrymandering "seems to me a perverse use of data sanctioned by the Supreme Court for use in efforts to *avoid* the dilution of individual votes cast in congressional elections."[7] I believe the third judge is correct.

The Effect on Minorities

The effect of the final redistricting plan on minority voters is discussed throughout this book. The unanimous recommendation of the professional staff of the Department of Justice's Voting Section to object to the plan clearly shows that the concerns of minority lawmakers in Texas were bona fide. However, as indicated in Chapter Eleven, the U.S. attorney general's final decision whether to object to the implementation of an election change (such as the Texas redistricting) is not reviewable by any court. I agree with most of the Voting Section's analysis, however, it is unlikely that the existence of the memorandum containing that analysis will affect the challenge to the Texas redistricting now pending at the U.S. Supreme Court.

As discussed above, the court challenge to the Texas redistricting plan is not an appeal of the department's action. Instead, it is a separate action in which the plaintiffs (Democrats and minority-advocacy groups) must show that the redistricting plan violates either the Constitution or Section 2 of the Voting Rights Act. The federal three-judge district court in 2005 spent virtually no time on the minority-voter issues because the case had been remanded on the issue of partisan gerrymandering. However, in its earlier opinion in 2003, a majority of the court rejected the arguments that the plan violated Section 2 or the Constitution; Judge Ward dissented. Essentially, the majority concluded that it was within the state's authority to determine how best to reflect minority interests in a state through redistricting, and rejected the claim that minority voters in Districts 24 and 25 were protected under the Voting Rights Act or the Constitution. The court majority accepted that Texas could legitimately choose to reduce minority voting strength in some districts (e.g., Districts 23 and 24) while creating new or enhanced minority strength in other districts (such as redrawn Districts 9 and 25) as long as the result (considered statewide) did not discriminate.

The Voting Rights Act

The Voting Rights Act of 1965 has been the primary cause of much of the success by minority candidates nationwide. However, the effect of the act on the drawing of state legislative and congressional districts in Texas has been less clear.

Texas was not included among the states covered by Section 5 of the act when it was adopted in 1965. As a result, none of the state's redistricting plans in the 1960s or in 1971 were required to be submitted for preclearance. As discussed in Chapter Three, the dramatic changes in minority representation that came through the equalizing of population among districts and the elimination of multimember districts in the 1970s resulted primarily from litigation based on the Constitution, not the Voting Rights Act.

Texas first became subject to Section 5 (and its preclearance requirement) in 1975. The section requires that election changes, such as redistricting, must not be retrogressive. The impact of this requirement on minority representation in Texas has been unclear. For example, there were fourteen African Americans in the Texas House of Representatives by 1981, before the legislature first drew a statewide districting plan that had to be reviewed under Section 5. The number of African Americans in the Texas House has dropped to thirteen after three decades and numerous redistrictings. It is possible, therefore, to argue that the Voting Rights Act has successfully prevented any substantial loss of African American seats in the state House, or alternately that by requiring the maintenance of African American majorities in these districts, the act (as interpreted and applied by Justice through the mid-1990s) has unnecessary lessened African American influence in other legislative districts and actually prevented the election of additional African Americans to the House. However, it also can be convincingly argued that the increases in African American representation in the Texas Senate (from no African American members in 1981 to two in 2001) and Congress (from one member in 1981 to two members in 2001) are at least partly attributable to the need perceived by the Texas legislature to draw African American–opportunity districts in order to comply with Sections 5 and 2 of the act.

The number of Hispanic state representatives and senators has significantly increased since 1981. Much of this increase is traceable to the dramatic growth of the Hispanic population over the past two decades rather than directly to the Voting Rights Act. However, Justice's objection to the compact districts in South Texas drawn by the legislature in 1981 has had a long-term enhancing effect on Hispanic congressional representation. The elongated districts subsequently adopted by the court for the 1982 election increased the number of congressional districts with Hispanic majorities by combining the overwhelmingly Hispanic areas of South Texas with the less Hispanic areas of Central Texas and provided a structure for those districts that prevails today. This effect has been maintained in subsequent redistrictings.

In assessing the effect of the Voting Rights Act, it is important to look beyond the official actions taken by the Justice Department on specific election changes. The greatest effect of Section 5 has been on the attitudes of state and local legislative bodies during the legislative process itself. For three decades Texas redistricting bodies have struggled to comply with the requirements of the act. I fault Justice for its needlessly counterproductive (although well-intentioned) interpretation and application of the act in the 1980s and early 1990s in an effort to maximize minority voting strength. In some ways the department's policy was outdated and actually worked against minority voting strength, especially when it resulted in the needless concentration of African American voters. The department's policy during this period was subsequently rejected by the U.S. Supreme Court.[8] Nevertheless, I believe that the need to comply with the requirements of the act played a major and generally positive role for over four decades in increasing or maintaining Hispanic and African American representation in Congress and the Texas legislature. Without such a constraint, Democratic-controlled legislatures of the past would likely have gone even further to avoid creating minority-opportunity districts.

At one time I doubted that Section 5 had much continuing importance, particularly for statewide redistricting in a state like Texas. I was confident that the gains of African American and Hispanic voters would be secure in the future. The 2003 redistricting has convinced me otherwise. The final redistricting bill went as far in creating Republican congressional districts as the Republican leadership thought the law would allow. Minority voting strength was equated with Democratic voting strength. Hispanic and African American advocacy organizations were described as being more Democratic than minority because they objected to reductions in minority voting strength in districts statewide. Whenever Republican decision makers were given an opportunity to choose between a minority priority and an additional Republican district, they chose adding to Republican power. Ultimately, Congressman DeLay and the other Republican leaders were deliberately willing to risk violating the Voting Rights Act to shore up Republican strength in District 23, to dismantle District 24, and to submerge smaller minority communities statewide in districts where their vote is insignificant. Whether their actions violated the Voting Rights Act remains disputed. However, if the act's requirements had not existed, there is little question in my mind that Republicans would have gone even further to reduce Democratic and minority voting strength.

It is reasonable to ask whether Republicans could have gone further in 2003 if not constrained by the Voting Rights act. The answer is yes. The most obvious means of further enhancing Republican strength at a cost to minorities would have been by eliminating the parallel congressional districts running north–south out of the Rio Grande Valley. Compact districts would further pack this very heavily Hispanic region into at least one less district having a majority Hispanic voting population. Other potential circumstances exist elsewhere, such as in Harris County, where it is doubtful if District 9 would have been designed with a predominantly African American voting population if not for the benefits such a district gave Republicans under the Voting Rights Act.

For these reasons, I believe the 2003 congressional redistricting in Texas supports a further extension of Section 5 of the Voting Rights Act beyond 2007 as a justifiable constraint on Democrats and Republicans. This recommendation assumes, however, that the Voting Section of the Department of Justice can review election changes and enforce the Voting Rights Act effectively and nonpartisanly. The events surrounding the department's action on the 2003 redistricting in Texas raise serious questions about the possibility of such non-partisan effectiveness.

The outcome before the United States Supreme Court in *LULAC v. Perry* is discussed in the Afterword.

CHAPTER 17

Criminal Investigations and Indictments

This act [the indictment of Congressman DeLay] is the product of a coordinated, premeditated campaign of political retribution, the all-too-predictable result of a vengeful investigation led by a partisan fanatic [District Attorney Ronnie Earle].
— CONGRESSMAN DELAY, SEPTEMBER 28, 2005

Being called vindictive and partisan by Tom DeLay is like being called ugly by a frog.
— DISTRICT ATTORNEY RONNIE EARLE, MARCH 6, 2005

At 9 a.m. on November 22, 2005, the ninth-floor courtroom for the 331st District Court of Travis County was packed.[1] Over 100 eager onlookers crammed together on the public pews in the courtroom to observe the proceedings. Most were representatives of print and television media. Another ten persons (mostly county and court employees) were seated in the jury box along the east side of the room. Six severe-looking men stood at the door to the courtroom. They were security for the court and for the most notable defendant on this day, Congressman Tom DeLay. Outside the courtroom, another fifty persons gathered with their still and television cameras and microphones, hoping for a worthwhile glimpse of or a statement from one of the notables now gathering in the courtroom.

Congressman DeLay and his two codefendants passed through this sea of media, microphones, and cameras to enter the courtroom by the front door. DeLay seated himself on the left side of the courtroom, on the first bench of the public section nearest the attorneys and the court dais. He obviously was aware of the many eyes focused on him, but he sat generally expressionless, watching the front of the courtroom and the court bench. He seldom spoke to those around him. Jim Ellis and John Colyandro, officials of the Texans for a Republican Majority Political Action Committee (TRMPAC), were in the courtroom too, but they were not seated alongside DeLay. Ellis remained outgoing and apparently confident, even in the face (or because) of the status of the legal proceedings. The much shorter Colyandro sat quietly, and was noticeably nervous. Five members of DeLay's legal team were seated in chairs around the table provided for the defense counsel. Ellis's two attorneys were seated together nearby on a bench between the attorneys' table and the public seating. Colyandro and his counsel were seated across the courtroom in the jury box.

The criminal charges against DeLay, Ellis, and Colyandro were brought of behalf of the State of Texas. Therefore, the cases were styled "The State of Texas" versus the three defendants. However, it was the district attorney of Travis County who was representing the state in these proceedings and who was responsible for securing the indictments and prosecuting the cases. District Attorney Ronnie Earle sat along with others from his office on the bench for legal staff and parties directly behind the prosecutors' table. Three of his assistant district attorneys were seated at the table. From his nearby position on the bench, Earle could pass suggestions to his assistants or, if necessary, rise to speak to the court himself, as he had done at a previous hearing.

Technically, the issues before the court on November 22 were the defendants' nonevidentiary pretrial motions to quash the indictments charging the defendants with felony violations of Texas law. In reality, however, much more was at stake. DeLay had been required by House Republican Conference rules to step down temporarily as majority leader of the U.S. House of Representatives because of his indictment. Congressman Roy Blunt (Missouri) had been named acting majority leader. If the charges were speedily dismissed, DeLay could reassume this position of power. On the other hand, the longer the indictments remained pending, the more likely it became that Republicans in Congress would replace him as majority leader. A trial could be months away. There was no assurance that the Republican majority in Washington would wait that long before again having a true majority leader. Therefore, even if eventually acquitted at a future trial, DeLay might not be able to reacquire his position as majority leader once he lost it. His best chance of staying majority leader was for this court to grant his motions and dismiss the indictments promptly.

This drama playing out in the courtroom on November 22, 2005, was a culmination of three years of criminal investigations and legal maneuvering.

The Criminal Investigations and Initial Indictments

The criminal investigation that began shortly after the 2002 election was initially focused a long way from Congressman DeLay. As discussed in Chapter

Four, Bill Hammond, president of the Texas Association of Business (TAB), bragged about the association's success in the 2002 election. Hammond's statements aroused the attention of persons in the Travis County district attorney's office and brought a formal complaint to the office in November 2002 from Common Cause, Public Citizen, and the League of Conservation Voters. It was soon clear that TAB had used corporate money for its campaign on behalf of Republican candidates, even though TAB, represented in the criminal and civil proceedings by Andy Taylor, tried to quash subpoenas intended to identify the corporations.

However, the role of TRMPAC and its principals, Jim Ellis and John Colyandro, was slow to come out. Initially, Hammond insisted that he acted alone in 2002, without coordinating his association's activities with TRMPAC or any other group. He denied working closely with Colyandro. As discovery in the civil lawsuits against TAB (discussed in Chapter Four) progressed, however, a trail to TRMPAC and, to a lesser extent, to Texans for Lawsuit Reform (TLR) and the Law Enforcement Alliance for America (LEAA) began to emerge. Records were found in the civil suits showing expenditures by TAB on behalf of TRMPAC. The district attorney found these same records and increasingly focused on TRMPAC and its principals. On March 31, 2003, the public watchdog group Texans for Public Justice requested in writing that Earle investigate possible illegal political expenditures by TRMPAC. The TPJ letter contained numerous specifics about the discrepancies between what TRMPAC had reported to the Texas Ethics Commission and what the organization had reported in its IRS filings. The TPJ letter alleged that TRMPAC had not raised enough noncorporate funds to pay for the expenditures and that TRMPAC had raised "at a minimum $602,300" in unreported corporate funds. It also was becoming increasingly clear to the district attorney's team that prosecuting TAB for its mailings would be difficult, despite the use of corporate money, because TAB, as an association of businesses, possibly had a constitutional right to spend money on behalf of its member corporations for a public-information campaign as long as it did not expressly advocate voting for or against specific candidates. Whether the wording of TAB's many mailings was enough to constitute express advocacy was problematic. However, TRMPAC, as a political action committee, was less well positioned to rely on this defense for its use of corporate funds.

For months the grand jury issued subpoenas and heard testimony as a part of its investigation into the conduct of certain organizations and persons before the 2002 election.[2] When the term of one grand jury ended in March 2004, another was empaneled to continue the probe. Some Republican officials, such as Governor Perry, labeled the subpoenas as part of a partisan "fishing expedition" and accused the district attorney of coordinating his investigation with the private attorneys in the civil lawsuits brought by Democrats against TRMPAC and TAB and leaking information about the investigation to them and the press.[3] Earle denied the charges. TAB attorney Andy Taylor pursued this issue by filing eighty-three open-records requests for material from the DA in an apparent effort to establish that the grand jury investigation and the civil lawsuits were part of a partisan conspiracy against TAB and TRMPAC.[4] When supplied to Taylor in April 2004, however, the material provided no evidence of leaks from the DA to the private attorneys. Earle withheld some records that he claimed would compromise grand jury secrecy if released. In an ironic turn of events, Earle asked Attorney General Abbott (a Republican, and Taylor's former boss and good friend) to determine that the documents were protected from disclosure under the open-records law.

Approximately twenty-two months after the criminal investigation began, the first indictments were returned. On September 21, 2004, the grand jury of the 403rd District Court of Travis County returned thirty-two indictments against three individuals and eight corporations. John Colyandro was indicted for knowingly accepting a political contribution of $25,000 from Westar Energy, Inc. in violation of Subchapter D (Restrictions on Contributions and Expenditures of Corporations and Labor Unions) of Chapter 253 of the Texas Election Code. In a separate cause, Jim Ellis was indicted for knowingly conducting and facilitating a transaction involving proceeds of criminal activity (i.e., delivering a check for $190,000 from the TRMPAC corporate account to the Republican National Committee, along with a list of candidates and the corresponding dollar amounts that the RNC was to contribute to each). The charge against Ellis was money laundering, a first-degree felony. This indictment also named six corporations (Diversified Collection Services, Inc.; Sears, Roebuck and Co.; the Williams Companies, Inc.; Cornell Companies; Bacardi USA, Inc.; and Questerra Corporation) that had contributed a total of $155,000 to TRMPAC. A separate indictment was against El Paso Energy Service Company for an unlawful political contribution of $50,000 to TRMPAC. This indictment also contained two counts against Warren M. Robold for knowingly soliciting the corporation's unlawful contribution and for knowingly accepting this unlawful political contribution on behalf of TRMPAC. Another indictment named Westar Energy, Inc. for an unlawful political contribution by a corporation. All of these charges were third-degree felonies except the money-laundering charge against Ellis. DeLay called the indictments against Ellis, Colyandro, and Robold "a joke," adding, "When you have lawyers advising you every step of the way in writing, it's very hard to make a case stick."[5]

According to a long-standing procedure adopted by the judicial district of Travis County, these criminal actions were transferred to the 331st Judicial Court of Travis County. Judge Robert Perkins, who specializes in hearing criminal cases, was the presiding judge. Each subsequent indictment discussed below was similarly transferred to the 331st Judicial Court regardless of which grand jury returned the indictment.

Both Ellis and Colyandro attacked the sufficiency of the indictments against them. They argued that the election-code provisions in question either did not apply or, if applicable, were unconstitutional constraints on free speech. Also, in a strategy that would have implications for 2005–2006, the attorneys for Colyandro and Ellis chose to draw out these criminal proceedings. They were in no hurry to proceed to trial. In July 2005, Colyandro was indicted on the same money-laundering charges that earlier had been brought against Ellis. Then the two were reindicted together for the money-laundering charge. At the end of July 2005, Judge Perkins ruled on the Colyandro and Ellis's challenges to the indictments. He refused to dismiss the charges. Colyandro and Ellis appealed this decision. As a result, the proceedings before the district court were stayed. This appeal remained pending in 2006.

Meanwhile, the district attorney was negotiating with the indicted corporations. Charges were dismissed over time against four (Sears Holdings Corp., Diversified Collection Services, Questerra, and Cracker Barrel/Old Store) in exchange for promises of cooperation in the ongoing investigations and future adherence to campaign-finance restrictions. The agreements also indicated that the corporations had contributed to TRMPAC based on "false and misleading information provided by the fund-raiser." The fund-raiser in question was Warren Robold. The extent to which evidence from these corporations will be important to any future criminal trials, however, remains unclear. Charges remained pending in 2006 against El Paso Energy Service Co., the Williams Cos., Westar Energy, the Alliance for Quality Nursing Home Care, and Bacardi USA.[6]

On September 8, 2005, indictments were announced against TAB and TRMPAC. One indictment charged TAB with eighty-three counts of "illegally funneling large amounts of corporate money into the 2002 elections through a series of mailers and televisions ads." TAB was also charged with coordinating these efforts with other groups, PACs, and individuals. A second indictment against TAB charged that Bill Hammond, as president and CEO of the organization, had illegally solicited corporate contributions for use in the 2002 elections. A third indictment charged TAB with fourteen counts of illegal corporate contributions—i.e., specifically that TAB had used corporate funds to pay Hammond and Jack Campbell, TAB's governmental affairs manager, for doing political work for various PACs. A fourth indictment charged TAB with making illegal corporate expenditures by spending $1.1 million in corporate money for political advertisements and campaign contributions. In a press release at that time, District Attorney Earle acknowledged that the investigation of TAB's activity had taken over two and half years, but he said that the primary factor delaying the investigation was "TAB's prolonged efforts to stymie the investigation and hide the details of the use of corporate money."[7] TAB's counsel, Andy Taylor, had repeatedly fought efforts by the DA and by counsel in the private lawsuits against TAB to learn more about TAB's 2002 activities, claiming that information about the identity of TAB's corporate contributors and the amount of their contributions as shielded by the First Amendment. TAB's appeals of orders for the production of the information in question had taken almost two years. In 2005 TAB was compelled by the Texas Supreme Court to produce the information. Another indictment announced on September 8 charged TRMPAC with illegally soliciting and accepting corporate contributions from AT&T and the Alliance for Quality Nursing Home Care.

On September 13, 2005, the grand jury for the 147th Judicial District reindicted both Colyandro and Ellis on the money-laundering charge. The reindictments essentially gathered the allegations from the previous money laundering indictments (including the names of the same six corporations alleged to have contributed $155,000 in unlawful corporate funds to TRMPAC) and combined them into a single document naming both Colyandro and Ellis. As discussed below, the district attorney refrained from asking the grand jury to include Congressman DeLay in this indictment in return for an agreement by DeLay to waive the three-year statute of limitations to allow further discussions between DeLay's attorneys and the prosecutors.

Those Who Escaped Indictment

Although both TRMPAC and TAB and several of the key participants in TRMPAC were indicted, two prominent figures remained unindicted by the fall of 2005 and were expected to avoid indictment.

Bill Hammond, the President of TAB, was a key figure in the 2002 election campaign. As discussed in Chapter Four, he led TAB in raising and spending corporate funds and coordinated his activities with TRMPAC and the TLR on behalf of candidates in the Republican primary and on behalf of Republican candidates in the general election. It was Hammond's braggadocio in November 2002 about TAB's success that had first drawn public and prosecutorial attention to the use of corporate funds in the 2002 election. However, Hammond escaped indictment. One reason was that TAB, as an association of business interests, was better positioned to argue in its defense that it was merely using the funds of its member corporations to advocate for the interests of its members, not to expressly advocate on behalf of specific candidates. Also, Hammond, through his attorneys (especially Roy Minton) made an ultimately persuasive case to prosecutors that he had sincerely believed in 2002, based on legal advice, that he was complying with applicable law and, therefore, lacked the requisite criminal intent.[8]

Ultimately, prosecutors decided that obtaining a criminal conviction of Hammond would be unlikely and would be a distraction from the other prosecutions. No indictment was presented to the grand jury. Much of the credit for Hammond avoiding indictment can be traced to the artful diplomacy and lobbying of his criminal counsel, Roy Minton. However, Hammond's organization (TAB) was indicted and faced the possibility of millions of dollars in fines for allegedly soliciting and spending corporate funds in violation of the election law.

Speaker Tom Craddick also escaped indictment. In the period after the 2002 election, he faced at least two possible bases for criminal charges. First, he faced the possibility of indictment along with Ellis and Colyandro because of his involvement in helping raise corporate contributions for TRMPAC. However, numerous other state officials theoretically faced similar liability, especially those who had served as members of the advisory board of TRMPAC. It appears that prosecutors determined that they were unable to prove that Craddick and these other officials had either sufficient involvement in TRMPAC or criminal intent to warrant indictment for their individual fund-raising activities.

Second, Craddick also faced the possibility of indictment for improperly using his connection to TRMPAC as a means of unlawfully influencing lawmakers and candidates to elect him Speaker. Texas law, Section 302.021 of the Government Code, imposes limitations on Speaker candidates and on persons and corporations in the context of a race for Speaker of the Texas House of Representatives. Another provision, Section 302.032, makes it an offense for a person to try to improperly influence a lawmaker or candidate's vote for Speaker. Some felt that Craddick's role in TRMPAC and as a go-between for some of TRMPAC's contributions to state House candidates might have violated these statutory provisions. In March 2004, Craddick and several Republican lawmakers were served with subpoenas by the grand jury. However, election-law experts questioned the constitutionality of these statutory provisions because of their breadth. Moreover, even if the individual acts by Craddick through or on behalf of TRMPAC ultimately aided his candidacy for Speaker, the circumstances surrounding those acts and Craddick's responsibility for the acts were sufficiently murky as to make prosecution difficult. And the Travis County district attorney probably lacked jurisdiction over some matters, such as Craddick's receipt of the $100,000 check from the Alliance for Quality Nursing Home Care at a restaurant in Houston. Austin attorney Roy Minton also represented Craddick and can be credited with helping him dodge this bullet. Ultimately no indictment was presented to the grand jury.

The Indictment of DeLay in 2005

Until the fall of 2005 it appeared that Congressman DeLay too might avoid indictment. DeLay acknowledged publicly that he had played a major role in the creation of TRMPAC and had been a participant in TRMPAC fund-raisers. However, he insisted that he had directed Ellis and Colyandro to get legal and accounting advice about running TRMPAC and that he (DeLay) had no involvement in the day-to-day operations of the political action committee. Moreover, the jurisdiction of the Travis County prosecutor appeared to effectively be limited under the election code to alleged violators residing within the county: venue for a violation of the code was in the county of residence of the defendant (Election Code, Section 251.004[a]). DeLay resided approximately 200 miles away to the southeast, in Fort Bend County. Although the district attorney of Fort Bend County had jurisdiction to prosecute charges against DeLay, he was not prepared to pursue him.[9] Finally, prosecutors had not yet found compelling evidence linking DeLay to specific misconduct. None of the persons who had earlier been indicted (Ellis, Colyandro, and Robold) had voluntarily implicated DeLay in any illegal acts. Therefore, as the three-year felony statute of limitations neared expiration for actions taken in the 2002 elections, it appeared that DeLay would escape indictment.

A Fateful Meeting on August 17, 2005

As the statute of limitations was running out, Congressman DeLay and his attorneys met quietly in Austin with District Attorney Earle and other prosecutors.[10] It was the first time that Earle had actually met DeLay. The Congressman was accompanied by his two Austin lawyers, as well as three attorneys from Washington. DeLay and his attorneys said later that they were tricked into attending the meeting by Earle's claim that he had a "runaway grand jury" that was going to indict DeLay before the statute of limitations expired. According to DeLay and his attorneys, Earle said he could possibly convince the jury not to do so if DeLay would waive the statute of limitations and allow

Earle to work longer with the grand jury. Earle denied these claims. DeLay came to Austin apparently expecting to put to rest any possibility of indictment by showing Earle and his prosecuting team that he had not been involved in the day-to-day running of TRMPAC. They brought DeLay's 2002 calendar and call record to show that he "was nowhere near Ellis and Colyandro" during 2002.

The meeting lasted approximately one and a half hours; accounts vary about precisely what occurred. DeLay said later that he had been led to believe that the matter "was pretty much over" after the meeting and that he would be spared indictment.[11] However, to Earle, DeLay at the meeting had implicated himself in a conspiracy regarding the use of the $190,000. Earle felt that DeLay had clearly admitted at the meeting that he knew beforehand about the transfer of $190,000 from TRMPAC's corporate-money account to the Republican National State Elections Committee (RNSEC) in return for $190,000 in contributions from RNSEC to seven state-representative candidates. This admission was enough in Earle's mind to make DeLay part of a conspiracy with Ellis and Colyandro. DeLay said publicly after the August 2005 meeting that he had meant to say that he had learned about the transfer after it happened. He told Fox News, "I knew about this after it happened because Jim Ellis in passing said, 'Oh, by the way, we sent some money to RNSEC,' and I said, 'OK.' That wasn't an approval. That was an acknowledgment."[12] DeLay charged, "I misspoke one sentence, and they [the district attorney prosecutors] have based all this on one sentence."

For the next few weeks things remained quiet. DeLay says that he was under the impression that he probably was not going to be indicted because "he (Earle) would have . . . called me to testify before the grand jury."[13] However, since Earle felt DeLay had admitted to personal involvement in the laundering of corporate money through RNSEC, and since he had other evidence as well, including grand-jury testimony by RNC official Terry Nelson and DeLay's schedule, showing he had met with Ellis on October 2, 2002 (the day the RNC memoranda approving the payments to the Texas candidates had been generated), Earle indicated to DeLay's attorneys that he anticipated presenting the matter to the grand jury in September for possible indictment. In an effort to head off such an indictment, DeLay agreed to waive the statute of limitations for a month to allow further discussions. As a result, DeLay was not included along with Ellis and Colyandro in the indictments returned on September 13, 2005.

DeLay's attorneys then tried to prevent any felony indictment from being returned. On September 23, former Arkansas congressman Ed Bethune (an attorney with the firm of Bracewell & Giuliani, he had overseen DeLay's response to ethics complaints in Congress) and Austin attorney Bill White met with Earle and his first assistant to discuss the possibility of DeLay's pleading guilty to a misdemeanor offense. Former Travis County Attorney Ken Oden served as intermediary. The meeting took place at night and lasted approximately four hours. Earle was willing to accept having DeLay plead to a misdemeanor (and thereby be able to remain majority leader), but he wanted DeLay and Ellis to enter their pleas immediately and to spend time in jail if their appeals on the constitutionality of the state laws were denied. DeLay's attorneys rejected this idea. They wanted an agreement based on DeLay's promise to plead (or to consider pleading) guilty later to a misdemeanor offense if his challenge to the state law failed. Either agreement would effectively have allowed DeLay to remain majority leader during the appeal (which could take years) and would have resulted in all charges being dismissed and the plea forgotten if the law were declared invalid. The two sides could not reach agreement.[14] Earle presented his case against DeLay to a grand jury.

The September 28 Indictments (First DeLay Indictment)

On September 28th, the grand jury for the 167th District Court in Travis County returned indictments against DeLay and two codefendants, Ellis and Colyandro. Shockwaves reached Washington because DeLay now faced the loss of his powerful position as majority leader. National print and television media turned their focus toward Austin. What previously had been a moderately interesting criminal prosecution of three of DeLay's associates now was a direct attack on a man whom many felt was the most powerful in Congress.

Congressman DeLay immediately stepped aside as majority leader on September 28 after the indictments were made public. At the same time, he labeled the indictment against him "a sham," demanded a quick trial, and lashed out at what he characterized as "politics at its sleaziest."[15] DeLay accused Democratic leaders in Washington of working with Earle to have him indicted. In addition, he directed his ire toward the *Austin American-Statesman,* which he accused of editorializing for his indictment. The editorial in question (published September 11) questioned the purpose of Earle's investigation if, after three years, it resulted in the indictment of only the organizations (TRMPAC and TAB), but not individuals. An editorial in the *Austin-American Statesman* on September 29 responded to DeLay's allegations: "DeLay was not mentioned by name, nor was there an allusion to him. It is either DeLay's hubris or his conscience that leads him to think that the editorial targeted him."

DeLay's harshest criticism, however, was directed at Earle: "This act [the indictment] is the product of a coordinated, premeditated campaign of political retribution, the all-too-predictable result of a vengeful investigation led by a partisan fanatic [Earle]."[16] DeLay's allies joined in the attack on Earle, portraying him as a "vendetta-obsessed partisan bumbler" who, according to well-known GOP operative Barbara Comstock, had a "history of using his office for attacks on his personal and political enemies."[17] The attack even reached Travis County, where the conservative Free Enterprise Fund sponsored ads on television likening Earle to a circling shark and a snarling dog. Earle and his staff largely remained silent in the face of this public attack.

The indictments on September 28 alleged felonies in violation of state law based on the transfer of corporate funds from TRMPAC to the RNSEC. However, the indictments took what some in the prosecutor's office thought was the easiest route for obtaining a felony conviction against DeLay. The indictments alleged that DeLay, Ellis, and Colyandro entered into an agreement that one or more of them would knowingly make a political contribution of $190,000 from TRMPAC's corporate funds "to the Republican National Committee, a political party" within a period of sixty days prior to the 2002 general election. Although the indictments also alleged that the RNC (through the RNSEC) subsequently contributed the same amount to state representative candidates, the criminal act alleged in the indictments did not require proving a connection between the two fund transfers. Instead, the mere transfer of the funds to RNC (the check actually was payable to RNSEC) from TRMPAC's corporate fund account was seen as sufficient to establish a violation of Section 253.104(b) of the Government Code, which prohibited a corporation from knowingly making any contribution to a "political party" within the period of sixty days before an election. By alleging that the three defendants had an agreement to engage in this criminal conduct, DeLay now became an indicted coconspirator.

These indictments offered several important advantages for the prosecutors. The alleged specific criminal act seemed easy to prove factually. Although the issue of the actors' requisite intent remained to be established, no one disputed the transfer of $190,000 from TRMPAC's corporate account to the RNC within the proscribed sixty days. There were numerous legal issues (e.g., was the RNSEC a "political party" within the scope of the Texas law? Was the transfer of funds the equivalent of a "corporation" making a contribution as prohibited by state law? Could Texas law constitutionally prohibit a corporation from contributing to a national political party if federal law permitted the contribution?), but there were few if any contested facts. Another advantage was that by alleging conspiracy, Earle hoped to be able to rely on venue and jurisdiction provisions of the state Penal Code (instead of the Election Code) that allowed him to indict and prosecute DeLay even though DeLay resided in distant Fort Bend County. Finally, DeLay's waiver of the statute of limitations allowed the indictment to be returned on September 28, even though the alleged criminal act (i.e., the transfer of corporate funds to the RNC) had occurred on or about September 13, 2002, over three years earlier.

On September 28, shortly after the indictments had been made public, the prosecutors learned that these indictments faced a legal hurdle that they had not foreseen. In 2005 the Texas legislature had adopted an amendment to Section 1.03 of the Texas Penal Code, specifically making the portion of the code (Title IV) containing the conspiracy provisions applicable to a violation of the state's election laws. This raised the legal question whether the conspiracy statute applied to violations of the election code in 2002, before the amendment was adopted. There are many theories as to how the prosecutors learned about this particular legal problem, but they immediately realized that the indictment might be invalid. They knew that they had to act quickly or face the possible dismissal of the only criminal charges against DeLay for his actions in 2002.

A possibility existed for an additional indictment. DeLay had withdrawn (or tried to withdraw) his waiver of the statute of limitations on September 29, but the statute would not run out on the money-laundering charge (that had earlier been brought against Ellis and Colyandro) until at least October 4, the three-year anniversary of the date that the checks had been sent by the RNSEC to the state-representative candidates.

However, prosecutors confronted a serious obstacle to any further indictments. The September 28 indictments had been returned by the grand jury of the 167th District Court, but the term of that grand jury had expired and the grand jury had been discharged. On September 29 and 30, prosecutors went to the still-convened 390th District Court grand jury and presented the money-laundering charges against the three defendants. According to the prosecutors, the foreman of that grand jury said that the grand jury had adopted a policy that a no-bill would be returned in all cases lacking nine votes for indictment, and that a no-bill would be returned on the money-laundering charges. Prosecutors prepared a no-bill, which the foreman signed and returned to the clerk of the court.

Over the weekend, October 1–2, an investigator for the district attorney's office telephoned several members of the now defunct 167th District Court grand jury to test whether they might have voted to indict DeLay along with Colyandro and Ellis, had they known about DeLay's apparent awareness of the funds transfer from TRMPAC to the RNSEC. Prosecutors say that they wanted an opinion whether the evidence was sufficient for an indictment of DeLay. The investigator did not tell the members of the grand jury about the earlier no-bill by the 390th District Court grand jury.

Early on Monday, October 3, prosecutors appeared before another sitting grand jury and presented charges of conspiracy and money laundering. The grand jury for the 403rd District Court voted indictments against DeLay, Ellis, and Colyandro. The new indictments were made public later on October 3, only hours after the defendants had filed their motion to quash the September 28 indictments.

The October 3 Indictments

The new indictments alleged essentially the same facts as the September 28 indictments. Count I of the new indictments was essentially a repeat of the previous conspiracy charges. However, Count II of the new indictments added a new offense against DeLay—money laundering—under Chapter 34 of the Texas Penal Code. Under this charge, it was no longer possible for the prosecutors to show a violation of state law solely because TRMPAC corporate funds were contributed to the RNC within sixty days of the election. Conviction under Count II for money laundering would be possible only if prosecutors could show that the RNSEC's state-candidate contributions were part of a conspiracy by DeLay, Ellis, and Colyandro to convert TRMPAC's legally restricted corporate funds to unrestricted "hard money" that was sent by the RNSEC to the candidates. The indictments alleged that these principals had committed a criminal conspiracy (Texas Penal Code, Section 15.02).

Critical facts were certain to be contested in relation to this new charge, such as whether the RNC contributions were sent in return for the TRMPAC funds, whether Ellis gave the RNSEC a list of candidates and contributions, and whether DeLay knew about the transaction beforehand and acted in furtherance of the money laundering, such as by prodding the RNSEC to send the contribution checks to the Texas candidates. TRMPAC and the RNC were also named as unindicted coconspirators in the new bill of indictment. Moreover, prosecutors maintained that the October 3 indictments were not in lieu of the September 28 indictments.[18] Therefore, defendants were left after October 3 facing charges of conspiring to violate the state election code (i.e., by contributing corporate funds to a political party [the RNC] within sixty days of the 2002 election) and conspiring to unlawfully launder monies. Conspiracy to commit money laundering is a second-degree felony punishable by anywhere from two years' probation to twenty years in prison and a fine.

Earle had waived normal booking procedures after the September 28 indictments. However, he was unwilling to do so again, probably because of the barrage of attacks earlier orchestrated by DeLay, questioning Earle's motives and competence. Therefore on October 19 the clerk of the 331st District Court issued a capias (arrest warrant) directing that DeLay be arrested and brought forth to the court. On October 20, DeLay "surrendered" to authorities at the Harris County sheriff's office. He was formally booked at that time, pointedly enduring being fingerprinted and posting $10,000 bail. If Democrats had hoped for an embarrassing mug shot, however, they were sorely disappointed. As shown in newspapers and on television nationwide, the mug shot showed a well-groomed DeLay appearing as a model of decorum, his congressional lapel pin prominently displayed on his jacket.

On November 7, DeLay filed a motion to consolidate all pleadings in both criminal actions.

The Legal Teams

In routine criminal cases, state prosecutors have a distinct and substantial advantage. However, when the defendant is a high-profile official or celebrity, the advantage often shifts if the defendant can afford to hire good counsel and to vigorously and simultaneously pursue many different defense strategies. A prosecutor's office may find itself handicapped by a lack of the time and resources sufficient to match a well-financed defense that can bombard it with novel motions. Moreover, the individual prosecutors (some of whom are young) may lack the experience of the defense counsel in the high-pressure circumstances of a strongly contested criminal case. The battle in Travis County matched two good legal teams.

The Prosecutor and His Team

The district attorney of Travis County is often described as one of the most important legal officers in Texas. Although not expressly given any additional statutory jurisdiction beyond that of his fellow local prosecutors, the Travis County district attorney maintains a special Public Integrity Unit for dealing with alleged crimes by public officials within his jurisdiction. The unit is partially funded (approximately $6 million every two years) by state appropriations. This state funding has remained despite numerous attempts over the years, including in 2005, to eliminate it from the state budget. Since the state capital, Austin, is within Travis County, the district attorney effectively has jurisdiction over many of the election and public-integrity issues affecting state and legislative officials.

Sixty-three-year-old Ronnie Earle had been Travis County district attorney since 1976, after serving several terms in the Texas House. He had won reelection relatively easily every four years. Over this same period he had prosecuted at least fifteen public officials (twelve Democrats and three Republicans) for allegedly violating the state's various election and ethics laws. Some of the prosecutions were successful; some were not. However, even when a particular investigation or prosecution did not end with a conviction, some of the targeted public officials felt a negative impact on their political careers. State lawmakers often describe the Travis County DA as "the third or fourth most powerful job in the state."[19] DeLay pointed out that "others in the past have been afraid of Earle. I'm not."

Earle is not a trial lawyer himself. He depends on his assistant district attorneys for the investigation and prosecution of alleged crimes. In the proceedings against DeLay, Colyandro, and Ellis, Earle relied on a team of attorneys and staff drawn from throughout his office. Assistant District Attorney Bryan Case headed the office's Appellate Division. Gregg Cox headed the Public Integrity Unit. However, it was Assistant District Attorney Rick Reed who took the lead in court on most matters. Throughout this proceeding, Reed suffered from chronic pain as a result of sinus surgery. Sometimes the pain interfered with his active participation in drafting pleadings. Assistant District Attorney Erik Nielsen also appeared on behalf of the state on particular issues. These attorneys were supported behind the scenes by many staffers who were eager to be involved in this high-profile prosecution.

The Defense Team

Jim Ellis was represented primarily by Jonathon D. Pauerstein of San Antonio. Pauerstein is a well-respected and effective attorney from the politically connected firm of Loeffler, Jonas and Tuggy.[20] Jim Colyandro was represented by Joe Turner of Austin. DeLay's defense team consisted of attorneys and public-relations experts. Former FBI agent and Arkansas congressman Ed Bethune was designated by DeLay early in the process to oversee his legal defenses nationwide.

Like many political figures involved recently in high-profile litigation, civil (e.g., involving election contests) or criminal, DeLay included public-relations experts on his defense team. Such experts are expected to package arcane legal arguments and confusing events into "messages" that can be communicated effectively to the media and the general public or to the political audience in Washington. A public-relations expert was necessary because DeLay confronted critical public-opinion battles on several fronts to salvage his political career. It was important for him to block any moves to remove him permanently as majority leader. Simultaneously, it was important for him to minimize or neutralize any adverse effect from the indictments on him personally or on the Republican Party generally, and to activate grassroots conservatives by portraying the indictments as baseless and politically motivated. Faced with the prospect of substantial legal fees, DeLay also needed to secure contributions to his defense fund. An aggressive public-relations campaign seemed an answer for all these needs.

However, combining a good legal defense with an aggressive public-relations campaign can cause unanticipated problems for the legal defense. Plain, unprovocative statements often used by an attorney are seldom the words that a public-relations expert can use to inspire the ire of a politician's allies. Therefore, the attorneys were under pressure to word their legal documents so as to provide combustible quotes that could be communicated to the media. A further problem can occur when the defendant himself insists on participating directly in the public-relations campaign. Such participation was a problem for Bill Gates when Microsoft was prosecuted for antitrust conduct. So too it initially was a problem for DeLay's defense team after he appeared on television (e.g., on Fox News) to dispute Earle's charges, thus leading to Earle's subpoena of the transcripts of these television programs in his search for inconsistent or incriminating statements that could be used later at trial. Eventually DeLay became more circumspect in his personal appearances and public comments, and his public-relations campaign continued through press statements that explained his view of each event as it happened and his Web site (*Stand with Tom*), which asked for contributions to his defense fund and conveyed regular messages to his supporters.

The attorneys on DeLay's legal team in Texas included Dick DeGuerin (lead counsel), William A. White (Austin), Stephen W. Brittain (Williams & Forsythe in Austin), Eric Storm (a recent law school graduate) and Richard Keeton (of counsel, from Houston). DeGuerin is a very able and well-respected criminal defense lawyer who conveys a dignified "Texan persona" with expensive western boots and western-style hats. He was added to the legal team immediately after the first indictment was returned against DeLay on September 28. He assumed the role of lead counsel in Texas and quickly sent notice to the prosecutors that DeLay was withdrawing his waiver of the statute of limitations.

DeGuerin and Earle had crossed swords a decade earlier in a political case. DeGuerin had secured the dismissal of charges against then–state treasurer (later U.S. Senator) Kay Bailey Hutchison for allegedly misusing her state employees for political purposes. In 2005, DeGuerin said that he welcomed a rematch. Quoting a phrase often attributed to Yogi Berra, DeGuerin said, "It's déjà vu all over again. That was a political prosecution, and this is a political prosecution."[21] Ironically, DeGuerin is a self-styled "Yellow Dog Democrat," but given his previous success on behalf of Hutchison, few were surprised when he was tapped to lead DeLay's defense.

DeGuerin was clearly lead counsel. He planned legal strategy, answered for the defendant in court, and handled most of the presentation of DeLay's case in court. However, Richard Keeton, the well-respected son of a legendary former dean of the University of Texas School of Law (Page Keeton), was responsible for the oral presentation of many of DeLay's primary legal arguments. DeLay's legal team seemed in court to work together well under DeGuerin's leadership and to deal respectfully with the court.

The Defense Strategy

The overriding defense strategy was to get a favorable resolution as quickly as possible. DeLay's political future hung in the balance. However, this objective was seen to depend necessarily on the defense team successfully maneuvering the criminal case away from Travis County and its judiciary. Therefore, the defense strategy was designed to balance the need to expedite proceedings with the need for at least a neutral judge and forum. The strategy encompassed the following:

1. Obtaining a speedy, favorable resolution
2. Obtaining the recusal of the assigned Travis County judge and the assignment of a favorable, or at least neutral, judge to the case
3. Undermining Earle's credibility and portraying in court and to the public that the prosecution was purely political
4. Obtaining a dismissal of the charges if possible
5. In the absence of winning a speedy dismissal of the charges, obtaining a change of venue and a speedy trial
6. Overwhelming the prosecutors with motions and briefs

In most circumstances, the attorneys for codefendants Ellis and Colyandro let the DeLay legal team take the lead. In several circumstances, the codefendants adopted DeLay's pleadings. However, one major difference in strategy existed. Ellis and Colyandro had been dragging out the criminal proceedings since 2004 in the hope that the Texas courts would declare the ban on corporate funds unconstitutionally vague. Their appeal of earlier indictments was pending. On October 14 their attorneys made it clear in a hearing before Judge Perkins that they did not want the speedy trial that DeLay was requesting. Instead, they wanted a separate trial from DeLay and wanted to postpone it until after the appellate courts ruled on their appeal. Prosecutors gave no sign at the time whether they would oppose trying the three codefendants separately.

Motions for a Speedy Resolution

As discussed above, Congressman DeLay stood to permanently lose his position as majority leader if the criminal proceedings were protracted (national publications reported that by November 2005 there was already a move afoot among some Republicans in Washington to permanently replace him as majority leader if he were still facing the criminal charges by January 2006). Therefore, the defense team continually pushed the judicial proceeding forward. DeGuerin said that he thought a trial before the end of 2005 was possible. On October 17, DeLay requested a speedy trial "consistent with the litigation of pretrial matters." On October 24, he asked for the expedited consideration of all pending motions. Attached to the motion were various "National Media Quotes" suggesting that "DeLay's removal from his post as majority leader could not have come at a worse time policy-wise for Republicans" and that Republicans would miss DeLay's "muscle" and "ability to pound reluctant colleagues into line," particularly on critical issues such as the budget. The prosecutors did not officially oppose DeLay's motions to expedite proceedings. Generally the courts moved expeditiously.

Motions to Recuse

Travis County district judge Robert Perkins had presided over the earlier (2004) indictments of Colyandro and Ellis. The indictments on September 28 and October 3, 2005 (including the indictments of DeLay) also were assigned to him. On October 25, DeLay moved to recuse Judge Perkins because he "is a Democrat and public records reveal he is very active in party politics at the State and Federal levels." Attached to the motion was an exhibit of "Travis County Criminal District Court Judges' Federal campaign contributions," showing that, among other things, Perkins was the only criminal court judge in Travis County to make a donation to John Kerry for President, to the Democratic National Committee, or to the political group MoveOn.org. The exhibit further showed that Perkins had contributed $3,400 to state Democratic candidates and organizations during 2000–2005. In 1994, Perkins had voluntarily recused himself from the criminal case against Kay Bailey Hutchison because he had contributed to her Democratic opponent. He was unwilling, however, to voluntarily do so in 2005 because he had not contributed to any of DeLay's opponents.

The prosecutors battled to keep Judge Perkins assigned to the case. They presented evidence that criminal-court judges of both parties from Travis, Tarrant, and Dallas counties commonly "provide financial support to candidates and organizations affiliated with the same political party with which they are affiliated." The prosecutors tried to portray the dispute as being whether a criminal defendant from one political party should be able to disqualify a judge solely because the judge contributes to another political party. In response, DeLay's team increasingly emphasized Judge Perkins's support of Moveon.org, an organization that specifically focused many of its attacks on DeLay.

The motion for recusal was heard on November 1 before Judge C. W. Duncan. He had been assigned to hear the case by B. B. Schraub, the presiding judge of the Third Administrative Judicial Region. DeGuerin led the defense. Rick Reed and Bryan Case led the prosecution team, but Earle also argued before the court. Both sides presented evidence and one or more witnesses. DeGuerin carefully avoided calling Judge Perkins biased. Instead, DeGuerin urged recusal because "a reasonable person, aware of all of the facts and circumstances in the public domain, would harbor reasonable doubts about the judge's impartiality." The most compelling argument came at the end of the hearing from defense counsel Richard Keeton, who, after reciting what he saw as uncontested facts about Perkins's political activity, posited that as long as Perkins presided in the case, both Republicans and Democrats nationwide would see the proceedings as political: Democrats would expect a favorable result, Republicans would see "a fix." Keeton urged Judge Duncan to take the "easy solution," to "save Perkins from himself," and to avoid the adverse impact on the judiciary that would come from allowing this proceeding to continue under a judge perceived as partisan. Duncan ruled from the bench at the end of the hearing. He ordered the recusal of Judge Perkins.

The next day lawyers and onlookers alike were treated to a fast round of musical chairs among judges. On the morning of November 2, the prosecutors asked Judge B. B. Schraub to recuse himself from presiding in DeLay's criminal case because "he may reasonably be perceived to have a personal bias in favor of Defendant, Thomas Dale DeLay, or against Ronald Earle." They pointed to numerous contributions by Schraub to Republican candidates for state office (e.g., $1,000 to Texans for Rick Perry) and federal office (e.g., $2,000 to Bush for President, Inc.). Schraub quickly and voluntarily recused himself and referred the matter to the chief justice of the Supreme Court of Texas. The hot potato landed on the plate of Chief Justice Wallace Jefferson.

Chief Justice Jefferson was prepared. Driving from San Antonio to Austin early on November 2, he heard news accounts of Schraub's ruling and knew that the case would pass to him. Judge Jefferson called from his car to his office in Austin and started his clerks researching his options. When the media spotlight fell on Jefferson, it was discovered that (as might be expected for a Republican candidate for statewide elective office) he had many ties to Republican organizations and even to some individuals and organizations directly or indirectly implicated in these specific criminal proceedings. For example, it was asserted that during the 2002 election cycle Jefferson had received $25,000 from the RNSEC, the same branch of the RNC that (as an unindicted coconspirator) in 2002 allegedly contributed $190,000 on behalf of TRMPAC to state legislative candidates; received a contribution from BACPAC, the unindicted PAC for the Texas Association of Business; named Bill Ceverha (the treasurer of TRMPAC) as his campaign treasurer; and hired TRMPAC fundraiser Susan Lilly as a paid consultant (paid $28,524). By 5 p.m. on November 3, the Travis County district attorney filed a motion to recuse Chief Justice Jefferson. The motion stressed that the prosecutors believed Jefferson "to be absolutely unimpeachable in character and integrity, fair and impartial, with a sterling reputation of honesty and integrity," but that a reasonable person could question the judge's impartiality.

Unbeknownst to the prosecutors, however, at 3 p.m. that afternoon Chief Justice Jefferson had moved the case along by assigning retired district judge Pat Priest of San Antonio to preside in the DeLay matter because (as he told my law school class in 2006) he considered Judge Priest a judge who would "do the right thing even under public pressure." Jefferson subsequently rejected the district attorney's recusal motion, indicating by letter: "It is imperative that I act in this matter" because the chief justice is the last official authorized to resolve the dispute and "The recourse is to challenge not the power to assign, but the assignment itself."[22] On November 7, Judge Perkins voluntarily recused himself from the pending cases against Ellis and Colyandro. A day later Chief Justice Jefferson also assigned these six cause numbers to Judge Priest.

Undermining the Credibility of the District Attorney

The defense team's strategy of attacking Ronnie Earle's credibility and motives was carried out not only by DeLay's public-relations consultants; lead counsel Dick DeGuerin joined in. Motions challenging the conduct of the district attorney were filed in court. However, DeGuerin also criticized Earle publicly through appearances on television talk shows and at press conferences. Simultaneously, however, he tried to pique Earle through occasional personal jabs in letters to Earle, calling on him to admit that the indictments had been a mistake and to dismiss them. On October 3, DeGuerin wrote to Earle: "Rumor has it that you are going to try and get another indictment against Tom DeLay," and asking Earle to keep in mind that DeLay had withdrawn his waiver of the statute of limitations. On that same date, he wrote to Earle, arguing that because Earle "professed not to be politically motivated in bringing his indictment," he should "immediately agree to dismiss this indictment so that the political consequences can be reversed."

Later, on October 17, DeGuerin wrote to Earle again: "Faced with the embarrassment of indicting for a crime that wasn't on the books, you sought a different indictment from another Grand Jury, but that Grand Jury refused you." DeGuerin also charged in this letter that Earle in the earlier meeting with DeLay on September 23 had tried to

> coerce a guilty plea from DeLay for a misdemeanor, stating that the alternative was indictment for a felony which would require his stepping down as Majority Leader . . . He [DeLay] turned you down flat so you had him indicted in spite of advice from others in your office that Tom DeLay had not committed a crime. In short, neither lack of evidence nor lack of law has deterred you.

DeGuerin concluded this letter by stating,

> [I]t should be clear that we're right on the law and the facts. The right thing, the courageous thing, for you to do is to admit you were wrong and dismiss this case right away. The longer you drag it out the more obvious it becomes that the result you care about most is the political damage your actions have done to Tom DeLay.

It is unlikely that these letters were intended to convince Earle to dismiss the indictments as much as to provide usable sound bites for the media and to provoke the prosecutors.

DeGuerin's public statements and efforts to provoke Earle were not unprecedented. In fact, such actions by defense attorneys have become a common tactic in many high-profile cases: to portray the prosecutors as, for example, engaged in a witch hunt or to distract or to badger them with personal insults. Any response by Earle to these charges would have enhanced the impression that this criminal proceeding was a personal or political vendetta against DeLay. Historically, Earle has not been shy about using the media: sitting for interviews with major publications, participating in a 2004 film (*The Big Buy*) on his investigation of DeLay, and even writing an op-ed for the *New York Times*. A few months earlier on March 6, on a segment of the television program *Sixty Minutes*, Earle had dodged questions about whether he was targeting DeLay, but in response to criticism from DeLay's congressional office, commented, "Being called vindictive and partisan by Tom DeLay is like being called ugly by a frog." In the fall of 2005, however, Earle and his staff refused to rise to the bait offered by DeGuerin. They remained largely silent. After all, as Bruce Oppenheimer, a Vanderbilt University political scientist, noted, "What are you going to say, 'No, it isn't politically motivated'?" Oppenheimer added, "I think responding to it gives the impression that it is politically motivated."[23] Earle apparently realized that, in the end, this battle was a legal contest, not a public-opinion fight.

The official attack on the district attorney's office came on October 7 through a motion to quash the October 3 indictment on the basis of prosecutorial misconduct. The motion recounted the events (described above) that occurred between September 29 and October 3 and led to the indictment. The motion alleged that Ronnie Earle and his staff unlawfully "participated in Grand Jury deliberations and attempted to browbeat and coerce the 390th Grand Jury"; unlawfully attempted to cover up that the 390th Grand Jury had no-billed Earle's "contrived charge of Money Laundering"; incited the foreman of the 167th Grand Jury to violate the grand-jury-secrecy law by speaking out to bias the public and sitting grand jurors; sought the opinion of members of the now-discharged 167th Grand Jury about whether they would have voted to indict DeLay on money-laundering charges; and submitted this additional information (i.e., the opinion of the former grand jurors) to yet another grand jury, the 403rd, which then issued an indictment. DeLay sought the disclosure of information, transcripts, and recordings made in connection with the grand-jury proceedings to support the accusations.

Since the prosecutors continued subpoenaing documents even after the indictments had been returned, Ellis's attorney, J. D. Pauerstein, commented, "It seems rather late in the day to be doing that, but I suppose after two years they're still looking for a case."[24]

Change of Venue

When I first spoke with Dick DeGuerin briefly in October 2005, he stressed that it was critical that DeLay find a way to move the criminal proceeding outside of Travis County. This conversation occurred before the recusal of Judge Perkins. Nevertheless, the prospect of a trial before a jury in Travis County was daunting for DeLay. There were several reasons why DeLay was unpopular in Travis County. The county historically has been one of the most liberal and Democratic in the state. For example, in 2004 the voters of Travis County preferred Kerry over Bush by 56 to 42 percent. Moreover, congressional redistricting had split Travis County among three districts, over the objection of county Republicans and Democrats alike, in an attempt to defeat Lloyd Doggett and to fracture the county's Democratic core. Many county residents held DeLay responsible.

On October 20, DeLay formally asked for a change of venue. He pointed to what he alleged was "massive and unrelenting media coverage" in Travis County, including the "unrelenting and highly unfavorable" coverage of the "seemingly interminable 'investigation' by Travis County District Attorney Ronnie Earle." DeLay also cited his unpopularity in the county because of the 2003 redistricting. He described Austin and Travis County as "one of the last enclaves of the Democratic Party in Texas." In support of his motion, DeLay attached affidavits from Travis County residents saying that DeLay could not obtain a fair and impartial trial in the county. During this period, a firm hired by DeLay's legal team began calling Travis County residents, apparently to prepare an expert report showing "so great a bias [among county residents] against DeLay that he could not obtain a fair and impartial trial." DeLay also claimed that he could not expect a fair trial in Travis County because there "is a dangerous combination instigated by influential persons." DeLay asked that venue be changed to another county.

DeLay also objected to venue in Travis County because the Texas Election Code specifically provides that venue for a criminal offense under the code is in the county of residence of the defendant, unless the defendant is not a Texas resident. By brief on November 9, DeLay asserted that the general venue provisions of the Code of Criminal Procedure (which would allow prosecution in Travis County) did not apply to his case, either because the specific provisions of the Election Code superseded the general provisions, or because (for the reasons discussed elsewhere in this chapter) the Penal Code's conspiracy statute did not apply at all to Election Code offenses in 2002. DeLay asked that either the indictments be dismissed or the venue transferred to Fort Bend County, his county of residence. Moreover, Fort Bend County could be counted upon to be a much more favorably partisan forum for DeLay. The voters there had supported Bush over Kerry by 57 to 42 percent.

By letter to the court on November 4, DeGuerin asked that the venue matters be addressed first. However, any decision on a change in venue would require evidence. Judge Priest preferred to go forward on the nonevidentiary motions at the hearing on November 22. Evidentiary hearings on the motions for a change in venue or dismissal for prosecutorial misconduct would have to wait.

Dismissal of the Indictments

DeLay's best chance for a quick and favorable disposition of the indictments lay in his motions to quash and dismiss the indictments for a failure to state an offense under Texas law. The original motion to quash was filed on October 3 against the September 28 indictment. Additional motions to quash were filed on October 17 challenging Counts I and II in the October 3 indictment.

There were many different grounds proffered by DeLay for quashing and dismissing the indictments. Some of these are discussed elsewhere in this chapter. However, the following issues and arguments were the ones most prominently presented by DeGuerin on November 22 and in the expert-opinion memorandum of law professor Susan Klein:

1. No corporation gave money to the RNSEC. The check for $190,000 was from TRMPAC, not a corporation. Moreover, "Neither Tom DeLay, nor John Colyandro, nor Jim Ellis, nor TRMPAC, nor the RNC is a corporation or an organization or a political party," and the indictments fail to allege that the defendants were acting as an agent or representative of a corporation.

2. There was no law in 2002 making it a crime to conspire to violate the Election Code or to launder money in violation of the Election Code. Title IV (conspiracy) of the Penal Code was expressly made applicable to offenses in the Election Code by an amendment to the Election Code in 2003. Since the legislature is assumed to never do a useless act, the 2003 amendment means that Title IV did not apply when the alleged conspiracy occurred in 2002.

3. Money laundering applied only to transfers of cash in 2002, not checks. Historically, the purpose of money-laundering provisions has been "to prevent criminals, especially drug traffickers, from moving the profits of their criminal activity into anonymous financial instruments that can then be pumped into the legitimate economy." Texas law was consistent with this purpose until 2005, when the legislature amended the statute to expand the definition of "funds" for the purposes of money laundering to include a list of financial instruments, including a "personal check."

4. There could not be any unlawful money laundering when the alleged criminal act came at the end of the series of transactions (i.e., the contributions by the RNSEC to the individual House candidates). Money laundering applies only when the funds being transferred are the proceeds of a criminal activity. If the money in question first became "dirty" when given by the RNSEC to the individual candidates, the prerequisites for a charge of money laundering could not be met.

5. The money given to the candidates by the RNSEC was not the "same money" received from TRMPAC. The check from TRMPAC's corporate account was properly deposited to the RNSEC's soft-money account. The checks from the RNSEC to the candidates properly came from the

RNSEC's "hard money" account: "The money from TRMPAC never got transferred." Trading soft money for hard money, or vice versa, was a common practice by both political parties before Congress passed campaign-finance-reform legislation in 2003.

6. The provisions of the Election Code are more specific than those of the Penal Code and exert control over the Penal Code. The prosecutors should not be allowed to use the higher offenses of conspiracy and money laundering under the Penal Code to avoid the venue requirements of the Election Code or to impose a higher penalty for essentially the same offense (i.e., statutes *in para material*).[25]

7. The provisions of the Election Code limiting corporate political contributions were unconstitutionally vague.

The defense arguments also included objections to the indictments based on the improper joinder of offenses, a lack of notice about the specific violations being alleged and the manner and means of the violations with which the defendants were charged, an improper tolling of the statute of limitations (i.e., not giving effect to DeLay's withdrawal of his waiver of the limitations period), and the improper elevation of election-code violations to a first-degree felony.

Overwhelming the Prosecutors with Motions and Briefs

By letter to Judge Priest on November 15, 2005, DeGuerin called attention to DeLay's nineteen different pleadings that remained pending. None of the motions or briefs were frivolous, but many would be beyond the means of most defendants. A common tactic used by well-financed civil and criminal defendants is to barrage opponents with motions and briefs, hoping to keep the opponent busy responding to the defendant's pleadings and to allow the defendant to control the momentum and tone of the proceedings. DeLay's legal team was able to use this tactic, which was even more potentially effective in the context of the expedited proceedings.

The Prosecution Strategy

Disguising Legal Theory and Strategy

Prosecutors generally disguise their legal theories and strategies until forced to disclose them. Neither the September 28 nor the October 3 indictments provided any specifics about the conduct that allegedly made DeLay a coconspirator in the transfer of the $190,000 from TRMPAC to the RNSEC, or in the RNSEC's payments to the Texas candidates. Defendants also complained that the indictments provided inadequate notice of precisely what provisions of the election code were allegedly violated or the "means" by which the provisions were allegedly violated. Prosecutors remained unresponsive, arguing that the indictments did not legally need to furnish such specifics.

The defendants were frustrated by the prosecutors' generalized statements and unresponsiveness to their requests for more detail. For example, the indictments stated that on or about September 13, 2002, Ellis had provided Terry Nelson of the RNC with a list of state-representative candidates and the amounts that Ellis and TRMPAC wanted contributed to each. The defendants asked the prosecutors for a copy of this alleged "list." The prosecutors responded that they had a list, but they did not know if it was "the" list. The prosecutors eventually gave defense counsel a copy of the list that they had obtained as a result of an earlier grand-jury subpoena of documents from TRMPAC, but without conceding that it was necessarily "the list" that Ellis allegedly gave to Nelson.

As the hearing on November 22, 2005, approached, DeGuerin complained to the court that the prosecutors were not filing responses to many of DeLay's motions. DeGuerin said that this lack of response by the prosecutors prevented the defense team from having an opportunity to study the prosecutors' rebuttal in preparation for the hearing. As DeGuerin concluded, "It's unusual. The problem may be that the law is on our side." [26]

The prosecutors largely saved the explanation of their legal theory and their rebuttal to the defense's key arguments for a sixty-four-page brief filed at 2:52 p.m. on the afternoon before the November 22 hearing. The timing was perfect. At least some of the defense attorneys had not even seen the prosecutors' filing by the time of the hearing on the 22nd. Some of defense counsels' oral argument at the hearing missed the nuanced positions now laid out by the prosecutors in their brief and, even more particularly, in ADA Rick Reed's oral presentation at the hearing.

DeGuerin, however, had prepared his own last-minute surprise. At 5 p.m. on the day before the hearing, DeLay's defense team also filed a major pleading, entitled "Final Pre-Submission Memoranda." This filing included a twenty-one-page, single-spaced, small-font, heavily footnoted "expert opinion" from University of Texas law professor Susan Klein in support of several of the key defense contentions. It was an interesting tactic—to file an expert legal opinion at the last minute (literally) rather than a brief. However, since the prosecutors' disguised their legal theories until the last minute, much of Professor Klein's able writing appeared to simply miss the mark. Moreover, in a pleading filed later, the prosecutors objected to Professor Klein's "expert testimony" as hearsay and not subject to cross-examination.

Avoiding Dismissal of the Charges

The prosecutors' sixty-four-page brief filed on November 21 offered a first look at the prosecutors' theory of their case for criminal conspiracy and money laundering.

In response to the defendants' argument that criminal conspiracy (in Title IV of the Penal Code) did not apply to an offense under the Election Code until 2003, the prosecutors argued that Section 15.02 of the Penal Code as it existed in 2002 was clear on its face that it applied to any felony. They asserted that the court should not look to the legislative history of the 2003 amendment (as the defendants urged), since the 2002 law was clear on its face. Moreover, they argued that the most meaningful legislative history was at the time of the enactment of the Election Code in 1951. The prosecutors urged that criminal conspiracy had existed as an offense since at least the adoption of the first Penal Code in 1856 and that it had applied to the felony offense of corporate contributions to aid or defeat a candidate when that offense was added to the Penal Code in 1907.

Prosecutors argued that this did not change when the legislature adopted the Penal Code of 1973 and deleted the felony offenses related to elections from the new code, because the 1973 enactment was meant solely to clarify the law, not to change it. Similarly, the prosecutors argued that the 2003 amendment to the Election Code relied upon by defendants was itself merely an effort to clarify the law, not to change it, since (according to their theory) criminal conspiracy and the other provisions of Title IV of the Penal Code had always applied to felony offenses affecting elections.

In response to the defendants' argument that the offense of money laundering in 2002 applied only to the transfer of cash, the prosecutors initially relied on the fact that the indictments contained the essential elements of money laundering because they duly alleged transactions involving "funds" or "proceeds of criminal activity" as required by the Penal Code (Section 34.01). The prosecutors' brief downplayed the significance of "check." They emphasized that the transaction in question was not the delivery of the check for $190,000, but "the withdrawal—'coin or paper money of the United States'—from the bank account owned by" TRMPAC. They also argued that "funds" as defined in Section 34.01 of the Penal Code "includes" cash. The prosecutors relied on the plain, nonexclusive meaning of "includes" and on the state's statutory-construction act for the proposition that when used in a law, "includes" is a term of enlargement, not of limitation or exclusion. In a subsequent brief, prosecutors pointed to several cases decided under the Penal Code prior to 2005 in which the money-laundering crime rested on the use of checks.

In response to the defendants' argument that the offense of money launder-ing was inapposite because the alleged illegal activity occurred at the end of a series of transactions, prosecutors argued that there were numerous legal theo-ries under which the funds transferred to the RNC from the TRMPAC corpo-rate account were already "criminal proceeds." At the hearing on the 22nd, Rick Reed sent the defense lawyers scurrying in a search for a response when he sug-gested that the funds initially became criminal proceeds when they were con-tributed by the corporations, since the Election Code permitted corporations to "expend" money directly only for the administrative expenses of a political action committee, not to lose control over those funds by "contributing" to the political action committee. Defense attorneys were caught off guard by this ar-gument. They wondered whether the prosecutors had held back this theory as a strategy or were grasping at any theory. In a subsequent brief, the prosecutors added that the corporate funds became illegal when contributed to TRMPAC for political purposes, when the defendants encouraged corporations to make the contributions to TRMPAC, or when TRMPAC and the defendants con-tributed the corporate funds to the RNC with the intent of having the RNC send the funds to state-legislative candidates. The prosecutors also pointed out that TRMPAC failed to report its corporate contributions to the Texas Ethics Commission.

Although the prosecutors ultimately addressed DeLay's specific arguments, the basic prosecutorial position was that the arguments being raised by the de-fendants were ones appropriately addressed at trial, not in pretrial dispositive motions. Essentially, the prosecutors argued, DeLay was trying to go behind the indictments to contest the adequacy of the prosecutors' evidence, which a defendant should not be allowed to do at this early stage of the proceeding.

The Hearing on November 22

The hearing on November 22 lasted somewhat over four hours. DeGuerin led the defense, but the attorneys for both Ellis and Colyandro added to the de-fense argument. Rick Reed took the lead for the prosecutors, with help from Bryan Case and Erik Nielsen.

The arguments presented at the hearing were the arguments described above. There were, however, several events on the 22nd that should be noted:

1. Judge Priest had been asked by the national television channel Court TV to be allowed to bring cameras into the courtroom and possibly to broadcast

some of the proceedings live. Priest rejected the idea for the November 22 hearing, but indicated that if this matter went to trial, he probably would allow a single camera for use by all broadcasters.

2. Judge Priest indicated that he was taking the extraordinary step of providing a Web site on which he would post notice of developments in the case, and if given the e-mail addresses of interested media, he would send them notices. He even gave out his home telephone number in San Antonio. Judge Priest warned that the telephone number should be used only in emergencies and that he was never going to discuss the case with anyone. He reminded the attorneys and onlookers that he was a retired judge, without staff or an office outside his home, and that his wife "doesn't have a staff either."

3. Turner, on behalf of Colyandro, said that the case was simple because the money sent by the RNSEC to the state legislative candidates was not "the same money" sent to the RNC by TRMPAC. DeGuerin picked up on this argument that the key to the prosecution's case was that this was the same money. The prosecutors spent a significant amount of time protesting that their theory of the case did not turn on the funds' being the identical money, like money marked with red dye in a bank robbery or kidnapping.

4. Richard Keeton again presented DeLay's closing argument. However, he was not nearly as effective as at the November 1 hearing. The prosecutors' brief and oral argument had presented legal theories that the defense had not anticipated and that were not addressed in Keeton's concluding comments. Moreover, Keeton personalized his argument at the end by talking about the prosecutors' "sloppiness" (a reference to the circumstances that produced the October 3 indictment) and attributing this to a political motive for this prosecution. Under other circumstances this argument may have been fruitful, but it seemed to fall flat with Judge Priest, who seemed disinclined to be drawn in to the politics of the case.

5. Judge Priest was very matter-of-fact in his handling of the hearing and the proceeding. He seemed to be trying to handle this emotion-charged matter as nearly like a normal criminal prosecution as possible. He explained that he was conscious of the urgency felt by DeLay for a quick resolution, but that he (Judge Priest) also had other commitments that he could not ignore. As a result, if he did not dismiss the indictments, trial could not begin before January 2006 at the earliest. Finally, he warned lawyers that although he was not imposing a gag order, he expected them to stop talking about the citizens of Travis or Fort Bend counties or otherwise making public statements that could "poison the jury pool." The warning was framed broadly, but since the prosecutors had been mostly silent, it

seemed clearly aimed at the public statements being made by DeLay's legal team.

The Court made no immediate ruling.

Judge Priest

Chief Justice Jefferson's selection as judge for the criminal proceeding, sixty-four-year-old Pat Priest, was from Jefferson's hometown, San Antonio. Although elected to the judiciary in the past as a Democrat, Priest was not connected to any high-profile candidates or causes and, in comparison to the displaced Judge Perkins, gave only a small amount ($450) in 2004 to Democratic candidates. Neither the prosecutors nor the defendants officially objected to Judge Priest as the presiding judge. Jim Ellis's counsel, J. D. Pauerstein (who was also from San Antonio) said, "Pat Priest has the reputation of being one of the finest judges in the state, and he's a Democrat, and he has a reputation for being a scholar. He has a reputation of being scrupulously fair."[27] Dick DeGuerin in 2006 described Judge Priest to me as "cautious, fair and studious," even though DeGuerin has been disappointed with some of the judge's rulings. District Attorney Earle agreed that Priest is fair.

Litigation Tactics and Misjudgments?

At one of the hearings in this case, a reporter for one of the major national newspapers joked that I, as a former trial lawyer, was getting unfair pleasure from watching the proceedings. Using a baseball analogy, he accused me of enjoying a pitchers' duel while the reporters were looking for a slugfest. He is correct about my pleasure in watching the legal proceedings. In a complex legal battle involving good lawyers, I do not expect to find one side or the other suddenly winning an obviously lopsided victory. Instead, I enjoy looking for the sometimes small and nuanced events that may ultimately determine an outcome. It is in this context (and with admittedly unfair hindsight) that I offer the following observations on some decisions or actions that may have a significant impact on the outcome of this proceeding.

A Flawed First Indictment

The indictment returned on September 28 had several potentially determinative flaws. Prosecutors were given a second chance when they quickly learned about the possibility that a conspiracy charge might not exist for the allegations in the first indictment of violations of the election code in 2002. Prosecutors have indicated to me that they were aware of the legal issues before pursuing the September 28 indictment, but thought that the law ultimately was on their side. However, sometime after the indictment became public, the prosecutors decided that they needed a second indictment. The validity of the subsequent, October 3 indictment rests in part on whether the prosecutors' rush to obtain it withstands the challenge that it was a result of prosecutorial misconduct. Perhaps the October 3 indictment will survive, but it was needlessly jeopardized because it was not presented and returned earlier along with the conspiracy indictment.

Meeting with the Prosecutors

Any meeting of a potential defendant with prosecutors during the course of an investigation is a chancy business. Trying to convince prosecutors to not bring charges can prove successful, as shown by the success of Austin attorney Roy Minton on behalf of Bill Hammond and Tom Craddick. However, DeLay may identify his August 2005 meeting with prosecutors and his attempt to persuade them of his lack of involvement in TRMPAC as the key moment that was to lead to his political downfall and possible conviction for conspiracy or money laundering. Perhaps, as DeLay claims, he merely misspoke about his involvement in the transfer of funds from TRMPAC to the RNC. Nevertheless, it appears that the meeting as well as DeLay's statements and documents from the meeting persuaded prosecutors that DeLay had felonious involvement in the transfer of monies to the RNC and in the payments by the RNSEC to the Texas House candidates.

A Leak of Strategy?

The indictment returned on September 28 may turn out to be legally flawed. If so, the dismissal of that indictment, in conjunction with the passage of a few days and the withdrawal by DeLay of the waiver of the statute of limitations, would have left the prosecutors blocked by the statute of limitations from bringing any further charges against DeLay. However, somehow the prosecutors learned of the vulnerability of the first indictment on the day that it was made public and were able to secure a second indictment by October 3. DeLay's motion to quash the first indictment was filed long before it was required under pleading guidelines. On November 22, Richard Keeton stated that the motion was filed "within a few hours or a day" of the return of the indictment, "thereby leading the D.A. to go back to the grand jury" for a second bite at the apple.

It appears that the actual motion to quash was not filed until October 3, too late to be the cause of the prosecutors' efforts, beginning on September 28th, to secure a second indictment. Did anyone on the defense team unintentionally leak the substance for the motion to quash beforehand, perhaps to the press? DeGuerin says definitely not.[28] If a leak from the DeLay team about the flaws in the indictment allowed Earle to obtain a second indictment in time to continue his prosecution of DeLay, such a leak probably led directly to DeLay's need subsequently to step aside as majority leader. (The press knew the grounds for the motion by at least Friday, September 30, because I was called by one reporter for my take as to whether the grounds were sufficient for dismissal.

Please Sit Down!

Mark Stevens, instead of J. D. Pauerstein, presented argument on behalf of Ellis at the November 22 hearing. Stevens is a well-respected criminal defense attorney. On this day, he faced a difficulty. He was presenting oral argument as a courtesy to Pauerstein, whose father had died shortly before the hearing. Stevens, who previously had focused on the criminal-procedural questions, lacked time to familiarize himself with the substantive issues at stake in the motions to quash. Two problems developed. First, Stevens in his oral argument acknowledged that he had not read the prosecutors' brief filed the previous afternoon. As a result, his statement that he "could not imagine" any legitimate argument that the prosecutors could offer sounded hollow.

A second statement by Stevens made DeGuerin squirm. Obviously DeLay's attorneys wanted an immediate ruling if possible on the motions to quash. Stevens, however, asked the court for time to file a written response to the prosecutors' brief. DeGuerin's body language showed his concern: Stevens's request opened the door to further delay without any request from the prosecutors. DeGuerin tried to shut the door by convincing Judge Priest that any additional briefs should be filed by noon on the following day. However, with the door ajar, Judge Priest allowed a week for filing supplemental briefs.

The Outcome on DeLay's Motions to Quash

By written opinion on December 5, 2005, Judge Priest ruled on the defense motions to quash the outstanding indictments. He quashed the specific charges based on conspiracy to violate the election code (i.e., the September 28 indictment and Count I of the October 3 indictment). He accepted the defendants' argument that the conspiracy provisions of the Penal Code did not apply to a violation of the Election Code occurring before the amendment of the Election Code in 2003. He agreed that the legislature is assumed to not do a useless act, and, therefore, the amendment in 2003 changed the prior law.

However, Priest found that the Election Code prohibited contributing corporate funds to be used to finance a candidate, soliciting corporate contributions with the unlawful intent to divert the funds to a candidate, or diverting lawful corporate contributions to a candidate: "If funds were sought and obtained from corporations in order to channel the funds to individual candidates, or if money was so channeled though originally lawfully received, once the candidates received the funds the crime is complete." The court noted that showing such a violation of the Election Code would be a necessary predicate for money laundering.

Priest denied the defendants' motions to quash the indictments for money laundering or conspiring to launder money because the "funds" allegedly laundered were really "cash," not "checks." Priest said that he did not perceive the $190,000 check to be "the funds" allegedly laundered: "Not only is the money in Texans for a Republican Majority PAC bank account intuitively 'funds,' it is also legally so," because the word "includes" as used in Section 34.01 of the Penal Code is a term of enlargement and not of limitation or exclusive enumeration. He found it unnecessary to depend on the applicability of the Code Construction Act to support such a conclusion. Although he did not feel compelled to specifically answer the defendants' argument that the money-laundering statute does not apply to checks, Priest presented ten separate state and federal cases that he said involved the use of checks to launder money.[29] Finally, he found that since money laundering and conspiracy are both in the penal code, there was no reason to believe that conspiracy did not apply to money laundering.

Priest's ruling was a substantial setback for DeLay. It meant that he would not be in a position to reassume his position as majority leader in early 2006. Without a dismissal of the money-laundering indictment on the basis of prosecutorial misconduct, DeLay faced the prospect of a trial on money-laundering charges sometime in 2006 (at the earliest) or a possibly time-consuming appeal of the court's rulings. DeLay's enemies and ambitious competitors within the Republican Party in Washington now had a rationale for moving to elect a new majority leader. DeLay's position soon worsened.

The State Court Case: December 2005–March 2006

Most of the legally significant events in the criminal litigation following Judge Priest's decision on December 5 were predictable. The momentum went out of DeLay's effort to obtain a quick resolution of the criminal charges. The clear advantage thereafter lay with the prosecutors, who initially indicated that they had not yet decided whether to appeal the judge's adverse ruling on the first indictment and Count I of the second indictment. DeGuerin continued to try to press the judge for rulings on his other pending motions. On December 7, he asked Priest to isolate the money-laundering charges in Count II of the October 3 indictment and to proceed to hear motions affecting that count.

The state had until December 20 to announce whether it would appeal Priest's dismissal of the charges discussed above. Priest indicated that he was not going to set any additional hearings in the case until the state decided whether to appeal. On December 12, Earle announced that the state would appeal the ruling; the official notice of appeal was filed on that day. DeGuerin had already anticipated the appeal and on December 7 had moved to sever the charges against DeLay in Count II of the second indictment (i.e., conspiracy to launder money) from the dismissed charges. If granted, a severance would allow DeLay to pursue his challenges to the money-laundering charges and, if necessary, efforts to obtain a possible trial on those charges even while the state appealed the dismissal of the other charges.

Under Section 3.04 of the Texas Penal Code, a defendant has an almost unlimited right to sever charges. Initially it appeared that Judge Priest was persuaded that DeLay should at least have a hearing on these issues before the state perfected its appeal. He said that he would address the issues during the week of December 27. On December 15, Priest indicated that if he were to sever the counts (a decision that he emphasized that he had not yet made), he would lean toward proceeding to trial on the unappealed counts. He ordered the clerk to not send the case files to the appellate court until after the upcoming hearing. However, most of the files had already been sent to the Third Court of Appeals as part of the state's appeal. Perfection of this appeal effectively froze all legal proceedings against DeLay.

On December 17, Priest acknowledged that jurisdiction now rested with the appellate court, and announced that further proceedings on the remaining motions and charges would be frozen pending the outcome of the state's appeal. Priest explained his apparent change of mind by indicating that he was now convinced that both of the indictments involved essentially the same evidence. Moreover, DeLay's codefendants did not want to proceed to trial quickly, so any severance would have to be as to the parties as well as to the charges. With these considerations in mind, Priest said that trying the charges and defendants separately on the money-laundering charges while the other charges were on appeal would be "illogical" and a lack of "judicial economy." DeGuerin disagreed that judicial economy could trump his client's right to sever the charges against him. However, there apparently was no dispute over whether, with the record now at the appeals court, the trial court had lost jurisdiction of the case.

Priest indicated that his order to the clerk to not send the records to the appellate court was "improvident" and apologized for confusing the proceedings. He rescinded his order to the clerk and cancelled the hearing for December 27.[30]

From DeGuerin's perspective, the events described in the paragraphs above were critical to the ultimate need for DeLay to step aside as majority leader. When I spoke with DeGuerin in early 2006, he was angry that, in his view, the prosecutors had lied to Judge Priest and rushed to deprive the trial court of jurisdiction of the case before Priest could grant DeLay's motion for severance. DeGuerin believed that if the hearing had gone ahead on December 27 as planned, Priest would at least have severed the pending charges from the appeal and may have reconsidered his earlier decision and dismissed all charges. DeGuerin blamed the prosecutors for "lying" to Priest. DeGuerin said that persons from the DA's office (including ADA Brian Case) were "standing over the personnel in the clerk's office rushing them to finish forwarding the files to the appeals court" on December 15 to deprive Priest of jurisdiction, because (DeGuerin said) Earle knew that Priest was likely to rule for the defense on December 27. DeGuerin indicated that the DA's staff even went behind the clerk's counter to improperly rush along the preparation of the files. According to DeGuerin, the defense counsel learned of the activity in the clerk's office and immediately tried to contact Priest by e-mail, asking him to enter an order stopping the clerk. Priest apparently was presiding over a trial in Dallas and did not see the messages. DeGuerin then telephoned Priest that evening. He emphasized to me in 2006 that he asked Judge Priest only to read the e-mails. Judge Priest shortly thereafter issued the order halting the preparation of the record for appeal. However, three boxes of records already had been sent by the clerk that day to the Court of Appeals.

This exchange of communications with Judge Priest by DeGuerin and the prosecutors had come outside of public view, the e-mails being copied only to the other parties. Priest's responses also came primarily by e-mail to the attorneys. The prosecutors challenged this practice with a motion on December 16 objecting to the handling of the court's business through e-mail, charging that DeGuerin was using these unofficial e-mails to try to influence the judge on substantive matters. In response, DeGuerin charged that the prosecutors were being "dishonest" with the judge in their e-mails by denying that they were trying to deprive the trial court of jurisdiction while at the same time hurriedly filing the record on appeal to achieve just that end. DeGuerin filed the prosecutors' e-mails publicly in his pleadings with the Third Court of Appeals to "expose their [the prosecutors'] misconduct."[31] In an e-mail to reporters on Saturday, December 18, Priest assured them that all e-mail communications had been sent timely to both sides and that any suggestion that he had been improperly communicating with the defense attorneys "is not the case and will not be the case." [32]

Once the prosecutors filed their appeal of Priest's dismissal of the conspiracy charges, DeGuerin faced an appeal process that under normal circumstances could take ninety days just for the parties to file their briefs at the Third Court of Appeals (an intermediate state-appellate court). Expediting matters at that intermediate court could do little to help Delay's situation in Washington. Therefore, DeGuerin sought to jump over the intermediate court by seeking immediate relief from the highest criminal court in Texas, the Court of Criminal Appeals. This court is the equivalent for criminal matters of the state supreme court for civil matters. DeLay's pleadings asked the Court of Criminal Appeals to dismiss all of the charges against him or to order an immediate trial on the money-laundering charges in Count II of the second indictment.

However, the plea to the highest criminal court was a long shot. The court rarely intervenes to reverse a trial judge on pretrial matters. The prosecutors opposed DeLay's motion by arguing that DeLay's extraordinary request was "a bold attempt to bully his way to the very front of the line simply and solely to serve his own political interests and ambitions." The Texas Court of Criminal Appeals (all of its members Republican) on January 8 rejected DeLay's request without comment. This left the state's appeal pending at the Third Court of Appeals and the case at the trial level frozen, pending the outcome of the state's appeal.

Judge Priest's Effect on the Proceedings

The replacement of Judge Perkins with Judge Priest had brought mixed results for Congressman DeLay. Priest was not as politically active as Perkins and seemed during the last months of 2005 to preside over the criminal case without attention to partisan events. However, by ignoring the potential partisan effects of the criminal case against DeLay, Priest was also not allowing the schedule and rulings in the case to be driven by their potential effects on DeLay's future in Washington. In one sense, DeLay got what he wanted—a nonpolitical judge ruling in a nonpartisan manner. However, the result of being treated like other criminal defendants instead of as the majority leader of the U.S. House of Representatives meant that DeLay found it harder to convince the judge that the Texas judicial system should move in extraordinary ways to accommodate his concerns about his political future.

Some attorneys have even speculated that DeLay may ultimately have been better off before Judge Perkins, who, although more politically active as a Democrat than Judge Priest, was very conscious of the political significance of the case on the scale of a national events. Both Judge Perkins and Judge Priest were expected to rule fairly in the criminal case and probably would have reached similar conclusions on the key legal issues on the motions to quash. However, by replacing Judge Perkins, DeLay lost his opportunity to criticize the adverse rulings as a product of partisanship and the possibility that Perkins, concerned about appearing partisan, would have been more willing to move the criminal case ahead as fast as possible. These judgmental musings are, of course, really possible only after the fact. There were many good reasons why DeLay may have thought it wise to remove Perkins (e.g., concern over how he might rule on the motion to change the venue outside of Travis County). There was no way to predict in November 2005 that Chief Justice Jefferson would replace Perkins with Priest or how any new judge would manage the case. Nevertheless, by the end of 2005 it was clear to all but the most hopeful DeLay supporters that being treated like other defendants in a criminal case meant that there would be no quick, favorable resolution to the criminal charges in Texas.

District Attorney Earle and Attorney Dick DeGuerin

Although there is almost inevitably an acrimonious atmosphere around intense litigation, the animosity between Earle and DeGuerin was more bitter than usual. Earle had always portrayed his investigation and prosecution of the principals in TRMPAC and TAB as a proper attempt to enforce what he felt was a clear requirement of state law (i.e., no corporate contributions are allowed to go to candidates). However, he also saw a higher purpose: "Democracy is at stake here. If we allow corporations to control elections, we will destroy democracy. It will be the death knell of democracy."[33] Earle spoke out in 2003: "I think people are beginning to understand we are in danger of turning into a banana republic with a few wealthy people and many who are hungry and forlorn." He saw the risk of a "takeover of state government by wealthy corporate interests."[34] By the time in 2005 when indictments were pending against DeLay and his codefendants, Earle was more circumspect.

However, Earle's relative silence in 2005 did nothing to convince DeGuerin that Earle's pursuit of DeLay had anything to do with enforcement of the state's laws. To DeGuerin, Earle's prosecution was a vengeful partisan effort to destroy DeLay because of what DeLay had done to pass the congressional redistricting in 2003. DeGuerin felt that the prosecutors had misled the courts, manipulated the grand juries, bullied the clerk's staff, and generally misused the criminal process. He felt that by compelling DeLay to step aside as majority leader and leaving him vulnerable to possible defeat in the 2006 elections, Earle had achieved his primary goal. DeGuerin remained confident that DeLay would be exonerated of the criminal charges. At the same time, however, it was clear in our interview at the end of January 2006 that DeGuerin was bitter, angry at Earle, and disappointed that he had been unable to save DeLay's post as majority leader.

Commentary

During the fall of 2005 the criminal proceedings in Texas were often treated with skepticism and even ridicule by national writers. For example, Jonathan Gurwitz on December 7 hailed DeLay's partial victory before Judge Priest and described the October 3 indictment as "wafer-thin," the chances of a conviction as slight, and the criminal proceedings in Austin as a "carnival sideshow led by a charlatan masquerading as a defender of public integrity."[35] To some extent, these comments were a result of the effort by DeLay and his supporters to portray the criminal proceedings as baseless and partisan.[36] Allegations that the Travis County district attorney was motivated by partisan and personal objectives were unintentionally helped by some of Earle's own statements and actions, such as his videotaped interview with the producers of the anti-DeLay film *The Big Buy,* and his comments on national television about the DeLay investigation. It was clear to even the most casual and objective viewer that the personal relationship between Earle and DeLay was vitriolic. Nevertheless, many of these national writers lacked a firm understanding of the nature of the charges and evidence in the criminal cases against DeLay and his fellow defendants. Also, many of these national writers seemed to share a perception common to some national political writers that political events of importance happen primarily in Washington, not as a result of a county prosecutor's actions out in the hinterland of Austin, Texas. Contrary to Mr. Gurwitz's assessment of the proceedings in Austin, Judge Priest's ruling on December 5 was not a reason for "holiday cheer for the DeLay camp."[37]

Even when DeLay was forced to permanently step aside as majority leader in January 2006, some national political writers continued to belittle the criminal prosecution in Texas. For example, Gurwitz continued his assault on the Texas proceedings by commenting that DeLay's troubles were "likely to have very little to do with Mr. Earle's legal charades in Austin and everything to do with Mr. DeLay's ethical quandary in Washington."[38]

National political writers who have dismissed the Texas criminal proceedings as frivolous are wrong. TRMPAC's solicitation and use of approximately $600,000 in unreported corporate funds in 2002 were unprecedented in Texas. As discussed in Chapter Four, attempts to justify the PAC's actions as merely "business as usual" for Republicans and Democrats alike is wrong. The acrimonious personal relationship between DeLay and Earle makes for a distracting media show but does not change the facts of what happened in 2002. The following simple analysis persuades me that an investigation and eventual prosecution of TRMPAC, along with DeLay and his codefendants, was appropriate:

1. Whatever ambiguities existed in state election law about what constitutes allowable "administrative expenses" of a PAC on which corporate funds may be spent, TRMPAC's aggressive solicitation of corporate monies in 2002 made clear that it intended to do something different with corporate funds from what had been done in the past. This is discussed further in Chapter Four. TRMPAC never intended business as usual.

2. All attorneys agreed that Texas election law prohibits the contribution of corporate funds to a candidate. I have listened closely to several very able Republican lawyers try in various forums to explain why the transfer of $190,000 in corporate money to the RNC and the virtually simultaneous payment by the RNC of $190,000 in hard-dollar contributions to state House candidates did not violate any law. I have never found the arguments credible. The facts of the transfer negate any chance that the transactions were coincidental. The Republican lawyers' technical arguments about why this apparent attempt to avoid the restrictions of Texas law was okay because "it was not the same money" seem likely to fail a jury's test of common sense.

3. The issue whether DeLay was part of a conspiracy to launder money through the transfer of $190,000 in corporate funds from TRMPAC to the RNSEC in return for an equivalent amount in contributions to seven state House candidates is a bit more problematic. Contrary to his indication to the prosecutors at the August 2005 meeting that he knew about plans for the transfer in 2002 before it occurred, DeLay now says that he earlier misspoke and that he did not learn about the transfer until October 2, 2002, or later—after it had occurred. DeGuerin told me that Ellis will testify to this fact at trial. I do not know the extent of DeLay's involvement in the funds transfer.

It would be foolish to predict whether DeLay or any of his codefendants ultimately will be convicted. As demonstrated many times in the history of this country, good lawyers, the ambiguities of law, and the vagaries of a trial can produce unexpected results. Moreover, the heart of the defense is that the state law violates the First Amendment. However, the question whether the Texas Election Code restriction on the use of corporate funds on behalf of candidates is constitutional is a far cry from the question whether TRMPAC knowingly ignored this proscription. The criminal charges in Austin were never frivolous.

I see no reason to believe that DeLay would have stepped aside as majority leader in January 2006 except for the indictments and pending criminal proceedings in Texas. The progress of the corruption investigation[39] in Washington was an important factor in DeLay's decision, particularly since it adversely affected the support he could expect from Republican supporters for his battle against the criminal charges in Texas. However, other Washington lawmakers potentially implicated in the corruption investigation remained in their congressional positions. DeLay had not been indicted in Washington, and in early 2006 continued to insist on his innocence of all charges and on a claimed representation from prosecutors that he was not a target of the ongoing criminal investigation. It was the criminal proceedings in Texas that made the difference. As long as those state criminal charges remained pending, DeLay was barred from being majority leader. By January 2006, it was clear that the charges in Texas were not going to go away soon. Neither DeLay nor the Republican conference had much of an option but to "move on separately."

Another question that arises particularly in this chapter, but also exists elsewhere in this book, is whether the decisions of the various state and federal courts were impartial or were a result of partisan bias. I believe that the actions of the courts throughout this matter have been a bright spot in an otherwise dark journey. Judge Priest is discussed earlier in this chapter. However, many other courts were drawn into this story. None of their decisions appeared in my opinion to be driven by political partisanship in disregard of impartiality and legal precedent. Specifically:

1. In August 2003, Republican state officials asked the Texas Supreme Court to compel the Democratic senators in Albuquerque to return to Austin to restore the Senate quorum. All nine of the justices on the Court were Republican. Nevertheless, as discussed in Chapter Ten, the Court very correctly denied the requested relief by refusing to become involved.

2. A few days earlier (July 28), a state district judge had been asked to ban the Texas Department of Safety from hunting the absent Democratic senators. The judge was a Democrat. Nevertheless, as discussed in Chapter Ten, he refused to grant a ban on hunting senators since no senator was a party to the litigation then before the court. Again, an absolutely correct decision.

3. In September 2003, a three-judge federal court heard the Democrats' claim that the Texas Senate should be enjoined from allowing a redistricting bill to be considered without a two-thirds vote. The court was composed of two judges appointed by Republican presidents and one appointed by a Democrat. As discussed in Chapter Ten, the Court correctly rejected the Democrats' argument. In fact, the sole Democrat on the Court had earlier indicated that he was very skeptical of the Democrats' argument.

4. The three-judge federal court that heard the legal challenge to the merits of the Texas redistricting plan consisted of two judges appointed by Republican presidents and one appointed by a Democratic president. The members of the Court split 2–1, with the two Republican judges in the majority sustaining the redistricting. I was not present at the hearings in this case in 2003. The court subsequently reaffirmed its ruling in 2005. Although I disagree with the ruling and believe it should be reversed by the Supreme Court, I do not believe the court's opinions are clearly partial, given the law and facts argued to the court. I believe all members of the court took the various arguments seriously, especially the constitutional argument for equal representation (see Chapter Sixteen).

5. As detailed in this chapter, in early 2005 the Texas Supreme Court largely rejected (after a considerable delay) the mandamus request of the Texas Association of Business, challenging lower-court orders for the production of documents about contributions and expenditures in the 2002 election. The unsuccessful appeals were based on the First Amendment and were brought by attorney Andy Taylor. All nine justices on the Supreme Court of Texas at the time of the ruling were Republican.

6. In early 2005 Senior District Judge Joe Hart ruled against TRMPAC treasurer Bill Ceverha in a civil suit brought by defeated Democratic House candidates. I have known Judge Hart for years and have never known him to be politically active (although he won election to the judiciary in Travis County as a Democrat). Both sides in the litigation agreed that Judge Hart be assigned to hear the case. I was at the trial (discussed in Chapter Four) and believe that Judge Hart's ruling was fair and correct.

7. As discussed in this chapter, District Judge C. W. Duncan in November 2005 ordered the recusal of District Judge Bob Perkins in the criminal proceeding against Congressman DeLay. Perkins was a Democrat. No one challenged Judge Perkins as biased or unfair. However, I agreed with Judge Duncan at the time after hearing the arguments and evidence that a recusal of Perkins was appropriate because of the perception of partisanship and partiality that would likely exist if he remained as the presiding judge in the criminal cases. Judge Schraub, a Republican, recused himself from hearing

the case. Chief Justice Wallace Jefferson, a Republican, then appointed Senior Judge Pat Priest, a Democrat, to preside. As discussed above, I believe that Judge Priest has presided in a nonpolitical manner.

8. As discussed in this chapter, in January 2006, the Texas Court of Criminal Appeals (all its members Republican) rejected the request by DeLay to dismiss the charges against him or order the trial judge to proceed immediately to trial on the money-laundering charges. Legal precedent and practice was heavily against DeLay's extraordinary request for relief. Nevertheless, if influenced only by partisan concerns, the court could have intervened on DeLay's behalf. To its credit, it did not do so.

9. On April 19, 2006, the Third Court of Appeals affirmed Judge Priest's dismissal of the charge that DeLay had been part of a conspiracy to violate the election code. The court agreed with Judge Priest that the conspiracy provisions of the Penal Code did not apply to violations of the election code until after the 2003 amendments. The court panel consisted of two Republicans and one Democratic. The ruling was unanimous. I believe it was correct.

10. Another test of the effects of partisanship on the judiciary in this affair will occur when the U.S. Supreme Court hears the appeal of the challenge to the 2003 redistricting in Texas. The Supreme Court's ruling is discussed in the Afterword.

11. Perhaps a final test of the effects of partisanship will come when the Texas appellate courts rule on the constitutionality of the state campaign-finance laws at issue in the civil and criminal proceedings involving TRMPAC, TAB, and the principals of those organizations.

Some readers are certain to disagree with my assessment of the effect of partisanship on the court rulings in this matter. Some lawyers will also disagree, especially those attorneys affected by the adverse rulings of the federal district court in the challenge to the lawfulness of the 2003 redistricting. However, I believe that in this society some persons have a mistaken view of what type of impartiality can realistically be expected from our judges. For thirty years I have tried cases involving important public issues, such as elections, public-school finance, prison overcrowding, state programs to reduce pollution, etc. As I explain to my students in law school, I have never in thirty years felt that I had a level playing field in any court. Sometimes the field was tilted toward me, sometimes away from me, because the judge or judges virtually always had some personal, ideological, or even political opinions that they brought to the courtroom and the case. Most judges, whether elected or appointed, are intelligent, informed individuals who are interested in and have opinions on legal issues and important social issues and policies. They cannot simply jettison these opinions when assigned to hear a case. In an opinion on behalf of the U.S. Supreme Court in a case involving the constitutional authority of states to limit the right of judicial candidates to speak about their views publicly on disputed legal or political issues while campaigning for office, Justice Scalia said:

> One meaning of "impartiality" in the judicial context—and of course its root meaning—is the lack of bias for or against either party to the proceeding. Impartiality in this sense assures equal application of the law. . . .
>
> A judge's lack of predisposition regarding the relevant legal issues in a case has never been thought a necessary component of equal justice, and with good reason. For one thing, it is virtually impossible to find a judge who does not have preconceptions about the law. . . . Indeed, even if it were possible to select judges who did not have preconceived views on legal issues, it would hardly be desirable to do so. 'Proof that a Justice's mind . . . was a complete *tabula rasa* in the area of constitutional adjudication would be evidence of lack of qualification, not a lack of bias' [authority deleted]. . . .
>
> A . . . possible meaning of "impartiality" . . . might be described as open-mindedness. This quality in a judge demands, not that he have no preconceptions on legal issues, but that he be willing to consider views that oppose his preconceptions, and remain open to persuasion, when the issues arise in a pending case. This sort of impartiality seeks to guarantee each litigant, not an *equal* chance to win the legal points in the case, but at least *some* chance of doing so.[40]

From my experience, virtually all judges want to rule correctly and will not ignore the law for partisan or ideological reasons despite their preconceptions. There is ordinarily in any case, however, a broad range of legally correct outcomes from which a judge may choose. It is the job of the attorney to develop and pursue the best strategy for winning in front of each judge. This strategy must vary in accordance with the judge. It serves no purpose for an attorney to gripe or complain because the presiding judge is conservative or liberal, Republican or Democrat, or to blame an unfavorable outcome on the philosophical or political mindset of the judge. The court rulings in the Texas redistricting saga were not in my view a result of partisan bias.[41]

It will be interesting in the coming months to observe whether any of the TRMPAC defendants (Colyandro, Ellis, or Robold) agree to give evidence against Congressman DeLay in return for a lesser sentence or probation. Some writers speculated about this possibility as long ago as 2004. However, there was little chance of such a plea as long as the constitutional questions about the state law remained unanswered and DeLay remained in power, or likely to return to power, in Washington. With DeLay's decision to step down as majority leader, the landscape has changed; how much so remains to be seen. Moreover, the silence and inactivity since 2004 with regard to the pending charges against Warren Robold, the principal TRMPAC corporate fund-raiser, could be significant.

Finally, there is a bit of irony in the outcome in Texas as it stands in early 2006. For several years, Congressman DeLay had been openly critical of members of the judiciary for being too activist. He even suggested that Congress look at the possibility of impeaching federal judges for such activism. DeLay's political future ultimately turned on the willingness of the courts of Texas to grant extraordinary relief by intervening in the grand jury and pretrial process. DeLay found himself in the position in late 2005 and early 2006 of asking first Judge Priest and then perhaps the most conservative court in the state (the Court of Criminal Appeals) to take the extraordinary "activist" step of intruding into the pretrial criminal process and dismissing charges against him or ordering an immediate trial so that he could remain majority leader. Such a request for court intrusion coming from an ordinary criminal defendant would almost certainly have been doomed. Yet with the able representation of Dick DeGuerin, Congressman DeLay took his shot at convincing the courts to act. The courts, however, were unmoved.

CHAPTER 18

The Fall of Congressman DeLay

I have no fear whatsoever about any investigation into me or my personal or professional activities.
— CONGRESSMAN TOM DELAY, *WASHINGTON POST*, APRIL 4, 2006

Congressman DeLay's aggressive effort to shed the Texas criminal proceedings during the fall of 2005 failed. Over this same period, events elsewhere in the country turned against the congressman. DeLay did not directly face criminal charges outside Texas. Instead, as discussed below, he confronted a cascade of events and news stories that implied wrongdoing and led to his decisions to step aside as majority leader and later to resign from Congress.

Events in Washington

Events in Washington also rapidly turned against Congressman DeLay. Another book will need to be written by someone else to detail those events. For the purposes of this book, however, the cascade of events affecting Congressman DeLay included:

1. Contributions to DeLay's defense fund proved disappointing at the same time that the costs of his legal representation were escalating because of both the criminal proceeding in Texas and the events in Washington.[1]
2. Nick Lampson, one of the Democratic incumbents defeated in 2002, announced his intention to run against DeLay in the 2006 general election. It also appeared that DeLay would face opposition in the Republican primary. Ultimately three opponents filed against DeLay for the primary. Polls by USA Today/CNN showed that only 36 percent of the registered voters in DeLay's district indicated that they would vote for him in 2006. Some

observers suggested that demographic changes in DeLay's district were making it more Asian and African American and more Democratic.[2]

3. On October 5, 2005, a Washington grand jury indicted David Safavian, the federal government's chief procurement officer, on five counts of making false statements and obstructing investigations into his relationship with Washington lobbyist Jack Abramoff. Safavian pleaded not guilty and resigned from his post. On June 20, 2006, he was found guilty by a jury on four of the five counts.

4. On November 28, 2005, California congressman Randall "Duke" Cunningham pleaded guilty to accepting over $2.4 million in bribes. Defense contractor Brent Wilkes was identified as unindicted coconspirator #1 in the case. News stories disclosed that Wilkes also had connections with Congressman DeLay (e.g., financial support, golfing together, DeLay flying on Wilkes's private airplane) and that one of Wilkes's California-based companies, Perfect Wave Technologies, had contributed $15,000 in corporate money to TRMPAC in 2002.[3] Earle immediately subpoenaed records from Wilkes and several of his associates and companies. A DeLay spokesman dismissed Earle's subpoenas as "comical." He accused Earle of "grasping at straws" and "literally trying to make this up as he goes along."[4]

5. On November 21, 2005, Michael Scanlon, a former DeLay press secretary and Abramoff law partner, pleaded guilty to conspiracy to corrupt public officials and agreed to cooperate with prosecutors in their investigation of undisclosed public officials. Scanlon had worked with Abramoff and also had operated his own "grass roots and public relations services" firm (Capitol Campaign Strategies) with ties to Abramoff and his clients.

6. On January 3, 2006, Jack Abramoff pleaded guilty to conspiracy to corrupt public officials, mail fraud, and tax evasion and agreed to pay almost $27 million in restitution to former clients he had defrauded and in back taxes to the Internal Revenue Service. Abramoff faced a possible term of eleven years in jail. Abramoff also agreed to cooperate with prosecutors investigating whether he had bought specific actions from any members of Congress, congressional aides, or members of the Bush administration.[5] Newspapers reported many connections between Abramoff and DeLay.[6] Travis County DA Ronnie Earle swiftly issued subpoenas for records from two of Abramoff's former law firms and two former Indian tribe clients that had contributed to TRMPAC in 2002.[7]

7. Abramoff's plea agreement focused attention on the Alexander Strategy Group, a Washington lobbying and political consulting firm founded in the late 1990s by former DeLay chief of staff Edwin A. Buckham. The firm had grown to approximately twenty lobbyists and was considered a lucra-

tive landing spot for many former DeLay staffers. The firm, which at one time shared offices with DeLay's national PAC (ARMPAC) in a residential neighborhood, was alleged to have promoted the idea that it could deliver special access to Congressman DeLay. It also had shared at least one Indian tribe client (the Choctaw tribe from Mississippi) with Abramoff. News stories reported that ARMPAC had paid the Alexander Strategy Group over $300,000 for fund-raising and consulting services from 2000 to 2003. These stories also reported that the Alexander Strategy Group during that same period had paid DeLay's wife, Christine, approximately $115,000 in consulting fees.[8]

8. Former DeLay staffer Buckham also ran another organization that began to attract attention as a result of the Abramoff plea agreement. The U.S. Family Network (USFN) was ostensibly a grassroots nonprofit organization dedicated to promoting family values. In reality, however, it received most of its money from Republican sources or Abramoff's clients (including Russian interests) and spent the money for the benefit of Republican lawmakers or on ads targeting Democratic candidates. Almost immediately after this connection was announced, Earle subpoenaed documents relating to a $500,000 transfer of corporate funds from the Republican Congressional Committee to the U.S. Family Network and Robert G. Mills, a former DeLay campaign chairman who oversaw the Washington townhouse shared by ARMPAC and the USFN.[9]

9. The Abramoff plea agreement also highlighted the activities of Tony Rudy, a former DeLay deputy chief of staff. After leaving DeLay's legislative staff, Rudy had worked for Abramoff before joining the Alexander Strategy Group. Prosecutors indicated that they were investigating whether Rudy, while DeLay's aide, had secured legislative favors for Abramoff's clients in exchange for gifts and the promise of a job.[10]

10. By January 6th, some House Republicans were circulating a petition in the Republican conference calling for the election of a new majority leader. The petition had twenty-five signatures by that Friday, but was expected to gain the necessary fifty signatures by the following week.

11. Conservative editorial writers abandoned DeLay. For example, on January 6, the *Wall Street Journal* said, "The prospect that Mr. DeLay might still return as leader has contributed to the GOP's recent dysfunction; he and they should move on separately."[11]

Although none of these developments resulted in any criminal charge against Congressman DeLay or amounted to any legal reason for him to step aside as majority leader, DeLay found himself at the center of the widest-ranging congressional-corruption investigation in more than two decades. By Saturday, January 7, Congressman DeLay's political fortunes were in free fall.

Buffeted by the ongoing Texas criminal proceedings, his potential role in future criminal proceedings at the federal level, the apparent disarray of House Republicans on major policy issues for lack of a permanent majority leader, and the possibility of a serious challenge for reelection, DeLay consulted with several colleagues and advisers before deciding what action to take. Former Republican Party chairman Ed Gillespie proposed to fly to Texas for a private meeting, but the meeting never took place.[12] On Saturday morning, January 7, DeLay called Speaker Dennis Hastert from Texas. Hastert added his voice to those who counseled DeLay to step aside as majority leader.

That afternoon, in Sugar Land, Texas, DeLay released the contents of letters that he had sent that day to Hastert and his Republican congressional colleagues announcing that he was permanently stepping aside as majority leader. The letters made no specific mention of the pending federal investigation. Instead, DeLay told Hastert in the letter:

> I am writing to inform you of my decision to permanently step aside as majority leader, and of my belief that the best interests of the conference would be served by the election of a new leader as soon as possible. The job of majority leader and the mandate of the Republican majority are too important to be hamstrung, even for a few months, by personal distractions.

In the second letter, to his House Republican colleagues, DeLay insisted, "I have always acted in an ethical manner within the rules of our body and the laws of our land. I am fully confident time will bear this out."[13] DeLay's spokesperson added, "Mr. DeLay did the noble thing by calling for new leadership elections at this time since the legal schedule in Austin could have been a distraction for the Republican conference."[14]

Dick DeGuerin told me in January 2006 that he believes if DeLay had held off from stepping down for a few more days, the Texas Court of Criminal Appeals would have ruled in his favor and possibly dismissed all charges—thus making it possible for DeLay to reoccupy the position of majority leader. DeGuerin believes that once DeLay stepped down, the "pressure was off the court," and the Texas Court of Criminal Appeals two days later rejected DeLay's request for relief. I told DeGuerin that I knew of no way to test this opinion.[15]

After DeLay announced his permanent departure from the post of majority leader, some of DeLay's Republican colleagues in Washington praised him and expressed regret about what had happened. However, the race to replace

DeLay as majority leader started in earnest immediately. Very little loyalty to DeLay was on display among the many Republicans whom DeLay had helped in the past. DeLay was gone from the Republican leadership, and the members of the party conference moved quickly to replace him. The issue of ethics reform was an important public topic among the lawmakers competing for the majority leader post. On February 2, 2006, Congressman John Boehner of Ohio was elected majority leader by the Republican conference. He defeated Congressman Roy Blunt of Missouri, who remained as majority whip. The vote on the second ballot was 122–109; Blunt had led the first ballot, but failed by six votes to achieve a majority. Most of the freshmen Republican lawmakers from Texas voted for Blunt.

A Decision to Resign

DeLay's fight for reelection in the March 2006 Republican primary proved easier than some had expected. DeLay (with 62 percent of the vote) handily defeated three opponents. Nevertheless, it still appeared after the primary that DeLay would face a tough fight for reelection in the 2006 general election against the Democratic nominee, former congressman Nick Lampson. Still, few persons expected that DeLay would resign.

Little or nothing that occurred in the Texas criminal proceedings during the spring of 2006 seemed likely to influence DeLay's resignation decision. There were related pretrial hearings in several cases, including the federal case against LEAA[16] and the criminal prosecution of TAB[17], and a hearing on the district attorney's appeal of the dismissal of the conspiracy charge against DeLay,[18] but none of these matters had been decided by April 15. DeLay's attorneys were no longer pushing for an early trial on the state charges, seeming to adopt the same strategy as DeLay's codefendants: wait for an appellate ruling on the constitutionality of the corporate-ban provisions of the Texas Election Code.

Elsewhere, however, developments in federal criminal investigations continued to make headlines and, implicitly, to affect DeLay. On March 29, former Washington lobbyist Jack Abramoff and a former business partner, Adam Kidan, were sentenced in Miami for their earlier convictions for business fraud. Abramoff was sentenced to five years and ten months in prison, but was allowed to remain free for three months to assist on the ongoing Miami investigation, including the slaying of a business associate.[19] Abramoff was also ordered to pay $21 million in restitution. Neither DeLay nor other members of Congress were implicated in this Miami case, but news stories generally used the occasion of the sentencing in Florida to remind readers of the ongoing congressional corruption investigation also involving Abramoff.

The *Washington Post* continued its focus on nonprofit organizations related to DeLay. On March 26 the paper reported that the "pro-family" organization U.S. Family Network had provided a steady stream of payments to DeLay's former chief of staff, Edwin Buckham, and his wife. The newspaper reported that the Buckhams' consulting firm had been paid $996,754 during a five-year period ending when the organization folded in 2001. The newspaper also claimed that most of the organization's $3.23 million in revenue over this period came from clients of former lobbyist Jack Abramoff, and that the FBI had subpoenaed the organization's records, possibly to explore "links between the payments and favorable legislative treatment of Abramoff clients by DeLay's office." The *Washington Post* also reported that for at least three years of this period, the Buckhams' consulting firm paid DeLay's wife, Christine, for consulting services.

Soon another federal criminal plea agreement struck close to DeLay. News stories in December 2005 had suggested that Tony Rudy, a former DeLay deputy chief of staff[20] and Abramoff associate, was a focus of the ongoing congressional corruption investigation. On March 31, 2006, Rudy pleaded guilty to a charge of conspiracy to violate federal mail- and wire-fraud laws. He also pleaded guilty to violating the postemployment restrictions for former congressional staffers by lobbying DeLay's office within one year of leaving as deputy chief of staff.[21] The agreed-upon factual basis for the guilty plea indicates that beginning in 1997, Rudy voluntarily participated along with Abramoff and others:

> in a course of conduct through which one or more of them corruptly offered and provided a stream of things of value to public officials with the intent to influence or reward a series of official actions and agreements to perform official action, and public officials corruptly accepted the stream of things of value knowing that they were given with the intent to influence or reward official action.

Among the "rewards or benefits" identified by the agreed facts were "all-expense-paid trips," tickets for sporting events, use of a box suite at Washington Redskins football games, regular meals at expensive restaurants, and "frequent" golf and related expenses at courses in Washington and elsewhere. The agreed-upon facts also indicate that Abramoff paid Rudy's consulting firm, Liberty Consulting, for consulting services to be provided by Rudy's wife even while

Rudy was DeLay's deputy chief of staff. The agreement further indicates that, in return, Abramoff and others received Rudy's assistance, beginning "at least in 1997," with providing services for Abramoff's clients, enhancing Abramoff's reputation in order to help him secure additional clients, stopping legislation adverse to the interest of Abramoff's clients, and supporting or opposing actions to be taken by other governmental agencies and departments. Rudy also agreed that he had, once in private practice as a lobbyist, secured payments for certain organizations by falsely representing that some of the organizations were charities and without disclosing that he, Abramoff, and others would personally benefit from the payments (e.g., through golfing excursions to Scotland and payments to Rudy's consulting firm).

DeLay apparently had considered resigning for several months. During the last part of March, after winning the Republican primary, DeLay began privately discussing the possibility of resignation with his friends and Republican colleagues in Washington. Most or all apparently made no effort to convince him not to resign.[22] On April 4, DeLay released to his constituents a video listing his accomplishments in office and explaining that he had decided to resign from Congress. He said that his decision had come after "many weeks of personal prayerful thinking." Defiant in his decision, DeLay indicated to his constituents, "I refuse to allow liberal Democrats an opportunity to steal this seat [in Congress] with a negative, personal campaign." In an interview later that day with Fox News, DeLay explained that "every leftist organization in America is down here in Houston" and that the political campaign to oust him had turned "very nasty." He said, "I'm more interested in growing the Republican majority than my own future."[23]

Many politicians and writers speculated about why DeLay would resign instead of battling the Democrats in the general election. DeLay associates said privately that DeLay had considered resigning on several occasions in the past, but had wanted to do so only after vanquishing his Republican foes in the March primary. These associates pointed to recent DeLay-sponsored poll results showing that DeLay faced a stiff reelection challenge from Democrat Nick Lampson[24] and to DeLay's frustration with no longer being part of the House Republican leadership.[25] The prospect of possibly needing to raise $10 million for his reelection campaign conflicted with his need to raise money with which to pay his lawyers in Texas and Washington. One former aide, John Feehery, said, "He needed to raise money for his defense fund. That was the bottom line."[26] It also is likely that few of his Republican colleagues wanted a high-profile DeLay election campaign in the fall, one in which allegations of corruption and abuse of power could spill over to other Republican reelection campaigns. DeLay was a "lightning rod" for negative publicity and voter opposition. It was better for Republicans nationwide if, by November, DeLay (even if not indicted by the federal task force) were a memory rather than a day-to-day target of Democrats and media.

DeLay rejected any possibility that he was resigning because of any of the pending criminal investigations. In regard to the criminal charges pending in Texas, DeLay explained that he had expected the charges to be dismissed before now, but that "in the end, we're going to give him [DA Ronnie Earle] a pretty good Texas whopping." As to the federal congressional corruption investigation in Washington, he said, "The Abramoff affair has nothing to do with me. The Justice Department has told my lawyers I'm not the target of this investigation. What these men did has greatly disappointed me, but it has nothing to do with me."

DeLay indicated that he would officially resign in June. Texas governor Perry indicated that if he receives DeLay's resignation in June, the congressional seat will remain vacant until a special election in November, to be held simultaneously with the general election. This will allow the Republican Party to select the party's candidate for the congressional race in the general election, which, in the view of some observers, means that DeLay will effectively be able to select his Republican successor. On the other hand, the election to fill the vacancy for the unexpired term will be an open election, possibly attracting multiple candidates from both political parties. Under this unusual circumstance, the winner of the seat to fill the vacancy for the unexpired term (i.e., November–January) may be different from the winner of the contest for the two-year term beginning in January 2007.

Commentary

For some writers, DeLay's problems were proof of the price of hubris in politics. For example, David Broder in the *Washington Post* commented that DeLay's decline from power was "a classic case of pride going before a fall, with a hard-edged, arrogant political operative tripped up by his own tactics."[27] Nevertheless, even though I am no fan of Congressman DeLay, it was painful for me to watch as the edifice of power that DeLay had built over many years crumbled piece by piece over a few months. By the middle of January, this man who only a few months earlier was considered the most powerful man on Capitol Hill and invincible in the congressional district that he had insisted be drawn for him in 2003 had become someone largely stripped of his official and unofficial power and prestige and faced with the possibility of electoral defeat and a lengthy prison term in state or federal prison.

I do not know how federal prosecutors will proceed in the congressional corruption investigation. DeLay may eventually be indicted—or not. As Senator John McCain commented at the time of DeLay's retirement announcement, "I think there are other aspects of the Abramoff scandal that will be unfolding in the weeks ahead."[28] None of the plea agreements to this point name Congressman DeLay as a coconspirator or suspected lawbreaker. Nevertheless, most of the convicted persons have connections back to DeLay; the plea agreements all indicate the involvement of "others" in the criminal conspiracy; DeLay or members of his family received benefits from the persons or organizations implicated in the plea agreements; some of the favorable official actions that Abramoff achieved for himself or his clients were taken by DeLay or his office; and, by giving Abramoff, Scanlon, and Rudy reduced prison sentences in return for their cooperation, the federal task force appears to be trying to gather testimony that will lead to the indictment and prosecution of one or more high-ranking government officials. Whether DeLay is now or will become a target of the federal corruption investigation is unknown to me. Time will provide an answer.

CHAPTER 19

Conclusion

The events of 2001–2003 in Texas make up an amazing tale that continues to have a significant effect on national and state politics. I have tried to present those events in a straightforward and nonpolitical manner. Ultimately, however, I think the story is a tragedy. It is tragic not because one side won or lost, but because it illustrates the misplaced priorities of our government officials and institutions at a time when the future of this country demands more.

One reason why the events are tragic is obvious. They show national and state officials losing sight of the needs of Texans while focusing on the misbegotten priority of partisan dominance. Like most states, Texas in 2003 was struggling with many serious state issues, including an increasingly inadequate public school system and a serious shortfall in available revenues. The editorial board of the *Houston Chronicle* was correct in February 2003 when, on hearing about the possibility of redistricting, it observed: "At a time when Texas is grasping for pennies to immunize Texas children, legislators don't need to waste resources giving booster shots to political power plays."

The outlay of energy by the partisan participants in 2003 was enormous. Politicians of both parties put aside other personal and state affairs in favor of warring over an unnecessary redistricting. For lawmakers who seldom have time to focus intently on a single subject for a few hours, much less for days, it was extraordinary for eleven Democratic senators to encamp themselves together for forty days in a hotel over a thousand miles from the Texas Capitol because of partisan rancor. For most of that time, Republican senators remained gathered in Austin, restricted to their offices and apartments and seething with a similar rancor, while Republican congressmen shuttled in and out of the city lobbying for partisan district lines. Altogether the state officials and lawmakers spent almost 140 days (June–October) plotting and fretting almost solely about congressional redistricting. The personal sacrifice by these officials and lawmakers was great. Yet Texans realized no bona fide gain. It was a time of great personal and institutional waste.

Both national and state politicians' priorities were wrongly placed. The romanticism of high-profile partisan war games prevailed over the unexciting and sometimes obscure task of actually governing. Millions of dollars were raised for partisan election campaigns, but none for public schools. Elected officials found it more thrilling to grandstand on partisan issues than to toil in possible obscurity while trying to find and sell a bipartisan plan for adequately funding public schools, fixing Medicare, reforming taxes, fighting racial discrimination in its seemingly infinite forms, or addressing the many other pressing national and state issues. Texans had a right to expect their elected officials to do more than play partisan games, but the real needs of both Republican and Democratic Texans were lost amidst the grandstanding of members of both political parties.

The events in Texas further will be a tragedy if they become legal and practical precedent for other states. Redistricting is always a messy, divisive business that too often shows our legislative bodies and state leaders at their worst. Partisan or other special interests may inevitably be a part of an otherwise necessary redistricting, but such interests should never justify redistricting, especially when the legislative body is left to use inaccurate population data that can be manipulated by a legislative majority to the detriment of a partisan or political minority. Moreover, the creators of TRMPAC saw it in 2002 as a model for use in other states: a way for national parties and party officials, such as DeLay, to gain increased influence over state politics, state politicians, and state redistricting. It is not in the national interest to see the highly partisan, gridlocked environment of Washington purposefully spread to the states. Whether the subsequent events surrounding DeLay will forestall or prevent similar attempts in other states is yet to be seen.

The events in 2003 also showed a patronizing racism by Republican officials and lawmakers. At one point while writing this book, I thought that Democratic claims of racial and ethnic discrimination were part of an ill-conceived strategy that backfired on the Democratic senators. I still believe that over the summer of 2003 the Democratic senators' claims of racial discrimination in the redistricting plan and in the actions of the Republican officials and lawmakers became redundant and were widely perceived as unavailing whining. I have become convinced, however, that, rather than being part of a poor media or issues strategy, the claims of racism were the product of a legitimate emotional response from the African American and Hispanic senators.

Republican officials never understood what was driving the response of the minority senators. For Republicans, the effect of the proposed redistricting was purely a partisan or legal issue. The Republicans maneuvered and played for the victory. For the minority lawmakers, the issue of racial discrimination was not solely or even primarily a legal issue. The African American and Hispanic senators were incensed when their Senate Republican colleagues and other Republican officials declared that Republicans were redistricting in the best interest of minority voters. The Democratic senators saw a group of white men and women from generally wealthy and racially segregated neighborhoods purporting to tell Hispanics and African Americans in Texas what was best for them. Republicans claimed to be enhancing racial and ethnic voting strength by creating overwhelmingly minority election districts and defeating Anglo Democratic incumbents. They were doing so while ignoring the opinions of minority lawmakers elected from those same minority areas of the state. To the African American and Hispanic senators, the redistricting plan and the Senate sanctions were objectionable, but the greatest hurt came from the perceived audacity of Republicans claiming to be better qualified to decide what was beneficial for Hispanic and African American voters than the lawmakers who were elected by them. Even conservative and moderate minority senators became enraged.

The Republicans' patronizing attitude toward minority voters is indicative of a serious systemic problem within the Republican Party. Every Republican lawmaker was entitled to express his or her views on whether the redistricting benefited racial and ethnic minorities and to have those views be respected. However, the views of the minority senators, even if they were Democrats, were also entitled to respect. So also, the views of the bona fide minority advocacy organizations such as MALDEF, LULAC, the NAACP, and the GI Forum were entitled to consideration. Republicans dismissed all these views as being "more Democratic than minority" whenever the organizations or lawmakers disagreed with some aspects of what the Republicans were doing. Republicans had no legitimate or credible standing to insist that they alone knew what was in the best interest of minority voters in Texas. Designing districts to increase the possibility that minority candidates instead of Anglo candidates will win elections is neither a legal requirement nor a good policy for minority voters or the public interest, especially when doing so results in racially segregated districts and in minority voters being packed into a minimal number of election districts. Nevertheless, Republicans insisted that they knew that this was the right thing to do for Texas minorities. Even if Republicans claim that their patronizing attitude toward minority voters in 2003 was no worse than a similar attitude shown in the past by Anglo Democrats when Democrats controlled the redistricting process, such patronizing (whether by Anglo Republicans or Democrats), although possibly kinder and gentler than *de jure* exclusion of minorities from the election process, is still racism.

A further tragic aspect of the Texas redistricting was the hypocrisy that permeated the process. Congressman DeLay is the best example of an actor who publicly proclaimed one set of priorities and acted on another. The *Houston Chronicle* in 2002 criticized DeLay for his "situational principles and win-at-all costs lust for power," even before congressional redistricting became a reality. The events of 2001–2003 amply demonstrated these personal characteristics. When the outcome of redistricting was in doubt, Republicans urged fairness in redistricting and promoted the impression of a thoughtful process that was sensitive to neutral criteria, minority representation, and partisan balance. However, these representations were made against the background of a now documented, but then secret, strategy of "cobbling together" a map to win initial legislative approval and then changing the plan later in the unrestricted circumstances of a conference committee. Once the outcome on redistricting was no longer in doubt and Republicans were in a position to configure the final districts at will, these earlier "priorities" were forgotten. Instead of being compact and based on recognized communities of interest, the districts of the final plan were misshapen, intertwined, and elongated in an effort to maximize Republican voting strength and privileges at the cost of election opportunities for Democrats, independents, and minority and rural Texans. The plan was as partisan as the law was thought to allow.

I am not claiming that the Democrats might not have done the same thing if given such an extraordinary opportunity to meticulously design a congressional plan in secret during the final stages of a long process. I do not know. My objection is that elected officials of either party should act for partisan gain in such disregard of the publicly professed interests of the state's citizens and of their own publicly announced priorities. Perhaps the American public has become so cynical that it expects hypocrisy and lies from its elected leaders at the expense of truth and the public interest. However, the possibility that we as a citizenry may resign ourselves to such conduct from elected officials does not justify it. Americans have a right to expect truth and integrity from our public officials.

The president too was guilty of hypocrisy. Whether the congressional redistricting in Texas was good or bad policy, it was never merely a state matter, as claimed by President Bush. I cannot answer whether the president played a significant direct role in the decision to proceed with the redistricting or in maintaining the determination of state officials to proceed in the face of constant Democratic opposition. However, the redistricting was done in President Bush's name, expressly for his benefit, and affirmatively supported by his closest aides. The president's effort to maintain "plausible deniability" for the 2003 redistricting was political silliness.

The events in Texas demonstrated new ways in which money can affect how government officials make decisions. The potentially illegal use of corporate funds by TRMPAC, TAB, and LEAA to affect the 2002 general election and the use of TRMPAC funds and opportunities to aid the Speaker campaign of Tom Craddick have understandably attracted the most public attention. However, other and perhaps even more significant uses of money were apparent in the Republican 2002 primary, when these organizations controlled who would be the Republican candidate, and at the end of the redistricting process in 2003, when major Republican donors helped persuade reluctant Republican senators to support the most aggressively partisan plan possible. As Senator Ratliff recalled being told by one of these TRMPAC donors: "Redistricting is not *an* issue, it is *the* issue."

The impact of these wealthy donors and party activists comes both from the importance of their contributions to selected candidates and from Republican officeholders' fear that a failure to follow the donors' lead on important issues, such as redistricting, will mean a well-funded opponent in the Republican primary. Even Dewhurst with his personal fortune was not immune to these pressures. These major donors and party activists helped enforce discipline within the Republican Party and furthered their own ideological goals through the fear of retribution. Redistricting was not, of course, their only issue, but the 2003 redistricting in Texas showed how such donors, and their money, can affect policy issues behind the scenes and beyond those in which they have a known business interest.

The 2003 redistricting also demonstrated how the redistricting process can be co-opted and controlled to allow a few powerful persons to carefully engineer congressional district lines for immediate and long-term partisan and personal advantage. Much has been written about a need to create competitive districts in which voters choose the lawmaker, rather than districts drawn to allow a lawmaker to effectively choose his or her voters. In 2001, Congressman DeLay publicly was an advocate for such "competitive districts." In 2003, however, he did all that he could to destroy them.

The final redistricting plan makes it possible for a small group of like-minded staunch Republicans to control the primary and, ultimately, the general elections. The 2003 redistricting plan resulted in the election of five freshmen Republicans, all beholden to the same political and financial interests and personalities who made their victories possible; they have voted in lockstep with the priorities of the national party. The redistricting plan adopted in 2003 virtually ensures their reelection for the foreseeable future. So a subset of Republican voters (who are overwhelmingly Anglo) is poised to effectively control twenty-one or twenty-two of the state's thirty-two congressional districts, even though they constitute only a subset of a minority of the Texas population. This result is contrary to the best interest of all Texans.

Finally, the events of 2003 are tragic because they show how readily elected officials may abuse government power for personal or partisan benefit. On one level the spasmodic actions of the Republican leadership on May 12–13, 2003, in their effort to find and return the absent House Democrats were comical. At a more meaningful level, however, the readiness with which the Speaker of the Texas House and the chief assistants (chief of staff and legal counsel) to the arguably most powerful man in Congress (majority leader Tom DeLay) called on state and federal officials and agencies to help in a purely partisan war game is alarming. On this occasion, Americans were lucky that many of the federal officials said no to these entreaties—or called them "wacko"—from powerful people. There is no assurance that future efforts will be similarly rebuffed if partisanship becomes more important than integrity among government actors.

Given the apparent readiness of these officials to call on state and federal agencies for partisan assistance, it is unlikely that these few disclosed contacts were the only times when these or other officials have made such requests. However, no politicizing of any federal agency is as consequential as what has occurred in the Voting Section of the Department of Justice. This section has historically been an independent and generally active voice for minority voting rights under both Republican and Democratic presidents. The section's past effectiveness has made it a target for conservatives, who saw it as run by a professional staff of "liberal bureaucrats" biased in favor of minority voters—thus, in the eyes of these critics, of Democratic interests. The current administration has set out to destroy the historic independence of the Voting Section and to weed out these long-term professional staffers. Control of critical decisions has increasingly been entrusted to partisan appointees. Internal hiring policies have been changed to allow the partisan appointees to control hiring; over time, the professional staff will consist of persons who embody the same partisan and conservative ideological values. The changes in personnel and policy are substantial and long-term. The effects reach beyond the Voting Rights Act to other election laws of broader application, such as the Help America Vote Act. The danger to our democracy is very real. Our nation's voting laws are essential to maintaining the foundation of a free society. Politics should have no role in the enforcement or implementation of those laws. The outcome in Texas provides a frightening glimpse inside a Department of Justice that has lost its way because of partisanship.

In four months in 1787, representatives in Philadelphia were able through persuasion and compromise to fashion a constitution for a nation. In five months in 2003, the congressmen and state lawmakers of Texas could do no more than draw wasteful and mutable lines in the sand.

Afterword

The story of the Texas redistricting continued in 2006. Several significant developments occurred after this book was in production.

The Supreme Court Rules in *LULAC v. Perry*

In 2004, in *Vieth v. Jubelirer* (a redistricting case from Pennsylvania), the United States Supreme Court split over the justiciability of claims that a redistricting plan could be unconstitutional for being too partisan. The Texas case presented the Court (and its new members, Chief Justice Roberts and Justice Alito) with an opportunity to again consider the justiciability of a partisan gerrymandering claim.

The unique legal aspect of the Texas redistricting was that the new plan was adopted "mid-decade" to replace an existing valid redistricting plan drawn by a federal district court in 2001. No prior reported federal or state redistricting decision had ever dealt with such a circumstance. The challengers to the plan attempted to take advantage of this aspect of the Texas redistricting. Democrats urged that it was wrong for the Republican-controlled Texas Legislature to replace an existing valid redistricting plan solely for partisan reasons. Other challengers urged that the Texas redistricting violated the constitutional mandate for districts of equal population because the Texas Legislature used inaccurate, outdated census data to replace a valid existing redistricting plan without state rather than partisan justification for doing so. Minority advocacy organizations, such as the G.I. Forum and LULAC, challenged the Texas redistricting plan as violative of Section 2 of the Voting Rights Act.

The Texas redistricting case *LULAC v. Perry* was argued before the United States Supreme Court on March 1, 2006. The Court expanded the time for oral argument to two full hours. The argument did not go well for the challengers. Texas Solicitor General Ted Cruz was excellent in defense of the redistricting. The Justices asked him few questions. Justices acknowledged being impressed with the state's argument that the redistricting was justified by the Republican desire to overcome the effects of prior Democratic gerrymanders. By contrast, the attorney for the Democrats (Paul Smith of the Washington based law firm, Jenner and Block) was beset from the beginning by questions from the Justices. Smith was reprising his role as the Democrat's attorney from *Vieth*. Most of his forty minute dialogue with the Justices in the Texas case seemed at times to be merely a continuation of dialogue on the earlier case that Smith had lost. Smith spent less than a minute at the end of his rebuttal on the equal population/mid-decade issue (which ironically the attorney general of Texas had privately acknowledged beforehand was the only issue that the state feared). Democrats left the Supreme Court chamber disappointed and depressed about their chances of success.

The Supreme Court Ruling [1]

On June 28, 2006, a divided Supreme Court upheld the redistricting plan statewide, but found that Texas had violated Section 2 of the Voting Rights Act by reducing the opportunity of Hispanic voters to elect the candidate of their choice in District 23. The Justices split on the various legal issues with six different opinions stretching over 130 pages.[2] As expected, it was Justice Kennedy who was the deciding vote and the author of the Court's opinion. The justices again agreed to disagree on the justiciability of the partisan gerrymandering claim, leaving that constitutional issue hanging, but with the state winning on the facts in this case. At least seven of the justices rejected the argument that the redistricting plan violated the one person, one vote mandate of the Constitution, finding that the Court in the past had repeatedly held that a legislative body can replace a court plan (such as the one drawn in Texas in 2001). By 5-4, however, the Court concluded that the changes to District 23 curtailed the emerging political power of a Hispanic majority in the district and that "In sum, appellants have established that Latinos could have had an opportunity district in District 23 (to elect the candidate of their choice) had its lines not been altered and that they do not have one now."[3]

This author joined with Professor Scot Powe, a colleague at the University of Texas School of Law, in July 2006, in a short article that was critical of Justice Kennedy's Court opinion.[4] The thrust of the criticism was that Justice Kennedy and the Court made a grave error by rejecting what we believed was a

clean standard and a clean set of facts for restricting the ability of state and local legislative bodies to engage in wasteful, acrimonious and unnecessary "rolling redistricting" for partisan or special interests.[5] We would like to believe that
one day the Justices will regret their decision. In the meantime, the door has
been opened by the Supreme Court for mid-decade redistricting by state and
local governments nationwide.[6]

The Political Implications of the Supreme Court Decision

The final 2003 redistricting plan was a partisan gerrymandering masterpiece.
Only three of the ten Democratic incumbents survived as Democrats after the
2004 election. Two of these three won by running in neighboring Hispanic
majority districts (an action which Republicans attacked as effectively denying
Hispanic voters an opportunity to elect the candidate of their choice). The
effect of the redistricting plan was to immediately replace six Democratic congressmen with Republicans, to leave a seventh Democrat fighting a continuing
battle for survival in a heavily Republican district, and to assure the continued
election of a Republican in an endangered eighth district. Altogether, the plan
changed the probable partisan outcomes in eight districts to favor Republicans.
The Republican success in Texas was felt by the nation as a whole.[7]

On the day after the Supreme Court decision in *LULAC* was announced,
the district court in Texas ordered the parties to submit proposed remedial
plans and responses in July for a hearing on August 3rd. The court sensed
correctly that the governor and legislature had no intention to meet in special
session to draw a plan.

Fourteen proposed remedial plans were submitted by July 14th. Although
the object was to address the Voting Rights Act violation, the significant differences in the plans were political. Political game-playing came front and center.
The key issues among the plans were (1) whether Webb County would be
in District 23 (pairing Bonilla and Cuellar) or wholly in District 28 (avoiding a pairing), and (2) whether a district would be drawn including part of
Travis County that Democratic incumbent Lloyd Doggett might win.[8] All of
the plans presented the court with an opportunity to create at least seven districts statewide (including the Hispanic majority district remaining in Harris
County) with Hispanic voting majorities.

The district court drew its own remedial plan.[9] Under an obligation to affect as few districts as possible, the court began by placing all of Webb County
in District 28 and moving counterclockwise to reconfigure four other districts
(Districts 15, 25, 21 and 23). The plan left incumbent Republican Henry Bonilla

at risk politically in a District 23 redrawn to restore an SSRV percentage above 54 per cent. Judge Higginbotham reminded Solicitor General Cruz during the August 3rd hearing that the voting rights violation in 2003 occurred because of the legislature's "aggressive" effort to save Bonilla, therefore it seemed appropriate that any remedy would leave Bonilla at risk of defeat.

A major loser with this outcome was Texas Attorney General Greg Abbott. His office had successfully defended the highly partisan statewide redistricting. However, in 2003, no attorney but the most gung-ho Democrat had thought that the Republican partisan gerrymander was illegal. The primary legal dispute in 2003 was over how far the redistricting could go in adversely affecting the state's minority districts. Legal counsel for both the Texas House and Senate advised against reducing Hispanic voting strength in District 23; but DeLay insisted on this result to protect Republican incumbent Bonilla. Texas Attorney General Abbott ultimately played the critical role. In October, 2003, he intervened to convince the legislative leaders to go along with DeLay's aggressive plan. Abbott personally assured Republican leaders that he could successfully defend DeLay's plan against any alleged violation of the Voting Rights Act. Abbott was wrong. DeLay and the Republicans had overreached. Abbott then compounded this mistake by proposing a highly partisan remedial map in 2006 that even the heretofore friendly district court would not accept.[10]

The political effect of the court's remedial plan as compared to the outcome in 2004 was to provide a safe seat for Democrat Doggett (District 25) based in Travis County and to create an opportunity for Democrats to win one additional congressional district (District 23) by defeating incumbent Bonilla or on Bonilla's retirement from Congress. Democrats in 2006 also appeared likely to win District 22 because of DeLay's political problems and resignation that had their origin with the 2003 redistricting.[11] Otherwise, Democrats may find it difficult to hold on to the eleven seats that they won in 2002.[12]

Other Court Decisions

The criminal proceedings arising from the 2002 election progressed slowly in 2006. District Attorney Ronnie Earle appealed the adverse ruling of the Texas appellate court on the conspiracy (for violation of the election code) indictment against Congressman DeLay. The appeal was likely to take months, leaving the money laundering charge pending without resolution. DeLay's attorneys were no longer trying to expedite proceedings.[13]

On June 29th, a state district court in Travis County threw out most of the criminal charges against the Texas Association of Businesses (TAB). District

Judge Mike Lynch ruled that the organization's ads in 2002 were not "express advocacy" and thus did not constitute a violation of the state law ban on corporate contributions in an election campaign. This dismissal won for TAB by Austin lawyer Roy Minton was another indication of the prowess of Minton (a Democrat) in working within the Travis County judicial system to win victories for his Republican clients. He earlier had successfully avoided indictments for Speaker Tom Craddick and TAB President Bill Hammond.[14] In dismissing most of the charges against TAB, Judge Lynch called some of the organization's ads "patently offensive," but found that they did not expressly advocate the election or defeat of candidates. He described the Texas Election Code as "an archaic, cumbersome, confusing, poorly written document in need of serious legislative overhaul." This ruling does not apply directly to the civil or criminal proceedings against Texans for a Republican Majority (TRMPAC) or Tom DeLay and his associates. Moreover, TAB was better positioned than these defendants to make use of the "express advocacy" defense. However, DeLay's attorney Dick DeGuerin hailed Judge Lynch's decision as strengthening his client's argument that the election code provisions are "unconstitutionally vague." The remaining charges against TAB concerned whether TAB or its officers effectively contributed corporate funds to the organization's PAC by paying expenses for the PAC or by spending time on behalf of the PAC.

Tom DeLay's Farewell

DeLay's final day in Congress was Monday, June 12, 2006. Four days earlier he had given his farewell address on the House floor before a packed house chamber. Democrats tried unsuccessfully to prevent DeLay from making his final remarks before the full House, but DeLay was not to be denied.[15]

In his farewell address, DeLay praised partisanship and conservatism, while attacking liberalism and compromise.[16] He saw partisanship as a sign of a democracy's "health and strength." He said, "You show me a nation without partisanship, and I'll show you a tyranny." He credited conservatism with furthering "human freedom and human dignity" through: lower taxes; welfare reform; an opposition to abortion, cloning, and euthanasia; and a foreign policy supporting the spread of democracy in the world. Democrats hissed and, at one point, most of the fifty who had stayed in the House walked out.

DeLay's farewell address was full of self-laudatory bravado. He portrayed himself as a principled partisan fighting for conservative values. DeLay said, "It is not the principled partisan, however obnoxious he may seem to his opponents, who degrades our public debates, but the preening, self-styled statesman who elevates compromise to a first-principle. For true statesmen, Mr. Speaker, are not defined by what they compromise, but what they don't compromise." "Here on this floor, I have thrown or caught spears of every sort . . . [for legislation] that I believed in my heart would protect human freedom and defend human dignity." "I have done so at all times honorably and honestly. . . ." "For twenty-two years, I have served as best I could. In this House I found my life's calling and my soul's Savior." DeLay also called attention to his personal efforts (and those of his wife, Christine) on behalf of foster children.

DeLay's farewell address was characterized by some as unconventional because it was confrontational rather than humble, and because it praised the value of partisanship instead of cooperation.[17] However, as with the whole story of the Texas redistricting, it too seemed tragic and hollow. DeLay had been lauded by his Republican colleagues. He had been feted at a French restaurant in Washington and given a standing ovation during a luncheon on June 7th. Many Republicans had publicly lamented DeLay's departure.[18] Nevertheless, relief at his departure was almost palpable among many Republicans who feared for their own chances for reelection in 2006 if DeLay remained in Congress and Democrats could continue to hammer publicly on DeLay and his claimed misdeeds.

The figure alone at the microphone on June 8th seemed to me to be an insecure and pitiable figure. DeLay tried to appear fearless in the face of his opponents, unbothered by his personal setbacks and sudden loss of power and prestige. He tried to find a meaningful, worthwhile legacy as he prepared to depart from the institution (the United States House of Representatives) in which only months earlier he had been so powerful. DeLay was proud of his uncompromising service in the past to the Republican Party and to his concept of "conservatism." However, despite evoking the images of Washington, Lincoln,[19] and Reagan in his farewell address, DeLay's search for a positive legacy for himself was fruitless beyond the ranks of the Republican Party faithful. The appropriate goal of governance in this country is not the success or failure of a political party or even of a particular political ideology. It is the welfare of the American people and the American state. No single party or person always has the right answer for serving that goal. Congressman Tom DeLay's intense and ruthless pursuit of success for his adopted party and ideology (even if heartfelt) blinded him to the destructive effects of that success on the welfare of this nation, and to the negative legacy that he eventually would leave behind.

Maps, Photos, and Resources

Maps

Map 1. State of Texas

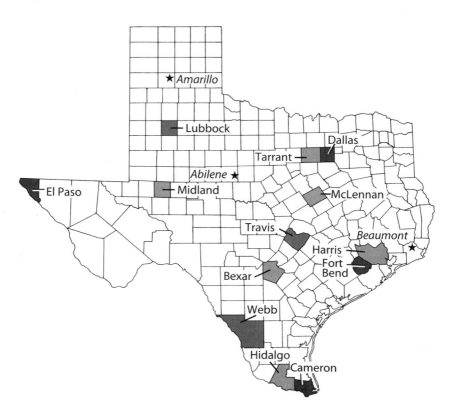

Map 2. Texas Congressional Districts in 2002 before the 2003 Redistricting

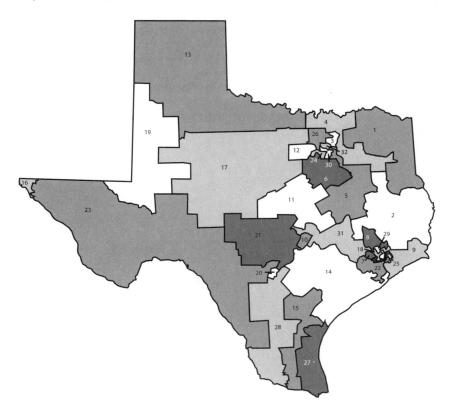

Map 3. Texas Congressional Districts after the 2003 Redistricting in 2004

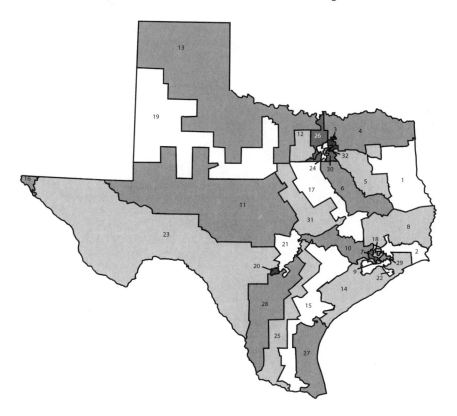

Map 4. Congressional Districts in Dallas and Tarrant Counties in 2002 before the 2003 Redistricting

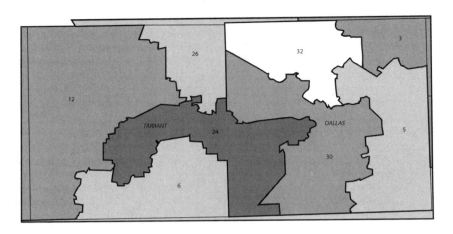

Map 5. Congressional Districts in Dallas and Tarrant Counties in 2004

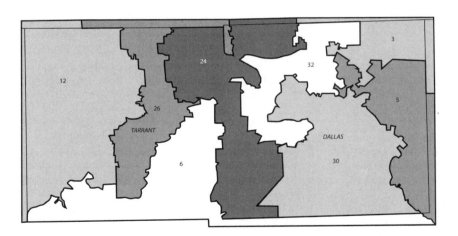

Map 6. Congressional Districts in Harris County in 2002

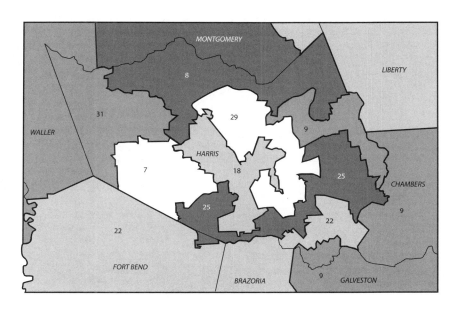

Map 7. Congressional Districts in Harris County in 2004

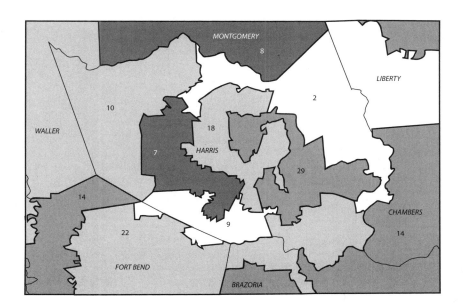

Map 8. Congressional Plan 1438C Showing Districts Redrawn by the Court in 2006

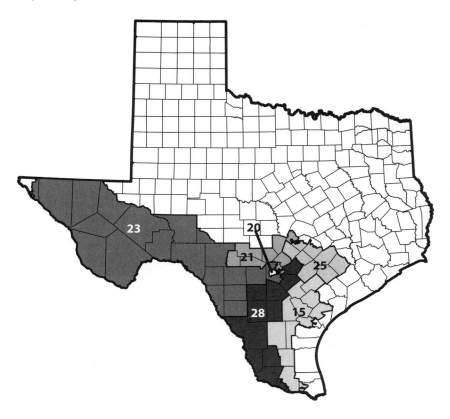

Photos

(Unless noted otherwise, courtesy of Texas Senate Media or Texas House Photography.)

The boycotting Texas House members gathered in front of the Holiday Inn in Ardmore, Oklahoma, on May 14, 2003, shortly before their return to Austin.

Speaker Tom Craddick (*left*) at the dais, May 12, 2003; in the background, the House voting board shows that a quorum is not present.

Two leaders of the House Democratic Caucus, Reps. Jim Dunnam (*left*) and Pete Gallego, on July 7, 2003, during the first special session.

State Reps. Ron Wilson (*right*) and Terry Keel conversing on the House floor on May 12, 2003, the first day of the Democratic boycott.

Republican lawmakers on the House floor, gathered around a television set on May 12, 2003, to watch news coverage of the Democratic boycott.

Democratic state representative Richard Raymond (*right*) discusses strategy in May 2003 with two W-D40s (white Democrats over 40), representatives Robbie Cook (*left*) and Craig Eiland (*rear*).

(*Left to right*) State Reps. Sylvester Turner, Harold Dutton, Helen Giddings, and Al Edwards at a news conference on May 12, 2003, explaining why they were not part of the boycott.

Lieutenant Governor David Dewhurst (*right*), making his point to Senator Robert Duncan during the first special session in 2003.

Lieutenant Governor David Dewhurst (*right*) and Senator Bill Ratliff, summer 2003.

Senators Royce West (*left*) and Robert Duncan, summer 2003.

Senators John Whitmire (*left*) and Bill Ratliff, summer 2003.

(*Left to right*) Lieutenant Governor David Dewhurst, Senator Jeff Wentworth, and Dewhurst's chief of staff, Bruce Gibson, in the Capitol.

The boycotting senators: (*left to right*) Judith Zaffirini, Eddie Lucio, Gonzalo Barrientos, Mario Gallegos (face partially hidden), Rodney Ellis, Frank Madla, and Leticia Van de Putte, at a press conference after their return to the Senate. Other senators (not pictured) participating in the boycott were Royce West, Eliot Shapleigh, Juan Hinojosa, and John Whitmire.

The public gallery of the Senate, packed with cheering supporters for the return of the ten boycotting Democratic senators, who entered the chamber together on September 15, 2003, after being gone since July 28, and were mobbed by the press.

The Republican triumph: (*left to right*) State Rep. Phil King, Speaker Tom Craddick, Senator Todd Staples, Lieutenant Governor David Dewhurst, and Governor Rick Perry at a press conference, announcing passage of the final redistricting map.

DeLay associate Jim Ellis (*left*) and TRMPAC Executive Director John Colyandro (*right*) at the Travis County Courthouse on July 12, 2003, facing criminal charges.

DeLay triumphant: Congressman Tom DeLay on the floor of the Texas Senate, October 2003, shortly after the redistricting deal was completed. Photo by Ralph Barrera, courtesy of the *Austin American-Statesman*.

DeLay prosecuted: Congressman DeLay and his wife, Christine, entering the district courtroom in Travis County, Texas, 2005. Photo by Jay Janner, courtesy of the *Austin American-Statesman*.

Answering questions amid a sea of reporters: Dick DeGuerin and other members of DeLay's defense team in front of the Travis County Courthouse. Photo by Ricardo B. Brazziell, courtesy of the *Austin American-Statesman*.

Travis County District Attorney Ronnie Earle, answering questions about the criminal investigation into alleged violations of Texas campaign-finance laws. Photo by Jay Janner, courtesy of the *Austin American-Statesman*.

Resources

This book relies on information obtained principally from the following sources:

1. Testimony, exhibits, depositions, and pleadings from *Paul Clayton v. Bill Ceverha*, (Cause No. GN-301481, Travis County District Court), the state-court civil suit by defeated state House candidates against Bill Ceverha, the treasurer of Texans for a Republican Majority. The author attended the five days of the trial in 2005.

2. Testimony, exhibits, depositions, and pleadings from the consolidated federal lawsuits challenging the lawfulness of the 2003 congressional redistricting. The case was styled *Session v. Perry* when tried in 2003. Due to a change in named plaintiffs, the case later became identified as *Henderson v. Perry*. The case number (Civil Action 2:03-CV-354 [E.D. Tex.]) has remained the same. The court's 2005 opinion appears at 300 F. Supp. 2d 756 (E.D. Tex.). At the United States Supreme Court the case is styled *LULAC v. Perry*. Of greatest value as a resource are the memoranda sent in 2003 by Jim Ellis to Congressman Tom DeLay, describing the redistricting process as it happened. All of the memoranda are grouped under a single exhibit, Plaintiff Jackson Exhibit 136.

3. Interviews in 2005 and 2006 by the author with approximately fifty persons who participated in the events covered by this book. A few of the interviews with defeated Republican primary candidates were conducted by the author's research assistant, law student Mason Hestor. The interviews are listed below. A few interviewees asked not to be identified, and therefore are not listed.

4. Official journals from the Texas House of Representatives and Texas Senate from the regular and special sessions of the 78th Texas Legislature in 2003. The major debates in the legislature were reduced to writing and included in these journals. Some oral recordings and videotapes were reviewed from 2001 and 2003. Information on the history of politics in Texas and on the state's elected officials (past and present) is generally available from multiple sources available at the Texas Legislative Reference Library.

5. Official maps and demographic and political data produced by the Texas Legislative Council during the process in 2003. These reports are available from the council. Some materials were obtained from Patsy Spaw, the secretary of the Texas Senate, regarding the history of events and procedures in that legislative body.

6. Official campaign financial reports filed with the Texas Ethics Commission, along with ethics opinions from the commission. Some of this information was obtained directly by the author. Some of it was compiled at the author's request by the nonprofit organization Texans for Public Justice, which routinely monitors and reports on campaign-finance filings.

7. Newspaper articles from the periods in question, describing the events as they occurred and quoting the participants. The articles reviewed for this book came from over twenty daily periodicals in Texas. Several of these newspapers had reporters in Austin and covered the story daily. These newspapers usually carried the same coverage of a day's events, but often with added twists or quotes not offered in the other papers. National publications also were reviewed for specific

articles that might offer a different perspective on the topics in this book. A list of the publications appears below.

8. Indictments, pleadings, and oral arguments from the state criminal proceedings against Congressman Tom DeLay, John Colyandro, and James Ellis. The author attended all of the hearings in 2005.

9. The personal experience and observations of the author, who previously served as parliamentarian of the Texas Senate and special assistant state attorney general, and has been involved in state redistricting in Texas since 1975.

Drafts of this manuscript were sent at various times during 2005 and early 2006 to many of the Republican and Democratic officials mentioned and quoted in this book for their review and comment. I am grateful to the many persons who submitted comments, recommendations, or corrections.

For online access to some of the materials, I suggest beginning at the home page of the Texas Legislative Reference Library, www.lrl.state.tx.us. Much information is available directly through the library. Links also are available from the library home page to other sources, such as the Texas Legislature Online, www.capitol.state.tx.us (for official journals, current lawmaker profiles, etc.), and the Texas Legislative Council (for redistricting maps and reports). Individual newspaper and magazine articles since 1980 are maintained by subject on a database at the Legislative Reference Library. I used this valuable database; unfortunately, it is not accessible online through the state library. These articles generally can be found through the Web sites of the individual publications. The author reviewed hard copies of the testimony, depositions, exhibits, oral arguments, and pleadings in the various civil and criminal cases, usually acquired from the court or from attorneys involved in the litigation. This information is not generally accessible online. However, many of the filings in the criminal proceedings are available at this time on the Web site of the *Austin American-Statesman* (www.austin-statesman.com/TRMPAC). Many of the pleadings for *LULAC v. Perry* at the United States Supreme Court are available at this time at www.jennerblock.com. Other potentially useful Web sites include www.tpj.org (the Web site of Texans for Public Justice) and www.defenddelay.com. Obviously the content of all of these Web sites changes over time.

Interviews

The following persons were kind enough to cooperate with me on this book and to assist me through interviews: Lieutenant Governor David Dewhurst; former lieutenant governor William P. Hobby; former congressmen Jim Turner and Nick Lampson; former state senator Bill Ratliff; State Senators Robert Duncan, Leticia Van de Putte, Juan Hinojosa, Rodney Ellis, Royce West, Jon Lindsay, John Whitmire, Jeff Wentworth, Eliot Shapleigh, and Mario Gallegos; former Speaker Pete Laney; State Representatives Jim Dunnam, Richard Raymond, Phil King, and Mike Krusee; former state representative Ron Wilson; Texas solicitor general Ted Cruz; Jim Ellis, executive director of ARMPAC; Bruce Gibson, Lieutenant Governor Dewhurst's chief of staff; Mike Toomey, Governor Perry's former chief of staff; attorneys Cris Feldman, Buck Wood, Gerald Hebert, Roy Minton, Hugh Brady, Ed Shack, and Dick DeGuerin; Nina Perales, regional council for MALDEF; Jose Garza, an attorney for LULAC; Dave Mc-Neely, former reporter for the *Austin American-Statesman;* reporters Laylan Copelin (*Austin American Statesman*) and Christy Hoppe (*Dallas Morning News*); Harvey Kronberg, editor of the *Quorum Report;* House Democratic Caucus chief of staff Dean Rindy; Senate Democratic Caucus chief of staff Harold Cook; Kirk Watson, attorney, former Austin mayor, and candidate for attorney general; Craig McDonald, director of Texans for Public Justice; political consultant Ed Martin; Matt Angle, former aide to Congressman Martin Frost; Joe Rich and Robert Kengle, formerly attorneys with the U.S. Department of Justice; Jeff Archer and David Hannah, attorneys with the Texas Legislative Council; Bob Richardson, attorney and defeated Republican Primary candidate, District 50; defeated Republican primary candidates Clayton Downing (District 58), John R. Roach, (District 67), Sue Ann Harding (District 2), Fred Moses (District 66), and W. H. Vitz (District 70); District Attorney Ronnie Earle (Travis County), Assistant District Attorney Rick Reed (Travis County), and Professor Susan Klein. A few other participants asked not to be identified.

Unfortunately, the following persons rejected or failed to respond to my requests for an interview: Congressman Tom DeLay, Speaker Tom Craddick, State Senator Todd Staples, presidential adviser Karl Rove, and first assistant attorney general Barry McBee.

Publications

Austin American-Statesman, Houston Chronicle, Dallas Morning News, Fort Worth Star-Telegram, San Antonio Express-News, El Paso Times, Waco Tribune-Herald, Beaumont Enterprise, Laredo Morning Times, Lubbock Avalanche-Journal, San Angelo Standard-Times, Amarillo Globe-News, Longview News-Journal, Corpus Christi Caller-Times, Abilene Reporter-News, Wichita Falls Times Record News, Texarkana Gazette, Valley Morning Star, Bryan–College Station Eagle, Austin Chronicle, New York Times, New Yorker, Washington Post, Washington Post Weekly, Wall Street Journal, National Journal, Texas Observer, Texas Lawyer, Newsweek, Texas Monthly, Fox News.com, Bloomberg.com, and the Associated Press.

Notes

Chapter 1

1. The legislative sponsor of the redistricting bill, Texas Republican lawmaker Phil King, explained, "If we send four, five or six more representatives to Congress from Texas, it would make it difficult for Democrats to make up the difference" (*Dallas Morning News,* Aug. 18, 2003). David Bositis, a senior analyst for the Washington-based Joint Center for Political and Economic Studies, commented, "Democrats know that without Texas, they won't be able to take back the House. They are both fighting for the same thing" (ibid.). There was also speculation that the addition of six or seven new Republicans from Texas could allow Congressman DeLay to seek the speakership.

2. *Dallas Morning News,* July 6, 2003.

3. Their fiscally conservative views were missed on issues such as deficit reduction, which passed the U.S. House by two votes on November 15, 2005. The Central America Free Trade Act (HR 3045), which passed by two votes on July 28, 2005, is another example of legislation potentially affected by the outcome in Texas, since all the Texas freshmen congressmen supported the legislation.

4. The Gasoline for America's Security Act (HR 3893), sponsored by Texas congressman Joe Barton, passed the U.S. House by two votes (212–210) on October 7, 2005, after House leadership left voting open for nearly an hour. The legislation was opposed by groups such as the Sierra Club, which described it as "yet another energy bill that fails to solve America's energy crisis" and as one that "eliminates environmental safeguards to benefit the oil and other polluting industries" by weakening the Clean Air Act. Twenty Texas Republicans voted for passage; one did not vote.

5. *Austin American-Statesman,* Aug. 21, 2003, quoting a profile of Rove by Nicholas Lemann in the *New Yorker* (May 12, 2003). See also the *Dallas Morning News,* June 30, 2003, which described Rove as "criss-crossing the nation" to boost Republicans' chances.

6. *Houston Chronicle,* Aug. 17, 2003.

7. Interview with State Senator Rodney Ellis (2005).

8. *Texas Observer,* June 6, 2003, quoting Norquist in the *Denver Post,* May 26, 2003.

9. *Fort Worth Star-Telegram,* May 7, 2003.

10. *Washington Post,* Oct. 19, 2003.

11. *Dallas Morning News,* Aug. 18, 2003.

12. This was the finding of the U.S. Census Bureau's 2004 American Community Survey. The results for Texas can be found online at http://factfinder.census.gov/servlet/ADPTable?_bm=y&-context=adp&-ds_name=ACS_2004_EST_G00_&-tree_id=304&-all_geo_types=N&-_caller=geoselect&-geo_id=04000US48&-format=&-_lang=en. According to the survey estimates, there were 10,851,505 non-Hispanic whites out of a total population of 21,912,164—or 49.5 percent of the total.

13. Many powerful lobbying firms have their offices on K Street in Washington.

Chapter 2

1. Hamilton was a Unionist and former congressman from Texas. The historical information on Republicans in the nineteenth and early twentieth century is derived from various materials maintained at the Texas Legislative Reference Library. Some of the specifics in the different sources varied as to the events surrounding Governor Edmund Davis.

2. Pease had also been elected governor in 1853 and 1855.

3. The office of lieutenant governor remained vacant from 1867 until 1874, but the position of Speaker of the House was held by a Republican from 1871 through 1873.

4. For example, at least one African American (Nathan H. Haller of Brazoria County) served in the Texas Legislature in 1893 and 1895. At least two (A. Asberry and Elias Mayes) served in 1889.

5. Information about the gains of Republicans during the twentieth century is derived from various data maintained by the Texas Legislative Reference Library.

6. *Bush v. Martin,* 224 F. Supp. 499, 506 (S.D. Tex 1963). The disparity at issue in the 1957 redistricting ran from 216,371 in rural District 4 to 951,527 in District 5 in Dallas, according to the 1960 census (ibid.). The court ordered that elections occur statewide until a new plan was enacted. The order was stayed on appeal. The court further stayed implementation on remand in 1964, giving the legislature until 1965 to come up with a valid plan.

7. Any measure of the voting strength of a political party in Texas is problematic. There is no registration of voters by political party. This particular measure of "statewide voting strength" is derived from the 2005 opinion of the federal court in *Henderson v. Perry,* which upheld the 2003 redistricting plan. However, the vote for Republican candidates as a percentage of the total vote in congressional races is far less in past elections (e.g. 1992, 2002) than for the statewide offices. This result reflects the degree of ticket splitting present in these congressional races. Republicans would argue, however, that this result merely reflects the "incumbency advantage" of the Democratic incumbent congressmen.

8. The offices are governor, lieutenant governor, attorney general, commissioner of the general land office, comptroller of public accounts, commissioner of agriculture, the members of the state railroad commission (3), the members of the state supreme court (9), the members of the state court of criminal appeals (9), and the two U.S. Senators. A thirtieth statewide elective office (state treasurer) was eliminated by constitutional amendment in 1996.

9. Interview with former lieutenant governor William P. Hobby (2006).

10. An interesting side note is that Laney's Texas Partnership PAC, formed to counter Craddick's effort, aided Democratic lawmakers, but also indirectly assisted Republican incumbents (especially those supporting Laney) by not aiding Democrats aiming to unseat incumbent Republicans (interview with former Speaker Pete Laney, 2006).

11. The author was personally involved in many of the redistricting efforts described in this section. Various materials, including news articles, from the periods in question served as resources. These materials are available at the Texas Legislative Reference Library.

12. *White v. Weiser*, 412 U.S. 783, 791 (1973).

13. Interview with Senator Bill Ratliff (2005).

14. Interview with Senator Jeff Wentworth (2005).

15. Ratliff interview.

16. *Balderas v. Perry*, Civil Action No. 6:01-CV-158, Memorandum Opinion (E.D. Tex. Nov. 14, 2001).

17. *New York Times*, Nov. 15, 2001.

18. *Session v. Perry*, Civil Action No. 2:03-CV-354 (E.D. Tex. Nov. 12, 2003); 298 F. Supp. 2d 451 (E.D. Tex. 2004).

19. *Henderson v. Perry*, Civil Action No. 2:03-CB-354, Memorandum Opinion (E.D. Tex. June 9, 2005).

Chapter 3

1. MALDEF regional counsel Nina Perales strongly disputes this claim and attributes it to "Bush campaign spin" (interview with Nina Perales, 2005).

2. U.S. Census Bureau, 2004 American Community Survey. The figures for Texas: state population—21,912,164; non-Hispanic whites—10,851,505 (49.5 percent of the total); Hispanic or Latino—7,656,151 (34.9 percent); black—2,379,453 (10.8 percent); Asian—692,360 (3.1 percent); all others made up the remaining 1.7 percent.

3. The racial and ethnic breakdown reported in the 2000 census for all Texas counties can be found at http://factfinder.census.gov/servlet/GCTTable?_bm=n&_lang=en&mt_name=DEC_2000_PL_U_GCTPL_ST2&format=ST-2&_box_head_nbr=GCT-PL&ds_name=DEC_2000_PL_U&geo_id=04000US48.

4. Multimember districts covered an area with enough population to elect several members to a legislative body. Usually the districts were countywide, so all of the voters in the county voted on all legislative members from the county. As a result, a majority that voted as a bloc within the county could always elect its favored candidates to multiple legislative seats. Similar discriminatory election systems functioned to maintain Anglo control over local offices. At-large election systems were widespread at the local level for cities, school districts, and other local governments, and allowed Anglo majorities to control these local governing boards. Many of these systems were successfully challenged in the courts in the 1970s and 1980s. So too, many county-commissioner districts were malapportioned, to the detriment of minority voters. This book makes no attempt to deal with the state's experience with at-large districts or malapportionment at the local level. Another election structure that harmed Hispanics in particular at the local level in Texas was the actual drawing of county boundaries in South Texas during the early twentieth century to segregate the predominantly Hispanic areas from the

more heavily Anglo areas. The number of counties in this region increased from seven to thirteen over the span of a few years as parts of existing counties were carved away to form new counties and voting districts.

5. As a result of the state legislature's failure to redraw congressional districts timely after being apportioned extra congressional seats in the first half of the twentieth century, Texas elected some of its congressmen at-large statewide. These at-large races were won overwhelmingly by candidates from the largest cities (Houston and Dallas), since those were the centers of population. These results partly offset the rural advantage derived from the malapportioned single-member congressional districts. Nine congressmen were elected at-large (i.e., statewide) between 1910 and 1965 in Texas (*Bush v. Martin* [1963]).

6. The House plan was struck down by the Texas courts for violating the Texas Constitution. The Senate plan was vetoed by Governor Clements.

7. The partisan battle in 1981 was similar in its intensity to the battle over congressional districts in 2003. Clements's obvious goal in 1981 was to elect more Republicans to Congress by concentrating African American voters in a single district, thereby reducing Democratic votes in surrounding districts. At least one Democratic incumbent congressman was expected to be sacrificed, even as a Democratic legislature was drawing the other district boundaries. Partisan passions ran high as the Republican governor and Democratic-controlled legislature were caught in a standoff. Initially, most African American witnesses from the Dallas–Fort Worth region supported maintaining the maximum number of Democratic districts in Dallas County. As the issue lingered before the legislature in special session, however, this support began to shift. Increasingly, African Americans in Dallas spoke out in favor of creating a congressional district in which they could elect the candidate of their choice. This apparent shift in public opinion (although of only a few of the African American witnesses at the public hearings in Austin), along with increasing concern that a plan without a predominantly African American district in Dallas County would not win Voting Rights Act preclearance, moved the legislature eventually to accept a congressional plan that included a district acceptable to Governor Clements.

8. The court never found the legislative districts to be unlawful, but found that the Democratic congressmen from Dallas had been responsive historically to their minority constituents and that since the African American voting population in the legislatively drawn district was less than 50 percent, there was no guarantee that an African American candidate would be elected from the district.

9. These two judges were intelligent, caring judicial officers who strongly supported minority civil rights throughout their judicial careers. However, in my opinion there is no good way to defend this decision except on the basis of partisan politics. Governor Clements's partisan reasons for creating the African American–dominated congressional district in Dallas were not, in my opinion, sufficient justification for the court's insistence on redrawing the legislatively adopted district.

Chapter 4

1. Much of the information in this chapter was derived from the testimony, exhibits, and depositions in *Paul Clayton et al. v. Bill Ceverha*, Cause No. GN-301481, Travis

County District Court, a civil lawsuit against Bill Ceverha as treasurer of TRMPAC. The case was tried before a state judge during the spring of 2005. The author was present throughout the five-day hearing.

2. Some of the dollar amounts given in this chapter must be treated as approximate amounts. Sources and exhibits differ slightly based on differences in record keeping. For example, some records show that TRMPAC fundraiser Warren Robold raised $603,000 in corporate funds for TRMPAC. Other records show the amount to be nearer $578,000. Similar small differences exist for other amounts shown in this chapter. Most of these small differences are unlikely ever to be reconciled. However, none of these differences are consequential for the story.

3. *Dallas Morning News,* June 29, 2003.

4. Interview with Jim Ellis (2005).

5. *Austin American-Statesman,* Nov. 25, 2001.

6. Colyandro deposition (2004).

7. In addition to receiving compensation from TRMPAC in 2002 ($65,936 in unreported corporate funds), Colyandro received additional reported monies from other sources, including the Texas Conservative Coalition ($26,020), Texans for Greg Abbott ($12,551), and Texans for Kenn George ($10,000).

8. In addition to receiving compensation from TRMPAC in 2002 ($39,162 in unreported corporate funds and $15,000 in reported funds), Brannon also received additional reported monies from other sources, including Phil King ($8,000) and Texans for Government Integrity ($30,000), the political action committee of Republican stalwart James Leininger.

9. *Dallas Morning News,* Mar. 30, 2005. The article also reports that TRMPAC lined up a breakfast for Tom Craddick in Washington with some of TRMPAC's largest corporate donors.

10. Brannon deposition (2004).

11. Interview with State Representative Phil King (2006).

12. Colyandro deposition (2004).

13. Brannon deposition (2004).

14. Interview with Bob Richardson (2005).

15. A similar meeting (perhaps with a different outcome) may also have occurred with candidate Laubenberg.

16. Interview with Clayton Downing (2005).

17. Interview with John R. Roach (2006).

18. Thomas Graphics was an operation that had ties to Republican election efforts in Texas since at least the early 1980s. Initially it was closely tied to Karl Rove's election-campaign mailing service. Subsequently it became a key source for the design of campaign mailers, the printing and mailing of such materials, and the addresses and contact information for targeted Republican voters. For the election in 2002, Thomas Graphics was where the election activities of many of the individual Republican candidate campaigns and the political committees or organizations, such as TRMPAC and TAB, converged. The full extent of these activities is unknown. For example, in 2006 it was disclosed that at the time he was serving as the executive director of TRMPAC, Colyandro was also being paid by Thomas Graphics to design mailers for at least one Republican candidate, Ben Bentzin. Were there others? I do not know. The candidates paid Thomas Graphics; Thomas Graphics paid Colyandro. Only the payment

from a candidate to Thomas Graphics as an expense of the candidate's campaign was reported.

19. *Quorum Report,* June 27, 2002.

20. Colyandro deposition (2004).

21. *Austin American-Statesman,* Mar. 10, 2005.

22. Colyandro deposition (2004).

23. A partial listing of these companies is included in Chapter Fifteen.

24. *Quorum Report,* June 27, 2002, quoting Republican strategist Royal Masset.

25. At the time of Hammond's solicitation of funds in 2002, the insurance companies were under considerable scrutiny because of high rates for home insurance and malpractice coverage. In 2003, the insurance industry was successful in convincing the Texas legislature (including the lawmakers elected in 2002 through the efforts of TAB) that it was not responsible for the higher rates.

26. *Texas Observer,* July 30, 2004.

27. Interview with Kirk Watson (2005).

28. Interview with Buck Wood (2005).

29. *Austin American-Statesman,* May 16, 2004.

30. Colyandro deposition (2004).

31. Attorney Ed Shack had explicitly advised TAB about the dangers of "coordination." In our interview in 2006, Toomey carefully avoided using the word "coordination" to describe the relationship among the organizations, because of the potential legal significance attached to the word in the context of federal campaign-finance law (e.g., the "coordination" of an ostensibly independent expenditure with a candidate could make an expenditure an unlawful contribution). Toomey left no doubt, however, that these organizations worked actively together toward a common goal—Republican control of the Texas House.

32. In 2006, it was disclosed that while serving as executive director of TRMPAC and attending these group meetings, John Colyandro was also being paid as a political consultant for Republican state-senatorial candidate Ben Bentzin. Colyandro reportedly prepared Bentzin's mailers for Thomas Graphics and shared in the fee paid by the Bentzin campaign to Thomas Graphics. Bentzin said he knew nothing about the arrangement (*Austin American-Statesman,* Jan. 8, 2006).

33. These expenses paid from corporate money were particularly problematic, even under federal law. Using corporate money to fund the solicitation of hard dollars is a clear no-no.

34. Apparently it was common for members of the DeLay family to be paid by PACs close to the lawmaker. The *New York Times* (Apr. 6, 2005) reported: "The wife and daughter of Tom DeLay . . . have been paid more than $500,000 since 2001 by Mr. DeLay's political action and campaign committees."

35. *Austin American-Statesman,* Feb. 5, 2005.

36. In 2004, Colyandro's lawyer explained that the check was blank because Colyandro wanted to make a round $200,000 donation "for party building activities at the state and federal level," but wasn't sure he would receive the necessary last-minute donations (*Austin American-Statesman,* Apr. 6, 2004).

37. Ellis said that he does not recall whether he discussed the state candidates when he met with Nelson (*New York Times,* Feb. 16, 2004).

38. *Texas Observer,* Oct. 21, 2005.

39. *Bloomberg.com,* Oct. 14, 2005 (http://www.bloomberg.com/apps/news?pid=1000 0103&sid=acqTIqpGJWG0&refer=us); *Washington Post,* July 12, 2004.

40. Some Democrats wonder whether TRMPAC was as much a vehicle for Craddick as for DeLay.

41. *Dallas Morning News,* Mar. 30, 2005.

42. This source requested to remain anonymous.

43. Maloney was later rewarded for his support of the Republican effort when his lobbying firm was awarded a contract to represent the State of Texas with lawmakers in Congress.

44. *Quorum Report,* Nov. 2002.

45. Interview with Cris Feldman (2005).

46. Cause No. GN-301481, Travis County District Court.

47. Ellis interview (2005).

48. Travis County District Attorney Ronnie Earle to State Senator Robert F. Deuell (July 30, 2004).

49. Interview with State Rep. Pete Laney (2006).

50. FEC Advisory Opinion Nos. 1995-25 and 1998-9 (May 22, 1998).

51. Texas Ethics Commission Opinion No. 132 (1993).

52. Under 11 CFR 106.5(a)(2)(i) at the time, administrative expenses were defined to include such expenses as rent, utilities, office supplies, and salaries.

53. For example, in 2002 the Texas Republican Party's federal committee ran a $12.3 million general-election effort using both individual and corporate contributions, and the Texas Democratic Party received more than $5 million from the national party, approximately $197,000 of which was treated as "restricted" funds that could be used to pay only administrative costs (*Houston Chronicle,* Apr. 25, 2004).

54. Interview with Dick DeGuerin (2006).

55. *Buckley v. Valeo,* 524 U.S. 1 (1976).

56. See, for example, *McConnell v. Federal Election Commission,* 124 S. Ct. 619 (2004).

Chapter 5

1. Associated Press, Apr. 26, 2003.

2. *Fort Worth Star-Telegram,* May 7, 2003; Associated Press, May 7, 2003.

3. *Houston Chronicle,* Feb. 16, 2003.

4. The 1991 districts in Dallas and Harris Counties were the most bizarrely shaped districts ever used in Texas elections. The shapes of these districts were the direct result of the effort by the Texas legislature to draw new minority districts in Dallas County (African American [District 30]) and Harris County (Hispanic [District 29]) after Texas had been apportioned three new congressional seats following the 1990 census. An explanation of what happened in 1991 can provide a useful tutorial on the mechanics of drawing minority districts in response to the Voting Rights Act. Both Dallas and Harris counties had sufficient minority population for the creation of the minority dis-

trict proposed for each county. Most of this minority population was concentrated in a contiguous, racially homogenous core area within each county. The total population of this core area, however, was insufficient to provide the constitutionally required population of a congressional district. To expand beyond this core minority area by taking swaths of contiguous geography would have significantly diluted the minority percentage of the proposed district's population and voters. Lawyers felt that the Department of Justice would almost certainly object under Section 5 of the Voting Rights Act to any redistricting plan that did not create in each of these counties a district (or an additional district in Harris) that had a sufficient minority percentage to allow the minority voters to elect the person of their choice. Therefore, working outward from these core concentrations of minority voters, the map drawers added census geography and population on a block-by-block basis, according to the percentage of minority persons within each individual census block, until the proposed district had the required total population with the desired (achievable) percentage of minority population. The by-product of this method of creating the minority districts in Dallas and Harris counties was the creation of truly bizarre districts, characterized by a core area and many very narrow tentacles (some only a block wide at points) extending outward to capture pockets of minority population in nearby parts of the county that were not necessarily contiguous with the core of the district. An additional complication was that this search for minority population and voters had to be primarily for either Hispanic or African American voters, depending on the district that the drawers were trying to create. Because of low levels of Hispanic voter participation (discussed in Chapter Three), the presence of predominantly African American areas in a district with even a majority of Hispanic residents could leave African Americans in a position to control election outcomes. The federal court plan in 1996 eliminated these bizarre tentacles and smoothed the boundaries of these minority districts, but kept the basic nature of the districts as minority districts intact. The Supreme Court decision in the case is *Bush v. Vera*, 517 U.S. 952 (1996).

5. By this time in 1991 it was largely futile for Democrats to search the rural areas of Texas for concentrations of dependably Democratic voters. Most of the Hispanic voters were already in the predominantly Hispanic districts in El Paso and Bexar Counties extending northward and westward from the Mexican border. The few, widely separated African American communities outside the urban areas were not large enough to provide the basis for any district. Essentially, no predominantly Anglo areas outside of Travis County could be counted upon to vote Democratic. Therefore, any districts drawn outside the urban areas (other than in heavily Hispanic areas along the Mexican border) were certain to be predominately Republican in most elections. When these rural districts from 1991 were essentially preserved in the 2001 *Balderas* court plan, the court counted twenty of thirty-two congressional districts in Texas that could be expected to vote primarily Republican.

6. Interview with State Rep. Mike Krusee (2005).

7. Interview with Bruce Gibson (2005).

8. Jim Ellis interview.

9. Ibid.

10. *Austin American-Statesman*, Aug. 21, 2003, quoting from an article by Nicholas Lemann in the *New Yorker*, May 12, 2003.

11. *Fort Worth Star-Telegram*, May 11, 2003.

12. *Dallas Morning News*, Aug. 1, 2003.

13. Ibid., Sept. 21, 2001.

14. *Houston Chronicle*, July 23, 2003.

15. Ibid.

Chapter 6

1. The judicial outcome was reached only after months of litigation in state and federal court. There were times when the outcome was not clear. Ultimately, however, the Democratic strategy in 2001 of leaving congressional redistricting to the courts played out as predicted to the Democrats' benefit.

2. This description apparently originated with U.S. Senator Phil Gramm (*Austin American-Statesman*, Aug. 25, 2002).

3. Byrd was averting an adjournment for lack of a quorum on a cloture vote on campaign-finance legislation (National Civic League, *Federal Campaign Finance: The Long and Winding Road* [2001]; www.ncl.org/publications).

4. Ellis interview (2005).

5. The absence of a calendar committee means ostensibly that any senator who can move legislation out of a substantive committee can have that legislation heard by the Senate if he or she has twenty-one votes. The legislation cannot be bottled up indefinitely by an unfavorable calendar committee.

6. The Senate uses several calendars. Legislation reported out of committee is placed at the bottom of the appropriate calendar for Senate bills, House bills, Senate resolutions, or House resolutions. Different days of the week are set aside to consider primarily Senate or House legislation. Legislation returning to the Senate as a Senate bill passed with House amendments or through a conference-committee report is not placed on the regular calendars. Such legislation takes priority, and usually can be considered without the need to suspend Senate rules, once it has been printed and timely distributed to senators.

7. The two-thirds vote requirement to take up bills out of order dates back over 100 years. The regular use of the requirement as a device of parliamentary convenience and issue management probably became common in the 1950s after the Senate's regular order of business was formalized in 1947. For over five decades, since it was first instituted by then Lieutenant Governor Ben Ramsey, the Senate has relied on this practice. Any suspension of a Senate rule requires a vote of two-thirds of the senators present (i.e., usually twenty-one of the thirty-one senators). Therefore, a senator wanting to move to suspend the rule setting the Senate order of business ordinarily must have the support of twenty-one senators and be able to show the lieutenant governor that he has the necessary votes. Also, the senator must have given timely notice of his or her intention to request a suspension to consider the legislation in question. (The Senate in 1975 began requiring senators to give notice on the prior day and printing a list of all bills on which they had given notice of an intention to suspend the rules. I was Senate parliamentarian at the time and wrote this requirement. This "intent calendar" is still used.) Once the order of business is suspended by a two-thirds vote to take up a specific bill, the bill

passes or fails based on the vote of a majority of the senators voting on the bill, just as though the bill had come up for consideration at the top of the calendar.

8. Nevertheless, there have been numerous occasions over the past decades in which bills (especially House bills on the House bill calendar) have been considered in their order on the calendar rather than by a suspension of the rules.

9. The first intentional blocker bill (although called at the time a "silly bill" that "was never going to be laid out") apparently appeared in 1949 at the behest of Lieutenant Governor Allan Shivers. Other lieutenant governors used the same practice in subsequent sessions. One bill in particular, dealing with a "County Park Beautification and Improvement Program," appeared regularly at the top of the Senate calendar through the 1990s and up through the 2004 special session. This presence of a blocker bill at the top of the appropriate Senate calendar meant that any other bill below it on that calendar could be considered only by a suspension of the Senate rule specifying that the bills be taken up in order.

10. *Austin Chronicle,* Aug. 22, 2003.

11. Interviews with Lieutenant Governor David Dewhurst (2005 and 2006).

12. Dewhurst interview, 2005.

13. Dewhurst interview, 2006.

Chapter 7

1. *Austin American-Statesman,* Dec. 12, 2002.

2. Interview with Senator Eliot Shapleigh (2006).

3. Dewhurst interview, 2006.

4. *Houston Chronicle,* Feb. 2, 2003, quoting the *Quorum Report.*

5. *Dallas Morning News,* Jan. 30, 2003; *Houston Chronicle,* Feb. 2, 2003.

6. *Waco Tribune-Herald,* June 8, 2003; interview with Mike Toomey (2006).

7. *Dallas Morning News,* Jan. 30, 2003.

8. Ibid.

9. *Austin American-Statesman,* Apr. 24, 2003.

10. *Houston Chronicle,* Feb. 10, 2003.

11. Jim Ellis interview.

12. Dewhurst interview, 2006. Senator Hinojosa later charged that Dewhurst assured him in early 2003 that he would not bring up redistricting (*McAllen Monitor,* July 30, 2003).

13. Jim Ellis interview.

14. This description of the considerations of the Republican congressmen during the spring of 2003 is taken from Ellis's memoranda at the time, describing the nature and status of the effort to achieve a consensus redistricting plan. All of Ellis's memoranda from 2003 are contained in Plaintiff Jackson Exhibit 136 from *Session v. Perry,* the lawsuit filed in 2003 to challenge the redistricting.

15. *Houston Chronicle,* Feb. 10, 2003.

16. Ibid., Feb. 16, 2003.

17. *Austin American-Statesman,* Feb. 26, 2003.

18. Associated Press, Apr. 16, 2003.

19. *Houston Chronicle,* Feb. 10, 2003.

20. Ibid.
21. Interview with Rep. Richard Raymond (2005).
22. Rep. Joe Crabb to Attorney General Abbott, Feb. 11, 2003.
23. *Houston Chronicle,* Apr. 23, 2003.
24. *Austin American-Statesman,* Apr. 24, 2003.
25. A spokesman for the attorney general told me in 2006 that he doubted whether there had been any coordination.
26. *Fort Worth Star-Telegram,* May 11, 2003; Ellis memoranda.
27. *Austin American-Statesman,* Apr. 25, 2003.
28. *Dallas Morning News,* Apr. 25, 2003.
29. Ibid.
30. Ibid., May 2, 2003.
31. Ibid., Apr. 25, 2003.
32. Ibid., Apr. 23, 2003.
33. Ibid.
34. Ibid., Apr. 25, 2003.
35. Raymond interview.
36. *Laredo Morning Times,* May 6, 2003; *Austin American-Statesman,* May 8, 2003.
37. Raymond interview.
38. Ibid.
39. *San Antonio Express-News,* May 23, 2003.
40. Raymond interview.
41. Jim Ellis interview.
42. Raymond interview.
43. *Houston Chronicle,* May 8, 2003.

Chapter 8

1. Much of the information in this chapter about the organization and execution of the walkout of Democrats in the Texas House came from a series of interviews with State Representatives Jim Dunnam and Richard Raymond in 2005, as supplemented by interviews with several other Democratic House lawmakers and Democratic Caucus staff members. The excellent articles of Jake Bernstein in the *Texas Observer* also helped document what happened at this stage of the 2003 regular session. Information about the role of the Texas attorney general's office, Congressman DeLay, and his staff in trying to locate and return the boycotting Texas lawmakers is derived from the reports submitted to the U.S. House Ethics Committee by the United States Department of Justice and the Federal Communications Commission. In addition, I talked with a spokesman for the Texas attorney general.
2. Raymond interview.
3. *Houston Chronicle,* May 14, 2003.
4. The Texas Constitution (Article III, Sec. 5) prescribes the length of the biannual regular session. State law prescribes when the session will begin and when it must end. The 2003 legislative session had to adjourn sine die by June 2, 2003.
5. Interview with Rep. Pete Laney (2005).
6. *Houston Chronicle,* May 7, 2003.

7. Ibid.

8. *Texas Observer,* June 6, 2003.

9. Interview with Rep. Jim Dunnam (2005).

10. *Texas Observer,* June 6, 2003.

11. Raymond interview.

12. *Texas Observer,* June 6, 2003.

13. Interview with Rep. Ron Wilson (2005).

14. Interview with Hugh Brady (2005).

15. *Texas Observer,* June 6, 2003.

16. Rodney Ellis interview.

17. Brady interview.

18. *Texas Observer,* June 6, 2003.

19. *Fort Worth Star-Telegram,* May 13, 2003.

20. U.S. Department of Justice, Office of the Inspector General, *An Investigation of the Department of Justice's Actions in Connection with the Search for Absent Texas Legislators* (Aug. 12, 2003). Available online at http://www.usdoj.gov/oig/special/0308a/index.htm.

21. In an interview in 2006, a spokesman for the Texas attorney general stressed that once that office had concluded that the Texas House had a right to "arrest" the absent lawmakers, it was reasonable for Barry McBee and other assistant attorneys general to seek the cooperation of other state and federal law enforcement agencies in an attempt to arrest the Democrats.

22. Justice Department, *Search for Absent Texas Legislators,* note 8.

23. Ibid., sections 6a and 6c.

24. This statement was attributed by one source to Jim Ellis (*The Hill,* May 13, 2003). DeLay said, "It is so Texas contrary" (Associated Press, May 13, 2003).

25. *Fort Worth Star-Telegram,* May 13, 2003.

26. Ibid.

27. *Dallas Morning News,* May 13, 2003.

28. Ibid.

29. *Fort Worth Star-Telegram,* May 14, 2003.

30. Ibid., May 13, 2003.

31. The information and quotations in this paragraph and the next one come from Justice Department, *Search for Absent Texas Legislators,* section 4.

32. *Fort Worth Star Telegram,* May 13, 2003.

33. *Austin American-Statesman,* May 13, 2003.

34. Ibid., May 15, 2003.

35. *Dallas Morning News,* May 13, 2003.

36. Ibid., May 14, 2003.

37. Raymond interview.

38. *Houston Chronicle,* May 14, 2003.

39. *Dallas Morning News,* May 13, 2003.

40. *Houston Chronicle,* May 14, 2003.

41. *Fort Worth Star-Telegram,* May 13, 2003.

42. *Dallas Morning News,* May 14, 2003.

43. Ibid.

44. Ibid.
45. *San Antonio Express-News,* May 14, 2003.
46. *Austin American-Statesman,* May 14, 2003.
47. *Fort Worth Star-Telegram,* May 13, 2003.
48. *Austin American-Statesman,* May 14, 2003.
49. *Fort Worth Star-Telegram,* May 14, 2003.
50. *Dallas Morning News,* May 15, 2003.
51. Ibid.
52. *Austin American-Statesman,* May 16, 2003.
53. Jim Ellis interview.
54. Gibson interview.
55. Wentworth interview.

Chapter 9

1. Lieutenant Governor Dewhurst's biographical information is available at www.lrl.state.tx.us.
2. Senator Ratliff's biographical information is available at www.lrl.state.tx.us.
3. *San Antonio Express-News,* Aug. 20, 2003. This comment was attributed to Bill Ratliff as early as 2001. He repeated it to me in one of our interviews in 2005.
4. Ratliff interview. It is probable that this statement referred at the time to state legislative as well as congressional redistricting.
5. Ibid.; *Dallas Morning News,* Mar. 7, 2002.
6. *Quorum Report,* Mar. 7, 2002; *Austin Chronicle,* Mar. 15, 2002.
7. Ratliff interview.
8. Senator Duncan's biographical information is available at www.lrl.state.tx.us.
9. *Lubbock Avalanche-Journal,* Aug. 3, 2003.
10. *Houston Chronicle,* June 24, 2003.
11. *Lubbock Avalanche-Journal,* Sept. 3, 2003.
12. Interview with Senator Robert Duncan (2005).
13. Ibid.
14. *Fort Worth Star-Telegram,* May 18, 2003.
15. *Dallas Morning News,* May 31, 2003; *Congress Daily,* June 19, 2003.
16. *Dallas Morning News,* May 31, 2003.
17. Redistricting Recap Memorandum from Jim Ellis to Congressman Tom DeLay (Oct. 5, 2003).
18. Jim Ellis interview.
19. Ibid.
20. *Dallas Morning News,* June 20, 2003.
21. Ibid., Aug. 20, 2003; Ratliff interview.
22. Ratliff interview.
23. *Dallas Morning News,* June 20, 2003.
24. Ibid., June 19, 2003. In 1948, Duval County was the source of controversial last-minute (likely fraudulent) votes that first elected Lyndon Baines Johnson to the U.S.

Senate. Current election practices in Duval County are not tainted by claims of illegality, but a reference to "Duval County" remains synonymous in Texas with electoral fraud.

25. *Houston Chronicle*, June 24, 2003.

26. Duncan interview.

27. *Laredo Morning Times*, June 27, 2003; *Austin American-Statesman*, June 27, 2003.

28. *Houston Chronicle*, June 29, 2003; *Austin American-Statesman*, June 29, 2003.

29. *Austin American-Statesman*, June 27, 2003.

30. Ibid., July 2, 2003.

31. *Houston Chronicle*, June 29, 2003; *Austin American-Statesman*, July 7, 2003.

32. *Laredo Morning Times*, July 3, 2003.

33. Duncan interview.

34. Ibid.

35. *Dallas Morning News*, June 19, 2003.

36. *Austin American-Statesman*, June 27, 2003.

37. One of the attorneys raising concerns about the prior plan was Legislative Council attorney Jeff Archer. The apparent concern was about the plan's breakup of the 24th District in Dallas–Fort Worth. This issue would pervade discussions and negotiations throughout the redistricting process.

38. *Austin American-Statesman*, July 3, 2003.

39. Ibid., July 4, 2003.

40. King interview.

41. Krusee interview; *Austin American-Statesman*, July 7, 2003.

42. *Texas House Journal*, July 7, 2003; *Houston Chronicle*, July 8, 2003; *Austin American-Statesman*, July 8, 2003.

43. King interview; *Houston Chronicle*, July 8, 2003; *Abilene Reporter-News*, July 9, 2003. King said that he did not understand at the time why fellow lawyer, Democrat Steven Wolens, told him that he was surprised at the openness of the Republicans' acknowledgment that they were acting solely for partisan reasons. King said that in view of the Democrats' court challenge, he now understood Wolens's comment. However, King said that Republican lawyers were advising him and other Republican leaders that the safest legal course was to emphasize that the redistricting was only for partisan reasons (King interview).

44. *House Journal*, July 7, 2003.

45. *Houston Chronicle*, July 13, 2003.

46. *Austin American-Statesman*, July 8, 2003.

47. Dewhurst interview, 2005.

48. Interestingly, a blocker bill sat atop the House Bill calendar in the Senate because the House passed several other bills in addition to the redistricting bill (HB 3). There would have been no blocker bill on the House Bill calendar in the Senate if the House had passed only HB 3.

49. Memorandum from Jim Ellis to Congressman Tom DeLay (June 15, 2003); Jim Ellis interview.

50. *Dallas Morning News*, June 20, 2003.

51. Ibid.

52. Rodney Ellis interview.

53. *Texas Observer*, Nov. 22, 2002.

54. *Fort Worth Star-Telegram,* May 11, 2003.
55. Memorandum from Jim Ellis to Congressman Tom DeLay (Feb. 5, 2003).
56. *Texas Observer* (July 2003).
57. *Houston Chronicle,* July 8, 2003.
58. Ibid., July 9, 2003.
59. *Dallas Morning News,* July 9, 2003.
60. Ibid., July 11, 2003.
61. *Houston Chronicle,* July 9, 2003.
62. *Wichita Falls Times Record News,* July 15, 2003.
63. *Dallas Morning News,* July 9, 2003.
64. Ibid.
65. *Austin American-Statesman,* July 9, 2003.
66. *Houston Chronicle,* July 13, 2003.
67. Ibid.
68. Rodney Ellis interview.
69. Dewhurst said that supporters of Senator Gallegos had earlier approached him about redrawing District 29 in Harris County to make it more likely that Gallegos could win a congressional seat (Dewhurst interview, 2006).
70. *Texarkana Gazette,* July 11, 2003.
71. Dewhurst interview, 2006.
72. Senator Ratliff would not divulge to me the names of these other three senators. It has been possible to confirm their names through other sources. However, in accordance with Ratliff's promise of anonymity for these senators, I will not give their names in this book.
73. *Dallas Morning News,* July 16, 2003.
74. Ratliff interview.
75. Interview with John Whitmire, 2005.
76. Ratliff interview.
77. *Austin American-Statesman,* July 15, 2003.
78. Ratliff interview.
79. *Austin American-Statesman,* July 15, 2003.
80. Ibid.; *Dallas Morning News,* July 15, 2003.
81. Dewhurst interview, 2005; *Dallas Morning News,* July 15, 2003; *Wichita Falls Time Record News,* July 15, 2003.
82. *Dallas Morning News,* July 15, 2003.
83. Ibid., July 16, 2003.
84. *Austin American-Statesman,* July 16, 2003.
85. *Dallas Morning News,* July 15, 2003.
86. Interview with Senator Royce West (2005).
87. Ratliff interview.
88. *Austin American-Statesman,* July 16, 2003. Armbrister changed his position on July 23. After considering the lieutenant governor's explanation of prior precedent, Armbrister concluded that not having blocker legislation in a special session was not changing the rules. He explained that he would not lead a boycott because there was no way to win, "How do you win if everybody walks? You can't be gone 60 days; you can't be gone 180 days" (*Austin American-Statesman,* July 24, 2003).

89. *Austin American-Statesman,* July 18, 2003; *Bryan–College Station Eagle,* July 18, 2003; *Dallas Morning News,* July 18, 2003.

90. Dewhurst has known Ms. Hughes for many years. He insists that in the meeting in July with her "there was no discussion of the President or Rove" (Dewhurst interview, 2006). Democrats generally see Hughes's visit as key and believe that Dewhurst changed his position on the two-thirds requirement in direct response to her request or recommendation (see, for example, Gerald Hebert's interview with me).

91. *Austin American-Statesman,* July 18, 2003.

92. Dewhurst interview, 2005.

93. *Austin American-Statesman,* July 17, 2003. The plans were drawn by Dewhurst aides, the father-son team of Bob Davis and Doug Davis. Allegedly, Attorney General Abbott and two of his aides had reviewed the plans for possible legal problems before Harris was to present them. Both the office of the attorney general and the lieutenant governor emphasized later, however, that the attorney general's office was not responsible for drawing the maps. The maps were seen as legally vulnerable because they eliminated the majority-minority in District 24 and weaken Hispanic strength in District 23 (*Houston Chronicle,* July 17, 2003).

94. *Lubbock Avalanche-Journal,* July 17, 2003. The attorney general's office was quick to deny that it had drawn any maps (ibid.).

95. *Austin American-Statesman,* July 17, 2003; *Houston Chronicle,* July 17, 2003.

96. *Austin American-Statesman,* July 18, 2003.

97. Among the significant differences between the Staples map and the House version: (1) the division of Hidalgo County into three districts, with a new district running from southeast of Travis County to the Rio Grande Valley to create a new Hispanic-opportunity district while splitting Travis County among three districts; (2) the addition of Republican areas to District 23 and the elimination of heavily Hispanic Webb County from it in an attempt to help Republican congressman Henry Bonilla; (3) the splintering of the majority-minority district in Dallas (District 24) into four pieces to pair Congressman Frost with Congressman Barton in a probable Republican district while pushing more Democrats into the predominately African American District 30 and other Republican districts; (4) keeping Midland and Lubbock in the same congressional district rather than creating a Midland-dominated district, as sought by Craddick; and (5) increasing the African American voting age population in the renumbered 25th (now 9th) District in Houston from 22 percent to 36 percent while leaving the Anglo Democratic incumbent (Chris Bell) paired in a nearby heavily Republican district. The plan paired two other sets of incumbents: Democrats Gene Green and Nick Lampson in a probable Republican district and Democrats Chet Edwards and Jim Turner in a probable Republican district. The plan would have essentially the same effect as the plan approved in April by the Republican congressmen and a very similar effect as the final plan adopted in October, except for the treatment of the Midland-Lubbock districts in West Texas.

98. *Austin American-Statesman,* July 18, 2003.

99. The two districts were a new majority-Hispanic district running from southeast Travis County to the Rio Grande Valley and a Houston district with an increased percentage of African American voters. However, it also splintered District 24 in Dallas–Forth Worth and greatly reduced Hispanic voting strength in District 23.

100. *McAllen Monitor,* July 17, 2003.

101. *Dallas Morning News,* July 9, 2003.

102. *Austin American-Statesman,* July 17, 2003.

103. *McAllen Monitor,* July 18, 2003.

104. *Dallas Morning News,* July 19, 2003.

105. Interviews with Dewhurst (2005), Whitmire, State Senator Leticia Van de Putte (2005), and West.

106. *Austin American-Statesman,* July 19, 2003.

107. Ibid.

108. Wentworth interview.

109. *Houston Chronicle,* July 19, 2003.

110. Wentworth interview; Van de Putte interview.

111. For example, *Dallas Morning News,* July 21, 2003.

112. Dewhurst specifically pointed to what he called "the Bullock precedent." In 1992 the Texas legislature met in special session to adopt a senatorial redistricting plan in response to a federal district court's plan for the Senate that was anticipated to favor Republicans. The only subject in the 1992 special session was redistricting. Dewhurst proposed a similar approach in a second special session in 2003. The Senate redistricting bill in 1992 was considered without the necessity of a two-thirds vote; it passed eighteen to twelve. The federal court, however, never let the legislative plan go into effect. The 1992 election for the Senate was held using the court's plan, and four seats changed hands from Democrat to Republican (*Dallas Morning News,* July 19, 2003).

113. It is impossible to say with certainty what such a compromise would have looked like. From the Senate view, such a plan would have left Frost and Stenholm in position to win reelection, the districts in northeast Texas largely unchanged, and Republican Bonilla's District 23 intact, with a Hispanic voting majority. However, whatever DeLay's willingness to accept such a compromise, any plan without a "Midland district" was certain to face Speaker Craddick's opposition.

114. Dewhurst interview, 2006.

115. Van de Putte interview.

116. *Dallas Morning News,* July 24, 2003.

117. *Houston Chronicle,* July 22, 2003.

118. *Austin American-Statesman,* July 26, 2003.

119. *Amarillo Globe-News,* July 20, 2003.

120. *Houston Chronicle,* Aug. 3, 2003.

121. *Dallas Morning News,* Aug. 4, 2003.

122. Laney interview.

123. Patricia Kilday Hart, "The Unkindest Cut," *Texas Monthly,* Oct. 2003.

124. Dewhurst confirmed this observation in an interview in 2006, but also said that he genuinely believed that fairness demanded redrawing the state's congressional districts to give Republicans a majority.

Chapter 10

1. Van de Putte interview.

2. *Dallas Morning News,* July 25, 2003.

3. *Austin American-Statesman,* July 24, 2003.

4. *Houston Chronicle,* July 25, 2003.

5. Van de Putte interview.

6. Interview with Harold Cook (2005).

7. The events on the morning of July 28 were discussed with me by Dewhurst and five of the Democratic senators present at the meeting.

8. Whitmire interview.

9. Former lieutenant governor Bill Hobby pointed out to me in 2006 that a call on the Senate would not have been in order if a quorum had been present as a result of the presence of Democrats in the Senate when it convened.

10. Whitmire interview.

11. *Austin American-Statesman,* July 29, 2003.

12. Ibid; *Dallas Morning News,* July 29, 2003.

13. *Austin American-Statesman,* July 30, 2003.

14. Ibid.

15. *Houston Chronicle,* July 29, 2003; *Austin American-Statesman,* July 29, 2003. Ironically, this dispute between the Democrats and Dewhurst, Craddick, and Perry had intra–Republican Party implications because the state comptroller, Republican Carole Keeton Strayhorn, had urged several weeks earlier (to the apparent unconcern on the part of her fellow state officials) that the legislature needed to act in order to be sure that the federal funds could be spent on health and human services. Strayhorn was known to be a potential opponent of Perry for the governorship. A writer for the *Fort Worth Star-Telegram* (July 31, 2003) accused both Perry and the Democrats of not telling the truth about the effect of the boycott on state finances.

16. *Dallas Morning News,* Aug. 7, 2003.

17. Dewhurst interview, 2006.

18. Much of the information about the events in Albuquerque was obtained through interviews with six of the senators and several staff members who were present.

19. *Houston Chronicle,* July 29, 2003.

20. "Governor Bill Richardson Statement Regarding Texas Senators' Arrival in New Mexico," July 28, 2003; available online at www.governor.state.nm.us/press/2003/july/072803_2.pdf.

21. *El Paso Times,* July 30, 2003.

22. *Fort Worth Star-Telegram,* July 30, 2003.

23. Kilday, "Unkindest Cut," *Texas Monthly,* Oct. 2003.

24. Whitmire interview.

25. The attorney fees totaled an estimated $300,000. Apparently these fees were paid primarily (or entirely) from funds of the Democratic congressional delegation.

26. *Dallas Morning News,* July 31, 2003.

27. Both Dewhurst and Duncan talked in their interviews about this trip. Democratic senators confirmed the events.

28. *Fort Worth Star-Telegram,* Aug. 9, 2003.

29. *Dallas Morning News,* Aug. 9, 2003.

30. *San Antonio Express-News,* Aug. 14, 2003; *Dallas Morning News,* Aug. 15, 2003.

31. MoveOn.org is a corporation functioning under Section 527 of the federal tax code. Such "527 corporations" became prominent in 2004 because they were not subject to the contribution and spending limits set by the new Bipartisan Campaign Reform Act.

32. *Dallas Morning News,* Aug. 24, 2003.

33. Ibid., Aug. 4, 2003.

34. *Houston Chronicle,* Aug. 3, 2003.

35. *Dallas Morning News,* Aug. 4, 2003.

36. *McAllen Monitor,* July 30, 2003.

37. Ibid.

38. *Corpus Christi Caller-Times,* Aug. 11, 2003.

39. Ibid.

40. Ibid.

41. *Dallas Morning News,* Aug. 18, 2003.

42. Ibid.

43. *Laredo Morning Times,* Aug. 20, 2003.

44. *Austin American-Statesman,* Aug. 6, 2003; *Dallas Morning News,* Aug. 7, 2003.

45. *Austin American-Statesman,* Aug. 7, 2003.

46. Republicans filed another action in state district court in Travis County to compel the senators to return. This lawsuit too was dismissed on August 26 when Judge Darlene Byrne determined that she lacked jurisdiction to decide the issue. Both sides claimed victory after the dismissal.

47. *San Antonio Express-News,* Aug. 15, 2003.

48. *Dallas Morning News,* Aug. 15, 2003.

49. *Austin American-Statesman,* Aug. 16, 2003.

50. Ibid.

51. John Hermann, a political science professor at Trinity University in San Antonio, said, "I see (the fines) as a political maneuver, rather than a sanction. The symbolism is unmistakable: Republicans are telling the public we won't stand for this" (*San Antonio Express-News,* Aug. 15, 2003).

52. In 2006, former lieutenant governor Bill Hobby pointed out to me that any such change in the Senate rules almost certainly would require initiation of a calendars committee to set bills for consideration. He doubted that a majority of the Senators would support such a result.

53. *Houston Chronicle,* Aug. 3, 2003.

54. Ibid.

55. Wentworth interview.

56. *Dallas Morning News,* Sept. 6, 2003; *Houston Chronicle,* Sept. 10, 2003.

57. *Dallas Morning News,* Aug. 27, 2003.

58. *Wichita Falls Times Record News,* Aug. 12, 2003.

59. *El Paso Times,* July 30, 2003; *Dallas Morning News,* July 30, 2003.

60. *McAllen Monitor,* July 30, 2003.

61. Ibid.

62. *Fort Worth Star-Telegram,* July 29, 2003.

63. *Houston Chronicle,* July 31, 2003.

64. *Lubbock Avalanche-Journal,* July 30, 2003 (calling Perry's actions "disappointing" and asking, "Has he been promised a cabinet position in President Bush's administration if he presses forward?"); *Waco Tribune-Herald,* July 30, 2003 (suggesting that the governor was a profile in hypocrisy).

65. *Austin American-Statesman,* Aug. 28, 2003.

66. Ibid.

67. Whitmire interview.

68. *Austin American-Statesman,* Sept. 12, 2003.

69. Ibid.

70. *Barrientos v. Texas,* 290 F. Supp. 2d 740 (S.D. Tex. 2003); affirmed, 541 U.S. 984 (2004).

71. *Dallas Morning News,* Aug. 6, 2003.

72. *Houston Chronicle,* July 29, 2003.

73. Ibid., Aug. 16, 2003.

74. *San Antonio Express-News,* Aug. 17, 2003.

75. *Austin American-Statesman,* Aug. 14, 2003.

76. *Houston Chronicle,* Aug. 16, 2003; *San Antonio Express-News,* Aug. 17, 2003.

77. All but one of the Democrats represented districts that are at least 61 percent minority; only Gonzalo Barrientos from Travis did not. All the Republicans senators were from districts with a minority population of 40 percent or less. Eleven Republicans served from districts with a minority population of less than 26 percent (Estes had the least with 16 percent).

78. Van de Putte interview.

79. *San Antonio Express-News,* Aug. 17, 2003.

80. Ibid.

81. *Dallas Morning News,* Aug. 11, 2003.

82. Ibid.

83. *Amarillo Globe-News,* Aug. 12, 2003.

84. *Dallas Morning News,* Aug. 12, 2003.

85. Jim Ellis interview.

86. *Houston Chronicle,* July 18, 2003.

87. *Fort Worth Star-Telegram,* Aug. 5, 2003.

88. *Dallas Morning News,* July 26, 2003.

89. Ibid.

90. *Austin American-Statesman,* Aug. 10, 2003.

91. *Corpus Christi Caller-Times,* Aug. 26, 2003.

92. Ibid.

93. *Houston Chronicle,* Aug. 25, 2003.

94. Ibid., Aug. 17, 2003.

95. *San Antonio Express-News,* Aug. 17, 2003.

96. *Abilene Reporter-News,* Aug. 22, 2003.

97. *Dallas Morning News,* Aug. 23, 2003.

98. Ibid.

99. *Austin American-Statesman,* Aug. 27, 2003.

100. *Houston Chronicle,* Sept. 1, 2003.

101. *Dallas Morning News,* Aug. 28, 2003.

102. *Houston Chronicle,* Sept. 1, 2003.

103. *Dallas Morning News,* Aug. 28, 2003.

104. *Houston Chronicle,* Aug. 28, 2003.

105. Ibid.

106. Whitmire interview. Whitmire denied to me that he had received any pressure from his law firm to end the boycott. He also specifically denied speaking with his former law partner Harriet Miers, now counsel to President Bush.

107. *Lubbock Avalanche-Journal,* Sept. 3, 2003.

108. Van de Putte interview.

Chapter 11

1. *Austin American-Statesman,* Sept. 4, 2003.

2. Lieberman called the Texas redistricting attempt "an arrogance of power that goes all the way up to the Oval Office" (Associated Press, Sept. 4, 2003).

3. Senator Ellis said that MoveOn.org became involved after he contacted the group's cofounder, which he had done at the suggestion of Mark Strama, a former Ellis staffer who in 2004 won election to the Texas House of Representatives.

4. *Dallas Morning News,* Sept. 8, 2003.

5. *Austin American-Statesman,* Sept. 4, 2003.

6. Ibid.

7. *Dallas Morning News,* Sept. 5, 2003.

8. *Houston Chronicle,* Oct. 8, 2003; *Dallas Morning News,* Oct. 8, 2003.

9. *Austin American-Statesman,* Sept. 4, 2003.

10. *Dallas Morning News,* Sept. 6, 2003.

11. *Houston Chronicle,* Sept. 4, 2003.

12. *Dallas Morning News,* Sept. 6, 2003.

13. Whitmire interview; *Houston Chronicle,* Aug. 7, 2003.

14. *Austin American-Statesman,* Sept. 6, 2003.

15. *Houston Chronicle,* Sept. 4, 2003.

16. *Dallas Morning News,* Sept. 6, 2003.

17. Whitmire interview.

18. *Austin American-Statesman,* Sept. 6, 2003.

19. *Dallas Morning News,* Sept. 6, 2003.

20. For example, *Texas Lawyer* magazine reported that the firm earned more money than any other ($1.755–3.155 million) for lobbying during the 2003 session. One client was Texans for Lawsuit Reform, which fought in 2003 to get damage caps on medical malpractice suits and had played a critical role alongside TRMPAC in the 2002 election (see Chapter Four). Some critics also pointed out that Harriet Miers, counsel to President Bush, was a former Whitmire law partner and could have exerted pressure on him. Whitmire denied speaking with Miers.

21. *Houston Chronicle,* Sept. 7, 2003.

22. Ibid., Sept. 4, 2003.

23. Ellis's initial memoranda presented four plans. Attention focused, however, on only two, the so-called 8–3 and 7–2–2 plans.

24. *San Antonio Express-News,* Sept. 5, 2003.

25. *Dallas Morning News,* September 10, 2003.

26. Ibid.

27. Ibid., Sept. 9, 2003.

28. Senator Harris said that the conduct "did not meet the decorum of the Senate" (*Houston Chronicle,* Aug. 16, 2003).

29. *Dallas Morning News,* Sept. 9, 2003.

30. Ibid., Sept. 16, 2003.

31. Ibid., Sept. 17, 2003.

32. Ibid.; *Houston Chronicle,* Sept. 17, 2003.

33. Dewhurst interview, 2005.

34. Hobby interview.

35. *Houston Chronicle,* Sept. 19, 2003.

36. *San Antonio Express-News,* Oct. 8, 2003.

37. Ibid.

38. Wentworth interview.

39. *San Antonio Express-News,* Oct. 13, 2003.

40. Duncan confirmed this statement to me in 2005.

41. *Houston Chronicle,* Oct. 13, 2003.

42. *Austin American-Statesman,* Sept. 20, 2003.

43. Ibid.

44. *Dallas Morning News,* Sept. 24, 2003.

45. For example, Democrats tried unsuccessfully to force the reading of the seventy-seven-page bill. The Democrats also argued that since HB 3 was a House bill, it could not be considered under Senate rules on any day other than Wednesday or Thursday; Dewhurst overruled these points of order. His ruling on consideration of the House bill on Tuesday was appealed to the full Senate, but was upheld by a vote along party lines.

46. *Senate Journal,* Sept. 24, 2003.

47. *Houston Chronicle,* Sept. 25, 2003.

48. Wentworth interview.

49. *San Antonio Express-News,* Oct. 5, 2003.

Chapter 12

1. *Houston Chronicle,* Sept. 25, 2003.

2. Dewhurst interview.

3. There are not, of course, any fixed boundaries defining this region. At various times in Texas history, much more of Texas has been described as being in West Texas. For some people, the general dividing line remains Interstate 35 from Dallas/-Fort Worth, through Austin, through San Antonio, and on to the Rio Grande Valley. For purposes of this redistricting dispute, the region encompasses the less populated counties of the rural western portion of the state, and a few contiguous counties in central and north-central Texas.

4. Kent Hance in 1984 lost the Democratic primary election for nomination to the U.S. Senate. He subsequently changed parties and ran unsuccessfully for the Republican nomination for governor in 1998. In 2005 he practiced law in Austin, Texas. It was Terry Scarborough of his firm who represented Bill Ceverha in the civil litigation against TRMPAC. This litigation is discussed in Chapter Four.

5. Conaway is a certified public accountant who met Bush in the late 1970s. He audited Bush's company for three years before joining it as vice president. Conaway later became senior vice president and chief financial officer of the United Bank of Midland. The bank loaned Bush $500,000 so that he could purchase his share of the Texas Rangers baseball team. As governor, Bush appointed Conaway to the State Board of Public Accountancy. Conaway later became chairman of that agency. Conaway said in 2003 that he never talked to Bush about making his run for Congress.

6. *San Angelo Standard-Times,* Sept. 10, 2003.

7. *Amarillo Globe-News,* Sept. 23, 2003.

8. *El Paso Times,* Sept. 21, 2003.

9. *Abilene Reporter-News,* Sept. 14, 2003.

10. Duncan interview.

11. *Houston Chronicle,* Sept. 17, 2003.

12. Ibid.

13. *San Angelo Standard-Times,* Oct. 14, 2003.

14. *Senate Journal,* Oct. 10, 2003.

15. *Austin American-Statesman,* Sept. 26, 2003.

16. Dewhurst recalls that he met with the Senate members of the conference committee in his office at least once.

17. According to Senator Todd Staples, one of the regular attendees at the meetings was Dale Oldham, redistricting counsel for the Republican National Committee.

18. Bob Davis is a former Republican lawmaker. As a state representative he played a major role in the state House districts drawn by the legislature in 1981. In 2001 he was an adviser to then commissioner of the General Land Office, David Dewhurst, when Dewhurst served on the Texas Legislative Redistricting Board that drew the heavily partisan state Senate and House legislative districts. He is very knowledgeable about Republican political strength statewide, especially in the Dallas area. He was paid $300 an hour for his work in 2003.

19. For example, at one point a map under consideration paired Republican Kevin Brady and Democrat Jim Turner. Brady was concerned about the pairing (*Dallas Morning News,* Sept. 21, 2003). The map was changed, and Turner ended up paired with Republican Steve Barton and Democrat Martin Frost.

20. *Abilene Reporter-News,* Oct. 10, 2003.

21. Working with the data was described to me by one participant as being akin to playing for hours on a computer game. Often the map was projected on a wall-size screen to allow additional participants to observe the changes and to suggest others.

22. *Abilene Reporter-News,* Sept. 29, 2003.

23. *Dallas Morning News,* Sept. 27, 2003.

24. *Houston Chronicle,* Oct. 3, 2003; *Fort Worth Star-Telegram,* Oct. 3, 2003.

25. *Fort Worth Star-Telegram,* Oct. 3, 2003.

26. In his deposition, Senator Staples explained the inclusion of District 23 among the eight Hispanic districts counted by the Republicans: "I mean it is represented by a Hispanic representative."

27. Ellis had described an earlier and similar version of this redrawn District 9 as one designed to defeat incumbent Chris Bell (*Houston Chronicle,* July 23, 2003).

28. Interview with Senator Robert Duncan (2006).

29. Toomey interview.

30. *Houston Chronicle,* Oct. 10, 2003.

31. According to a spokesperson for the office of the attorney general, that state official had insisted from the beginning of 2003 that the office's attorneys should merely provide advice on legal issues and not try to influence the shape of the redistricting plan.

32. A representative from the attorney general challenged me in 2006 by asking, "Hasn't this legal advice proven correct?" Other Republican state officials also pointed with pride to the fact that the aggressive redistricting plan was subsequently upheld by Justice and the federal district court.

33. *Dallas Morning News,* Sept. 24, 2003.

34. *Abilene Reporter-News,* Oct. 10, 2003; *San Angelo Standard-Times,* Oct. 10, 2003.

35. *Lubbock Avalanche-Journal,* Oct. 19, 2003.

36. Jim Ellis interview.

37. Compiled at the author's request by Texans for Public Justice from individual candidate filings with the Texas Ethics Commission for the 2002 election cycle. These same ten contributors also gave slightly over $100,000 to Democratic senators during this period, including slightly over $30,000 to John Whitmire.

38. Jim Ellis interview.

39. In his deposition, Staples said that Ellis and RNC counsel Alden brought this map.

40. King interview.

41. *Austin American-Statesman,* Oct. 4, 2003.

42. *Houston Chronicle,* Oct. 7, 2003.

43. Ibid., Oct. 12, 2003.

44. *Fort Worth Star-Telegram,* Oct. 7, 2003.

45. *Midland Reporter-Telegram,* Oct. 10, 2003.

46. *Houston Chronicle,* Oct. 9, 2003; *San Antonio Express-News,* Oct. 9, 2003.

47. *Dallas Morning News,* Oct. 9, 2003.

48. Ibid.

49. Ibid.

50. Ibid., Oct. 10, 2003.

51. Jim Ellis interview. He would not identify which state leaders took this position.

52. *San Antonio Express-News,* Oct. 8, 2003.

53. *Austin American-Statesman,* Oct. 11, 2003.

54. *Houston Chronicle,* Oct. 8, 2003.

55. *Austin American-Statesman,* Oct. 10, 2003.

56. Ibid., Sept. 26, 2003.

57. *Houston Chronicle,* Oct. 10, 2003.

58. *Austin American-Statesman,* Oct. 10, 2003.

59. *Abilene Reporter-News,* Oct. 10, 2003.

60. Ibid.

61. *House Journal,* Oct. 11, 2003.

62. Ibid.

63. Ibid. The roll-call vote is on page 466.

64. *Senate Journal,* Oct. 10, 2003. The debate was reduced to writing and included in the journal.

65. Ibid.

66. Ibid.

67. *San Angelo Standard-Times,* Oct. 2003.

68. *Austin American-Statesman,* Oct. 13, 2003.

69. *Houston Chronicle,* Oct. 16, 2003.

70. The e-mail is included among the exhibits in the lawsuit challenging the 2003 redistricting.

71. The information in this section is derived primarily from the following sources: interviews with personnel who were in the Justice Department at the time the redistricting was considered; a series of articles in the *Washington Post* during the fall of 2005 and early 2006 about the changes in the voting section of the department; and the internal Justice staff memorandum prepared on the redistricting plan in 2003.

72. *Dallas Morning News*, Oct. 17, 2003.

73. Quoted in the *Houston Chronicle*, Dec. 3, 2005. I could not locate a contemporary news report of this statement from Abbott. In 2006, I wrote to Attorney General Abbott, asking him to confirm or deny that he made this statement. I received no response.

74. Hans von Spakovsky was rewarded for his service at Justice when President Bush in late 2005 bypassed the U.S. Senate to appoint him during a congressional recess to a seat on the Federal Election Commission. Several Democratic senators objected because the interim appointment meant that von Spakovsky could avoid answering questions during his confirmation about the Texas redistricting and other decisions within the Voting Section of Justice (*Austin American-Statesman*, Jan. 5, 2006).

75. Democratic attorney Gerald Hebert acknowledged in April 2006 in a speech at the University of Texas Law School that he was the person who obtained a copy of this Justice memorandum and made it public.

Chapter 13

1. *Dallas Morning News*, July 9, 2003.

2. Ibid., May 31, 2003.

3. The statistics in this chapter are derived from various reports prepared by the Texas Legislative Council in October 2003, comparing the districts in the new plan to the districts used in 2002 and to the districts in the plans passed by the House and Senate.

4. Jim Ellis interview.

5. Perales interview.

6. *Senate Journal*, Oct. 10, 2003.

7. Wilson interview.

8. Nina Perales, regional counsel for MALDEF, reminded me, however, that geography necessarily plays a major role in achieving this effect. It would be difficult or impossible to draw congressional districts in south Texas that were not overwhelmingly Hispanic and Democratic.

9. Democratic incumbent Chet Edwards won reelection in 2004 in a District 17 that had been redrawn in 2003 with an expected Republican vote of 64 percent. Edwards is facing a very strong Republican challenge in 2006 from a veteran of the Iraq war.

10. *San Antonio Express-News*, Aug. 17, 2003.

Chapter 14

1. LULAC, however, in 2003 favored keeping the existing congressional districts and was responsible for the turnout of many at the legislative hearings opposed to redistricting.

2. Perales interview.

3. I interviewed State Senator Ellis twice in 2005.

4. Rodney Ellis interview.

5. The 2003 internal Justice Department memoranda objecting to the Republican redistricting plan supported Ellis's opinion by concluding, based on historical voting, that District 25 as it existed in 2002 was one in which African-American voters could

elect the candidate of their choice by virtue of the control they exercised over the outcome of the Democratic Primary.

6. *El Paso News,* July 30, 2003.

7. *Senate Journal,* Oct. 10, 2003.

8. Ibid.

9. Ibid.

10. *Dallas Morning News,* May 27, 2003.

Chapter 15

1. The information in this chapter is derived primarily from the TRMPAC documents made available in the civil trial *Paul Clayton v. Bill Ceverha,* newspaper articles covering the activities of Congressman DeLay over this period, the reports of the federal agencies asked for help by Congressman DeLay in finding and returning the Democratic House lawmakers, the memoranda prepared for Congressman DeLay by Jim Ellis during the 2003 legislative sessions, and an interview with Jim Ellis in 2005.

2. *Washington Post Weekly,* Oct. 3–9, 2005.

3. Ibid.

4. Ibid., Oct. 17–23, 2005.

5. Ratliff interview; *Dallas Morning News,* Aug. 20, 2003.

6. Ratliff interview.

7. DeLay said, "Yes, it was my idea, or it was our idea—those of us that wanted to enhance the Republicans who served in the House of Representatives of the Texas Legislature" (*New York Times,* Mar. 10, 2005).

8. Ellis interview.

9. *Austin American-Statesman,* Nov. 23, 2001.

10. Colyandro deposition (2004).

11. Associated Press, Apr. 12, 2005.

12. Ibid.

13. E-Mail exchange between Warren Robold and John Colyandro (2003).

14. *Houston Chronicle,* March 16, 2005.

15. *Austin American-Statesman,* Feb. 20, 2005.

16. Ibid.

17. Texans for Public Justice reports that 54 percent of the corporate contributions to TRMPAC came from businesses represented by Washington lobbying firms, "including some with close ties to House Majority Leader Tom DeLay" (TPJ "Lobby Watch," October 11, 2004). For example, the Alexander Strategy Group, led by former DeLay chief of staff Ed Buckham, represented AT&T and Questerra Corporation in 2002. Former DeLay aides Drew Maloney and Chris Lynch at the Federalist Group represented El Paso Energy and Reliant Energy.

18. For example, Preston, Gates Ellis & Rouvelas Meeds, the lobbying arm of Preston Gates & Ellis (Abramoff and Scanlon's former law firm), gave $25,000 to TRMPAC and at least two of their Indian tribe clients gave small amounts. I do not recall seeing any direct reference to either Abramoff or Scanlon in the TRMPAC documents that I reviewed for this book. It is likely, however, that one of the reasons for the surge in subpoenas by the Travis County district attorney in late 2005 and early

2006 was his effort to discover documents linking TRMPAC or DeLay to these former lobbyists.

19. Wilkes has been identified as "co-conspirator No. 1" in Congressman Randy "Duke" Cunningham's federal plea agreement on bribery charges, which led to his resignation from the U.S. House of Representatives (*Austin American-Statesman*, Dec. 14, 2005).

20. Lake later faced fraud charges for allegedly trying to loot Westar. Lake, along with David Wittig, the chief executive of Westar, left the company late in 2002. A federal fraud trial against the pair ended in a mistrial in December 2004.

21. In 2003, columnist Molly Ivins suggested that DeLay had planned to "slip an amendment into the defense authorization bill" to benefit Bacardi (*Texas Observer*, Nov. 7, 2003).

22. A "letter of admonition," as opposed to an "admonishment" or "censure" is not considered a penalty. Such a letter is essentially a caution from the Ethics Committee, stating that it believes that the particular member has exercised "bad judgment."

23. The information in this section is derived primarily from the reports of the Department of Justice, the Department of Homeland Security, and the Federal Aviation Agency on the contacts that state and federal officials made with these agencies in May 2003 during the hunt for the Democratic House members.

24. *Houston Chronicle*, May 23, 2003.

25. *Fort Worth Star-Telegram*, May 15, 2003.

26. *Houston Chronicle*, May 23, 2003.

27. I am grateful to Jim Ellis for agreeing to an interview in 2005. The information in this section is derived primarily from that interview.

28. Ratliff interview.

29. *Austin American-Statesman*, May 7, 2003.

30. *El Paso News*, July 30, 2003.

31. *New York Times*, May 15, 2003.

32. Associated Press, May 13, 2003.

33. *Houston Chronicle*, May 13, 2003.

34. Ibid., May 14, 2003.

35. Ibid., May 13, 2003.

36. *National Journal*, May 13, 2003.

37. *Los Angeles Times*, May 14, 2003.

38. Associated Press, July 15, 2003.

39. *Fort Worth Star-Telegram*, May 16, 2003.

40. DeLay made the statement on Fox News on Sunday, August 17, 2003. It was reported in various newspapers, including the *Houston Chronicle*, the following day.

41. *Houston Chronicle*, Aug. 18, 2003.

42. *Dallas Morning News*, Sept. 17, 2003.

43. Ibid., Sept. 26, 2003.

44. *Houston Chronicle*, Oct. 7, 2003.

45. *San Antonio Express-News*, Oct. 9, 2003.

46. *Houston Chronicle*, Oct. 9, 2003.

47. *Austin American-Statesman*, July 16, 2003.

48. Ibid.

49. *Dallas Morning News*, Sept. 5, 2003.

50. Ibid., May 14, 2003.

51. *Austin American-Statesman,* Oct. 16, 2003.

52. Ibid., Sept. 4, 2003.

53. Ibid., Sept. 17, 2003.

54. *Fort Worth Star-Telegram,* May 11, 2003.

55. Ratliff interview.

56. *Dallas Morning News,* June 20, 2003.

57. *Fort Worth Star-Telegram,* May 11, 2003.

58. *Dallas Morning News,* July 8, 2003.

59. Wentworth interview.

60. *McAllen Monitor,* July 17, 2003.

61. *Dallas Morning News,* Sept. 5, 2003.

62. Ibid.

63. Ibid.

64. Dewhurst interview, 2006. Democrats believe that Hughes was responsible for Dewhurst's change on the two-thirds requirement.

65. *Houston Chronicle,* Oct. 2, 2003.

66. Ibid., Oct. 17, 2003.

67. *Lubbock Avalanche-Journal,* May 11, 2003.

68. *Dallas Morning News,* Sept. 5, 2003.

69. Ibid., Oct. 10, 2003.

70. Ibid., Oct. 16, 2003.

71. The information in this section comes from the experience of the author, interviews with current and former members of the Voting Section of the Department of Justice, and a series of articles in the *Washington Post* and *New York Times* about changes taking place in the Department of Justice.

72. *Washington Post,* Jan. 23, 2006.

73. For example, when Democrats went to federal court in August 2003 to try to block a change in the state Senate's two-thirds vote requirement, Justice responded in writing in less than a week that eliminating the vote requirement was not a voting change subject to review under Section 5. While the substance of this decision is probably correct, the department acted so quickly to undermine the Democrats' legal position that it did not even allow them to submit substantive written comments on the state's request for Justice Department aid. According to Joe Rich, such action by Justice apparently was unprecedented.

A further possibility of partisan influence occurred in May 2003, when Democratic state representative Richard Raymond submitted a complaint about the lack of redistricting hearings in Latino areas of Texas. Raymond says that he was told by at least one Republican colleague that DeLay had assured Texas Republicans that he would personally see that Justice dismissed Raymond's complaint. I could not substantiate whether DeLay actually made such a promise or contacted the department about Raymond's complaint. Raymond withdrew his complaint after hearing of DeLay's promise of intervention.

74. A spokesperson for the Texas attorney general's office told me that the question for that office in 2003 was whether Justice would have the nerve to preclear the Texas plan, given the adverse media attention that would "certainly" follow the decision. The spokesperson said that he believed the legal decision by Justice on the Texas redistrict-

ing plan was correct and dismissed any contention that partisanship played a role at Justice as probably being untrue.

Chapter 16

1. Governor Arnold Schwarzenegger proposed that California adopt a state commission to redraw districts before the 2006 election; in November 2005 the voters of California rejected this proposal.

2. *Connor v. Finch*, 431 U.S. 407, 416n13 (1977).

3. For example, areas thought by some legislators to have grown in Anglo population since the census was taken could be added to minority-majority districts to dilute minority voting strength, and the result would be disguised through the use of old census data. So also, areas thought to have changed from Anglo to minority since the census was taken could be added to existing majority-minority districts to pack minority voters and minimize their vote. Similarly, partisan objectives can be achieved using current election results as a basis, and the new gerrymandered boundaries could be justified on the basis of old census data. The possibilities for abuse are almost unlimited.

4. Professor Michael McDonald, professor of government and politics at George Mason University (*Fort Worth Star-Telegram*, May 11, 2005).

5. *Vieth v. Jubelirer*, 541 U.S. 267 (2004).

6. *Henderson v. Perry*, 399 F. Supp. 2d 756.

7. Ibid., dissent of Judge Ward, 399 F. Supp. 2d at 779–785.

8. *Miller v. Johnson*, 515 U.S. 900 (1995).

Chapter 17

1. Much of the information in this chapter is derived directly from the pleadings and oral arguments in the criminal proceedings against Congressman Tom DeLay, Jim Ellis, and John Colyandro. The author was present at all of the hearings. Many of the statements attributed to persons in this chapter are derived from those hearings or the legal documents filed in the criminal proceedings. This author interviewed Tom DeLay's counsel, Dick DeGuerin (twice), Roy Minton, and the Travis County district attorney, Ronnie Earle. All were helpful. However, Earle in particular was cautious not to make any statements about pending or potential charges or defendants, since doing so might violate his duty as a prosecutor. Therefore, the accounts of the August meeting with DeLay, the decision-making process regarding Craddick and Hammond, etc. are primarily a result of a review of pleadings and newspaper accounts and my own conjecture based on my experience as a litigator and knowledge of the principal attorneys.

2. By the spring of 2004 the grand jury had subpoenaed approximately two dozen persons and piles of documents (*Dallas Morning News*, Mar. 26, 2004). Among those persons ordered to appear before the grand jury were Kevin Shuvalov (regional director for the RNC), Danielle Ferro (DeLay's daughter), Demetrius McDaniel (an Austin lobbyist whose clients had contributed to TRMPAC), and Terry Nelson (former dep-

uty chief of staff to the RNC and director of the Bush-Cheney reelection campaign in 2004). Subpoenas from the grand jury gathered a wide range of documents from TRM-PAC, TAB, Texas lawmakers, Speaker Craddick, and the office of Governor Perry.

3. *Houston Chronicle,* Feb. 28, 2004.

4. In 2006, documents released pursuant to a freedom of information request showed that Texas Republican congressman Sam Johnson asked the IRS to conduct an audit of Texans for Public Justice (TPJ) for actions inconsistent with its status as a nonprofit, tax-exempt organization. The apparent concern by Johnson was that TPJ was engaged in political activities by coordinating with the Texas Democratic Party in a "witch hunt" against DeLay. Specifically, the allegation was that the TPJ was providing information to District Attorney Earle in his investigation. Congressman Johnson's actions had been requested by an attorney whose law firm at one time represented ARMPAC and whose partner had been subpoenaed by the Travis County grand jury investigating TRMPAC and TAB. The IRS conducted the audit, but found nothing in TPJ's conduct that jeopardized its tax status (*Austin American-Statesman,* Feb. 27, 2006).

5. *Austin American-Statesman,* Mar. 10, 2005.

6. Ibid., Nov. 6, 2005.

7. Press Statement, Travis County District Attorney (Sept. 8, 2005).

8. *Austin American-Statesman,* Nov. 6, 2005.

9. DeLay's defense counsel Susan Klein urged to me in 2006 that the Fort Bend DA did not believe that a crime had been committed. I do not know the reason for his inaction.

10. Interview with Travis County district attorney Ronnie Earle (2006). Another source has indicated that DeLay decided to meet with Earle to head off a subpoena from the grand jury that DeLay's attorneys understood was imminent.

11. Associated Press, Sept. 29, 2005.

12. *Austin American-Statesman,* Nov. 6, 2005.

13. Associated Press, Sept. 29, 2005.

14. Interview with Travis County District Attorney Ronnie Earle and Assistant District Attorney Rick Reed (2006).

15. DeLay made this comment on *Fox News Sunday* in an interview with Chris Wallace, and it was widely reported in newspapers the next day; see, for example, *USA Today,* Oct. 3, 2005.

16. *Austin American-Statesman,* Sept. 29, 2005.

17. Ibid., Oct. 23, 2005.

18. One effect of leaving the September 28 indictment in place even though these charges were essentially repeated in Count I of the October 3 indictments was to allow the charges to survive DeLay's efforts to withdraw his waiver of the statute of limitations (i.e., the September 28 indictments came before DeLay attempted to withdraw his waiver).

19. *Austin American-Statesman,* Oct. 25, 2005.

20. The name of the law firm was later changed to Loeffler, Tuggy and Pauerstein.

21. *Austin American-Statesman,* Sept. 29, 2005.

22. Ibid., Nov. 4, 2005.

23. Ibid., Oct. 23, 2005.

24. Ibid., Nov. 8, 2005.

25. The defense argument was that the two statutes were "on the same subject" and that, to the extent they differed, the more specific (i.e., the Election Code) should control.

26. *Austin American-Statesman,* Nov. 16, 2005.

27. Associated Press, Nov. 4, 2005.

28. DeGuerin interview, 2006. He believes that the district attorney of Harris County alerted Earle to the deficiencies of the first indictment. Earle said absolutely not. Earle insisted to me that the second indictment was simply obtained out of an abundance of caution.

29. Law professor and DeLay counsel Susan Klein believes that these federal court cases are inapposite because federal law now specifically includes "checks" as a basis for money laundering charges. I believe she is correct.

30. *Austin American-Statesman,* Dec. 20, 2003. The quotes are taken from the actual e-mails and orders.

31. Ibid., Dec. 18 and 20, 2003, and various e-mails and pleadings available at www.statesman.com/trmpac.

32. Ibid., Dec. 19, 2005.

33. Earle interview; *Dallas Morning News,* Dec. 4, 2004.

34. *Austin American-Statesman,* Oct. 25, 2003.

35. *Wall Street Journal,* Dec. 7, 2005.

36. For example, DeLay spokesperson Kevin Madden said on December 13, 2005, that Earle "has turned a three-year political vendetta against Mr. DeLay into a zany, careless subpoena bazaar that has legal observers and legitimate prosecutors across the country using the Travis County district attorney's office as a case study on how not to run a governmental office" (*Austin American-Statesman,* Dec. 14, 2005).

37. *Wall Street Journal,* Dec. 7, 2005.

38. Ibid., Jan. 9, 2006.

39. Prosecutions for bribery have historically been difficult to win because of the need to show a specific quid pro quo in which the public official agreed to give a specific vote or to perform a specific act in return for a gift or payment. Public officials historically have defended their actions by claiming that they had other good reasons for voting or acting in the requested manner and that the relationship was a legal, mutually beneficial relationship.

40. *Republican Party of Minnesota v. White,* 536 U.S. 765, 777–778 (2002). Emphasis in original.

41. As indicated in Chapter Fifteen, however, I believe that the decisions by the Department of Justice in regard to the 2003 redistricting plan were attributable to partisanship.

Chapter 18

1. *Wall Street Journal,* Dec. 30, 2005. DeLay's PAC fund report for November showed $69,322.79 in cash and $145,931.81 in debts.

2. *Austin American-Statesman,* Dec. 8, 2005.

3. *New York Times,* Jan. 8, 2006.

4. *Austin American-Statesman,* Jan. 14, 2005.

5. *Wall Street Journal,* Jan. 5, 2006.

6. For example, Jonathan Gurwitz in the *Wall Street Journal* (Dec. 7, 2005) described the ties as "numerous," specifically referencing expenses associated with a "political jun-

ket and golfing trip to the United Kingdom," DeLay's "frequent use of Abramoff's sky-box at MCI Center," and Christine DeLay's role with the Alexander Strategy Group, to which Abramoff referred clients. Gurwitz concluded that these ties "only scratch the surface of a relationship between Mr. Abramoff, Mr. DeLay, and Mr. DeLay's office that stretches back a decade and involves some of the lobbyist's most noxious efforts."

7. *Austin American-Statesman*, Jan. 4, 2006.

8. *New York Times*, Jan. 8, 2006.

9. *Austin American-Statesman*, Jan. 10, 2003, and Jan. 24, 2006.

10. *New York Times*, Jan. 8, 2006. en.wikipedia.org/wiki/Tony_Rudy

11. *Wall Street Journal*, Jan. 6, 2006.

12. Ibid., Jan. 9, 2006.

13. *Washington Post*, Jan. 8, 2006; *Austin American-Statesman*, Jan. 8, 2006.

14. *Austin American-Statesman*, Jan. 9, 2006.

15. Interview with Dick DeGuerin, 2006.

16. *Austin American-Statesman*, Mar. 28, 2006.

17. Ibid., Mar. 30, 2006.

18. Ibid., Mar. 22, 2006.

19. Ibid., Mar. 30, 2006.

20. Rudy joined DeLay's staff as press secretary in 1995. He became deputy chief of staff in 1998 and served until 2006.

21. For this section, I reviewed the Indictment, Plea Agreement, and Factual Basis for the Plea in *United States of America v. Tony C. Rudy*, Crim. No. 06-082 (U.S. Dist. Court, District of Columbia).

22. *Washington Post*, Apr. 5, 2006.

23. Fox News.com, Apr. 4, 2006.

24. Nick Lampson told me in 2006 that his polls during this period showed him leading DeLay by 44 percent to 36 percent among likely voters in the general election in District 22.

25. *Washington Post*, Apr. 5, 2006.

26. Ibid.

27. Ibid., Jan. 11, 2006.

28. Ibid., Apr. 14, 2006. McCain has played a major role in the Senate investigation of Abramoff.

Afterword

1. *League of United Latin American Citizens v. Perry*, No. 05-204 (June 28, 2006), Slip Opinion.

2. It may turn out that the opinion of Justice Scalia, joined by Justice Thomas, holds the greatest long-term significance. Scalia accepted for the first time the proposition earlier advanced by Justice O'Connor (but never expressly adopted by the Court) that election districts can be drawn using race, even as a predominant consideration, when necessary to comply with Section 5 of the Voting Rights Act because compliance with that Act is a compelling state interest. This interesting proposition now appears to have majority support on the Court.

3. Slip Opinion, Opinion of the Court at 22. Justice Kennedy for a majority of the Court rejected the state's argument that the reduction of Hispanic voting strength in District 23 was offset by the creation of a Hispanic opportunity district in District 25. Kennedy saw this new district as not "reasonably compact." It is doubtful that Kennedy's newfound legal penchant for "compact" minority districts adds any meaningful principle to election law jurisprudence.

4. Powe and Bickerstaff, "Anthony Kennedy's Blind Quest", *University of Michigan Law Review* [students.law.umich.edu/mlr].

5. Many eyes nationwide were fixed on the outcome of the Texas case. If the Republican-controlled Texas Legislature could redraw election districts during a decade to enhance partisan or special interests without current or accurate population enumerations, then other state or local governments should also be able to do so. Colorado tried to redraw its congressional districts for partisan reasons in 2003, but the state supreme court declared mid-decade redistricting unlawful under the state constitution. Georgia in 2006 followed the Texas precedent and redrew congressional districts to increase Republican representation from that state. An initiative for redrawing state legislative and congressional districts prior to the 2006 election was defeated in 2005 by the voters of California. Other states and local governments have also shown interest in following the Texas precedent. Republicans in Texas urge that the risk of a wave of mid-decade redistricting is slight. They posit that mid-decade redistricting is only likely to occur in circumstances like Texas where there is a significance imbalance between the makeup of the congressional delegation and the popular vote and where partisan control of the legislature has recently changed.

6. The decision literally applies only to a circumstance when a legislative body replaces a court drawn plan. Kennedy repeatedly puts the decision in this context. Whether a mid-decade redistricting plan that replaces an earlier valid legislatively enacted redistricting plan would meet the same fate is left at least theoretically to another date.

7. Six new Republicans (five freshmen Republicans and one Democratic incumbent who switched parties) joined congress in 2005 as a result of the redistricting, thereby increasing the thin Republican majority in the House by twelve. All of the new Republican congressmen consistently voted in 2005–2006 with the Republican House leadership on issues such as CAFTA, drilling on the north slope of Alaska, ethics reform, tax cuts, immigration, funding for health and social programs, and other controversial legislation. These new congressmen on July 13, 2006, voted in favor of proposed amendments that would have weakened the Voting Rights Act by changing the formula for application of the Act or allowing an expedited procedure for bailing out from coverage by the Act, but only one (Conaway) ultimately voted against passage of the extension of the Act.

8. The primary plans were the following:

- MALDEF/GI Forum proposal paired Bonilla and Cuellar in District 23, leaving the redrawn District 28 (Cuellar's prior district) as an open seat with a Hispanic majority. Also, the proposed MALDEF/GI Forum plan redrew District 25 into a razor thin district running only from Travis County to northern Bexar County. This redrawn District 25 remained heavily Democratic and was one in which incumbent Lloyd Doggett could probably win.

- The State's proposal joined Webb County with the area stretching west to El Paso (that had previously been in District 23) and renumbered the district as District 28. Bonilla and the predominately Anglo and Republican remainder of prior District 23 were joined with Travis County in a heavily Republican District 23, thereby protecting Bonilla. The portion of Travis County previously in District 25 was added to District 21, pairing Democratic incumbent Lloyd Doggett with Republican Lamar Smith in a heavily Republican district with most of its voters in Smith's home county, Bexar. This left a redrawn District 25 with a large Hispanic majority and no incumbent. The State's plan fractured the Democratic stronghold of Travis County and was an obvious attempt to prevent Democrat Lloyd Doggett from again escaping defeat.
- LULAC offered two plans. Both reunited Webb County, but one placed it in District 23 (pairing Cuellar and Bonilla), and the other placed the whole county in District 28.
- The Democratic plan placed Webb County in District 23 (pairing Cuellar and Bonilla), protected Doggett, and left an open seat in District 28.
- Three incumbents (Bonilla, Cuellar, and Lamar Smith) also submitted a plan that had been negotiated in Washington. It avoided pairing any incumbents, but left Webb County split between Districts 23 and 28. Doggett had participated in these negotiations, but, at the last minute, was unwilling to join with his colleagues on the proposed plan. Nevertheless, the plan retained District 25 in Travis County and gave Doggett the opportunity to win reelection in that district.

9. This plan (1438C) (as well as all of the proposed remedial plans) was available on the Texas Legislature website www.tlc.state.tx.us/redist. A map of the plan is included in this book. As discussed, the plan makes important changes that aided Democrats (and Doggett) in District 25 and addressed the voting rights violation in District 23. However, for the Hispanic advocacy organizations, the court plan was a disappointment. While it restored Hispanic voting strength in District 23, it eliminated District 25 as a majority Hispanic district. Moreover, for these groups, the plan also "packed" Hispanic voters unnecessarily into redrawn Districts 15 (73% Hispanic VAP) and District 28 (74% Hispanic VAP). Although "prevailing parties" in the litigation and eligible for attorney fees, the end result was not what these organizations had wanted.

10. At various places in this book I have been willing as a matter of courtesy to repeat the Attorney General's position that throughout 2003 and thereafter he and his office were merely giving legal advice as the state's attorney and took no position on partisan issues. However, both the events themselves and the statements of other Republicans say otherwise. Attorney General Abbott was a critical partisan force during the 2003 redistricting.

11. Neither the courts nor the Democrats would allow DeLay to go away quietly. Republican efforts to replace DeLay on the District 22 ballot were frustrated by Democratic attorney Cris Feldman, who earlier had sued TRMPAC and TAB on behalf of defeated Democratic state legislative candidates. Feldman filed suit to keep DeLay on the ballot in Congressional District 22 despite DeLay's resignation from Congress. DeLay had won the Republican primary before announcing his intention to resign. Feldman's argument was that, by doing so, DeLay had tried to manipulate the primary process to allow him to effectively control who would be the Republican candidate. DeLay expected that with his resignation after the primary and his announced plan

to move to Virginia, the Texas Republican Party (with ample help from DeLay) could select a Republican nominee favored by DeLay. Feldman, however, argued that this attempted manipulation of the process by DeLay to prevent selection of the Republican nominee at the party primary violated state law and that, once DeLay was nominated, he could not thereafter be replaced by the Republican Party for the general election ballot. Federal district judge Sam Sparks (a Republican appointee) was persuaded by this argument and wrote an outstanding opinion. A rushed appeal by the Republican Party was unsuccessful as the Fifth Circuit agreed with Spark's ruling and, on August 8th, Justice Scalia refused to block it. There was speculation (fueled somewhat by DeLay himself) that, if required to remain on the ballot, DeLay would run an aggressive race to recapture his congressional seat. (*Time Magazine* [July 17, 2006]). Through an e-mail sent on August 8th by his daughter, Dani DeLay Ferro, however, DeLay made clear that he would not attempt to run. He described his decision as based on his residency in Virginia and blamed the federal courts for "slam[ming] the door on a fair ballot." It is likely that DeLay's decision was driven in large part by his loss of his usual money raising strengths, which had been sapped by his large attorney fees and his departure from Congress. Democratic candidate Nick Lampson (well funded by Democratic sources nationwide) says the polls showed him to have been a likely winner over DeLay even if DeLay had stayed in the race. Republicans were left to trying to mount a write-in campaign on behalf of an agreed candidate; but such a campaign was unlikely to be successful. District 22, however, was drawn in 2003 to have a Republican voting majority, so, even if successful in 2006, Democrats may have a difficult time holding on to the district in future elections.

12. The Democrat at risk under the current plan is Chet Edwards in the heavily Republican-leaning District 17.

13. The appeal of Ellis and Colyandro was set for consideration in August, 2006. Ellis counsel, J. D. Pauerstein told me that he was optimistic that he would secure dismissal of the criminal charges against these defendants by January, 2007.

14. Minton told me in 2006 that as a Democrat himself he faced critical comments at home because of his success on behalf of the Republicans and the TAB. However, as with any good lawyer, he said he could put aside his political affiliations when representing his clients. Minton is primarily a criminal defense attorney who has been practicing before the Travis County courts for over forty years. He has been the attorney to whom Republican and Democratic state office-holders have historically turned when implicated in possibly unlawful conduct. Over this long span, Minton has nurtured a respectful relationship with the Travis County District Attorney's Office that allows him to work with prosecutors in that office to try to resolve disputes and to avoid criminal indictments by convincing the prosecutors that there is no offense that can be proven. During the criminal investigations over 2003–2006, he voluntarily presented his clients privately, Craddick and Hammond, to answer prosecutors' questions. These individual clients avoided indictment. Minton emphasized to me that, in his experience, there was much more to be gained by building credibility, trust, and respect with prosecutors over time than in trying to hammer prosecutors into submission as occurred in the DeLay case.

15. Some Democrats refused to remain for the speech.

16. Farewell Address of Congressman Tom DeLay. I originally obtained the address through DeLay's congressional office. The text remains available at as of August 2006 at www.chron.com/dsp/story.mpl/politics/3951854.html

17. Michael Crowley of the *New Republic* called the speech "a melodramatic soliloquy" and (quoting the *Wall Street Journal* from a year earlier) said that DeLay "had become the living exemplar of some of (government's) worst habits." (Available at www.tnr.com/blog/theplank?/pid=19846). Other commentators were kinder, e.g., the *Washington Times,* available at the Deschutes County Republican Party website www. deschutesrepublicans.org/170787.aspt

18. *Austin American-Statesman,* June 9, 2006.

19. DeLay fixated on the clenched fist of Lincoln at the Lincoln monument as an indication of partisan principle.

Glossary of Redistricting Terms

Reapportionment: The allocation of seats in a legislative body (e.g., Congress) among political entities. Seats in Congress are reapportioned among the states at the beginning of each decade according to the relative population of the states. Some states also reapportion state legislative seats at the beginning of each decade among political subdivisions, such as counties. Sometimes, the words reapportionment and redistricting are used interchangeably, but they actually have different meanings.

Redistricting: The designation of the geographical boundaries of the election districts from which members of a legislative body will be elected. For Congress, one member is elected from each such district nationwide. Each district within a state must be equal in population. Only voters within the boundaries of a given district may vote in an election from which the congressman from that district is elected. Therefore, in a politically nonhomogeneous state where voters often are grouped in neighborhoods or communities alongside persons with similar voting tendencies, the location of the boundaries of the district may determine which political party or interest group is likely to win in a particular district. Redistricting occurs for congressional, state legislative, and many local government seats.

One Person, One Vote: The United States Supreme Court has required since the 1960s that election districts must be equal in population. For congressional districts, this means that all districts within a state must essentially be absolutely equal in population, with many states having a difference of only one or two persons among districts (out of a population of over 650,000). The requirement of equality in population is not quite as rigid for state and local government districts.

Neutral Factors: Theoretically, election district boundaries are drawn in furtherance of state policies or interests. For example, congressional district boundaries are likely to follow natural boundaries, like rivers, and political subdivision boundaries, such as county lines or city limits. However, adherence to these neutral factors must yield to the requirement of equal population, so district boundaries seldom are determined solely by these neutral factors (e.g., a county will be split among districts).

Member-Constituent Relations: The recognized, legitimate state interest of drawing the boundaries of districts to maintain the relationship between an incumbent and his or her constituents. The interest is seen as a proper state interest because it maintains continuity for the voters, avoids voter confusion, and, in the case of congressional districts, can help preserve a state's seniority in Congress by avoiding the unnecessary pairing of incumbents. Critics call the policy "incumbent protection." Texas redistricting consistently embodied this policy until 2003. In 2003, the legislature deliberately set out to defeat certain Democratic incumbents in Congress by destroying the existing member-constituent relations and, in many cases, pairing Democratic incumbents with Republican incumbents in districts drawn to elect the Republican.

Gerrymandering: The drawing of the boundaries of an election district to further the interests of a political group. The group may be partisan or may be another special interest (e.g., racial, ethnic, or economic). Usually the boundaries of a gerrymandered district are not compact. Many are bizarre or strange in appearance because the drawer has tried to carefully shape the district to place voters from certain political groups in or out of certain districts to achieve a particular political goal.

Partisan Gerrymandering: The gerrymandering of districts to further partisan interests.

Racial Gerrymandering: The gerrymandering of districts to enhance or minimize racial interests.

Packing: The technique in redistricting of trying to minimize the overall electoral strength of an opposing political group by drawing district boundaries so as to crowd as many of the group's voters into as few districts as possible. The political group is virtually certain to elect the candidate of its choice in the packed districts but is without an effective voice in electing candidates in the remaining districts.

Cracking or Fracturing: The technique in redistricting of trying to minimize the overall electoral strength of an opposing political group by drawing boundaries so as to divide an otherwise compact area of the group's voters and to scatter the group's voters among several districts, leaving them as a voting minority in those districts and unable to elect a candidate of their choice.

Voting Rights Act of 1965: This Act has had a very significant effect on redistricting. Section 2 of the Act applies nationwide and prohibits an election practice (such as redistricting) that has the "result" of denying or abridging the right to vote on the basis of race or national origin. Section 5 of the Act applies only to certain states and parts of states. Texas has been subject to Section 5 since 1975. Section 5 generally requires that before any change in an election procedure or practice (e.g., a redistricting of election districts) may become effective, the government adopting the change must show that the change has neither the "purpose" nor the "effect" of denying or abridging the right to vote on the basis of race or national origin. Most states and local governments covered by Section 5 seek to make this claim by submitting the change to the U.S. Attorney General (Department of Justice), where it is reviewed by the Voting Section of that agency. The government may submit it instead to a special District of Columbia district court.

Preclearance: When a state or local government makes the requisite showing under Section 5 to the U.S. Attorney General or the D.C. court, the election change is "precleared" and can take effect. If the state or local government fails to make a showing sufficient to meet its burden under the Act, the change is subject to an objection under the Act and cannot become effective.

Retrogressive: The standard that must be met by the state or local government under Section 5 of the Voting Rights Act is to show that the change does not have the purpose or effect of worsening (i.e., retrogressing) the position of the protected minority voters.

Spanish Surname Registered Voters (SSRV): The percentage of registered voters within a district who bear a Spanish surname. This percentage of voters is compiled annually from a state's voter lists and is generally seen as the best resource available (at least at the beginning of a decade) for measuring actual Hispanic voting strength within a district. Hispanic population totals are problematic because a disproportionate number of Hispanics are not citizens of the United States and cannot register to vote. Citizenship figures (such as Citizen Hispanic Voting Age Population [CHVAP]) are not available from the census bureau until several years after the census is taken and then are only an estimate based on a sample of census enumerations. SSRV numbers and percentages can change during each election cycle and are a means for showing the growth or decline of Hispanic voting strength in a district over time.

Political Performance: It is possible to determine the past voting patterns of persons within a particular geographical area and to use those patterns to project how the persons in the area will vote in the future. State and local governments maintain the results of past elections. These results are available for each local election precinct (usually 1,000–2,500 voters). Although the exact boundaries of these election precincts may change slightly from election cycle to election cycle, it remains possible to aggregate these election precinct results to measure generally how voters in a particular geographical area have voted in the recent past. It is easy to then use computer programs to manipulate this past election data to show how any proffered new district has "performed" (e.g., partisan tendency, turnout, etc.) in recent elections, and therefore how it is likely to "perform" for future elections. Past and future potential performance is measured using recent statewide elections because a result is available for these elections from every election precinct. Potential election results can be shown instantaneously for any proffered district, and the potential political effect of any change of geography for the district can be measured by the click of a computer mouse. Potential "performance" can vary depending on the closeness of the specific past race results selected for the analysis. Therefore, sometimes the data from all statewide elections for a particular year will be aggregated to provide the measure for the prediction of performance.

Index

Italic page numbers refer to tables.

Index